THE 1908 OLYMPIC GAMES

THE 1908 OLYMPIC GAMES

Results for All Competitors in All Events, with Commentary

by Bill Mallon
and Ian Buchanan

RESULTS OF THE EARLY MODERN OLYMPICS, 5

McFarland & Company, Inc., Publishers
Jefferson, North Carolina, and London

Library of Congress Cataloguing-in-Publication Data

Mallon, Bill, 1952–
    The 1908 Olympic Games : results for all competitors in all
events, with commentary / by Bill Mallon and Ian Buchanan.
       p. cm. — (Results of the early modern Olympics ; 5)
    Includes bibliographical references (p.) and index.
    ISBN 0-7864-0598-8 (library binding : 50# alkaline paper) ∞
    1. Olympic Games (4th : 1908 : London, England)
    2. Olympics — Records. I. Buchanan, Ian. II. Title.
    III. Series : Mallon,Bill. Results of the early modern Olympics ; 3
    GV721.8.M35   2000 vol. 5
    [GV722 1908]
    796.48 — dc21   99-57985

British Library Cataloguing-in-Publication data are available

Manufactured in the United States of America

McFarland & Company, Inc., Publishers
  Box 611, Jefferson, North Carolina 28640
   www.mcfarlandpub.com

For Wolf Lyberg

Table of Contents

Introduction

This is the fifth in a series of seven books giving complete summaries of the earliest Olympic Games. The series has run chronologically and the earlier books covered, in order, the 1896, 1900, 1904, and 1906 Olympic Games. The 1896 book was co-authored by Bill Mallon and Ture Widlund, while the 1900–1906 books were the sole work of Bill Mallon. Two further books planned for the series will deal with the 1912 and 1920 Olympic Games.

This book was written jointly by Bill Mallon and Ian Buchanan. It is an apt pairing and our fourth major book we have written together on the history of the Olympic Games. The pairing is apt because of our nationalities — Mallon is American, while Buchanan is British. Those who know little of the 1908 Olympic Games will shortly learn that these Olympics featured almost constant bickering between the American team and the British officials. In fact, because of the controversies, the 1908 Olympics have been termed "The Battle of Shepherd's Bush," referring to the site of the Olympic stadium. We have been able to look at the controversies from the eyes of both nations' media to present a balanced outlook concerning the various arguments that transpired.

This series of books covers the earliest Olympics because these are the Olympic Games for which results are not well recorded. Currently, at the end of each Olympic Games, the Organizing Committee is required by the International Olympic Committee to produce a detailed *Official Report* of the Olympic Games. At the end of the first century of the Modern Olympic Movement, these *Official Reports* are often exhaustive, covering in great detail every aspect of the organization and the results of the Olympics. This was not the case in the early years.

Official Reports did exist for all the Olympic Games between 1896 and 1920 but they were of varying quality. Some of them barely contained results at all; the medalists were usually mentioned, but often nothing further. Thus, this series is an attempt to complete and re-create the Olympic record, as it were, by filling in the many gaps in the record left by several of the less than complete early *Official Reports*.

The *Official Reports* of 1908 and 1912 are by far the best of that era. In fact, both contain almost complete results of all the events and sports. So what then is the need for this book?

It should be noted that we have relied on the 1908 *Official Report* primarily, but not exclusively. And we have greatly expanded on it in terms of the results of the 1908 Olympic Games. We have found results for several sports (archery, athletics [track & field], football [soccer], gymnastics, motorboating, shooting) which are not contained in the *1908 Official Report*, whose complete, unwieldy title is *The Fourth Olympiad: Being the Official Report of the Olympic Games of*

1908 Celebrated in London Under the Patronage of His Most Gracious King Edward VII and by the Sanction of the International Olympic Committee. In addition, we have tried to expand on the results by giving complete statistics for the Games, as much background information as a student of the Olympics will need to understand the political milieu, and in particular, we have tried to cover the controversies more completely than previous works have.

Finally, please note that students of Olympic history will not find the 1908 report or any of the early reports with ease. Copies are rare and few libraries have them. The 1908 report does show up for sale in certain auctions of Olympic memorabilia from time to time, but expect to pay at least $1,500 (American) or £1,000 (British).

The study of Olympic history has undergone a renaissance in the past decade, partly sparked by the formation of the International Society of Olympic Historians (ISOH). ISOH was formed on 5 December 1991 at a meeting at a pub called the Duke of Clarence in the Kensington section of London. Both Mallon and Buchanan were present, were founding members, and have served as officers since its inception. In particular, Ian Buchanan has been the group's only president to date.

We would like to thank the various members of ISOH, many of whom have helped us with this project. Notably, we give very special thanks to another founding member, David Wallechinsky (United States), who provided us with an unusual set of newspaper clippings he found in the archives of the British Olympic Association. This set contained clippings from many British and American papers in 1908 and was invaluable in our research.

We also give thanks to the following for helping answer specific question relating to the topic of this book: Peter Diamond (United States), Hardy Fink (Canada — Gymnastics), Josef Goehler (Germany — Gymnastics), Harry Gordon (Australia), Hubert Hamacher (Germany), Paul Jenes (Australia), Rupert Kaiser (Germany), Ove Karlsson (Sweden), Jiří Kössl (CZE), Hans Larsen (Denmark), Karl Lennartz (Germany), Alan Little (Great Britain — Tennis), John Lucas (United States), Jos Luypaers (Belgium), Bill McNulty (Canada), Giuseppe "Beppe" Odello (Italy), Ted Radcliffe (Canada), Ralf Regnitter (Germany), Jonathan Rosenthall (Great Britain), Daniel Schamps (France), Markku Siukonen (Finland), Gabriel Szabó (Hungary), Magne Teigen (Norway), Floris J. G. Van Der Merwe (RSA), Lewis Waller (Canada — Gymnastics), and Ture Widlund (Sweden).

Naturally we both give thanks to our wives, Karen Mallon and Jeanne Buchanan, for putting up with this crazy "hobby" of ours.

Bill Mallon
Durham, North Carolina
October 1998

Ian Buchanan
Burgh Next Aylsham, England
October 1998

Abbreviations and Usage Notes

General Abbreviations

A:	athletes competing	ICAAAA	Intercollegiate Association of
AAA	Amateur Athletic Association		Amateur Athletes of America
AAU	Amateur Athletic Union	kg.	kilogram(s)
AB	abandoned	km.	kilometer(s)
AC*	also competed (place not known)	ko	knockout
AE	also entered	lbs.	pounds
ASA	Amateur Swimming Association	m.	meter(s)
bh	behind	mi.	mile(s)
C:	countries competing	NCU	National Cycling Union
d.	defeated	NH	no-height
D:	date(s) of competition	NM	no mark
dec	decision	NP	not placed
DNF*	did not finish	or	Olympic Record
DNS	did not start	Q	qualified for the next round
DQ	disqualified	r	round
E	entered	S:	site of competition
est	estimate(d)	T:	time competition started
f	final	vs.	versus
F	foul	wo	walkover (won by forfeit)
F:	format of competition	WR	World Record
h	heat	yd(s).	yard(s)
IAAF	International Amateur Athletic Federation		

National Abbreviations

AUS	Australasia (Australia and New Zealand) or Australia	AUT	Austria
		BEL	Belgium

These abbreviations appear in lowercase in Appendix III.

xi

BOH	Bohemia		ITA	Italy
CAN	Canada		NED	Netherlands
DEN	Denmark		NOR	Norway
ENG	England		NZL	New Zealand
FIN	Finland		RUS	Russia
FRA	France		SAF	South Africa
GBR	Great Britain and Ireland		SCO	Scotland
GER	Germany		SUI	Switzerland
GRE	Greece		SWE	Sweden
HUN	Hungary		USA	United States
IRL	Ireland		WLS	Wales
ISL	Iceland			

Sports Abbreviations

ARC	Archery		POL	Polo
ATH	Athletics (Track & Field)		RAQ	Racquets
BOX	Boxing		ROW	Rowing & Sculling
CYC	Cycling		RUG	Rugby Union Football
DIV	Diving		SHO	Shooting
FEN	Fencing		SWI	Swimming
FSK	Figure Skating		TEN	Tennis (Lawn)
FTB	Football (Soccer)		TOW	Tug-of-War
GYM	Gymnastics		WAP	Water Polo
HOK	Hockey (Field)		WLT	Weightlifting
JDP	Jeu de Paume (Court Tennis)		WRE	Wrestling (Greco-Roman)
LAX	Lacrosse		YAC	Yachting
MTB	Motorboating			

Sources and Names

The primary source for the 1908 Olympics must be the _Official Report_, or properly, _The Fourth Olympiad: Being the Official Report of the Olympic Games of 1908 Celebrated in London Under the Patronage of His Most Gracious King Edward VII and by the Sanction of the International Olympic Committee_, edited by Theodore Andrea Cook, and published in late 1909. In all cases, we started with this report, which is the first _Official Report_ to give detailed summaries of the results.

However, after very close examination of the 1908 _Official Report_, we consider the reputation to be better than the reality. Many results are omitted, or are incorrect, or are not fully explained to any degree. What the 1908 _Official Report_ did superbly was list complete rules and regulations for all events. But its summary of the results was less than we would hope for. We hope to correct this failing herein. We used numerous sources to aid in this expansion of our understanding of the Games of the IVth Olympiad.

Sporting Life was a daily sporting newspaper which was published every day of the Olympics and gave very detailed results. In addition, after the Olympics, _Sporting Life_ published a report of the Olympic Games, giving results for most of the sports, although it was apparently published before the later autumn sports were finished. We were fortunate to have access to both of these sources, which are difficult to find. It should be noted, however, that these sources are somewhat redundant. The *Sporting Life* report, published after the Games, is taken almost verbatim from the *Sporting Life* newspaper reports and further, the *Official Report* also used these reports almost exclusively. Therefore, although it would seem that if a fact is confirmed by *Sporting Life*, *Sporting Life*'s report, and the *Official Report,* it would be irrefutable, in fact, we have often used other sources to confirm or deny facts listed in these three similar sources.

These primary sources were supplemented by a collection we refer to as "BOADW" which stands for "British Olympic Association/David Wallechinsky Collection." David Wallechinsky, an outstanding Olympic historian, found a scrapbook in the archives of the British Olympic Association which contained newspaper clippings concerning the 1908 Olympic Games. He kindly provided both of us with complete copies of this scrapbook which contains clippings from both British and American newspapers. The British papers do predominate, including *Sporting Life* as well as *The Sportsman*, another daily sporting journal. The scrapbook was an invaluable resource which we scoured multiple times for information. Our bound copies include three volumes and include 600 pages of clippings.

One source not contained in BOADW, strangely, is the British weekly sporting journal *The Field*, which we also used extensively. Other sources we checked were American, British, and Canadian newspapers, as well as specialty sporting journals, such as those devoted to cycling, tennis, rugby, football, shooting, and gymnastics. Finally, we supplemented our research by looking at Olympic reference books, especially national Olympic histories, primarily in an effort to be certain of name spellings and vital dates. All of these sources are listed in the bibliography.

We have extensively footnoted corrections and additions to other Olympic statistical works. This is not in an effort to embarrass or demean those authors, upon whose pioneering work we have relied for years. There are two main reasons for our notes. First of all, by cross-checking all our figures against others, we have been able to find many of our own mistakes. Whenever a discrepancy was found, we would then go back to all the sources to be as sure as possible that we had the correct data. Secondly, many readers will know of those other works and wonder, "But it says in this other source that the time/distance/athlete/data was something else " These footnotes simply point out to those readers that we know of that information, but feel it is incorrect, and we usually point out why and give our sources.

In athletics [track & field], the field events contain marks given both in metric and Imperial measure. First, it should be pointed out that the 1908 field event distances were definitely measured Imperially — of that we are sure. Second, we are not certain if a metric mark was also taken concurrently. Metric marks are given in the *Official Report* and *Sporting Life*, but these may be conversions. For metric conversions in all cases, we have used the *Official Report/Sporting Life* marks. Since those sources do not contain many of the marks listed Imperially in other sources, for those we have used the *International Metric Conversion Tables*, compiled by Bob Sparks (President, Association of Track & Field Statisticians) and officially approved by the International Amateur Athletic Federation. Some extrapolation was necessary from those tables in the long throws (discus, hammer, javelin) because the current tables only allow marks to the nearest even centimeter or inch.

In 1908, especially in Great Britain, it was *de rigueur* not to list first names, but to simply list the first initial of the Christian (first) name and the last name, e.g., "I. Buchanan and B. Mallon." We have tried to find full names in all cases, and for the index, this includes complete names, including any middle names. We think it is important for future researchers to be able to identify Olympic athletes as completely as possible. Many National Olympic histories have been used in this search and many members of ISOH (see above) have also edited the index as it concerns athletes from their own nations.

References

with Their Abbreviations as Cited in Text

Primary Sources from Circa 1908

AATM   *Arms and the Man*, weekly American (New York) shooting magazine.

AKTZ   *Amerikanische Turnzeitung*, weekly American (Milwaukee, Wisconsin) gymnastics (turner) magazine.

Answer   *The Olympic Games: An Answer to Mr. Francis Peabody, Jr., and "A Member of the British Olympic Committee"* by "A Member of the American Olympic Committee" ns: np, [1908–09].

AR   *The Archer's Register*, monthly British (London) archery magazine.

ARCC   Cook, Theodore Andrea. *The Olympic Games of 1908 in London: A Reply to Certain Criticisms.* London: British Olympic Council, 1908.

ASZ   *Allgemeine Sport Zeitung*, weekly Germany (Berlin) sporting magazine.

BDG   *Boston Daily Globe*, daily American (Boston) newspaper (later *Boston Globe*), 1908.

BET   *Boston Evening Transcript*, daily American (Boston) newspaper, 1908.

Blue   *The Olympic Games: Their Origin and Their Organization.* by "An Old Blue" of "The Daily Telegraph." London: Daily Telegraph, 1908.

BMP   *Birmingham Morning-Post*, daily British (Birmingham) newspaper.

BOADW   British Olympic Association/David Wallechinsky newspaper clipping files. In many cases we can identify the newspaper or magazine from which the clipping was taken. In cases where we cannot it is listed as "BOADW/source uncertain."

Burlford   Burlford, Thomas R. *American Hatred and British Folly.* London: np, 1911.

CDT   *The Chicago Daily Tribune*, daily American (Chicago) newspaper.

CRH   *Chicago Record-Herald*, daily American (Chicago) newspaper.

Cyclist   *Cyclist*, weekly British (London) cycling magazine.

Desb   Clipping files in Lord Desborough's Archives, held at Hertfordshire County Record Office, Hertfordshire, England (under D/ERv F25).

DG   *Daily Graphic*, daily British (London) newspaper.

DM   *The Daily Mirror*, daily British (London) newspaper.

DMail   *The Daily Mail*, daily British (London) newspaper.

DT   *Das Turner*, weekly German (Berlin) gymnastics (turner) magazine.

DTZ   *Deutsche Turnzeitung*, weekly German (Berlin) gymnastics (turner) magazine.

GH   *Glasgow Herald*, daily Scottish (Glasgow) newspaper.

Kirby   Kirby, Gustavus Town. *To the Inter-Collegiate Association of Amateur Athletes of Amer-
           ica: An answer to statements of the Amateur Athletic Association of Great Britain con-
           cerning the Olympic games of 1908*. New York: privately printed, 1909.

LGym   *Le Gymnaste*, weekly French (Paris) gymnastics magazine.

NYEW   *New York Evening World*, daily American (New York) newspaper.

NYH   *New York Herald*, daily American (New York) newspaper.

NYHP   *New York Herald (Paris Edition)*, daily French (Paris) newspaper published by the
           American company, this is the forerunner of the *International Herald Tribune*.

NYS   *New York Sun*, daily American (New York) newspaper.

NYT   *The New York Times*, daily American (New York) newspaper.

OR   1908 *Official Report*; the proper title is *The Fourth Olympiad: Being the Official Report
           of the Olympic Games of 1908 Celebrated in London Under the Patronage of His Most
           Gracious King Edward VII and by the Sanction of the International Olympic Com-
           mittee*, edited by Theodore Andrea Cook. London: British Olympic Association,
           1908.

Outing   *Outing Magazine*, weekly American (New York) sporting magazine.

People   *The People*, daily British (London) newspaper.

Ref   *The Referee*, weekly British (London) sporting newspaper.

SF   *The Scottish Field*, weekly Scottish (Glasgow) sporting newspaper.

SL   *The Sporting Life*, daily British (London) sporting newspaper.

SLHG   *South London Harriers Gazette*, bi-weekly journal of leading British (London) ath-
           letics club.

SLR   The Sporting Life, *Olympic Games of London. 1908. A Complete record with photo-
           graphs of winners of the Olympic Games held at the Stadium, Shepherd's Bush, London,
           July 13–25, 1908, Along with Accounts of other Olympic Events*. London: *Sporting
           Life*, 1908. This is the summary report published by *The Sporting Life* after the
           Olympic Games. *The Sporting Life* also published a daily sporting newspaper dur-
           ing the Olympics, which we also consulted — our versions were contained in
           BOADW (see above) — see that paper listed above as SL.

SM   *The Sportsman*, daily British (London) sporting newspaper.

SMR   *The Sportsmen's Review*, weekly American (Cincinatti, Ohio) shooting journal.

STBS   *Shooting Times and British Sportsman*, weekly British (London) shooting journal.

TF   *The Field*. Weekly British (London) sporting newspaper.

Times   *The Times*. Daily British (London) newspaper.

TRS   *The Rifle Shot*, monthly British (London) shooting magazine.

YBM   *The Yachting and Boating Monthly*, monthly British (London) sailing magazine.

YM   *The Yachtsman*, monthly British (London) sailing magazine.

YW   *Yachting World*, weekly British (London) sailing magazine.

Olympic and Sporting Historical and Statistical Works after 1908

Bailey   Bailey, Steve. "A Noble Ally and Olympic Disciple: The Reverend Robert S. de
           Courcy Laffan, Coubertin's 'Man' in England," *Olympika*, VI: 51–64, 1997.

Barcs   Barcs, Sándor. *The Modern Olympics Story*. Budapest: Corvina Press, 1964.

British   Matthews, Peter and Buchanan, Ian. *Guinness All-Time Greats of British and Irish
           Sport*. London: Guinness, 1995.

CA3992   McNulty, Bill and Radcliffe, Ted. *Canadian Athletics 1839–1992*. ns: np, 1992.

Charter   International Olympic Committee. *Olympic Charter*. 1997 edition. Lausanne: IOC, 1997.

Coates   Coates, James R., Jr. "London 1908: The Games of the IVth Olympiad," In: *Historical Dictionary of the Modern Olympic Movement*, Press, 1996.

Cornfield   Cornfield, Susan. *The Queen's Prize: The Story of the National Rifle Association*. London: National Rifle Association, 1987.

Coub1   Coubertin, Pierre de. *Une Campagne de vingt-et-un ans (1887–1908)*. Paris: Librairie de l'Education Physique, 1909.

Coub2   Coubertin, Pierre de. *Mémoires olympiques*. Lausanne: Bureau International de Pédagogie Sportive, 1931. Trans. by Geoffrey de Navacelle, published in 1979.

DW   Wallechinsky, David. *The Complete Book of the Olympics*. Fourth edition. New York: Little, Brown, and Company, 1996.

Dyreson   Dyreson, Mark Sanford. *America's Athletic Missionaries: The Olympic Games and the Creation of a National Culture, 1896–1936*. Ph.D. Thesis, University of Arizona, 1989.

EK   Kamper, Erich. *Enzyklopädie der olympischen Spiele*. Dortmund: Harenberg, 1972. Parallel texts in German, French, and English. American edition issued as *Encyclopaedia of the Olympic Games* by McGraw-Hill (New York) in 1972.

EzM   zur Megede, Ekkehard. *Die olympische Leichtathletik*. Bands 1-3. Darmstadt: Justus von Liebig Verlag, 1984.

FJGVDM   Van Der Merwe, Floris J. G. "Formation of the South African National Olympic Association," In: *The Olympic Games Through the Ages: Greek Antiquity and its Impact on Modern Sport*. R. Renson, M. Lämmer, J. Riordan, D. Chassiotis, eds. Athens: Hellenic Sports Research Institute, 1991. pp. 251–259.

FW   Wasner, Fritz. *Olympia-Lexikon*. Bielefeld, Germany: Verlag E. Gunglach Aktiengesellschaft, 1939.

Gillmeister   Gillmeister, Heiner. *Olympisches Tennis. Die Geschichte der olympischen Tennisturniere (1896–1992)*. Sankt Augustin, Germany: Academia Verlag, 1993.

Grasso   Grasso, John. *Olympic Games Boxing Record Book*. Guilford, New York: International Boxing Research Organization, 1984.

Guiney   Guiney, David. *Ireland's Olympic Heroes*, Dublin: David Roderick, 1969.

Gynn   Gynn, Roger. *The Guinness Book of the Marathon*. London: Guinness, 1984.

Henry   Henry, Bill. *An Approved History of the Olympic Games*. First edition. New York: G. P. Putnam, 1948.

H/A   Hugman, Barry J. and Peter Arnold. *The Olympic Games: Complete Track & Field Results 1896–1988*. London: The Arena Press, 1988.

IFFHS   "Die olympischen Fußball-Turniere (1900–1920)," In: *IFFHS Fußball-Weltzeitschrift*, 16: 4-5 (January/June 1989): 4–5.

JAL   Lucas, John A. *The Modern Olympic Games*. South Brunswick, New Jersey: A. S. Barnes, 1980.

Johnson   Johnson, William Oscar. *All That Glitters is Not Gold*. New York: Putnam, 1972.

KLWT   Lennartz, Karl and Teutenberg, Walter. *Die Olympischen Spiele 1906 in Athen*. Kassel: Kasseler Sportverlag, 1992.

Kossl   Kössl, Jiří. "Origin and Development of the Czech and Czechoslovak Olympic Committee," In: *Citius, Altius, Fortius*, 2(3) (Autumn 1994): 11–26.

Lovesey   Lovesey, Peter. *The Official Centenary History of the AAA: Amateur Athletic Association*. Enfield, Middlesex: Guinness, 1979.

Lyberg   Lyberg, Wolf. *The History of the IOC Sessions. I. 1894–1939*. Lausanne: International Olympic Committee, October 1994.

Matthews   Matthews, George. "The Controversial Olympic Games of 1908 as Viewed by the *New York Times* and the *Times* of London," *J Sport History*, 7(2) (Summer 1980): 40–53.

MRH   Howell, Max and Reet. *The Olympic Movement Restored: The 1908 Games*. Québec (CAN): np, 1976.

Müller   Müller, Norbert. *One Hundred Years of Olympic Congresses: 1894–1994*. Lausanne: International Olympic Committee, 1994.

Nurmberg   Nurmberg, Reet. "A History of Competitive Gymnastics in Canada," Masters Thesis, University of Edmonton (Alberta, Canada).

Olympiadebogen   Andersen, Peder Christian and Hansen, Vagn. *Olympiadebogen. De Olympiske Lege 1896–1948*. København: np, 1948.

OS   Crossman, Colonel Jim. *Olympic Shooting*. Washington: National Rifle Association, 1978.

OSVK   Kluge, Volker. *Olympische Sommerspiele. Die Chronik I: Athen 1896–Berlin 1936*. Berlin: Sport Verlag, 1997.

OTAF   *Olympic Track and Field*. Editors of *Track & Field News*. Los Altos, Calif: Tafnews Press, 1979.

Phillips   Phillips, Bob. *100 Years of the Olympic Marathon*. London: National Union of Track Statisticians, 1996.

POE   Associated Press and Grolier. *Pursuit of Excellence: The Olympic Story*. New York: Franklin Watts, 1979.

Polley   Polley, Martin. "'No business of ours'?: The Foreign Office and the Olympic games, 1896–1914," *Int J History Sport*, 13(2): (August 1996): 96–113.

Schaap   Schaap, Richard. *An Illustrated History of the Olympics*. New York: Knopf, 1963.

Scot   Scot, Alan. "Gångsport i Olympiska Spel," In: *SOF-Bulletinen*, 34 (July 1997).

SG   Greenberg, Stan. *The Guinness Olympics Fact Book*. Third edition. Enfield, Middlesex, England: Guinness, 1983.

Sheridan   Sheridan, Michael. *Good Reasons: 100 Years of Olympic Marathon Races*. Somerset, England: author, 1996.

Skating   Terták, E., Wright, B., Teigen, M., and Markland, W. L., eds. *Skating in the Olympic Games 1908–1994*. Davis Platz, Switzerland: International Skating Union, 1994.

Skating2   International Skating Union. *The Olympic Games. Results in Figure Skating 1908, 1920, 1924–1968. Results in Speed Skating 1924–1968*. Davos Platz, Switzerland: International Skating Union, [1972].

Tait   Tait, Robin. *The Politicization of the Modern Olympic Games*. Ph.D. Thesis, University of Oregon, 1984.

TMF   Martin, David E., Gynn, Richard W. H. *The Marathon Footrace*. Champaign, Ill., USA: C. C. Thomas, 1979.

VK   Kluge, Volker. *Die olympischen Spiele von 1896 bis 1980*. Berlin: Sportverlag, 1981.

Webster   Webster, Frederick A. M. *The Evolution of the Olympic Games 1829 B.C.–1914 A.D.* London: Heath, Cranton & Ouseley, [1914?].

Weyand   Weyand, Alexander. *The Olympic Pageant*. New York: Macmillan, 1952.

WW   Maritchev, Gennadi. *Who Is Who at the Summer Olympics: 1896–1992*. Riga: Demarko Sport Publishing, 1996.

Wright   Wright, Benjamin T. *Skating Around the World 1892–1952. The One Hundredth Anniversary History of the International Skating Union*. Davos Platz Switzerland: International Skating Union, May 1992.

National Olympic Histories

Bijkerk, Ton. and Paauw, Ruud. *Gouden Boek van de Nederlandse Olympiers.* Haarlem: Uitgeverij de Vrieseborch, 1996.

Buchanan, Ian. *British Olympians: A Hundred Years of Gold Medallists.* London: Guinness, 1991.

Charpentier, Henri. *La Grande Histoire des médaillés olympiques français de 1896 à 1988.* Paris: Editions Robert Laffont, 1993.

Colasante, Gianfranco. *La nascita del Movimento Olimpico in Italia. 1894–1914.* Rome: CONI, 1996.

Cosentino, Frank and Leyshon, Glynn. *Olympic Gold: Canadian Winners of the Summer Games.* Toronto: Holt, Rinehart, and Winston, 1975.

Glanell, Tomas; Huldtén, Gösta, et al., editors. *Sverige och OS.* Stockholm: Brunnhages Förlag, 1987.

Gordon, Harry. *Australia and the Olympic Games.* St. Lucia, Queensland: University of Queensland Press, 1994.

Guiney, David. *Gold, Silver, Bronze.* Dublin: Sportsworld, *ca* 1991.

Howell, Reet, and Howell, Max. *Aussie Gold: The Story of Australia at the Olympics.* South Melbourne: Brooks Waterloo, 1988.

Hungarian Olympic Committee. *Az Olimpiai Játékokon Indult Magyar Versenyzők Névsora 1896–1980.*

Klír M.; Kössl J. Martínkovi, A. M. *Almanach Ceskoslovenskych Olympioniku.* Praha: 1987.

Koryürek, Cüneyt E. *Atina Atlanta 1896–1996: 28 Asrlk Olimpiyadlar Tarihi.* Istanbul: Arcelik Gururla Sunar, 1996.

Kristensen, Preben, and Larsen, Hans Agersnap. *De Olympiske. Biografi af danske OL-deltagere 1896–1996.* København: Danmarks Idræts-Forbund, 1996.

Lester, Gary. *Australians at the Olympics: A Definitive History.* Sydney: Lester-Townsend Publishing, 1984.

Mallon, Bill, and Buchanan, Ian. *Quest for Gold: The Encyclopaedia of American Olympians.* New York: Leisure, 1984.

Mező, Ferenc. *Golden Book of Hungarian Olympic Champions/Livre d'or des champions olympiques hongrois.* Budapest: Sport Lap. És Könyvkiadö, 1955. Parallel texts in English and French.

Naughton, Lindie and Watterson, Johnny. *Irish Olympians.* Dublin: Blackwater Press, 1992.

"Norske deltakere i olympiske leker 1900–1980," In: *Norges Olympiske Komité 1977–80: XIII vinterleker Lake Placid 1980— XXII sommerleker Moskva 1980.* Aage Møst, editor. Oslo: Norges Olympiske Komité, 1980.

Palenski, Ron and Maddaford, Terry. *The Pride and Drama of New Zealanders at Olympic & Commonwealth Games: The Games.* Auckland: MOA Publications, 1983.

Pellissard-Darrigrand, Nicole. *La Galaxie Olympique.* Paris: J. & D. Editions, 1997.

Pettersson, Ulf, editor. *1896–1980 Guldboken om alla våra Olympiamästare.* Stockholm: Brunnhages Förlag, 1980.

Roxborough, Henry. *Canada at the Olympics.* Third edition. Toronto: Ryerson Press, 1975.

Tarasouleas, At[hanassios]. *Helliniki simmetokhi stis Sinkhrones olympiades.* [transliterated title] Athens: author, 1990.

"Turkey and Olympism," In: *Olympic Review*, 89-90 (March-April 1975): 117–128.

Other Sources

Hamm, Charles, ed. *Irving Berlin. Early Songs. I. 1907–1911*. Volume 2, Part I of *Music of the United States of America*, Richard Crawford, editor-in-chief; Jeffrey Magee, executive editor. Madison, Wisconsin: A-R Editions, 1994.

Kidd, Bruce. *Tom Longboat*. Richmond Hill, Ontario: Fitzhenry & Whiteside, 1992.

Sparks, Bob. *International Metric Conversion Tables*. Second ed. London: Arena Publications Limited, 1979.

1908 Olympic Games — Background

Early History of the British Influence on the Modern Olympic Games

At the beginning of the twentieth century, Great Britain was the most powerful nation in the world. A quarter of the world's land mass and a quarter of the world's population owed allegiance to the Union Jack, the British navy was twice the size of the next largest fleet and commercial prosperity had been assured by the phenomenon of the Industrial Revolution.

Occasional setbacks such as the British defeat by the guerrilla tactics of an amateur army of Dutch settlers in the Boer War (1899–1902) could be taken in their stride but increasing German power in Europe was of more concern. After France had suffered a humiliating defeat in the Franco-Prussian war (1870–71), the British saw them as natural allies in curbing German influence in Europe. The Anglo-French alliance prospered and in 1904 the *entente cordiale*, which gave the British and the French jurisdiction over Egypt and Morocco respectively, was signed. In 1905 the two countries jointly began planning a vast trade fair in London. Only Britain and France and their colonies were to be permitted as exhibitors and the Franco-British Exhibition was to play a major role in the staging of the 1908 Olympic Games.

The British had a deep-rooted interest in the Olympic Games and from as early as the fifteenth century many festivals describing themselves as "Olympic" or "Olympian" were staged around the country. The most significant attempt at revival of the ancient Olympic Games, prior to Baron de Coubertin's efforts, came in England in the form of the Much Wenlock Olympian Games. Much Wenlock is a small town in Shropshire, England, 12 miles south of Shrewsbury and 40 miles west of Birmingham. On 22 October 1850, these Games were held for the first time. They were the brainchild of the British sports enthusiast, Dr. William Penny Brookes (1809–1895).

The Games were only national in nature and the events were more those of a British medieval country fair enriched by modern athletic sports disciplines. The original events in 1850 consisted of cricket, 14-a-side football, high and long jumping, quoits, a hopping race, and a running race. However, several athletic events were added in the next few years. The most popular event became tilting-at-the-ring, which was first held in 1858. The competitors, dressed in medieval costumes, rode horses, and used lances to spear a small ring, suspended from a bar over the course.

The Much Wenlock Olympian Games, altogether 45 in number up to 1895, achieved their high point in the 1860s and 1870s. In those years, representatives of the German Gymnastic Society (which was based in London) competed regularly. In 1860, 1861, 1862, and 1864, Brookes also organized the Shropshire Olympian Games on a regional level in, respectively, Much Wenlock, Wellington, Much Wenlock, and Shrewsbury. These were followed by the other "Olympian" Games organized by the National Olympic Association: 1866 (London), 1867 (Birmingham), 1868 (Wellington), 1874 (Much Wenlock), 1877 (Shrewsbury), and 1883 (Hadley).

The Much Wenlock Olympian Games were held more sporadically after Brookes' death in 1895, but are still held today, sponsored by the Much Wenlock Olympian Society, which celebrated the one hundredth Much Wenlock Olympian Games in 1986. The Much Wenlock Olympian Games are important in the history of Olympic revivals because of their influence on Pierre de Coubertin. Coubertin knew of Brookes' efforts and visited the Much Wenlock Olympian Games as a guest of honor in October 1890, and in 1891, he donated a gold medal which was given to the winner of tilting-at-the-ring.

Dr. William Penny Brookes was educated at various schools in Shropshire. He began his study of medicine at Guy's and St. Thomas's Hospitals in London in about 1827, but finished his studies in Paris and Padua, returning to Much Wenlock in 1831 to carry on the general practice of medicine which his father had started. He founded the National Olympian Association in 1865, the forerunner of the British Olympic Association. Brookes was an invited dignitary to Coubertin's Sorbonne Congress of 1894 which founded the Modern Olympic Games, but was unable to attend because of illness. However, in 1881, William Penny Brookes was the first person to propose an International Olympic Festival to be staged in Athens.

In more modern times, both Charles Herbert and Lord Ampthill were founding members of the International Olympic Committee (IOC) and, after hosting the 1904 IOC Session in London, the British finally established their interest in Olympic matters on a more formal basis. At a meeting at the Houses of Parliament on 24 May 1905, the British Olympic Association (BOA) was formed[1]* but the founding members had no way of knowing that within one year they would assume the responsibility of organizing the 1908 Olympic Games. The circumstances which brought about this unexpected turn of events are unique in the history of the Games.

Choice of the Host City for the 1908 Olympic Games

At the 1904 Session of the IOC held in London, the Games of the IVth Olympiad were awarded to Rome but due to unforeseen circumstances, more than 50 years would pass before Italy actually hosted the Games. On 4 April 1906, Mount Vesuvius, near Naples, erupted, devastating the surrounding area; the reason usually given for Rome's withdrawal as host for the 1908 Games is that the Italian government felt that all available funds should be used to provide relief for the victims. This was only a small part of the story.

Baron de Coubertin was a strong advocate for the 1908 Games going to Rome and was supported by such luminaries as Pope Pius X, King Victor Emanuel III and, not surprisingly, the mayor of Rome. Their main opponent was Prime Minister Giovanni Gioletti, who held the purse strings for many new government projects, such as the building of the Simplon Tunnel between Switzerland and Italy, the construction of the aqueduct in the Puglia region and land reclamation projects in many parts of the country. It was clear that the Italian Government simply could not afford to subsidize the Games and, under pressure from Rome's rival cities of Milan and Turin, Prime Minister Gioletti decided to withhold the promised Government funds and effectively ended Rome's hopes of staging the 1908 Games.[2]

In an effort to salvage some of his country's lost prestige the Italian IOC member, Count Eugenio Brunetta d'Usseaux, advised the IOC members at the Intercalated Olympic Games at Athens in 1906 that because of the eruption of Mount Vesuvius, which could not possibly have been foreseen, Rome no longer had the financial resources to honor its commitment. In reality, the decision had been made some time before the volcanic eruption. Interestingly, Baron de Coubertin must have known the true reason for the withdrawal as, in a circular letter to IOC members dated 9 December 1906, he mysteriously referred to "certain specific difficulties we encountered in Rome and which we had to keep secret."[3] Since the disaster at Mount Vesuvius had received worldwide press coverage, de Coubertin can hardly have considered this particular event to be secret.

Faced with the dilemma of finding an alternative host city with both the facilities and inclination to stage the Olympics in only two years, the IOC acted with commendable speed. They immediately approached Lord Desborough, who was in Athens as a British member of the IOC and as a competitor in the épée team event, in which he won a silver medal. Desborough sounded out King Edward VII, who was also in Athens for the Games, and he had the added advantage of being able to discuss the matter in greater depth with his fellow members of the fencing team who were all staying aboard Lord Howard de Walden's private yacht, the *SS Branwen*, which was anchored in the Bay of Athens for the period of the Games.

The fencers on board the *Branwen* were Charles Newton-Robinson and Theodore Cook, both members of the Council of the British Olympic Association, and Lord Howard de Walden, a future President of the Amateur Fencing Association, together with two future Vice-Presidents of the Association, Sir Cosmo Duff-Gordon and Edgar Seligman.[4]

The consensus of opinion from this experienced group was that the IOC invitation for London to host the 1908 Games should be accepted, provided support from the governing bodies of British sport was forthcoming. From his earlier conversations, Desborough knew that the King shared this view and the IOC was advised accordingly. On his return to London, Desborough put the matter of hosting the 1908 Games before the British Olympic Association (BOA). It was agreed that a letter should be sent to the governing bodies of all the major sports in the United Kingdom and when the replies were in favor of hosting the Games, a British Olympic Council was formed, within the BOA, whose sole responsibility was the organization of the 1908 Olympic Games. On 19 November 1906, a letter was sent to the IOC advising them that London was prepared to take over the Games.

The Olympic Movement is fortunate that a man of the calibre of William Henry Grenfell, Baron Desborough of Taplow, K.C.V.O. was available at that time. An Olympic fencer, he both ran and rowed for Oxford against Cambridge University, stroked an eight across the English Channel, swam across Niagara twice, and climbed the Matterhorn three times by different routes. He was also a renowned big game hunter in India and the Rockies, and was a successful tarpon fisherman off the coast of Florida. There were few sporting pursuits at which he did not excel. He was elected a Member of Parliament at the age of 25, was offered the governor-generalship of Canada, but declined, and at one time he served on as many as 115 sporting and civic committees. A tall, imposing man whose austere appearance hid a generous character, he sent flowers to Dorando Pietri wishing him a speedy recovery after his marathon ordeal and, after the gold medals of the American shooting team had been stolen, he personally paid for them to be replaced. By any standards his achievements were phenomenal and no man was better qualified, or better placed in society, to further the cause of Olympism in Britain.

Lord Desborough brought an intellectual authority to the task and gathered an influential, efficient, and enthusiastic Organizing Committee around him. With his fellow IOC member, the Rev. Robert Stuart de Courcy Laffan, acting as General Secretary and Captain F. Whitworth Jones as Assistant Secretary, work began immediately. The contribution of the Reverend de Courcy Laffan to the work of the British Olympic Council was inestimable, and has recently been well documented by Steve Bailey in *Olympika*.[5] Only eight days after the agreement to stage the Olympics in London a letter appeared in the British press giving a broad outline of the arrangements for the Games.

The Franco-British Exhibition and the White City Stadium

Although such splendid and well-established venues as Wimbledon for tennis, Bisley for shooting, and Henley for rowing were immediately available, the major problem which faced the Organizing Committee was the lack of a suitable main stadium and it had already been made clear that no government funds would be made available for such a project.

By a fortunate coincidence the vast Franco-British Exhibition was planned for London in the summer of 1908 and the British Olympic Association was able to come to a highly satisfactory arrangement with organizers. The Franco-British Exhibition opened on 14 May 1908, with its express purpose being to further the feeling of *entente cordiale*. At the time, French relationships with the Germans were at a low ebb and the Exhibition was designed to build and strengthen a new trading partnership between France and Great Britain.

Planning for the Exhibition had begun in 1905. It was based on a 140-acre site in West London called Shepherd's Bush, and was laid out in a cross pattern. The prevailing architectural pattern was brilliant white buildings, which lent the exhibition site its nickname of the "White City." Only exhibitors from France, Britain, and their respective colonies were allowed to participate and it was planned that the Exhibition should be far more than just a "trade fair."

Displays were set amid gardens with lakes and fountains and exhibitors were keen to display the indigenous characteristics of their country and not just their wares. The size of the delegations was significant and on Saturday, 9 May, nearly 150 men, women, and children, natives of India and Ceylon, arrived at the Ceylon village with a large contingent of elephants, dromedaries, antelopes, bears, and monkeys. Among the party was a dwarf from Colombo named Maricar who stood only 3' 6" (1.06 meters) tall, and who was said to have a great reputation as a doctor. With the Edwardian macabre fascination for physical freaks he proved a great attraction. The Franco-British Exhibition lasted until 31 October 1908, with a total attendance of 8.4 million spectators and receipts of over £420,000. Contemporary opinion was that the event was an outstanding success.[6]

The Olympic Organizing Committee pulled off a notable coup when they persuaded the Exhibition authorities to build an entire stadium complete with running and cycling tracks, swimming pool, dressing rooms, and spectator accommodations. Not only was the Exhibition to pay for all this, at a cost of "not less than £44,000," they were also to make a grant of £2,000 towards the preliminary costs of the British Olympic Association. In return the Exhibition was to receive 75 percent of the gate receipts. This remarkably beneficial contract — from an Olympic viewpoint — was signed by both parties on 14 January 1907. Some sources suggest that the actual cost of construction of the Shepherd's Bush facilities subsequently rose to £220,000 and that the grant made to the British Olympic Association was increased to £20,000.

The next problem to be faced was the raising of funds for the day-to-day running expenses of the Games.[7] A public appeal was duly launched, but by the end of June only £2,840 had been raised from 200 subscribers, most of them personal friends of Desborough's. With just two weeks to go before the start of the Games a further £10,000 was still urgently needed, mainly to provide suitable hospitality for the visiting competitors and officials. Lord Northcliffe, the owner of the *Daily Mail*, was approached and at a meeting with Lord Desborough he reluctantly agreed that his newspaper group would sponsor a final appeal. The response was phenomenal and donations poured in from all corners of Britain and from abroad. The Prince of Wales, the Maharajah of Cooch Behar, and the American millionaire, Cornelius Vanderbilt all sent donations. The professional strongman, Eugen Sandow, gave £1,500, the French Government sent £680, the classical dancer Maud Allan passed on the proceeds of a special matinee performance, and hundreds of donations of just a few pence came from the readers of Lord Northcliffe's newspapers. In little more than one week over £12,000 had been subscribed and the newspapers had to beg their readers not to send any more money. To the total donations of almost £16,000 the organizers could add £6,000 as their share of the gate receipts. Out of a total sum of £15,000 for expenses, the £5,300 spent on entertainment and hospitality was the largest single item and the British Olympic Association finished with a profit of more than £6,000. The Franco-British Exhibition was not so fortunate and their only return on a substantial capital outlay was just £18,000 as their share of the gate receipts. The largest single individual contribution came from well-known strongman/bodybuilder Sandow, with his £1,500.

The Exhibition authorities were as good as their word and duly subsidized the construction of what was then the finest stadium in the world. The main features of the impressive new facility were a cinder running track of three laps to the mile (586.67 yds. [536.44 m.]), a banked concrete cycling track of 660 yards (603.5 meters), and a swimming pool 100 meters in length, twice the size of the standard modern Olympic pool. A special tower, 55 feet (16.76 meters) in height, which could be lowered below the water when not in use, was built for the high diving event. There was also room inside the running track for a full-sized pitch on which the soccer (association football), hockey (field), rugby football, and lacrosse matches were played; platforms for wrestling and gymnastics were erected; and the archery competitions were held in the grass infield. The stadium, which became known as the White City because of the white plaster buildings in the adjoining Exhibition, was years ahead of its time and was used as a model for the stadium which was built in Berlin for the ill-fated 1916 Olympic Games. A unique feature of the London stadium was that spectators could watch athletics, cycling, gymnastics, swimming and wrestling all at the same time.

Ten miles of seating provided accommodation for 63,000 spectators in the grandstands with standing room for another 30,000 and everything was built with miraculous speed. The first foundation was laid by Lord and Lady Desborough on 2 August 1907, and work began under the supervision of Charles Perry, the London Athletic Club groundsman at Stamford Bridge; Perry had not only laid down the track at Athens in 1896 but also took charge at Stockholm in 1912 and Antwerp in 1920 and thus claimed the unique record of being responsible for four Olympic running tracks.

In addition to the Royal Box, five other boxes were placed in a prime position. The Franco-British Exhibition, the International Olympic Committee and the British Olympic Committee each had their own box as did the Comité d'Honneur which was made up of three representatives from each competing country. Alongside these privileged viewing areas was the press box and a separate area for the judges, both of which were open to the elements.

The more affluent and socially prominent spectators became members of the Imperial Sports Club which had been founded in February 1908 and which boasted a fine clubhouse, with direct access to the stadium, within the Exhibition grounds. With two large dining rooms, drawing, smoking, and waiting rooms, all of which were surrounded by a sheltered terrace, the clubhouse provided the privileged membership with everything they needed to feel at home and it was an ideal venue for the IOC to hold their meetings.

The area underneath the banked seating for spectators was fully utilized. There were 14 large dressing rooms for upwards of 3,000 competitors, separate rooms for the police and ambulance services and five temperance restaurants. According to the plans of the stadium there were no refreshment facilities for those spectators who were not of a temperate persuasion. Surrounding the whole area at ground level were 167 stands for the Sports Exhibition which was an appropriate adjunct to the main Franco-British Exhibition. This area, known as the Sportsmen's Parade, was 5,000 feet (1,500 meters) in length, and exhibits were divided into thirteen categories: angling & fishing, archery, athletics, cycling, fencing, games, gymnastics & physical culture, life saving, riding, rowing, shooting, swimming, and touring.

On 14 May 1908, less than one year after the first stone had been laid, the Franco-British Exhibition was formally opened by the Prince and Princess of Wales and on the same day, with Lord Desborough and other members of the Organizing Committee drawn up in front of the Royal Box, the Royal couple dedicated the adjoining stadium to International Sport. Before the Games began, ten meetings were held in the stadium, including the British championships for athletics, cycling, and swimming. These served mainly as rehearsals for the Games although the international fly and bait casting tournament held in the swimming pool on 9–10 July could hardly be considered as a rehearsal.

After the Games, Britain took a well deserved rest from Olympism and one of the tragedies of the reaction was that the magnificent stadium fell into disuse. The surrounding Exhibition buildings were demolished; the seating capacity of the sporting arena was reduced but no major meetings were held there for many years. In 1927 the newly formed Greyhound Racing Association took over the stadium and in 1932 a 440 yard cinder track replaced the old one-third of a mile circuit and the White City became the center of British athletics. Mindful of the history of the White City, the Greyhound Racing Association staged a "Dorando Marathon" for dogs each year and after the stadium closed the event was moved to the Wimbledon dog track where it is still an annual event. Apart from greyhound racing, such sports as speedway, boxing, soccer (association football), rugby football, American football, show jumping, and even cheetah racing were staged at the White City, and American evangelist Billy Graham once addressed a crowd of 65,000 in the stadium.

In 1971 the Amateur Athletic Association moved their championships to a new athletics center at Crystal Palace and this finally marked the end of what was once the finest stadium in the world. The last event at the White City Stadium was a greyhound race held at 10:15 P.M. (2215) on 22 September 1984, which was won by the blue brindle bitch Hastings Girl. Demolition work on the stadium began a few days later. The site is now the headquarters of BBC television and no trace of the stadium remains although, ironically, television films of the 1908 Games are still occasionally transmitted from the site.

The Olympic Program and Early Plans

In the area of organization, the 1908 Olympics were seminal Games. From an entry list of 2,666, the actual number of competitors from 21 countries was 2,022 (1,978 men; 44 women) and no organized sports gathering had ever before been faced with such large numbers of overseas visitors. The committee of the London Games did not have the experience of any comparable celebration on which to base their plans and, under the circumstances, they showed superb organizational skills from which many future Games were to benefit.

At their session at the Hague in 1907 the IOC gave their general approval to the arrangements being made by the British organizers and various specific points were resolved. The design of the medals to be awarded was left to the absolute discretion of the British committee, it was agreed that the British colonies should have separate representation both at the Games and on the IOC and, significantly, that the judges at the Games should be British. A Greek motion that an International Jury of Appeal should be appointed was not carried.

A provisional program, based on the 1906 Games, was approved during the Hague session although some events originally scheduled to form part of the London Games were never held. Notable among these sports were motor racing, flying machines (including models), golf, and military (horse) riding.

An individual and team event was planned for golf in early June, with play to be at three leading courses in Kent, but this failed to materialize. The matter of the inclusion of military riding was deferred pending a report from the Swedish IOC member, Count Clarence von Rosen. Evidently, the report was not favorable as no equestrian events were held in 1908. Conversely, it should be noted that boxing was not one of the original sports but eventually found its way into the Olympic program. There was also talk of including cricket and bandy in the program but nothing came of these preliminary suggestions.

The organizing committee was also asked to promote competitions for architecture, literature, music, painting, and sculpture and although these events were never held, the rules which had been drawn up were used as the basis for the arts competitions at Stockholm in 1912.

The organizers, with the approval of the IOC, decided to stage the Games in two parts. The Summer Games, including the major part of the program, were to begin with the official Opening Ceremony on 13 July while the Autumn or Winter Games comprising association football (soccer), rugby football, hockey, lacrosse, figure skating, and, rather surprisingly, boxing, were held in October. This convenient division does, however, overlook the fact that a number of events had been held much earlier in the year. The 1908 Olympic competitions actually began on 27 April with the racquets tournament and then the jeu de paume (real tennis), covered court tennis, and polo events were all held before the Games were officially declared open in July.

Admission prices in the stadium ranged from sixpence to one guinea with the cost of admission being doubled for the Opening Ceremony. This tariff was generally considered to be too high for the average spectator and this factor, allied with the abysmal weather, resulted in some very disappointing audiences. On Thursday, 16 July, a cold rainy day when a not particularly attractive program was offered, it is estimated that there were no more than 4,000 people in the vast stadium. The press urged the organizers to reduce prices and the President of the City of London Athletic Association, Mr. George Pragnell, explained to Lord Desborough that his members, who were essentially "working class," not only found the prices beyond their means but because of their work commitments they could not get to the stadium during the day. They therefore asked that the prime events be held in the evening. They had no success with their second request but the organizers eventually bowed to the growing pressure and reduced most admission prices by half. By Saturday (18 July), although the weather was still overcast, it had stopped raining, prices had been reduced, and with the presence of the Queen the number of spectators rose spectacularly to 45,000. Attendance figures remained satisfactory throughout the second week and on the day of the marathon every ticket was sold and with £10 being offered for a seat, no matter where it was placed, there was a brisk trade in black market tickets outside the stadium.

With Olympic Villages still a thing of the future, the problem of accommodating almost 1,500 competitors from overseas and their accompanying officials was immense. Hundreds of booklets listing recommended small hotels and boarding houses were sent to governing bodies and competitors overseas and the overall arrangements were entrusted to the Polytechnic Institute. Most countries found the arrangements quite acceptable but the Americans chose to stay in the coastal town of Brighton, 53 miles south of London, and travel to the stadium daily.

Large numbers of copies of the rules and regulations for the various sports were printed in the English, German and French language and after they had been approved by the IOC they were dispatched around the world.

An extensive program of hospitality was arranged for visiting competitors and officials and there was a special religious service at St. Paul's Cathedral on Sunday, 19 July. It was here that the Bishop of Central Pennsylvania, Ethelbert Talbot, preached "that the Games themselves are better than the race and the prize." These words, slightly adapted, are often erroneously attributed to Baron de Coubertin and form the basis for the Olympic Creed.

The Opening Ceremony

With little more than one week to go before the opening of the Games King Edward VII finally consented to appear at the Opening Ceremony and the stage was set for a grand State occasion. Traveling by horse-drawn carriage from Buckingham Palace, the King and Queen entered the stadium at 3:49 P.M.[8] on Monday, 13 July. The royal children were in attendance and many members of the royal households of Europe were in the party together with numerous noblemen, statesmen, and high ranking officers from the armed forces. Also present were the ambassadors and representatives of all the competing countries together with other senior members of the diplomatic corps. The IOC members were presented to His Majesty by Baron de Coubertin.

After a fanfare from the trumpeters of the Life guards, who were stationed on the wrestling stage, Lord Desborough bowed to the King, and asked him, "Will your Majesty graciously declare the fourth Olympiad open?" With the words "I declare the Olympic Games of London open," the King began two weeks of competition and controversy in the stadium.

The band of the Grenadier guards then played the national anthem and the standard bearers of the teams, who were lined up in the center of the stadium, lowered their national ensigns in salute. The 18 nations then marched in a parade around the stadium and again saluted the King as they passed the royal box.

The Continental teams marched in alphabetical order with Austria leading the file and these were followed by the British Empire nations — Australasia, Canada, and South Africa, with Great Britain, as the host country, bringing up the rear. All teams, except for Finland, were headed by a standard bearer carrying their national flag. The Finns, still considered a part of Russia, were refused permission by the Russian officials to march under the Finnish flag, and they refused to march under the Russian flag, preferring to join the parade with only a standard bearer and no flag. The Games had started badly for the Finns and they were lucky to make the Opening Ceremony at all after the boat bringing them to England was stranded off the port of Hull with a defective boiler.

The Opening Ceremony was marred by several controversies involving the flags of the nations, including the problem with Finland and Russia. When lined up in the center field and on passing the royal box, all teams, with the notable exception of the Americans, observed the protocol of dipping their flag as a salute to the King. Although this is now one of the better-known stories from the Games the incident was never widely reported in the British press at the time even though the Americans failed to make the salute that was expected of them on *two* separate occasions. Due to an embarrassing administrative error, the flags of Sweden and the United States were not flown during the Opening Ceremony and, although the matter was quickly rectified, it got things off to a bad start particularly as far as the Americans were concerned. Matters were not helped by the fact that the flags of China and Japan, who were not even taking part in the Games, were flying in their appointed places. In charge of the arrangements for the display of national standards in the stadium was Mr. Imre Kiralfy, the Director-General of the Franco-British Exhibition, who had a close affiliation with America after spending some years in New York where three of his sons were born. All three became United States citizens and one son, Edgar, was actually a sprinter on the 1908 U.S. Olympic team. It seems inconceivable that a man with such strong American connections would deliberately arrange for the Stars and Stripes not to be flown.

The Games of the IVth Olympiad — Glory and Controversy

After the ceremonies, the program began with the heats of the 1,500 meters track race, the heats of the men's 400 meters freestyle swimming race, and the tandem cycling event held on the opening day. Interspersed among these competitions were diving and gymnastic displays and a busy first day in the stadium closed with an exhibition bicycle polo match in which the Irish Bicycle Polo Association beat the Deutscher Radfahrerbund from Germany by three goals to one.

From 13 to 25 July, the main portion of the Olympic Games was conducted at the White City Stadium. The Games were marred by controversies and protests, mainly involving the Americans protesting against the behavior of the British officials, although no nations were immune to the contagion and protests from many countries were made. The greatest controversies occurred in three events — the tug-of-war, the 400 meters, and the marathon — and all were between the American team and the British officials. It has been conjectured that the animosity began at the outset, with the Opening Ceremony problems in which the American flag was not flown at the stadium, and the American flag bearer, Ralph Rose, then refused to dip the American flag to King Edward. We will discuss these three controversies briefly here, although full descriptions are found in the summaries of the events themselves. In addition, Appendix II is devoted completely to a detailed description of the many controversies, including contemporary newspaper opinions.

The tug-of-war preliminaries were scheduled for Friday, 17 July. After withdrawals there were only five teams entered and the only quarter-final match was to be between the American team and a British team representing the Liverpool police. The match was to be the best two of three pulls, but the Americans were thoroughly outmatched by the Liverpudlians in the first pull. They then refused to compete further, protesting that the police were wearing illegal footwear. The rules stated that spikes or other projections from the shoes were not permitted. The Liverpool Police wore what was standard footwear for them, with thick metal rims, which the Americans considered to embroach the rules. The subsequent American protest was disallowed, but they refused to pull further, and the Liverpool Police team advanced to the semi-final where they defeated Sweden, before losing in the final to another British team representing the London Police.

Of the three major protests, we basically agree with the decision of the British officials on the next two. We are slightly more ambivalent in the matter of the tug-of-war although it is difficult to be precise because pictures of the footwear have not survived in any source we could find. We suspect that the Liverpool team followed the letter of the law, but that they pushed the envelope of the rules somewhat.

The 400 meter controversy occurred in the final, originally held on 23 July (Thursday). The favorite was the British runner, Wyndham Halswelle, who was opposed by three Americans — John Carpenter, John Taylor, and William Robbins. Carpenter was leading going into the last turn, with Halswelle close behind. Entering the final straight, Halswelle moved outside Carpenter to pass him, and Carpenter then ran almost diagonally across the track to obstruct Halswelle, who pulled up somewhat. The tape at the finish was pulled down as the British officials immediately noted the foul. The race was ordered to be re-run and Carpenter was, we feel, properly disqualified. American Olympic officials protested against this and refused to allow the other Americans to participate in the re-run of the final. Thus, Halswelle ran by himself to collect the Olympic gold medal.

The final major controversy occurred in the marathon race which was conducted on Friday, 24 July, starting at Windsor Castle and finishing in the White City Stadium. The leader entering the stadium was the tiny Italian candymaker, Dorando Pietri. But Pietri was spent and collapsed shortly after beginning his final lap around the track. He was helped to his feet by British officials, who were cheered on by the sympathetic British crowd. Pietri eventually collapsed four more times while rounding the track, but he was able to finally cross the finish line, although basically held up by the British officials. The next finisher was the American, Johnny Hayes, who finished relatively fresh and unaided. Initially, Pietri was declared the winner of the race, but the Americans protested that decision because of his receiving assistance. Pietri was correctly disqualified, and Hayes was eventually declared the marathon champion.

It is difficult at this distance to apportion the blame fairly for the strained relations which developed between the Americans and the British. During the two weeks when the main events were held at the stadium, the total American protests averaged almost one per day. This was undoubtedly an excessive number but the American anger was likely increased by the seemingly condescending manner with which their complaints were received. The British reserve was probably prompted by the aggressive manner in which James Edward Sullivan, Secretary of the American Olympic Committee, lodged the American complaints.

It is usually said that much of the animosity which developed between the Americans and the British teams can be attributed to the anti-English feeling among the Irish members of both teams, but this is a dangerous over-simplification. There is little evidence that the athletes themselves felt particularly strongly on what was, essentially, a political matter, and in a number of the disputes, notably the 400 meters final, no Irish athlete was involved. The U.S. officials saw things differently and Sullivan felt that, in order to consolidate his position in the sporting hierarchy at home, he felt that he must be seen as a dedicated team leader fighting for the rights of his charges. While the image he sought to convey was reported to his liking in the sensational newspapers the more respected and responsible journals took a quite different view of Sullivan's behavior in London.

Then, as now, tabloid-type newspapers would print a "story" regardless of the facts and Casper Whitney, the President of the American Olympic Committee and the influential editor of *Outing Magazine,* provided an interesting and informed viewpoint in a letter he sent to Lord Desborough on his return to New York.[9] Whitney wrote "I want to tell you that we Americans understand the highly colored and sensational newspaper stories that correspondents have been sending over. We have in America the same fault-finding, suspicious and bickering class that you have in England, but we know how much stock to take of the output; and I suppose you (i.e., your kind) in England also know." In his letter to Desborough, Caspar Whitney also passed on his forthright views on the Olympic Movement in general. He referred to de Coubertin as a "well-meaning, fussy and incompetent little Frenchman" and on the question of national representation he said "… the IOC has members from Mexico, Peru, Russia and Turkey (Good Lord, think of it) and yet ignores Canada entirely."

Sullivan, the son of an Irish-born construction worker, left school at the age of 16 and took a variety of jobs as he set out to improve his lot in life. He wrote a column for the *New York Morning Journal* but his controversial writings failed to meet with the approval of his peers and the *Spirit of the Times* was moved to comment "Mr. J. E. Sullivan degrades modern journalism. He is a renegade Irishman, the purveyor of shameful and malicious falsehoods." An early supporter of the Amateur Athletic Union (AAU) Sullivan used the AAU as his power base and after being appointed Secretary in 1889 he was elected President in 1906. Undoubtedly the most powerful man in American sport at this time, he made as many enemies as he did friends but, most importantly, he remained in power. Sullivan's relationship with Coubertin fluctuated constantly but, even at the best of times, they were never really on friendly or intimate terms and once Sullivan realized that he had no chance of being invited to join the magic inner circle of the IOC, he set up a commission within the AAU to look into the possibility of forming a new IOC.[10]

Unfortunately, James Sullivan seemed to encourage, rather than try to restrain, the press in their sensational reporting and he made no effort to set the record straight, even when the competitors themselves pointed out that certain reports were simply not true, (e.g. swimmer Charles Daniels' denial that the 100 meters freestyle had been started before he was ready).[11] In his *Mémoires olympiques* Coubertin wrote, "I just could not understand Sullivan's attitude. He shared his team's frenzy and did nothing to try and calm them down."[12]

Perhaps the most telling insight into Sullivan's character came at a reception for the returning Olympic team at New York City Hall. Sullivan chose the occasion to parade a "British Lion" in chains and on a leash and considerable diplomatic skills were needed to prevent a major international incident from developing.

Whatever the reasons and whatever the rights and wrongs, a serious rift in Anglo-American sporting relationships developed. Under the editorship of Theodore Cook, a member of the British Olympic Council, the British Olympic Association published the pamphlet *A Reply to Certain Criticisms* which set out to answer the more serious of the American complaints. The publication adopted a strictly factual tone with signed statements from officials and competitors but confessed that it was at a loss to fully understand the complaint of James E. Sullivan that there were too many events at the London Games. Theodore Cook no doubt took pleasure in pointing out that there were 110 events on the program in London compared to the 390 events at St. Louis in 1904 when Sullivan himself was in charge of the arrangements. For the Americans, Gustavus Town Kirby, a staunch ally of Sullivan's, produced his own pamphlet which was addressed to the Intercollegiate American Amateur Athletic Association and a copy was mailed to every college newspaper in the United States. This did nothing to lower the tension and at their 1909 Convention the Amateur Athletic Union voted to break off relations with the Amateur Athletic Association in England. In practice, this did little to restrict competition between athletes of the two countries but it was not until 1922 that a letter of agreement was signed formally restoring amicable relationships between the two bodies.

Fortunately, the 1908 Games were considered a great success by every other country and, on their return home, their chief delegates wrote effusive letters of thanks to Lord Desborough expressing their appreciation of the hospitality and fair play they had encountered in London. Just one chief delegate failed to send such a letter and that, as one might expect, was James Edward Sullivan of the United States.

Despite all the difficulties between America and Britain, the 1908 Olympic Games were highlighted by some wonderful performances. Mel Sheppard won three gold medals on the track, winning the 800 meters, the 1,500 meters, and running on the winning U.S. medley relay team. Britain's Henry Taylor also won three golds in the stadium, but these were in the swimming pool, as he was victorious in the 400 freestyle, the 1,500 freestyle, and swimming the anchor leg on the 4 × 200 freestyle relay. Other outstanding individual performances were achieved by Ben Jones (GBR) who won two gold medals and one silver on the cycling track, Martin Sheridan (USA), who garnered two gold medals and one bronze in the weight-throwing events and the standing broad jump, and Oscar Swahn (SWE) who won three shooting medals, two gold and one bronze.

In the measured events, numerous world records were set. On the track, Melvin Shepperd's 1:52.8, set in winning the 800 meters, bettered the best mark on record for 800 meters or 880 yards, although it was probably slightly inferior to Charles Kilpatrick's world record of 1:53.4 for 880 yards. Both hurdle races saw new world records by American hurdlers, Forrest Smithson winning the 110 hurdles in 15.0 and Charles Bacon the 400 hurdles in 55.0. Both marks would become the initial world records for those distances at the establishment of the International Amateur Athletic Federation in 1912. George Larner (GBR) established a world record of 1-15:57.4 in winning the 10 mile walk and en route, also broke the 9-mile walking world record with 1-07:37.8.

In the classical discus throw, Martin Sheridan won the event with a new world mark of 124-8 (38.00), although the crowd did not realize it because the world record in the program was listed as the one for the freestyle discus throw. Sheridan led four finishers past the world record. Another world record set at the White City Stadium during the 1908 Olympic Games came in the 100 kilometer cycling event, which was won by Charles Bartlett in 2-41:48.6.

The swimming events saw the world record broken in all six events on the program, probably due to the quality of the pool. The records set were as follows: 100 meter freestyle–1:05.6 Charles Daniels (USA); 400 meter freestyle–5:36.8 Henry Taylor (GBR); 1,500 meter freestyle–22:48.4 Henry Taylor (GBR); 100 meter backstroke–1:24.6 Arno Bieberstein (GER); 200 meter breaststroke–3:09.2 Fred Holman (GBR); and 4 x 200 meter freestyle relay–10:55.6 by the Great Britain team of John Derbyshire, Paul Radmilovic, William Foster, and Henry Taylor. Thus Taylor not only won three gold medals in the swimming pool, but did so in world record time in each event.

In both 1900 and 1904, the Olympic Games were spread out over several months, as they were arranged to take advantage of their nexus with the World's Fairs held concurrently with those Olympics. In 1908, a somewhat similar situation existed, both with the Franco-British Exhibition, and the length of the Olympics. The events began in late April with the racquets tournament and ended over six months later.

But the bulk of the competition was conducted in July. The White City Stadium saw competition held from 13–25 July, save for Sunday, 19 July. During this period, spectators could watch track & field athletics, swimming, diving, water polo, cycling, wrestling, archery, gymnastics, tug-of-war, and even fencing, which was held in the periphery of the stadium. There were also events in July both before and after the stadium competitions. From 6–11 July, shooting and lawn tennis competitions were held, and rowing and yachting competition took place from 27–31 July, with one yachting event, the 12-meter, finished in Glasgow, Scotland on 11–13 August.

That an Olympic event in 1908 was held in Glasgow was quite unusual. In 1896 and 1906 all the Olympic events were held in the center of Athens or in the bay just off Athens, near Piraeus. In 1900 and 1904, the events were slightly more spread out, but with the exception of one yachting class in 1900 held at Le Havre, all the Olympic events in those years were held basically in the centers of Paris and St. Louis.

The 1908 "London" Olympic Games were really the first Olympics to begin the modern style of spreading the events around, so that not all were held in the host city proper. This trend really began just after the close of the stadium events, when the yachting events were held at the Royal Victoria Yacht Club in Ryde, on the Isle of Wight. The Isle of Wight is a small island off the southernmost coast of England, and the nearest large mainland town is Southampton. Olympic events were also held in the waters of Southampton as well, when the motorboat races were conducted there on 28–29 August. The 12-meter yacht racing events were moved to Glasgow because there were no foreign entries in the 12 meter class and both the British entries were racing on the River Clyde in Glasgow that summer. Finally, even the rowing competitions were held about 36 miles (58 km.) from central London at Henley-on-Thames.

The Closing and Awards Ceremony

Having officially opened the Games, it had been planned that King Edward would also preside over the awards ceremony which brought to a close the two weeks of activity in the stadium. But the King, angered and hurt by what he saw of the American behavior and the way they impugned the integrity of British officials, decided that he wanted nothing further to do with the Games. A brief announcement was made from Buckingham Palace stating "The King would not give the prizes, as had been planned, nor participate in the finish of the Games."

In the King's absence, the duty of presenting the prizes on Saturday, 28 July fell to Queen Alexandra and the ceremony began immediately after the medley relay race concluded the program in the stadium. The Queen awarded the gold medals. Silver medals were given out by the Duchess of Rutland, bronze medals by Catherine, Duchess of Westminster, and Lady Desborough presented the diplomas of merit and commemorative medals.

With the rowing and yachting events and the Autumn Games still to come, only 86 of the 110 events on the program had been decided but even so there was a formidable number of prizes to be presented. There were gold, silver, and bronze medals for the three place winners, each of whom also received a diploma, with the winners also getting a smaller diploma for presentation to their Club or Association. Diplomas of Merit were awarded to athletes who achieved a standard of excellence but failed to win a medal and a number of officials also received this award. Participants in the various demonstration events were each awarded a commemorative medal. For some sports, even more medals were awarded, and in the épée and sabre individual events after the customary gold and silver medals had been awarded to the winner and the runner-up all the other six finalists received a bronze medal.

This proliferation of awards meant that no less than 1,320 presentations had to be made. Separate tables with different categories of prizes were set out and prior to the arrival of the Queen, the silver medals were presented by the Duchess of Rutland, the bronze medals by the Duchess of Westminster, and the commemorative medals and merit certificates by Lady Desborough.

At 4:00 P.M. (1600) the Queen arrived to present the gold medals to the winners. As the band of the Grenadier Guards struck up "See, the Conquering Hero Comes" the newly-crowned Olympic champions advanced across the grass to receive their awards and each was also presented with a sprig of oak leaves from Windsor Forest tied with red, white and blue ribbons.

In view of the numbers involved, it is hardly surprising that not all the prize winners were able to be at the stadium for the ceremony. This prompted the British Olympic Council to announce that they would be prepared to accept duly authorized postal claims for the prizes which had not been collected.

In addition to the multitude of medals and diplomas, which remained the property of the recipients, 12 perpetual Challenge Cups or Trophies had been donated and these formed an impressive display on a separate table in front of the Queen.

The Brunetta Trophy for the men's 1,500 meters swimming race had not arrived in time for the prize giving ceremony but the Queen presented The Hurlingham Trophy for the winners of the polo tournament; The International Cup for Fencing for the épée team event; The Prince of Wales Cup for the 100 kilometer cycling race; Lord Westbury's Cup for individual clay pigeon shooting; The Greek Trophy for the marathon race; The Prague Trophy for individual gymnastics; The Montgomerie Statuette for the discus throw and The Goldsmith's Trophy for the winner of the Greco-Roman heavyweight wrestling event. Three additional events, for which trophies had been donated, had not yet taken place and the Brunetta Statuette for the rowing eights, The Football Association Trophy and The French President's Vase for yachting were all presented at a later date. Count Eugene Brunetta d'Usseux, the IOC member for Italy, gave trophies for both swimming and rowing, one of which was originally intended to be awarded to the "Champion Nation" but the idea was abandoned half-way through the Games when it was realized that a satisfactory points scoring system could not be agreed on. Except for polo and the 100 kilometers cycling event, which were not on the program in 1912, all the other perpetual trophies were presented for a second time in Stockholm.

In contrast to the previous two weeks, the prize ceremony was a thoroughly happy occasion with many pleasant interludes. Amid cheers and laughter Lord Desborough was presented with his commemorative medal by his wife, and as Charles Kingsbury, the winner of the 20 kilometers cycling race, had left for the world championships in Leipzig, the Queen presented his gold medal to his infant daughter. Dorando Pietri was the center of attention and seemed fully recovered from his trials of the previous day. The Italian was feted and Queen Alexandra presented him with a trophy which was the exact replica of the one given to the marathon winner, Johnny Hayes. As there had been no time to get the cup engraved it was presented with an accompanying card in the Queen's own hand bearing the words "For P. Dorando, In Remembrance of the Marathon Race from Windsor to the Stadium, From Queen Alexandra." The eventual winner of the marathon, Johnny Hayes, also received his due share of attention, and after being presented with the handsome Marathon Trophy donated by the Greek Olympic Committee he was carried around the stadium, shoulder-high on a table, by his teammates.

Summary and Retrospective

In the cool mist of a British autumn afternoon, on 31 October, slightly more than six months after they had begun in April 1908, the London Olympic Games finally ended when the umpire blew his whistle to end the hockey final between England and Ireland. The time had come to assess the success — or failure — of the Games.

There was no true closing ceremony at the end of October. But that night, the final official function of the 1908 Olympics occurred when a banquet was given at Holborn Restaurant for the Olympic officials and any remaining competitors. It was chaired by Lord Desborough, President of the British Olympic Council, and the attendance was about 450. A description of the event is found in *The Times*[13]:

> The company, numbering about 450, included Lord Selby, Lord Kinnaird, Count Brunetta d'Usseaux, the Mexican Minister, Sir John Cockburn, Mr. Hayes Fisher, the Rev. R. S. de Courcy Laffan, Sir H. Mackworth Praed, Captain Muirhead Collins, Mr. T. A. Coghlan, Mr. Imre Kiralfy, Mr. C. Freeman Murray (secretary, British Empire League), and the Mayors of Oxford, Windsor, Reading, High Wycombe, Maidenhead, and Hammersmith.
>
> After the toast of "The King and Foreign Rulers,"
>
> LORD DESBOROUGH proposed "The Olympic Games." He said that both the summer and the winter games of 1908 had been a great success. They had brought together from nearly every civilized country a trained body of athletes who had fought amicably in, he thought, the finest arena ever constructed for the purpose in the history of athletics. (Hear, hear.) In the course of the games, 3,000 picked athletes had represented 21 different countries and there had been 800 officials engaged in the management of the games. The programme had been criticized, to some extent, but it began to be drawn up two years ago, and was submitted to the International Olympic Committee at The Hague, and discussed in its entirety for a week. It was, therefore, a programme which received the endorsement of all the

distinguished gentlemen belonging to different countries who formed the great International Committee which, under Baron Pierre de Coubertin, started and had since carried on the Olympic Games. (Cheers.) He thought these games had completed two great objects in the sphere of athletics. They had brought foreign athletes of various countries into close comradeship with each other, and they had also made them realize that they must set aside their local jealousies and enter as teams representing their particular countries as a whole. (Hear, hear.) Without the hearty co-operation of the great athletic associations which governed sports in this country it would have been impossible to carry out the programme. Having expressed regret at the absence of Mr. Eugen Sandow, who, he reminded them, contributed £1,500 to the fund for the entertainment of the competitors, he said they were greatly indebted to the executive of the Franco-British Exhibition and to Mr. Imre Kiralfy, the designer for the splendid building in which the sports took place. (Cheers.) He spoke of the successes of the different countries in the winter games, and said that France, Germany, Sweden, the United States, Australia, and South Africa were represented at the dinner. (Cheers.)

Mr. E. B. DENNEY, replying on behalf of the French competitors, said that he and his friends had been surprised at the results obtained in organizing such an enormous athletic meeting. (Cheers.)

Mr. SALCHOW, on behalf of Sweden, said that his countrymen were more than satisfied with the splendid arrangements made, especially in connexion with the skating competition.

Mr. COGHLAN (Agent-General for South Australia) said that the people of Australia were athletes. They did not pay their shillings to see others contend in the arena, but contended themselves, with the result that they produced the greatest scullers in the world, and in England's own game, cricket, they were well able to hold their own. (Cheers.)

LORD DESBOROUGH, on behalf of the members of the British Olympic Council, then presented to the Rev. R. S. de Courcy Laffan a specially prepared autograph album and a brass lantern clock in recognition of the kindly, tactful, and whole-hearted manner in which he had discharged the arduous duties of hon. secretary. The clock was made about 1647 by Thomas Wheeler, who was an apprentice of the Clockmakers' Company, in the parish of Walbrook, in which Mr. Laffan's church is situated.

The REV. R. S. DE COURCY LAFFAN, in acknowledging the gifts, said that but for Lord Desborough's prestige as a sportsman it would have been practically impossible to have held the Olympic Games in London at all. The Olympic movement was one with great ideals — the perfect physical development of a new humanity, the spreading all over the world of the spirit of sport, which was the spirit of the truest chivalry, and the drawing together of all the nations of the earth in the bonds of peace and mutual amity. They were at the beginning of one of those great world movements which was going to develop long after all present had passed away. (Cheers.)

Mr. HAYES FISHER next made a presentation of an illuminated address to Lord Desborough in appreciation of the zeal and untiring energy and good will displayed by him as president of the British Olympic Council. At the top of the address appears the Olympic badge: half-way down on each side, surrounded by laurel leaves, are reproductions of the obverse and reverse of the commemorative medal, while at the lower corners are the obverse and reverse of the prize medal. Between these are shown the arms of Lord Desborough. A suitable inscription is enclosed in a border of red roses, symbolical of England, among which are entwined the names of the 21 countries which have taken part in the Fourth International Olympiad.

LORD DESBOROUGH expressed his warm thanks for the presentation, and testified to the valuable assistance given by every member of the British Olympic Council. He also alluded to the splendid personal efforts of Lord Northcliffe, who, he said, came to their help at a critical time and secured the success of the hospitality fund. (Cheers.) He afterwards proposed "The Fifth International Olympiad."

COUNT BRUNETTA D'USSEAUX (hon. secretary, International Olympic Committee) responded to the toast. Before separating the whole company joined enthusiastically in singing "Auld Lang Syne," followed by "God Save the King."

And thus it ended — hardly with a bang, though not exactly a whimper, either. The London Games brought the Olympic Movement back onto the track of Coubertin's ideal. Had the debacles of the 1900 and 1904 Games been repeated, the Olympic Movement probably would not have survived or, at best, deteriorated into little more than a minor sporting organization with little influence. The Games of Paris (1900) and St. Louis (1904) suffered from the overbearing influence of the World's Fairs with which they were associated. Although the London Games also had a strong affiliation with a major exhibition, Lord Desborough and his colleagues on the British Olympic Council deserve the utmost credit for the way in which they kept the Franco-British Exhibition on an equal footing with the Olympic Games and never allowed it to assume a dominant role in what was essentially a joint venture.

In retrospect, it is clear that the London Olympic Games helped to resurrect the flagging Olympic Movement, after the failures in Paris and St. Louis. Many innovations introduced in London were developed and refined for use at future Games and lessons were also learned from the mistakes made in London. Disputes over judging in certain sports had the ultimate advantage of bringing about the introduction of international judges. Similarly, the unfortunate incident in the 400 meters resulted in the race being run in lanes in Stockholm. Improvements such as the provision of a planting hole and a soft landing area for the pole vaulters and a stop-board for the shot putters were also introduced in Stockholm but these were due more to normal technical evolution within the sport rather than to any specific lessons learned from the London Games.

The ever-present problem of amateurism was again in evidence. The organizers were guided by the General Regulations approved at the IOC Congress at the Hague in 1907 but the resolution was loosely worded and there was plenty of scope for misunderstanding. In essence, the rules drawn up at the Hague placed the onus of establishing amateur credentials on the governing bodies of different sports in the participating countries. The most publicized amateur dispute arose over the Canadian marathon runner, Tom Longboat, who was considered an amateur in his native Canada but was classified as a professional across the border in America. The organizers had no alternative but to accept the assurances of the Canadians but the whole situation was far from satisfactory. The complexity of the amateur problem was underlined in the *Official Report* which listed separate definitions of an amateur for seventeen different sports in England alone, and additional interpretations were given for sports in Scotland and Ireland.

After the Games, the English journal *The Sporting Life* took an interest in the subject of amateurism and, after collecting information from around the world, they turned over a file of 150 documents to the IOC. Coubertin wasn't particularly interested in the findings and passed the file on to Baron Bertier de Sauvigny who prepared an exhaustive report for the 1909 session in Berlin which, in turn, decided to send out a questionnaire to all the interested parties. Coubertin felt that the issue was getting too complicated and that every possible situation could not be covered by legislation. He maintained, perhaps naively, that the concept of amateurism could be adequately covered in a few paragraphs.

A major step was taken towards clarifying, in an Olympic context, the definition of a "country" and a "sovereign state." At previous Games any members of athletic clubs were permitted to represent the country where that club was domiciled, irrespective of their own nationality, but for the 1908 Games more stringent rules were introduced. A complex set of new regulations permitted British Dominions to enter separate teams and countries such as Finland could enter separately from Russia. The IOC was well aware that the decision they had reached was no more than a compromise and that they would have to review their position if, for example, Bavaria or Saxony made representations to compete as separate entities.

Another positive factor to come out of the London Games was the formation of an International Swimming Federation, but on the debit side the Games marked the first significant exodus to the professional ranks by successful Olympians.

Still, despite all the acrimony for which they are known, the 1908 Olympic games presaged the bright future of the Olympic Movement. Perhaps the truest summary of the early years of the Olympic Movement, exemplified by the 1908 Olympic Games, the finest held to that date, was noted by the Rev. de Courcy Laffan at the banquet on the night the 1908 Olympic Games ended, "The Olympic movement was one with great ideals — the perfect physical development of a new humanity, the spreading all over the world of the spirit of sport, which was the spirit of the truest chivalry, and the drawing together of all the nations of the earth in the bonds of peace and mutual amity. They were at the beginning of one of those great world movements which was going to develop long after all present had passed away."[14]

NOTES

1. Writing in the April-July 1902 issue of *Revue Olympique* Coubertin refers to a National Olympic Committee of Great Britain. There was certainly no formally constituted body at the time and he was in all probability referring to the group of individuals who founded the British Olympic Association three years later.

2. Background information from Giuseppe Odello.

3. Coub2, p. 97.

4. Cook, Theodore Andrea. *Cruise of the Branwen.*

5. Bailey, Steve. "A Noble Ally and Olympic Disciple: The Reverend Robert S. de Courcy Laffan, Coubertin's 'Man' in England," *Olympika*, VI: 51–64; 1997.

6. Jeens C. "London 1908: The Franco-British Exhibition." In: Findling/Pelle.

7. Most of our facts concerning the fund raising efforts are contained in the OR, in various pages near the introduction.

8. The time is usually listed as 3:30 P.M., but *NYHP* carefully described the opening ceremony, noting, "At twelve minutes to four o'clock, the Grenadier Guards' band, resplendent in scarlet, struck up 'God Save the King,' and the gathering arose and uncovered and a minute later their Majesties made their appearance."

9. The letter dated 31 July 1908 is held in the Desborough files at the Hertford County Record Office, England.

10. *The International Journal of the History of Sport.* Vol. 11(3), (December 1994.)

11. *ARCC,* p. 12.

12. Coub2, p. 57.

13. Times, 2 November 1908, p. 17.

14. *Ibid.,* p. 17.

Summary and Statistics

Dates:	27 April–31 October 1908.[1]*
Site:	London, England, United Kingdom
Candidate Cities:	Berlin, Germany; Milan, Italy; Rome, Italy (Rome was originally selected but the site was later moved to London)
Official Opening By:	King Edward VII
Number of Countries Competing:	23[2] [23 Men — 3 Women]
Number of Athletes Competing:	2,023 [1,979 Men — 44 Women]
Number of Sports:	23 [23 Men — 5 Women]
Number of Events:	110 [103 Men — 4 Women — 3 Mixed]

Members of the International Olympic Committee in 1908[3] [36] (years on IOC in brackets)

President:	Pierre Frédy, Baron Pierre de Coubertin [1894–1925]
Secretary-General:	Count Eugenio Brunetta d'Usseaux [1897–1919]
Treasurer:	Ernst Callot [1894–1913]

Argentina	Manuel Quintana [1907–1910]
Australia	Richard Coombes [1905–1932]
Austria	Prince Alexander von Solms Braunfels [1905–1909]
Belgium	Count Henri de Baillet-Latour [1903–1942]
Bohemia	Dr. Jiří Stanislav Guth-Jarkovský [1894–1943]
Bulgaria	Dimitry Tzokov [1906–1913]
Denmark	Torben Grut [1906–1912]
Finland	Baron Reinhold Felix von Willebrand [13 July 1908–1919][4]
France	Pierre Frédy, Baron Pierre de Coubertin [1894–1925]
	Ernst Callot [1894–1913]
	Henri Hébrard de Villeneuve [1900–1911]

*See Notes on pages 36–38.

18

	Count Albert de Bertier de Sauvigny [1904–1920]
Germany	Karl August Willibald Gebhardt [1896–1909]
	Count Julius Caesar Karl Oskar Erdmann von Wartensleben [1903–1914]
	Count Egbert Hoyer von der Asseburg [1905–1909]
Great Britain	Reverend Robert Stuart de Courcy Laffan [1897–1927]
	William Henry Grenfell, Lord Desborough of Taplow [1906–1913]
Greece	Count Alexandros Merkati [1897–1925]
Hungary	Count Géza Andrassy [1907–1938]
Italy	Count Eugenio Brunetta d'Usseaux [1897–1919]
	Prince Scipion Borghese [1908–1909]
Mexico	Miguel de Beistegui [1901–1931]
Monaco	Count Albert Gautier Vignal [1908–1939]
The Netherlands	Baron Frederik Willem Christiaan Hendrik van Tuyll van Serooskerken [1898–1924]
Norway	Thomas Heftye [1907–1908][5]
	Captain Johan Tidemann Sverre [1908–1927][6]
Peru	Carlos F. de Candamo [1903–1922]
Portugal	Duke Antonio de Lancastre [1906–1912]
Russia	Count Nikolao Ribeaupierre [1900–1916]
	Prince Simon Andreyevich Trubetsky [1908–1910]
Spain	Count Antonio Gonzalo Mejorada del Campo, Marquis de Villamejor [1902–1921]
Sweden	Colonel Viktor Gustaf Balck [1894–1921]
	Count Carl Clarence von Rosen [1900–1948]
Switzerland	Baron Godefroy de Blonay [1899–1937]
United States	Professor William Milligan Sloane [1894–1924]
	James Hazen Hyde [1903–1908]

Co-opted in 1908 After the Olympic Games Ended

Romania	Gheorghe A. Plagino [1908–1949][7]
Turkey	Selim Sirri Bey Tarcan [1908–1920][8]
United States	Allison Vincent Armour [1908–1920][9]

Council of the British Olympic Association, 1908

Chairman: The Right Honorable Lord Desborough of Taplow
Honorary Secretary: The Reverend Robert Stuart de Courcy Laffan
Assistant Secretary: Captain F. Whitworth Jones
Members: The Right Honorable Lord Montagu of Beaulieu (Automobile Club)
Major General Right Honorable Lord Cheylesmore (Chairman of Council, National Rifle Association)
Sir Lees Knowles (Ex-President, Cambridge University Athletic Club)
Francis Philip Armstrong, Esquire (Chairman, Motor Yacht Club)
Henry Benjamin, Esquire (Ex-President, Amateur Swimming Association)
Edwin Anthony Biedermann, Esquire (Honorary Secretary, Tennis and Racquets Association)

James Blair, Esquire (Scottish Cyclists' Union)

T. W. J. Britten, Esquire (Honorary Treasurer, National Cyclists' Union)

Michael J. Bulger, Esquire, M.D. (Irish Amateur Athletic Association)

Guy M. Campbell, Esquire (F.R.G.S.)

Theodore Andrea Cook, Esquire (F.S.A., Amateur Fencing Association)

Lieutenant Colonel C. R. Crosse (Secretary, National Rifle Association)

John H. Douglas, Esquire (President, Amateur Boxing Association)

David Scott Duncan (Honorary Secretary, Scottish Amateur Athletic Association)

William Hayes Fisher, Esquire (President, National Skating Association)

Percy L. Fisher, Esquire (Honorary Secretary, Amateur Athletic Association)

Major Francis Egerton Green (Hurlingham Club)

Reginald Claude M. Gillett Gridley, Esquire (Honorary Secretary, Amateur Rowing Association)

F. B. O. Hawes, Esquire (Honorary Secretary, Lacrosse Union)

William Henry (né Nawrocki), Esquire (Honorary Secretary, Royal Life Saving Society)

George Rowland Hill, Esquire (Past President, Rugby Football Union)

Captain Alfred Hutton (F.S.A., President, Amateur Fencing Association)

W. J. Leighton, Esquire, M.B. (Vice-President, Irish Amateur Swimming Association)

Edward Lawrence Levy, Esquire (Honorary Secretary, Amateur Gymnastics Association)

George Richmond Mewburn, Esquire (Honorary Secretary, Lawn Tennis Association)

Colonel G. M. Onslow (National Physical Recreation Society)

E. J. O'Reilly, Esquire (Irish Cyclists' Association)

William Ryder Richardson, Esquire (Honorary Secretary, Amateur Golf Championship Committee)

George Stuart Robertson, Esquire (British Representative Juror at the Olympic Games of Athens, 1906)

Charles Newton Robinson, Esquire (Yacht Racing Association)

Brooke Heckstall-Smith, Esquire (Secretary, Yacht Racing Association)

Andrew Ernest Stoddart, Esquire (Secretary, Queen's Club)

E. H. Stone, Esquire (Secretary, The Clay Bird Shooting Association)

A. H. Sutherland, Esquire (Chairman, Amateur Wrestling Association)

Edgar Morris Wood Syers, Esquire (Honorary Secretary, Figure Skating Club)

Henry Moncrief Tennent, Esquire (Honorary Secretary, Hockey Association)

Frederick Joseph Wall, Esquire (F.C.I.S., Secretary, Football Association)

Colonel Henry Walrond (Honorary Secretary, Royal Toxophilite Society)

Comité d'Honneur

Australia	Dr. W. Camac Wilkinson
	William Hill
	Charles Campbell

Austria	Dr. Gustav Magy
	H. Robert Deutsch
	Felix Graf
Belgium	Baron Édouard-Émile de Laveleye
	Oscar Grégoire
	Albert Feyerick
	F. Van den Carput
Bohemia	Count Dr. Frankisch von Lützow
	Dr. Karel Grös
	Captain A. Wentworth Forbes
	Jiří Rössler-Ořovský
Canada	Leslie Boyd
	William Stark
	John Howard Crocker
	Emmanuel Tassé
Denmark	Captain Fritz Hansen
	Ivar Nyholm
	Captain Hans Henrik Bondo
	Colonel Sigfred Otto Rudolph Meyer
Finland	Axel Fredrik Londen
	Gösta Wasenius
	Frederik Hackman
France	Daniel Mérillon
	General — — Brugère
	Jean Charcot
Germany	General Count Egbert Hoyer von der Asseburg
	Dr. Paul Martin
	P. Joseph Müller
Greece	Spiridon Lambros
	Miltiades Negropontes
	Anastasios Metaxas
Hungary	Gyula de Mező
	Désiré Lauber
	Alfred Brüll
Italy	Marquis Compans de Brichanteau
	Marquis Charles Collobrini
	Prince Scipion Borghese
The Netherlands	Franciscus Jacobus Johannes Cremer
	Jacob Pieter Crommelin
	Jan Herman van Royen
Norway	Captain Jacob P. Grøttum
	Anton A. Frisch
	Captain Jean Louis Adolph Bentzen
Russia	Count Nikolao Ribeaupierre
	Nikolaos de Babine
	Charles de Petion
South Africa	Harry Sidney Howard Farrer
	Gustov Imroth
	J. B. Reynolds

	J. P. Taylor
Sweden	Johannes Sigfrid Edström
	Bernhard Fredrik Burman
	Fred Löwenadler
Switzerland	Walther de Bonstetten
	Marcel Guinand
	Maxime de Stoutz
United States	James Edward Sullivan
	Bartow Sumner Weeks
	Gustavus Town Kirby
	General James Andrew Drain

Flag Bearers at the Opening Ceremonies[10] (18 nations[11]; 11 bearers known)

Austria	not known
Belgium	not known
Bohemia	Miroslav Šustera [Athletics]
Denmark	Aage Vilhelm Holm [Swimming]
France	not known[12]
Germany	Wilhelm Kaufmann [Gymnastics]
Greece	not known[13]
The Netherlands	not known[14]
Hungary	István Mudin [Athletics]
Italy	not known[15]
Norway	Oskar Wilhelm Bye [Gymnastics]
Sweden	Erik Granfelt [Gymnastics]
Finland	Bruno W. Zilliacus[16] [Athletics]
United States	Ralph Rose [Athletics]
South Africa	Douglas Stupart[17]
Canada	not known[18]
Australasia	Henry St. Aubyn Murray (New Zealand) [Athletics]
Great Britain	John Edward Kynaston Studd [Official]
Argentina	did not march in the opening ceremony
Iceland	did not march in the opening ceremony[19]
Russia	did not march in the opening ceremony[20]
Switzerland	did not march in the opening ceremony

Attendance and Weather at the White City Stadium[21]

13 July (Monday)	30,000	Windy, cool, drizzling rain
14 July (Tuesday)	18,000	Cold, rain all day
15 July (Wednesday)	15,000	Drizzling rain all day
16 July (Thursday)	4,000	Cold, rain all day
17 July (Friday)	15,000	Cool rain and windy in A.M., clearing in P.M.
18 July (Saturday)	45,000	Drizzling rain in A.M., sunny in P.M.

19 July (Sunday)	— —	Non-competition day
20 July (Monday)	30,000	Gloomy with threatening rain
21 July (Tuesday)	50,000	Warm and sunny
22 July (Wednesday)	45,000	Ideal summer weather
23 July (Thursday)	60,000	Warm and sunny
24 July (Friday)	80,000	Warm (78° F. [26° C.]), calm, sunny, and dry
25 July (Saturday)	60,000	Bright and warm

Competition Sites[22]

Archery	White City Stadium, Shepherd's Bush, London
Athletics	White City Stadium, Shepherd's Bush, London
Boxing	Northampton Institute, Clerkenwell, London
Cycling	White City Stadium, Shepherd's Bush, London
Diving	White City Stadium, Shepherd's Bush, London
Fencing	Fencing Grounds on the periphery of the White City Stadium, Shepherd's Bush, London
Figure Skating	Prince's Skating Club, Knightsbridge, London
Football (Soccer)	White City Stadium, Shepherd's Bush, London
Gymnastics	White City Stadium, Shepherd's Bush, London
Hockey (Field)	White City Stadium, Shepherd's Bush, London
Jeu de Paume	Queen's Club, West Kensington, London
Lacrosse	White City Stadium, Shepherd's Bush, London
Motorboating	Southampton Water, Southampton, Southern Coast of England
Polo	Hurlingham Polo Grounds, London
Racquets	Queen's Club, West Kensington, London
Rowing & Sculling	Henley-on-Thames
Rugby Football	White City Stadium, Shepherd's Bush, London
Shooting	Bisley Rifle Range (rifle, pistol, and running deer shooting) Uxendon School Shooting Club (trap shooting)
Swimming	White City Stadium, Shepherd's Bush, London
Tennis (Lawn)	All-England Lawn Tennis & Croquet Club (Wimbledon), London
Tennis (Indoor)	Queen's Club, West Kensington, London
Tug-of-War	White City Stadium, Shepherd's Bush, London
Water Polo	White City Stadium, Shepherd's Bush, London
Wrestling	White City Stadium, Shepherd's Bush, London
Yachting	Royal Victoria Yacht Club, Ryde, Isle of Wight Royal Clyde Yacht Club, Hunter's Quay, Glasgow, Scotland

SUMMARY STATISTICS

1908 Olympic Games — Medals Won by Countries

	Gold	Silver	Bronze	Medals
United Kingdom[23]	56	51	39	146
United States	23	12	12	47

	Gold	Silver	Bronze	Medals
Sweden	8	6	11	25
France	5	5	9	19
Canada	3	3	10	16
Germany	3	5	5	13
Hungary	3	4	2	9
Norway	2	3	3	8
Belgium	1	5	2	8
Finland	1	1	3	5
Denmark	–	2	3	5
Italy	2	2	–	4
Australia	1	2	1	4
Greece	–	3	–	3
Russia	1	2	–	3
South Africa	1	1	–	2
The Netherlands	–	–	2	2
Bohemia	–	–	2	2
New Zealand	–	–	1	1
Austria	–	–	1	1
Totals (110 events)	110	107	106	323
Great Britain/England	54	46	36	136[24]
Ireland	2	5	1	8[25]
Scotland	–	–	1	1[26]
Wales	–	–	1	1[27]

Note: *No second/third in 400 meters (athletics—men); three seconds/no third in high jump (athletics—men); two firsts/no second/three thirds in pole vault (athletics—men); two seconds/no third in standing high jump (athletics—men); no medals in match sprint (cycling); two thirds in springboard diving; two thirds in hockey (field); no third in lacrosse; no second/third in class A motorboating; no second/third in class B motorboating; no second/third in class C motorboating; two seconds/no third in polo; two thirds in men's singles racquets; two thirds in single sculls (rowing); two thirds in pairs without coxswain (rowing); two thirds in fours without coxswain (rowing); two thirds in eights (rowing); no third in rugby football; no third in running deer, single shot, team shooting; no second/third in 7 meter class (yachting); and no third in 12 meter class (yachting).*

Most Medals (2 or more) [65: 64 Men, 1 Woman]

Men	Gold	Silver	Bronze	Medals
Melvin Sheppard (USA-ATH)	3	–	–	3
Henry Taylor (GBR-SWI)	3	–	–	3 [2]
Benjamin Jones (GBR-CYC)	2	1	–	3 [3]
Martin Sheridan (USA-ATH)	2	–	1	3
Oscar Gomer Swahn (SWE-SHO)	2	–	1	3 [5]
Major Josiah Ritchie (GBR/IRL-TEN)	1	1	1	3 [6]
Thomas "Ted" Ranken (GBR-SHO)	–	3	–	3 [7]
Gaston Alibert (FRA-FEN)	2	–	–	2

Men	Gold	Silver	Bronze	Medals
Raymond Ewry (USA-ATH)	2	–	–	2
Capt. John Field-Richards (GBR-MTB)	2	–	–	2 [10]
Jenő Fuchs (HUN-FEN)	2	–	–	2
Arthur "Wentworth" Gore GBR-TEN)	2	–	–	2
Albert Helgerud (NOR-SHO)	2	–	–	2
Clarence Kingsbury (GBR-CYC)	2	–	–	2
George Larner (GBR-ATH)	2	–	–	2
Eric Lemming (SWE-ATH)	2	–	–	2
Paul Radmilovic (GBR-SWI/WAP)	2	–	–	2
Bernard Redwood (GBR-MTB)	2	–	–	2
Isaac Thornycroft (GBR-MTB)	2	–	–	2 [19]
Kellogg Casey (USA-SHO)	1	1	–	2 [20]
Walter Ewing (CAN–SHO)	1	1	–	2
Reginald Fenning (GBR-ROW)	1	1	–	2
Harry Humby (GBR-SHO)	1	1	–	2
Alexandre Lippmann (FRA-FEN)	1	1	–	2
Maurice Matthews (GBR-SHO)	1	1	–	2
George de Relwyskow (GBR-WRE)	1	1	–	2
Arthur Robertson (GBR-ATH)	1	1	–	2
Maurice Schilles (FRA-CYC)	1	1	–	2
Gordon Thomson (GBR-ROW)	1	1	–	2
Paul Van Asbroeck (BEL-SHO)	1	1	–	2 [30]
Edward Amoore (GBR-SHO)	1	–	1	2
John Jacob Astor (GBR-RAQ)	1	–	1	2
André Auffray (FRA-CYC)	1	–	1	2
Edward Barrett (GBR/IRL-TOW/WRE)	1	–	1	2
Nathaniel Cartmell (USA-ATH)	1	–	1	2
Charles Daniels (USA-SWI)	1	–	1	2
James Gorman (USA-SHO)	1	–	1	2
Robert Kerr (CAN-ATH)	1	–	1	2
Alexander Maunder (GBR-SHO)	1	–	1	2
Evan Noel (GBR-RAQ)	1	–	1	2 [40]
Eugène Olivier (FRA-FEN)	1	–	1	2
Ole Sæther (NOR-SHO)	1	–	1	2 [42]
George Beattie (CAN-SHO)	–	2	–	2
George Caridia (GBR-TEN)	–	2	–	2
Zoltán von Halmay (HUN-SWI)	–	2	–	2
Réginald Storms (BEL-SHO)	–	2	–	2
Konstantin Tsiklitiras (GRE-ATH)	–	2	–	2
Ernest Webb (GBR-ATH)	–	2	–	2 [48]
Frank Beaurepaire (AUS-SWI)	–	1	1	2
Hanns Braun (GER-ATH)	–	1	1	2 [50]
John Eisele (USA-ATH)	–	1	1	2
Walter Ellicott (GBR-SHO)	–	1	1	2
John Garrells (USA-ATH)	–	1	1	2
Arne Halse (NOR-ATH)	–	1	1	2
Marquis "Bill" Horr (USA-ATH)	–	1	1	2

Men	Gold	Silver	Bronze	Medals
Henry Leaf (GBR-RAQ)	–	1	1	2
Karl Neumer (GER-CYC)	–	1	1	2 [57]
Gordon Balfour (CAN-ROW)	–	–	2	2
Becher Gale (CAN-ROW)	–	–	2	2
Vilém Goppold von Lobsdorf (BOH-FEN)	–	–	2	2 [60]
Pontus Hanson (SWE-SWI/WAP)	–	–	2	2
Harald "Julie" Julin (SWE-SWI/WAP)	–	–	2	2
Charles Riddy (CAN-ROW)	–	–	2	2
Geoffrey Taylor (CAN-ROW)	–	–	2	2 [64]

Woman	Gold	Silver	Bronze	Medals
Florence "Madge" Syers (GBR-FSK)	1	–	1	2 [1]

Most Gold Medals (2 or more) [17:17 Men, 0 Women]

Men	Gold	Silver	Bronze	Medals
Melvin Sheppard (USA-ATH)	3	–	–	3
Henry Taylor (GBR-SWI)	3	–	–	3 [2]
Benjamin Jones (GBR-CYC)	2	1	–	3 [3]
Martin Sheridan (USA-ATH)	2	–	1	3
Oscar Gomer Swahn (SWE-SHO)	2	–	1	3 [5]
Gaston Alibert (FRA-FEN)	2	–	–	2
Raymond Ewry (USA-ATH)	2	–	–	2
Capt. John Field-Richards (GBR-MTB)	2	–	–	2
Jenő Fuchs (HUN-FEN)	2	–	–	2
Arthur "Wentworth" Gore (GBR-TEN)	2	–	–	2 [10]
Albert Helgerud (NOR-SHO)	2	–	–	2
Clarence Kingsbury (GBR-CYC)	2	–	–	2
George Larner (GBR-ATH)	2	–	–	2
Eric Lemming (SWE-ATH)	2	–	–	2
Paul Radmilovic (GBR-SWI/WAP)	2	–	–	2
Bernard Redwood (GBR-MTB)	2	–	–	2
Isaac Thornycroft (GBR-MTB)	2	–	–	2 [17]

Youngest Competitors, Men (10 athletes/13 performances)

Yrs-days[28]
16-001   Erik "Loppan" Adlerz (SWE-DIV, plain high diving)
16-026   Mario Massa (ITA-SWI, 400 meter freestyle)
16-031   Ödön Toldi (HUN-SWI, 200 breaststroke)
16-124   Amilcare Beretta (ITA-SWI, 100 meter backstroke)
16-125   Beretta (ITA-SWI, 200 meter breaststroke)

16-132   Victor Jacquemin (BEL-ATH, 100 meters)
16-135   Jacquemin (BEL-ATH, 400 meters)
16-205   Stanislao Di Chiara (ITA-GYM, Combined exercises, team)
16-212   Ferenc Szpts (HUN-GYM, Combined exercises, individual)
16-296   Christian Marius Hansen (DEN-GYM, Combined exercises, team)
16-312   Adamo Bozzani (ITA-GYM, Combined exercises, team)
17-035   Harry Hebner (USA-SWI, 100 meter freestyle)
17-039   Hebner (USA-SWI, 4 × 200 meter relay)

Youngest Competitors, Men, Individual (5 athletes/7 performances)

Yrs-days
16-001   Erik "Loppan" Adlerz (SWE-DIV, Plain high diving)
16-026   Mario Massa (ITA-SWI, 400 meter freestyle)
16-031   Ödön Toldi (HUN-SWI, 200 breaststroke)
16-124   Amilcare Beretta (ITA-SWI, 100 meter backstroke)
16-125   Beretta (ITA-SWI, 200 meter breaststroke)
16-132   Victor Jacquemin (BEL-ATH, 100 meters)
16-135   Jacquemin (BEL-ATH, 400 meters)

Youngest Medalists, Men (10 athletes/11 performances)

Yrs-days
17-039   Harry Hebner (USA-SWI, 4 × 200 meter relay)
17-064   Frank Beaurepaire (AUS-SWI, 400 meter freestyle)
17-073   Beaurepaire (AUS-SWI, 1,500 meter freestyle)
17-207   Pál Simon (HUN-ATH, 1,600 meter medley relay)
17-237   József Munk (HUN-SWI, 4 × 200 meter relay)
17-298   Hermann Bohne (NOR-GYM, Combined exercises, team)
17-303   Sverre Grøner (NOR-GYM, Combined exercises, team)
18-014   William Foster (GBR-SWI, 4 × 200 meter relay)
18-073   John Skrataas (NOR-GYM, Combined exercises, team)
18-074   Imre Zachár (HUN-SWI, 4 × 200 meter relay)
18-095   Béla Las Torres (HUN-SWI, 4 × 200 meter relay)

Youngest Medalists, Men, Individual (5 athletes/6 performances)

Yrs-days
17-064   Frank Beaurepaire (AUS-SWI, 400 meter freestyle)
17-073   Beaurepaire (AUS-SWI, 1,500 meter freestyle)
18-111   Arvid "Sparven" Spångberg (SWE-DIV, Plain high diving)
18-115   Harald "Julie" Julin (SWE-SWI, 100 meter freestyle)
18-170   Albert Zürner (GER-DIV, Fancy high diving)
18-217   Otto Scheff (AUT-SWI, 400 meter freestyle)

Youngest Gold Medalists, Men (10 athletes/performances)[29]

Yrs-days
18-014   William Foster (GBR-SWI, 4 × 200 meter relay)
18-131   "Gustaf" Johnsson (SWE-GYM, Combined exercises, team)
18-170   Albert Zürner (GER-DIV, Fancy high diving)
18-228   Rolf Johnsson (SWE-GYM, Combined exercises, team)
18-240   Edward Cook, Jr. (USA-ATH, Pole vault)
18-272   Carl Bertilsson (SWE-GYM, Combined exercises, team)
19-110   Carl Folcker (SWE-GYM, Combined exercises, team)
19-128   "Reggie" Walker (SAF-ATH, 100 meters)
19-265   Jay Gould, Jr. (USA-JDP, Singles)
19-300   A. Henry Thomas (GBR-BOX, Bantamweight)

Youngest Gold Medalists, Men, Individual (5 athletes/performances)

Yrs-days
18-170   Albert Zürner (GER-DIV, Fancy high diving)
18-240   Edward Cook, Jr. (USA-ATH, Pole vault)
19-128   "Reggie" Walker (SAF-ATH, 100 meters)
19-265   Jay Gould, Jr. (USA-JDP, Singles)
19-300   A. Henry Thomas (GBR-BOX, Bantamweight)

Oldest Competitors, Men (10 athletes/22 performances)

Yrs-days
61-004   Joshua Millner (GBR-SHO, Free rifle, 1,000 yards)
61-004   Millner (GBR-SHO, Running deer, double shot, individual)
61-004   Millner (GBR-SHO, Running deer, single shot, individual)
60-263   Oscar Gomer Swahn (SWE-SHO, Running deer, double shot, individual)
60-263   Swahn (SWE-SHO, Running deer, single shot, individual)
60-263   Swahn (SWE-SHO, Running deer, team)
58-242   István Móricz (HUN-SHO, Free rifle, 3 positions)
58-183   George Barnes (GBR-SHO, Small bore rifle, prone)
58-074   John Penrose (GBR-ARC, Double York round)
56-114   John Bridges (GBR-ARC, Double York round)
56-110   William Milne (GBR-SHO, Small bore rifle, disappearing target)
56-110   Milne (GBR-SHO, Small bore rifle, moving target)
56-110   Milne (GBR-SHO, Small bore rifle, prone)
56-097   Walter Winans (USA-SHO, Small bore rifle, disappearing Target)
56-097   Winans (USA-SHO, Small bore rifle, moving target)
56-096   Winans (USA-SHO, Free pistol)
56-095   Winans (USA-SHO, Running deer, double shot, individual)
56-095   Winans (USA-SHO, Running deer, single shot, individual)
56-012   John Butt (GBR-SHO, Trap shooting, individual)
56-012   Butt (GBR-SHO, Trap shooting, team)
56-012   Daniel Mérillon (FRA-SHO, Military rifle, team)
56-010   Mérillon (FRA-SHO, Free rifle, 1,000 yards)

Oldest Competitors, Men, Individual (5 athletes/8 performances)

Yrs-days
61-004   Joshua Millner (GBR-SHO, Free rifle, 1,000 yards)
61-004   Millner (GBR-SHO, Running deer, double shot, individual)
61-004   Millner (GBR-SHO, Running deer, single shot, individual)
60-263   Oscar Gomer Swahn (SWE-SHO, Running deer, double shot, individual)
60-263   Swahn (SWE-SHO, Running deer, single shot, individual)
58-242   István Móricz (HUN-SHO, Free rifle, 3 positions)
58-183   George Barnes (GBR-SHO, Small bore rifle, prone)
58-074   John Penrose (GBR-ARC, Double York round)

Oldest Medalists, Men (10 athletes/12 performances)

Yrs-days
61-004   Joshua Millner (GBR-SHO, Free rifle, 1,000 yards)
60-263   Oscar Gomer Swahn (SWE-SHO, Running deer, single shot, individual)
60-263   Swahn (SWE-SHO, Running deer, double shot, individual)
60-263   Swahn (SWE-SHO, Running deer, team)
58-183   George Barnes (GBR-SHO, Small bore rifle, prone)
56-095   Walter Winans (USA-SHO, Running deer, double shot, individual)
56-012   John Butt (GBR-SHO, Trap shooting, team)
55-161   Charles Rivett-Carnac (GBR-YAC, 7-meter class)
55-322   Blair Cochrane (GBR-YAC, 8-meter class)
54-096   Maurice Lecoq (FRA-SHO, Free rifle, team)
53-094   Léon Lécuyer (FRA-SHO, Small bore rifle, team)
50-182   Charles Benedict (USA-SHO, Military rifle, team)

Oldest Medalists, Men, Individual (5 athletes/6 performances)

Yrs-days
61-004   Joshua Millner (GBR-SHO, Free rifle, 1,000 yards)
60-263   Oscar Gomer Swahn (SWE-SHO, Running deer, double shot, individual)
60-263   Swahn (SWE-SHO, Running deer, single shot, individual)
58-183   George Barnes (GBR-SHO, Small bore rifle, prone)
56-095   Walter Winans (USA-SHO, Running deer, double shot, individual)
47-159   Alexander Maunder (GBR-SHO, Trap shooting, individual)

Oldest Gold Medalists, Men (10 athletes/11 performances)

Yrs-days
61-004   Joshua Millner (GBR-SHO, Free rifle, 1,000 yards)
60-263   Oscar Gomer Swahn (SWE-SHO, Running deer, single shot, individual)
60-263   Swahn (SWE-SHO, Running deer, team)
56-095   Walter Winans (USA-SHO, Running deer, double shot, individual)
55-161   Charles Rivett-Carnac (GBR-YAC, 7-meter class)
55-322   Blair Cochrane (GBR-YAC, 8-meter class)
50-193   Charles Benedict (USA-SHO, Military rifle, team)

49-163   James Gorman (USA-SHO, Free pistol, team)
48-193   Charles Axtell (USA-SHO, Free pistol, team)
47-159   Alexander Maunder (GBR-SHO, Trap shooting, team)
46-112   Arthur Carnell (GBR-SHO, Small bore rifle, prone)

Oldest Gold Medalists, Men, Individual (5 athletes/performances)

Yrs-days
61-004   Joshua Millner (GBR-SHO, Free rifle, 1,000 yards)
60-263   Oscar Gomer Swahn (SWE-SHO, Running deer, single shot, individual)
56-095   Walter Winans (USA-SHO, Running deer, double shot, individual)
46-112   Arthur Carnell (GBR-SHO, Small bore rifle, prone)
41-000   William Dod (GBR-ARC, Double York round)

Youngest Competitors, Women (5 athletes/performances)

Yrs-days
21-326   Phyllis Johnson (GBR-FSK, Pairs)
22-302   Else Rendschimdt (GER-FSK, Ladies' individual)
23-006   Elna Montgomery (SWE-FSK, Ladies' individual)
23-311   Anna Hübler (GER-FSK, Pairs)
24-271   Gladys Eastlake-Smith (GBR-TEN, Singles [covered court])

Youngest Medalists, Women (3 athletes/performances)

Yrs-days
21-326   Phyllis Johnson (GBR-FSK, Pairs)
22-302   Else Rendschimdt (GER-FSK, Ladies' individual)
23-311   Anna Hübler (GER-FSK, Pairs)

Youngest Medalists, Women, Individual (3 athletes/performances)

Yrs-days
22-302   Else Rendschimdt (GER-FSK, Ladies' individual)
24-271   Gladys Eastlake-Smith (GBR-TEN, Singles [covered court])
26-312   "Madge" Syers (GBR-FSK, Ladies' individual)

Youngest Gold Medalists, Women (2 athletes/performances)

Yrs-days
23-311   Anna Hübler (GER-FSK, Pairs)
24-271   Gladys Eastlake-Smith (GBR-TEN, Singles [covered court])

Youngest Gold Medalists, Women, Individual (2 athletes/performances)

Yrs-days
23-311   Anna Hübler (GER-FSK, Pairs)
26-312   "Madge" Syers (GBR-FSK, Ladies' individual)

Oldest Competitors, Women (5 athletes/performances)

Yrs-days
54-093   Sybil "Queenie" Newall (GBR-ARC, Double national round)
53-201   Margaret Weedon (GBR-ARC, Double national round)
45-201   Albertine Thackwell (GBR-ARC, Double National Round)
43-201   Jessie Wadworth (GBR-ARC, Double national round)
43-201   Lillian Wilson (GBR-ARC, Double national round)

Oldest Medalists, Women (3 athletes/performances)

Yrs-days
54-093   Sybil "Queenie" Newall (GBR-ARC, Double national round)
40-330   Märtha Adlerstråhle (SWE-TEN, Singles [covered court])
36-298   "Lottie" Dod (GBR-ARC, Double national round)

Oldest Medalists, Women, Individual (3 athletes/performances)

Yrs-days
54-093   Sybil "Queenie" Newall (GBR-ARC, Double national round)
40-330   Märtha Adlerstråhle (SWE-TEN, singles [covered court])
36-298   "Lottie" Dod (GBR-ARC, Double national round)

Oldest Gold Medalists, Women (2 athletes/performances)

Yrs-days
54-093   Sybil "Queenie" Newall (GBR-ARC, Double national round)
33-209   Frances Rivett-Carnac (GBR-YAC, 7-meter class)

Oldest Gold Medalists, Women, Individual (2 athletes/performances)

Yrs-days
54-093   Sybil "Queenie" Newall (GBR-ARC, Double national round)
29-342   Dorothea Lambert Chambers (GBR-TEN, singles [lawn])

Total Known Competitors (Men and Women)

	Arc	Ath	Box	Cyc	Div	Fen	Fsk	Ftb	Gym	Hok	Jdp	Lax	Mtb	Pol	Rag	Row	Rug	Sho	Swi	Ten	Tow	Wap	Wre	Yac	Sub/	Totals
Argentina	–	–	–	–	–	–	1	–	–	–	–	–	–	–	–	–	–	–	–	–	–	–	–	–	1	1
Australia	–	6	1	–	1	–	–	–	–	–	–	–	–	–	–	–	15	1	5	–	–	–	–	–	29	27
Austria	–	2	–	–	1	–	–	–	–	–	–	–	–	–	–	–	–	–	1	3	–	–	–	–	7	7
Belgium	–	6	–	6	1	18	–	–	2	–	–	–	–	–	–	10	–	10	7	–	–	7	4	3	74	70
Bohemia	–	3	–	–	–	6	–	–	2	–	–	–	–	–	–	–	–	–	–	4	–	–	4	–	19	18
Canada	–	27	–	5	1	1	–	–	2	–	–	12	–	–	–	13	–	22	1	3	–	–	1	–	88	87
Denmark	–	8	2	–	–	8	–	13	24	–	–	–	–	–	–	–	–	10	5	–	–	–	10	–	80	78
Finland	–	15	–	–	–	–	–	–	31	–	–	–	–	–	–	–	–	9	3	–	–	–	6	–	64	62
France	15	19	7	23	–	22	–	22	59	–	–	–	1	–	–	3	–	20	4	1	–	–	9	3	208	208
Germany	–	20	–	8	5	10	3	–	11	–	–	–	–	–	–	3	–	1	5	5	–	–	1	–	83	81
Great Britain	41	126	32	37	16	23	11	11	65	45	9	12	13	12	7	30	15	67	28	22	24	7	53	40	746	736
Greece	–	12	–	1	–	–	–	–	–	–	–	–	–	–	–	–	–	7	–	–	–	–	–	–	20	20
Hungary	–	19	–	–	–	8	–	–	6	–	–	–	–	–	–	11	–	2	10	3	–	–	7	–	66	65
Iceland	–	–	–	–	–	–	–	–	–	–	–	–	–	–	–	–	–	–	–	–	–	–	1	–	1	1
Italy	–	12	–	4	1	11	–	–	32	–	–	–	–	–	–	1	–	–	4	–	–	–	1	–	66	66
The Netherlands	–	19	–	5	–	13	–	12	23	–	–	–	–	–	–	4	–	17	7	2	–	9	7	–	118	113
New Zealand	–	3	–	–	–	–	–	–	–	–	–	–	–	–	–	–	–	–	–	–	–	–	–	–	3	3
Norway	–	11	–	–	–	1	–	–	30	–	–	–	–	–	–	9	–	13	–	–	–	–	1	5	70	69
Russia	–	1	–	–	–	–	1	–	–	–	–	–	–	–	–	–	–	–	–	–	–	–	4	–	6	6
South Africa	–	6	–	4	–	–	–	–	–	–	–	–	–	–	–	–	–	–	–	4	–	–	–	–	14	14
Sweden	–	31	–	2	10	7	4	–	38	–	–	–	–	–	–	19	–	19	12	4	8	7	9	13	178	168
Switzerland	1	–	–	–	–	–	–	–	–	–	–	–	–	–	–	–	–	–	–	–	–	–	–	–	1	1
United States	–	84	–	2	2	–	1	–	–	–	–	–	–	–	–	8	–	17	8	–	8	–	6	–	131	122
Totals	57	431	42	97	39	130	21	72	325	68	11	24	14	12	7	81	30	215	100	50	40	28	115	64	2,073	2,023
Nations	3	21	4	11	9	14	6	5	13	3	2	2	2	1	1	8	2	14	14	10	3	4	15	5	23	23

Women

	Arc	Fsk	Mtb	Ten	Yac	Totals
Germany	–	2	–	–	–	2
Great Britain	25	4	1	8	1	39
Sweden	–	1	–	2	–	3
Totals	25	7	1	10	1	44
Nations	1	3	1	2	1	3

Known Competitors by Nation

	Sub-Total Men	Men 2-sport	Men 3-sport	Total Men	Total Women	Total
Argentina	1	–	–	1	–	1
Australia	29	–	1	27	–	27
Austria	7	–	–	7	–	7
Belgium	74	4	–	70	–	70
Bohemia	19	1	–	18	–	18
Canada	88	1	–	87	–	87
Denmark	80	2	–	78	–	78
Finland	64	2	–	62	–	62
France	208	–	–	208	–	208
Germany	81	2	–	79	2	81
Great Britain	707	8	1	697	39	736
Greece	20	–	–	20	–	20
Hungary	66	1	–	65	–	65
Iceland	1	–	–	1	–	1
Italy	66	–	–	66	–	66
The Netherlands	118	5	–	113	–	113
New Zealand	3	–	–	3	–	3
Norway	70	1	–	69	–	69
Russia	6	–	–	6	–	6
South Africa	14	–	–	14	–	14
Sweden	175	8	1	165	3	168
Switzerland	1	–	–	1	–	1
United States	131	7	1	122	–	122
Totals	2,029	42	4	1,979	44	2,023
Nations	23	12	4	23	3	23

Competitors, Nations, and Events by Sports

	Total Comp.	All Nations	Events	Men Comp.	Men Nations	Men Events	Women Comp.	Women Nations	Women Events	Mixed Events
Archery	57	3	3	32	3	2	25	1	1	–
Athletics	431	21	26	431	21	26	–	–	–	–

	Total Comp.	Nations	All Events	Men Comp.	Men Nations	Men Events	Women Comp.	Women Nations	Women Events	Mixed Events
Boxing	42	4	5	42	4	5	–	–	–	–
Cycling	97	11	7	97	11	7	–	–	–	–
Diving	39	9	2	39	9	2	–	–	–	–
Fencing	130	14	4	130	14	4	–	–	–	–
Figure Skating	21	6	4	14	6	2	7	3	1	1
Football (Soccer)	72	5	1	72	5	1	–	–	–	–
Gymnastics	325	13	2	325	13	2	–	–	–	–
Hockey (Field)	68	3	1	68	3	1	–	–	–	–
Jeu de Paume	11	2	1	11	2	1	–	–	–	–
Lacrosse	24	2	1	24	2	1	–	–	–	–
Motorboating	14	2	3	13	2	2	1	1	–	1
Polo	12	1	1	12	1	1	–	–	–	–
Racquets	7	1	2	7	1	2	–	–	–	–
Rowing & Sculling	81	8	4	81	8	4	–	–	–	–
Rugby Football	30	2	1	30	2	1	–	–	–	–
Shooting	215	14	15	215	14	15	–	–	–	–
Swimming	100	14	6	100	14	6	–	–	–	–
Tennis	50	10	6	40	10	4	10	2	2	–
Tug-of-War	40	3	1	40	3	1	–	–	–	–
Water Polo	28	4	1	28	4	1	–	–	–	–
Wrestling	115	15	9	115	15	9	–	–	–	–
Yachting	64	5	4	63	5	3	1	1	–	1
Sub-Totals	2,073	23	110	2,029	23	103	44	5	4	3
Multi-Sport Athletes	50	–	–	50	–	–	–	–	–	–
Totals	2,023	23	110	1,979	23	103	44	5	4	3

Athletes Competing in Multiple Sports in 1908 (46)

Three Sports (4)

Australia (1)
   Reginald "Snowy" Baker, Boxing/Diving/Swimming.
Great Britain (1)
   Edward Barrett, Athletics/Tug-of-War/Wrestling.
Sweden (1)
   Robert "Robban" Andersson, Diving/Swimming/Water Polo.
United States (1)
   Leander "Lee" Talbott, Jr., Athletics/Tug-of-War/Wrestling.

Two Sports (42)

Belgium (4)
   Victor Boin, Swimming/Water Polo.
   Fernand Feyaerts, Swimming/Water Polo.
   Oscar Grégoire, Swimming/Water Polo.
   Herman Meyboom, Swimming/Water Polo.

Bohemia (1)
  Miroslav Šustera, Athletics/Wrestling.
Canada (1)
  Robert Zimmerman, Diving/Swimming.
Denmark (2)
  Poul Holm, Gymnastics/Swimming.
  Harald Klem, Gymnastics/Swimming.
Finland (2)
  Johan Kemp, Gymnastics/Athletics.
  Aarne Salovaara, Gymnastics/Athletics.
Germany (2)
  Paul Fischer, Gymnastics/Athletics.
  Friedrich Rahe, Hockey, Tennis (Lawn).
Great Britain (8)
  Arthur Hawkins, Gymnastics/Wrestling.
  William Hoare, Diving/Gymnastics.
  Frederick Humphreys, Tug-of-War/Wrestling.
  Albert Ireton, Boxing/Tug-of-War.
  Evan Noel, Jeu de Paume/Racquets.
  Vane Pennell, Jeu de Paume/Racquets.
  Kenneth Powell, Lawn Tennis/Athletics.
  Paul Radmilovic, Swimming/Water Polo.
Hungary (1)
  György Luntzer, Athletics/Wrestling.
The Netherlands (5)
  Bouke Benenga, Swimming/Water Polo.
  Johan Cortlever, Swimming/Water Polo.
  Hermanus van "Herman" Leeuwen, Gymnastics/Athletics.
  Eduard Meijer, Swimming/Water Polo.
  Pieter Ooms, Swimming/Water Polo.
Norway (1)
  Conrad Maurentius Carlsrud, Gymnastics/Athletics.
Sweden (8)
  Eric Carlberg, Fencing/Shooting.
  Pontus Hanson, Swimming/Water Polo.
  Hjalmar Johansson, Diving/Swimming.
  Harald "Julie" Julin, Swimming/Water Polo.
  Torsten Kumfeldt, Swimming/Water Polo.
  Gustaf "Gösta" Olson, Fencing/Gymnastics.
  Axel Runström, Diving/Water Polo.
  Gunnar Wennerström, Swimming/Water Polo.
United States (7)
  Wilbur Burroughs, Athletics/Tug-of-War.
  William Coe, Jr., Athletics/Tug-of-War.
  Arthur Dearborn, Athletics/Tug-of-War.
  John Flanagan, Athletics/Tug-of-War.
  Marquis "Bill" Horr, Athletics/Tug-of-War.
  Matthew McGrath, Athletics/Tug-of-War.
  Ralph Rose, Athletics/Tug-of-War.

NOTES

1. The dates are not completely inclusive. Specifically, events only took place on the following dates: 27–30 April; 1, 6–9, 11, 18–21, 23, 28 May; 18, 21 June; 6–11, 13–19, 20–25, 27–31 July; 11–13, 28–29 August; 19–20, 22–24, and 26–31 October 1908. See Appendix I for a detailed chronology of the 1908 Olympic program.

2. The number of nations competing varies in different sources, and a precise number cannot be given, because it depends on one's interpretation of what constituted a "nation" in 1908 and several other controversial decisions. We will mention all of them, in alphabetical order.

Australasia is usually listed as the nation representing both Australia and New Zealand. However, New Zealand could certainly be considered a separate nation, as it became independent from Australia in 1905.

Bohemia was not an independent nation in 1908, as it was a part of the Austro-Hungarian Empire and Hapsburg Monarchy. But Coubertin was on friendly terms with Bohemian IOC Member Jiří Guth, and arranged for Bohemia to compete at the Olympics as an independent nation in both 1906 and 1908.

Finland was still strictly a part of Russia, and was not independent until 6 December 1917, and Russia insisted that the Finnish flag not be displayed. Finland could be considered not to have competed by crediting their athletes' performances to Russia, but this is not done in any sources.

Great Britain obviously competed, but it could also be considered that Scotland, Wales, and even England also competed as separate nations. In hockey (field), four teams represented Great Britain — one each from England, Ireland, Scotland, and Wales.

Irish participation was hotly disputed in 1908 as Ireland wished to compete as an independent nation. The ruling British Olympic officials did not allow this, however, as Ireland was still a portion of the United Kingdom and would remain so until 6 December 1922 when it was established as a Dominion of the Crown.

In a similar vein, no problems were found with South Africa competing as a separate nation although the Union of South Africa would not become an independent nation until 1910. In 1908 it still consisted of four British colonies, all with separate governments: Cape Colony, Natal, Transvaal, and the Orange River Colony (later the Orange Free State).

Iceland was represented at the 1908 Olympics by one athlete, the wrestler Johannes Jósefsson. But in 1908, Iceland was still considered a Danish protectorate and not an independent nation. Similar to the situation with Russia, one could consider Iceland not to have competed, and credit Jósefsson's participation to Denmark. Again this is not usually done.

Switzerland is usually considered to have competed at the 1908 Olympic Games but it was represented by only one athlete, Julius Wagner, who competed in the hammer throw. Wagner was born a German citizen who competed at the 1906 Olympics for Germany. Shortly after those Olympics, he married a Swiss woman on 6 July 1906, and applied for Swiss citizenship. He did not have Swiss citizenship approved until 1917, but his 1908 and 1912 participation is usually credited to Switzerland. It is of some importance in Olympic history as Switzerland claims to be one of the five nations (Australia, France, Great Britain and Greece) to have competed in every Olympic Games. If Wagner's participation in 1908 was as a German representative, then Switzerland was not represented at these Olympic Games and cannot be considered to have competed at every Olympics. However, it should be noted that in the entry lists given in *The Sporting Life*, Wagner is listed as representing Switzerland.

Turkey is usually listed as competing in the 1908 Olympic Games (see Kluge [OSVK], Koryürek, and the *Olympic Review*, Vol. 89–90, March-April 1975, p. 119), represented by a single gymnast, Aleko Mulos. However, our research shows he almost certainly did not compete. Now it should be noted that the only event for which we have been unable to find complete results is the individual gymnastics competition. But entry lists for that event exist in the OR and in SL, as do the list of final competitors in the OR, and there is no evidence that Mulos competed or was even entered. Turkey should not be considered to have competed at the 1908 Olympic Games.

For the record, our final decision considered the following nations to have competed as independent nations: Australia, Bohemia, Finland, Iceland, New Zealand, and South Africa. We considered Switzerland to have competed and Turkey to have not competed. We listed England, Ireland, Scotland, and Wales as portions of Great Britain rather than as independent nations, except for the separate teams entered in hockey (field) and polo.

3. The following main list includes only members of the IOC during the "main body" of the 1908 Olympic Games.

4. Von Willebrand was co-opted as a member of the IOC during the IOC session (on 13 July) held in London during the 1908 Olympic Games.

5. Heftye resigned from the IOC at the session held in London during the 1908 Olympic Games (specifically on 13 July).

6. Von Willebrand was co-opted as a member of the IOC during the IOC session (on 13 July) held in London during the 1908 Olympic Games.

7. Co-opted 15 December 1908 by postal vote.

8. Co-opted 15 December 1908 by postal vote.

9. Co-opted 15 December 1908 by postal vote.

10. Listed in the order of entering the stadium.

11. The list of nations marching, and the order, is given in several daily newspapers and varies slightly. This list is as given on pp. 46–47 of the OR. It is noted in several newspapers that the nations marched in alphabetical order, except that the "English-speaking nations" brought up the rear. There is no mention in any source of Argentina, Iceland, Russia, or Switzerland taking part in the opening ceremony.

12. According to Daniel Schamps, French Olympic historian and the Comité Nationale Olympique et Sportif Français (CNOSF).

13. According to Athanassis Tarassouleas, Greek Olympic historian.

14. According to Tony Bijkerk, Dutch Olympic historian. The Netherlands marched after Greece and before Hungary because the London Organizing Committee used Holland as the name of the country.

15. According to Giuseppe Odello, Italian Olympic historian.

16. Zilliacus carried a name-plate and not the flag of Finland. In 1908 Finland was a subject of Russia and although Russia allowed Finnish athletes to compete independently, they were not allowed to march under their own flag. Finland also marched out of alphabetical order, whether they were listed under "Finland" or "Russia." This was due to the tardy arrival of their steamer to England. They arrived in the country only on the day of the ceremony, and barely made it to the ceremony at all.

17. See the earlier note concerning South Africa, which notes that South Africa did not become an independent nation until 1910. In 1908, it consisted of four British Crown colonies — Cape Colony, Natal, Transvaal, and the Orange River Colony (later the Orange Free State). It is not known which flag that Stupart carried in leading the South African contingent.

18. The Canadian Olympic Association states that Canada had no flag bearer in 1908, but this contradicts newspaper evidence stating that all the nations, save Finland, marched behind the flag of their country. It is possible that Australasia, Canada, and South Africa all marched under the Union Jack, as members of the British Empire, but this contradicts evidence given in Australian Olympic books (Howell and Lester) that Henry St. Aubyn Murray of New Zealand carried the flag for Australasia.

19. According to the Olympic Committee of Iceland the only Icelandic athlete in 1908 was Johannes Jósefsson. However, Iceland was not an independent nation in 1908, being a part of Denmark. Jósefsson marched with the Danish team.

20. Non-participation of the Russian athletes in the opening ceremony has been confirmed by the Russian Olympic Committee.

21. Figures are estimates based on newspaper reports.

22. Maps of the competition sites can be found in Appendix IV.

23. Includes all medals won by Great Britain, England, Ireland, Scotland, and Wales.

24. Includes separate medals won by Great Britain athletes, and the medal won by the English

team in hockey (field), but does not include medals won by Scottish and Welsh teams in hockey (field) and by Irish athletes.

25. Ireland was a part of Great Britain in 1908, but did compete separately in hockey (field) and polo.

26. Competed separately only in hockey (field).

27. Competed separately only in hockey (field).

28. All ages are listed as years-days. Italicized numbers indicate that the exact day of birth is not known, only the year of birth. In all such cases, a "worst case" assumption is made, i.e., for oldest records, we assigned a date of 31 December, while for youngest records, the date assigned was 1 January.

29. Daniel Carroll's (AUS-RUG) date of birth is usually listed as 17 February 1892, but research by Buchanan and his British colleagues who study rugby history has shown this year to be incorrect. The erroneous 1892 year of birth made him only 16 in 1908 and the youngest gold medalist in 1908, and one of the youngest gold medalists ever.

Archery

Archery had been contested at the 1900 and 1904 Olympic Games. In 1900, the sport was held virtually as a French national archery contest, with thousands of entrants qualifying from around the country. In 1904, only Americans competed at the St. Louis Olympic archery events. It was only marginally different in 1908. There were three events, two for men and one for women. Most of the competitors were British with a number of Frenchmen shooting in the men's events. One American also competed. The events were all held on the grass in the center of the main stadium infield.

The first day of shooting, Friday, 17 July, was devoted to the Gentlemen's Double York round and the Ladies' Double National round. Competition began at 10 in the morning, and was frequently interrupted by rain, with a strong wind also bothering the contestants. Still, the day's shooting finished by 2 P.M. (1400). The next morning, competition started at 11, as those two events were finished. It did not rain, but *The Archer's Register* noted that "For the time of year it was bitterly cold, the wind being again very strong and trying, as it eddied round the huge arena with its towering array of seats."

The third event, shooting in the Continental style, took place on Monday, 20 July. As the name would suggest, most of the competitors were from the continent — France. Officially, of the 17 archers, there was only one from Britain and one from the United States. However, eight British archers took part unofficially. Their scores are found in *The Archer's Register*, not having been published in the *Official Report*.

Site:	White City Stadium
Dates:	17–18, 20 July
Events:	3 [2 Men — 1 Women]
Competitors:	57 [32 Men — 25 Women]
Nations:	3 [3 Men — 1 Women]

	Competitors	1st	2nd	3rd	Totals
France	15	1	1	1	3
Great Britain	41	2	2	1	5
United States	1	–	–	1	1
Totals	57	3	3	3	9
Nations	3	2	2	3	3

39

Men	Competitors	1st	2nd	3rd	Totals
France	15	1	1	1	3
Great Britain	16	1	1	–	2
United States	1	–	–	1	1
Totals	32	2	2	2	6
Nations	3	2	2	2	3
Women	Competitors	1st	2nd	3rd	Totals
Great Britain	25	1	1	1	3
Totals	25	1	1	1	3
Nations	1	1	1	1	3

Officials

Judges: Colonel Henry Walrond, Eyre W. Hussey, Count Albert de Bertier de Sauvigny
Stewards: General Frederick Ernest Appleyard, C. E. Nesham, G. B. S. Walrond

Men

Gentlemen's Double York Round

A: 27; C: 3; D: 17–18 July; T: 1000 each day; F: 72 arrows at 100 yards, 48 arrows at 80 yards, and 24 arrows at 60 yards on each day (288 arrows in all).

William Dod led after the first day, scoring 403 with 91 hits, to lead Reginald Brooks-King, who posted marks of 393 and 93. John Penrose was third after day one, with Henry Richardson only in fifth place. On Saturday, Richardson had the highest score, with 417 points and 93 hits, followed by Dod who scored 412 with 94 hits. However, Dod's marks sufficed to keep him in the lead and earn him the gold medal.

William Dod was certainly not favored. Since 1900, the British National Championship had been divided among Brooks-King (five titles —1900, 1902–03, 1906, 1908), with John Penrose, John Bridges, Eyre Hussey, and Hugh Nesham each winning a single championship. Dod would win his only British title in 1909. He was the brother of Lottie Dod, the runner-up in the women's archery, and likely the greatest female all-around athlete in British sporting history. They were appropriately descended from Sir Antony Dod of Edge, who commanded the English archers at Agincourt. From a wealthy family, William Dod never had to worry about school or work, and spent his time in the pursuit of his sporting interests. He was also quite accomplished in golf and big game hunting.

		100y	80y	60y	Hits	Pts.	Golds
1. William Dod	GBR	70/292	71/299	44/224	185	815[1]*	13
2. Reginald Brooks-King	GBR	68/250	72/300	44/218	184	768	7
3. Henry Richardson	USA	60/248	67/291	43/221	170	760	8
4. John Penrose	GBR	69/259	62/244	41/206	175	709	9

*See Notes on page 43.

			100y	80y	60y	Hits	Pts.	Golds
5.	John Bridges	GBR	54/194	67/253	44/240	165	687	15
6.	Harold James	GBR	58/212	61/275	37/165	156	652	–[2]
7.	Theodore Robinson	GBR	63/267	48/188	42/192	153	647	17
8.	Hugh Nesham	GBR	54/181	61/267	41/195	153	643	7
9.	John Keyworth	GBR	68/244	64/234	30/144	162	622	9
10.	C. J. Perry Keene	GBR	44/166	50/204	37/173	131	543	6
11.	Capel Pownall	GBR	63/237	46/184	35/111	141	532	7
12.	John Stopford	GBR	44/182	48/204	32/144	124	530	17
13.	Robert Backhouse	GBR	28/100	54/222	40/194	122	516	9
14.	Robert Heathcote	GBR	34/118	44/198	40/160	118	476	7
15.	Geoffrey Cornewall	GBR	37/165	42/144	33/121	112	430	7
16.	H. Berton	FRA	28/128	38/156	29/141	95	425	8
17.	Eugène Richez	FRA	38/142	43/157	29/119	110	418	3
18.	Charles Coates	GBR	36/148	47/165	26/100	109	413	3
19.	Eugène Grisot	FRA	21/89	42/162	37/159	100	410	10
20.	Louis Vernet	FRA	30/104	36/138	37/143	103	385	5
21.	R. H. Bagnall-Oakley	GBR	30/104	33/149	31/121	94	374	4
22.	L. A. Salingne	FRA	11/39	40/158	36/150	87	347	6
23.	Albert Dauchez	FRA	21/95	20/86	27/99	68	280	4
24.	Charles Quervel	FRA	7/21	24/90	32/130	63	241	1
25.	E. Baudoin	FRA	16/42	26/92	17/81	59	215	4
26.	Gustave Cabaret	FRA	19/71	6/14	28/106	53	191	4
27.	A. Poupart[3]	FRA	5/19	5/17	--/-	10	36	–

Continental Style

A: 17 [25]; C: 3[4]; D: 20 July; F: 40 arrows shot at 50 meters.

Continental style refers to the fact that the arrows for this distance were shot one at a time, as opposed to proper rounds in which the arrows are shot in flights of three. Eight British archers competed unofficially in this event, at the request of the French archers, according to the Official Report. We have listed them among the official contestants to indicate approximately where they would have placed, but they had no official placings. All eight had also competed in the Gentlemen's Double York round. The leader among the unofficial contestants, Robert Backhouse, would have finished second and was awarded a Diploma of Merit for his efforts.

Little is known about the winner, Eugène Grisot. But 12 years later, at the 1920 Olympics in Antwerp, Grisot competed in the Olympics again in archery, winning three medals in the team events that year, finishing his Olympic career with one gold, two silvers, and one bronze medal.

			Hits	Score	Golds
1.	Eugène Grisot	FRA	39	263	9
	Robert Backhouse	*GBR*	40	260	9
2.	Louis Vernet	FRA	40[5]	256	7
3.	Gustave Cabaret	FRA	39	255	10
4.	Charles Aubras	FRA	39	231	8
5.	Charles Quervel	FRA	37	223	9
6.	Albert Dauchez	FRA	37	222	10

			Hits	*Score*	*Golds*
	Hugh Nesham	GBR	37	221	7
7.	L. A. Salingne	FRA	39	215	7
	R. H. Bagnall-Oakley	GBR	34	214	5
8.	H. Berton	FRA	40	212	8
9.	Eugène Richez	FRA	38	210	9
10.	E. Baudoin	FRA	34	206	3
11.	C. Vallie	FRA	37	193	5
12.	John Keyworth	GBR	38	190	4
13.	Émile Fisseux	FRA	37	185	6
	Robert Heathcote	GBR	37	183	4
	John Stopford	GBR	34	182	4
14.	L. S. de la Croix	FRA	37	177	3
	Capel Pownall	GBR	35	171	2
15.	Henry Richardson	USA[6]	33	171	4
16.	A. Poupart	FRA	35	155	3
	John Bridges	GBR	35	155	3
	Geoffrey Cornewall	GBR	32	144	–
17.	O. Jay	FRA	34	134	–

Women

Ladies' Double National Round

A: 25; C: 1; D: 17–18 July; T: 1100 each day; F: 48 arrows shot at 60 yards and 24 arrows shot at 50 yards on each day (144 arrows in all).

Lottie Dod took the lead on the first day with a score of 348 points and 66 hits, with Queenie Newall trailing, scoring 338 despite hitting the same number of targets. Nobody else was really close. On Saturday, the eighteenth, Queenie Newall scored well, leading the archers that day with 350 points but by a slim margin, as Beatrice Hill-Lowe was second on the day with 343. Lottie Dod collapsed completely on the second day, scoring only 294, which trailed five other archers.

Sybil Fenton "Queenie" Newall's victory still allows her the claim of being the oldest woman to win an Olympic medal or gold medal — she was four months short of her fifty-fourth birthday during the archery event. Newall won the British championship in archery in both 1911 and 1912 but she was far from the top female shooter of the era. That honor falls to Alice Legh, the greatest British archer ever, who won 23 national championships between 1886 and 1922. Legh elected not to compete at the Olympic event, which she almost certainly would have won. The following week at Oxford, she defeated Newall by 151 points.

The runner-up, Lottie Dod, who was the sister of the men's 1908 Olympic champion, never won a British title in archery. But she is certainly the greatest all-around British sportswoman. She remains the youngest ever champion at Wimbledon, having won the ladies' singles in 1887 when she was aged only 15. It was her first of five Wimbledon singles' titles, but she retired from tennis in 1893 and turned to other sports. She played hockey (field) for England in 1899-1900 and in golf, won the British Ladies' Amateur Championship in 1904, after reaching the semi-finals in 1898 and 1899.

			60y	*50y*	*Hit*	*Pts.*	*Golds*
1.	Sybil "Queenie" Newall	GBR	84/398	48/290	132	688[7]	23
2.	Charlotte "Lottie" Dod	GBR	80/388	46/254	126	642	16
3.	Beatrice Hill-Lowe	GBR/IRL	76/390	42/228	118	618	15
4.	Jessie Wadworth	GBR	79/357	44/248	123	605	13
5.	Mrs. G. W. H. Honnywill	GBR	79/377	44/210	123	587	10
6.	Mrs. S. H. Armitage	GBR	73/393	39/189	112	582	13
7.	Mrs. C. Priestley Foster	GBR	74/324	43/229	117	553	9
8.	Lillian Wilson	GBR	75/367	37/167	112	534	8
9.	Miss Mary Wadworth	GBR	79/321	43/201	122	522	3
10.	Mrs. Boddam Whetham	GBR	67/305	47/205	114	510	11
=11.	Gertrude Appleyard	GBR	65/281	42/222	107	503	9
	Mrs. E. Nott Bower	GBR	69/297	40/206	109	503	11
13.	Mrs. Norman Robertson	GBR	74/328	38/172	112	500	8
14.	Margaret Weedon	GBR	69/301	35/197	104	498	10
15.	Albertine Thackwell	GBR	65/303	39/181	104	484	11
16.	Doris Day	GBR	72/322	37/161	109	483	7
17.	K. G. Mudge	GBR	67/237	44/228	111	465	8
18.	Mrs. S. C. Babington	GBR	64/258	39/193	103	451	9
19.	Christine Cadman	GBR	67/233	40/194	107	427	3
20.	Martina Hyde	GBR	66/256	37/163	103	419	8
21.	Mrs. Everett Leonard	GBR	57/261	35/149	92	410	8
22.	Ina Wood	GBR	57/217	36/170	93	387	4
23.	J. Vance	GBR	58/228	37/157	95	385	7
24.	Mrs. H. Rushton	GBR	52/222	37/201	89	323	6
25.	Hilda Williams	GBR	51/179	31/137	82	316	4

NOTES

1. FW gave the scores for the first three by the numbers of hits made.
2. Number of golds for James is not given in any source.
3. Listed as DNF by OSVK, which, since he did not shoot at 60 yards, depends on one's interpretation.
4. DW and OSVK have two nations. OSVK incorrectly lists Henry Richardson (USA) as GBR.
5. FM incorrectly has 39 hits.
6. Incorrectly listed as GBR in OSVK.
7. FW gave the scores for the first three by the numbers of hits made.

Athletics (Track & Field)

For the first time virtually all the world's best track & field athletes competed at the Olympic Games and 430 athletes from 21 countries took part. The United States won 16 gold medals, Great Britain and her dominions won 9, and the only other country to win a gold medal was Sweden for whom Eric Lemming won both styles of the javelin.

Stringent qualifying conditions applied and for events up to 1,500 meters and both hurdle races only the winners advanced to the next round. This "sudden death" qualifying system produced some inconsistent results and in a number of cases athletes who would have been comfortable winners of other heats were eliminated. Certainly a system whereby a limited number of fastest losers advanced to the next rounds would have been preferable.

There is no evidence that all the marks in the qualifying round of the throwing events were actually measured. It seems likely that, if it was obviously apparent that a competitor had a better earlier mark, the officials did not bother to measure any subsequent inferior marks. Performances in the field events were measured in both the Imperial and Metric Systems.

The track was one-third of a mile in circumference — 586 yards, 2 feet (536.45 meters). It was within the huge White City Stadium and was surrounded by the 660-yard cycle track, but surrounded the infield which contained the swimming pool, and the areas for the field events, wrestling, gymnastics, archery, and football (soccer) matches.

Site:	White City Stadium, Shepherd's Bush, London	
Dates:	13–18, 20–25 July	
Events:	26	
Competitors:	431	
Nations:	21	

	Competitors	1st	2nd	3rd	Totals
Australia	6	–	–	–	–
Austria	2	–	–	–	–
Belgium	6	–	–	–	–
Bohemia	3	–	–	–	–
Canada	27	1	1	4	6

Denmark	8	–	–	–	–
Finland	15	–	–	1	1
France	19	–	1	1	2
Germany	20	–	1	1	2
Great Britain	126	7	7	3	17
Greece	12	–	3	–	3
Hungary	19	–	1	1	2
Italy	12	–	1	–	1
The Netherlands	19	–	–	–	–
New Zealand	3	–	–	1	1
Norway	11	–	1	2	3
Russia	1	–	–	–	–
South Africa	6	1	1	–	2
Sweden	31	2	–	3	5
Switzerland	1	–	–	–	–
United States	84	16	10	8	34
Totals	431	27	27	25	79
Nations	21	5	10	9	13

Notes: *400 meters — no second/no third; High jump — three seconds/no third; Pole vault — two firsts/no second/three thirds; Standing high jump — two seconds/no third.*

Officials

Referee (racing): T. M. Abraham, David Scott Duncan, Ernest Henry Pelling, George V. A. Schofield, Montague Shearman

Referee (field events): Harry J. Barclay, Arthur Roscoe Badger, A. J. Eggleston, A. Hannah, E. B. Holmes, Ernest Henry Pelling

Judges (racing): S. Anstey, J. Bartleman, David Basan, H. B. Butler, J. P. Ellis, Percy L. Fisher, R. W. Gale, W. Garbutt, J. T. Graham, S. J. Hardy, E. B. Holmes, Charles Val Hunter, W. Mabbett, –– O'Connell, Edward W. Parry, Ernest Henry Pelling, C. Pennycook, A. Ross Scott

Judges (field events): Harry J. Barclay, W. A. Brommage, –– Bryson, Michael J. Bulger, T. S. Cheesbrough, A. J. Eggleston, J. T. Green, P. Harding, C. T. W. Hickman, Frederick W. Parker, J. H. A. Reay, George Stuart Robertson, Montague Shearman, W. J. B. Tippetts, F. Wessenberg, –– Whitton, J. Yorkston

Judges (walking): Harry Venn, G. Duxfield, A. Smith, E. Ion Pool

Timekeepers: William W. Alexander, William M. Barnard, C. J. Pratt

Starters: J. M. Andrew, C. Harry Goble, Charles L. Lockton, W. Tripp

Starters' Stewards: I. Davidson

Timekeepers: William W. Alexander, William M. Barnard, B. R. Clayton, David Scott Duncan, Anthony Fattorini, A. Hannah, Joseph H. Hardwick, D. Lucas, A. E. Machin, D. McKeog, –– Osborne, Arthur Ovenden, Ernest Henry Pelling, C. J. Pratt, H. J. Rothery, G. M. Todd, A. J. Urry

Umpires: F. W. Baker, George F. Brewill, W. A. Brommage, M. Curry, J. S. Dutton, A. J. Eggleston, J. T. Green, F. Harrison, H. W. G. Haslegrave, William J. Morgan, E. F. Nicholls, Charles Otway, G. Stratton, G. Talbot, Harry Venn, Jack White

Competitors' Stewards: Harry J. Barclay (chief), H. W. G. Haslegrave (chief), Charles Otway (chief), Arthur Ovenden (chief), J. Allan, J. M. Andrew, F. W. Baker, David Basan, J. Bennett, Michael J. Bulger, E. O. Cheshire, W. Coles, E. Dutton, Frederick T. Elborough, C. W. Garnham, E. Gavin, J. E. Greenwood, C. T. W. Hickman, A. B. Horner, H. A. Mears, E. F. Nicholls, D. Prosser, W. P. Sparks, C. R. Staines, Jack White, A. W. Wilkie

Press Steward: E. O. Cheshire, W. Greenwood, Frederick W. Parker, P. W. B. Tippetts, F. W. Yexley

Hon. Secretary, AAA: Percy L. Fisher

Asst. Secretary, AAA: Sidney G. Moss

100 Meters

A: 60[1]*; C: 16; D: 20–22 July.

The top British sprinter of the era was John Morton, who had won the Amateur Athletic Association (AAA) championships four years consecutively, 1904–07, but he failed to make the Olympic final, finishing third and last in his semi-final. There was no dominant American sprinter, as since Bernie Wefers had won three straight titles in 1895–1897, 12 different sprinters had claimed the AAU (Amateur Athletic Union) championship. South Africa sent two good sprinters, Edward Duffy and the 1907 South African champion, Reggie Walker.

The Olympic record was 10.8, having been set in 1900 by Frank Jarvis (USA) and Walter Tewksbury (USA). The world mark was 10.6, set in 1906 by Sweden's Knut Lindberg. Though Lindberg competed in this event, he failed to get by the first round, finishing second in heat 8 to Lester Stevens (USA).

James Rector (USA) and Reggie Walker both equalled the Olympic record, Rector doing it in both rounds. Walker's record-equalling run came in the final when he beat Rector by one yard. At 19 years, 128 days, he set a record, which still stands, of being the youngest ever winner of the Olympic 100 meters.

It is often stated that Walker was not actually a member of the South African team in 1908, but travelled to London on his own. South African Olympic historian Lappe Laubscher has shown that this is not the case and that he was chosen for the team at the first opportunity.[2] He notes that Walker was recommended for the team on 1 May 1908 at a meeting of the South African Amateur Athletic and Cycling Union, but he initially could not make the trip because of a lack of funds. Walker was a native of Natal and Jim Wallace, a Natal sportswriter, started a successful campaign to raise funds for Walker's trip.[3]

Final A: 4; C: 3; D: 22 July; T: 1615.

1.	Reggie Walker	SAF	10.8		=OR
2.	James Rector	USA	11.0est[4]	at 1½ feet	
3.	Robert Kerr	CAN/IRL	11.0est	inches bh 2nd	
4.	Nathaniel Cartmell	USA	11.2est	few yards bh	

Semi-Finals A: 15; C: 4; D: 21 July; T: 1535; F: Winner of each heat advances to the final.

Heat 1 A: 4; C: 2.

1.	Reggie Walker	SAF	10.8	
2.	William May	USA	11.0est	at one yard
3.	Patrick Roche	GBR/IRL[5]		
4.	Lester Stevens	USA		

Heat 2 A: 3; C: 3.

1.	Robert Kerr	CAN	11.0	
2.	Nathaniel Sherman	USA	11.3est	at 3 yds
3.	John Morton	GBR		

Heat 3 A: 4; C: 3.

1.	James Rector	USA	10.8	=or
2.	Harold Huff	USA	11.1est	at 3 yds
3.	Edward Duffy	SAF		
4.	Robert Duncan	GBR		

Heat 4 A: 4; C: 2.

1.	Nathaniel Cartmell	USA	11.2	
2.	Lawson Robertson	USA	11.2est	at 1 ft
3.	James Stark	GBR		
4.	John George	GBR		

Round One A: 60; C: 16; D: 20 July; T: 1500; F: Winner of each heat advances to the semi-finals.

Heat 1 A: 3; C: 3.

1.	Edward Duffy	SAF	11.6	easy win
2.	Georgios Skoutaridis	GRE		
3.	Victor Henny	NED		

6

Heat 2 A: 2; C: 2.

1.	John George	GBR	11.6	
2.	Oscar Guttormsen	NOR	12.0est	at 3 yds

7

Heat 3 A: 4; C: 4.

1.	Nathaniel Cartmell	USA	11.0	
2.	Georges Malfait	FRA	11.2est	at 2 yds
3.	Arthur Hoffmann	GER	11.4est	
4.	Evert Koops	NED		

8

Heat 4 A: 5; C: 5.

1.	Reggie Walker	SAF	11.0	
2.	Jean Konings	BEL	11.6est	at 4 yds
3.	Denis Murray	GBR/IRL		

| AC. | Edgar Kiralfy | USA | | |
| | Ernestus Greven | NED | | |

Heat 5 A: 4; C: 4.

1.	Robert Cloughen	USA	11.0	
2.	John Johansen[9]	NOR	11.7est	at 5 yards
3.	David Beland	CAN		
	Henry Harmer[10]	GBR	DNF	

Heat 6 A: 4; C: 4.

1.	William May	USA	11.2	
2.	Victor Jacquemin	BEL	11.5est	at 3 yds
3.	L. Lescat	FRA		
4.	Mikhail Paskhalidis	GRE		

[11]

Heat 7 A: 5; C: 5.

1.	Robert Duncan	GBR	11.4	
2.	Knut Stenborg	SWE	11.5est	at 1 yd
3.	Hans Eicke	GER	11.6est	
4.	Umberto Barozzi	ITA		
5.	Ragnar Stenberg	FIN		

[12]

Heat 8 A: 4; C: 4.

1.	Lester Stevens	USA	11.2	
2.	Knut Lindberg[13]	SWE	11.2est	inches behind
3.	Heinrich Rehder	GER	11.8est	
4.	William Murray	GBR/IRL		

[14]

Heat 9 A: 3; C: 3.

1.	John Morton	GBR	11.2	
2.	Axel Petersen	DEN	11.5est	at 3 yds
3.	Jacobus Hoogveld	NED		

[15]

Heat 10 A: 3; C: 3.

1.	Robert Kerr	CAN	11.0	
2.	M. Chapman	GBR	11.3est	at 3 yds
	Paul Fischer[16]	GER	DNF	

[17]

Heat 11 A: 4; C: 4.

1.	William Hamilton	USA	11.2	
2.	Pál Simon	HUN	11.5est	at 3 yds
3.	G. Lamotte	FRA		
4.	Herbert Phillips	SAF	DNF	

[18]

Heat 12 A: 3; C: 3.

1.	Harold Huff	USA	11.4	
2.	Henry Pankhurst	GBR	11.5est	at 1 yd
3.	Karl Fryksdahl	SWE		

19

Heat 13 A: 4; C: 4.

1.	Lawson Robertson	USA	11.4	
2.	Frank Lukeman	CAN	11.7est	at 3 yds
3.	Henri Meslot	FRA		
4.	Eduard Schönecker	AUT		

20

Heat 14 A: 5; C: 5.

1.	Nathaniel Sherman	USA	11.2	
2.	Louis Sebert	CAN	11.7est	at 4 yds
3.	Harold Watson	GBR		
4.	Frigyes Mezei Wiesner	HUN		
5.	Hermann von Bönninghausen	GER	12.0est	

Heat 15 A: 3; C: 3.

1.	James Rector	USA	10.8	=OR
2.	Vilmos Rácz	HUN	11.4est	
3.	Willy Kohlmey	GER	12.0est	

21

Heat 16 A: 2; C: 2.

1.	James Stark	GBR	11.8
2.	Gaspare Torretta	ITA	12.0est

22

Heat 17 A: 2; C: 2.

1.	Patrick Roche	GBR/IRL	11.4	
2.	Carl Bechler	GER	11.7est	at 2 yds

23

200 Meters

A: 43; C: 14; D: 21–23 July.

The Olympic record was 22.2, set by Walter Tewksbury (USA) in winning the gold medal at Paris in 1900. Though there was no official body to recognize world records, the fastest time on record was the 21.4 by John Maybury of the United States, set at the Western Intercollegiate Athletic Meet in 1897. Neither the United States nor Great Britain had produced a dominant long sprinter, as the most recent AAA and AAU championships had been spread among several different runners. But the 1908 AAA title had recently been won by the Irish-born Canadian, Bobby Kerr, who had also won the Canadian AAU title from 1906–08. Kerr's family had moved to Hamilton, Ontario, when he was 17 years old, in 1899. By 1907 he was the greatest Canadian sprinter to date, winning over 40 events in that year alone.

The two fastest heat winners were Kerr (22.2) and the American William Hamilton (22.4). Both runners were drawn in the same heat in the semi-finals where Kerr was the winner in a close race and Hamilton was eliminated. Kerr went on to win the final and with the South African, Walker, winning the 100 meters, the United States failed to win either sprint for the first time. This is a relatively rare occurrence at the Olympics and has only been repeated in 1928, 1960, 1972, and 1980.

Final A: 4; C: 4; D: 23 July; T: 1600.

1.	Robert Kerr	CAN	22.6	
2.	Robert Cloughen	USA	22.6est	at 2 ft
3.	Nathaniel Cartmell	USA	22.7est	
4.	George Hawkins	GBR	22.9e	

Semi-Finals A: 14; C: 6; D: 22 July; T: 1015; F: Winner of each heat advances to the final.

Heat 1 A: 4; C: 4.

1.	Robert Kerr	CAN	22.6	
2.	William Hamilton	USA	22.7est	
3.	Károly Radóczy	HUN	22.8est	at 1 ft
4.	Oscar Guttormsen	NOR		

Heat 2 A: 3; C: 1.

1.	Nathaniel Cartmell	USA	22.6	
2.	Nathaniel Sherman	USA	22.9est	at 1½ yds
3.	Harold Huff	USA	23.0est	"close"

Heat 3 A: 4; C: 2.

1.	Robert Cloughen	USA	22.6	
2.	Lionel Reed	GBR	22.8est	at 1 yd
3.	John George	GBR		
4.	Samuel Hurdsfield	GBR		

Heat 4 A: 3; C: 2.

1.	George Hawkins	GBR	22.6	
2.	Patrick Roche	GBR/IRL	22.6est	at 1 ft
3.	Georges Malfait	FRA		

24

Round One A: 43; C: 14; D: 21 July; T: 1100; F: Winner of each heat advances to the semi-finals.

Heat 1 A: 2; C: 2:

1.	John George	GBR	23.4	
2.	Victor Henny	NED	24.6est	at 10 yds

25

Heat 2 A: 4; C: 4.

1.	Harold Huff	USA	22.8	
2.	Edward Duffy	SAF	23.2est	at 1½ yds
3.	Hendrik van der Wal	NED		
4.	Knut Stenborg	SWE		

26

Heat 3 A: 4; C: 4.

1.	Patrick Roche	GBR/IRL	22.8	
2.	Lawson Robertson	USA	23.0est	at 1 yd
3.	Frank Lukeman	CAN		
4.	Evert Koops	NED		

27

Heat 4 A: 3; C: 3.

1.	Nathaniel Cartmell	USA	23.0	
2.	Vilmos Rácz	HUN	23.3est	at 2 yds
3.	Ragnar Stenberg	FIN		

28

Heat 5 A: 2; C: 2.

1.	Georges Malfait	FRA	22.6	
2.	Robert Duncan	GBR	23.1est	at 4 yds

29

Heat 6 A: 3; C: 3.

1.	Sven Laftman	SWE	23.8	
2.	Frigyes Mezei Wiesner	HUN	24.0est	at 2 yds
3.	Ernestus Greven	NED		

30

Heat 7 A: 1; C: 1.

1.	Károly Radóczy	HUN		wo

31

Heat 8 A: 2; C: 2.

1.	Robert Cloughen	USA	23.4	
2.	Umberto Barozzi	ITA	24.1est	at 6 yds

32

Heat 9 A: 2; C: 2.

1.	Samuel Hurdsfield	GBR	23.6	
2.	Mikhail Paskhalidis	GRE	24.0est	at 1½ yds

33

Heat 10 A: 5; C: 5.

1.	William Hamilton	USA	22.4	
2.	Louis Sebert	CAN	22.8est	at 3 yds

3.	Henry Pankhurst	GBR
4.	Pál Simon	HUN
5.	Fernand Halbart	BEL[34]

Heat 11 A: 5; C: 5.

1.	Robert Kerr	CAN	22.2	OR
2.	William May	USA	22.7est	at 2½ yds
3.	James Stark	GBR		
4.	Knut Lindberg	SWE		
5.	Emilio Brambilla	ITA		

Heat 12 A: 4; C: 4.

1.	Nathaniel Sherman	USA	22.8	
2.	John Morton	GBR	23.1est	at 2 yds
3.	Eduard Schönecker	AUT		
4.	Cornelis den Held	NED		

35

Heat 13 A: 2; C: 2.

| 1. | Lionel Reed | GBR | 23.2 | |
| 2. | Arthur Hoffmann | GER | 23.5est | at 2½ yds |

36

Heat 14 A: 1; C: 1.

| 1. | Oscar Guttormsen | NOR | | wo |

37

Heat 15 A: 3; C: 3.

1.	George Hawkins	GBR	22.8	
2.	Henri Meslot	FRA	23.2est	at 3 yds
3.	Jacobus Hoogveld	NED		

38

400 Meters

A: 37[39]; C: 11; D: 21–23 July, 25 July.

At the beginning of 1908 Edgar Bredin's 48½, set in 1885, was still the world's fastest ¼-mile on a curved track. The Olympic record was Harry Hillman's 49.2, set in winning the gold medal at St. Louis in 1904. Hillman was in London in 1908 but only ran the 400 hurdles. The top British one-lapper was Wyndham Halswelle, who had been AAA champion in 1905–06 and 1908, and earlier in July, had run 48.4 in Glasgow to break Bredin's world best time for 440 yards.

After setting an Olympic record of 48.4 in the second round, Halswelle was easily the fastest of the qualifiers. In the final he faced three Americans, John Carpenter, John Taylor, and William Robbins, and the race resulted in possibly the most controversial finish in Olympic track & field history. Carpenter was drawn on the inside with Halswelle, Robbins, and Taylor outside him in that order, and after Robbins had been involved in some over-rigorous jockeying for position, Carpenter entered the home straight with Halswelle at his shoulder. At this point, Carpenter, in order to prevent Halswelle from passing him, moved progressively farther towards the outside of the track, forcing Halswelle to within 18 inches of the outside curb. By this time the British officials had seen enough and Dr. Arthur Roscoe Badger, the judge on the final bend, ran up the track signalling the judges to break the tape. Carpenter crossed the line in an unofficial 48.4[40], while Halswelle slowed to a jog.

After a lengthy inquiry on the evening after the race, Carpenter was disqualified and the race was ordered to be re-run two days later, in lanes (then termed strings, as strings separated each lane), but without Carpenter. The precise statement was, "The judges have decided that the race is void, and order same to be re-run in strings on Saturday next [25 July], at 12 o'clock. J. C. Carpenter is disqualified."[41] American officials ordered Robbins and Taylor not to take part in the re-run and Halswelle ran alone to take the Olympic title.

Even before the U.S. team left for home they announced that, as Carpenter had crossed the line first, they would consider him to be the Olympic champion. There is no recorded response to a reader's letter in a British newspaper inquiring if, by the same reasoning, the Americans would consider Pietri to be the Olympic marathon champion. Unfortunately, the ill-feeling lingered and at the 1909 AAU Convention a motion was passed refusing to recognize Carpenter's disqualification.

Photographs exist of the race and one, published on 24 July 1908 in *The Daily Mirror*, is quite telling, showing the footprints of the runners as they entered the home straight. From this photograph and the footprints, there is little doubt that Carpenter ran extremely wide coming off the turn. Another photograph of the finish confirms that he forced Halswelle to the very outside of the track. Amos Alonzo Stagg, a member of the American Olympic Committee, and later a famous football coach, attempted to assuage both sides when he noted that Carpenter "certainly took the route complained of but that he didn't commit a deliberate foul as it would have been considered an acceptable tactic at a track meet in America."

But the rules in force at the 1908 Olympics were British, those of the Amateur Athletic Association. Their rule regarding obstruction during a race was quite explicit.

> Any competitor willfully jostling, or running across, or obstructing another competitor, so as to impede his progress, shall forfeit his right to be in the competition, and shall not be awarded any position or prize that he would otherwise have been entitled to.

The 400 meter controversy received huge play in both the American and British press, with feelings running along nationalistic lines. The pamphlet published by the British, *A Reply to Certain Criticisms*, also devoted an entire chapter to the race. In it they quoted a letter from David Scott Duncan which was published in *The Field* on 29 August 1908, which also disputes Stagg's statement that Carpenter's tactics would have been allowed in the United States. Duncan had been the referee of the 400 meters.

> That Halswelle was badly bored and obstructed is, of course, beyond question, and the American rules as to such tactics are even more explicit than those obtaining in Britain. Here they are:—
> Rule III.—The Referee.—When in a final heat a claim of foul or interference is made, he (the referee) shall have power to disqualify the competitor who was at fault if he considers the foul intentional or due to culpable carelessness, and he shall also have the power to order a new race between such competitors as he thinks entitled to such a privilege.

Rule XVIII.— The Course.— Each competitor shall keep in his respective position from start to finish in all races on straightaway tracks, and in all races on track with one or more turns he shall not cross to the inner edge of the track except when he is at least six feet in advance of his nearest competitor. *After turning the last corner into the straight in any race each competitor must keep a straight course to the finish line, and not cross, either to the outside or the inside, in front of any of his opponents.*

In the face of the above rules of Union of which Mr. Sullivan is president, he is surely left "without a leg to stand upon." I may add that I was referee of the Four Hundred Metres.

David Scott Duncan

Wyndham Halswelle did address the situation in a letter he sent to *The Sporting Life.*

As regards the Four Hundred Metres Race, Carpenter did not strike me any vigorous blows with his elbow, nor were there any marks on my chest, nor did I say that Carpenter struck me or show the marks to any Press representative.[42] I did not attempt to pass the Americans until the last corner, reserving my effort for the finishing straight. Here I attempted to pass Carpenter on the outside, since he was not far enough from the curb to do so on the inside, and I was too close up to have crossed behind him. Carpenter's elbow undoubtedly touched my chest, for as I moved outwards to pass him he did likewise, keeping his right in front of me.

In this manner he bored me across quite two-thirds of the track, and entirely stopped my running. As I was well up to his shoulder, and endeavouring to pass him, it is absurd to say that I could have come up on the inside. I was too close after half way round the bend to have done this; indeed, to have done so would have necessitated chopping my stride, and thereby losing anything from two to four yards.

When about thirty to forty yards from the tape I saw the officials holding up their hands, so slowed up, not attempting to finish all out.

John Carpenter also gave his version of events, which was published in *The Daily Mail* on 24 July 1908:[43]

I started with the inside berth. Halswelle was next to me; Robbins next [to him] and Taylor on the outside. Up the final straight away Robbins led, and I was running second. Halswelle was close behind me, I imagine.

At the first curve the positions were unchanged. Then, at the second bend right at the top of the course I, because of my long stride, was unable to stick to the inside berth. It was at this point that I attempted to pass Robbins, and [moved] wide into the straight, Halswelle was still behind me.

From this point my path was absolutely straight to the finish line. For about [10] or 15 yards — at eighty yards from the finish — Halswelle was running absolutely abreast of me, with plenty of room on the outside of him, and he could have passed on the inside of me if necessary.

I do not know of any contact between us at any point during the race. I always know exactly what I do during a race, and I am perfectly certain we did not touch. I do not see how a race could have been more fairly run.

Wyndham Halswelle had a short, but meteoric track career. It began in 1904 when he won the Army 880 yards championship. After winning medals at the 1906 Olympics in Athens in both the 400 meters (silver) and 800 meters (bronze), he won the 100 yards, 220 yards, 440 yards, and 880 yards at the 1906 Scottish AAA Championships — all in the same afternoon. The actions and attitudes of the Americans at the 1908 Olympics so soured Halswelle's outlook that he ran just one more race before retiring from the sport in late 1908. A career Army officer, he tragically died from a sniper's bullet in France while fighting World War I.

John Carpenter's track career was also short and there is no record that he ever competed again after the 1908 Olympics. He attended Cornell and won one IC4A title in 1906, that at 880 yards. Over 440 yards he was fourth as a freshman in 1905 and third in 1908 at the IC4A's. As the 1908 IC4A was considered one of the American Olympic Trial Meets, he was named to the 1908 Olympic team. Carpenter never competed at the AAU Championship.

Re-run Final A: 1; C: 1; D: 25 July; T: 1200.

1.	Wyndham Halswelle	GBR	50.0	wo

Original Final A: 4; C: 4; D: 23 July; T: 1730.

1.	John Carpenter	USA	48.4[44]	DQ
2.	Wyndham Halswelle	GBR		
3.	William Robbins	USA[45]		
4.	John Taylor	USA		

Semi-Finals A: 15; C: 4; D: 22 July; T: 1730; F: Winner of each heat advances to the final.

Heat 1 A: 4; C: 2.

1.	John Carpenter	USA	49.4	49.8/440y
2.	Charles Davies	GBR	49.8est	at 3 yds
3.	Ned Merriam	USA		
4.	G. W. Young	GBR		

Heat 2 A: 4; C: 2.

1.	Wyndham Halswelle	GBR	48.4	OR 48.8/440y
2.	Edwin Montague	GBR	49.8est	at 12 yds
3.	George Nicol	GBR		
4.	William Prout	USA		

Heat 3 A: 4; C: 3.

1.	John Taylor	USA	49.8	50.2/440y
2.	Horace Ramey	USA	50.5est	at 5 yds
3.	Edward Ryle	GBR		
4.	Georges Malfait	FRA		

Heat 4 A: 3; C: 2.

1.	William Robbins	USA	49.0	49.8/440y
2.	Louis Sebert	CAN	49.5est	at 3 yds
3.	John Atlee	USA		

Round One A: 37; C: 11; D: 21 July; F: Winner of each heat advances to the semi-final.

Heat 1 A: 2; C: 2.

1.	Edwin Montague	GBR	50.2	
2.	Paul Pilgrim	USA	51.4est	at 8 yds

46

Heat 2 Voided — no starters.

47

Heat 3 A: 1; C: 1.

1.	Edward Ryle	GBR		wo

48

Heat 4 A: 3; C: 3.

1.	John Taylor	USA	50.8	
2.	Roberto Penna	ITA	52.4est	at 12 yds
3.	Sven Laftman	SWE		

49

Heat 5 A: 2; C: 2.

1.	George Nicol	GBR	50.8	
2.	Oscar Guttormsen	NOR	52.4est	at 12 yds

50

Heat 6 A: 2; C: 2.

1.	Georges Malfait	FRA	50.0	
2.	Donald Buddo	CAN	51.2est	at 8 yds

51

Heat 7 A: 4; C: 4.

1.	William Robbins	USA	50.4	easy win
2.	József Nagy	HUN		
3.	Noel Chavasse[52]	GBR		
4.	Victor Henny	NED		

53

Heat 8 A: 2; C: 2.

1.	William Prout	USA	50.4	
2.	Christopher Chavasse	GBR	50.7est	at 2 yds

54

Heat 9 A: 2; C: 2.

1.	Horace Ramey	USA	51.0	
2.	Arthur Astley	GBR	51.4est	at 1½ yds

55

Heat 10 A: 3; C: 3.

1.	Louis Sebert	CAN	50.2	
2.	Massimo Cartasegna	ITA	52.7est	at 20 yds

	Victor Jacquemin[56]	BEL	DNF	

[57]

Heat 11 A: 3; C: 3.

1.	John Atlee	USA	50.4	
2.	Alan Patterson	GBR	50.6est	at 1 yd
3.	Giuseppe Tarella	ITA		

[58]

Heat 12 A: 2; C: 2.

1.	Charles Davies	GBR	50.4	
2.	Cornelis den Held	NED	51.0est	at 4 yds

[59]

Heat 13 A: 2; C: 2.

1.	Ned Merriam	USA	52.2	
2.	R. C. Robb	GBR/IRL	52.5est	at 2 yds

[60]

Heat 14 A: 4; C: 4.

1.	John Carpenter	USA	49.6	
2.	Otto Trieloff	GER	50.9est	at 10 yds
3.	Arvid Ringstrand	SWE		
4.	Hendrik van der Wal	NED		

[61]

Heat 15 A: 3; C: 3.

1.	Wyndham Halswelle	GBR	49.4	
2.	Frederick de Selding	USA	50.8est	at 10 yds
3.	Brand "Bram" Evers	NED		

[62]

Heat 16 A: 2; C: 2.

1.	G. W. Young	GBR	52.4	easy win
2.	Jacobus Hoogveld	NED		

[63]

800 Meters

A: 38[64]; C: 10; D: 20–21 July.

The heavy favorite was Melvin Sheppard of the United States who had won the AAU Championship in 1906–08. He had also won the American Eastern Olympic trial in 1:54.0, challenging the long-standing world record of 1:53.4 for 880 yards set by Charles Kilpatrick on 21 September 1895 in New York .

The eight heats were all won in modest times but in the final Sheppard posted a new world record of 1:52.8. It is, however, probable that Kilpatrick had passed the 800 meters mark in a slightly faster time when he set his world record. In anticipation of a fast Olympic final, a tape was also placed at 880 yards which Sheppard reached in 1:54.0. After 400 meter splits of 53.0 and 59.8, it is evident that Sheppard was slowing considerably towards the end of the race but even so, a differential of 1.2 seconds to cover the additional 4.68 meters between 800 meters and 880 yards seems unrealistic. Having won the 1,500 meters seven days earlier, Sheppard completed a notable middle distance double.

Melvin Sheppard would eventually win four gold medals in middle distance running at the Olympics. In 1908 he won the 800 and 1,500, and ran on the medley relay team, anchoring the 800 meter leg. In 1912, he also ran on the 4 × 400 meter relay. He eventually won five AAU titles over two laps —1906–08, and 1911–12, and three Canadian titles —1906, 1911–12.

Final A: 8; C: 5; D: 21 July; T: 1700.

1.	Melvin Sheppard	USA	1:52.8	OR, WR 1:54.0/880
2.	Emilio Lunghi	ITA	1:54.2est	
3.	Hanns Braun	GER	1:55.2est	
4.	Ödön Bodor	HUN	1:55.4est	
5.	Theodore Just	GBR	1:56.4est	
6.	John Halstead	USA		
	Ivo Fairbairn-Crawford	GBR	DNF	
	Clarke Beard	USA	DNF	

Round One A: 38; C: 10; D: 20 July; T: 1530 and 1730; F: Winner of each heat advances to the final.[65]

Heat 1 A: 6; C: 5.

1.	Ödön Bodor	HUN	1:58.6	
2.	George Butterfield	GBR	1:58.9est	at 2 yds
3.	Evert Björn[66]	SWE		
4.	James Lightbody	USA		
	Frederick Ashford	GBR	DNF	
	Hendrik van der Wal	NED	DNF	
	[67]			

Heat 2 A: 3; C: 3.

1.	Melvin Sheppard	USA	1:58.0	
2.	James Lintott	GBR	1:58.8est	at 4 yds
3.	R. Irving Parkes	CAN		
	[68]			

Heat 3 A: 4; C: 3.

1.	John Halstead	USA	2:01.4	
2.	John Lee	GBR	2:01.7est	at 2 yds
3.	George Morphy	GBR/IRL		
4.	József Nagy	HUN		
	[69]			

Heat 4 A: 5; C: 4.

1.	Emilio Lunghi	ITA	1:57.2	
2.	Harry Coe	USA	1:58.0est	at 2 yds

3.	Lloyd Jones	USA		
	Stefanos Dimitrios	GRE	DNF	
	L. J. Manogue [70]	GBR	DNF	

Heat 5 A: 6; C: 5.

1.	Clarke Beard	USA	1:59.8	
2.	Arthur Astley	GBR	1:59.9est	at 1 yd
3.	Donald Buddo	CAN		
4.	M. Oskar Quarg	GER	2:10.0est	
	Charles French	USA	DNF	
	Edward Dahl [71]	SWE	DNF	

Heat 6 A: 4; C: 4.

1.	Theodore Just	GBR	1:57.8	
2.	Andreas Breynck[72]	GER	2:06.0est	at 50 yds
	Frank Gösta Danielson	SWE	DNF	
	Ary Vosbergen [73]	NED	DNF	

Heat 7 A: 6; C: 5.

1.	Hanns Braun	GER	1:58.0	
2.	Joseph Bromilow	USA	1:58.3est	at 1 yd
3.	Harold Holding	GBR	1:58.5est	
	Horace Ramey	USA	DNF	
	Fredrik Svanström	SWE	DNF	
	Brand "Bram" Evers [74]	NED	DNF	

Heat 8 A: 4; C: 4.

1.	Ivo Fairbairn-Crawford	GBR	1:57.8	
2.	Kristian Hellström	SWE	2:00.0est	at 15 yds
3.	Harvey Sutton[75]	AUS		
4.	Francis Sheehan [76]	USA		

1,500 Meters

A: 44; C: 15; D: 13–14 July.

George Butterfield was the top British miler, having won the AAA title in 1905–07. Unfortunately, because of the qualifying system which advanced only one runner to the next round, Butterfield did not make the final. In his heat he drew Melvin Sheppard, who set a new Olympic record of 4:05.0 to advance to the final. Norman Hallows (GBR) improved the record to 4:03.4 in the next heat. Hallows narrowly defeated Emilio Lunghi (ITA) whose estimated time of 4:03.8 would have won any of the other seven heats. These were yet further examples of the inequity of a qualifying system whereby only heat winners advanced to the next round.

Despite the fast qualifying times of Sheppard and Hallows, the favorite for the final was Harold Wilson (GBR) who had won the British Trials in a world record 3:59.8 in May. The final was held on a terrible day for running. It was noted, "The temperature was low, and a strong wind, laden with moisture, blew across the field, where the athletes sat shivering in blankets. The atmosphere was muggy and occasional showers, never attaining the dignity of real rain, now and then sprinkled the spectators and competitors."[77]

As expected, Wilson led the field into the home straight but was caught a few meters from the tape by Sheppard who equalled the Olympic record of 4:03.4 set by Hallows in the heats. With an estimated time of 4:03.6, a disappointed Wilson was almost four seconds outside his new British record.

Final A: 8; C: 3; D: 14 July; T: 1720.

1.	Melvin Sheppard	USA	4:03.4	OR
2.	Harold Wilson	GBR	4:03.6est	
3.	Norman Hallows	GBR	4:04.0est	
4.	John Tait	CAN	4:06.8est	
5.	Ivo Fairbairn-Crawford	GBR	4:07.6est	
6.	Joseph Deakin	GBR	4:07.9est	
	James Sullivan	USA	DNF	
	Vincent Loney	GBR	DNF	

Round One A: 44; C: 15; D: 13 July; T: 1600; F: Winner of each heat advances to the final.

Heat 1 A: 9; C: 7.

1.	James Sullivan	USA	4:07.6	
2.	James Lightbody	USA	4:08.6	at 6 yds
3.	Frederick Meadows	CAN	4:12.2	at 14 yds
4.	Francis Knott	GBR		run out
5.	Joseph Smith	GBR		
6.	Louis Bonniot de Fleurac	FRA		
7.	Nils Dahl	NOR		
8.	Ödön Bodor	HUN		
9.	Jacques Keyser	NED		

[78]

Heat 2 A: 7; C: 4.

1.	Melvin Sheppard	USA	4:05.0	OR
2.	John Halstead	USA	4:05.6	at 1 yd
3.	George Butterfield	GBR	4:11.8	
4.	John Lee	GBR	4:12.4est	at 3 yds
5.	Joseph Lynch	AUS		
6.	Kjeld Nielsen	DEN		
7.	Arno Hesse	GER		

[79]

Heat 3 A: 5; C: 4.

1.	Norman Hallows	GBR	4:03.4	OR
2.	Emilio Lunghi	ITA	4:03.8[80]	at 2 yds

81	Massimo Cartasegna	ITA	DNF	
	Frank Riley	USA	DNF	
	Evert Björn	SWE	DNF	
	Charles Swain[82]	AUS	DNF	
83				

Heat 4 A: 5; C: 4.

1.	Vincent Loney	GBR	4:08.4	
2.	Harry Coe	USA	4:09.2	at 2 yds
3.	John McGough	GBR/IRL	4:16.4	at 30 yds
4.	Stefanos Dimitrios	GRE		bad 4th
5.	Joseph Dreher	FRA		
84				

Heat 5 A: 4; C: 4.

1.	John Tait	CAN	4:12.2	
2.	József Nagy	HUN	4:19.6	at 50 yds
3.	Fredrik Svanström	FIN	4:25.2	long way bh
	A. Gaston Ragueneau	FRA	DNF[85]	
86				

Heat 6 A: 3; C: 3.

1.	Joseph Deakin	GBR	4:13.6	
2.	Andreas Breynck	GRE	4:30.0	at 75 yds
3.	Ary Vosbergen	NED	4:38.6	at 125 yds
87				

Heat 7 A: 3; C: 3.

1.	Harold Wilson	GBR	4:11.4	
2.	Jean Bouin	FRA	4:17.0	at 30 yds
3.	William Galbraith	CAN	4:20.2	
88				

Heat 8 A: 7; C: 6.

1.	Ivo Fairbairn-Crawford	GBR	4:09.4	
2.	Edward Dahl	SWE	4:10.4	at 4 yds
3.	Hanns Braun	GER	4:18.2	at 20 yds
4.	Oscar Larsen	NOR		
5.	François Delloye	BEL		
6.	Axel Andersson	SWE		
7.	John Fitzgerald	CAN		
89				

5-Mile (8,045 meters) Run

A: 36[90]; C: 14; D: 15, 18 July.

Only twice has a 5-mile race been contested at the Olympics, in 1906 and 1908. The world record for this distance was 24:33.4, set by Britain's Alfred Shrubb in London on 12 May 1904.

Shrubb was the greatest long distance runner in the world but had since turned professional and could not compete at the 1908 Olympics. The Olympic record had been set in 1906 at Athens by another British runner, Henry Hawtrey, who had recorded 26:11.8 on the tight Athens track. With Shrubb ineligible no real favorite existed. America had no top distance runners, and Britain had failed to produce a dominant distance man to replace Shrubb.

Edward Owen (GBR), Charles Hefferon (SAF), who was later to finish second in the marathon, and Johan Svanberg (SWE) shared the early lead but 700 yards from home, Emil Voigt made his move and left the pack to win by 70 yards, although his winning time was almost 40 seconds outside Shrubb's world record. The splits and leaders were as follows: one mile–4:26.2 (Owen); two miles–9:54.2 (Hefferon); three miles–15:05,6 (Hefferon); four miles–20:19.2 (Svanberg).

Four athletes who had competed in the final of the 3-mile team race also started in the heats of the 5 miles which began less than three hours after the team race final. Deakin and Coales (both GBR) and Trube (USA) failed to finish in the heats but "Archie" Robertson (GBR), who had individually finished second in the team race final, won his heat in the 5 miles and then finished fifth in the final three days later.

Emil Voigt had won the AAA title at four miles only ten days before the Olympics. He repeated as AAA champion in 1909 and then won the one mile race in 1910 before retiring from competition. He claimed his athletic success was due to his vegetarianism.

Final A: 10; C: 5; D: 18 July; T: 1730.

1.	Emil Voigt	GBR	25:11.2	
2.	Edward Owen	GBR	25:24.0	
3.	Johan Svanberg	SWE	25:37.2	
4.	Charles Hefferon	SAF	25:44.0	
5.	Arthur "Archie" Robertson	GBR	26:13.0	
6.	Frederick Meadows	CAN	26:16.2	
7.	John Fitzgerald	CAN		
8.	Frederick Bellars	USA		
9.	Seth Landqvist	SWE		
	James Murphy	GBR/IRL	DNF	
	91			

Round One A: 36; C: 14; D: 15 July; T: 1430; F: Winner and runner-up in each heat advance to the final.

Heat 1 A: 5; C: 5.

1.	Johan Svanberg	SWE	25:46.2	92
2.	Charles Hefferon	SAF	26:05.0	
3.	George Blake	AUS		
	William Coales	GBR	DNF	at 4+ miles
	A. Gaston Ragueneau	FRA	DNF	at 1 lap
	93			

Heat 2 A: 7; C: 7.

1.	Emil Voigt	GBR	26:13.4	94
2.	Frederick Bellars	USA	26:49.0	
3.	Pericle Pagliani	ITA	26:56.4	

4.	Kjeld Nielsen	DEN	27:04.8	
	Willem Wakker	NED	DNF	
	Georgios Koulouberdas	GRE	DNF	
	Edward Dahl	SWE	DNF	
95				

Heat 3 A: 6; C: 5.

1.	Seth Landqvist	SWE	27:00.2	[96]
2.	Edward Carr	USA	27:24.4	
3.	Julius Jørgensen	DEN	28:08.8	
4.	Charles Hall	USA	28:24.0	
5.	Paul Nettelbeck	GER	28:31.6	
	Wilhelmus Braams	NED	DNF	
97				

Heat 4 A: 7; C: 5.

1.	James Murphy	GBR/IRL	25:59.2	[98]
2.	Frederick Meadows	CAN	26:16.2	
3.	J. Georg Peterson	SWE	26:50.4	
4.	Paul Lizandier	FRA	27:10.8	
	Joseph Deakin	GBR	DNF	
	John Tait	CAN	DNF	
	Jacques Keyser	NED	DNF	
99				

Heat 5 A: 7; C: 6.

1.	Arthur "Archie" Robertson	GBR	25:50.2	[100]
2.	John Fitzgerald	CAN	26:05.8	
3.	Samuel Stevenson	GBR	26:17.0	at 70 yds
	Axel Wiegandt	SWE	DNF	
	Joseph Lynch	AUS	DNF	
	Ary Vosbergen	NED	DNF	
	Herbert Trube[101]	USA	DNF	
102				

Heat 6 A: 4; C: 4.

1.	Edward Owen	GBR	26:12.0	[103]
2.	William Galbraith	CAN	27:23.3	
3.	Arnošt Nejedlý[104]	BOH	28:29.8	
	Antal Lovas	HUN	DNF	
105				

Marathon (42,195 meters)

A: 55[106]; C: 16; D: 24 July; T: 1433[107]; F: Point-to-point course of 42.195 km (26 miles, 385 yards).[108]

At the request of Princess Mary, the race, which was started by Lord Desborough, began under the windows of the nursery by the East Terrace at Windsor Castle so that the young Princes could have a good view of the runners. The distance to the finish in front of the Royal Box in the White City Stadium was precisely 26 miles, 385 yards (42,195 meters) and this rather arbitrary distance, which had no particular historical or athletic significance, eventually (1924) became the internationally accepted distance for the marathon footrace.

With a field of 55 runners from 16 nations this was by far the most international field yet assembled for a marathon and the British, quite unrealistically, entertained hopes of considerable success but eight of the twelve British starters failed to finish the race. Another fancied runner who also dropped out was the Canadian, Tom Longboat, who was competing in the face of American protests. The Americans claimed that Longboat was a professional but the Organizing Committee eventually allowed Longboat to compete (See Appendix II). Other starters included Georg Lind (nineteenth), a London-based Russian from Estonia who became the first Russian to compete in an Olympic track & field event, and the English-born Canadian, George Goulding (twenty-second), who would win the 10 km. walk at the 1912 Games. All of the runners were accompanied by two attendants on bicycles, many of them Olympic cycling competitors, who met them at the Crooked Billet Inn at the six-mile mark.

It was a very warm day for long-distance running, the temperature eventually reaching 78° F. (26° C.). Scotsman Thomas Jack led for the first five miles, but dropped out shortly thereafter. Fred Lord and Jack Price, both British, then ran together in the lead through 10 miles. At that mark Price pulled away, closely followed by the English-born South African, Charles Hefferon, who had always been near the lead. Tom Longboat was in second as far out as 17 miles, but he withdrew by 20 miles. After the excessive heat had taken its toll, the race came down to three runners by the 20 mile mark: Hefferon, the American John Hayes, and Italy's Dorando Pietri. Hefferon had control of the race from 15 through 25 miles, leading Pietri by over 3½ minutes at 20 miles.

A little more than one mile from the finish Pietri moved into the lead, passing Hefferon. However, the effort cost him dearly and Pietri entered the White City Stadium in an advanced state of exhaustion. He stumbled and fell, but doctors and attendants revived him, administering stimulants[109], and helping him to his feet. He then fell four more times over the final lap, each time being helped by his handlers. He eventually staggered across the finish line, while surrounded by officials, doctors, and attendants.[110] John Hayes crossed the line, unaided, more than 30 seconds later and, after Pietri had been disqualified for receiving assistance, the American was rightly declared the Olympic champion.

The official statement read, "That, in the opinion of the judges, M. P. Dorando would have been unable to finish the race without the assistance rendered on the track, and so, therefore, the protest of the U.S.A. is upheld, and the second man, Mr. J. Hayes, is the winner, the protest being made by the South African team being withdrawn."[111] Pietri quickly recovered from his ordeal and returned to the stadium the next day to receive a special award from the Queen.

Gynn and Martin described the assistance given Pietri, "The assistance given to Pietri was primarily by Jack Andrew, the Honorary General Secretary of the Polytechnic Harriers and the key organizer of the race. He followed instructions of the medical officer for the race, Doctor Bulger. He [Andrew] reported, in the August, 1908, issue of *The Polytechnic Magazine*, 'As regards the actual finish, most of the reports of same are absolutely erroneous regards my assisting the winner — the doctor's instructions were emphatic, carrying them out caused disqualification; as the animated photographs show, I only caught Dorando as he was falling at the tape. What I did then I would do again under similar circumstances.'"[112]

After the Olympic Games both Hayes and Pietri turned professional and Pietri won each of their four subsequent encounters in New York and San Francisco. To this day, Dorando Pietri is better remembered than the Olympic champion, John Hayes. Born 16 October 1885 in Mandrio, Reggio Emilia, Italy, Dorando Pietri is the most famous loser in Olympic history. But he had an excellent career as a marathon runner. He won his first marathon in 1906 in Rome, but failed to finish the 1906 Olympic marathon a month later. He had won a 40 km. marathon in Carpi, Italy only 17 days before the Olympic marathon. As a professional marathoner he won 7 of 12 of his professional races. He retired in 1911, having won 38 of 59 amateur races and 50 of 69 professional races.

Although the 1908 Olympic marathon is best remembered for the disqualification of Pietri, this does less than justice to John Hayes, who was correctly determined to be the champion, and was an excellent marathon runner in his own right. He had been born in America soon after his parents emigrated from Ireland, and his initial success came when he took third place in the 1907 Boston Marathon. Later in the season he won the Yonkers Marathon, then, by finishing second in the 1908 Boston race, Hayes won a spot on the Olympic team.

After his Olympic victory, Hayes paid a brief visit to his grandparents in Ireland and then returned to New York where Bloomingdale's had plastered their department store with photographs of Hayes and announced that their employee, who had been rumored to train on the store track on the roof, had been promoted to manager of sporting goods. Years later, Hayes laid to rest this oft-repeated bit of Olympic lore. He never did actually work at Bloomingdale's or train on the roof. He drew a salary from Bloomingdale's but most of his time was spent training at a track outside Manhattan.

Hayes was interviewed on the night of the race, "I took nothing to eat or drink on the journey. I think to do so is a great mistake. Before starting I partook of a light lunch, consisting of two ounces of beef, two slices of toast and a sup of tea. During the race I merely bathed my face with Florida water and gargled my throat with brandy.

"I ran my own race throughout, covering in almost mechanical fashion the first five or six miles at a rate of six minutes a mile. After that I went as hard as I could to the finish. Ten miles from home I was ten minutes behind the leader, and then I began to go through the field. I passed Hefferon on nearing the stadium, but saw nothing of Dorando until I entered the arena. I do not smoke and I drink only in moderation."[113]

Hefferon also commented, "The conditions of the race — weather, roads, &c. — suited me exactly, and I should have won the event. Two miles from home, however, I accepted a draught of champagne and this mistake cost me the race. The drink gave me a cramp a mile from the finish and then I lost my lead."[114]

The tragic sight of Dorando Pietri attempting to finish the 1908 marathon race, despite a body that had betrayed him, touched many people. One of those people was a young, aspiring songwriter who wrote a song about Pietri. Entitled simply "Dorando"[115] it was one of the first of many hits for Irving Berlin.
[116]

1.	John Hayes	[#26/3]	USA	2-55:18.4
2.	Charles Hefferon	[#8/4]	SAF	2-56:06.0
3.	Joseph Forshaw	[#24/3]	USA	2-57:10.4
4.	Alton Welton	[#34/1]	USA	2-59:44.4
5.	William Wood	[#68/3]	CAN	3-01:44.0
6.	Frederick Simpson	[#64/1]	CAN	3-04:28.2
7.	Harry Lawson	[#65/2]	CAN	3-06:47.2
8.	Johan Svanberg	[#40/4]	SWE	3-07:50.8
9.	Lewis Tewanima	[#33/3]	USA	3-09:15.0
10.	Kaale Nieminen	[#11/1]	FIN	3-09:50.8

11.	John Peter Caffrey	[#71/3]	CAN	3-12:46.0
12.	William Clarke	[#63/2]	GBR	3-16:08.6
13.	Ernest Barnes	[#58/1]	GBR	3-17:30.8
14.	Sydney Hatch	[#25/1]	USA	3-17:52.4
15.	Fred Lord	[#54/3]	GBR	3-19:08.8
16.	William Goldsboro	[#66/1]	CAN	3-20:07.0
17.	James Beale	[#53/2]	GBR	3-20:14.0
18.	Arnošt Nejedlý	[#48/2]	BOH	3-26:26.2
19.	Georg Lind	[#12/2]	RUS	3-26:38.8
20.	Willem Wakker	[#15/3]	NED	3-28:49.0
21.	Gustaf Törnros	[#39/1]	SWE	3-30:20.8
22.	George Goulding	[#67/2]	CAN	3-33:26.4
23.	Julius Jørgensen	[#50/2]	DEN	3-47:44.0
24.	Arthur Burn	[#74/3]	CAN	3-50:17.0
25.	Emmerich Rath	[#46/3]	AUT	3-50:30.4
26.	Rudy Hansen	[#49/4]	DEN	3-53:15.0
27.	George Lister	[#73/2]	CAN	4-22:45.0
	Dorando Pietri	[#19/4]	ITA	DQ	[2-54:46.4]
	W. Victor Aitken	[#2/3]	AUS	DNF	[21½ miles]
	Tom Longboat	[#72/1]	CAN	DNF	[20 miles]
	Fred Appleby	[#60/2]	GBR	DNF	[20 miles]
	Jack Price	[#55/4]	GBR	DNF	[17½ miles]
	John Tait	[#75/4]	CAN	DNF	[15 miles]
	Frederick Thompson	[#57/4]	GBR	DNF	[15 miles]
	Henry Barrett	[#56/4]	GBR	DNF	[12 miles]
	Fritz Reiser	[#37/2]	GER	DNF	[12 miles]
	Alexander Duncan	[#52/3]	GBR	DNF	[10 miles]
	Umberto Blasi	[#20/1]	ITA	DNF	[8 miles]
	Thomas Jack	[#61/4]	GBR	DNF	[7 miles]
	George Blake	[#3/3]	AUS	DNF	[5+ miles]
	Joseph Lynch	[#1/2]	AUS	DNF	[5 miles]
	Wilhelmus Braams	[#13/4]	NED	DNF	[4¼ miles]
	Albert Wyatt	[#59/2]	GBR	DNF	[3 miles]
	François Celis	[#18/3]	BEL	DNF	
	Edward Cotter	[#69/4]	CAN	DNF	
	Frederick Noseworthy	[#70/1]	CAN	DNF	
	Georgios Koulouberdas	[#9/1]	GRE	DNF	
	Anastasios Koutoulakis	[#10/2]	GRE	DNF	
	George Buff	[#17/1]	NED	DNF	
	Ary Vosbergen	[#14/1]	NED	DNF	
	J. N. Mitchell-Baker	[#4/3]	SAF	DNF	
	Johan Lindqvist	[#43/3]	SWE	DNF	
	Seth Landqvist	[#42/4]	SWE	DNF	
	Tom Morrissey	[#29/1]	USA	DNF	
	Michael Ryan	[#31/1]	USA	DNF	

Mileposts, Leaders, and Splits

1	Barnespool Bridge, Eton	Jack	5:01.4
2	Windsor Road	Jack	10:11
3	Corner High Street, Slough and Uxbridge Road	Jack	15:42
4	Road to Uxbridge	Jack	21:18
5	Furze Lodge, on road to Uxbridge	Jack	27:01
6	Just past Crooked Billet Inn	Lord	33:09
7	Near Ivy Lodge, Iver Heath	Lord	38:57
8	Long Bridge, Uxbridge Moor	Lord	44:52
9	The Lodge, High Street, Uxbridge	Lord	50:50
10	Near Uxbridge Common, on road to Ickenham	Price	56:53
11	Road to Ickenham	Price	1-02:44
12	Bridge approach (Ruislip and Ickenham Station)	Price	1-08:56
13	On Eastcote Road (near Ruislip School)	Price	1-15:13
14	Near Eastcote Post Office	Price	1-22:03
15	Rumens Farm, near Pinner Gas Works	Hefferon	1-28:22
16	Pinner Road, opposite Penhurst Villa	Hefferon	1-35:00
17	Pinner Road, opposite Hawthorne Villas	Hefferon	1-41:47
18	Kenton Road, Harrow	Hefferon	1-48:51
19	Near Harrow Nursery	Hefferon	1-55:29
20	Sudbury and Harrow Road Station	Hefferon	2-02:26
21	Wembley and Sudbury Station	Hefferon	2-08:58
22	Near sixth milestone at Stonebridge Park	Hefferon	2-17:20
23	Midland Railway, Stonebridge Park Goods Office	Hefferon	2-25:20
24	No. 28, Railway Cottages, Willesden Junction	Hefferon	2-33:28
25	On Wormwood Scrubs	Hefferon	2-41:44
26	Entrance of White City Stadium	Pietri	2-51:36[117]
26+	1 circuit of White City Stadium	Hayes	2-55:18.4

110 Meter Hurdles

A: 25; C: 10; D: 21–22, 25 July.

The Olympic record was 15.4, set by Alvin Kraenzlein in Paris in 1900. The world record was 15.2, co-held by America's John Garrells and Arthur Shaw. The Americans were the top hurdlers in the world, and it is instructive to look at the winners of their recent major meets. Forrest Smithson had won the 1907 AAU title, while in 1908, Arthur Shaw won that event. At the 1908 American Olympic Trial Meets, four different hurdlers won: Smithson (Western), Garrells (Central), Shaw (IC4A), and Leonard Howe of Yale (Eastern). Garrells had also won the IC4A crown in 1907.

This race was not run on the cinder track but on a grass track in the infield of the White City Stadium. Fourteen heats resulted in the elimination of only 11 competitors. In the second round, Forrest Smithson equalled the Olympic record and then set a world record of 15.0 in the final. The four American finalists were undoubtedly the best in the field but, surprisingly, they had never raced against each other before.

A well-known photograph suggests that Smithson won the final carrying a Bible in his left hand, and this false rumor has been oft repeated. But this was actually a posed photograph taken to support Smithson's protest against Sunday competition. Precisely to whom this protest was directed is not clear. The Olympic final was held on a Saturday, and Sunday competition was virtually unknown in England at the time. Smithson was a devoutly religious man and, after winning the 1909 AAU hurdles title, he became a minister.

Final A: 4; C: 1; D: 25 July; T: 1130.

1.	Forrest Smithson	USA	15.0	OR, WR
2.	John Garrells	USA	15.7est	
3.	Arthur Shaw	USA	15.8est	
4.	William Rand	USA	16.0est	

Semi-Finals A: 13; C: 2; D: 22 July; T: 1130; F: Winner of each heat advances to the final.

Heat 1 A: 4; C: 2.

1.	Arthur Shaw	USA	15.6	
2.	Eric Hussey	GBR	16.5est	at 6 yds
3.	Wallis Walters	GBR	16.9est	at 2 yds
4.	Oswald Groenings	GBR		

Heat 2 A: 3; C: 2.

1.	Forrest Smithson	USA	15.4	=OR
2.	William Knyvett	GBR	15.6est[118]	
3.	Leonard Howe	USA	15.8est	

Heat 3 A: 4; C: 2.

1.	William Rand	USA	15.8	
2.	Alfred Healey	GBR	15.9est	at 1 ft
3.	Laurence Kiely	GBR/IRL		
4.	Timothy Ahearne	GBR/IRL		

Heat 4 A: 2; C: 2.

1.	John Garrells	USA	16.2	
2.	Cecil Kinahan	GBR/IRL	17.5est	at 10 yds
	[119]			

Round One A: 25; C: 10; D: 21 July; T: 1530; F: Winner of each heat advances to the semi-finals.

Heat 1 A: 3; C: 3.

1.	Alfred Healey	GBR	15.8	
2.	Henry St. A. Murray	NZL	16.3est	at 4 yds
3.	Douglas Stupart	SAF		
	[120]			

Heat 2 A: 2; C: 2.

1.	John Garrells	USA	16.2	
2.	Arthur Halligan[121]	GBR	17.1est	at 7 yds
	[122]			

Heat 3 A: 2; C: 2.

1.	Oswald Groenings	GBR	16.4	
2.	Georgios Skoutaridis	GRE	17.0est	at 5 yds
123				

Heat 4 A: 1; C: 1.

1.	Laurence Kiely	GBR/IRL	wo
124			

Heat 5 A: 3; C: 3.

1.	William Rand	USA	15.8	
2.	Kenneth Powell	GBR	16.2est	at 3 yds
3.	Frank Savage	CAN		
125				

Heat 6 A: 2; C: 2.

1.	Wallis Walters	GBR	17.8
	Oscar Lemming	SWE	DNF
126			

Heat 7 A: 1; C: 1.

1.	William Knyvett	GBR	wo
127			

Heat 8 A: 1; C: 1.

1.	Fernand Halbart	BEL	wo
128			

Heat 9 A: 1; C: 1.

1.	Timothy Ahearne	GBR/IRL	wo
129			

Heat 10 A: 2; C: 2.

1.	Forrest Smithson	USA	15.8	
2.	Nándor Kováts	HUN	17.2est	at 10 yds
130				

Heat 11 A: 2; C: 2.

1.	Eric Hussey	GBR	16.8
	Wilhelm Blystad	NOR	DNF
131			

Heat 12 A: 2; C: 2.

1.	Cecil Kinahan	GBR/IRL	16.8	
2.	Oscar Guttormsen	NOR	18.2est	at 10 yds
132				

Heat 13 A: 2; C: 2.

1.	Leonard Howe	USA	15.8	
2.	Edward Leader[133]	GBR	16.1est	at 1½ yds

Heat 14 A: 1; C: 1.

1.	Arthur Shaw[134]	USA		wo

400 Meter Hurdles

A: 15; C: 6; D: 20–22 July.

In 1908 this event was rarely held at major national meets, though it had been contested at the Olympics of 1900 and 1904. Unlike the 400 meter flat race, this event was run in lanes. As in the 110 meter hurdles, an excessive number of heats was scheduled. Seven of the heats had just one starter, one heat was declared void as there were no starters at all, and the remaining four heats had just two starters. Hence, after 12 heats, only four runners had been eliminated.

In the first round, Charles Bacon (USA) set a new Olympic record of 57.0 and Harry Hillman (USA) improved the record to 56.4 in the second round. Hillman had been Olympic champion in this event in 1904. Bacon recaptured the Olympic record and set a new world record of 55.0 in winning the final. There was a delay in announcing the result as Bacon had taken a wrong hurdle during the race. He regained the proper course at the next hurdle and the judges, after due consideration, decided that he had covered the correct distance.[135] In third place in the final was Jimmy Tremeer (GBR) who had won the British 100 yard title in 1897.

Final A: 4; C: 2; D: 22 July; T: 1530.

1.	Charles Bacon	USA	55.0	OR, WR
2.	Harry Hillman	USA	55.3est	at 2 yds
3.	Jimmy Tremeer	GBR	57.0est	at 15 yds
	Leslie Burton[136]	GBR		

Semi-Finals A: 11; C: 4; D: 21 July; T: 1600; F: Winner of each heat advanced to the final.

Heat 1 A: 3; C: 2.

1.	Harry Hillman	USA	56.4	OR
2.	Harry Coe	USA	57.0est	
	Evert Koops	NED	DNF	

Heat 2 A: 3; C: 3.

1.	Charles Bacon	USA	58.8
	Oswald Groenings[137]	GBR	DNF
	Nándor Kováts	HUN	DNF

Heat 3 A: 3; C: 1.

1.	Leslie Burton	GBR	59.8	
2.	Frederick Harmer	GBR	1:00.3	at 6 yds
3.	Wyatt Gould	GBR		

Heat 4 A: 2; C: 1.

1.	Jimmy Tremeer	GBR	1:00.6
	G. Burton	GBR	DNF

Round One A: 15; C: 6; D: 20 July; T: 1645; F: Winner of each heat advanced to the semi-finals.

Heat 1 A: 1; C: 1.

1.	Evert Koops	NED	wo
	138		

Heat 2 A: 2; C: 2.

1.	Harry Coe	USA	58.8	
2.	John Densham	GBR	59.2est	at 1½ yds
	139			

Heat 3 A: 2; C: 2.

1.	Charles Bacon	USA	57.0	OR
2.	Henry St. A. Murray	NZL	59.8est	at 20 yds
	140			

Heat 4 A: 1; C: 1.

1.	Frederick Harmer	GBR	wo
	141		

Heat 5 A: 1; C: 1.

1.	G. Burton	GBR	wo
	142		

Heat 6 A: 2; C: 2.

1.	Harry Hillman	USA	59.2
	O. Georges Dubois	FRA	DNF
	143		

Heat 7 A: 1; C: 1.

1.	Oswald Groenings	GBR	wo
	144		

Heat 8 A: 1; C: 1.

1.	Wyatt Gould	GBR	wo
	145		

Heat 9 A: 1; C: 1.

1.	Nándor Kováts	HUN	wo
	146		

Heat 10 A: 1; C: 1.

1.	Jimmy Tremeer	GBR	wo
	147		

Heat 11 Voided — no starters.

148

Heat 12 A: 2; C: 2.

1.	Leslie Burton	GBR	1:00.6	
2.	Henri Meslot	FRA	1:01.0est	at 2 yds
	149			

3,200 Meter Steeplechase

A: 24; C: 6; D: 17–18 July.

Steeplechase racing was mostly popular in Great Britain, although steeplechase events had been on the Olympic program in both 1900 and 1904. But because the event was not held frequently outside of Britain, it was difficult to consider any challenger other than the British runners. The last five AAA titles in steeplechase had been won by Arthur Russell (1904–06), Joseph English (1907), and Reginald Noakes (1908). Noakes would later win the 1909 and 1911 AAA titles and English won again in 1910. English competed at the 1908 Olympics but did not finish the second heat. Noakes did not compete because of an injury.

Four Britons, one American, and one Canadian qualified for the final. A notable non-qualifier was James Lightbody (USA), the 1904 Olympic champion, who finished second to Harry Sewell in heat 6. In the final, at the bell, Arthur Russell, "Archie" Robertson, and John Eisele were together. Halfway through the last lap, Robertson took the lead, and Eisele was dropped with 220 yards remaining. Russell passed Robertson at the water jump and held on to win by two yards. Eisele did well to finish third as he had torn away a toenail in training and it was not certain he would compete.

Final A: 6; C: 3; D: 18 July; T: 1430.

1.	Arthur Russell	GBR	10:47.8	
2.	Arthur "Archie" Robertson	GBR	10:48.8	at 4 yds
3.	John Eisele	USA	11:00.8	at 35 yds
4.	Guy Holdaway	GBR	11:26.0est	
5.	Harry Sewell	GBR		
6.	William Galbraith	CAN		

Round One A: 24; C: 6; D: 17 July; T: 1700; F: Winner of each heat advances to the final.

Heat 1 A: 5; C: 4.

1.	Arthur Russell	GBR	10:56.2
2.	Massimo Cartasegna	ITA	11:15.0
	A. Gaston Ragueneau	FRA	DNF

	Edward Carr	USA	DNF	
	Thomas Downing	GBR/IRL	DQ	
150				

Heat 2 A: 5; C: 4.

1.	John Eisele	USA	11:13.6	
	Antal Lovas	HUN	DNF	
	Louis Bonniot de Fleurac	FRA	DNF	
	Frank Buckley	GBR/IRL	DNF	
	Joseph English	GBR	DNF	
151				

Heat 3 A: 2; C: 2.

1.	William Galbraith	CAN	11:12.4	
	Henry Barker	GBR	DNF	
152				

Heat 4 A: 4; C: 2.

1.	Arthur "Archie" Robertson	GBR	11:10.0	
2.	Gale Dull	USA	11:50.0est	at 220 yds
	George Bonhag	USA	DNF	
	Richard Yorke	GBR	DQ	
153				

Heat 5 A: 4; C: 2.

1.	Guy Holdaway	GBR	11:18.8	
2.	Joseph Kinchin	GBR	11:44.0est	at 100 yds
3.	Roger Spitzer	USA		
4.	Charles Hall	USA		
154				

Heat 6 A: 4; C: 3.

1.	Harry Sewell	GBR	11:30.2	
2.	James Lightbody	USA	11:41.0	at 10 yds
	John Fitzgerald	CAN	DNF	
	W. Grantham	GBR	DNF	
155				

1,600 Meter Medley Relay

A: 28; C: 7; D: 24–25 July; F: Four runners covering 1,600 meters in the following order: 200 meters, 200 meters, 400 meters, 800 meters.

This was the first Olympic relay race and evidence that the event was still in its infancy is confirmed by the fact that the runners did not carry a baton and transfer was by "touch." The United States was untroubled in both rounds. After winning their heat in 3:27.2, they were comfortable winners of the final in a time more than two seconds slower. The U.S. margin was 8 yards at the first exchange, 15 yards at the second exchange, and 20 yards on the final exchange.

With Emilio Lunghi, the silver medalist in the individual 800, running the vital 800 anchor leg, the Italians, who had been drawn in the second heat, were viewed as likely finalists but they withdrew at the last minute to lend their support to their countryman, Dorando Pietri, who was approaching the stadium in the closing stages of the marathon.

The 400 meter leg for the United States was run by John Taylor, who was a black man. His gold medal in this race makes him the first black to win a gold medal. He was considered the top American at 400 meters, having won three IC4A 440 yard titles while at the University of Pennsylvania; he had also won the Eastern Olympic Trials in 1908. He had trained in veterinary medicine, but practiced only briefly. After returning to the United States, he contracted typhoid fever and died only a few months after the Olympics, on 2 December 1908.

Final A: 12; C: 3; D: 25 July; T: 1230.

1.   United States   3:29.4
        (William Hamilton [22.0], Nathaniel Cartmell [22.2], John Taylor [49.8],
           Melvin Sheppard [1:55.4])

2.   Germany   3:32.4
        (Arthur Hoffmann [22.9est], Hans Eicke [22.8est], Otto Trieloff [50.5e],
           Hanns Braun [1:56.2est])

3.   Hungary   3:32.5
        (Pál Simon, Frigyes Mezei Wiesner[156], József Nagy, Ödön Bodor)

        Round One A: 28; C: 7; D: 24 July; T: 1200; F: Winner of each heat
           advances to the final.

        Heat 1 A: 8; C: 2.[157]

1.   Hungary   3:32.6
        (Pál Simon, Frigyes Mezei Wiesner, József Nagy, Ödön Bodor)

2.   Sweden   3:33.0   at 3 yds
        (Sven Laftman, Knut Lindberg, Knut Stenborg, Evert Björn)

        Heat 2 A: 8; C: 2.[158]

1.   Germany   3:43.2
        (Arthur Hoffmann, Hans Eicke, Otto Trieloff, Hanns Braun)

2.   The Netherlands   at 90 yards
        (Evert Koops, Jacobus Hoogveld, Victor Henny, Brand "Bram" Evers)

        Heat 3 A: 12; C: 3.[159]

1.   United States   3:27.2
        (William Hamilton, Nathaniel Cartmell, John Taylor, Melvin Sheppard)

2.   Great Britain   3:32.0   at 25 yds
        (George Hawkins, Henry Pankhurst, Edwin Montague, Theodore Just)

3.   Canada
        (Frank Lukeman, Donald Buddo, Louis Sebert, R. Irving Parkes)

3-Mile Team Race

A: 28; C: 6; D: 14–15 July; F: Five men running for each team with three to count. Scoring by a point-for-place system.

Great Britain was the only team to finish three runners in the first heat and in the second heat, the United States and France eliminated Sweden. In the final, the British runners filled the first three places to give them the victory with the minimum score of 6 points (1 + 2 + 3). Joseph Deakin's official winning time was 14:39.6 but the *Official Report* mentions that as he finished 30 yards in front of "Archie" Robertson, so in all probability, his actual time was nearer 14:35.

Final A: 14[160]; C: 3; D: 15 July; T: 1130.

1. Great Britain 6 points [1-2-3]
    (Joseph Deakin [1], Arthur "Archie" Robertson [2], William Coales [3], Harold Wilson [ns/5], Norman Hallows [ns/7])
2. United States 19 points [4-6-9]
    (John Eisele [4], George Bonhag [6], Herbert Trube [9], Gale Dull [ns/10], Harvey Cohn [ns/12])
3. France 32 points [8-11-13]
    (Louis Bonniot de Fleurac [8], Joseph Dreher [11], Paul Lizandier [13], Jean Bouin [ns/dnf])

Individual Placings

1.	Joseph Deakin	GBR	14:39.6	[14:35.6est][161]
2.	Arthur "Archie" Robertson	GBR	14:41.0	
3.	William Coales	GBR	14:41.6	
4.	John Eisele	USA	14:41.8	
5.	Harold Wilson	GBR	14:57.0est	
6.	George Bonhag	USA	15:05.0est	
7.	Norman Hallows	GBR	15:08.0est	
8.	Louis Bonniot de Fleurac	FRA	15:08.4est	
9.	Herbert Trube	USA	15:11.0est	
10.	Gale Dull	USA	15:27.0est	
11.	Joseph Dreher	FRA	15:40.0est	
12.	Harvey Cohn	USA	15:40.2est	
13.	Paul Lizandier	FRA	16:03.0est	
	Jean Bouin[162]	FRA	DNF	

Round One A: 28; C: 6; D: 14 July; T: 1555.

Heat 1 A: 13[163]; C: 3.

1. Great Britain 6 points [1-2-3] Q
    (Harold Wilson [=1], Arthur "Archie" Robertson [=1], William Coales [=1], Joseph Deakin [=1], Norman Hallows [ns/dnf])
2. Italy DNF [5-6-DNF]
    (Pericle Pagliani [5], Massimo Cartasegna [6], Emilio Giovanoli [ns/dnf], Dorando Pietri [ns/dnf], Emilio Lunghi [ns/dnf])
3. The Netherlands DNF [7-8-DNF]
    (Ary Vosbergen [7], Willem Wakker [8], Wilhelmus Braams [dnf])

Individual Placings

=1.	Harold Wilson	GBR	15:05.6
	Arthur "Archie" Robertson	GBR	15:05.6
	William Coales	GBR	15:05.6
	Joseph Deakin	GBR	15:05.6
5.	Pericle Pagliani	ITA	15:22.6
6.	Massimo Cartasegna	ITA	16:26.0
7.	Ary Vosbergen	NED	17:15.8
8.	Willem Wakker	NED	17:46.4
	Norman Hallows	GBR	DNF
	Emilio Giovanoli	ITA	DNF
	Dorando Pietri	ITA	DNF
	Emilio Lunghi	ITA	DNF
	Wilhelmus Braams	NED	DNF

Heat 2 A: 15; C: 3.

1. United States   10 points   [2-3-5]   Q
   (John Eisele [2], Herbert Trube [3], George Bonhag [5], Gale Dull [ns/11],
   Harvey Cohn [ns/dnf])

2. France   15 points   [1-4-10]   Q
   (Jean Bouin [1], Louis Bonniot de Fleurac [4], Joseph Dreher [10], Alexandre
   Fayollat [ns/13], Paul Lizandier [ns/14])

3. Sweden   21 points   [6-7-8]
   (Johan Svanberg [6], J. Georg Peterson [7], Edward Dahl [8], Axel Wiegandt
   [ns/9], Seth Landqvist [ns/12])

Individual Placings

1.	Jean Bouin	FRA	14:53.0
2.	John Eisele	USA	14:55.0
3.	Herbert Trube	USA	14:55.0
4.	Louis Bonniot de Fleurac	FRA	14:56.0
5.	George Bonhag	USA	14:56.4
6.	Johan Svanberg	SWE	14:57.0
7.	J. Georg Peterson	SWE	15:14.4
8.	Edward Dahl	SWE	15:21.0
9.	Axel Wiegandt	SWE	15:33.0
10.	Joseph Dreher	FRA	15:37.2
11.	Gale Dull	USA	15:37.4
12.	Seth Landqvist	SWE	15:46.4
13.	Alexandre Fayollat	FRA	15:52.2
14.	Paul Lizandier	FRA	15:56.6
	Harvey Cohn	USA	DNF

3,500 Meter Walk[164]

A: 23[165]; C: 8; D: 14 July.

Ernest Webb led on the first lap but was caught on lap two by George Larner. They pulled away from the field and walked together for the first mile. At that point, Larner slowly drew away and eventually won by 12 seconds, a margin of about 45 yards.

George Larner did not begin race walking until 1903 when he was already 28 years old. He quickly won four AAA walking championships and set nine world records, and then retired. He was convinced to return for the 1908 Olympics where he won both walk races. He competed sporadically after the Olympics both as a cross-country runner and in race walking, but he retired shortly before the 1912 Olympics.

Final A: 9; C: 5; D: 14 July; T: 1530.

1.	George Larner	GBR	14:55.0
2.	Ernest Webb	GBR	15:07.4
3.	Harry Kerr	NZL	15:43.4
4.	George Goulding	CAN	15:49.8
5.	Arthur Rowland	NZL	16:07.0
6.	Charles Vestergaard	DEN	17:21.8
7.	Einar Rothman	SWE	17:50.0
	William Palmer	GBR	DNF
	Richard Harrison	GBR	DQ

Round One A: 23; C: 8; D: 14 July; T: 1100; F: First three finishers in each heat advance to the final.

Heat 1 A: 8; C: 5.

1.	George Larner	GBR	15:32.0
2.	Harry Kerr	NZL	16:02.2
3.	William Palmer	GBR	16:33.0
4.	Paul Gunia	GER	16:38.0
5.	Sydney Sarel	GBR	17:06.0
6.	Arne Højme	DEN	17:23.4
7.	Jo Goetzee	NED	17:37.8
	William Brown	GBR	DQ

Heat 2 A: 8; C: 5.[166]

1.	Ernest Webb	GBR	15:17.2
2.	Charles Vestergaard	DEN	17:07.0
3.	Einar Rothman	SWE	17:40.2
4.	Willem Winkelman[167]	NED	17:57.6
5.	István Drubina	HUN	18:44.6
6.	Petrus Ruimers	NED	18:44.6
	Richard Quinn	GBR	DQ
	John Reid	GBR/IRL	DQ

Heat 3 A: 7; C: 5.

1.	George Goulding	CAN	15:54.0
2.	Richard Harrison	GBR	16:04.4
3.	Arthur Rowland	NZL	16:08.6
4.	Ernest Larner	GBR	16:10.0

5.	John Butler	GBR	16:17.0
6.	Richard Wilhelm	GER	17:33.8
7.	Johan Huijgen	NED	17:43.0

10-Mile (16.09 km.) Walk

A: 25[168]; C: 8; D: 16–17 July.

Five of the finalists from the 3,500 meter walk (held two days earlier) also qualified for the final of the 10-mile walk. Over the longer distance, the British walkers, George Larner and Ernest Webb, repeated their first and second places from the shorter event, with Larner setting a new world record of 1-15:57.4. En route to his victory, Larner also broke the 9-mile world record. Webb (1-17:31.0) was also inside the old world record of 1-17:38.8, which had been set by W. J. Sturgess at Stamford Bridge and had stood since 3 October 1896. Splits for Larner and Webb, and, in his world record race, Sturgess, were as follows:

Mile	Larner	Webb	Sturgess
1	7:01.6	7:02.0	7:27.4
2	14:11.0	14:13.0	15:13.2
3	21:20.4	21:38.0	22:58.8
4	28:43.4	29:05.4	30:38.8
5	36:16.4	36:36.4	38:15.8
6	43:54.0	44:21.0	46:01.2
7	51:37.4	52;16.4	53:41.2
8	59:33.0	1-00:23.8	1-01:36.4
9	1-07:37.8	1-08:35.8	1-09:31.4
10	1-15:57.4	1-17:31.0	1-17:38.8

Final A: 7; C: 2; D: 17 July; T: 1430.

1.	George Larner	GBR	1-15:57.4	OR, WR
2.	Ernest Webb	GBR	1-17:31.0	
3.	Edward Spencer	GBR	1-21:20.2	
4.	Frank Carter	GBR	1-21:20.2[169]	
5.	Ernest Larner	GBR	1-24:26.2	
	William Palmer	GBR	DNF	
	Richard Harrison	GBR	DNF	

Round One A: 25; C: 8; D: 16 July; T: 1000; F: First four in each heat advance to the final.

Heat 1 A: 12; C: 5.

1.	Ernest Webb	GBR	1-20:18.8
=2.	Frank Carter	GBR	1-21:25.4
	Edward Spencer	GBR	1-21:25.4
	Ernest Larner	GBR	1-21:25.4
5.	Arthur Rowland[170]	NZL	1-21:57.6

6.	Thomas Hammond	GBR	1-23:44.0
7.	Paul Gunia	GER	1-26:09.4
AC.	Jo Goetzee	NED	DNF
	Willem Winkelman	NED	DNF
	Piet Soudyn	NED	DNF
	Arne Højme	DEN	DNF
	Alfred Yeoumans	GBR	DQ

171

Heat 2 A: 13; C: 6.

1.	George Larner	GBR	1-18:19.0
2.	Richard Harrison	GBR	1-18:21.2
3.	Harry Kerr	NZL	1-18:40.2
4.	William Palmer	GBR	1-19:40.4
5.	Gadwin Withers	GBR	1-19:22.4
6.	Sydney Schofield	GBR	1-21:07.4
7.	Petrus Ruimers	NED	1-27:38.8
8.	Emmerich Rath	NED	1-30:33.8
AC.	Johan Huijgen	NED	DNF
	John Butler	GBR	DNF
	George Goulding	CAN	DNF
	Einar Rothman	SWE	DNF
	Charles Vestergaard	DEN	DNF

172

High Jump

A: 22[173]; C: 10; D: 21 July.

The high jump world record was still held by the United States' Mike Sweeney, who had cleared 6-5⅝ (1.97) in 1895. He had long since turned professional and subsequently retired. The Olympic record was the 6-2¾ (1.90) which had won the 1900 gold medal for Irving Baxter (USA). The favorite for the 1908 Olympics was probably the great Irish jumper, Cornelius "Con" Leahy, who had won the AAA title from 1905–08. He had also won the American AAU championship in 1907, and was also the defending Olympic champion, having won in 1906. The best American jumper was Harry Porter, who in 1908 won the AAU title and the Eastern Olympic Trial. Porter had also been second at the 1905 IC4A Meet.

The *Official Report* makes no mention of qualifying conditions but there were eight scheduled qualifying sections, which were consolidated into four pools. After pool 1 had been completed at the south end of the stadium, the officials decided that the slippery conditions were unsuitable and moved the remaining three pools to another jumping area at the north end of the stadium. Herbert Gidney (USA), who had not qualified in the first pool, then lodged a protest, claiming that the original results of the first pool should be declared void and the competition held again under more favorable conditions at the north end. Despite the fact that all the competitors had been equally affected by the original adverse conditions, the judges, rather surprisingly, upheld Gidney's protest.

Otto Monsen (NOR) and Edward Leader (GBR) had shared first place in the original competition, but Monsen refused to take part in the re-scheduled event, while Leader failed to match the height he had achieved in the less favorable conditions. The only beneficiary of the protest was Gidney himself.

Having won the competition, Harry Porter made three unsuccessful attempts at the world record height of 6-5¾ (1.97). For these world record attempts, Porter removed his sweater for the first time in the competition. In the final, István Somodi (HUN) was the only competitor to improve on his qualifying mark in the morning. Leahy, Somodi, and André had a jump-off for the silver and bronze medals, but none could equal their earlier marks so they were declared equal seconds.

After the Olympics, Harry Porter continued to be a top jumper. He led the 1909 world lists with 6-4 (1.93), and tied for first in 1911 at the AAU Meet, but he did not compete at the 1912 Olympics.

Final Standings

					6-2	6-3	6-5¾
1.	Harry Porter	USA	6-3	OR [1.90][174]	o	o	xxx
=2.	Cornelius "Con" Leahy	GBR/IRL	6-2	[1.88]	o	xxx	
	István Somodi	HUN	6-2	[1.88]	xo	xxx	
	Georges André	FRA	6-2	[1.88]	xxo	xxx	
=5.	Herbert Gidney	USA	6-1	[1.85][175]			
	Tom Moffitt	USA	6-1	[1.85][176]			
7.	Norman Patterson	USA	6-0	[1.83]			
8.	Axel Hedenlund, Jr.[177]	SWE	5-10⅞	[1.80]			
9.	Patrick Leahy	GBR/IRL	5-10	[1.78]			
=10.	Edward Leader	GBR	5-9¾	[1.77]			
	George Barber	CAN	5-9¾	[1.77]			
	George Wilson	GBR	5-9¾	[1.77]			
=13.	Jøzsef Haluzsinszky	HUN	5-7¾	[1.72]			
	Henry Olsen	NOR	5-7¾	[1.72]			
	J. Garfield MacDonald	CAN	5-7¾	[1.72]			
=16.	Léon Dupont	BEL	5-6	[1.67]			
	Folke Hellstedt	SWE	5-6	[1.67]			
	Lauri Pihkala	FIN	5-6	[1.67]			
19.	Herman van Leeuwen	NED	5-5	[1.65]			
20.	Alfred Bellerby	GBR	5-2½	[1.59]			
AC.	Otto Monsen	NOR	WD				
	Lauri Wilskman	FIN	WD				

Final A: 8; C: 5; D: 21 July; T: 1430.

1.	Harry Porter	USA	6-3	[1.90]
=2.	Cornelius "Con" Leahy	GBR/IRL	6-2	[1.88]
	Georges André	FRA	6-2	[1.88]
	István Somodi	HUN	6-2	[1.88]
=5.	Herbert Gidney	USA	6-1	[1.85]
	Tom Moffitt	USA	6-1	[1.85]
7.	Norman Patterson	USA	6-0	[1.83]
	Axel Hedenlund, Jr.	SWE	DNS	

Qualifying Rounds A: 22; C: 10; D: 21 July; T: 1030; F: The eight leading competitors in the qualifying round go forward to the final. The eight scheduled qualifying sections were consolidated into four pools. Marks from the qualifying round carry forward to the final.

Pool 1 (Sections 1 and 2) A: 6; C: 5.

=1.	Otto Monsen	NOR	5-10⅞	[1.79]	
	Edward Leader	GBR	5-10⅞	[1.79]	
3.	Herbert Gidney	USA	5-9¾	[1.77]	
4.	József Haluzsinszky	HUN	5-7⅞	[1.72]	
5.	Lauri Wilskman	FIN	5-6	[1.67]	
6.	Alfred Bellerby	GBR	5-1	[1.55]	

178

Pool 1 Re-Jump (Sections 1 and 2) A: 4; C: 3.

1.	Herbert Gidney	USA	6-1	[1.85]	Q
2.	Edward Leader	GBR	5-9¾	[1.77]	
3.	József Haluzsinszky	HUN	5-7⅞	[1.72]	
4.	Alfred Bellerby	GBR	5-2½	[1.59]	

179

Pool 2 (Sections 3 and 4) A: 8; C: 7.

=1.	Cornelius "Con" Leahy	GBR/IRL	6-2	[1.88]	Q
	Georges André	FRA	6-2	[1.88]	Q
3.	Norman Patterson	USA	6-0	[1.83]	Q
4.	Axel Hedenlund, Jr.	SWE	5-10⅞	[1.80]	Q
5.	Patrick Leahy	GBR/IRL	5-10	[1.78]	
=6.	Henry Olsen	NOR	5-7¾	[1.72]	
	J. Garfield MacDonald	CAN	5-7¾	[1.72]	
8.	Lauri Pihkala	FIN	5-6	[1.67]	

180

Pool 3 (Sections 5 and 6) A: 6; C: 5.

1.	Harry Porter	USA	6-3	OR	[1.90]	Q
=2.	Tom Moffitt	USA	6-1		[1.85]	Q
	István Somodi[181]	HUN	6-1		[1.85]	Q
=4.	Folke Hellstedt	SWE	5-6		[1.67]	
	Léon Dupont	BEL	5-6		[1.67]	
6.	Herman van Leeuwen	NED	5-5		[1.65]	

182

Pool 4 (Sections 7 and 8) A: 2; C: 2.

=1.	George Barber	CAN	5-9¾	[1.77]	
	George Wilson	GBR	5-9¾	[1.77]	

183

Pole Jump (Vault)

A: 15[184]; C: 7; D: 24 July.

The world record of 12-9½ (3.90) had recently been set by Walter Dray (USA) on 13 June 1908. The Olympic record had been set by Charles Dvorak at St. Louis in 1904, with 11-6 (3.50).

Neither Dvorak nor Dray competed, although Dray had finished in a four-way tie for first at the 1908 IC4A Meet on 30 May. Dray had tied with A. C. Gilbert, Frank Nelson, and Charles Campbell, and all four competed for Yale University's track team. Dray withdrew because his mother was concerned that he might be injured if he competed.[185] Gilbert had also won the Eastern Olympic Trial with Dray and Nelson tying for second. Among other nations, the top vaulters were Sweden's Bruno Söderström, 1907 AAA champion and silver medalist in 1906, and Canada's Edward Archibald, who had cleared 12-5½ (3.80) in Canada earlier in the season and three weeks before the Games had won the British title at 12-0 (3.66).

Five competitors broke the Olympic record, and two more equalled the former record. The Americans, Alfred "A. C." Gilbert and Edward Cook shared first place at 12-2 (3.71) with Archibald and Söderström tying with Charles Jacobs (USA) for third. The closing stages of the competition were considerably delayed as they coincided with the dramatic happenings at the finish of the marathon. Because of the time factor, the officials decided against holding jump-offs for first and third places and, in an unusual decision, two gold and three bronze medals were awarded.

For the last time in Olympic competition, the "climbing" technique was permitted although it remained legal in England until 1920. Among their numerous protests, the Americans argued about the fact that there was no pit or hole in which to plant the pole and also that there was no sandpit or bales of straw to break the competitors' falls. This protest was understandable and the organizers were definitely behind the times in these matters as similar facilities had been provided at the two previous Olympic Games.

Edward Cook was a fine all-around jumper and hurdler. He won the IC4A long jump in 1908 and 1909, the AAU pole vault in 1907 and tied for first in the AAU pole vault in 1911. Gilbert spread his athletic talents even farther, winning the 1905 Yale gymnastics championship and was intercollegiate wrestling champion in 1906. Gilbert earned an M.D. degree from Yale but never practiced medicine. He later made a fortune as president of the toy company that bore his name and manufactured Erector Sets, American Flyer electric trains, and other popular toys.

Final Standings

=1.	A. C. Gilbert	USA	12-2	[3.71]	=OR
	Edward Cook	USA	12-2	[3.71]	=OR
=3.	Charles Jacobs	USA	11-9	[3.58]	
	Bruno Söderström	SWE	11-9	[3.58]	
	Edward Archibald	CAN	11-9	[3.58]	
=6.	Georgios Banikas	GRE	11-6	[3.50]	
	Sam Bellah	USA	11-6	[3.50]	
8.	Károly Szathmáry	HUN	11-0	[3.35]	
9.	Stefanos Kountouriotis	GRE	10-9	[3.27]	
=10.	Robert Pascarel	FRA	10-6	[3.20]	
	Carl Silfverstrand	SWE	10-6	[3.20]	
=12.	Thomas Jackson	USA	10-0	[3.05]	
	G. Koeger	FRA	10-0	[3.05]	
14.	Coenraad van Veenhuijsen	NED	9-6	[2.89]	
15.	Brand "Bram" Evers	NED	9-3	[2.82]	

Final A: 8; C: 5; D: 24 July; T: 1730.

1.	A. C. Gilbert	USA	12-2	[3.71]	=OR

2.	Edward Cook	USA	12-0	[3.66]	
=3.	Charles Jacobs	USA	11-9	[3.58]	
	Bruno Söderström	SWE	11-9	[3.58]	
	Edward Archibald	CAN	11-9	[3.58]	
=6.	Georgios Banikas	GRE	11-6	[3.50]	
	Sam Bellah	USA	11-6	[3.50]	
8.	Károly Szathmáry	HUN	11-0	[3.35]	

Qualifying Rounds A: 15; C: 7; D: 24 July; T: 1100; F: The eight leading competitors from the qualifying round advance to the final. The six scheduled qualifying sections were consolidated into three pools. Qualifying marks carry through to the final.

Pool 1 (Sections 1 and 2) A: 4; C: 4.

1.	Bruno Söderström	SWE	11-9	[3.58]	Q
2.	Charles Jacobs	USA	11-6	[3.50]	Q
3.	Stefanos Kountouriotis	GRE	10-9	[3.27]	
4.	Brand "Bram" Evers	NED	9-3	[2.82]	

186

Pool 2 (Sections 3 and 4) A: 5; C: 4; D: 24 July.

1.	Edward Cook	USA	12-2	[3.71]	Q	OR
2.	A. C. Gilbert	USA	12-0	[3.66]	Q	OR
3.	Edward Archibald	CAN	11-9	[3.58]	Q	
4.	Georgios Banikas	GRE	11-3	[3.43]	Q	
5.	Robert Pascarel	FRA	10-6	[3.20]		

187

Pool 3 (Sections 5 and 6) A: 6; C: 5; D: 24 July.

1.	Sam Bellah	USA	11-3	[3.43]	Q
2.	Károly Szathmáry	HUN	11-0	[3.35]	Q
3.	Carl Silfverstrand	SWE	10-6	[3.20]	
=4.	Thomas Jackson	USA	10-0	[3.05]	
	G. Koeger	FRA	10-0	[3.05]	
5.	Coenraad van Veenhuijsen	NED	9-6	[2.89]	

188,189

Broad (Long) Jump

A: 32[190]; C: 9; D: 22 July; T: 1030—Qualifying, 1530—Final.

The British Isles had no top jumper since Ireland's Peter O'Connor had retired after the 1906 Olympics. America also was lacking a dominant long jumper as Meyer Prinstein was no longer competing. O'Connor was the holder of the world record of 24-11¾ (7.61), which he had set in 1901 and which, amazingly, remained an Irish record until 1990.

Francis Irons (USA) easily surpassed his best form at home and his victory was one of the major upsets of the 1908 Olympics. He led the qualifying with 24-5 (7.44) and improved to 24-6½ (7.48) in the final. He was the only one of the three finalists to improve on his performance in the qualifying round and his winning mark placed him third on the all-time list behind O'Connor and Prinstein. Irons later won the AAU long jump title in both 1909 and 1910 and in 1909 also won the triple jump. He competed at the 1912 Olympics as well, but finished ninth in the long jump.

Final Standings: A: 32; C: 9; D: 22 July; T: 1530.

1.	Francis Irons	USA	24-6½	[7.48]
2.	Daniel Kelly	USA	23-3¼	[7.09]
3.	Calvin Bricker	CAN	23-3	[7.08][191]
4.	Edward Cook	USA	22-10½	[6.97]
5.	John Brennan	USA	22-6¼	[6.86]
6.	Frank Mount Pleasant[192]	USA	22-4½	[6.82]
7.	Albert Weinstein	GER	22-2¾	[6.77]
8.	Timothy Ahearne	GBR/IRL	22-0¾	[6.72]
9.	Denis Murray	GBR/IRL	22-0¼	[6.71]
10.	Gunnar Ronström	SWE	21-10½	[6.67][193]
11.	Charles Williams	GBR	21-10	[6.65]
12.	Sam Bellah	USA	21-9½	[6.64]
13.	Frank Lukeman	CAN	21-7½	[6.59]
14.	Ödön Holits	HUN	21-5½	[6.54][194]
15.	Arthur Hoffmann	GER	21-4	[6.50]
16.	Alfred Bellerby	GBR	21-1¾	[6.44]
17.	Wilfred Bleaden	GBR	21-1½	[6.43]
18.	William Watt	GBR/IRL	21-0 ¾	[6.42]
19.	George Barber	CAN	21-0½	[6.41]
20.	Carl Silfverstrand	SWE	20-9½	[6.34]
AC.	"Ludwig" Uettwiller	GER	19-10¼	[6.05][195]
	Brand "Bram" Evers	NED		
	John O'Connell	USA		
	Jacobus Hoogveld	NED		
	Hugo Wieslander	SWE		
	Hermann von Bönninghausen	GER		
	Henri Guttierez	FRA		
	Lionel Cornish	GBR		
	Géza Kovesdi	HUN		
	J. Garfield MacDonald	CAN		
	Arvid Ringstrand	SWE		
	Henry Olsen	NOR		

Qualifying Rounds A: 32[196]; C: 9; D: 22 July; T: 1030; F: Each competitor was allowed three jumps, after which the leading three were allowed a further three trials. The nine scheduled qualifying sections were consolidated into five pools.

Pool 1 (Sections 1 and 2) A: 4?; C: 3.

1.	Edward Cook	USA	22-10½	[6.97]
2.	Sam Bellah	USA	21-9½	[6.64]
3.	Ödön Holits	HUN	21-5½	[6.54]
4.	Wilfred Bleaden	GBR	21-1½	[6.13]

197

Pool 2 (Sections 3 and 4) A: 7?; C: 5.

1.	Daniel Kelly	USA	23-3¼	[7.09]	Q
2.	John Brennan	USA	22-6¼	[6.86]	
3.	Albert Weinstein[198]	GER	22-2¾	[6.77]	
4.	Timothy Ahearne	GBR/IRL	22-0¾	[6.72]	
5.	Alfred Bellerby	GBR	21-1¾	[6.44]	
6.	George Barber	CAN	21-0½	[6.41]	
7.	Carl Silfverstrand	SWE	20-9½	[6.34]	

199

Pool 3 (Sections 5 and 6) A: 5?; C: 3.

1.	Francis Irons	USA	24-5	[7.44]	Q
2.	Frank Mount Pleasant	USA	22-4½	[6.82]	
3.	Charles Williams	GBR	21-10	[6.65]	
AC.	Brand "Bram" Evers	NED			
	John O'Connell	USA			

200

Pool 4 (Section 7) A: 6?; C: 5.

1.	Denis Murray	GBR/IRL	22-0¼	[6.71]	
2.	Frank Lukeman	CAN	21-7½	[6.59]	
3.	William Watt	GBR/IRL	21-0¾	[6.42]	
AC.	Jacobus Hoogveld	NED			
	Hugo Wieslander	SWE			
	Hermann von Bönninghausen	GER			

201

Pool 5 (Sections 8 and 9) A: 9?; C: 7.

1.	Calvin Bricker	CAN	23-3	[7.08]	Q
2.	Gunnar Ronström	SWE	21-10½	[6.67]	
3.	Arthur Hoffmann	GER	21-4	[6.50]	
AC.	Henri Guttierez	FRA			
	Lionel Cornish	GBR			
	Géza Kovesdi[202]	HUN			
	J. Garfield MacDonald	CAN			
	Arvid Ringstrand	SWE			
	Henry Olsen	NOR			

203

Hop, Step, and Jump (Triple Jump)

A: 20[204]; C: 8; D: 25 July; T: 1000—Qualifying; Finals immediately followed qualifying jumps.

There could be no favorite as this event was rarely contested at national meets in this era. The world record had stood since 1893 when Edward Bloss (USA) had jumped 48-6 (14.78) when the event was on the AAU program for the only time prior to 1908. The Olympic record was 47-5¾ (14.47), set by Meyer Prinstein (USA) in 1900.

Three qualifying sections were held in the morning with the three leading competitors taking three further jumps in the afternoon. The Irishman Timothy Ahearne and J. Garfield MacDonald, a Canadian from Nova Scotia, waged a fierce battle and completely dominated the competition. They were both drawn in the same qualifying section and both produced their best performances in the final three jumps. With his final jump Ahearne set a new Olympic record to take the gold medal and MacDonald was unable to match Ahearne's effort. Contrary to most reports, Ahearne did *not* win with the last jump of the competition. He was ahead of MacDonald in the jumping order.

Tim Ahearne and his brother, Dan Ahearn, hailed from Dirreen, County Limerick in Ireland. Shortly after the Olympics, they emigrated to the United States, where Daniel dropped the final "e" from his name. Tim Ahearne won the 1909 AAA long jump championship, but in the United States he was eclipsed by his younger brother. Daniel Ahearn set the first IAAF-recognized triple jump with 50-11 (15.52) in May 1911. He won the AAU triple jump in 1911 and 1913–1918, usually defeating Tim, who was runner-up in 1911, 1913–14, and 1916.

1.	Timothy Ahearne	GBR/IRL	48-11¼ OR [14.92][205]	(1392, 1472, f, 1462, f, 1492)
2.	J. Garfield MacDonald	CAN	48-5¼ [14.76]	(?, 1476, ?, ?, 1459, ?)[206]
3.	Edvard Larsen	NOR	47-2¾ [14.39][207]	(?, 1439, ?, ?, 1434, ?)[208]
4.	Calvin Bricker	CAN	46-3 [14.10][209]	
5.	Platt Adams	USA	46-2 [14.07]	
6.	Frank Mount Pleasant	USA	45-10 [13.97]	
7.	Karl Fryksdahl	SWE	44-9½ [13.65]	
8.	John Brennan	USA	44-7 [13.59]	
9.	Martin Sheridan	USA	44-0¼ [13.42]	
10.	Douglas Stupart	SAF	43-11½ [13.40]	
11.	Cyril Dugmore	GBR/IRL	43-8 [13.31]	
12.	Michael Dineen	GBR/IRL	43-5 [13.23]	
13.	Henry Olsen	NOR	43-2¾ [13.17]	
14.	Oscar Guttormsen	NOR	43-2 [13.16]	
15.	Dimitrios Muller	GRE	42-11½ [13.09]	
16.	Francis Irons	USA	41-7 [12.67]	
17.	Sam Bellah	USA	41-2 [12.55]	
AC.	Nathaniel Sherman	USA		
	George Mayberry	GBR/IRL		
	Juho Halme	FIN		

Qualifying Rounds A: 20; C: 8; D: 25 July; T: 1000; F: Each competitor was allowed three jumps, after which the leading three were allowed a further three trials.

Section 1 A: 7; C: 5.

1.	Platt Adams	USA	46-2	[14.07]
2.	Karl Fryksdahl	SWE	44-9½	[13.65]
3.	Martin Sheridan	USA	44-0¼	[13.42]
4.	Cyril Dugmore	GBR/IRL	43-8	[13.31]
5.	Henry Olsen	NOR	43-2¾	[13.17]
6.	Dimitrios Muller	GRE	42-11½	[13.09]
7.	Francis Irons	USA	41-7	[12.67]

210

Section 2 A: 9; C: 6.

1. Timothy Ahearne	GBR/IRL	48-3¾	[14.72]	Q
2. J. Garfield MacDonald	CAN	46-4	[14.12]	Q
3. John Brennan	USA	44-7	[13.59]	Q
4. Douglas Stupart	SAF	43-11½	[13.40]	
5. Oscar Guttormsen	NOR	43-2	[13.16]	
6. Sam Bellah	USA	41-2	[12.55]	
AC. Nathaniel Sherman	USA			
George Mayberry	GBR/IRL			
Juho Halme[211]	FIN			

212

Section 3 A: 4; C: 4.

1. Edvard Larsen	NOR	47-2	[14.37]	Q
2. Calvin Bricker	CAN	46-3	[14.10]	
3. Frank Mount Pleasant	USA	45-10	[13.66]	
4. Michael Dineen[213]	GBR/IRL	43-5	[13.23]	

214

Standing High Jump

A: 23[215]; C: 11; D: 23 July.

Ray Ewry concluded his remarkable Olympic career with his fourth successive "double" in the standing high jump and long jump. He also won the standing triple jump in 1900 and 1904 to bring his total of individual gold medals to ten, a record which has never been surpassed.

Final Placings

1. Ray Ewry	USA	5-2	[1.57][216]
=2. John Biller	USA	5-1	[1.55]
Konstantin Tsiklitiras	GRE	5-1	[1.55]
4. LeRoy Holmes	USA	5-0	[1.52][217]
=5. Platt Adams	USA	4-10	[1.47]
Georges André	FRA	4-10	[1.47]
Alfred Motte	FRA	4-10	[1.47]
=8. Léon Dupont	BEL	4-8	[1.42]
Walter Henderson	GBR	4-8	[1.42]
Wilhelm Blystad	NOR	4-8	[1.42]
Francis Irons	USA	4-8	[1.42]
Arthur Mallwitz	GER	4-8	[1.42]
Svend Langkjær	DEN	4-8	[1.42]
=14. Karl Fryksdahl	SWE	4-7	[1.40]
Allan Bengtsson	SWE	4-7	[1.40]
16. Martin Sheridan	USA	4-6	[1.37]
=17. Lancelot Stafford	GBR	4-4	[1.32]
Ludwig Uettwiller[218]	GER	4-4	[1.32]

AC. Alfred Flaxman　　　　GBR
　　　Ernest Hutcheon　　　NZL[219]
　　　George Barber　　　　CAN
　　　Henri Jardin　　　　　FRA
　　　Lawson Robertson　　USA

　　Qualifying Rounds A: 23; C: 11; D: 23 July; F: Each competitor was allowed three jumps, after which the leading eight were allowed a further three trials. The eight qualifying sections were consolidated into four pools.

　　　Pool 1 (Section 1) A: ?; C: ?.

1.	Konstantin Tsiklitiras	GRE	5-1	[1.55]	Q
2.	Platt Adams	USA	4-10	[1.47]	
3.	Léon Dupont	BEL	4-8	[1.42]	
AC.	Alfred Flaxman	GBR			

220

　　　Pool 2 (Sections 2 and 3) A: ?; C: ?.

1.	Ray Ewry	USA	5-1	[1.55]	Q
2.	John Biller	USA	4-11	[1.50]	Q
=3.	Walter Henderson	GBR	4-8	[1.42]	
	Wilhelm Blystad	NOR	4-8	[1.42]	
5.	Martin Sheridan	USA	4-6	[1.37]	
=6.	Lancelot Stafford	GBR	4-4	[1.32]	
	"Ludwig" Uettwiller	GER	4-4	[1.32]	

221

　　　Pool 3 (Sections 4 and 5) A: ?; C: ?.

1.	LeRoy Holmes	USA	5-0	[1.52]	Q
2.	Francis Irons	USA	4-8	[1.42]	
3.	Arthur Mallwitz	GER	4-8	[1.42]	
AC.	Ernest Hutcheon	NZL			
	George Barber	CAN			

222, 223

　　　Pool 4 (Sections 7 and 8) A: ?; C: ?.

1.	Alfred Motte	FRA	4-8	[1.42]	
2.	Allan Bengtsson	SWE	4-7	[1.40]	
AC.	Lawson Robertson	USA			
	Henri Jardin	FRA			

224

Standing Broad Jump

　　A: 25; C: 11; D: 20 July; T: 1430—Qualifying; Finals immediately following the qualifying jumps.

In winning the first leg of his "double" in the standing jumps, Ray Ewry defeated Konstantin Tsiklitiras (GRE), who was to succeed Ewry as Olympic champion in this event in 1912. It was Ewry's fourth successive Olympic title in this event.

Final Placings

1. Ray Ewry	USA	10-11¼	[3.33][225]
2. Konstantin Tsiklitiras	GRE	10-7¼	[3.22][226]
3. Martin Sheridan	USA	10-7	[3.22][227]
4. John Biller	USA	10-6½	[3.21][228]
5. Ragnar Ekberg	SWE	10-5¾	[3.19][229]
=6. Platt Adams	USA	10-2½	[3.11]
LeRoy Holmes	USA	10-2½	[3.11]
AC. Francis Irons	USA		
Evert Koops	NED		
Jacobus Hoogveld	NED		
Brand "Bram" Evers	NED		
Lionel Cornish	GBR		
Lancelot Stafford	GBR		
Walter Henderson	GBR		
Frederick Kitching	GBR		
Timothy Ahearne	GBR/IRL		
Wilfred Bleaden	GBR		
Jarl Jakobsson	FIN		
George Barber	CAN		
Svend Langkjær	DEN		
Henri Jardin	FRA		
Alfred Motte	FRA		
Léon Dupont	BEL		
Arthur Mallwitz	GER		
Sigmund Muenz	USA		

Qualifying Rounds A: 24; C: 11; D: 20 July; T: 1430; F: Each competitor was allowed three jumps, after which the leading eight were allowed a further three trials. The eight scheduled qualifying sections were consolidated into four pools.

Pool 1 (Sections 1 and 2) A: ?; C: ?.

1. Konstantin Tsiklitiras	GRE	10-7¼	[3.23]
2. Martin Sheridan	USA	10-7	[3.22]
3. Platt Adams	USA	10-2½	[3.11]

230

Pool 2 (Sections 3 and 4) A: ?; C: ?.

1. Ray Ewry[231]	USA	10-11	[3.32]
2. LeRoy Holmes	USA	10-2½	[3.11]
AC. Sigmund Muenz	USA		

Pool 3 (Sections 5 and 6) A: ?; C: ?.

Pool Four (Sections 7 and 8) A: ?; C: ?.
232,233

Shot Put

A: 25[234]; C: 8; D: 16 July; T: 1430 — Qualifying; Finals immediately followed the qualifying throws.

Ralph Rose was the greatest shot putter of the pre–World War I era. For the time he was a massive 6' 6¾" (2.00), weighing up to 285 lbs. (130 kg.). Rose was AAU shot put champion in 1907–1910 and had won the Olympic shot put gold medal at St. Louis in 1904. In his career, he set eight world records, ending with the first IAAF-recognized mark of 51-0 (15.54), set in San Francisco on 21 August 1909. Prior to Rose, the top putter in the world had been the Irishman, Denis Horgan. Born in Banteer, County Cork, Horgan's career would see him win 13 British AAA shot put crowns — 1893–1899, 1904–05, 1908–10, and 1912. He was also AAU champion in 1900. He also won 17 Irish titles with the shot and 11 in other weight-throwing events. Horgan would possibly have won the shot put gold medal in the Olympics of 1900, 1904, and 1906 if he had competed at those Olympics.

At London in 1908, Rose and Horgan competed against each other for the only known time, but Rose had little difficulty in turning back the aging Horgan's challenge. Surprisingly, Rose did not approach his Olympic record of 48-7¼ (14.81) from St. Louis in 1904, or his world record of 49-7¼ (15.12). In an exhibition throw after the competition had entered, he recorded 47-2. Interestingly, no toe board was used in shot putting.

1. Ralph Rose	USA	46-7½	[14.21]
2. Denis Horgan	GBR/IRL	44-8¼	[13.62]
3. John Garrells	USA	43-3	[13.18]
4. Wesley Coe	USA	42-10½	[13.07]
5. Edward Barrett	GBR/IRL	42-3½	[12.89]
6. Marquis "Bill" Horr	USA	42-1	[12.83][235]
7. Jalmari Sauli	FIN	41-3½	[12.58]
8. Leander Talbott	USA	38-2[236]	[11.63]
AC. Juho Halme	FIN		
Charles Lagarde	FRA		
Henry Leeke	GBR		
István Mudin	HUN		
Wilbur Burroughs	USA		
Martin Sheridan	USA		
Thomas Nicolson	GBR		
John Barrett	GBR/IRL		
Mikhail Dorizas	GRE		
Verner Järvinen	FIN		
Hugo Wieslander	SWE		
Elmer Niklander	FIN		
Bruno Zilliacus	FIN		
André Tison	FRA		
Mór Kóczán	HUN		
Nikolaos Georgantas	GRE		

Arne Halse	NOR

237

Qualifying Rounds A: 25; C: 8; D: 16 July; T: 1430; F: Each competitor was allowed three throws, after which the leading three were permitted a further three throws. The scheduled eight qualifying sections were consolidated into four pools.

Pool 1 (Sections 1 and 2) A: 8; C: 5.

1. Wesley Coe	USA	42-10½	[13.07]
2. Jalmari Sauli	FIN	41-3½	[12.58]
3. Leander Talbott	USA	38-2	[11.63]
AC. Juho Halme	FIN		
Charles Lagarde	FRA		
Henry Leeke	GBR		
John Barrett	GBR/IRL		
István Mudin	HUN		

238

Pool 2 (Sections 3 and 4) A: 8; C: 5.

1. John Garrells	USA	43-3	[13.18]	Q
2. Marquis "Bill" Horr	USA	42-1	[12.83]	
AC. Wilbur Burroughs	USA			
Martin Sheridan	USA			
Thomas Nicolson	GBR			
Mikhail Dorizas	GRE			
Verner Järvinen	FIN			
Hugo Wieslander	SWE			

239

Pool 3 (Sections 5 and 6) A: 4; C: 3.

1. Denis Horgan	GBR/IRL	43-8¾	[13.33]	Q
2. Edward Barrett[240]	GBR/IRL	42-3½[241]	[12.89]	
AC. Elmer Niklander	FIN			
Bruno Zilliacus	FIN			

242

Pool 4 (Sections 7 and 8) A: 5; C: 5.

1. Ralph Rose	USA	46-2½	[14.08]	Q
AC. André Tison	FRA			
Mór Kóczán	HUN			
Nikolaos Georgantas	GRE			
Arne Halse	NOR			

243

Discus Throw, Freestyle

A: 42[244]; C: 11; D: 16 July; T: 1000 — Qualifying; Finals immediately followed the qualifying round.

The discus was thrown from a 7-foot circle without follow, and it was noted "three turns being allowed before the missile leaves the thrower's hand."[245]

The world record holder, and two-time defending Olympic champion, Martin Sheridan (USA), won his third successive Olympic discus title but failed to match his winning mark from the 1906 Olympics. Sheridan was at this time unequaled as a discus thrower and an all-around athlete. Born in Bohola, County Mayo, Ireland, Martin Sheridan emigrated to the United States in 1900, and quickly became the best discus thrower in the world. He stood 6' 3" and weighed 195 lbs. in his prime.

Sheridan is credited with as many as 16 world records, although it is difficult to be precise in the pre-IAAF period. Sheridan's Olympic fame rests primarily on winning the Olympic gold medal in the discus in 1904, 1906, and 1908. Overall, he won nine Olympic medals, including five gold, counting those from the 1906 Olympics.

Sheridan was a superb jumper and weight thrower, and displayed his other talents in the all-around championship, the early American forerunner of the decathlon. Sheridan entered three all-arounds in his athletic career, the AAU National Championships of 1905, 1907, and 1909. He won each of them easily, and set a world record each time, finally leaving it at 7,385 points, a mark which Jim Thorpe broke by only a few points in 1912.

1. Martin Sheridan	USA	134-2	[40.89][246]
2. Merritt Giffin	USA	133-6½	[40.70][247]
3. Marquis "Bill" Horr	USA	129-5	[39.45][248]
4. Verner Järvinen	FIN	129-4½	[39.43][249]
5. Arthur Dearborn	USA	126-4½[250]	[38.52]
6. Leander Talbott[251]	USA	126-0	[38.40]
7. György Luntzer	HUN	125-9	[38.34]
8. André Tison	FRA	125-8	[38.30]
9. John Flanagan[252]	USA	124-0	[37.80]
10. Wilbur Burroughs	USA	122-9½[253]	[37.43]
11. Emil Welz	GER	121-5	[37.02][254]
AC. Platt Adams[255]	USA		
Charles Lagarde	FRA		
Henry Leeke	GBR		
Ernest May	GBR		
Walter Henderson	GBR		
Alfred Flaxman	GBR		
Ferenc Jesina	HUN		
Mór Kóczán	HUN		
Lauri Pihkala	FIN		
Aarne Salovaara	FIN		
Michael Collins	GBR		
Lauri Wilskman	FIN		
John Garrells	USA		
Hugo Wieslander	SWE		
Miroslav Šustera	BOH		
John Murray	GBR/IRL		
Simon Gillis	USA		
Theodor Neijström	SWE		
František Souček	BOH		
Nikolaos Georgantas	GRE		

Imre Mudin[256]	HUN			
Jalmari Sauli	FIN			
Elmer Niklander	FIN			
Folke Fleetwood	SWE			
"Ludwig" Uettwiller	GER			
Edward Barrett	GBR/IRL			
Otto Nilsson	SWE			
Eric Lemming	SWE			
Mikhail Dorizas	GRE			
Umberto Avattaneo	ITA			
John Falchenberg	NOR			

Qualifying Rounds A: 42; C: 11; D: 16 July; T: 1000; F: Each competitor was allowed three throws, after which the first three from the pools were allowed a further three throws. The eight scheduled qualifying sections were consolidated into six pools.

Pool 1 (Sections 1 and 2) A: 8; C: 4.

1. Wilbur Burroughs	USA	122-9½	[37.43]	
AC. Platt Adams	USA			
Charles Lagarde	FRA			
Henry Leeke	GBR			
Ernest May	GBR			
Walter Henderson	GBR			
Alfred Flaxman	GBR			
Ferenc Jesina	HUN			
257

Pool 2 (Section 3) A: 6; C: 3.

1. Arthur Dearborn	USA	126-4½	[38.52]	
2. György Luntzer	HUN	125-9	[38.34]	
3. John Flanagan	USA	124-0	[37.80]	
AC. Mór Kóczán	HUN			
Lauri Pihkala	FIN			
Aarne Salovaara	FIN			
258

Pool 3 (Section 4) A: 6; C: 5.

1. Merritt Giffin	USA	133-6½	[40.71]	Q
AC. Michael Collins	GBR			
Lauri Wilskman	FIN			
John Garrells	USA			
Hugo Wieslander	SWE			
Miroslav Šustera	BOH			
259

Pool 4 (Section 5) A: 7; C: 6.

1. Marquis "Bill" Horr	USA	129-5	[39.44]	Q
2. André Tison	FRA	125-8	[38.30]	

AC. John Murray   GBR/IRL
    Simon Gillis   USA
    Theodor Neijström   SWE
    František Souček   BOH
    Nikolaos Georgantas   GRE
    260

Pool 5 (Section 6) A: 5; C: 4.

AC. Imre Mudin   HUN   261
    Jalmari Sauli   FIN
    Elmer Niklander   FIN
    Folke Fleetwood   SWE
    "Ludwig" Uettwiller GER
    262

Pool 6 (Sections 7 and 8) A: 10; C: 8.

1. Martin Sheridan   USA   133-1½   [40.58]   Q
2. Verner Järvinen   FIN   129-4   [39.42]
3. Leander Talbott   USA   126-0   [38.40]
4. Emil Welz   GER   121-5   [37.02]
AC. Edward Barrett   GBR/IRL
    Otto Nilsson   SWE
    Eric Lemming   SWE
    Mikhail Dorizas   GRE
    Umberto Avattaneo   ITA
    John Falchenberg   NOR
    263

Discus Throw, Classical

A: 23[264]; C: 8; D: 18 July; T: 1440—Qualifying; Finals immediately following the qualifying throws.

Classics scholars maintain that this event was based on a mistranslation of a corrupt text and does not truly represent the style actually used by the Ancient Greeks. Although the first four competitors beat the world record for this event, the fact was not appreciated by the spectators due to an error in the program. The world record listed in the program was that for the freestyle event (128-10½ [39.29]), rather than the 115-4 (35.16) world record for the Greek-style event, which had been set by Verner Järvinen (FIN) at the 1906 Olympics.

Martin Sheridan completed his "double" of winning both discus events at the same Olympics. This also was his last Olympic medal in a storied career which saw him win five gold, three silver, and one bronze medal for nine Olympic medals in all.

1. Martin Sheridan   USA   124-8   [37.99][265]   OR, WR
2. Marquis "Bill" Horr   USA   122-5½   [37.32][266]
3. Verner Järvinen   FIN   119-8¼   [36.48][267]
4. Arthur Dearborn   USA   116-11½   [35.65]

5. Mikhail Dorizas	GRE	109-4½	[33.34][268]
6. Nikolaos Georgantas	GRE	108-11¼	[33.21][269]
7. István Mudin	HUN	108-7½	[33.11]
8. Wilbur Burroughs	USA	107-7¾	[32.81][270]
9. Elmer Niklander	FIN	106-6	[32.46]
10. Umberto Avattaneo	ITA	93-7¼	[29.15]
AC. Miroslav Šustera	BOH		
Henry Leeke	GBR		
Walter Henderson	GBR		
Imre Mudin	HUN		
John Garrells	USA		
Ernest May	GBR		
Alfred Flaxman	GBR		
György Luntzer	HUN		
Eric Lemming	SWE		
271			
Platt Adams	USA		
Folke Fleetwood	SWE		
Mór Kóczán	HUN		
John Barrett	GBR/IRL		
272			

Qualifying Rounds A: 23; C: 8; D: 18 July; T: 1440; F: The eight scheduled qualifying sections were consolidated into four pools. Contestants threw from a forward sloping pedestal and were required to follow a restricted set of movements. The discus had to be released from a standing position and no turning or spinning was allowed.

Pool 1 (Sections 1 and 2) A: 7; C: 5.

1. Mikhail Dorizas	GRE	109-4½	[33.34]
2. Wilbur Burroughs	USA	107-7¾	[32.81]
3. Umberto Avattaneo	ITA	93-7¼	[28.53]
AC. Platt Adams	USA		
Miroslav Šustera	BOH		
Henry Leeke	GBR		
Walter Henderson	GBR		
273			

Pool 2 (Sections 3 and 4) A: 4; C: 4.

1. Arthur Dearborn	USA	116-11½	[35.65]
2. Nikolaos Georgantas	GRE	108-11¼	[33.21]
AC. Folke Fleetwood	SWE		
Imre Mudin	HUN		
274			

Pool 3 (Sections 5 and 6) A: 5; C: 4.

1. István Mudin	HUN	108-7½	[33.11]
2. Elmer Niklander	FIN	106-6	[32.46]
AC. John Garrells	USA		

Ernest May GBR
Alfred Flaxman GBR
275

Pool 4 (Sections 7 and 8) A: 7; C: 5.

1. Martin Sheridan	USA	122-8¾	[37.40]	Q
2. Marquis "Bill" Horr	USA	120-4	[36.68]	Q
3. Verner Järvinen	FIN	119-8¼	[36.48]	Q
AC. Mór Kóczán	HUN			
John Barrett	GBR/IRL			
György Luntzer	HUN			
Eric Lemming	SWE			
276

Hammer Throw

A: 19[277]; C: 8; D: 14 July; T: 1000—Qualifying; Finals immediately followed the qualifying throws.

Matthew McGrath (USA) led the qualifiers with 167-11 (51.18), while John Flanagan (USA) was in second place with 165-2½ (50.36). In the final, Flanagan improved on his last throw to 170-4¼ (51.92) to repeat his victories of 1900 and 1904. Flanagan commented on his victory 20 years later, "It was, without doubt, one of the most satisfying competition wins of my life. Matt McGrath tended to be a little arrogant and I had the feeling he believed he was certain to win. When it all came down to my last throw I knew I had to put everything into it and as it turned out I did. If I have any regret at all now, it is that I was not competing for Ireland on that day."[278]

John Flanagan had won the Olympic title in 1900 and 1904 and was then considered the greatest hammer thrower of the twentieth century. He set 18 marks considered as world records between 1896 and 1909. Flanagan would win seven AAU hammer championships and six titles with the 56-lb. weight. Of Irish birth (Kilbreedy, County Limerick), he had emigrated to the United States in 1897. Amazingly for a man of his size (5' 10" [1.78 meters], 220 lbs. [100 kg.]), he finished second in both the high and long jump and the all-around at the 1895 Irish Championships.

By 1908, Matt McGrath (USA) was becoming Flanagan's rival for hammer throw supremacy. He first appeared on the national scene in 1907, finishing second in the AAU championship, but he was a world-class hammer thrower until 1928, winning seven AAU titles (the last in 1926), setting two world records, and winning three Olympic medals — silvers in 1908 and 1924, and a gold in 1912. In his defense, it was noted that he had injured his knee in the spring of 1908 and was not fully recovered from that by the time of the Olympics.

Interestingly, all three medal winners were born in Ireland and with Scotsman Tom Nicolson finishing in fourth place, it was a memorable day for Celtic throwers. The bronze medalist, Con Walsh, had been born in Carriganimma, County Cork, but spent most of his athletic career in Canada, and may have had the most potential of any of the throwers. The 1920 Olympic hammer champion, Paddy Ryan (USA), commented on Walsh in a 1958 interview, "Con liked the good life and as far as he was concerned training was not part of the good life. He could have beaten the lot of us but he never bothered with any serious training. He was lazy but thoroughly enjoyed competition and was a wonderful man to know at all times."[279]

1.	John Flanagan	USA	170-4¼	[51.92][280]	
2.	Matthew McGrath	USA	167-11	[51.18]	
3.	Cornelius "Con" Walsh	CAN	159-1½	[48.51][281]	
4.	Thomas Nicolson	GBR	157-9¼	[48.09][282]	
5.	Leander Talbott	USA	157-0¼	[47.86][283]	
6.	Marquis "Bill" Horr	USA	154-0¼	[46.95][284]	
7.[285]	Simon Gillis	USA	149-6½	[45.59][286]	
8.	Eric Lemming	SWE	141-3	[43.06]	
9.	Alan Fyffe	GBR	122-6¼	[37.35]	
AC.	Robert Lindsay-Watson	GBR			
	Benjamin Sherman[287]	USA			
	John Murray	GBR/IRL			
	Carl Olsson	SWE			
	Harald Agger[288]	DEN			
	Ernest May	GBR			
	István Mudin	HUN			
	Julius Wagner	SUI			
	"Ludwig" Uettwiller	GER			
	Henry Leeke	GBR			

Qualifying Rounds A: 19; C: 7; D: 14 July; T: 1000; F: Each competitor allowed three throws, after which the three leading competitors were allowed a further three trials.[289]

Section 1 A: 6; C: 4.[290]

1.	Cornelius "Con" Walsh	CAN	159-1½	[48.51]	Q
2.	Leander Talbott	USA	157-0¼	[47.87]	
3.	Eric Lemming	SWE	141-3	[43.06]	
AC.	Robert Lindsay-Watson	GBR			
	Benjamin Sherman	USA			
	John Murray	GBR/IRL			

Section 2 A: 9; C: 6.

1.	Thomas Nicolson	GBR	157-9¼	[48.09]	
2.	Marquis "Bill" Horr	USA	154-0¼	[46.95]	
3.	Alan Fyffe	GBR	122-6¼	[37.35]	
AC.	Carl Olsson	SWE			
	Harald Agger	DEN			
	Ernest May	GBR			
	István Mudin	HUN			
	Julius Wagner	SUI			
	"Ludwig" Uettwiller	GER			

Section 3 A: 4; C: 2.

1.	Matthew McGrath	USA	167-11	[51.18]	Q
2.	John Flanagan	USA	165-2½	[50.36]	Q
3.	Simon Gillis[291]	USA	149-6½	[45.59]	
AC.	Henry Leeke	GBR			

292

Javelin Throw, Freestyle

A: 33[293]; C: 9; D: 15 July; T: 1000 — Qualifying; Finals immediately followed the qualifying throws.

This was only the second Olympic javelin event, as it first appeared on the Olympic program in 1906, when the title was won by Eric Lemming (SWE). The holder of the world record, who would set 11 world marks in his career, Lemming was the heavy favorite. He had set the current record at the 1908 Swedish championships on 7 June, recording 57.33 (188-1).

The three finalists failed to improve their qualifying marks and Lemming was a comfortable winner. Although the contestants were free to use any style they chose, the majority of the competitors used the orthodox center-grip technique. Hence, there was little difference between the two javelin competitions and the freestyle event was dropped from the Olympic program.

1.	Eric Lemming	SWE	178-7½	[54.44][294]
2.	Mikhail Dorizas	GRE	168-6	[51.36]
3.	Arne Halse	NOR	163-1¾	[49.73]
4.	Kharalambos Zouras	GRE	159-5¾	[48.61]
5.[295]	Hugo Wieslander	SWE	156-0	[47.56][296, 297]
6.	Armas Pesonen	FIN	151-0½	[46.04][298]
7.	Imre Mudin	HUN	150-9	[45.96][299]
8.	Jalmari Sauli	FIN	142-1	[43.30][300]
9.	Juho Halme	FIN	130-10	[39.88]
AC.	Henry Leeke	GBR		
	Walter Henderson	GBR		
	Ernest May	GBR		
	Nikolaos Georgantas	GRE		
	Conrad Carlsrud	NOR		
	István Mudin	HUN		
	Alfred Flaxman	GBR		
	Edward Barrett	GBR/IRL		
	Johan Kemp	FIN		
	Aarne Salovaara	FIN		
	Evert Jakobsson	FIN		
	Ferenc Jesina	HUN		
	György Luntzer	HUN		
	Bruno Söderström	SWE		
	Knut Lindberg	SWE		
	Otto Nilsson	SWE		
	František Souček	BOH		
	Jarl Jakobsson	FIN		
	Verner Järvinen	FIN		
	"Ludwig" Uettwiller	GER		
	Emil Welz[301]	GER		
	Mór Kóczán	HUN		
	Emilio Brambilla	ITA		
	John Johansen	NOR		

Qualifying Rounds A: 33; C: 9; D: 15 July; T: 1000; F: Each competitor allowed three throws, after which the leading three were allowed a further three trials. The scheduled eight qualifying sections were consolidated into five pools.

Pool 1 (Section 1) A: 6; C: 2.

1.	Armas Pesonen	FIN	151-0½	[46.04]
2.	Jalmari Sauli	FIN	142-1	[43.30]
3.	Juho Halme	FIN	130-10	[39.88]
AC.	Henry Leeke	GBR		
	Walter Henderson	GBR		
	Ernest May	GBR		

Pool 2 (Section 2 and 3) A: 8; C: 4.

1.	Mikhail Dorizas	GRE	168-6	[51.36]	Q
2.	Arne Halse	NOR	163-1¾	[49.73]	Q
3.	Kharalambos Zouras	GRE	159-5¾	[48.61]	
AC.	Nikolaos Georgantas	GRE			
	Conrad Carlsrud	NOR			
	István Mudin	HUN			
	Alfred Flaxman	GBR			
	Edward Barrett	GBR/IRL			

Pool 3 (Section 4 and 5) A: 6; C: 2.

1.	Imre Mudin	HUN	150-9	[45.96]
AC.	Johan Kemp	FIN	302	
	Aarne Salovaara	FIN		
	Evert Jakobsson	FIN		
	Ferenc Jesina	HUN		
	György Luntzer	HUN		

Pool 4 (Section 6) A: 5; C: 2.

1.	Eric Lemming	SWE	178-7½	[54.45][303]	Q
AC.	Bruno Söderström	SWE			
	Knut Lindberg	SWE			
	Otto Nilsson	SWE			
	František Souček	BOH			

Pool 5 (Section 7 and 8) A: 8; C: 6.

1.	Hugo Wieslander	SWE	156-0	[47.56]
AC.	Jarl Jakobsson	FIN		
	Verner Järvinen	FIN		
	"Ludwig" Uettwiller	GER		
	Emil Welz	GER		
	Mór Kóczán	HUN		
	Emilio Brambilla	ITA		
	John Johansen	NOR		

304

Javelin Throw (held in middle)[305]

A: 16; C: 6; D: 17 July; T: 1430—Qualifying; Finals immediately following the qualifying throws.

Eric Lemming led the qualifiers with 176-1½ (53.68) and improved by more than one meter in the final to repeat his victory in the freestyle event from two days earlier.

1.	Eric Lemming	SWE	179-10½	[54.83][306]
2.	Arne Halse	NOR	165-11	[50.57][307]
3.	Otto Nilsson	SWE	154-6¼	[47.11][308,309]
4.	Aarne Salovaara	FIN	150-6¾	[45.89][310]
5.	Armas Pesonen	FIN	148-2¾	[45.18][311]
6.[312]	Juho Halme	FIN	147-6	[44.96]
7.	Jalmari Sauli	FIN	[313]	
AC.	John Johansen	NOR		
	Kharalambos Zouras	GRE		
	Hugo Wieslander	SWE		
	Henry Leeke	GBR		
	Jimmy Tremeer	GBR		
	Ernest May	GBR		
	Evert Jakobsson	FIN		
	Jarl Jakobsson	FIN		
	Carl Bechler	GER		

Qualifying Rounds A: 16; C: 6; D: 17 July; T: 1430; F: The four scheduled qualifying sections were consolidated into two pools. Each competitor allowed three throws, after which the leading three were allowed a further three throws.

Pool 1 (Sections 1 and 2) A: 11; C: 6.

1.	Otto Nilsson	SWE	154-6¼	[47.11]	Q
2.	Aarne Salovaara	FIN	153-6¾	[46.81]	
3.	Armas Pesonen	FIN	148-2¾	[45.17]	
	Carl Bechler	GER			
	John Johansen	NOR			
	Juho Halme	FIN			
	Kharalambos Zouras	GRE			
	Henry Leeke	GBR			
	Hugo Wieslander	SWE			
	Jimmy Tremeer	GBR			
314					

Pool 2 (Sections 3 and 4) A: 5; C: 4.

1.	Eric Lemming	SWE	176-1½	[53.69]	Q
2.	Arne Halse	NOR	165-11	[50.58]	Q
AC.	Evert Jakobsson	FIN			
	Jarl Jakobsson	FIN			
	Ernest May	GBR			
315					

NOTES

1. DW, EK, and VK/OSVK have 57. Notably, OSVK lists 59 competitors, omitting only Henry Harmer in heat 5 of round one. See the footnotes concerning Harmer after his heat.

2. Laubscher, Lappe. *South African Sport Cummunico, 8(2)*: June/July 1987.

3. *Ibid.*

4. DW, EK, and VK list the time as 10.9, which is certainly also an estimate.

5. NYH has the positions reversed, with Stevens third and Roche in fourth.

6. Also entered in this heat, but not competing, were Francis Rod (SUI), Ervin Déry (HUN), and Emilio Brambilla (ITA).

7. Also entered in this heat, but not competing, were Dimitrios Muller (GRE), Erik Majunke (HUN), and Pierre Failliot (FRA).

8. Knut Lindberg (SWE) was also entered in this heat, but did not compete.

9. John Johansen was not entered in this heat nor, to our knowledge, can he be found in the list of entrants prior to the start of this event.

10. Harmer is not listed in OSVK. SL and SLR both list him, however, and note, "Harmer broke down." The OR also lists Harmer, and also notes, "Harmer broke down." SM lists only two starters with Cloghen first and N[ils] Dahl (NOR) second. Dahl is not listed in any other source; he competed in the 1,500 meters and was more of a middle-distance runner than a sprinter.

11. Also entered in this heat, but not competing, were Gustav Krojer (AUT) and Nils Dahl (NOR).

12. Ernest H. Hutcheon (AUS) was also entered in this heat, but did not compete.

13. Lindberg was not entered in this heat. However, he was entered in heat 3 of this event, but did not compete. The reason for his changing heats is not known.

14. Also entered in this heat, but not competing, were C. Vondracek (BOH) and I. Neumann (SWE).

15. Also entered in this heat, but not competing, were István Kiss (HUN) and Vincent Duncker (SAF/GER). Duncker competed in the AAA Championships a few weeks before, but during the Olympic Games he was noted by SL to be sick with rheumatic fever.

16. Fischer is listed in OR and SL as a competitor in this heat, but according to EzM he did not start.

17. Also entered in this heat, but not competing, were Cornelis den Held (NED) and Gaszton Töldi (HUN).

18. C. Schwarz (GER) was also entered in this heat, but did not compete.

19. Also entered in this heat, but not competing, were Kornél Scheer (HUN) and Charles M. Hervoche (FRA).

20. Ernő Schubert (HUN) was also entered in this heat, but did not compete.

21. Also entered in this heat, but not competing, were Kenneth G. Macleod (GBR) and Lóránd. Hamos (HUN).

22. Also entered in this heat, but not competing, were Forrest Smithson (USA), Heinrich Rehder (GER), and Lajos Ludinszky (HUN).

23. Also entered in this heat, but not competing, were Jenő Bartkó (HUN), Eino Railio (FIN), and Jay D. Whitham (USA).

24. Sven Laftman (SWE), the winner of heat 6, did not start in the semi-finals.

25. Also entered in this heat, but not competing, were Jay D. Whitham (USA), Gaszton Toldy (HUN), and Otto Trieloff (GER).

26. Jenő Bartkó (HUN) was also entered in this heat, but did not compete.

27. Kornél Scheer (HUN) was also entered in this heat, but did not compete.

28. Also entered in this heat, but not competing, were William Murray (GBR/IRL) and O. Georges Dubois (FRA).

29. Also entered in this heat, but not competing, were Dimitrios Muller (GER), James Rector (USA), and Willy Kohlmey (GER).

30. Also entered in this heat, but not competing, were Wyndham Halswelle (GBR) and L. Hussak (AUT).

31. Also entered in this heat, but not competing, were Vincent Duncker (SAF/GER), John Atlee (USA), Heinrich Rehder (GER), and G. Lamotte (FRA).

32. Also entered in this heat, but not competing, were Carl Bechler (GER), Sándor Veres (HUN), and Charles M. Hervoche (FRA).

33. Also entered in this heat, but not competing, were Eino Railio (FIN), C. Vondracek (BOH), and Ernő Schubert (HUN).

34. The OR and SL incorrectly show Halbart as being Hungarian.

35. Géza Gráber (HUN) was also entered in this heat, but did not compete.

36. Also entered in this heat, but not competing, were Pierre Failliot (FRA), Edgar Kiralfy (USA), and László Lichteneckert (HUN).

37. Also entered in this heat, but not competing, were Reggie Walker (SAF), Harold Watson (GBR), Richard Mason (USA), and Hermann von Bönninghausen (GER).

38. Also entered in this heat, but not competing, were Herbert Phillips (SAF), and Ervin Déry (HUN).

39. DW, EK, and VK/OSVK have 36. OSVK omitted Victor Jacquemin (BEL), who competed in heat 10 of round one. See the footnote after that heat.

40. There is some controversy concerning this figure — see note 44 below.

41. SL, 24 July 1908.

42. In one newspaper report, it was stated that Halswelle had marks on his chest from Carpenter's elbows and that he showed these marks to other competitors in the dressing room.

43. Our version of this is not legible on the right in a few sentences and where we are not certain, we have added words in brackets that appear to be Carpenter's comments.

44. One American newspaper (BOADW/source uncertain) gives the time as "47 4/5." OSVK also lists this (47.8) as the time for this race, but we do not know the source. Our source is *The Sportsman*. DMail had the time as 49 seconds. OTAF noted "There are two versions of the unofficial winning time for Carpenter. American sources give 47.8 while British sources gave 48.6."

45. The positions in which Robbins and Taylor finished are given variably in the many newspapers which gave accounts of this race. This is a best guesstimate, and is probably not of great importance due to this final being declared "no race." OSVK has Taylor third and Robbins fourth. Reports by Kirby during the post-race controversy have Robbins third and Taylor fourth.

46. Also entered in this heat, but not competing, were A. Rax (FRA), Géza Gráber (HUN), and Kristian Hellström (SWE).

47. Entered in this heat, but not competing, were Nathaniel Cartmell (USA), G. Defnas (FRA), Károly Radóczy (HUN), Edward Duffy (SAF), and Ragnar Stenberg (FIN).

48. Also entered in this heat, but not competing, were Carl Alfred Pedersen (NOR), Knut Lindberg (SWE), Sándor Veres (HUN), and Karl Lampelmayer (AUT).

49. Also entered in this heat, but not competing, were Henry St. A. Murray (NZL) and Ödön Bodor (HUN). In SL, Bodor is incorrectly listed as Italian.

50. Also entered in this heat, but not competing, were Richard Mason (USA), Gyula Vangel (HUN), and M. Oskar Quarg (GER).

51. Also entered in this heat, but not competing, were Harry Hillman (USA), Vincent Duncker (SAF/GER), and Jenő Bartko (HUN).

52. Noel Chavasse and his brother, Christopher, who competed in the next heat of this event, were twin brothers.

53. Emilio Lunghi (ITA) was also entered in this heat, but did not compete.

54. Also entered in this heat, but not competing, were Herbert Phillips (SAF), Uuno Railo (FIN), and Gaszton Toldy (HUN).

55. Also entered in this heat, but not competing, were R. Irving Parkes (CAN), O. Georges Dubois (FRA), and József Bernegh (HUN).

56. Jacquemin is not listed in OSVK. OR, SL, and SLR list him in this heat as "retired." SM also lists him, but has him finishing third.

57. Also entered in this heat, but not competing, were Hanns Braun (GER) and George Morphy (GBR/IRL).

58. Also entered in this heat, but not competing, were Mikhail Paskhalidis (GRE) and Ödön Holits (HUN).

59. Also entered in this heat, but not competing, were G. Lamotte (FRA), Knut Stenborg (SWE), and Lauri Pihkala (FIN).

60. Also entered in this heat, but not competing, were Robert Kerr (CAN), Evert Koops (NED), and Henri Meslot (FRA).

61. C. Vondracek (BOH) was also entered in this heat, but did not compete.

62. László Lichteneckert (HUN) was also entered in this heat, but did not compete.

63. Also entered in this heat, but not competing, were Pierre Failliot (FRA) and A. Quinn (CAN).

64. DW, EK, FW, and VK/OSVK have 39 starters. The difference is certainly our make-up of heat 4 in round one, and the "missing" athlete is the fact that we did not count Irving Parkes (CAN) as having competed twice. See the extensive footnote after heat 4 for a discussion of this problem.

65. Melvin Sheppard and John Halstead (both USA) were presumably drawn for heat 3, but the entry list for heat 3 is not listed in the papers of 20 July. The United States protested the draw for this event, however, noting that their best two runners were drawn in the same heat, and they both could not advance, because of the unusual system of advancing only the winners. The Americans noted that no American runner had been drawn for heat six and asked that either Halstead or Sheppard be changed to that heat. Although that was not done as requested, the heats were changed slightly. The Swedish team also protested, noting that in two heats, two Swedish runners would have to compete against each other. In the redraw, a number of the entrants appear to have been "shuffled around" in the heats, leading to some confusion when looking at the original entries. We have tried to footnote all of these below. Interestingly, in the 1,500 meter race, which preceded the 800, Sheppard and Halstead were also drawn in the same heat, which presumably inspired some of the American officials' ire at the similar draw in the 800, and led to the protest.

66. Evert Björn was not entered in this heat, but was entered in heat 6 of this event.

67. Also entered in this heat, but not competing, were Paul Pilgrim (USA), Carl G. Andersson (SWE), and Jean Bouin (FRA).

68. Also entered in this heat, but not competing, were Joseph Lynch (AUS), John McGough (GBR/IRL), John Halstead (USA), A. Rax (FRA), and Ragnar Stenberg (FIN). Lynch is listed in some sources as having competed in heat 4, but we feel he did not compete. See the footnotes at the end of heat 4.

69. The original entry list is not in SL or *Times* on 20 July 1908.

70. The entry list as given in SL on the day of this heat was as follows: Emilio Lunghi (ITA), Harry Coe (USA), Lloyd Jones (USA), Stefanos Dimitrios (GRE), Gyula Vangel (HUN), Joseph English (GBR), Pierre Failliot (FRA), and L. J. Manogue (GBR). The result of this event is quite confusing and is usually not given as we have above. The OR, SL, and several other newspapers (BOADW) give the result as follows: (1) Emilio Lunghi (ITA); (2) Harry Coe (USA); (3) Lloyd Jones (USA); (4) J. Parkes (CAN); and AC: Joseph English (GBR) and Joseph Lynch (AUS). We think this result is wrong for several reasons. Our result is given in only one source, SM, which we found in BOADW. The key to our using this result, even though it contradicts multiple other sources, is because of our research into J. Parkes, Stefanos Dimitrios, and L. J. Manogue.

We think J. Parkes is simply a non-existent athlete. R. Irving Parkes (CAN) competed in heat 2 of the 800 metres and finished third. That is certain and is given in all sources, including every Canadian newspaper we examined. No athlete named Parkes is entered in heat 4. At the Canadian Olympic Trials, only one athlete named Parkes is mentioned — R. Irving Parkes. The Canadian newspaper descriptions of the Canadian Olympic team mention only one athlete named Parkes. In CA 3992, the only Parkes listed is Irving Parkes, with marks recorded for him in 1907–1909. In personal communication with McNulty and Radcliffe both confirm that only one Parkes was a competitive runner in Canada at that time, and also note that the 1908 Canadian Olympic Report did not mention a second Parkes. H/A and EzM both list two Parkeses in their index of 1908 athletes, but we think they are simply copying the incorrect OR.

L. J. Manogue is not listed in OR or SL, but he definitely competed. A member of the South London Harriers, he is listed as having competed in heat 4 of the 800 meters in the SLHG (August 1908, p. 5). Manogue and Stefanos Dimitrios (GRE) were also both entered in this heat per SL. Also, all of the five athletes given in our (i.e., SM) result were entered in this heat per SL. In the result we consider erroneous, Parkes and Lynch were not entered in the heat; in fact, both were entered in heat 2 per SL. Finally, Dimitrios is listed as running in the 800 meters in *Helliniki simmetokhi stis Sinkhrones olympiades*, and he definitely did not compete in any other heat.

Thus, due to these findings concerning Parkes, Manogue, Lynch, and Dimitrios, we are certain that the above result is the correct one.

71. Also entered in this heat, but not competing, were Arnošt Nejedlý (BOH) and Henri Meslot (FRA).

72. Breynck was not entered in this heat, but was entered in heat 7 of this event.

73. Also entered in this heat, but not competing, were Henry St. A. Murray (NZL), Evert Björn (SWE), O. Georges Dubois (FRA), Géza Bruger (HUN), and John Fitzgerald (CAN).

74. Also entered in this heat, but not competing, were Andreas Breynck (GER) and József Bernegh (HUN). Breynck competed in heat 6 of this event — see above.

75. *Australia at the Olympic Games* (Blanch/Jenes) gives Sutton third in 1:58.0, but that would have been a faster time than Kristian Hellström who finished second at 15 yards.

76. Also entered in this heat, but not competing, were Guy Haskins (NZL), Ödön Holits (HUN), A. Pouillot (FRA), and Erwin von Sigel (GER).

77. BOADW source uncertain.

78. Hendrik van der Wal (NED) was also entered in this heat, but did not compete.

79. Also entered in this heat, but not competing, were Antal Lovas (HUN) and Kristian Hellström (SWE).

80. Time given as 4:04.8 in SM.

81. OSVK lists Cartasegna third, Riley fourth, and Björn fifth, implying that they finished. OR, SL, and SLR do not really address their places, listing them as "also ran." However, SM notes, "Lunghi, who had faltered on being collared, finishing in 4 min. 4 4-5 sec., *no one else completing the distance*," which implies that Cartasegna, Riley, and Björn did not finish.

82. Swain is listed as entrant in this heat but is not listed in the results of any British or American newspaper. We originally did not include him as a competitor in this event. But Brisbane and Queensland, Australia, claim that he did compete and has provided a reference in the 1908 *Brisbane Courier*, which states that Swain started in the 1,500 but could not stand the pace and did not finish. Based on this we have included him in the results.

83. Also entered in this heat, but not competing, were R. Daubin (SUI) and George Morphy (GBR/IRL).

84. Also entered in this heat, but not competing, were J. Georg Peterson (SWE), Imre Veres (HUN), and John C. Blankenagel (USA).

85. OSVK lists Ragueneau as fourth, implying that he finished. SL, SLR, and OR all note that he "retired." SM is less definite, not describing his exact finish, but listing it as "0" which in the 1908 British sources usually implied that the athlete did not finish.

86. Also entered in this heat, but not competing, were Lloyd Jones (USA), Arthur "Archie" Robertson (GBR), Guy Haskins (NZL), Floyd A. Rowe (USA), and Carl G. Andersson (SWE).

87. Also entered in this heat, but not competing, were Charles Hefferon (SAF), Marcel Quilbeuf (FRA), Gale Dull (USA), Johan Svanberg (SWE), George Blake (AUS), and Donald Buddo (CAN).

88. Also entered in this heat, but not competing, were Herbert Trube (USA), W. A. Shee (SAF), Felix Kwieton (AUT), Frank Gösta Danielson (SWE), and Kálmán Becske (HUN).

89. George Hoynes (USA) was also entered in this heat, but did not compete.

90. DW, EK, FW, and VK/OSVK have 35. OSVK does not list Herbert Trube (USA) in heat 5 of round one. See the footnote in that heat concerning Trube.

91. Edward Carr (USA) and William Galbraith (CAN), who had qualified, did not start.

92. Mile splits were as follows: 4:52.0 (Coales)/10:02.8 (Hefferon)/15:10.4 (Svanberg)/20:29.4 (Svanberg).

93. Also entered in this heat, but not competing, were Dorando Pietri (ITA), Harvey Cohn (USA), Hendrik van der Wal (NED), George Bonhag (USA), A. Henry Thomas (FRA), and Rudolf Hansen (DEN).

94. Mile splits were as follows: 5:06.2 (Bellars)/10:40.0 (Bellars)/16:06.0 (Bellars)/21:16.0 (Voigt).

95. Also entered in this heat, but not competing, were Joseph Dreher (FRA), A. C. Young (USA), Imre Veres (HUN), Tom Longboat (CAN), W. A. Shee (SAF), and Thomas Downing (GBR).

96. Mile splits were as follows: 5:07.6 (Nettelbeck)/10:32.6 (Nettelbeck)/15:53.4 (Landqvist)/21:26.2 (Landqvist).

97. Also entered in this heat, but not competing, were Jean Bouin (FRA), Alexander Duncan (GBR), Guy Haskins (NZL), Kálmán Becske (HUN), Francis Edwards (GBR), and Edward Cotter (CAN).

98. Mile splits were as follows: 4:49.6 (Murphy)/9:59.8 (Murphy)/15:12.4 (Murphy)/20:31.4 (Murphy).

99. Also entered in this heat, but not competing, were Louis Bonnoit de Fleurac (FRA), R. G. Carr (USA), Floyd A. Rowe (USA), Felix Kwieton (AUT), and W. F. Theunissen (NED).

100. Mile splits were as follows: 4:52.8 (Robertson)/10:02.6 (Robertson)/15:18.4 (Robertson)/20:37.4 (Robertson).

101. OSVK does not list Herbert Trube as competing. He is not listed by OR, SL, or SLR, but *The Sportsman* does list him, and notes that Stevenson finished third, with "no else completing the distance."

102. Also entered in this heat, but not competing, were Emilio Giovanoli (ITA), Gale Dull (USA), B. Millerot (FRA), and William Wood (CAN).

103. Mile splits were as follows: 4:46.6/9:56.0/15:19.2/20:37.4.

104. Nejedlý was not entered in this heat, nor in any heat of the 5 mile race.

105. Also entered in this heat, but not competing, were Johan Lindqvist (SWE), Alexandre Fayollat (FRA), Harold Wilson (GBR), John Eisele (USA), W. Victor Aitken (AUS), J. R. Armour (USA), Anastasios Koutoulakis (GRE), Arthur Burn (CAN), and Frederick Simpson (CAN).

106. DW, EK, FW, and OSVK have 56. OSVK lists Samuel Stevenson (GBR) as competing — see below for our discussion of this. VK has 75, which is the number of original entries. It is difficult to know the exact number of original entrants. The papers mentioned 75 entrants several times, and the starting numbers ran from 1 to 75. But there were most likely only 72 or 73 entrants. The OR listed 75 entrants, giving numbers for all 75. However, #20 and #21 were both listed as U. Blasi, who was Umberto Blasi, who did compete. Also, #19 was P. Dorando, while #23 was P. Durando, most likely both referring to Dorando Pietri, who eventually wore #19. In addition, #7, . — — Vincent (SAF) is not listed in any of the entry lists given in the papers, from which we could identify only 72 entrants. He would be the seventy-third entrant, although his name is given in no other source, including the index of athletes in the OR.

Several different entry lists appeared in various newspapers, and a few days after the original entry lists were released, revised versions were again printed in the papers, listing 58 remaining entries. The following athletes were listed in the original entry lists, but not the revised ones — presumably they withdrew: Felix Kwieton (AUT), Hermann Müller (GER), Lajos Merényi (HUN), Augusto Cocca (ITA), A. B. Moie (SAF), G. E. Stevens (SAF), Ivar Lundberg (SWE), J. Georg Peterson (SWE), J. Thure Bergvall (SWE), Alexander Thibeau (USA), Fred Lorz (USA), James J. Lee (USA), James W. O'Mara (USA), and William Wood (USA). The day before the race, a final draw was released. Of the revised entries, all were included in the final draw except one — W. F. Theunissen of the Netherlands.

Finally, of the 57 athletes included in the final draw, two did not actually start — Samuel Stevenson (GBR) and Paul Nettelbeck (GER) — eventually leaving 55 starters in the marathon. Several sources, including the OR, do include Stevenson as having started, but this appears to be an error. SL gave a list of the final starters, and also specifically stated, "It was a great disappointment to find S. Stevenson (the Scotsman) an absentee from the British team."

107. Scheduled for 2:30 P.M. [1430], the race actually started at 2:33 P.M. [1433].

108. A map of the marathon course can be found in Appendix IV.

109. BOADW/source uncertain.

110. TMF, p. 30.

111. SL, 25 July 1908.

112. TMF, p. 31, referenced to A.E.H. Winter, *From the Legend to the Living*, Rugeley: Benhill Press, Ltd., 1969.

113. BOADW, source uncertain.

114. BOADW, source uncertain.

115. Many sources list the name as "Dorando — He's Good-a For Not!" which is incorrect. However, that phrase was the last line of the song. The music and lyrics can be found in Appendix V.

116. After each athlete's name we have listed his starting number followed by the starting row. The draw separated the runners into four rows, with 15 runners in the first three rows and 12 in the fourth row. Because Samuel Stevenson (GBR) and Paul Nettelbeck (GER) did not start, there were actually only 10 runners in row four.

117. This time is an estimate. It is actually listed as 2-54:36 in BOADW, which cannot be correct given Pietri's final finishing time of 2-54:46.4. Given the description of Pietri's struggle around the track, it is likely he entered the stadium at around 2-51. In addition, 1 and 4 can often be mistaken for one another, creating a typographical error.

118. The times for Knyvett and Howe are taken from the Index to Volume III of EzM. The OR says that Smithson won "very easily" which makes the above times for second and third places rather suspect.

119. Fernand Halbart (BEL), who had qualified for the semi-finals by his win in heat 8 of round one, did not start.

120. Edward Cook (USA) was also entered in this heat, but did not compete.

121. Halligan was a New Zealander living in Scotland in 1908. He later returned home and became New Zealand champion in the 120 yard hurdles in 1915.

122. Also entered in this heat, but not competing, were Francis Rod (SUI), and Ragnar Stenberg (FIN).

123. Also entered in this heat, but not competing, were J. Frere (BEL) and F. A. Natwick (USA).

124. Also entered in this heat, but not competing, were Norman Patterson (USA), Evert Koops (NED), and Karl Fryksdahl (SWE).

125. Emile Hautekeet (BEL) was also entered in this heat, but did not compete.

126. Also entered in this heat, but not competing, were Iván Medgyessy (HUN) and Douglas R. Robbins (USA).

127. Also entered in this heat, but not competing, were Eugène Choisel (FRA), Knut Lindberg (SWE), and John L. Hartranft (USA).

128. Also entered in this heat, but not competing, were E. Steiner (FRA), Axel Ljung (SWE), and A. Gordon (GBR).

129. Also entered in this heat, but not competing, were G. Durbee (FRA), J. Garfield MacDonald (CAN), and Alfredo Pagani (ITA).

130. Also entered in this heat, but not competing, were Henri Meslot (FRA) and George Barber (CAN).

131. Also entered in this heat, but not competing, were L. Lescat (FRA) and Emilio Brambilla (ITA).

132. Also entered in this heat, but not competing, were Vincent Duncker (SAF/GER) and Julius Wagner (SUI).

133. Also entered in this heat, but not competing, were Ernő Kéméndy (HUN) and E. Casenave (FRA).

134. Also entered in this heat, but not competing, were Calvin Bricker (USA), Charles M. Hervoche (FRA), and Ödön Holits (HUN).

135. SL, p. 59.

136. EK, SL, SLR, and OR list Burton as DNF. SM lists him as fourth, as does OSVK.

137. OSVK has Groenings in second and finishing. DM and SM note that Bacon "finished alone." SL, SLR, and OR note that Groenings and Kováts "retired."

138. Also entered in this heat, but not competing, were Tom Kiely (GBR/IRL), Ragnar Stenberg (FIN), and Joseph Bromilow (USA).

139. Also entered in this heat, but not competing, were E. Steiner (USA) and Oscar Guttormsen (NOR).

140. Also entered in this heat, but not competing, were Vincent Duncker (SAF/GER) and Eugène Choisel (FRA).

141. Also entered in this heat, but not competing, were Pierre Failliot (FRA), Douglas Stupart (SAF), and Charles French (FRA).

142. Also entered in this heat, but not competing, were John Halstead (USA), G. A. Chavez (FRA), and George Barber (CAN).

143. Also entered in this heat, but not competing, were Jenő Bartkó (HUN) and Fernand Halbart (BEL).

144. Also entered in this heat, but not competing, were William Hamilton (USA), Carl Alfred Pedersen (NOR), and Ödön Bodor (HUN).

145. Also entered in this heat, but not competing, were A. Gaston Ragueneau (FRA) and John L. Hartranft (USA).

146. Also entered in this heat, but not competing, were Leonard Howe (USA) and Emile Hautekeet (BEL).

147. Also entered in this heat, but not competing, were James Lightbody (USA) and Calvin Bricker (CAN).

148. The entries in this heat were József Nagy (HUN), Edwin Montague (GBR), and Ned Merriam (USA).

149. Melvin Sheppard (USA) was also entered in this heat, but did not compete.

150. A. C. Young (USA) was also entered in this heat, but did not compete.

151. Lloyd Jones was also entered in this heat, but did not compete.

152. Also entered in this heat, but not competing, were John Halstead (USA), John Daly (GBR/IRL), Guy Haskins (NZL), and Herbert Trube (USA).

153. Also entered in this heat, but not competing, were Charles Hefferon (SAF) and Emilio Lunghi (ITA).

155. Also entered in this heat, but not competing, were John Tait (CAN) and Hermann Wraschtil (AUT).

155. Also entered in this heat, but not competing, were Paul Lizandier (FRA) and Floyd Rowe (USA).

156. OR, FW have Rácz instead of Mezei Wiesner. FM has Vilmos Rácz instead of Mezei Wiesner. EK notes that Rácz is incorrect and Mezei Wiesner is correct. The source is not known but is likely from Hungarian sources corresponding with Kamper. All current sources have Mezei Wiesner and no Hungarians have corrected this as an error.

157. In the original entry list, the four teams entered in this heat were Sweden, the United States, South Africa, and Greece. Greece and South Africa did not compete in this event. The United States eventually started in heat 3. Hungary was actually entered in heat 2 of this event.

158. In the original entry list, the four teams entered in this heat were Great Britain, Germany, Hungary, and Italy. Italy did not compete in this event. Great Britain started in heat 3, while Hungary had already started in heat 1.

159. In the original entry list, the four teams entered in this heat were Canada, Finland, the Netherlands, and Norway. Finland and Norway did not compete in this event. The Netherlands had already started in heat 2. The United States was originally entered in heat 1, and Great Britain was originally entered in heat 2.

160. Only four French runners started.

161. The mile splits were as follows: 4:42.6/9:44.8.

162. OSVK does not list Bouin as a starter. He is not listed by SL, SLR, or OR. However, SM noted, "The Frenchman, Bouin, alone did not finish, dropping out at the end of the first mile."

163. Only three Dutch runners started.

164. We have not been able to find entry lists for this event.

165. DW, and OSVK have 24 starters and 9 nations. There were only eight nations represented, unless Great Britain and Great Britain/Ireland are counted as separate nations.

166. OSVK appears to list seven walkers, but on closer inspection he has Rothman and Winkelman both in third, then Drubina in fourth. He actually has eight walkers in the heat.

167. OSVK incorrectly lists Rothman and Winkelman both as third, and has the other finishers one place higher than their actual finish. Kluge did have the correct times for Rothman and Winkelman, however, and the error is certainly a typo.

168. VK has 28.

169. VK has 1-21:20.4, which is likely a typo, as all 1908 sources give Spencer and Carter the same time.

170. Rowland was not entered in this heat, nor even in this event.

171. Also entered in this heat, but not competing, were F. Preiss (GER), György Sztantics (HUN), J. Eugen Spiegler (AUT), A. Claro (GER), George Bonhag (USA), W. Victor Aitken (AUS), and Antal Lovas (HUN).

172. Also entered in this heat, but not competing, were Richard Wilhelm (GER), Hermann Müller (GER), Ferenc Manglitz (HUN), István Drubina (HUN), and Lajos Tumbácz (HUN).

173. DW, FW, and VK/OSVK have 20. The difference is likely to be he re-start of pool 1, in which two of the original starters did not compete.

174. DW and OSVK have 1.905. OR has 1.90.

175. DW and OSVK have 1.855. OR has 1.85.

176. DW and OSVK have 1.855. OR has 1.85.

177. Hedenlund is not listed as eighth in DW, but SM (in BOADW) definitely supports his mark of 5-10⅞ [1.80] which would place him eighth. He withdrew and did not compete in the final, however, which may lead to the omission in DW.

178. The original section entries were as follows: section 1— Douglas Stupart (SAF), Konstantin Tsiklitiras (GRE), Lauri Wilskman (FIN), Coenraad van Veenhuijsen (NED), Otto Monsen (NOR), John Brennan (USA), Oswald Groenings (GBR), and Edward Leader (GBR); section 2 — Robert Pasemann (GER), Conrad Rehder (GER), Hugo Wieslander (SWE), József Haluzsinszky (HUN), Béla Szabó (HUN), Alfred Bellerby (GBR), John B. Milne (GBR), and Herbert Gidney (USA).

179. Otto Monsen (NOR) and Lauri Wilskman (FIN) did not start.

180. The original section entries were as follows: section 3 — Axel Hedenlund, Jr. (SWE), Lajos Gönczy (HUN), Francis Irons (USA), Géza Vadon (HUN), Georges André (FRA), Norman Patterson (USA), Lauri Pihkala (FIN), Henry Olsen (NOR); section 4 — Robert Pascarel (FRA), István Somodi (HUN), Otto Muhl (GER), Cornelius "Con" Leahy (GBR/IRL), Patrick Leahy (GBR/IRL), J. Garfield MacDonald (CAN), Géza Szegedy (HUN), and Jeremiah Mahoney (USA).

181. Somodi was actually entered in section 4, which was part of pool 2. It is not known why he competed in this pool. In addition, it was quite difficult to even determine his qualifying mark and the pool in which he competed. We knew he had qualified, since he eventually finished second, but he is listed in only one source, which was difficult to find — an obscure American newspaper listed in BOADW, and whose source is uncertain.

182. The original section entries were as follows: section 5 — J. Lynn Miller (USA), Harry Porter (USA), Léon Dupont (BEL), Gustav Krojer (AUT), Albert Weinstein (GER), Carl Silfverstrand (SWE), Timothy Ahearne (GBR/IRL), and Károly Szathmáry (HUN); section 6 — A. Berthet (FRA), Tom Moffitt (USA), Herman van Leeuwen (NED), Gaspare Torretta (ITA), Folke Hellstedt (SWE), Dr. Paul Weinstein (GER), Georges André (FRA), and Baron Ivan Wardener (HUN).

183. The original section entries were as follows: section 7 — György Domokos (HUN), József Zöld (HUN), George Mayberry (GBR/IRL), John Schommer (USA), Oscar Lemming (SWE), Georges Martin (FRA), and George Barber (CAN); section 8 — Gunnar Ronström (SWE), Elemér

Szigeti-Polyákovics (HUN), Béla Danér (HUN), E. Cazenave (FRA), George Wilson (GBR), and Benjamin Stephenson (USA).

184. DW, FW, and VK/OSVK have 14. OSVK does not list Thomas Jackson (USA) as a competitor and there is some controversy concerning this — see our footnote after pool 3.

185. BOADW, source uncertain.

186. The original section entries were as follows: section 1— Claude Allen (USA), Otto Franke (GER), György Páhy (HUN), E. C. Mercer (USA), V. Blois (FRA), Brand "Bram" Evers (NED), and Stefanos Kountouriotis (GRE); section 2 — Lauri Pihkala (FIN), E. A. Hansson (NOR), A. Petrovsky (RUS), Charles Jacobs (USA), M. Rank (GER), Charles Campbell (USA), and Bruno Söderström (SWE).

187. The original section entries were as follows: section 3 — Kálmán Szabó (HUN), G. Robin (FRA), Edward Archibald (CAN), Alfred Flaxman (GBR), Hans Liesche (GER), A. C. Gilbert (USA), and Douglas Stupart (SAF); section 4 — B. Haggard (USA), Georgios Banikas (GRE), Edward Cook (USA), Robert Pasemann (GER), Emil Kazár (HUN), Georg Karth (GER), and Robert Pascarel (FRA).

188. The original section entries were as follows: section 5 — M. Cobert (FRA), Sam Bellah (USA), P. Monstey (FRA), Walter Dray (USA), Wilhelm Weber (GER), Károly Szathmáry (HUN), and Coenraad van Veenhuijsen (NED); section 6 — G. Koeger (FRA), Frank Nelson (USA), A. G. Parker (USA), Rudolf Kallmeyer (GER), Carl Silfverstrand (SWE), G. Monstey (FRA), and Thomas Jackson (USA).

189. There are different listings for the pools in various 1908 newspapers, as noted in the BOADW and Desb. SM lists only two pools as follows: pool 1 (Sections 1–3): (1) Gilbert, (=2) Söderström and Archibald, (4) Jacobs, (5) Kountouriotis, (6) Evers; and pool 2 (Sections 4–6): (1) Cook, (=2) Banikas and Bellah, (4) Szathmáry, (=5) Pascarel and Silfverstrand, (7) Jackson, and (8) van Veenhuijsen. SL does not list the pool results, but lists only 14 athletes as having competed, omitting Thomas Jackson (USA). A clipping in Desb (source uncertain) and DG give the above result, but also omitted Thomas Jackson.

Based on a majority of newspaper reports we have chosen the above result listing for the pools, although we cannot be positive it is fully correct. It is difficult to know what to do with Thomas Jackson. He is not listed in two of the above reports. However, it should be noted that DG listed only the top three finishers in each pool, so strictly speaking, Jackson was not omitted in that source, but the results were not deep enough to list him, if he competed. But SM definitely listed him as competing, giving him a mark of 10-0 (3.05) as noted above. He was entered in section 6, which would have placed him in pool 3 in the above listing. We have included him based on the mark given in SM, but it is not certain that he competed.

190. DW, FW, VK have 30 starters.

191. VK has 7.085, while OSVK has 7.09. OR has 7.08.

192. OR and SLR do not list Mount Pleasant as sixth, giving that place to Albert Weinstein (GER), but Mount Pleasant's mark is well documented in 1908 sources, found in several places in BOADW.

193. OSVK has 6.66.

194. OSVK has 6.45. Our metric mark is based on the Imperial measurement in BOADW.

195. EzM (Vol. III, p. 233) lists "Ludwig" Uettwiller as competing in this event and gives him a mark of 19-10¼ (6.05), with no place given. We can find no 1908 source in English listing Uettwiller as having competed in this event; specifically he is not in the entry lists, not in the pool entry lists, and no result is given for him in OR, SL, and BOADW. The source for Uettwiller's participation is apparently the 1908 yearbook of the German athletics federation (DFBsA) per German statisticians.

196 See previous footnote. Because we do not know in which pool Uettwiller competed, we cannot be certain about the number of competitors in each pool.

197. The original section entries were as follows: section 1— Platt Adams (USA), Armas Pesonen (FIN), Károly Szathmáry (HUN), Ödön Holits (HUN), Henri Meslot (FRA), Wilfred Bleaden (GBR), Frank Savage (CAN), and Edvard Larsen (NOR); section 2 — Eino Railio (FIN), Douglas

Stupart (SAF), Evert Koops (NED), Gaston Martens (BEL), Sam Bellah (USA), E. Steiner (FRA), Edward Cook (USA), and Sándor Veres (HUN).

198. Albert Weinstein (GER) was not entered in either section of this pool (he was entered in section 9/pool 5), but O. Weinstein (GER) was entered in section 4. This is likely Paul Weinstein, who was entered but did not compete, as there was no prominent athlete named "O. Weinstein" in Germany at the time, per German statisticians.

199. The original section entries were as follows: section 3 — Oswald Groenings (GBR), F. Young (USA), Benjamin Stephenson (USA), Alfred Bellerby (GBR), Carl Bechler (GER), Sven Laftman (SWE), Erik Majunke (HUN), and George Barber (CAN); section 4 — John Brennan (USA), Paul Weinstein (GER) (see prvious footnote), Ede Rökk (HUN), Daniel Kelly (USA), Carl Silfverstrand (SWE), Cornelius "Con" Leahy (GBR/IRL), Timothy Ahearne (GBR/IRL), and Andor Szende (HUN).

200. The original section entries were as follows: section 5 — Robert Pascarel (FRA), Cyril Dugmore (GBR), István Csurgay (HUN), Georges André (FRA), Charles Williams (GBR), John O'Connell (USA), Frank Mount Pleasant (USA), and Juho Halme (FIN); section 6 — Ragnar Stenberg (FIN), Brand "Bram" Evers (NED), Francis Irons (USA), Gustav Krojer (AUT), Martin Brustmann (GER), Knut Stenborg (SWE), and Nándor Kováts (HUN).

201. The original pool/section entries were as follows: pool 4/section 7 — William F. C. Watt (GBR/IRL), Frank Lukeman (CAN), Hugo Wieslander (SWE), Hermann von Bönninghausen (GER), Nathaniel Sherman (USA) (this is almost certainly Nathaniel Sherman [USA]), Jacobus Hoogveld (NED), Karl Fryksdahl (SWE), and Denis Murray (GBR/IRL). Nathaniel Sherman apparently attempted to compete in this pool. BOADW (source uncertain) notes "Sherman, who was running in the semi-finals of the 200 metres at the same time that the running broad jump was being contested. After the sprint he hastened to the official at the broad jump, but was told that he could not compete, as he had not been there a few minutes earlier to answer to his name." This is likely correct. Sherman ran in heat 2 of the semi-finals of the 200 on 22 July at around 1025, and the pools for the broad jump started at 1030.

202. Kovesdy is definitely entered in this pool (section 9) and is listed as competing by all the pertinent sources (OR, SL, BOADW), but he is not listed among Hungarian Olympians in the best source for that information - *Az Olimpiai Játékokon Indult Magyar Versenyzők Névsora 1896-1980*. His full name was identified by Hungarian ATFS member, Gabriel Szabó.

203. The original section entries were as follows: section 8 — Henry Olsen (NOR), Ernest H. Hutcheon (AUS), Arthur Hoffmann (GER), A. Gordon (GBR), J. Garfield MacDonald (CAN), Calvin Bricker (CAN), István Somodi (HUN), and Arvid Ringstrand (SWE); section 9 — Gaspare Torretta (ITA), Jeremiah Mahoney (USA), Karl Lampelmayer (AUT), Julius Wagner (SUI), Albert Weinstein (GER), Gunnar Ronström (SWE), Géza Kovesdy (HUN), Henri Guttierez (FRA), and Lionel Cornish (GBR).

204. DW, FW, and VK/OSVK have 19 from 7 nations. The difference is surely Juho Halme (FIN) in section 2; see the footnote concerning him in that section.

205. VK has 14.915. OR has 14.92.

206. The exact order of MacDonald's jumps is unknown, but it is known that he recorded 14.76 in qualifying and 14.59 in the finals.

207. VK has 14.395. OR has 14.39.

208. The exact order of Larsen's jumps is unknown, but it is known that he recorded 14.39 in qualifying and 14.34 in the finals.

209. VK has 14.095. OR has 14.10.

210. Also entered in this section, but not competing, were Frank Lukeman (CAN), A. Quinn (CAN), Eino Railio (FIN), Ernest H. Hutcheon (NZL), Emilio Brambilla (ITA), F. Young (USA), Albert Weinstein (GER), and Cornelius "Con" Leahy (GBR/IRL).

211. OSVK does not list Halme as competing. He is not listed in OR or SLR. People and SM both listed him as competing in this section.

212. Also entered in this section, but not competing, were John O'Connell (USA), Karl Lampelmayer (AUT), Arthur Hoffmann (GER), Sven Laftman (SWE), and Frank Savage (CAN).

213. Dineen was not entered in this section, nor in this event in the final pool entries. He was in the original entry list, however.

214. Also entered in this section, but not competing, were Knut Stenborg (SWE), Edward Cook (USA), John Schommer (USA), Benjamin Stephenson (USA), Gustav Krojer (AUT), Paul Weinstein (GER), Martin Brustmann (GER), Carl Silfverstrand (SWE), N. S. Jacobsson (SWE), and George Barber (CAN).

215. DW, FW, and VK/OSVK have 22. They certainly do not include "Ludwig" Uettwiller (GER), for whom a mark does exist from pool 2; see below.

216. DW, and VK/OSVK have 1.575. OR has 1.57.

217. DW, VK have 1.525. OR has 1.52.

218. OSVK does not list Uettwiller as competing, but BOADW gives a mark for him in pool 2.

219. Listed in some sources as a New Zealander, current Australian Olympic experts list Hutcheon as Australian. He is also not listed in the New Zealand book on Olympics by Palenski and Maddaford.

220. Also entered in this section/pool, but not starting, were Róbert Abarbanell (HUN) and A. Berthet (FRA).

221. The original section entries were as follows: section 2 — Walter Henderson (GBR), István Mudin (HUN), Herman van Leeuwen (NED), John Biller (USA), Martin Sheridan (USA), and "Ludwig" Uettwiller (GER); section 3 — Douglas Stupart (SAF), Wilhelm Blystad (NOR), Géza Vadon (HUN), Lancelot Stafford (GBR), Ray Ewry (USA), and Georges André (FRA).

222. The original section entries were as follows: section 4 — John Brennan (USA), George Barber (CAN), Timothy Ahearne (GBR/IRL), Coenraad van Veenhuijsen (NED), LeRoy Holmes (USA), and Nándor Kováts (HUN); section 5 — Ernest H. Hutcheon (NZL), Francis Irons (USA), Arthur Mallwitz (GER), Ferenc Blazsek (HUN), and Pierre Durand (FRA).

223. The following athletes were entered in section 6, but none of them actually competed in this event: Lajos Gönczy (HUN), Sigmund Muenz (USA), E. Cazenave (FRA), Edward Leader (GBR), and A. Quinn (CAN). Also entered in section 6 was Karl Fryksdahl (SWE), who competed but we are uncertain in which pool.

224. The original section entries were as follows: section 7 — Cornelius "Con" Leahy (GBR/IRL), Lawson Robertson (USA), Svend Langkjær (DEN), István Mudin (HUN), Andor Horner (HUN), and Alfred Motte (FRA); Section 8 - Robert Pasemann (GER), J. K. Macmeekan (GBR), John Schommer (USA), Andor Szende (HUN), Allan Bengtsson (SWE), and Henri Jardin (FRA).

225. DW, VK have 3.35. OR has 3.33.

226. DW has 3.235.

227. DW, VK have 3.225. OR has 3.22.

228. DW has 3.215. OR has 3.21.

229. DW, VK have 3.195. OR has 3.19.

230. The original section entries were as follows: section 1 — Ernest H. Hutcheon (NZL), Boldizsár Horváth (HUN), Francis Irons (USA), Pierre Failliot (FRA), Evert Koops (NED), and Lionel Cornish (GBR); section 2 — Platt Adams (USA), Douglas Stupart (SAF), Martin Sheridan (USA), Lancelot Stafford (GBR), Konstantin Tsiklitiras (GRE), and Nándor Kováts (HUN).

231. Ewry was not entered in this pool/section, but was entered in section 7. It is not known why he competed in pool 2.

232. The original section entries were as follows: section 3 — Jarl Jakobsson (FIN), Brand "Bram" Evers (NED), Walter Henderson (GBR), Andor Horner (HUN), Sigmund Muenz (USA), and F. Vyskocik (BOH); section 4 — LeRoy Holmes (USA), "Ludwig" Uettwiller (GER), O. Georges Dubois (FRA), John Schommer (USA), Frederick Kitching (GBR), and George Barber (CAN).

233. We have no results available in any source for the remaining two pools, Pool Three and Pool Four. They were made up from sections 5–6 (pool 3), and sections 7–8 (pool 4). The entries in these four sections were as follows, and we have also listed if the athlete competed in this event [ac] or not [dnc]: section 5 — Timothy Ahearne [ac] (GBR/IRL), A. Quinn [dnc] (CAN), Karl Lampelmayer [dnc] (AUT), John Biller [ac] (USA), Arthur Radó [dnc] (HUN), and Ragnar Ekberg [ac] (SWE); section 6 — Svend Langkjær [ac] (DEN), Henri Jardin [ac] (FRA), Arthur Mallwitz [ac]

(GER), Lawson Robertson [dnc] (USA), and Wilfred Bleaden [ac] (GBR); section 7 — Jacobus Hoogveld [ac] (NED), Ray Ewry [ac-pool 2] (USA), Wilhelm Blystad [dnc] (NOR), Andor Szende [dnc] (HUN), Patrick Leahy [dnc] (GBR/IRL), and Pierre Durand [dnc] (FRA); section 8 — Léon Dupont [ac] (BEL), John Brennan [dnc] (USA), Hermann von Bönninghausen [dnc] (GER), Cornelius "Con" Leahy [dnc] (GBR/IRL), Alfred Motte [ac] (FRA), and Imre Mudin [dnc] (HUN).

234. DW, FW, and VK/OSVK have 26. The discrepancy deals with whether or not Imre Mudin (HUN) competed. See footnotes at the end of the final standings and pool 3.

235. VK has 12.825. OSVK has 12.82.

236. DW has 38-1¾, but agrees with 11.63.

237. OSVK also lists Imre Mudin (HUN) as competing, with no mark. We cannot find him listed in 1908 sources, notably the newspapers in BOADW. He is listed in OR, SL, and SLR as a competitor. He was entered in section 5, which competed in pool 3, but SM results for that pool do not include Mudin.

238. The original section entries were as follows: section 1— Lauri Pihkala (FIN), Juho Halme (FIN), Wesley Coe (USA), Leander Talbott (USA), Eric Lemming (SWE), F. Vyskocik (BOH), Lajos Veres (HUN), and András Kozla (HUN); section 2 — Charles Lagarde (FRA), G. Baillard (FRA), Henry Leeke (GBR), Edward Barrett (GBR/IRL), István Mudin (HUN), Mihály David (HUN), Svend Langkjær (DEN), and Jalmari Sauli (FIN).

239. The original section entries were as follows: section 3 — Aarne Salovaara (FIN), Lauri Wilskman (FIN), Martin Sheridan (USA), John Flanagan (USA), Otto Nilsson (SWE), Karl Jank (AUT), Mikhail Dorizas (GRE), and Ferenc Jesina (HUN); section 4 — John Garrells (USA), Marquis "Bill" Horr (USA), Johan Kemp (FIN), Verner Järvinen (FIN), Hugo Wieslander (SWE), Hans Tronner (AUT), Tom Kirkwood (GBR), and Thomas Nicolson (GBR).

240. Edward Barrett (GBR/IRL) was entered in pool 1, but started in pool 3, for unknown reasons.

241. Barrett recorded this on his only throw. Another competitor dropped his shot on Barrett's ankle prior to the second round of throws, and Barrett had to withdraw.

242. The original section entries were as follows: section 5 — John Barrett (GBR/IRL), Denis Horgan (GBR), Cornelius "Con" Walsh (CAN), Douglas Stupart (SAF), Elmer Niklander (FIN), William Krueger (USA), and Imre Mudin (HUN); section 6 — Henri Jardin (FRA), P. Gouvert (FRA), Evert Jakobsson (FIN), Bruno Zilliacus (FIN), Wilbur Burroughs (USA), Simon Gillis (USA), György Luntzer (HUN), and Otto Franke (GER).

243. The original section entries were as follows: section 7 — Jarl Jakobsson (FIN), John Schommer (USA), Benjamin Stephenson (USA), Theodor Neijström (SWE), István Szekelyhidy (HUN), Kálmán Kirchhoffer (HUN), Raoul Paoli (FRA), and André Tison (FRA); section 8 — Nikolaos Georgantas (GRE), H. Hubinen (BEL), Arne Halse (NOR), Umberto Avattaneo (ITA), Miroslav Šustera (BOH), František Souček (BOH), M. Rasmussen (DEN), Mór Kóczán (HUN), and André Delfarges (FRA).

244. DW, FW, and VK/OSVK have 41. The difference is Platt Adams (USA) — see below.

245. BOADW, source uncertain.

246. FM has 40.89 and 134-1¹³⁄₁₆.

247. FM has 40.70 and 133 6⅜. DW also has 133-6. OR has 133-6½.

248. FM has 39.45 and 129 5⅛. VK has 39.445. OR has 129-5.

249. DW has 39.42 and 129-4.

250. DW has 126-4.

251. The marks of Talbott and Flanagan have not been noted in previous compilations of Olympic performances but they were reported in the *Chicago Tribune* of 17 July. Hence, Talbott is shown, for the first time, as placing in the first six. All previous sources have Luntzer in sixth.

252. See previous footnote.

253. DW has 122-9 and 37.43.

254. OSVK has 37.00.

255. OSVK does not list Platt Adams (USA). He is listed in the pool results in SM from BOADW.

256. OSVK has István Mudin instead of Imre Mudin (HUN). It is almost impossible to be certain when looking at 1908 sources in English. Usually, two Mudins are listed as "I. Mudin" and "E. Mudin." It would seem that "E. Mudin" is "Étienne Mudin," or in Hungarian, "István Mudin." But this is not exactly correct. Sometimes E. Mudin seems to correlate with a placement we know to be István Mudin, and sometimes I. Mudin correlates with Imre Mudin (HUN). We have not had a chance to look at Hungarian 1908 sources, notably *Sport-Világ*.

257. The original section entries were as follows: section 1— Harald Agger (DEN), Karl Jank (AUT), F. Vyskocik (BOH), Pál Antal (HUN), Károly Halmos (HUN), Charles Lagarde (FRA), Henry Leeke (GBR), and Ernest May (GBR); section 2 — M. Rasmussen (DEN), Hans Tronner (AUT), Ferenc Jesina (HUN), Károly Kobulszky (HUN), Walter Henderson (GBR), Alfred Flaxman (GBR), Platt Adams (USA), and Wilbur Burroughs (USA).

258. Also entered in this pool/section, but not competing, were Cornelius "Con" Walsh (CAN) and André Delfarges (FRA).

259. Also entered in this pool/section, but not competing, were G. Baillard (FRA) and Juho Halme (FIN).

260. Also entered in this pool/section, but not competing, were Raoul Paoli (FRA) and Edward Archibald (CAN).

261. No marks are known from this pool.

262. Also entered in this pool/section, but not competing, were Douglas Stupart (SAF) and Nikolaos Georgantas (GRE).

263. The original section entries were as follows: section 7 — Mikhail Dorizas (GRE), Verner Järvinen (FIN), Matthew McGrath (USA), Ralph Rose (USA), C. Rehder (GER), Julius Wagner (SUI), István Muller (HUN), Gyula Strausz (HUN), and Edward Barrett (GBR/IRL); section 8 — Lajos Veres (HUN), Johan Kemp (FIN), Umberto Avattaneo (ITA), John Falchenberg (NOR), Martin Sheridan (USA), Leander Talbott (USA), Emil Welz (GER), Eric Lemming (SWE), and Otto Nilsson (SWE).

264. DW, FW, and VK/OSVK have 24 from 9 nations. See the footnote at the end of the final standings, which discusses discrepancies in various sources listing all competitors.

265. FM has 124 7¹¹⁄₁₆.

266. FM has 122 5¼. VK has 37.325.

267. FM has 119 8³⁄₁₆.

268. DW has 33.35 but agrees with 109-4½. OSVK has 33.35.

269. DW has 33.20 but agrees with 108-11¼. OSVK has 33.20.

270. DW has 32.73 and 107-4¾ OSVK has 32.73. Our source from 1908 is SM, found in BOADW, which gave 107-7¾ and 32.8.

271. Platt Adams, Folke Fleetwood, Mór Kóczán, and John Barrett did not compete per the OR. But SM gives the most complete results and these four are listed as competing. Further, they are listed as competing in the pools in which they were entered.

272. OSVK lists Lauri Wilskman (FIN), Jalmari Sauli (FIN), Leander Talbott (USA), Ralph Rose (USA), and Ferenc Jesina (HUN) as competing, with no marks. He does not list Platt Adams (USA), Folke Fleetwood (SWE), Mór Kóczán (HUN), nor John Barrett (GBR/IRL) as competing. The only 1908 source which gave complete pool summaries and results was SM, found in BOADW. We have followed it exactly.

273. The original section entries were as follows: section 1— Douglas Stupart (SAF), Kharalambos Zouras (GRE), Aarne Salovaara (FIN), Umberto Avattaneo (ITA), Platt Adams (USA), Harald Agger (DEN), Miroslav Šustera (BOH), and Henry Leeke (GBR); section 2 — Mikhail Dorizas (GRE), Juho Halme (FIN), Wilbur Burroughs (USA), Károly Kobulszky (HUN), Lajos Veres (HUN), Charles Lagarde (FRA), Julius Wagner (SUI), and Walter Henderson (GBR).

274. The original section entries were as follows: section 3 — Gyula Strausz (HUN), Arthur Dearborn (USA), Otto Nilsson (SWE), Edward Barrett (GBR/IRL), Cornelius "Con" Walsh (CAN), Karl Jank (AUT), Arthur Mallwitz (GER), and André Delfarges (FRA); section 4 — Károly Halmos (HUN), John Flanagan (USA), František Souček (BOH), Folke Fleetwood (SWE), István Mudin (HUN), G. Baillard (FRA), Conrad Rehder (GER), and Nikolaos Georgantas (GRE).

275. The original section entries were as follows: section 5 — Lauri Wilskman (FIN), John Garrells (USA), Merritt Giffin (USA), István Mudin (HUN), Nándor Kováts (HUN), Ernest May (GBR), André Tison (FRA), and F. Vyskocik (BOH); section 6 — Elmer Niklander (FIN), Jalmari Sauli (FIN), Michael Collins (GBR), Alfred Flaxman (GBR), Edward Archibald (CAN), Hugo Wieslander (SWE), Raoul Paoli (FRA), Leander Talbott (USA), and Ralph Rose (USA).

276. The original section entries were as follows: Section 7 — Theodor Neijström (SWE), Mór Kóczán (HUN), Ferenc Jesina (HUN), John Barrett (GBR/IRL), Verner Järvinen (FIN), Marquis "Bill" Horr (USA), Simon Gillis (USA), M. Rasmussen (DEN), and Hans Tronner (AUT); Section 8 — Johan Kemp (FIN), Emil Welz (GER), Martin Sheridan (USA), György Luntzer (HUN), Pál Antal (HUN), John Murray (GBR/IRL), Matthew McGrath (USA), "Ludwig" Uettwiller (GER), and Eric Lemming (SWE).

277. DW, FW, and VK/OSVK have 18. The discrepancy concerns Benjamin Sherman (USA) — see below.

278. Guiney, David. *Gold, Silver, Bronze*, p. 9.

279. *Ibid*, p. 53.

280. FM has 170 4⁄₁₆. DW has 170-4. OR has 170-4¼.

281. VK/OSVK have 48.50. DW has 159-1, but agrees with 48.51.

282. DW has 157-9 but 48.09.

283. DW has 157-0. OR has 157-0¼.

284. VK/OSVK have 46.94. DW has 46.94 and 154-0.

285. Only the first seven places are given in the OR, but the section results are given in SL, CDT, and NYH.

286. DW and OSVK have 45.58 and 149-6.

287. OR and OSVK does not list Benjamin Sherman as competing. Sherman is listed as competing in Section One in SL, which gave complete section results.

288. OSVK lists Agger as fifteenth with no mark, but does not list the places for 9–14. Our source for the pool results is SL, which did not list a mark for Agger.

289. According to *Nordiskt Idrottslif* (25 July 1908), throws of less than 110 feet (100.6 meters) were not measured.

290. We have been unable to find entry lists for the hammer throw. Through an American newspaper (BOADW) we know that Ralph Rose was entered in the first section and Wilbur Burroughs in the second section, but neither competed.

291. Gillis was noted to be troubled with a felon (infection) of his finger, which prevented a better effort on his part.

292. The precise entries by section are not available in any source. However, the complete entry list, not separated into sections, is available. Also entered in this event, but not competing, were Mikhail Dorizas (GRE), Nikolaos Georgantas (GRE), Wilbur Burroughs (USA), Ralph Rose (USA), M. Rasmussen (DEN), Emil Welz (GER), Dennis Carey (GBR), Laurence Kiely (GBR), Edward Archibald (CAN), and C. Sandberg (SWE).

293. DW, and VK/OSVK have 31, although OSVK lists 32 athletes. The "missing" athlete is likely Emil Welz (GER) — see below.

294. FM has 178 7¼. VK has 54.445.

295. The OR has only the top four places. OVSK gave only the top eight places. Our results are from SM, whch gave complete section results.

296. DW and OSVK have 47.55.

297. Weislander also had the second best throw of the competition —170-11 (52.10 meters), but it was not allowed. Swedish Olympic historian Ture Widlund has noted (no source given), "Weislander's way of holding the javelin was not allowed. Wieslander, and other Swedes, were upset and could not understand the decision as the rules explicitly said [that] 'the manner of holding the javelin is left to the absolute discretion of each competitor.'" Considering that it was a "freestyle event," it is difficult to explain how Wieslander's method could have been disallowed.

298. VK/OSVK have 46.08.

299. DW and OSVK have 45.95.

300. DW and OSVK have 43.31.

301. OSVK does not list Emil Welz as having competed, but he is listed in pool 5 in SM.

302. Only the winner's throw was measured.

303. Lemming's first throw was noted to be in the range of 176 feet [53.64].

304. It appears probable that in pools 4 and 5 only the winner's throw was measured. This was the case in pool 3 and it is logical that the same situation pertained in the two succeeding pools.

305. Listed as the freestyle javelin by FW.

306. VK has 54.825. DW has 54.825 and 179-10. OR has 179-10½ and 54.83.

307. FM has 165-10¹⁵⁄₁₆ . OR has 165-11 and 50.57.

308. DW and VK have 47.105. DW also has 154-6. OSVK has 47.10.

309. In EzM, p. 216 Otto Nilsson, (SWE) is shown as having set an Olympic record of 49.09 in the qualifying round. This is not confirmed in any other source and is possibly a misreading of the accepted mark of 47.11. Whatever the reason, we have rejected this version.

310. DW has 150-6. OR has 150-6¾.

311. DW has 148-3. OR has 148-2¾.

312. Only the first five places were given in OR, but Halme's mark is found in NYH.

313. Distances were only measured for the first 6 competitors.

314. The original section entries were as follows: section 1— Douglas Stupart (SAF), Aarne Salovaara (FIN), Juho Halme (FIN), John Johansen (NOR), J. Lie (NOR), G. E. Stevens (SAF), Platt Adams (USA), Wilbur Burroughs (USA), Arthur Dearborn (USA), Carl Bechler (GER), Oscar Lemming (SWE), Bruno Söderström (SWE), István Mudin (HUN), Ferenc Jesina (HUN), Denis Horgan (GBR), and Alfred Flaxman (GBR); section 2 — Kharalambos Zouras (GRE), Mikhail Dorizas (GRE), Armas Pesonen (FIN), Jalmari Sauli (FIN), John Flanagan (USA), John Garrells (USA), Simon Gillis (USA), A. Struby (SUI), Julius Wagner (SUI), Otto Nilsson (SWE), Hugo Wieslander (SWE), Imre Mudin (HUN), Mór Kóczán (HUN), György Luntzer (HUN), Henry Leeke (GBR), Walter Henderson (GBR), Pierre Failliot (FRA), and Jimmy Tremeer (GBR).

315. The original section entries were as follows: section 3 — Evert Jakobsson (FIN), Jarl Jakobsson (FIN), Umberto Avattaneo (ITA), Vincent Duncker (SAF/GER), Matthew McGrath (USA), John Schommer (USA), Benjamin Sherman (USA), Miroslav Šustera (BOH), František Souček (BOH), Eric Lemming (SWE), Knut Lindberg (SWE), Gyula Strausz (HUN), Kálmán Czorna (HUN), Cornelius "Con" Walsh (CAN), George Barber (CAN), Raoul Paoli (FRA), and G. Baillard (FRA); section 4 — Verner Järvinen (FIN), Johan Kemp (FIN), Conrad Carlsrud (NOR), Arne Halse (NOR), Martin Sheridan (USA), Ralph Rose (USA), Leander Talbott (USA), Ernest May (GBR), "Ludwig" Uettwiller (GER), Emil Welz (GER), Arthur Radó (HUN), Lajos Veres (HUN), Alan Fyffe (GBR), Edward Archibald (CAN), André Delfarges (FRA), and Charles Lagarde (FRA).

Boxing

For the only time ever, the Olympic boxing tournament was contested in a single day. The matches began at 11:25 A.M. and lasted until late in the evening, finishing at 10:30 P.M. (2230). Remarkably, this forced two boxers, Frederick Spiller and Reginald "Snowy" Baker, to compete in four bouts in one day. The matches were all three rounds, with the first two rounds lasting three minutes each, and the last round lasting four minutes. A one minute break was allowed between each round. Spiller fought 11 rounds in one day; Baker fought 9.

There were semi-final round byes in the bantamweight, lightweight, and heavyweight divisions; thus only one bronze medalist is recorded in those events. The rules noted that any boxer drawing a bye was required to spar for the specified time with any opponent approved of by the judges and the referee. No evidence exists to determine if this rule was followed to the letter or not.

Site:	Northampton Institute, Clerkenwell, London
Date:	27 October
Events:	5
Competitors:	42
Nations:	4

	Competitors	1st	2nd	3rd	Totals
Australia	1	–	1	–	1
Denmark	2	–	–	–	–
France	7	–	–	–	–
Great Britain	32	5	4	5	14
Totals	42	5	5	5	15
Nations	4	1	2	1	2

Bantamweight Class (≦ 52.62 kg. [115¾ lbs./8 stone 4 lbs.])

A: 6; C: 2; D: 27 October; F: Single-elimination tournament.

There was only one non-British competitor, Pierre Mazior of France. Most of the top British bantams were present. Henry Perry had been Amateur Boxing Association (ABA) champion in 1903-1904, while William Webb won that title in 1905 and 1910, and John Condon would win it in 1909. Henry Thomas won two decisions to take the gold medal, receiving a bye in the semi-finals. He was also ABA Champion in 1908. Thomas turned professional in 1909 and settled in the United States. He fought there and in Australia until his retirement in 1916.

1.	A. Henry Thomas	GBR
2.	John Condon	GBR
3.	William Webb	GBR
=4.	Frank McGurk	GBR
	Pierre Mazior	FRA
	Henry Perry	GBR

Tournament Draw

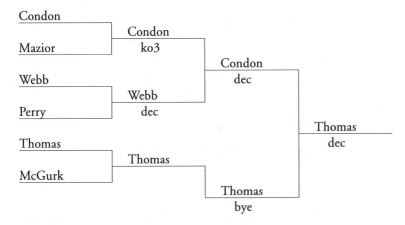

Featherweight Class (≦ 57.15 kg. [125¾ lbs./9 stone])

A: 8; C: 2; D: 27 October; F: Single-elimination tournament.

The winner, Richard Gunn, had two decisions and one knock-out in his three bouts. He was 37 years old in 1908, having won the ABA featherweight championship in 1894-1896. He then retired at the request of the boxing officials because of his superiority over all his competitors, but he came out of retirement for the 1908 Olympics. The runner-up, Charles Morris, had been ABA champion in this class in 1904. In the final, Gunn won the first round and Morris the second, but Gunn, despite his age, outpointed Morris in the third round for the decision.

1.	Richard Gunn	GBR
2.	Charles Morris	GBR
3.	Hugh Roddin	GBR[1]*
4.	Thomas Ringer	GBR

*See Notes on page 121.

=5.	Louis Constant	FRA
	Etienne Poillot	FRA
	John Lloyd	GBR
	Edward Adams	GBR

Tournament Draw

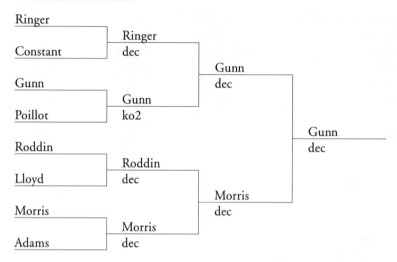

Lightweight Class (≦ 63.50 kg. [139¾ lbs./10 stone])

A: 12; C: 3; D: 27 October; F: Single-elimination tournament.

The eventual winner was not highly considered. The favorites had to be Matt Wells, ABA Champion from 1904-1907, and later British and European pro champion in 1911, and Harold Holmes, champion in 1908. But Holmes lost in the quarter-finals to Harry Johnson and Wells lost a decision in the semi-finals to Frederick Grace. Grace was lightly regarded before the Olympic tournament began but he went on to win four ABA Championships at this weight — 1909, 1913, and 1919-1920. He also competed at the 1920 Olympics, where he won one match and then lost to the eventual champion, Sammy Mosberg (USA) in an overtime decision.

1.	Frederick Grace	GBR
2.	Frederick Spiller	GBR
3.	Harry Johnson	GBR
=4.	Matt Wells	GBR
	Harold Holmes	GBR
	George Jessup	GBR
=7.	Valdemar Holberg	DEN
	Edward Fearman	GBR
	Hemming Hansen	DEN
	André Bouvier	FRA
	Frank Osborne	GBR
	Patrick Fee	GBR

Tournament Draw

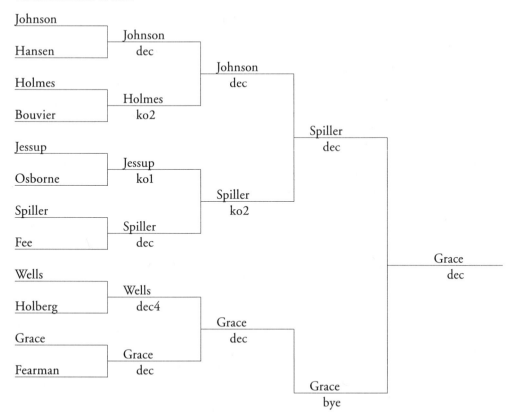

Middleweight Class (≦ 71.67 kg. [157¾ lbs./11 stone 4 lbs.])

A: 10; C: 3; D: 27 October; F: Single-elimination tournament.

This class produced the bext boxing of the day, with three Frenchmen and the Australian, Reginald "Snowy" Baker, contesting the title against six British boxers. The last four ABA Champions were present — John Douglas (1905), Arthur Murdoch (1906), Ruben Warnes (1907 and 1910), and William Childs (1908-09, and 1911).

The final came down to Douglas and Baker, and was described as the best match of the tournament. The first round was even. Douglas knocked Baker down in round two, but he continued in a closely fought battle. However, Douglas hung on in round three to win on points. Douglas was presented his gold medal by his father, who was then the President of the ABA. John Douglas, the son, was actually better known as a cricketer and later captained Essex County and England teams. He and his father died tragically in a sea disaster returning from Finland in December 1930.

Snowy Baker is the greatest all-around athlete ever produced by Australia. He competed at the 1908 Olympics in boxing, diving, and swimming. In addition to those three sports, he represented Australia at the international level in rugby union and water polo. He was also state or national caliber in cricket, track & field athletics, and rowing. In December 1908, he was appointed referee for the Jack Johnson vs. Tommy Burns heavyweight professional bout, which was held in Sydney, but Johnson objected to Baker's snow-white hair (hence his nickname), and he was replaced. Baker later became a movie star and stuntman.

1.	John Douglas	GBR
2.	Reginald "Snowy" Baker	AUS
3.	William Philo	GBR
4.	Ruben Warnes	GBR
5.	William Childs	GBR
=6.	Arthur Murdoch	GBR
	Charles Morard	FRA
	René Doudelle	FRA
	Gaston Aspa	FRA
	William Dees	GBR

Tournament Draw

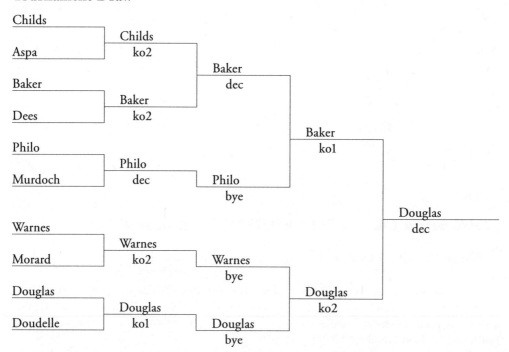

Heavyweight Class (Unlimited Weight)

A: 6; C: 1; D: 27 October; F: Single-elimination tournament.

This was the only class with no foreign entrants. Albert Oldman was a City of London policeman but was not highly regarded as a boxer prior to the 1908 Olympic tournament. The favorites were Frederick Parks, who had been ABA Champ in 1901-02 and 1905-06, and the two most recent ABA Champions, Harold Brewer (1907) and Sydney Evans (1908). But Oldman won both his matches by first-round knock-outs, fighting for a total of less than one round.

1. Albert Oldman   GBR
2. Sydney Evans   GBR
3. Frederick Parks   GBR
=4. Ian Myrams   GBR
     Albert Ireton   GBR
     Harold Brewer   GBR

Tournament Draw

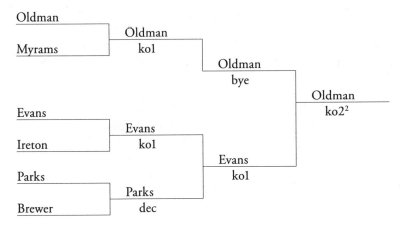

Oldman

Myrams

Oldman
ko1

Oldman
bye

Oldman
ko2[2]

Evans

Ireton

Evans
ko1

Evans
ko1

Parks

Brewer

Parks
dec

NOTES

1. Both Ringer and Roddin lost in the semi-finals. We know of no bout for third place which took place. Ringer lost to Gunn, the eventual champion, but third place in OR is definitely given as H. Roddin. The method by which he was determined to be the bronze medalist is not known.

2. Grasso has the result as "ko2" but the OR notes that "Evans was down and out in two minutes," implying that it was in the first round. The precise round was not mentioned.

Cycling

The cycling events were conducted during the first week of the stadium events at the 1908 Olympics. As *The Sporting Life* noted, "…the weather was the reverse of pleasant. As a matter of fact, it was the rule rather than the exception for the track to be flooded."[1]* The track in question was at the large White City Stadium which had been constructed for the 1908 Olympic Games. It was a concrete track measuring 660 yards (603.5 meters) in length and surrounding the running track.

Site:	White City Stadium, Shepherd's Bush, London
Dates:	13–18 July
Events:	7
Competitors:	97
Nations:	11

	Competitors	1st	2nd	3rd	Totals
Belgium	6	-	-	1	1
Canada	5	-	-	1	1
France	23	1	2	2	5
Germany	8	-	1	1	2
Great Britain	37	5	3	1	9
Greece	1	-	-	-	-
Italy	4	-	-	-	-
The Netherlands	5	-	-	-	-
South Africa	4	-	-	-	-
Sweden	2	-	-	-	-
United States	2	-	-	-	-
Totals	97	6	6	6	18
Nations	11	2	3	5	5

*See Notes on pages 138–140.

Officials

Judges: M. de Beukelaer (President, UCI), James Blair, A. Blakeborough, L. Breton, T. W. J. Britten, W. H. Halliwell, J. Hill (Scottish Cyclists' Union), T. Lonsdale, Dr. E. B. Turner, J. Wright

Assistant Judges: S. H. Ansell, T. W. Craig, C. Gösta Drake (SWE), T. Lonsdale, W. E. Cope, R. F. Davis, F. P. Low, W. Mitson, R. J. Owen, A. C. Rawson, J. R. Smiles

Umpires: S. H. Ansell, R. C. Bishop, W. R. Bond, Gerard Bousselot (Swiss Cyclists' Union), T. W. J. Britten, W. G. Chandler, F. Chick, H. L. Clark, O. Cole, P. Coleman, J. D. Douglas, R. R. Flint, R. B. Franklin, R. J. Gear, T. Grantham, R. C. Harris, W. F. Hartt, A. T. Heelas, T. R. Hensher, E. P. Hewkin, R. Johnstone (Scottish Cyclists' Union), A. E. Lumsden (USA), R. McLardy, G. Metcalfe (Irish Cyclists Association), P. Nix, F. O'Connor, M. Panard, E. Payne, E. Perman, Francis Portier (Swiss Cyclists Union), W. W. Ridley, C. E. Salt, R. G. Sangster (Scottish Cyclists' Union), A. W. Sawyer, J. Dalton Smith, Marcel Meyer de Stadelhöfen (Swiss Cyclists' Union), J. H. Stapley, W. F. Sutton, J. Teuton, R. H. Vessey, E. G. Warden, S. C. Winks, E. O. White, M. Young (Scottish Cyclists Union)

Starters: J. Brown, Charles Edgar Liles, W. Robinson, A. Vickers

Timekeepers: J. H. Burley, C. P. Glazebrook, H. H. Griffin, E. V. Ebblewhite, A. J. Wakeford, V. Waterhouse, C. H. Wheelwright, T. H. Woollen

Clerks of the Course: A. Barrett, W. E. Cope, P. Harding, J. R. Smiles, J. C. P. Tacagni

Stewards: S. H. Ansell, S. Ayres, E. Battersby, E. Blakesley, Ellis Bradshaw, F. Chick, T. W. Craig, S. S. Curra, R. F. Davis, A. Deacon, L. Ducrocq, R. R. Flint, R. B. Franklin, R. J. Gear, W. B. Goodwin, H. Hollands, W. R. James, C. K. Mills, W. Mitson, P. Nix, R. J. Owen, E. Payne, W. W. Ridley, C. E. Salt, H. Scott, J. R. Smiles, W. F. Sutton, R. H. Vessey, A. J. Wakeford, J. A. Walker, W. H. S. Walker, E. G. Warden, E. O. White, S. C. Winks, Z. Wheatley

Lap Scorers: V. Waterhouse (chief), E. Blakesley, W. A. Blofield, Ellis Bradshaw, W. E. Cope, S. S. Curra, A. Deacon, R. R. Flint, R. B. Franklin, R. J. Gear, W. B. Goodwin, H. C. Harris, D. Lucas, C. K. Mills, W. Mitson, P. Nix, H. Papps, W. T. Pearse, J. W. Ridley, C. E. Salt, J. H. Stapley, A. Vickers, J. A. Walker, H. E. Winks, Z. Wheatley

Members of the BOC: T. W. J. Britten (NCU), James Blair (NCU and Scottish Cyclists' Union), E. J. O'Reilly (Irish Cyclists Association)

Olympic Committee NCU: R. Bradley (Chairman), James Blair, T. W. J. Britten, S. H. Ansell, W. Mitson, T. Lonsdale, A. Vickers, J. R. Smiles, Dr. E. B. Turner, W. H. Halliwell, W. E. Ord

Secretary : S. R. Noble

One Lap (660 yards [603.49 meters]) Match Sprint

A: 46; C: 9; D: 14-15 July; F: Time limit of 70 seconds for each race. If this time limit was exceeded the race was declared void. Time standard = 46 seconds.

Later in the summer, Victor Johnson would win the world sprint championship at Leipzig (GER), with the other medals going to his countryman, Benjamin Jones, and the Frenchman, Émile Demangel. All three competed in the Olympic sprint, with Johnson winning there as well, this time narrowly defeating Demangel in the finals. In the final race, Karl Neumer jumped after one-third of a lap, gaining six lengths quickly. Just before the straight, Johnson and Demangel caught Neumer and they battled to the finish with Johnson winning by inches. During his career, Johnson would win six National Cycling Union (NCU) championships.

Final A: 4; C: 3; D: 15 July; T: 1630.

1.	Victor Johnson	GBR	51.2	
2.	Émile Demangel	FRA	by inches	
3.	Karl Neumer	GER	at 1 length	
4.	Daniel Flynn	GBR	close up	

Semi-Finals A: 15; C: 8; D: 15 July; T: 1530; F: Winners advance to the final.

Heat 1 A: 4; C: 4.

1.	Victor Johnson	GBR	59.2	Q
2.	Johannes van Spengen	NED	"easily"	
3.	Pierre Texier	FRA		
4.	Walter Andrews	CAN		

Heat 2 A: 4; C: 3.

1.	Émile Demangel	FRA	51.6	Q
2.	Clarence Kingsbury	GBR	at ⅔ length	
3.	William Bailey	GBR		
4.	F. D. Venter	SAF		

Heat 3 A: 4; C: 3.

1.	Daniel Flynn	GBR	54.8	Q
2.	André Auffray	FRA	at ½ wheel	
3.	George Cameron	USA		
4.	Ernest Payne	GBR		

Heat 4 A: 3; C: 3.

1.	Karl Neumer	GER	1:05.6	Q
2.	Lucien Renard	BEL	won easily	
3.	Benjamin Jones	GBR		

Round One A: 46; C: 9; D: 14 July; T: 1600; F: Winners advance to the semi-finals.

Heat 1 A: 2; C: 2.

1.	Benjamin Jones	GBR	59.0	Q
2.	Dorus Nijland [2]	NED		

Heat 2 A: 3; C: 3.

1.	William Bailey	GBR	50.8	Q
2.	Frederick McCarthy	CAN	at 1 length	
3.	Pierre Seginaud [3]	FRA		

Heat 3 A: 3; C: 3.

1.	Clarence Kingsbury	GBR	57.4	Q

2. Richard Katzer   GER   at 2 lengths
3. Georgius Damen   NED
4

Heat 4 A: 3; C: 3.

1. Victor Johnson   GBR   56.2   Q
2. Jean Patou   BEL   "easily"
3. R. Villepontoux   FRA
5

Heat 5 A: 2; C: 2.

AC. Maurice Schilles   FRA   Race declared void.
    F. Shore   SAF   Time limit exceeded.
6

Heat 6 A: 3; C: 3.

1. Émile Demangel   FRA   59.8   Q
2. George Summers   GBR   at 1 length
3. Andrew Hansson   SWE
7

Heat 7 A: 3; C: 3.

1. Johannes van Spengen   NED   58.2   Q
2. Hermann Martens   GER   by inches
3. J. L. Lavery   GBR/IRL
8

Heat 8 A: 3; C: 3.

1. Walter Andrews   CAN   55.8   Q
2. Joseph Werbrouck   BEL   at ½ wheel
3. Gaston Delaplane   FRA
9

Heat 9 A: 2; C: 2.

1. Pierre Texier   FRA   1:01.6   Q
2. T. H. E. Passmore   SAF   at 1 length
10

Heat 10 A: 3; C: 3.

1. F. D. Venter   SAF   1:03.2   Q
2. G. Perrin   FRA   at 1+ lengths
3. Bruno Götze   GER
11

Heat 11 A: 4; C: 4.

1. Karl Neumer   GER   54.2   Q
2. W. F. Magee   GBR/IRL   at 2 lengths
3. Émile Marechal   FRA
4. Antonie Gerrits   NED

Heat 12 A: 3; C: 3.

1.	Ernest Payne	GBR	57.2		Q
2.	André Poulain	FRA	at 1 length		
3.	Jean Van Benthem	BEL			

12

Heat 13 A: 3; C: 3.

1.	Daniel Flynn	GBR	55.0		Q
2.	Gerard Bosch van Drakestein	NED	by inches		
3.	Paul Schulze	GER			

13

Heat 14 A: 4; C: 4.

1.	Lucien Renard	BEL	55.2		Q
2.	G. Dreyfus	FRA	"easily"		
3.	William Morton	CAN			
4.	G. C. Anderson	GBR			

Heat 15 A: 2; C: 2.

| 1. | George Cameron | USA | 1:05.2 | | Q |
| 2. | Léon Coeckelberg | BEL | by inches | | |

14

Heat 16 A: 3; C: 3.

1.	André Auffray	FRA	58.4		Q
2.	Arthur Denny	GBR	at 1 length		
3.	P. T. Freylinck	SAF			

15

1,000 Meters Match Sprint

A: 40; C: 9; D: 16 July; F: Time limit–1:45.0. If this time limit was exceeded the race was declared void. Time standard–1:19.0. World record —1:16.0 by Jaap Eden (NED) at Bordeaux (FRA) on 14 May 1896.

No medals were awarded in this race because, in the final, the time limit was exceeded. The best description of the final comes from *The Sporting Life*, "This was a fiasco, for not only was the race declared void through the time limit being exceeded, but, in addition, Kingsbury and Johnson punctured. The former was thrown out of the race before half a lap had been covered, and Johnson's mishap occurred at the beginning of the last banking. Most of the work was done on the banks at a crawl, but in spite of the red flag being shown the competitors, they continued the same rate of progression. They were hopelessly outside the time limit when the sprint came, when, with Johnson puncturing, Schilles and Jones rode out an inches finish. The Frenchman got there by two or three inches. No official placing was given."[16] Other sources noted that Schilles won the race by a few inches.

Final A: 4 C: 2 D: 16 July T: 1730.

AC.	Maurice Schilles	FRA	Race declared void.	
	Victor Johnson	GBR	Time limit exceeded.	
	Benjamin Jones	GBR		
	Clarence Kingsbury	GBR		

Semi-Finals A: 14; C: 6; D: 16 July; T: 1645; F: Winners advance to the final.

Heat 1 A: 4; C: 4.

1.	Victor Johnson	GBR	1:27.4	Q
2.	Karl Neumer	GER	by inches	
3.	F. D. Venter	SAF		
4.	Pierre Texier	FRA		

Heat 2 A: 4; C: 3.

1.	Maurice Schilles	FRA	1:38.8	Q
AC.	Ernest Payne	GBR	over 1 length	
	Daniel Flynn	GBR		
	George Cameron	USA		

17

Heat 3 A: 3; C: 2.

1.	Benjamin Jones	GBR	1:40.8	Q
2.	Émile Demangel	FRA	at ½ wheel	
3.	J. L. Lavery	GBR/IRL		

Heat 4 A: 3; C: 2.

1.	Clarence Kingsbury	GBR	1:35.6	Q
2.	Guglielmo Morisetti	ITA	at 2 lengths	
3.	André Auffray	FRA		

Round One A: 40; C: 9; D: 16 July; T: 1500; F: Winners advance to the semi-finals.

Heat 1 A: 3; C: 3.

1.	Victor Johnson	GBR	1:33.8	Q
2.	Gerard Bosch van Drakestein	NED	at 2 lengths	
3.	Guglielmo Malatesta	ITA		

18

Heat 2 A: 3; C: 3.

1.	F. D. Venter	SAF	1:33.2	Q
2.	André Poulain	FRA	at one wheel	
3.	John Matthews	GBR		

19

Heat 3 A: 2; C: 2.

1.	Maurice Schilles	FRA	1:38.4	Q
2.	Andrew Hansson	SWE	at 1 length	

20

Heat 4 A: 4; C: 4.

1.	Daniel Flynn	GBR	1:30.2	Q
2.	Pierre Seginaud	FRA	at 2 lengths	
3.	Paul Schulze	GER		
4.	Frederick McCarthy	CAN		

21

Heat 5 A: 2; C: 2.

1.	Ernest Payne	GBR	1:32.0	Q
2.	Dorus Nijland	NED	at 1½ lengths	

22

Heat 6 A: 3; C: 3.

AC.	W. F. Magee	GBR/IRL	Race declared void.	
	Hermann Martens	GER	Time limit exceeded.	
	Johannes van Spengen	NED		

23

Heat 7 A: 3; C: 3.

1.	Karl Neumer	GER	1:33.2	Q
2.	R. Villepontoux	FRA	at 2 lengths	
3.	William Bailey	GBR		

24

Heat 8 A: 4; C: 4.

1.	George Cameron	USA	1:29.4	Q
2.	P. T. Freylinck	SAF	at 2 lengths	
3.	Herbert Crowther	GBR		
4.	G. Dreyfus	FRA		

25

Heat 9 A: 2; C: 2.

1.	Émile Demangel	FRA	1:35.2	Q
2.	William Morton	CAN	at 2½ lengths	

26

Heat 10 A: 1; C: 1.

1.	André Auffray	FRA	1:23.6	rode over	Q

27

Heat 11 A: 1; C: 1.

1.	Guglielmo Morisetti	ITA	1:21.4	rode over	Q

28

Heat 12 A: 3; C: 3.

1.	Benjamin Jones	GBR	1:35.0	Q
2.	Émile Marechal	FRA	at 1 length	
3.	Bruno Götze	GER		

29

Heat 13 A: 3; C: 3.

1.	Pierre Texier	FRA	1:31.0	Q
2.	George Summers	GBR	at nearly 2 lengths	
3.	Louis Weintz	USA		

30

Heat 14 A: 2; C: 2.

1.	J. L. Lavery	GBR/IRL	1:41.0	Q
2.	Antonie Gerrits	NED	"easily"	

31

Heat 15 A: 2; C: 2.

1.	Clarence Kingsbury	GBR	1:27.4	Q
2.	Gaston Delaplane	FRA		

32

Heat 16 A: 2; C: 2.

AC.	F. Shore[33]	SAF	Race declared void.
	G. Perrin	FRA	Time limit exceeded.

34

5,000 Meters

A: 42; C: 8; D: 17–18 July; F: Time limit-9:25.0. If this time limit was exceeded the race was declared void. Time standard-6:55.0.

This was a tremendous race. At the bell, the Dutchman, Gerard Bosch van Drakestein jumped the field and was not caught until the final straight. Benjamin Jones then passed him, taking a length's lead. But the Frenchmen Maurice Schilles and André Auffray were in rapid pursuit and only failed by inches to catch Jones at the line. Schilles entered a protest, claiming that Jones had collided with him on the last lap, but it was disallowed. This was Jones' second gold medal of the Olympics, as he helped the British pursuit team to the title.

Final A: 7; C: 3; D: 18 July; T: 1445.

1.	Benjamin Jones	GBR	8:36.2
2.	Maurice Schilles	FRA	by inches
3.	André Auffray	FRA	within inches
4.	Émile Marechal	FRA	
5.	Clarence Kingsbury	GBR	
6.	Johannes van Spengen	NED	
7.	Gerard Bosch van Drakestein	NED	

Round One A: 42; C: 8; D: 17 July; T: 1600; F: Winners advance to the final.

Heat 1 A: 5; C: 4.

1.	Johannes van Spengen	NED	8:39.8	Q
2.	Daniel Flynn[35]	GBR	at ⅔ length	
3.	Guglielmo Malatesta	ITA		
4.	Pierre Seginaud	FRA		
	William Bailey	GBR	DNF	

36

Heat 2 A: 5; C: 4.

1.	Émile Marechal	FRA	9:01.4	Q
2.	Frederick McCarthy	CAN		
3.	Antonie Gerrits	NED		
	Ernest Payne	GBR	DNF	
	Émile Demangel[37]	FRA	DQ	

38

Heat 3 A: 5; C: 4.

1.	André Auffray	FRA	8:56.8	Q
2.	Hermann Martens	GER	at 1 length	
3.	P. T. Freylinck	SAF		
4.	Bruno Götze	GER		
5.	William Morton	GBR		

39

Heat 4 A: 5; C: 4.

1.	Gerard Bosch van Drakestein	NED	8:42.8	Q
2.	W. F. Magee	GBR/IRL	by inches	
3.	Pierre Texier	FRA		
AC.	T. H. E. Passmore	SAF		
	André Poulain	FRA		

40

Heat 5 A: 9; C: 6.

1.	Benjamin Jones	GBR	9:08.8	Q
2.	Karl Neumer	GER	at 1 length	
3.	Luigi Arizini	ITA		
AC.	Georgius Damen	NED		
	Max Götze	GER		
	J. L. Lavery	GBR/IRL		
	Gaston Delaplane	FRA		
	F. Shore	SAF		
	R. Villepontoux	FRA		

41

Heat 6 A: 6; C: 5.

1.	Clarence Kingsbury	GBR	8:53.0	Q

2.	Guglielmo Morisetti	ITA	at 1½ lengths	
3.	Dorus Nijland	NED		
4.	G. Dreyfus	FRA		
AC.	Walter Andrews	CAN		
	A. E. Calvert	GBR		

42

Heat 7 A: 7; C: 6.

1.	Maurice Schilles	FRA	7:55.4	Q
2.	C. V. Clark	GBR	"just over 1 length"	
3.	William Anderson	CAN		
AC.	Guillaume Coeckelberg	BEL		
	Richard Katzer	GER		
	G. Perrin	FRA		
	F. D. Venter	SAF		

43

20,000 Meters

A: 44; C: 11; D: 14 July; F: Time limit-40:00.0. If this time limit was exceeded the race was declared void. Time standard-27:45.0. Unpaced.

The Sporting Life noted that Clarence Kingsbury "was undoubtedly favourite for this event"[44] but that is difficult to fathom given that Leon Meredith was in the field. Meredith was the greatest British long-distance track racer of this era, but he did not fare well at the 1908 Olympics. In the final, Meredith punctured early, his spare bike was not readily available, and he lost two laps before remounting and never figured again in the race.

Clarence Kingsbury did go on to win this race. A versatile rider, he won NCU titles every year from 1907 to 1912 at distances between ¼-mile and 50 miles.

Final A: 9; C: 5; D: 14 July; T: 1730.

1.	Clarence Kingsbury	GBR	34:13.6
2.	Benjamin Jones	GBR	at 3 inches
3.	Joseph Werbrouck	BEL	
4.	Louis Weintz	USA	
AC.	Leon Meredith	GBR	
	Arthur Denny	GBR	
	Andrew Hansson	SWE	
	François Bonnet	FRA	
	Octave Lapize	FRA	

Round One A: 43; C: 10; D: 14 July; T: 1000–1730; F: Winners advance to the final together with the leader for the greatest number of laps in the three fastest heats.

Heat 1 A: 9; C: 6; T: 1000.

1.	Leon Meredith	GBR	33:21.0	Q
2.	Hermann Martens	GER	33:21.2	

3.	Joseph Werbrouck	BEL	33:21.4	Q
4.	André Lapize	FRA		
5.	Georgius Damen	NED		
6.	Frederick McCarthy	CAN		
AC.	Pierre Hostein	FRA		
	Richard Katzer	GER		
	Daniel Flynn	GBR	DNF	

45

Heat 2 A: 9; C: 7; T: *circa* 1100.

1.	Clarence Kingsbury	GBR	32:33.8	Q
2.	Colin Brooks	GBR	32:34.0	
3.	F. D. Venter	SAF	32:34.4	
4.	G. C. Lutz	FRA		
5.	Gerard Bosch van Drakestein	NED		
AC.	François Bonnet	FRA		Q
	Walter Andrews	CAN		
	Jean Van Benthem	BEL		
	Paul Schulze	GER		

46

Heat 3 A: 8; C: 7; T: 1200.

1.	Louis Weintz	USA	33:39.8	Q
2.	F. Shore	SAF	33:40.0	
3.	Harry Young	CAN	33:45.2	
4.	Herbert Bouffler	GBR		
5.	Max Triebsch	GER		
AC.	H. Cunault	FRA		
	Dorus Nijland	NED		
	Frederick Hamlin	GBR	DNF	

47

Heat 4 A: 8; C: 6; T: *circa* 1300.

1.	Benjamin Jones	GBR	32:39.0	Q
2.	George Cameron	USA	32:39.2	
3.	T. H. E. Passmore	SAF	32:39.4	
4.	Octave Lapize	FRA		Q
5.	Henri Baumler	FRA		
AC.	Alwin Boldt	GER		
	Johannes van Spengen	NED		
	W. Lower	GBR	DNF	

48

Heat 5 A: 5; C: 5; T: 1430.

1.	Andrew Hansson	SWE	34:53.6	Q
2.	D. C. Robertson	GBR	34:53.8	
3.	William Anderson	CAN	34:55.6	
	Ioannis Santorinaios	GRE	DNF	
	Pierre Texier	FRA	DNF	

49

Heat 6 A: 4; C: 4; T: *circa* 1530.

1.	Arthur Denny	GBR	33:40.6	Q
2.	C. Avrillon	FRA	33:40.8	
3.	Gustaf Westerberg	SWE	33:41.4	
4.	Guglielmo Morisetti	ITA		
	Léon Coeckelberg	BEL	DQ	

50

100 Kilometers

A: 43; C: 11; D: 15–16, 18 July; F: Time limit-3-15:00. Time standard-2-30:00. Unpaced.

The 100 kilometer race was considered the "major" championship of the 1908 Olympic cycling program, and the Prince of Wales donated a cup to be presented to the winner. Leon Meredith was the heavy favorite. He would be World Champion seven times in the 100 kilometer motor-paced event — 1904–05, 1907–09, 1911, and 1913.

A potentially disastrous accident occurred in heat 2 of this event. At the beginning of the sprint, Mr. Harry Venn, a judge in the walking contests, wandered onto the track and Guillaume Coeckelberg (BEL) collided with him. Coeckelberg was thrown from his bike, and struck his head on the concrete curb of the track. Fortunately, neither was severely injured and Coeckelberg was able to remount and finish the race and qualify for the final as a result of having led the race for a sufficient number of laps.

The track was wet from rains at the start of the final of this event and intermittent rain saturated the riders for most of the race, which was marred by multiple punctures and accidents. At 13 miles, Meredith was involved in a crash with Walter Andrews and D. C. Robertson. He remounted but was off the back and could never rejoin the leading group. Meredith was lapped at 62 laps, and he dismounted within the next mile. The half-way mark (50 km.) was covered in 1-16:47.2, with Sydney Bailey (GBR) leading.

At 70 kilometers (115 laps) the leading pack numbered seven, including Charles Bartlett. But Bartlett punctured, only to be paced back to the pack in eight laps by the Canadian, Harry Young. The final lap came down to a pack of four — Bartlett, Charles Denny, Octave Lapize, and William Pett. With three British riders, Lapize stood little chance, and the Brits paced the quick sprinting Bartlett, leading him out for the final sprint, which he won by about one wheel to earn the Prince of Wales Cup. Bartlett had no other major international titles but won the NCU 50-mile tandem-paced championship in 1908 and 1909. His time in winning this race was a world record, bettering the mark of 2-49:00.8 set by Capelle in Dijon, France on 20 October 1898.

Although Octave Lapize "only" earned the bronze medal, in 1910 he became the first former Olympic rider to win the Tour de France. He also remains the only rider to win Paris-Roubaix in three consecutive years — 1909–11. His other major professional titles included Paris-Brussels in 1911–13 and Paris-Tours in 1911. Lapize was killed in a dogfight during World War I.

Pierre Texier (FRA) [38 laps], Lapize [31 laps], and Denny [23 laps], received Diplomas of Merit for leading the greatest number of laps. Bartlett led for only 16 laps.

Final A: 17; C: 5; D: 18 July; T: 1530.

1.	Charles Bartlett	GBR	2-41:48.6	OR, WR
2.	Charles Denny	GBR	at one wheel	

3.	Octave Lapize	FRA		
4.	William Pett	GBR		
5.	Pierre Texier	FRA		
6.	Walter Andrews	CAN		
7.	D. C. Robertson	GBR		
8.	Sydney Bailey	GBR		
AC.	Andrew Hansson	SWE	DNF	
	G. C. Lutz	FRA	DNF	
	François Bonnet	FRA	DNF	
	J. H. Bishop	GBR	DNF	
	Harry Mussen	GBR/IRL	DNF	
	Leon Meredith	GBR	DNF	
	Gustaf Westerberg	SWE	DNF	
	Guillaume Coeckelberg	BEL	DNF	
	Harry Young[51]	CAN	DNF	

Round One A: 43; C: 11; D: 15–16 July; F: The first six plus the two riders from each heat who led for the greatest number of laps advanced to the final.

Heat 1 A: 17; C: 7; D: 15 July; T: 1000.

1.	Andrew Hansson	SWE	2-50:21.4	Q
2.	G. C. Lutz	FRA	at ½ wheel	Q
3.	Sydney Bailey	GBR	at 2 lengths	Q
4.	Pierre Texier	FRA		Q
5.	J. H. Bishop	GBR		Q
6.	D. C. Robertson	GBR		Q
AC.	François Bonnet	FRA		q
	Harry Mussen	GBR/IRL		q
	William Anderson	CAN		
	André Lepere	FRA		
	Alwin Boldt	GER		
	Georgius Damen	NED		
	Gerard Bosch van Drakestein	NED		
	J. Norman	GBR		
	Ioannis Santorinaios	GRE	DNF	
	Frederick McCarthy	CAN	DNF	
	Richard Katzer	GER	DNF	

52

Heat 2 A: 26; C: 10; D: 16 July; T: 1000.

1.	Leon Meredith	GBR	2-43:15.4	Q
2.	Charles Bartlett	GBR	a short length	Q
3.	Gustaf Westerberg	SWE		Q
4.	Octave Lapize	FRA		Q
5.	Walter Andrews	CAN		Q
6.	William Pett	GBR		Q
7.	Charles Denny	GBR		q
8.	Guillaume Coeckelberg	BEL		q

9.	Harry Young	CAN		q
	William Morton	CAN	DNF	
	Pierre Hostein	FRA	DNF	
	Hermann Martens	GER	DNF	
	Bruno Götze	GER	DNF	
	Paul Schulze	GER	DNF	
	Max Triebsch	GER	DNF	
	Dorus Nijland	NED	DNF	
	Guglielmo Malatesta	ITA	DNF	
	Battista Parini	ITA	DNF	
	Luigi Arizini	ITA	DNF	
	T. H. E. Passmore	SAF	DNF	
	H. Cunault	FRA	DNF	
	C. Avrillon	FRA	DNF	
	J. Madelaine	FRA	DNF	
	R. Jolly	GBR	DNF	
	David Noon	GBR	DNF	
	Louis Weintz	USA	DNF	

53

2,000 Meter Tandem Match Sprint

A: 34; C: 7; D: 13, 15 July; F: Time limit–4:00.0. Time standard–2:22.0.

Maurice Schilles and André Auffray were both top sprinters individually, but they had never ridden together as a tandem prior to the first heat of this event. Both would win medals at the world sprint championships, Auffray a silver in 1907 and Schilles a bronze in 1909. The final was a slow race but the French tandem drew away gradually in the straight to win easily. Colin Brooks and Walter Isaacs lodged a protest, claiming that they had been cut off by the French pair on the last turn, but it was disallowed.

Final A: 6; C: 2; D: 15 July; T: 1745.

1.	France	3:07.6
	(Maurice Schilles, André Auffray)	
2.	Great Britain	at 1 length
	(Frederick Hamlin, Thomas Johnson)	
3.	Great Britain	
	(Colin Brooks, Walter Isaacs)	

54

Semi-Finals A: 16; C: 4; D: 15 July; T: 1700; F: Winners and the fastest losers advance to the final.

Heat 1 A: 8; C: 3.

1.	Great Britain	2:42.2	Q
	(Frederick Hamlin, Thomas Johnson)		
2.	Great Britain	at 6 lengths	q
	(Colin Brooks, Walter Isaacs)		

3. Germany
    (Max Götze, Otto Götze[55])
4. Belgium
    (Jean Patou, Léon Coeckelberg)

Heat 2 A: 8; C: 2.

1. France   2:46.2   Q
    (Maurice Schilles, André Auffray)
2. Great Britain   at 1 length
    (John Matthews, Leon Meredith)
3. Great Britain
    (John Barnard, Arthur Rushen)
4. France
    (Octave Lapize, François Bonnet)

Round One A: 34; C: 7; D: 13 July; F: Winners and the fastest losers advance to the semi-finals.

Heat 1 A: 4; C: 2; T: 1615.

1. Great Britain   3:09.4   Q
    (Colin Brooks, Walter Isaacs)
2. Germany   at 5 lengths
    (Max Triebsch[56], Alwin Boldt)
    [57]

Heat 2 A: 4; C: 2; T: 1615.

1. Great Britain   3:14.8   Q
    (Frederick Hamlin, Thomas Johnson)
2. France   at 4 lengths
    (Pierre Texier, Maurice Texier)
    [58]

Heat 3 A: 6; C: 3; T: 1615.

1. Germany   2:55.6   Q
    (Max Götze, Otto Götze[59])
2. France   at 1 wheel
    (C. Avrillon, J. Guyader)
3. Great Britain   at 2 lengths
    (C. McKaig, E. C. Piercy)
    [60]

Heat 4 A: 6; C: 3; T: 1615.

1. Belgium   2:25.0   Q
    (Jean Patou, Léon Coeckelberg)
2. Great Britain   at 1½ lengths   q
    (John Barnard, Arthur Rushen)
3. Sweden
    (Andrew Hansson, Gustaf Westerberg)
    [61]

Heat 5[62] A: 4; C: 2; T: 1715.

> 1. France   3:11.4   Q
>   (Maurice Schilles, André Auffray)
> 2. South Africa   at 1 length
>   (F. D. Venter, P. T. Freylinck)
>   [63]

Heat 6 A: 4; C: 2; T: 1715.

> 1. France   3:06.8   Q
>   (Octave Lapize, François Bonnet)
> 2. Great Britain   at 6 lengths
>   (R. Jolly, J. Norman)

Heat 7 A: 6; C: 3; T: 1715.

> 1. Great Britain   2:43.2   Q
>   (John Matthews, Leon Meredith)
> 2. France   at 2 lengths
>   (André Poulain, G. Dreyfus)
> 3. Canada   "beaten off"
>   (Frederick McCarthy, Walter Andrews)

Team Pursuit (3 laps = 1,980 yards [1,810.47 meters])

A: 20; C: 5; D: 17 July; F: The time for the third rider constituted the time for the team. Races were held over 3 laps of the track, totalling a distance of 1,980 yards (1,810.473 meters).

Final Standings

> 1. Great Britain
>   (Leon Meredith, Benjamin Jones, Ernest Payne, Clarence Kingsbury)
> 2. Germany
>   (Hermann Martens, Max Götze, Karl Neumer, Richard Katzer)
> 3. Canada
>   (William Morton, Walter Andrews, Frederick McCarthy, William Anderson)
> 4. The Netherlands
>   (Johannes van Spengen, Antonie Gerrits, Dorus Nijland, Gerard Bosch van Drakestein)
> 5. France
>   (André Auffray, Émile Demangel, Émile Marechal, Maurice Schilles)

Final A: 8; C: 2; D: 17 July; T: 1815.

> 1. Great Britain   2:18.6
>   (Leon Meredith, Benjamin Jones, Ernest Payne, Clarence Kingsbury)
> 2. Germany   2:28.6
>   (Hermann Martens, Max Götze, Karl Neumer, Richard Katzer)

Semi-Finals A: 16; C: 4; D: 17 July; T: 1745; F: Winners advance to the final.

Heat 1 A: 8; C: 2.

1. Great Britain   2:19.6
    (Leon Meredith, Benjamin Jones, Ernest Payne, Clarence Kingsbury)
2. Canada   2:29.6
    (William Morton, Walter Andrews, Frederick McCarthy, William Anderson)

Heat 2 A: 8; C: 2.

1. Germany   2:31.8
    (Hermann Martens, Max Götze, Karl Neumer, Richard Katzer)
2. The Netherlands   2:44.0
    (Johannes van Spengen, Antonie Gerrits, Dorus Nijland, Gerard Bosch van Drakestein)

Round One A: 16; C: 4; D: 17 July; T: 1700; F: Winners advance to semi-finals.

Heat 1[64] A: 4; C: 1.

1. Great Britain   rode over
    (Leon Meredith, Benjamin Jones, Ernest Payne, Clarence Kingsbury)

Heat 2[65] A: 4; C: 1.

1. Canada   rode over
    (William Morton, Walter Andrews, Frederick McCarthy, William Anderson)

Heat 3 not contested

The Netherlands   bye
    (Johannes van Spengen, Antonie Gerrits, Dorus Nijland, Gerard Bosch van Drakestein)

Heat 4[66] A: 8; C: 2.

1. Germany   2:25.4
    (Hermann Martens, Max Götze, Karl Neumer, Richard Katzer)
2. France   2:32.0
    (André Auffray, Émile Demangel, Émile Marechal, Maurice Schilles)

NOTES

1. SL, p. 92.
2. Also entered in this heat, but not competing, were C. Todt (GER) and Gustaf Westerberg (SWE).
3. Guillaume Coeckelberg (BEL) was also entered in this heat, but did not compete.
4. Louis Weintz was also entered in this heat, but did not compete.
5. Frederick Hill (USA) was also entered in this heat, but did not compete.
6. Also entered in this heat, but not competing, were Erich Dannenberg (GER) and William Anderson (CAN).

7. Max Triebsch (GER) was also entered in this heat, but did not compete.

8. William van den Dries (USA) was also entered in this heat, but did not compete.

9. Also entered in this heat, but not competing, was Otto Götze (GER).

10. Also entered in this heat, but not competing, were Max Götze (GER) and J. Martinsson (RUS).

11. Ioannis Santorinaios (GRE) was also entered in this heat, but did not compete.

12. Harry Young (CAN) was also entered in this heat, but did not compete.

13. V. Borchino (ITA) was also entered in this heat, but did not compete.

14. Also entered in this heat, but not competing, were H. D. Buck (GBR) and H. Gondero (FRA).

15. Alwin Boldt (GER) was also entered in this heat, but did not compete.

16. SL, p. 100.

17. Payne, Flynn, and Cameron finished in a line but no official placings were given.

18. Guillaume Coeckelberg (BEL) was also entered in this heat, but did not compete.

19. Alwin Boldt (GER) was also entered in this heat, but did not compete.

20. Also entered in this heat, but not competing, were William Anderson (CAN) and Luigi Arizini (ITA).

21. Joseph Werbrouck (BEL) was also entered in this heat, but did not compete.

22. Also entered in this heat, but not competing, were Richard Katzer (GER) and Léon Coeckelberg (BEL).

23. Jean Patou (BEL) was also entered in this heat, but did not compete.

24. Also entered in this heat, but not competing, were Frederick Hill (USA) and Ioannis Santorinaios (GRE).

25. Max Triebsch (GER) was also entered in this heat, but did not compete.

26. Also entered in this heat, but not competing, were Gustaf Westerberg (SWE) and G. Nairani (ITA).

27. Also entered in this heat, but not competing, were G. Brambilla (ITA), Harry Young (CAN), and Max Götze (GER).

28. Also entered in this heat, but not competing, were Georgius Damen (NED), Jean Van Benthem (BEL), and R. Condero (FRA).

29. Also entered in this heat, but not competing, were J. Martinsson (RUS) and Battista Parini (ITA).

30. Also entered in this heat, but not competing, were Max Götze (GER) and G. Calloni (ITA).

31. Also entered in this heat, but not competing, were T. Portioli (ITA) and Lucien Renard (BEL).

32. Also entered in this heat, but not competing, were William van den Dries (USA), Clarence Kingsbury (GBR), and T. H. E. Passmore (SAF).

33. Shore had finished first before the race was declared void.

34. Also entered in this heat, but not competing, were Walter Andrews (CAN), H. D. Buck (GBR), and C. Todt (GER).

35. Flynn was not entered in this heat.

36. Also entered in this heat, but not competing, were Alwin Boldt (GER), T. Portioli (ITA), Lucien Renard (BEL), Ioannis Santorinaios (GRE), and Harry Young (CAN).

37. Demangel beat Marechal by inches but was disqualified for fouling.

38. Also entered in this heat, but not competing, were -- Durand (ITA), Andrew Hansson (SWE), Jean Patou (BEL), C. Todt (GER), and Joseph Werbrouck (BEL).

39. Also entered in this heat, but not competing, were G. Brambilla (ITA), Léon Coeckelberg (BEL), R. Condero (FRA), William van den Dries (USA), and Leon Meredith (GBR).

40. Also entered in this heat, but not competing, were H. D. Buck (GBR), George Cameron (USA), Battista Parini (ITA), Paul Schulze (GER), and Carl Götze (GER).

41. Louis Weintz (USA) was also entered in this heat, but did not compete.

42. Also entered in this heat, but not competing, were Jean Van Benthem (BEL), J. Martinsson (RUS), Max Triebsch (GER), and Gustaf Westerberg (SWE).

43. Also entered in this heat, but not competing, were B. Andrews (GBR), Erich Dannenberg (GER), G. Galloni (ITA), and Frederick Hill (USA).

44. SL, p. 104.

45. Also entered in this heat, but not competing, were P. T. Freylinck (SAF), Guglielmo Malatesta (ITA), and Frederick Hill (USA).

46. Also entered in this heat, but not competing, were William van den Dries (USA), Karl Neumer (GER), and G. Galloni (ITA).

47. Also entered in this heat, but not competing, were Battista Parini (ITA), Lucien Renard (BEL), and A. Trousselier (FRA).

48. Also entered in this heat, but not competing, were Luigi Arizini (ITA), G. Brambilla (ITA), Guillaume Coeckelberg (BEL), and Erich Dannenberg (GER).

49. Also entered in this heat, but not competing, were Antonie Gerrits (NED), Bruno Götze (GER), Otto Götze (GER), J. Madelaine (FRA), G. Mairani (ITA), Harry Mussen (GBR/IRL), and Jean Patou (BEL).

50. Also entered in this heat, but not competing, were B. Andrews (GBR), O. Ginistry (FRA), Max Götze (GER), J. Martinsson (RUS), Guglielmo Morisetti (ITA), William Morton (CAN), and T. Portioli (ITA).

51. Young was permitted to start after he had satisfied the judges that he had not been lapped in heat 2 of the first round.

52. Also entered in this heat, but not competing, were Jean Van Benthem (BEL), Léon Coeckelberg (BEL), Lucien Renard (BEL), Henri Baumler (FRA), O. Ginistry (FRA), Max Götze (GER), Otto Götze (GER), Karl Neumer (GER), C. Todt (GER), G. Brambilla (ITA), G. Mairani (ITA), Guglielmo Morisetti (ITA), T. Portioli (ITA), W. F. Magee (GBR), George Cameron (USA), and Frederick Hill (USA).

53. Also entered in this heat, but not competing, were Joseph Werbrouck (BEL), Jean Patou (BEL), G. Galloni (ITA), A. Trousselier (FRA), A. Fontaine (FRA), Erich Dannenberg (GER), J. Martinsson (RUS), and William van den Dries (USA).

54. VK has GBR (Matthews, Meredith) in fourth, but there really was no fourth place.

55. The OR lists Karl Neumer, but all press reports show Otto Götze.

56. The OR lists Hermann Martens, but all press reports list Triebsch.

57. Also entered in this heat, but not competing, were France (R. Villepontoux, Émile Marechal) and the United States (Frederick Hill, William van den Dries).

58. Also entered in this heat, but not competing, were Belgium (Lucien Renard, Guillaume Coeckelberg) and Germany (Richard Katzer, Hermann Martens).

59. The OR lists Karl Neumer, but all press reports show Otto Götze.

60. Canada (Harry Young, William Anderson) was also entered in this heat, but did not compete.

61. Germany (Erich Dannenberg, Bruno Götze) was also entered in this heat, but did not compete.

62. We have not been able to locate the entry lists for the last three heats of the first round of the tandem match sprint. However, we do have the overall entry list for the event. Based on the entrants and competitors in heats 1–4, we can deduce that the following teams were entered in heats 5–7, but did not compete in any of the heats: Belgium (Joseph Werbrouck, Jean Van Benthem), France (Émile Demangel, C. Dauvergne), Germany (Karl Neumer, Paul Schulze), United States (Frederick Hill, William van den Dries), and United States (George Cameron, Louis Weintz).

63. According to SL, the original draw for the tandem first round had only four heats.

64. This was listed as heat 2 in SL entry lists. Belgium was entered but did not start.

65. This was listed as heat 3 in SL entry lists. The United States was entered but did not start.

66. This was listed as heat 1 in SL entry lists.

Diving

The two diving events at the 1908 Olympics were conducted as part of the swimming program, which also included water polo. They were held in the huge pool which had been built in the infield of the White City Stadium. At one side of the pool, a large diving tower was erected, which was retractable so that when in it was not in use, it was lowered below the surface of the water. The pool and the tower were designed by William Henry, Secretary of the Royal Life Saving Society, who had also competed in the 1900 and 1906 Olympic Games.

Two events were contested — a plain high diving, or platform-type diving, and fancy high diving off a springboard. In addition, on Saturday, 18 July, an exhibition of diving was given by two women — Valborg Florström of Finland and Ebba Gisico of Sweden. Women would not make their official Olympic début in swimming and diving until 1912 in Stockholm. This diving exhibition was the first appearance at the Olympics for women in the pool.

An unusual difference in the scoring systems is noted in the rules for the diving. In the plain high diving (platform) the judges' scores were multiplied by the degree of difficulty for each dive. But in the fancy diving (springboard), the degree of difficulty was added to the judges' scores. Also of note, the regulations stated that the final placements would be determined by an ordinal system of scoring, similar to figure skating, but the ordinal scores are not recorded in any source. In addition, the individual judges' scores are not known, so it is not possible to reconstruct the ordinal placements.

Site:	White City Stadium, Shepherd's Bush, London				
Dates:	14–18, 20–24 July				
Events:	2				
Competitors:	39				
Nations:	9				

	Competitors	1st	2nd	3rd	Totals
Australia	1	-	-	-	-
Belgium	1	-	-	-	-
Canada	1	-	-	-	-
Finland	2	-	-	-	-

Germany	5	1	1	1	3
Great Britain	16	-	-	-	-
Italy	1	-	-	-	-
Sweden	10	1	1	1	3
United States	2	-	-	1	1
Totals	39	2	2	3	7
Nations	9	2	2	3	3

Officials

Diving Judges: S. J. Monks, H. J. Grimwade, Hugo Stromberg, D. F. Cooke
Scorers: W. Burton, A. Barnes, S. Dixon
Stewards: J. H. Buckle, F. O. Venning, A. Richardson, H. T. Edney, J. H. Phipps, F. B. Howard, G. F. Simmons, W. G. Emery, R. W. Jones, W. S. Hankins, H. J. Johnson, H. Bolton, A. G. Chalmers, A. Freedman, A. Judkins, H. T. Bretton, H. C. Martin

Men's Plain High Diving

A: 24[1]*; C: 6; D: 20–24 July.

There were two platforms used, one of 5 meters and one of 10 meters. Each competitor made seven dives, four compulsory and three optional. Two compulsory dives were made from the 5-meter platform, a running plain dive and a backward somersault; and two were made from the 10-meter platform, a standing plain dive and a running plain dive. The optional dives were made from the 10-meter platform.

Sweden dominated this event, advancing seven to the semi-finals, and having the first four finishers in the final. America's Polish emigré George Gaidzik was a favorite, as he had won the 1908 British highboard championship earlier in the summer. Gaidzik had the highest total in the first round but he performed very poorly in the finals. Hjalmar Johansson dominated the finals, and had trailed only Gaidzik in the qualifying rounds. He was the diving champion of Sweden from 1897 through 1908, except for 1900 and 1903 when he lived in London. He was also an accomplished swimmer, holding the Swedish record for the 100 breaststroke at the time of the 1908 Olympics. The two other Swedish medalists, Karl Malmström and Arvid Spång-berg, were relative newcomers to diving.

In the preliminaries to this event, George Cane (GBR) had a poor dive and passed out upon landing. Spectators and officials were not certain why he was not leaving the pool. Hjalmar Johansson, the eventual gold medalist, realized what had happened and dove in to rescue Cane. Fortunately, Cane was quickly revived and sustained no major injuries.

In the semi-finals, George Gaidzik (USA), one of the favorites, finished third and did not qualify for the final. He was actually briefly disqualified, as one of the judges felt he was receiving signals (coaching) from a teammate on the ground. The judges' scores for Gaidzik were as follows: one gave him an 8, a 6, and a 9½; one gave him a 9 for each dive; while the third judge scored him 0 for each dive, and disqualified him, based on the above reasoning. The Americans

See Notes on page 146.

protested, and after consideration by the judges, the protest was upheld and Gaidzik was advanced as an extra diver to the final.[2]

Final A: 5; C: 2; D: 24 July; T: 1515.

1.	Hjalmar Johansson	SWE	83.75
2.	Karl Malmström	SWE	78.73
3.	Arvid Spångberg	SWE	74.00
4.	Robert Andersson	SWE	68.30
5.	George Gaidzik	USA	56.30

Semi-Finals A: 10; C: 5; D: 23 July; F: Top two finishers in each heat to advance to the final.[3]

Heat 1 A: 5; C: 2; T: 1130; F: Winners of heats 3, and 4 and the runners-up in heats 2, 4, and 5 in the first round to compete.

1.	Arvid Spångberg	SWE	72.30	Q
2.	Karl Malmström	SWE	67.00	Q
3.	Toivo Aro	FIN	62.70	
4.	Hilmer Löfberg	SWE	59.18	
5.	Harald Arbin	SWE	52.81	

Heat 2 A: 5; C: 4; T: 1130; F: Winners of heats 1, 2, and 5, and the runners-up in heats 1, and 3 in the first round to compete.

1.	Hjalmar Johansson	SWE	80.75	Q
2.	Robert Andersson	SWE	66.75	Q
3.	George Gaidzik	USA	61.05	Q
4.	Harald Goodworth	GBR	59.48	
5.	Heinz Freyschmidt	GER	48.80	

Round One A: 24; C: 6; D: 20-22 July; F: Top two finishers in each heat to advance to the final.

Heat 1 A: 5; C: 4; D: 20 July; T: 1130.

1.	George Gaidzik	USA	81.80	Q
2.	Harald Goodworth	GBR	76.00	Q
3.	Erik Adlerz	SWE	74.10	
4.	Oskar Wetzell	FIN	69.70	
5.	James Aldous	GBR	68.00	

[4]

Heat 2 A: 4; C: 3; D: 20 July; T: 1455.

1.	Hjalmar Johansson	SWE	78.40	Q
2.	Karl Malmström	SWE	73.95	Q
3.	William Hoare	GBR	65.20	
	Joseph Huketick	BEL	DNF	

[5]

Heat 3 A: 5; C: 3; D: 21 July; T: 1130.

1.	Hilmer Löfberg	SWE	68.90	Q
2.	Heinz Freyschmidt	GER	67.30	Q

3.	Sigfrid Larsson	SWE	64.80	
4.	William Webb	GBR	57.70	
5.	F. J. Collins	GBR	56.50	
6				

Heat 4 A: 4; C: 2; D: 22 July; T: 1130.

1.	Arvid Spångberg	SWE	79.20	Q
2.	Harald Arbin	SWE	76.80	Q
3.	George Cane	GBR	73.10	
4.	Karl Gustaf Vindqvist[7]	SWE	65.70	
8				

Heat 5 A: 6; C: 5; D: 22 July; T: 1430.

1.	Robert Andersson	SWE	73.55	Q
2.	Toivo Aro	FIN	69.50	Q
3.	Harold Grote	USA	62.80	
4.	Axel Runström	SWE	57.60	
5.	Fritz Nicolai	GER	54.50	
6.	Thomas Harrington	GBR	53.15	
9				

Fancy High (Springboard) Diving

A: 23; C: 8; D: 14–18 July.

There were two springboards used, one of 1 meter and one of 3 meters. Each competitor made seven dives, four compulsory and three optional. Two compulsory dives were made from the 1-meter springboard, a plain running dive and a running forward somersault; and two were made from the 3-meter springboard, a 1½ somersault and a backward spring with forward dive. The optional dives were made from the 3-meter springboard.

Germany dominated this event. In the first round, the top score was posted by Kurt Behrens, while in the semi-finals he was second to the United States' George Gaidzik. The winner in the finals, however, was the 18-year-old Albert Zürner, who narrowly defeated Behrens and whose main claim to fame was having been Champion of Hamburg (Germany) for the past four years. Tying for third with Gaidzik was Gottlob Walz, who was the heavy favorite. Walz had won the platform competition at the 1906 Olympic Games, was an 11-time German champion, and had won the European championship three times, first in 1903.

Final A: 4; C: 2; D: 18 July; T: 1455.

1.	Albert Zürner	GER	85.50
2.	Kurt Behrens	GER	85.30
=3.	George Gaidzik	USA	80.80
	Gottlob Walz	GER	80.80

Semi-Finals A: 11; C: 4; D: 17 July; F: Top two finishers in each heat to advance to the final.

Heat 1 A: 6; C: 3; T: 1525; F: Winners of heats 3, 4, and 5, and the runners-up in heats 1, and 3 in the first round to compete.[10]

1.	Kurt Behrens	GER	83.00	Q
2.	Gottlob Walz	GER	80.30	Q
3.	Herbert Pott	GBR	79.60	
4.	Heinz Freyschmidt	GER	79.30	
5.	Frank Errington	GBR	72.60	
6.	Oskar Wetzell	FIN	70.10	

Heat 2 A: 5; C: 3; T: 1525; F: Winners of heats 1 and 2, and the runners-up in heats 2, 4, and 5 in the first round to compete.

1.	George Gaidzik	USA	85.60	Q
2.	Albert Zürner	GER	82.80	Q
3.	Fritz Nicolai	GER	81.80	
4.	Harold Clarke	GBR	81.10	
5.	Harold Grote	USA	74.50	

Round One A: 23; C: 8; D: 14-16 July; F: Top two finishers in each heat to advance to the final.

Heat 1 A: 5; C: 4; D: 14 July; T: 1430.

1.	George Gaidzik	USA	82.80	Q
2.	Heinz Freyschmidt	GER	78.10	Q
3.	Robert Zimmerman	CAN	74.00	
4.	Harry Crank	GBR	70.30	
5.	Anthony Beckett	GBR	67.50	

11

Heat 2 A: 3; C: 2; D: 14 July; T: 1430.

1.	Albert Zürner	GER	83.60	Q
2.	Harold Clarke	GBR	78.60	Q
3.	Anthony Taylor	GBR	58.80	

12

Heat 3 A: 5; C: 4; D: 15 July; T: 1130.

1.	Kurt Behrens	GER	83.60	Q
=2.	Frank Errington	GBR	70.83	Q
	Oskar Wetzell	FIN	70.83	Q
4.	Karl Malmström	SWE	70.30	
5.	William Hoare	GBR	67.80	

13

Heat 4 A: 6; C: 5; D: 15 July; T: 1545.

1.	Herbert Pott	GBR	82.50	Q
2.	Fritz Nicolai	GER	67.10	Q
3.	William Bull	GBR	66.00	
4.	Carlo Bonfanti	ITA	65.80	
5.	Sigfrid Larsson	SWE	64.50	
6.	Reginald "Snowy" Baker	AUS	61.30	

14

Heat 5 A: 4; C: 3; D: 16 July; T: 1500.

1.	Gottlob Walz	GER	81.30	Q
2.	Harold Grote	USA	79.50	Q
3.	Harold Smyrk	GBR	78.30	
4.	Thomas Cross	GBR	64.50	

15

Exhibitions

Two diving exhibitions were given. One was held on Monday, 13 July at 5:00 P.M. (1700). The divers in this exhibition were Harold Smyrk (GBR), Reginald "Snowy" Baker (AUS), Carlo Bonfanti (ITA), Gottlob Walz (GER), Hjalmar Johansson (SWE), and Heinz Freyschmidt (GER).

On Saturday, 18 July at 4:30 P.M. (1630), a diving exhibition was also held between Miss Valborg Florström (FIN) and Miss Ebba Gisico (SWE). This was the first time women appeared at the Olympics in either swimming or diving.

NOTES

1. DW, FW, and VK/OSVK have 23. However, OSVK lists 24 divers, exactly the same competitors by heat as we have.
2. NYHP, 24 July 1908.
3. George Gaidzik (USA), third in the second heat, was also advanced to the final. The reason is given above in the description of the event.
4. Also entered in this heat, but not competing, were T. Norberg (SWE), and G. Meister (FRA).
5. Also entered in this heat, but not competing, were Albert Zürner (GER), Harold Smyrk (GBR), and –– Briard (FRA).
6. Also entered in this heat, but not competing, were Carlo Bonfanti (ITA) and Frank A. Bornamann (USA).
7. This athlete's full name has been difficult for us to find for some time, because both the OR and SL listed him as "Landqvist." Swedish historians knew of him, however, and his name is given as Karl Gustaf Vindqvist in *Sverige och OS*.
8. Also entered in this heat, but not competing, were A. W. Ullström (FIN) and R. Feret (FRA).
9. Also entered in this heat, but not competing, was .–– Viglietti (ITA).
10. Because Frank Errington and Oskar Wetzell tied for 2nd in Heat Three, they were both advanced to the semi-finals, and both placed in this heat, which gave six starters.
11. Also entered in this heat, but not competing, were Gérard Meister (FRA), and A. W. Ullström (FIN).
12. Also entered in this heat, but not competing, were E. Renou (FRA), Tor Norberg (SWE), Joseph Huketick (BEL), and Otto Satzinger (AUT).
13. Also entered in this heat, but not competing, were R. Feret (FRA) and Frank A. Bornamann (USA).
14. Also entered in this heat, but not competing, was –– Briard (FRA).
15. Also entered in this heat, but not competing, were Harald Arbin (SWE), and –– Viglietti (ITA).

Fencing

The fencing matches were held during the "main" portion of the Olympics, i.e., while the stadium events were being contested. However, they were held outside the stadium, although nearby, at a site described as "the fencing ground of the Franco-British Exposition." There were four events: épée for individuals and teams, and sabre for individuals and teams. As would be expected, the French dominated the two épée events, sweeping the individual medals, and the Hungarians dominated the sabre, beginning their Olympic dominance in that event.

Site:	The Fencing Ground of the Franco-British Exposition, just outside the White City Stadium, Shepherd's Bush, London
Dates:	17–18, 20–24 July
Events:	4
Competitors:	130
Nations:	14

	Competitors	*1st*	*2nd*	*3rd*	*Totals*
Austria	1	-	-	-	-
Belgium	18	-	-	1	1
Bohemia	6	-	-	2	2
Canada	1	-	-	-	-
Denmark	8	-	-	-	-
France	22	2	1	1	4
Germany	10	-	-	-	-
Great Britain	23	-	1	-	1
Hungary	8	2	1	-	3
Italy	11	-	1	-	1
The Netherlands	13	-	-	-	-
Norway	1	-	-	-	-
South Africa	1	-	-	-	-
Sweden	7	-	-	-	-
Totals	130	4	4	4	12
Nations	14	2	4	3	6

Officials

Committee: Sir Cosmo Duff-Gordon, A. Virgoe Buckland, G. H. Baillie, F. Legge, Colonel J. Leslie, A. G. Ross, Dr. G. H. Savage, J. Pollock, M. Silverston, Commander H. Watson, H. Montgomerie (Secretary)

British Judges: Gordon Reuben Alexander, Charles Henry Biscoe, F. J. Brett, Capt. E. C. Brierley, C. F. Clay, Capt. A. E. Cresswell, J. B. Cunliffe, Capt. S. de Joux, R. W. Doyne, A. Fellows, G. C. D. Gordon, G. L. Jacobs, John Jenkinson, E. B. Milnes, Major C. Moore, H. Pollock, Alfred Rawlinson, Colonel S. P. Rolt, Commander Royds, W. H. C. Staveley, Capt. Alfred Edward Syson, F. H. Townsend, Capt. C. Trueman, F. Moore, Capt. Warwick C. Wright

Belgian Judges: A. Feyerick and "three others"

Bohemian Judges: Dr. Gustav Magy and "another"

French Judges: G. Breittmayer, Marquis de Chasseloup-Laubat

Hungarian Judges: Désiré Lauber and "two others"

Italian Judges: Commandant Parise Masanilo, Baron Pontevani

Norwegian Judges: Capt. Jean Bentzen, Capt. Edvard Dahl, Capt. Johan Sverre

Swedish Judges: Lieut. Carl Hjörth

Scorers/Timekeepers: A. C. Amy, W. Bean, Rev. G. L. Blake, P. G. Doyne, Capt. S. Dyer, Capt. A. G. Hall, C. Montgomerie, E. Plowden, F. C. Reynolds, Major A. B. King, H. Turner, A. Todhunter

Épée, Individual

A: 85[1]*; C: 14; D: 17–18, 20, 23–24 July.

In the results of the various pools, the following abbreviations are used: o = won the match, giving a hit and receiving none; x = lost the match, receiving a hit and giving none; d = a double hit, considered as a hit received for both fencers;—= no match, as it refers to the same fencer. A blank space indicates a match was scheduled but did not take place.

The French dominated this event, placing three fencers in the final and sweeping the medals. The gold medalist, Gaston Alibert, was particularly impressive. In 25 matches, he had 20 outright wins, and 5 ties, or double hits. He was never defeated during the individual épée tournament. He also helped France win a gold medal in the team épée. In that event, he fought 12 matches, winning 11 and losing 1. Alibert never again competed at the Olympics. He was killed fighting in World War I.

Final A: 8; C: 4; D: 24 July; T: 1445.
[2]

			Ali	Lip	Oli	Mon	Ans	Hai	Lab	Hol	
1.	Gaston Alibert	FRA	–	o	o	d	o	o	d	o	5-0-2
2.	Alexandre Lippmann	FRA	x	–	o	x	o	o	d	o	4-2-1 (2-0)
3.	Eugène Olivier	FRA	x	x	–	o	o	o	x	o	4-3-0 (1-1)
4.	Robert Montgomerie	GBR	d	o	x	–	o	o	o	d	4-1-2 (0-2)
=5.	Paul Anspach	BEL	x	x	x	x	–	o	x	o	2-5-0
	Cecil Haig	GBR	x	x	x	x	x	–	o	o	2-5-0

See Notes on pages 166–167.

	Alfred Labouchere	NED	d	d	o	x	o	x	-	x	2-3-2
8.	Martin Holt	GBR	x	x	x	d	x	x	o	-	1-5-1

Barrage for places 2–4 A: 3; C: 2.

			Lip	Oli	Mon	
1.	Alexandre Lippmann	FRA	-	o	o	2-0
2.	Eugène Olivier	FRA	x	-	o	1-1
3.	Robert Montgomerie	GBR	x	x	-	0-2

Semi-Finals A: 16; C: 6; D: 23 July; F: First four in each pool advanced
to the final.

Pool 1 A: 8; C: 4; T: 1030.

			Ali	Hai	Lab	Mon	Rom	GBe	Ren	Bos	
1.	Gaston Alibert	FRA	-	o	o	o	d	o	o	d	5-0-2
=2.	Cecil Haig	GBR	x	-	x	o	x	o	o	o	4-3-0
	Alfred Labouchere	NED	x	o	-	x	o	x	o	o	4-3-0
4.	Robert Montgomerie	GBR	x	x	o	-	x	o	x	o	3-4-0
=5.	François Rom	BEL	d	o	x	o	-	d	x	d	2-2-3
	Henri-Georges Berger	FRA	x	x	o	x	d	-	o	d	2-3-2
	Gaston Renard	BEL	x	x	x	o	o	x	-	d	2-4-1
8.	Fernand Bosmans	BEL	d	x	x	x	d	d	d	-	0-3-4

Pool 2 A: 8; C: 5; T: 1600.

			Ans	Hol	Lip	Oli	Ste	Øst	Lin	LeB	
1.	Paul Anspach	BEL	-	x	o	o	x	o	o	o	5-2-0
2.	Martin Holt	GBR	o	-	o	x	x	o	x	o	4-3-0
3.	Alexandre Lippmann[3]	FRA	x	x	-	d	o	d	o	o	3-2-2 (2-0)
4.	Eugène Olivier	FRA	x	o	d	-	o	x	d	o	3-2-2 (1-1)
5.	Jean Stern	FRA	o	o	x	x	-	x	x	o	3-4-0 (0-2)
=6.	Lauritz Østrup	DEN	x	x	d	o	o	-	d	d	2-2-3
	Gustaf Lindblom	SWE	x	o	x	d	o	d	-	x	2-3-2
8.	Pierre Le Blon	BEL	x	x	x	x	x	d	o	-	1-5-1

Round Two A: 39; C: 8; D: 20 July; F: First two in each pool advance
to the semi-finals.

Pool 1 A: 5; C: 4; T: 1030.

			LeB	Ste	Doo	Stu	Lev	
1.	Pierre Le Blon	BEL	-	d	o	o	o	3-0-1
2.	Jean Stern[4]	FRA	d	-	o	o	d	2-0-2 (1-0)
3.	Jetze Doorman	NED	x	x	-	o	o	2-2-0 (0-1)
4.	François Stuyck	BEL	x	x	x	-	p	1-3-0
5.	Ejnar Levison	DEN	x	d	x	x	-	0-3-1

Pool 2 A: 5; C: 4; T: 1030.

			Øst	Ren	Osi	Rod	Amp	
1.	Lauritz Østrup	DEN	-	o	o	x	o	3-1-0
2.	Gaston Renard[5]	BEL	x	-	x	o	o	2-2-0 (2-0)
=3.	Ivan Osiier	DEN	x	o	-	o	x	2-2-0 (0-1)
	Jacques Rodocanachi	FRA	o	x	x	-	o	2-2-0 (0-1)
5.	Edgar Amphlett	GBR	x	x	o	x	-	1-3-0

Pool 3 A: 5; C: 4; T: 1030.

			Ali	GBe	vL	Spe	Dav	
1.	Gaston Alibert	FRA	-	o	o	o	o	4-0-0
2.	Henri-Georges Berger[6]	FRA	x	-	o	o	d	2-1-1 (1-0)
3.	Vilém Goppold von Lobsdorf	BOH	x	x	-	o	o	2-2-0 (0-1)
4.	Pietro Speciale	ITA	x	x	x	-	o	1-3-0
5.	Henry Davids	GBR	x	d	x	x	-	0-3-1

Pool 4 A: 5; C: 3; T: 1030.

			Hol	Mon	Tvr	Gra	Mar	
1.	Martin Holt	GBR	-	x	o	o	o	3-1-0
2.	Robert Montgomerie[7]	GBR	o	-	x	o	x	2-2-0 (2-0)
=3.	Vilém Tvrzský	BOH	x	o	-	x	o	2-2-0 (0-1)
	Bernard Gravier	FRA	x	x	o	-	o	2-2-0 (0-1)
5.	Joseph Marais	FRA	x	o	x	x	-	1-3-0

Pool 5 A: 5; C: 5; T: 1715.

			Lip	Lin	LD	Ber	LS	
=1.	Alexandre Lippmann	FRA	-	o	d	o	o	3-0-1
	Gustaf Lindblom	SWE	x	-	o	o	o	3-1-0
3.	Charles Leaf Daniell	GBR	d	x	-	o	o	2-1-1
4.	Marcello Bertinetti	ITA	x	x	x	-	o	1-3-0
5.	Vlastimil Lada-Sázavský	BOH	x	x	x	x	-	0-4-0

Pool 6 A: 5; C: 3; T: 1715.

			Rom	Bos	VLa	Now	Col	
1.	François Rom	BEL	-	x	o	o	o	3-1-0
2.	Fernand Bosmans	BEL	o	-	d	d	o	2-0-2
=3.	Marcel Van Langenhove	BEL	x	d	-	x	o	1-2-1
	Riccardo Nowak	ITA	x	d	o	-	x	1-2-1
	Charles Collignon	FRA	x	x	x	o	-	1-3-0

Pool 7 A: 5; C: 4; T: 1715.

			Ans	Lab	dMo	SMa	Šou	
1.	Paul Anspach	BEL	-	o	o	o	x	3-1-0
2.	Alfred Labouchere[8]	NED	x	-	o	x	o	2-2-0 (2-0)
=3.	Fernand de Montigny	BEL	x	x	-	o	o	2-2-0 (0-1)
	Sydney Martineau	GBR	x	o	x	-	o	2-2-0 (0-1)
5.	Jaroslav "Tuček" Šourek	BOH	o	x	x	x	-	1-3-0

Pool 8 A: 4; C: 3; T: 1715.

			Aol	Hai	Cag	Que	
=1.	Abelardo Olivier	ITA	-	x	o	o	2-1-0
	Cecil Haig	GBR	o	-	x	o	2-1-0
=3.	Giulio Cagiati	ITA	x	o	-	x	1-2-0
	René Quenessen	FRA	x	x	o	-	1-2-0

Round One A: 85; C: 14; D: 17–18 July; F: First three in each pool advance to the second round.

Pool 1 A: 7; C: 6; D: 17 July; T: P.M.

			Øst	Gra	Šou	Car	vRo	Stö	Fil	
1.	Lauritz Østrup	DEN	-	x	o	o	o	o	o	5-1-0
=2.	Bernard Gravier	FRA	o	-	x	x	o	o	o	4-2-0
	Jaroslav "Tuček" Šourek	BOH	x	o	-	o	x	o	o	4-2-0
4.	Eric Carlberg	SWE	x	o	x	-	o	x	o	3-3-0
5.	Pontus von Rosen	SWE	x	x	o	x	-	o	d	2-3-1
6.	Georg Stöhr	GER	x	x	x	o	x	-	d	1-4-1
7.	Luke Fildes	GBR	x	x	x	x	d	d	-	0-4-2

Pool 2 A: 7; C: 7; D: 17 July; T: P.M.

			LS	Col	Spe	San	vSc	Gat	Jac	
1.	Vlastimil Lada-Sázavský	BOH	-	x	o	o	o	o	o	5-1-0
2.	Charles Collignon	FRA	o	-	o	o	d	x	o	4-1-1
3.	Pietro Speciale	ITA	x	x	-	o	x	o	o	3-3-0
=4.	Herbert Sander	DEN	x	x	x	-	o	o	x	2-4-0
	Johan van Schreven	NED	x	d	o	x	-	d	o	2-2-2
=6.	Walter Gates	SAF	x	o	x	x	d	-	d	1-3-2
	Friedrich "Fritz" Jack	GER	x	x	x	o	x	d	-	1-4-1

Pool 3 A: 6; C: 6; D: 17 July; T: PM.

			Mar	Lev	Ren	Ada	Bla	Dwi	
1.	Joseph Marais	FRA	-	o	o	o	o	o	5-0-0
=2.	Ejnar Levison	DEN	x	-	o	o	o	x	3-2-0
	Gaston Renard	BEL	x	x	-	o	o	o	3-2-0
=4.	Johannes Adam	GER	x	x	x	-	x	o	1-4-0
	Jack Blake	GBR	x	x	x	o	-	d	1-3-1
	Marcus "Max" Dwinger	NED	x	o	x	x	d	-	1-3-1

Pool 4 A: 8; C: 8; D: 17 Jul; T: PM

			GBe	Hol	Tvr	Bec	Dia	HBe	Sar	vR	
1.	Henri-Georges Berger	FRA	-	o	o	o	o	o	o	o	7-0-0
=2.	Martin Holt	GBR	x	-	x	x	x	o	o	o	3-4-0 (2-2-0) (2-1-0)
	Vilém Tvrzský	BOH	x	o	-	o	x	x	o	d	3-3-1 (2-2-0) (2-1-0)
=4.	Otto Becker	DEN	x	o	x	-	x	o	d	o	3-3-1 (2-1-1) (1-2-0)
	Dino Diana	ITA	x	o	o	o	-	d	d	x	3-2-2 (2-1-1) (1-2-0)

6.	Hans Bergsland	NOR	x	x	o	x	d	-	o	o	3-3-1 (2-2-0)
=7.	André Sarens	BEL	x	x	x	d	d	x	-	o	1-4-2
	George van Rossem	NED	x	x	d	x	o	x	x	-	1-5-1

Barrage/Pool 4 for places 2–5 A: 5; C: 5; D: 17 July; T: P.M.

			Bec	Dia	Hol	Tvr	HBe	
=1.	Otto Becker	DEN	-	d	x	o	o	2-1-1
	Dino Diana	ITA	d	-	o	o	x	2-1-1
	Martin Holt	GBR	o	x	-	x	o	2-2-0
	Vilém Tvrzský	BOH	x	x	o	-	o	2-2-0
5.	Hans Bergsland	NOR	x	o	x	x	-	1-3-0

Second Barrage/Pool 4 for places 2–4 A: 4; C: 4; D: 17 July; T: P.M.

			Hol	Tvr	Bec	Dia	
=1.	Martin Holt	GBR	-	x	o	o	2-1-0
	Vilém Tvrzský	BOH	o	-	o	x	2-1-0
=3.	Otto Becker	DEN	x	x	-	o	1-2-0
	Dino Diana	ITA	x	o	x	-	1-2-0

Pool 5 A: 8; C: 8; D: 17 Jul; T: P.M.

			Ali	dMo	Osi	PDa	Cec	Lad	Krü	vLS	
1.	Gaston Alibert	FRA	-	o	o	o	o	o	o	d	6-0-1
=2.	Fernand de Montigny	BEL	x	-	o	x	d	o	o	o	4-2-1
	Ivan Osiier	DEN	x	x	-	o	o	o	o	d	4-2-1
=4.	Percival Davson	GBR	x	o	x	-	o	x	o	x	3-4-0
	Sante Ceccherini[9]	ITA	x	d	x	x	-	o	o	o	3-3-1
6.	Otakar Lada	BOH	x	x	x	o	x	-	d	o	2-4-1
=7.	Robert Krünert	GER	x	x	x	x	x	d	-	o	1-5-1
	Jacob van Löben Sels	NED	d	x	d	o	x	x	x	-	1-4-2

Pool 6 A: 6; C: 6; D: 17 July; T: P.M.

			Rom	Cag	SMa	Pey	Nau	Sch	
1.	François Rom	BEL	-	o	x	o	o	o	4-1-0
=2.	Giulio Cagiati	ITA	x	-	o	d	o	o	3-1-1
	Sydney Martineau	GBR	o	x	-	o	o	x	3-2-0
4.	Henry Peyron	SWE	x	d	x	-	o	o	2-2-1
=5.	Albert Naumann	GER	x	x	x	x	-	o	1-4-0
	Bedřich Schejbal	BOH	x	x	o	x	x	-	1-4-0

Pool 7 A: 7; C: 7; D: 17 July; T: P.M.

			LD	vL	Bos	Dub	ESc	Föl	vBl	
1.	Charles Leaf Daniell	GBR	-	x	o	o	o	o	o	5-1-0
2.	Vilém Goppold von Lobsdorf	BOH	o	-	x	o	x	o	o	4-2-0
3.	Fernand Bosmans[10]	BEL	x	o	-	d	x	o	o	3-2-1 (2-0)
=4.	Frédéric Dubordieu	FRA	x	x	d	-	o	o	o	3-2-1 (0-1)
	Emil Schön	GER	x	o	o	x	-	o	d	3-2-1 (0-1)
6.	Dezső Földes	HUN	x	x	x	x	x	-	o	1-5-0
7.	Willem Hubert van Blijenburgh	NED	x	x	x	x	d	x	-	0-5-1

Pool 8 A: 7; C: 7; D: 17 July; T: PM.

		Lab	Ans	Rod	Cha	EdB	PB	Šou	
1. Alfred Labouchere	NED	-	o	o	o	o	x	o	5-1-0
2. Paul Anspach	BEL	x	-	o	o	d	o	o	4-1-1
3. Jacques Rodocanachi[11]	FRA	x	x	-	o	x	o	o	3-3-0 (1-0)
4. Ralph Chalmers	GBR	x	x	x	-	o	o	o	3-3-0 (0-1)
=5. Jacob Erckrath de Bary	GER	x	d	o	x	-	d	o	2-2-2
Alessandro Pirzio Biroli	ITA	o	x	x	x	d	-	o	2-3-1
7. Jaroslav "Tuček" Šourek	BOH	x	x	x	x	x	x	-	0-6-0

Pool 9 A: 7; C: 7; D: 18 July; T: 1030.

		Mon	Lin	Que	Man	Jør	Pet	Nob	
1. Robert Montgomerie	GBR	-	o	o	o	o	o	d	5-0-1
=2. Gustaf Lindblom	SWE	x	-	o	d	d	o	o	3-1-2 (1-0)
René Quenessen	FRA	x	x	-	x	o	o	o	3-3-0 (1-0)
4. Giuseppe Mangiarotti	ITA	x	d	o	-	o	d	o	3-1-2 (0-2)
5. Frantz Jørgensen	DEN	x	d	x	x	-	o	o	2-3-1
=6. August Petri	GER	x	x	x	d	x	-	d	0-4-2
Percy Nobbs[12]	CAN	d	x	x	x	x	d	-	0-4-2

Pool 10 A: 6; C: 6; D: 18 July; T: 1030.

		Amp	Doo	Oli	Mol	PSa	Zul	
=1. Edgar Amphlett	GBR	-	o	o	o	o	x	4-1-0
Jetze Doorman	NED	x	-	o	o	o	o	4-1-0
3. Eugène Olivier	FRA	x	x	-	o	o	o	3-2-0
=4. Pietro Sarzano	ITA	x	x	x	o	-	d	1-3-1
Béla Zulavszky	HUN	o	x	x	x	d	-	1-3-1
Ernst Moldenhauer	GER	x	x	x	-	x	o	1-4-0

Pool 11 A: 5; C: 5; D: 18 July; T: 1030.

		Ber	LeB	Hai	Okk	Bra	
1. Marcello Bertinetti	ITA	-	o	x	o	o	3-1-0
=2. Pierre Le Blon[13]	BEL	x	-	o	d	o	2-1-1 (1-0)
Cecil Haig	GBR	o	x	-	x	o	2-2-0 (1-0)
4. Simon Okker	NED	x	d	o	-	o	2-1-1 (0-2)
5. Georg Branting	SWE	x	x	x	x	-	0-4-0

Pool 12 A: 6; C: 5; D: 18 July; T: 1030.

		Lip	Stu	Now	Cna	Sel	Ols	
=1. Alexandre Lippmann	FRA	-	x	o	o	o	o	4-1-0
François Stuyck	BEL	o	-	o	o	d	o	4-0-1
3. Riccardo Nowak	ITA	x	x	-	o	o	o	3-2-0
=4. Birger Cnattingius	SWE	x	x	x	-	x	o	1-4-0
Edgar Seligman	GBR	x	d	x	o	-	d	1-2-2
6. Gustaf "Gösta" Olson	SWE	x	x	x	x	d	-	0-4-1

Pool 13 A: 5; C: 5; D: 18 Jul; T: 1430

		Ste	Dav	VLa	Lic	Tót	
1. Jean Stern	FRA	–	o	o	d	o	3-0-1
=2. Henry Davids	GBR	x	–	x	o	o	2-2-0
Marcel Van Langenhove	BEL	x	o	–	o	x	2-2-0
=4. Julius Lichtenfels	GER	d	x	x	–	o	1-2-1
Péter Tóth	HUN	x	x	o	x	–	1-3-0

14,15

Épée, Team

A: 45[16]; C: 9; D: 20-24 July.

With the three medalists in the individual épée event, the French had to be the heavy favorites and they did not disappoint, winning fairly comfortably, although Belgium extended them somewhat in the final, 9-7. The winning French team was awarded, in addition to their gold medals, the International Cup for Fencing, which had been designated for the winning team in this event.

1. France
    (Gaston Alibert, Bernard Gravier, Alexandre Lippmann, Eugène Olivier, Henri-Georges Berger, Charles Collignon, Jean Stern)

2. Great Britain
    (Edgar Amphlett, Charles Leaf Daniell, Cecil Haig, Robert Montgomerie, Martin Holt, Edgar Seligman)

3. Belgium
    (Paul Anspach, Fernand Bosmans, Fernand de Montigny, François Rom, Victor Willems, Désiré Beaurain, Ferdinand Feyerick)

4. Italy
    (Marcello Bertinetti, Giuseppe Mangiarotti, Riccardo Nowak, Abelardo Olivier)

=5. Germany
    (Jacob Erckrath de Bary, Julius Lichtenfels, August Petri, Georg Stöhr)

    Denmark
    (Ejnar Levison, Lauritz Østrup, Ivan Osiier, Herbert Sander, Otto Becker)

    Bohemia
    (Otakar Lada, Vlastimil Lada-Sázavský, Vilém Goppold von Lobsdorf, Vilém Tvrzský)

    Sweden
    (Eric Carlberg, Gustaf Lindblom, Henry Peyron, Pontus von Rosen)

9. The Netherlands
    (Adrianus de Jong, Jetze Doorman, Alfred Labouchere, George van Rossem)

17

Tournament Draw Summary

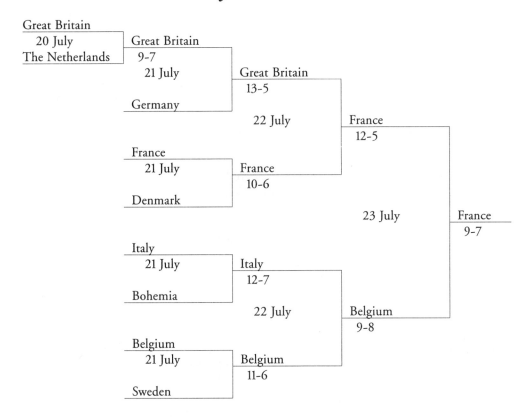

Great Britain
20 July
The Netherlands

Great Britain
9-7
21 July

Germany

Great Britain
13-5
22 July

France
12-5

France
21 July

Denmark

France
10-6

23 July

France
9-7

Italy
21 July

Bohemia

Italy
12-7

22 July

Belgium
9-8

Belgium
21 July

Sweden

Belgium
11-6

Match Summaries

Great Britain d. The Netherlands, 9-7. A: 8; C: 2; D: 20 July; T: 1500.

Netherlands	LD	Hol	Mon	Sel	Totals	Great Britain	dJ	Doo	Lab	vR	Totals
de Jong	x	x	o	o	2-2-0	Daniell	o	o	x	o	3-1-0
Doorman	x	o	o	o	3-1-0	Holt	o	x	o	o	3-1-0
Labouchere	o	x	x	o	2-2-0	Montgomerie	x	x	o	o	2-2-0
van Rossem	x	x	x	x	0-4-0	Seligman	x	x	x	o	1-3-0
Total					**7-9-0**	**Total**					**9-7-0**

Italy d. Bohemia, 12-7. A: 8; C: 2; D: 21 July; T: 1500.

Bohemia	Ber	Man	Now	AOl	Totals	Italy	Lad	LS	vL	Tvr	Totals
O. Lada	x	o	x	d	1-2-1	Bertinetti	o	x	o	x	2-2-0
V Lada-Sázavský	o	x	x	d	1-2-1	Mangiarotti	x	o	x	o	2-2-0
von Lobsdorf	x	o	x	x	1-3-0	Nowak	o	o	o	o	4-0-0
Tvrzský	o	x	x	d	1-2-1	Olivier	d	d	o	d	1-0-3
Total					**4-9-3**	**Total**					**9-4-3**

Great Britain d. Germany, 13-5. A: 8; C: 2; D: 21 July; T: 1600.

Germany	LD	Hai	Hol	Mon	Totals
de Bary	x	x	x	x	0-4-0
Lichtenfels	d	x	x	d	0-2-2
Petri	x	o	o	x	2-2-0
Stöhr	o	x	x	x	1-3-0
Total					**3-11-2**

Great Britain	EdB	Lic	Pet	Stö	Totals
Daniell	o	d	o	x	2-1-1
Haig	o	o	x	o	3-1-0
Holt	o	o	x	o	3-1-0
Montgomerie	o	d	o	o	3-0-1
Total					**11-3-2**

France d. Denmark, 10-6. A: 8; C: 2; D: 21 July; T: 1600.

Denmark	Ali	Ste	Li	pGra	Totals
Levison	x	o	x	x	1-3-0
Østrup	x	x	x	o	1-3-0
Osiier	o	o	o	x	3-1-0
Sander	x	x	o	x	1-3-0
Total					**6-10-0**

France	Lev	Øst	Osi	San	Totals
Alibert	o	o	x	o	3-1-0
Stern	x	o	x	o	2-2-0
Lippmann	o	o	x	x	2-2-0
Gravier	o	o	x	o	3-1-0
Total					**10-6-0**

Belgium d. Sweden, 11-6. A: 8; C: 2; D: 21 July; T: 1700.

Belgium	Car	Lin	Pey	vR	Totals
Anspach	o	o	x	o	3-1-0
Beaurain	x	o	o	o	3-1-0
de Montigny	o	o	d	x	2-1-1
Willems	x	x	o	o	2-2-0
Total					**10-5-1**

Sweden	Ans	Bea	dMo	Wil	Totals
Carlberg	x	o	x	o	2-2-0
Lindblom	x	x	x	o	1-3-0
Peyron	o	x	d	x	1-2-1
von Rossem	x	x	o	x	1-3-0
Total					**5-10-1**

Belgium d. Italy, 9-8. A: 8; C: 2; D: 22 July; T: 1500.

Italy	Ans	Bea	Fey	Rom	Totals
Bertinetti	x	x	o	o	2-2-0
Mangiarotti	x	o	x	d	1-2-1
Nowak	x	o	x	o	2-2-0
Olivier	x	o	o	x	2-2-0
Total					**7-8-1**

Belgium	Ber	Man	Now	AOl	Totals
Anspach	o	o	o	o	4-0-0
Beaurain	o	x	x	x	1-3-0
Feyerick	x	o	o	x	2-2-0
Rom	x	d	x	o	1-2-1
Total					**8-7-1**

France d. Great Britain, 12-5. A: 8; C: 2; D: 22 July; T: 1630.

France	LD	Hai	Hol	Mon	Totals
Alibert	o	o	o	o	4-0-0
Berger	o	o	d	x	2-1-1
Collignon	o	o	o	x	3-1-0
Olivier	o	o	x	x	2-2-0
Total					**11-4-1**

Great Britain	Ali	Ber	Col	Oli	Totals
Daniell	x	x	x	x	0-4-0
Haig	x	x	x	x	0-4-0
Holt	x	d	x	o	1-2-1
Montgomerie	x	o	o	o	3-1-0
Total					**4-11-1**

France d. Belgium, 9-7. A: 8; C: 2; D: 23 July; T: 1445.

France	Ans	Bea	Fey	Rom	Totals
Alibert	o	o	o	o	4-0-0
Gravier	o	x	o	x	2-2-0

Belgium	Ali	Gra	Lip	Oli	Totals
Anspach	x	x	x	o	1-3-0
Beaurain	x	o	o	o	3-1-0

Lippmann	o	x	o	x	2-2-0	Feyerick	x	x	x	o	1-3-0
Olivier	x	x	x	o	1-3-0	Rom	x	o	o	x	2-2-0
Total					**9-7-0**	**Total**					**7-9-0**

Second-Place Tournament Summary

Great Britain		
24 July	Great Britain	
Denmark	9-8	
	24 July	Great Britain
		9-5
	Belgium	

Match Summaries

Great Britain d. Denmark, 9-8. A: 8; C: 2; D: 24 July; T: 1030.

Denmark	LD	Hai	Hol	Mon	Totals	Great Britain	Bec	Lev	Osi	San	Totals
Becker	x	x	o	d	1-2-1	Daniell	o	o	x	x	2-2-0
Levison	x	x	o	x	1-3-0	Haig	o	o	x	o	3-1-0
Osiier	o	o	o	x	3-1-0	Holt	x	x	x	x	0-4-0
Sander	o	x	o	x	2-2-0	Montgomerie	d	o	o	o	3-0-1
Total					**7-8-1**	**Total**					**8-7-1**

Great Britain d. Belgium, 9-5. A: 8; C: 2; D: 24 July; T: 1730.

Great Britain	Ans	Bos	dM	Rom	Totals	Belgium	Amp	LD	Hai	Mon	Totals
Amphlett	x	o	o	o	3-1-0	Anspach	o		x	o	2-1-0
Daniell		d	o	o	2-0-1	Bosmans	x	d		x	0-2-1
Haig	o		o	x	2-1-0	de Montigny	x	x	x		0-3-0
Montgomerie	x	o		x	1-2-0	Rom	x	x	o	o	2-2-0
Total					**8-4-1**	**Total**					**4-8-1**

Sabre, Individual

A: 76; C: 11; D: 17–18, 20, 23–24 July.

Jenő Fuchs won his first gold medal in this event. He would eventually win four Olympic gold medals in sabre fencing—1908 individual and team, and 1912 individual and team. Fuchs was also a top ranked rower and bobsledder in Hungary.

Fuchs' individual victory began the Hungarian streak in this event. From 1908 through 1964 a Hungarian fencer always won the sabre gold medal at the Olympics, with the exception of 1920, when Hungary was not invited as they were considered an aggressor nation in World War I. Hungarians also won all the world championships in individual sabre from 1923 through 1937 and, after World War II, 1951–55.

Final A: 8; C: 4; D: 24 July; T: 1445.

			Fuc	Zul	vL	Szá	Tót	Wer	dlF	Doo	
1.	Jenő Fuchs	HUN	-	o	d	o	o	o	o	o	6-0-1
2.	Béla Zulavszky	HUN	x	-	o	o	o	o	o	o	6-1-0
3.	Vilém Goppold von Lobsdorf	BOH	d	x	-	o	x	o	o	o	4-2-1
4.	Jenő Szántay	HUN	x	x	x	-	o	o	o	d	3-3-1
5.	Péter Tóth	HUN	x	x	o	x	-	o	x	o	3-4-0
6.	Lajos Werkner	HUN	x	x	x	x	x	-	o	o	2-5-0
=7.	Georges de la Falaise	FRA	x	x	x	x	o	x	-	x	1-6-0
	Jetze Doorman	NED	x	x	x	d	x	x	o	-	1-5-1

Semi-Finals A: 16; C: 8; D: 23 July; F: First four in each pool advanced
to the final.

Pool 1 A: 8; C: 4; T: 1030.

			Fuc	Wer	Szá	dlF	Ber	Föl	Not	dLe	
1.	Jenő Fuchs	HUN	-	o	x	o	o	o	o	o	6-1
2.	Lajos Werkner	HUN	x	-	x	o	o	o	o	o	5-2
=3.	Jenő Szántay	HUN	o	o	-	x	o	o	x	x	4-3
	Georges de la Falaise	FRA	x	x	o	-	x	o	o	o	4-3
=5.	Marcello Bertinetti	ITA	x	x	x	o	-	x	o	o	3-4
	Desző Földes	HUN	x	x	x	x	o	-	o	o	3-4
7.	C. Barry Notley	GBR	x	x	o	x	x	x	-	o	2-5
8.	Bernard de Lesseps	FRA	x	x	o	x	x	x	x	-	1-6

Pool 2 A: 8; C: 6; T: 1600.

			vL	Zul	Tót	Doo	Ger	Øst	VdV	Cec	
=1.	Vilém Goppold von Lobsdorf	BOH	-	o	x	x	o	o	o	o	5-2
	Béla Zulavszky	HUN	x	-	x	o	o	o	o	o	5-2
	Péter Tóth	HUN	o	o	-	x	o	x	o		4-2
	Jetze Doorman	NED	o	x	o	-	x	o	o		4-2
5.	Oszkár Gerde	HUN	x	x	x	o	-	o	o	o	4-3
6.	Lauritz Østrup	DEN	x	x	o	x	x	-	o	o	3-4
7.	Joseph Van der Voodt	BEL	x	x	x	x	x	x	-		0-6
	Sante Ceccherini[18]	ITA	x	x			x	x		-	DNF

Round Two A: 38[19]; C: 10; D: 20 July; F: First two in each pool advance
to the semi-finals.

Pool 1 A: 5; C: 5; T: 1130.

			Fuc	Not	RSc	EGr	Lat	
1.	Jenő Fuchs	HUN	-	o	x	o	o	3-1
2.	C. Barry Notley[20]	GBR	x	-	o	o	x	2-2 (2-0)
=3.	Richard Schoemaker	NED	o	x	-	x	o	2-2 (0-1)
	Etienne Grade	BEL	x	x	o	-	o	2-2 (0-1)
5.	René Lateux	FRA	x	o	x	x	-	1-3

Pool 2 A: 5; C: 4; T: 1130.

		Wer	Föl	vR	Bad	Jac	
1.	Lajos Werkner	HUN	-	o	o	o	o	4-0
2.	Desző Földes	HUN	x	-	o	o	o	3-1
3.	George van Rossem	NED	x	x	-	o	o	2-2
4.	Richard Badman	GBR	x	x	x	-	o	1-3
5.	Friedrich "Fritz" Jack	GER	x	x	x	x	-	0-4

Pool 3 A: 5; C: 5; T: 1130.

		VdV	GvL	Mar	Now	dJ	
=1.	Joseph Van der Voodt	BEL	-	x	o	o	o	3-1
	Vilém Goppold von Lobsdorf	BOH	o	-	o	x	o	3-1
3.	William Marsh	GBR	x	x	-	o	o	2-2
=4.	Riccardo Nowak	ITA	x	o	x	-	x	1-3
	Adrianus de Jong	NED	x	x	x	o	-	1-3

Pool 4 A: 4; C: 3; T: 1130.

		dLe	Zul	Sch	Tvr	
1.	Bernard de Lesseps	FRA	-	o	o	o	3-0
2.	Béla Zulavszky	HUN	x	-	o	o	2-1
3.	Bedich Schejbal	BOH	x	x	-	o	1-2
4.	Vilém Tvrzský	BOH	x	x	x	-	0-3

Pool 5 A: 5; C: 5; T: 1615.

		Ger	Cec	Lad	ESc	Ans	
1.	Oszkár Gerde	HUN	-	o	o	o	o	4-0
2.	Sante Ceccherini	ITA	x	-	o	o	o	3-1
3.	Otakar Lada	BOH	x	x	-	o	o	2-2
4.	Emil Schön	GER	x	x	x	-	o	1-3
5.	Paul Anspach	BEL	x	x	x	x	-	0-4

Pool 6 A: 5; C: 3; T: 1615.

		Tót	Szá	Lab	Fle	HvB	
1.	Péter Tóth	HUN	-	o	o	o	o	4-0
2.	Jenő Szántay	HUN	x	-	o	o	o	3-1
=3.	Alfred Labouchere	NED	x	x	-	x	o	1-3
	Siegfried Flesch	AUT	x	x	o	-	x	1-3
	Willem Hubert van Blijenburgh	NED	x	x	x	o	-	1-3

Pool 7 A: 5; C: 4; T: 1615.

		Ber	Doo	Pet	PB	LS	
1.	Marcello Bertinetti	ITA	-	o	o	o	o	4-0
2.	Jetze Doorman[21]	NED	x	-	x	o	o	2-2 (1-0)
3.	August Petri	GER	x	o	-	o	x	2-2 (0-1)
=4.	Alessandro Pirzio Biroli[22]	ITA	x	x	x	-	o	1-3
	Vlastimil Lada-Sázavský	BOH	x	x	o	x	-	1-3

Pool 8 A: 4; C: 3; T: 1615.

		dlF	Øst	Apá	SN	
1.	Georges de la Falaise[23]	FRA	–	x	o	o	2-1 (2-0)
2.	Lauritz Østrup	DEN	o	–	x	o	2-1 (1-1)
3.	Jenő Apáthy	HUN	x	o	–	o	2-1 (0-2)
4.	Einar Schwartz-Nielsen	DEN	x	x	x	–	0-3

Round One A: 76; C: 11; D: 17-18 July; F: First three in each pool advance to the second round.

Pool 1 A: 6; C: 5; D: 17 July; T: A.M.

			Fle	Doo	LS	DML	Six	Šou	
1.	Siegfried Flesch	AUT	–	o	o	o	o	o	5-0
=2.	Jetze Doorman	NED	x	–	o	x	o	o	3-2
	Vlastimil Lada-Sázavskÿ	BOH	x	x	–	o	o	o	3-2
4.	Jean de Mas Latrie	FRA	x	o	x	–	o	x	2-3
=5.	Henri Six	BEL	x	x	x	x	–	o	1-4
	Jaroslav "Tuček" Šourek	BOH	x	x	x	o	x	–	1-4

Pool 2 A: 5; C: 5; D: 17 July; T: A.M.

			Lad	Tót	VdV	Mur	Ada	
1.	Otakar Lada	BOH	–	o	x	o	o	3-1
=2.	Péter Tóth[24]	HUN	x	–	o	o	x	2-2 (1-0)
	Joseph Van der Voodt	BEL	o	x	–	x	o	2-2 (1-0)
4.	Arthur Murray	GBR	x	x	o	–	o	2-2 (0-1)
5.	Johannes Adam	GER	x	o	x	x	–	1-3

Pool 3 A: 6; C: 6; D: 17 July; T: A.M.

			Lab	Gra	Jac	Ren	Dia	God	
1.	Alfred Labouchere	NED	–	o	o	o	x	o	4-1
=2.	Etienne Grade[25]	BEL	x	–	x	o	o	o	3-2 (1-0)
	Friedrich "Fritz" Jack	GER	x	o	–	x	o	o	3-2 (1-0)
4.	Jean-Joseph Renaud	FRA	x	x	o	–	o	o	3-2 (0-2)
5.	Dino Diana	ITA	o	x	x	x	–	o	2-3
6.	Douglas Godfree	GBR	x	x	x	x	x	–	0-5

Pool 4 A: 5; C: 5; D: 17 July; T: AM.

			Mar	Lat	RSc	Lic	Kre	
1.	William Marsh	GBR	–	o	x	o	o	3-1
=2.	René Lateux[26]	FRA	x	–	o	x	o	2-2 (1-0)
	Richard Schoemaker	NED	o	x	–	o	x	2-2 (1-0)
4.	Julius Lichtenfels	GER	x	o	x	–	o	2-2 (0-1)
5.	Harald Krenchel	DEN	x	x	o	x	–	1-3

Pool 5 A: 4; C: 4; D: 18 July; T: 1430.

			dJo	PB	SN	Lan	
=1.	Adrianus de Jong	NED	–	o	x	o	2-1
	Alessandro Pirzio Biroli	ITA	x	–	o	o	2-1

	Einar Schwartz-Nielsen	DEN	o	x	-	o	2-1
4.	Georges Langevin	FRA	x	x	x	-	0-3

Pool 6 A: 5; C: 5; D: 18 July; T: 1430.

			dlF	Szá	Pet	VT	vLS	
=1.	Georges de la Falaise	FRA	-	x	o	o	o	3-1
	Jenő Szántay	HUN	o	-	x	o	o	3-1
3.	August Petri[27]	GER	x	o	-	x	o	2-2 (1-0)
4.	Antoine Van Tomme	BEL	x	x	o	-	o	2-2 (0-1)
5.	Jacob van Löben Sels	NED	x	x	x	x	-	0-4

Pool 7 A: 6; C: 6; D: 18 July; T: 1430.

			Föl	Cec	Bad	vMi	EdB	IdL	
1.	Desző Földes	HUN	-	o	o	o	o	o	5-0
2.	Sante Ceccherini	ITA	x	-	o	o	o	o	4-1
3.	Richard Badman	GBR	x	x	-	o	x	o	2-3 (1-0)
4.	Lion van Minden	NED	x	x	x	-	o	o	2-3 (0-1)
=5.	Jacob Erckrath de Bary	GER	x	x	o	x	-	x	1-4
	Ignace de Lesseps	FRA	x	x	x	x	o	-	1-4

Pool 8 A: 6; C: 6; D: 18 July; T: 1600.

			Ber	BdL	Zul	Krü	CW	Gat	
=1.	Marcello Bertinetti	ITA	-	o	x	o	o	o	4-1
	Bernard de Lesseps	FRA	x	-	o	o	o	o	4-1
3.	Béla Zulavszky	HUN	o	x	-	x	o	o	3-2
=4.	Robert Krünert	GER	x	x	o	-	x	o	2-3
	Charles Wilson	GBR	x	x	x	o	-	o	2-3
6.	Walter Gates	SAF	x	x	x	x	x	-	0-5

Pool 9 A: 6; C: 6; D: 18 July; T: 1600.

			Ger	Øst	HvB	dBo	Kee	dSB	
=1.	Oszkár Gerde	HUN	-	x	o	o	o	o	4-1
	Lauritz Østrup	DEN	o	-	x	o	o	o	4-1
3.	Willem Hubert van Blijenburgh	NED	x	o	-	x	o	o	3-2
=4.	André du Bosch	BEL	x	x	o	-	x	o	2-3
	Alfred Keene	GBR	x	x	x	o	-	o	2-3
6.	Jacques de St. Brisson	FRA	x	x	x	x	x	-	0-5

Pool 10 A: 8; C: 8; D: 18 Jul; T: 1600.

			vL	Ans	Apá	Bro	vSc	PSa	Stö	Mik	
1.	Vilém Goppold von Lobsdorf	BOH	-	o	o	o	o	o	o	o	7-0
=2.	Paul Anspach	BEL	x	-	o	x	o	o	o	x	4-3
	Jenő Apáthy	HUN	x	x	-	x	o	o	o	o	4-3
=4.	Edward Brookfield	GBR	x	o	o	-	x	x	o	x	3-4
	Johan van Schreven	NED	x	x	x	o	-	o	x	o	3-4
=6.	Pietro Sarzano	ITA	x	x	x	o	x	-	[28]	o	2-4
	Georg Stöhr	GER	x	x	x	x	o	[29]	-	o	2-4
8.	Jean Mikorski	FRA	x	o	x	o	x	x	x	-	2-5

Pool 11 A: 6; C: 6; D: 18 July; T: 1600.

			Fuc	vHu	Tvr	Pin	Mol	Lei	
1.	Jen Fuchs	HUN	–	o	o	o	o	o	5-0
2.	Gustaaf Adolf van Hulstijn	NED	x	–	o	o	o	o	4-1
3.	Vilém Tvrzský	BOH	x	x	–	o	o	o	3-2
4.	Aroldo Pinelli	ITA	x	x	x	–	o	o	2-3
5.	Ernst Moldenhauer	GER	x	x	x	x	–	o	1-4
6.	Lockhart Leith	GBR	x	x	x	x	x	–	0-5

Pool 12 A: 6; C: 6; D: 18 July; T: 1730.

			vR	Not	Sch	LCh	Sim	Nau	
1.	George van Rossem	NED	–	o	o	x	o	o	4-1
=2.	C. Barry Notley	GBR	x	–	o	o	x	o	3-2
	Bedich Schejbal	BOH	x	x	–	o	o	o	3-2
4.	Louis Chapuis	FRA	o	x	x	–	o	o	3-2[30]
5.	Alexis Simonson	BEL	x	o	x	x	–	o	2-3
6.	Albert Naumann	GER	x	x	x	x	x	–	0-5

Pool 13 A: 7; C: 7; D: 18 Jul; T: 1730.

			Wer	Now	ESc	Per	dBe	Šou	ACh	
1.	Lajos Werkner	HUN	–	x	o	o	o	o	o	5-1
=2.	Riccardo Nowak	ITA	o	–	x	x	o	o	o	4-2
	Emil Schön	GER	x	o	–	o	x	o	o	4-2
4.	Marc Perrodon	FRA	x	o	x	–	x	o	o	3-3
=5.	Jan de Beaufort	NED	x	x	o	o	–	x	x	2-4
	Jaroslav "Tuček" Šourek	BOH	x	x	x	x	o	–	o	2-4
7.	Anthony Chalke	GBR	x	x	x	x	o	x	–	1-5

[31,32]

Sabre, Team

A: 35; C: 8; D: 21–24 July.

With the gold and silver medalists from the individual event, the Hungarians were particularly dominant in the team sabre competition. They won their opening match over Germany by 9-0, and the *Official Report* noted that nobody could remember a team fencing match in which one team never scored a hit.

This victory began the Hungarian streak of dominance in team sabre fencing at the Olympics. Hungary won all the gold medals in this event at the Olympics from 1908–1960, except for 1920 when the nation was not invited because of its role in World War I. David Wallechinsky has pointed out that Hungary won 46 consecutive matches during this streak.[33] Hungary has also been dominant in the team sabre at the world championships. World championships in the team sabre began in 1930, and were held through the 1950s in non-Olympic years. Hungary won the title in 1930–31, 1933–35, 1937, 1951, 1953–55, and 1957–58, failing to win the title only in 1938, 1947, and 1949–50.

1. Hungary
(Jenő Fuchs, Oszkár Gerde, Péter Tóth, Lajos Werkner, Dezső Földes)

2. Italy
(Riccardo Nowak, Alessandro Pirzio Biroli, Abelardo Olivier, Marcello Bertinetti, Sante Ceccherini)

3. Bohemia
(Vilém Goppold von Lobsdorf, Jaroslav "Tuček" Šourek, Vlastimil Lada-Sázavský, Otakar Lada, Bedřich Schejbal)

4. France
(Georges de la Falaise, Bernard de Lesseps, Marc Perrodon, Jean-Joseph Renaud)

=5. Belgium
(André du Bosch, Etienne Grade, Antoine Van Tomme, Joseph Van der Voodt)

Germany
(Jacob Erckrath de Bary, Robert Krünert, August Petri, Friedrich "Fritz" Jack)

The Netherlands
(Jetze Doorman, Adrianus de Jong, George van Rossem, Jacob van Löben Sels)

Great Britain
(H. Evan James, William Marsh, Arthur Murray, Charles Wilson)

Tournament Draw Summary

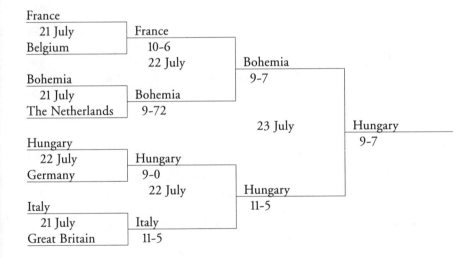

```
France
   21 July      France
Belgium          10-6
                 22 July      Bohemia
Bohemia                        9-7
   21 July      Bohemia
The Netherlands  9-72
                              23 July      Hungary
                                            9-7
Hungary
   22 July      Hungary
Germany          9-0
                 22 July      Hungary
Italy                          11-5
   21 July      Italy
Great Britain    11-5
```

Match Summaries

France d. Belguim, 10-6. A: 8; C: 2; D: 21 July; 1500.

Belgium	dlF	dLe	Per	Ren	Totals	France	dBo	EGr	VT	VdV	Totals
du Bosch	o	x	o	x	2-2	de la Falaise	x	x	o	x	1-3
Grade	o	o	x	x	2-2	de Lesseps	o	x	o	o	3-1

Van Tomme	x	x	x	x	0-4	Perrodon	x	o	o	o	3-1
Van der Voodt	o	x	x	o	2-2	Renaud	o	o	o	x	3-1
Total					**6-10**	**Total**					**10-6**

Italy d. Great Britain, 11-5. A: 8; C: D: 21 July; T: 1600.

Italy	Jam	WMa	Mur	CWi	Totals	Great Britain	Ber	Cec	AOl	PB	Totals
Bertinetti	o	o	x	o	3-1	James	x	x	o	x	1-3
Ceccherini	o	x	x	o	2-2	Marsh	x	o	x	x	1-3
Olivier	x	o	o	o	3-1	Murray	o	o	x	o	3-1
Pirzio Biroli	o	o	x	o	3-1	Wilson	x	x	x	x	0-4
Total					**11-5**	**Total**					**5-11**

Bohemia d. The Netherlands, 9-7[35]. A: 8; C: 2; D: 22 July[36]; T: 1000.

Bohemia	Doo	dJ	vR	vLS	Totals	Netherlands	Lad	LS	vL	Sch	Totals
Lada	x	x	o	x	1-3	Doorman	o	x	x	o	2-2
Lada-Sázavský	o	x	o	x	2-2	de Jong	o	o	x	o	3-1
von Lobsdorf	o	o	o	o	4-0	van Rossem	x	x	x	x	0-4
Schejbal	x	x	o	o	2-2	van Löben Sels	o	o	x	x	2-2
Total					**9-7**	**Total**					**7-9**

Hungary d. Germany, 9-0.[37] A: 8; C: 2; D: 22 July; T: 1000.

Germany	Fuc	Ger	Tót	Wer	Totals	Hungary	EdB	Krü	Pet	Jac	Totals
Erckrath de Bary	x	x	x		0-3	Fuchs	o			o	2-0
Krünert		x	x		0-2	Gerde	o	o			2-0
Petri			x	x	0-2	Tóth	o	o	o		3-0
Jack	x			x	0-2	Werkner			o	o	2-0
Total					**0-9**	**Total**					**9-0**

Bohemia d. France, 9-7. A: 8; C: 2; D: 22 July; T: 1500.

Bohemia	dlF	dLe	Per	Ren	Totals	France	Lad	LS	vL	Sch	Totals
Lada	x	o	x	x	1-3	de la Falaise	o	x	x	o	2-2
Lada-Sázavský	o	o	x	o	3-1	de Lesseps	x	x	o	o	2-2
von Lobsdorf	o	x	o	o	3-1	Perrodon	o	o	x	x	2-2
Schejbal	x	x	o	o	2-2	Renaud	o	x	x	x	1-3
Total					**9-7**	**Total**					**7-9**

Hungary d. Italy, 11-5. A: 8; C: 2; D: 22 July; T: 1630.

Italy	Föl	Fuc	Ger	Tót	Totals	Hungary	Ber	Cec	AOl	PB	Totals
Bertinetti	o	o	x	x	2-2	Földes	x	o	x	o	2-2
Ceccherini	x	x	x	x	0-4	Fuchs	x	o	x	o	2-2
Olivier	o	o	x	x	2-2	Gerde	o	o	o	x	3-1
Pirzio Biroli	x	x	o	x	1-3	Tóth	o	o	o	o	4-0
Total					**5-11**	**Total**					**11-5**

Hungary d. Bohemia, 9-7. A: 8; C: 2; D: 23 July; T: 1445.

Hungary	vL	Šou	LS	Sch	Totals	Bohemia	Fuc	Ger	Tót	Wer	Totals
Fuchs	x	o	o	o	3-1	von Lobsdorf	o	o	o	x	3-1
Gerde	x	o	x	o	2-2	Šourek	x	x	o	x	1-3
Tóth	x	x	o	x	1-3	Lada-Sázavský	x	o	x	o	2-2
Werkner	o	o	x	o	3-1	Schejbal	x	x	o	x	1-3
Total					**9-7**	**Total**					**7-9**

Second-Place Tournament Summary[38]

```
Italy
    24 July    | Italy
    Germany    | 10-4
```

Match Summary

Italy d. Germany, 10-4. A: 8; C: 2; D: 24 July; T: 1730.

Germany	Now	PB	AOl	Ber	Totals	Italy	EdB	Jac	Krü	Pet	Totals
Erckrath de Bary	x	o	x	x	1-3-0	Nowak	o		o	o	3-0-0
Jack		x	=	o	1-1-1	Pirzio Biroli	x	o		o	2-1-0
Krünert	x		x	x	0-3-0	Olivier	o	=	o		2-0-1
Petri	x	x		o	1-2-0	Bertinetti	o	x	o	x	2-2-0
Total					**3-9-1**	**Total**					**9-3-1**

EXHIBITIONS

Foil

Exhibitions of foil fencing were also given at the 1908 Olympics. The Committee of the Amateur Fencing Association (AFA) did not think that the foil was a suitable weapon for competition, considering its use an art form rather than a sport Thus, no formal competition was on the program.

The exhibition took place on the evening of 23 July at Prince's Galleries, Piccadilly, London, beginning at 9 P.M. (2100). The invited nations were allowed to have two foil fencers take part. Of note, a woman took part. This was Miss Millicent Hall of Great Britain, who had been ladies' foil champion of Britain for 1907–08. This was the first time that women fenced at the Olympics. Fencing for women would become a medal sport in 1924.

The program was as follows:

Part I

Belgium	Monsieur — Dolori
Belgium	Monsieur Marcel Berré
Bohemia	Herr Vilém Goppold von Lobsdorf

Bohemia	Herr Vlastimil Lada-Sázavskÿ
Denmark	Lieutenant Herbert Sander
Denmark	Mr. Ejnar Levison
Great Britain	Mr. John Jenkinson
Great Britain	Mr. Robert Montgomerie
Italy	Signor Abelardo Olivier
Italy	Signor Riccardo Nowak
The Netherlands	Monsieur Simon Okker
Norway	Mr. Hans Bergsland

Part II

Canada	Mr. Percy E. Nobbs
France	Dr. Eugène Olivier
France	Monsieur René Quenessen
Germany	Herr Albert Naumann
Germany	Herr Jacob Erckrath de Bary
Great Britain	Miss Millicent Hall
Great Britain	Mr. John Jenkinson
Hungary	Herr Béla Zulavszky
Hungary	Herr Péter Tóth
The Netherlands	Monsieur Marcus "Max" Dwinger
The Netherlands	Monsieur Simon Okker
South Africa	Mr. Walter P. Gates

NOTES

1. DW, EK, FW, and VK/OSVK have 84 from 13. OSVK lists 85 fencers in round one, however.

2. Places in all fencing pools were decided by the number of hits received. Thus, a fencer who lost four matches and a fencer who lost two and tied two (two double hits) would both be considered to have received four hits, and would be tied. Ties were fenced off in barrages when it was important for advancement to the next round, or for the medals. Otherwise, they were considered as ties.

3. In a barrage for places 3–5, Lippmann defeated both Olivier and Stern, and Olivier defeated Stern.

4. In a barrage for second place, Stern defeated Doorman.

5. In a barrage for places 2–4, Renard defeated both Osiier and Rodocanachi.

6. In a barrage for second place, Berger defeated von Lobsdorf.

7. In a barrage for places 2–4, Montgomerie defeated both Tvrzský and Gravier.

8. In a barrage for places 2–4, Labouchere defeated both de Montigny and Martineau.

9. Ceccherini was not entered in this event in SL.

10. In a barrage for places 3–5, Bosmans defeated both Dubordieu and Schön.

11. In a single-match barrage for third place, Rodocanachi defeated Chalmers.

12. Nobbs was not entered in this event in SL.

13. In the barrage for places 2–3, Le Blon and Haig both defeated Okker.

14. Exact details of the pool entrants are not available. However, the complete entry list is contained in SL. Also entered in this event, but not competing, were Josef Pfeiffer (BOH), B. A. Auza (ITA), G. Celano (ITA), Federico Cesarano (ITA), Adrianus de Jong (NED), Raphael Vigeveno (NED), Desiré Beaurain (BEL), J. de Vriendt (BEL), Emmanuel Fuchs (HUN), Bertalan Dunay (HUN), Jenő Szántay (HUN), Prospère Sénat (FRA), Georges A. Dillon-Kavanagh (FRA), J. Foule

(FRA), J. Aumont (FRA), T. Nieville (FRA), –– Pereard (FRA), –– Piugaud (FRA), Lucien Gaudin (FRA), and G. Anson (FRA).

15. Several of the French fencers above were not listed among the entrants in SL, but were listed as entered in the team épée event. They were as follows: Alexandre Lippmann, Bernard Gravier, Eugène Olivier, Frédéric Dubordieu, Henri-Georges Berger, Joseph Marais, and Jean Stern.

16. EK, FW, and VK/OSVK have 58 competitors, but correctly 9 teams from 9 nations. Also, OSVK lists all competitors, and has the same 45 as we have.

17. Hungary was also entered in this event, but did not compete.

18. Ceccherini retired after losing his first four matches, and the Toth–Ceccherini, Doorman–Ceccherini, and Van der Voodt–Ceccherini matches did not take place.

19. Gustaaf Adolf van Hulstijn did not compete in round two, although he was eligible from placing second in pool 11 of round one.

20. In a barrage for places 2–4, Notley defeated Schoemaker and Grade.

21. In a barrage for places 2–3, Doorman defeated Petri.

22. The OR has Lada-Sázavský with three hits against and Pirzio Biroli with four hits against, implying that Lada-Sázavský finished fourth and Pirzio Biroli fifth in this heat. However, they have a mistake, listing both of them as losing the match between them. SL has Pirzio Biroli in 4th, not listing Lada-Sázavský. This would imply that the correct result is that Pirzio Biroli defeated Lada-Sázavský. This would give them both records of 1-3, if the other match results are correct, and have them tied for fourth.

23. In the barrage for places 1–3, de la Falaise defeated Østrup and Apáthy, and Østrup defeated Apáthy.

24. In a barrage for places 2–4, Tóth and Van der Voodt defeated Murray.

25. In a barrage for places 2–4, Grade and Jack both defeated Renaud.

26. In a barrage for places 2–4, Lateux and Schoemaker both defeated Lichtenfels.

27. In a barrage for third place, Petri defeated van Tomme.

28. For some reason, the match between Sarzano and Stöhr did not take place.

29. For some reason, the match between Sarzano and Stöhr did not take place.

30. Notley, Schejbal, and Chapuis competed in a barrage for places 2–4, but it is not mentioned in OR. SL notes, "In the fight off, Notley and Schejbal qualified."

31. Šourek also started in pool 1, finishing tied for fifth and not qualifying for round 2. It is not known why he was allowed to compete again in pool 13.

32. Exact details of the pool entrants are not available. However, the complete entry list is contained in SL. Also entered in this event, but not competing, were Josef Pfeiffer (BOH), František Dušek (BOH), P. E. B. Feilmann (GBR), Henry James (GBR), Abelardo Olivier (ITA), E. Bossini (ITA), G. Pirzio Biroli (ITA), B. A. Auza (ITA), G. Celano (ITA), Raphael Vigeveno (NED), Fernand Bosmans (BEL), Victor Willems (BEL), Bertalan Dunay (HUN), Ervin Mészáros (HUN), A. Lichlineckert (HUN), Georg Erdmann (GER), and Federico Cesarano (ITA).

33. DW, p. 424.

34. Score given as 9-8 in OR, but the match scores indicate that Bohemia won by 9-7.

35. Score given as 9-8 in OR, but the match scores indicate that Bohemia won by 9-7.

36. Listed as 21 July in OR. But *Times* noted that, although it was scheduled for 1700 on that date, it was not held until the following morning at 1000.

37. The remaining matches were not fenced as Hungary had clinched a victory.

38. The second-place tournament was to be contested among teams which had lost to the champions, Hungary. This would have been Bohemia, Italy, and Germany. However, Bohemia declined to compete. Italy defeated Germany for the silver medals and Bohemia was awarded the bronze medals.

Figure Skating

The 1908 Olympic Games contained events in figure skating for both men and women. Pre-dating the first Olympic Winter Games by 16 years, these were the first Winter Olympic events contested at the modern Olympic Games.

This was the first time that an international figure skating competition saw men, women, and pairs compete at the same event. In addition, a fourth event, "Special Figures" was also held. This event never again appeared on the Olympic program but basically consisted of the school figures as a separate event.

Figure skating would not return to the Olympics until 1920 in Antwerp, as it was not held in 1912 at Stockholm.

Site:	Prince's Skating Club, Knightsbridge, London
Dates:	28–29 October
Events:	4 [2 Men, 1 Women, 1 Mixed]
Competitors:	21 [14 Men, 7 Women]
Nations:	6 [6 Men, 3 Women]

Total	Competitors	1st	2nd	3rd	Totals
Argentina	1	-	-	-	-
Germany	3	1	1	-	2
Great Britain	11	1	2	3	6
Russia	1	1	-	-	1
Sweden	4	1	1	1	3
United States	1	-	-	-	-
Totals	21	4	4	4	12
Nations	6	4	3	2	4

Men	Competitors	1st	2nd	3rd	Totals
Argentina	1	-	-	-	-
Germany	1	½	-	-	½

Men	Competitors	1st	2nd	3rd	Totals
Great Britain	7	-	1½	1½	3
Russia	1	1	-	-	1
Sweden	3	1	1	1	3
United States	1	-	-	-	-
Totals	14	2½	2½	2½	7½
Nations	6	3	2	2	4

Women	Competitors	1st	2nd	3rd	Totals
Germany	2	½	1	-	1½
Great Britain	4	1	½	1½	3
Sweden	1	-	-	-	-
Totals	7	1½	1½	1½	4½
Nations	3	2	2	1	2

Officials

Referee: Dr. Herbert G. Fowler (GBR)
Judges: Edvard Hörle (SWE), George Sanders (RUS), Gustav Hügel (SUI), Harry D. Faith (GBR), Henning Grenander (GBR), Hermann Wendt (GER), Horatio Torromé (ARG).

MEN

Gentlemen, Individual

A: 9[1*]; C: 5; D: 28–29 October; T: 28 October —1500 (Compulsory Figures); 29 October —1500 (Free Skating).

Ulrich Salchow of Sweden opened a large lead in the school figures. Although his countryman, Richard Johansson, defeated him in the free skating, it was not by a sufficient margin to prevent Salchow from winning the gold medal. Nikolay Panin was second after the compulsory figures, but withdrew before the free skating. Various reasons are given for the withdrawal, with two main possibilities: (1) he was upset at the judging which gave Salchow the lead, and (2) he became ill and was unable to continue.

Salchow was the dominant figure skater of the era. He was world champion in 1901–1905, and 1907–1911. He did not compete in 1906, the only year of the decade in which he failed to win the title. In his career, Salchow also won nine European championships: 1898–1900, 1904, 1906–1907, 1909–1910, and 1913. He retired after 1913 but returned for the 1920 Olympics, finishing fourth, before retiring for good. He is today remembered by the popular figure skating jump termed the Salchow, in which the skater takes off from the back inside edge of one foot and lands backwards on the outside edge of the opposite foot. He also served as President of the International Skating Union from 1925–1937.

See Notes on page 174.

			a	b	c	d	e	1	2
1.	Ulrich Salchow	SWE	1	1	2	2	1	7	1
			1	1	1	2	2	7	(1)
			3	2	2½	4	1½	13	(2)
			357.0	400.0	393.0	351.0	385.5	1,886.5	377.3
			224.0	253.0	246.0	218.0	231.5	1,172.5	234.5
			133.0	147.0	147.0	133.0	154.0	714.0	142.8
2.	Richard Johansson	SWE	2	2	3	1	2	10	2
			3	3	3	3	4	16	(4)
			1	1	2½	1	1½	7	(1)
			336.0	396.5	381.0	353.5	359.0	1,826.0	365.2
			196.0	235.5	234.0	199.5	205.0	1,070.0	214.0
			143.0	161.0	147.0	154.0	154.0	756.0	151.2
3.	Per Thorén	SWE	4	3	1	3	3	14	3
			4	2	2	4	3	15	(3)
			4	3	1	2	3	13	(3)
			318.0	387.5	397.0	341.0	343.5	1,787.0	357.4
			192.0	247.5	243.0	194.0	217.5	1,094.0	218.8
			126.0	140.0	154.0	147.0	126.0	693.0	138.6
4.	John Greig	GBR	3	4	4	4	4	19	4
			5	5	5	5	5	25	(5)
			2	4	4	3	4	17	(4)
			330.0	327.5	273.0	313.0	311.0	1,554.5	310.9
			190.0	201.5	175.0	173.0	199.0	938.5	187.7
			140.0	126.0	98.0	140.0	112.0	616.0	123.2
5.	Albert March	GBR	5	5	7	6	6	29	5
			6	6	8	7	6	33	(6)
			5½	7	7	7	7	33½	(7)
			224.0	257.5	208.5	228.0	242.0	1,160.0	232.0
			140.0	166.5	145.5	137.0	172.0	761.0	152.2
			84.0	91.0	63.0	91.0	70.0	399.0	79.8
6.	Irving Brokaw	USA	6	7	5	5	7	30	6
			8	8½	6½	6	9	38	(7)
			5½	5½	5½	5	5½	27	(5)
			207.0	246.5	240.0	266.0	241.5	1,201.0	240.2
			123.0	148.5	149.0	140.0	157.5	718.0	143.6
			84.0	98.0	91.0	126.0	84.0	483.0	96.6
7.	Horatio Torromé	ARG	7	6	6	7	5	31	7
			7	7	9	9	7	39	(8)
			7	5½	5½	6	5½	29½	(6)
			197.5	247.0	231.0	220.5	248.5	1,144.5	228.9
			127.5	149.0	140.0	122.5	164.5	703.5	140.7
			70.0	98.0	91.0	98.0	84.0	441.0	88.2
AC.	Nikolay Panin	RUS	-	-	-	-	-			DNF
			2	4	4	1	1	12	(2)	WD

		215.0	232.5	232.0	235.0	233.0	1,147.5	229.5

Herbert Yglesias GBR — — — — DNF

		9	8½	6½	8	8	40	(9)

		107.0	148.5	149.0	135.5	163.5	703.5	140.7

a = Scores from Judge Henning Grenander (GBR).
b = Scores from Judge Edvard Hörle (SWE).
c = Scores from Judge Gustav Hügel (SUI).
d = Scores from Judge George Sanders (RUS).
e = Scores from Judge Hermann Wendt (GER).
a-e = Columns a-e list, by line, (1) individual judge's total ordinals, (2) individual judge's ordinals for compulsory figures, (3) individual judge's ordinals for free skating, (4) individual judge's total scores, (5) individual judge's score for compulsory figures[2], and (6) individual judge's score for free skating[3].
1 = Column 1 lists, by line, (1) total judges' ordinals, (2) total judges' ordinals for compulsory figures, (3) total judges' ordinals for free skating, (4) totals judges' scores, (5) total judges' score for compulsory figures, and (6) total judges' score for free skating.
2 = Column 2 lists, by line, (1) final placing, (2) place in compulsory figures, (3) place in free skating, (4) adjusted total judges' score (total score/5), (5) adjusted total judges' score for compulsory figures, and (6) adjusted total judges' score for free skating.

Special Figures Competition, Men

A: 3; C: 2; D: 29 October; T: 1000.

The winner of this event was the interesting Russian skater and athlete, Nikolay Kolomenkin, who competed in figure skating under the pseudonym of Nikolay Panin, presumably because sports were considered undignified by the elite in Russian society in that era. He later (1910) wrote a landmark work on the international style of figure skating, although it was never translated into English. Kolomenkin-Panin also competed in shooting at the 1912 Olympic Games, finishing fourth in a team event.

			a	*b*	*c*	*d*	*e*	*1*
1.	Nikolay Panin	RUS	1	1	1	1	1	5
			44.0	44.0	44.0	42.0	45.0	219.0/43.8
2.	Arthur Cumming	GBR	2	2	2	2	2	10
			32.5	32.0	37.5	30.5	31.5	164.0/32.8
3.	George Hall-Say	GBR	3	3	3	3	3	15
			23.0	17.0	18.0	25.0	21.0	104.0/20.8[4]

5

a   =   Scores from Judge Henning Grenander (GBR)
b   =   Scores from Judge Edvard Hörle (SWE)
c   =   Scores from Judge Gustav Hügel (SUI)
d   =   Scores from Judge Hermann Wendt (GER)
e   =   Scores from Judge George Sanders (RUS)
a-e   =   Columns a-e list, by line, (1) individual judge's ordinals, and (2) individual judge's total score[6].
1   =   Column line lists, by line (1) total judges' ordinals, and (2) total judges' score/adjusted total score (total score/5).

WOMEN

Ladies, Individual

A: 5[7]; C: 3; D: 28–29 October; T: 28 October—1000 (Compulsory Figures); 29 October—1500 (Free Skating).

Madge Syers won this title quite comfortably. She was easily the top female skater of the era. Women's world championships did not begin until 1906, but Syers won the first two events in 1906 and 1907. Prior to that time, women competed against men and Syers won the British "men's" championship in 1903 and 1904. At the 1902 World Championship, Madge Syers placed second to Ulrich Salchow. The only other top female skater of the era who might have challenged Syers was Lily Kronberger of Hungary, World Champion from 1908–1911, but she did not compete at the 1908 Olympics.

			a	b	c	d	e	1	2
1. Madge Syers	GBR		1	1	1	1	1	5	1
			1	1	1	1	1	5	(1)
			1	1½	1	1	1	5½	(1)
			255.5	236.0	266.5	262.0	242.5	1,262.5	252.5[8]
			147.5	150.5	163.0	154.0	152.5	767.5	153.5
			108.0	85.5	103.5	108.0	90.0	495.0	99.0
2. Else Rendschimdt	GER		3	2	2	2	2	11	2
			3	2½	3	2	2	12½	(2)
			2	1½	2	2	2	9½	(2)
			201.5	211.0	211.0	211.5	220.0	1,055.0	211.0
			116.0	125.5	112.0	121.5	138.5	613.5	122.7
			85.5	85.5	99.0	90.0	81.5	441.5	88.3
3. Dorothy Greenhough-Smith	GBR		2	3	4	3	3	15	3
			2	2½	2	3	4	13½	(3)
			3	3	4½	4	3	17½	(3)
			210.0	206.5	182.0	180.5	181.5	960.5	192.1
			129.0	125.5	119.0	113.0	118.5	605.0	121.0
			81.0	81.0	63.0	67.5	63.0	355.5	71.1
4. Elna Montgomery	SWE		4	4	5	4	4	21	4
			4	4	4	4	3	19	(4)

		5	4	4½	5	4½	23	(5)
		167.5	166.5	174.5	170.0	173.0	851.5	170.3
		104.5	103.5	111.5	107.0	119.0	545.5	109.1
		63.0	63.0	63.0	63.0	54.0	306.0	61.2

5. Gwendolyn Lycett   GBR

5	5	3	5	5	23	5
5	5	5	5	5	25	(5)
4	5	3	3	4½	19½	(4)
164.0	152.0	187.5	160.0	156.5	820.0	164.0
87.5	93.5	97.5	88.0	102.5	469.0	93.8
76.5	58.5	90.0	72.0	54.0	351.0	70.2

a   =   Scores from Judge Harry D. Faith (GBR).
b   =   Scores from Judge Edvard Hörle (SWE).
c   =   Scores from Judge Gustav Hügel (SUI).
d   =   Scores from Judge George Sanders (RUS).
e   =   Scores from Judge Hermann Wendt (GER).
a-e =   Columns a-e list, by line, (1) individual judge's total ordinals, (2) individual judge's ordinals for compulsory figures, (3) individual judge's ordinals for free skating, (4) individual judge's total scores, (5) individual judge's score for compulsory figures[9], and (6) individual judge's score for free skating[10].
1   =   Column 1 lists, by line, (1) total judges' ordinals, (2) total judges' ordinals for compulsory figures, (3) total judges' ordinals for free skating, (4) totals judges' scores, (5) total judges' score for compulsory figures, and (6) total judges' score for free skating.
2   =   Column 2 lists, by line, (1) final placing, (2) place in compulsory figures, (3) place in free skating, (4) adjusted total judges' score (total score/5), (5) adjusted total judges' score for compulsory figures, and (6) adjusted total judges' score for free skating.

MIXED

Pairs Skating

A: 6[II]; C: 2; D: 29 October; T: 1500.

A world championship in pairs skating was held for the first time in 1908, in St. Petersburg, Russia, and it was won by the German pair of Anna Hübler and Heinrich Burger. Hübler and Berger also won the 1908 Olympic title, defeating two British pairs. In third place was the husband and wife team of Madge and Edgar Syers. Madge Syers' gold in ladies' singles and bronze in pairs makes her one of only two skaters to have medalled in pairs and an individual event at the same Olympics — the other being Ernst Baier of Germany in 1936. The second-place team of Phyllis and James Johnson (GBR) were also a married couple.

		a	*b*	*c*	*d*	*e*	*1*	*2*
1. Anna Hübler	GER	1	1	1	1	1	5	1
Heinrich Burger	GER	10.0	12.0	11.0	12.0	11.0	56.0	11.20
		4.0	6.0	5.0	6.0	5.0	26.0	(2)
		6.0	6.0	6.0	6.0	6.0	30.0	(1)

2. Phyllis Johnson	GBR	2½	2½	2	2	2	11[12]	2
James Johnson	GBR	9.0	11.5	10.5	10.5	10.0	51.5	10.30
		5.0	6.0	5.5	5.5	5.0	27.0	(1)
		4.0	5.5	5.0	5.0	5.0	24.5	(3)
3. Madge Syers	GBR	2½	2½	3	3	3	14[13]	3
Edgar Syers	GBR	9.0	11.5	10.0	8.0	9.5	48.0	9.60
		4.0	5.5	4.0	4.0	4.0	21.5	(3)
		5.0	6.0	6.0	4.0	5.5	26.5	(2)

a   =   Scores from Judge Hermann Wendt (GER)
b   =   Scores from Judge Gustav Hügel (SUI)
c   =   Scores from Judge Horatio Torromé (ARG)
d   =   Scores from Judge Harry D. Faith (GBR)
e   =   Scores from Judge George Sanders (RUS)
a-e   =   Columns a-e list, by line, (1) individual judge's ordinals, (2) individual judge's overall score, (3) individual judge's score for technical merit, and (4) individual judge's score for artistic impression.
1   =   Column 1 lists, by line, (1) total ordinals, (2) total judges' score, (3) total judges' score for technical merit, and (4) total judges' score for artistic impression.
2   =   Column 2 lists, by line, (1) final placing, (2) adjusted total judges' score, (3) place for technical merit, and (4) place for artistic impression.

NOTES

1. According to the Programme of the Figure Skating Competitions, there was one entered skater who did not compete, Heinrich Burger (GER).

2. The maximum possible score from each judge for compulsory figures was 264.0.

3. The maximum possible score from each judge for free skating was 168. Each judge scored each skater a maximum of 6.0 for technical merit and artistic impression, for a total possible from each judge of 12.0. The final score was multiplied by 14 to obtain the free skating score.

4. FM listed the score for Hall-Say as 15.8.

5. Per the Programme of the Figure Skating Competitions, the following were entered but did not compete: Irving Brokaw (USA) and Ulrich Salchow (SWE).

6. In the special figures event, each skater performed four voluntary special figures, and was graded from 0-6 for both technical merit and artistic impression, making a maximum score of 12.0 for each figure, or 48.0 for the event from any individual judge.

7. According to the Programme of the Figure Skating Competitions, there were no other entries than the five women who competed.

8. FW gives completely different point totals for all the ladies in this event. His scores are as follows, listing total first, followed by points for compulsories: Syers—1,074,50/1,767.50; Rendschmidt—858.90/1,477.00; Greenhough-Smith—847.00/1,344.70; Montgomery—763.70/1,192.10; Lycett—656.60/1,148.00. It is uncertain how these were derived. The scores listed herein are from the OR.

9. The maximum possible score from each judge for compulsory figures was 168.0.

10. The maximum possible score from each judge for free skating was 108. Each judge scored each skater a maximum of 6.0 for technical merit and artistic impression, for a total possible from each judge of 12.0. The final score was multiplied by 9 to obtain the free skating score.

11. According to the Programme of the Figure Skating Competitions, there were no other entries than the three pairs which competed.

12. VK/OSVK have 10 ordinals.

13. VK/OSVK have 14 ordinals. Our sources for the ordinal scores are Skating and Skating2.

Football (Soccer)

Hungary and Bohemia were the only world class soccer nations who did not take part in the 1908 Games. Their late withdrawal reduced the number of competing teams to six and the *Official Report* gives the reason for their absence as "political troubles in the Balkans." This was a rather laconic way of describing the annexation of Bosnia and Herzegovina by Austria, an action which ultimately led to the outbreak of World War I six years later.

Unlike hockey, in which the four countries comprising the United Kingdom entered separate teams, a single British team represented the United Kingdom of Great Britain and Ireland. However, only English players were considered for selection. The reason for this was that the Olympic competition was staged under the authority of FIFA (Fédération Internationale de Football Association) and Ireland, Scotland, and Wales had not become members of the international governing body. These three countries became FIFA members in 1910.

Surprisingly, France, who could hardly be rated as a leading soccer nation, entered two teams, and Denmark, Holland and Sweden completed the entries. The early rounds produced some high scoring matches and with their 17-1 defeat of France "A," Denmark set an Olympic scoring record which has never been beaten. The Danish center-forward, Sofus Nielsen, also set an Olympic record by individually scoring 10 goals in Denmark's overwhelming victory.

Before a crowd of 8,000, Great Britain met Denmark in the final. In a classic match, Britain scored a goal in each half to give them a 2–0 victory but the Danes were highly praised for their skill and commitment. In a playoff match for third place Holland beat Sweden 2–1. Great Britain and Denmark maintained their pre-eminent position in world soccer and met again in the 1912 Olympic final when the British were again the winners (4–2).

Six Danes and two Britons played in both the 1908 and 1912 finals and as the Danish players, Charles von Buchwald and Oscar Nielsen-Norland, had also played in the 1906 final they became the only players in history to take part in three Olympic soccer finals.

Site:	White City Stadium, Shepherd's Bush, London
Dates:	19–20, 22–24 October
Events:	1
Competitors:	72
Nations:	5

	Competitors	1st	2nd	3rd	Totals
Denmark	13	–	1	–	1
France	22	–	–	–	–
Great Britain	11	1	–	–	1
The Netherlands	12	–	–	1	1
Sweden	14	–	–	–	–
Totals	72	1	1	1	3
Nations	5	1	1	1	3

Final Standings

A: 73[1]*; C: 5; D: 19–20, 22–24 October

		W	T	L	Pts	GF	GA
1.	Great Britain	3	0	0	6	18	1
2.	Denmark	2	0	1	4	26	3
3.	The Netherlands	1	0	1	2	2	4
4.	Sweden	0	0	2	0	1	14
=5.	France "A"	0	0	1	0	1	17
	France "B"	0	0	1	0	0	9

Team Rosters

Great Britain
(Horace Bailey, Walter Corbett, Herbert Smith, Kenneth Hunt, Frederick Chapman, Robert Hawkes, Arthur Berry, Vivian Woodward, Henry Stapley, Clyde Purnell, Harold Hardman)

Denmark
(Ludwig Drescher, Charles von Buchwald, Harald Hansen, Harald Bohr, Christian Middelboe, Nils Middelboe, Oscar Nielsen,[2] August Lindgren, Sofus Nielsen, Vilhelm Wolfhagen, Bjørn Rasmussen, Peter Marius Andersen, Johannes Gandil)

The Netherlands
(Reinier Beeuwkes, Karel Heijting, Louis Otten, Johan Sol, Johannes de Korver, Emil Mundt, Johan Kok, Jan Welcker, Edu Snethlage, Gerard Reeman, Jan Thomée, George de Bruyn Kops)

Sweden
(Oskar Bengtsson, Åke Fjästad, Teodor Malm, Nils Andersson, Sven Olsson, Hans Lindman, Olle Olsson, Valter Lidén, Sune Almkvist, Gustaf Bergström, Sven Ohlsson, Karl Ansén, Arvid Fagrell, Karl Gustafsson)

France "A"
(Maurice Tillette, Jules Dubly, V. Wibaut, Georges Bayrou, Roland Schubart, C. Renaux, Jean Fenouillere, Gaston Cypres, Albert François, Yves Albert, Émile Sartorius)

*See Notes on page 179.

France "B"

(François Desrousseaux, Jules Verlet, E. Morillon, Serge Dastarac, Victor Denis, Charles Bilot, Adrien Filez, P. Mathaux, H. Holgart, Fernand Jenicot, Marcel Eucher)

Tournament Summary

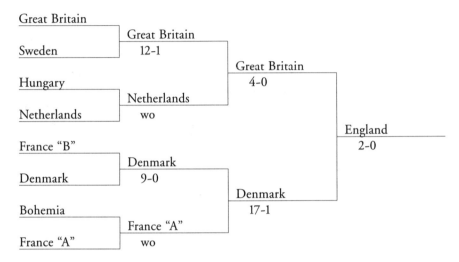

Third-Place Tournament

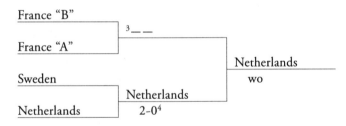

Match Summaries

19 October

Denmark   9   France "B"   0

   Time: 1500
   Attendance: 2,000
   Referee: Thomas Kyle
   Linesmen: E. C. Jarvis, L. F. Morrison
   Halftime: 4–0
   Goals: N. Middelboe [10: 1-0], Wolfhagen [2-0], Bohr [3-0], Wolfhagen [4-0], N. Middleboe [5-0], Bohr [6-0], S. Nielsen [7-0], Wolfhagen [8-0], Wolfhagen [9-0]
   Denmark (Drescher [G], von Buchwald [FB], Hansen [FB], Bohr [HB], Ch. Middelboe [HB], N. Middelboe [HB], O. Nielsen [F], Lindgren [F], S. Nielsen [F], Wolfhagen [F], Andersen [F])
   France "B" (Desrousseaux [G], Verlet [FB], Morillon [FB], Dastarac [HB], Denis [HB], Bilot [HB], Filez [F], Mathaux [F], Holgart [F], Jenicot [F], Eucher [F])

20 October

Great Britain   12   Sweden   1
  Time: 1500
  Attendance: 2,000
  Referee: John T. Ibbotson
  Linesmen: M. C. Frowde, Lt. W. C. Clover
  Halftime: 7–0
  Goals: Stapley [15: 1-0], Woodward [2-0], Berry [3-0], Chapman [4-0], Purnell [5-0], Stapley [6-0], Woodward [7-0], Bergström [65: 7-1], Purnell [8-1], Purnell [9-1], Hawkes [10-1], Hawkes [11-1], Purnell [12-1]
  Great Britain (Bailey [G], Corbett [FB], Smith [FB], Hunt [HB], Chapman [HB], Hawkes [HB], Berry [F], Woodward [F], Stapley [F], Purnell [F], Hardman [F])
  Sweden (Bengtsson [G], Fjästad [FB], Malm [FB], S. Olsson [HB], Lindman [HB], O. Olsson [HB], Almkvist [F], Bergström [F], Sv. Ohlsson [F], Ansén [F], Gustafsson [F]).

22 October

Great Britain   4   The Netherlands   0
  Time: 1300
  Attendance: 6,000
  Referee: John T. Howcroft
  Linesmen: H. Gray, W. E. Roberts
  Halftime: 1–0
  Goals: Stapley [37: 1-0], Stapley [60: 2-0], Stapley [64: 3-0], Stapley [75: 4-0]
  Great Britain (Bailey [G], Corbett [FB], Smith [FB], Hunt [HB], Chapman [HB], Hawkes [HB], Berry [F], Woodward [F], Stapley [F], Purnell [F], Hardman [F])
  The Netherlands (Beeuwkes [G], Heijting [FB], Otten [FB], Sol [HB], de Korver [HB], Mundt [HB], Welcker [F], Snethlage [F], Reeman [F], Thomée [F], de Bruyn Kops [F])

Denmark   17   France "A"   1
  Time: 1500
  Attendance: 1,000
  Referee: Thomas P. Campbell
  Linesmen: F. Lockwood, A. C. Hines
  Halftime: 6–1
  Goals: S. Nielsen [3: 1-0], S. Nielsen [4: 2-0], S. Nielsen [6: 3-0], Sartorius [16: 3-1], Lindgren [18: 4-1], Lindgren [37: 5-1], S. Nielsen [39: 6-1], S. Nielsen [46: 7-1], S. Nielsen [48: 8-1], S. Nielsen [52: 9-1], Wolfhagen [60: 10-1], S. Nielsen [64: 11-1], S. Nielsen [66: 12-1], N. Middelboe [68: 13-1], Wolfhagen [72: 14-1], S. Nielsen [76: 15-1], Wolfhagen [82: 16-1], Wolfhagen [89: 17-1]
  Denmark (Drescher [G], von Buchwald [FB], Hansen [FB], Bohr [HB], Ch. Middelboe [HB], N. Middelboe [HB], Gandil [F], Lindgren [F], S. Nielsen [F], Wolfhagen [F], Rasmussen [F])
  France "A" (Tillette [G], Dubly [FB], Wibaut [FB], Bayrou [HB], Schubart [HB], Renaux [HB], Fenouillere [F], Cypres [F], François [F], Albert [F], Sartorius [F])

23 October

The Netherlands   2   Sweden   0
  Time: 1500

Attendance: 1,000
Referee: John Hargreaves Pearson
Linesmen: unknown
Halftime: 1–0
Goals: Reeman [6: 1-0], Snethlage [58: 2-0]
The Netherlands (Beeuwkes [G], Heijting [FB], Otten [FB], Sol [HB], de Korver [HB], Kok [HB], Welcker [F], Snethlage [F], Reeman [F], Thomée [F], de Bruyn Kops [F])
Sweden (Bengtsson [G], Fjästad [FB], Andersson [FB], Olsson [HB], Lindman [HB], Lidén [HB], Fagrell [F], Bergström [F], Olle Olsson [F], Gustafsson [F], Ansén [F])

24 October

Great Britain   2   Denmark   0
Time: 1500
Attendance: 8,000
Referee: John Lewis
Linesmen: F. Styles, H. Woollett
Halftime: 1–0
Goals: Chapman [20: 1-0], Woodward [46: 2-0]
Great Britain (Bailey [G], Corbett [FB], Smith [FB], Hunt [HB], Chapman [HB], Hawkes [HB], Berry [F], Woodward [F], Stapley [F], Purnell [F], Hardman [F])
Denmark (Drescher [G], von Buchwald [FB], Hansen [FB], Bohr [HB], Ch. Middelboe [HB], N. Middelboe [HB], O. Nielsen [F], Lindgren [F], S. Nielsen [F], Wolfhagen [F], Rasmussen [F])

Goal Scoring Summary

Sofus Nielsen [DEN]	11	Robert Hawkes [GBR]	2
Vilhelm Wolfhagen [DEN]	8	August Lindgren [DEN]	2
Henry Stapley [GBR]	6	Gustaf Bergström [SWE]	1
Clyde Purnell [GBR]	4	Arthur Berry [GBR]	1
Nils Middelboe [DEN]	3	Gerard Reeman [NED]	1
Vivian Woodward [GBR]	3	E. Sartorius [FRA]	1
Harald Bohr [DEN]	2	Edu Snethlage [NED]	1
Frederick Chapman [GBR]	2		

NOTES

1. FW has 68. EK and OSVK have 72.
2. Often listed as Oscar Nielsen-Nørlund, but Oscar Nielsen did not change his name to Nielsen-Nørlund until 1914.
3. Neither team showed for this match which was cancelled.
4. FW incorrectly lists the score of this match as 2-1.

Gymnastics

Very little is known about the gymnastics events of the 1908 Olympic Games. There was an individual and a team event, both held in the infield of the White City Stadium. The contests were conducted under the rules of the Amateur Gymnastic Association of Great Britain.

It should be noted that in the team competition, it does not appear that the current system of distributing Olympic medals was followed. According to the *Official Report*, the first place team received a gold medal, and the team members each received silver medals. The second place team received a silver medal and the team members each received bronze medals. No prize is mentioned for the third place team.

We have not been able to obtain complete results for the individual gymnastics event, and it is the only event at the 1908 Olympic Games for which these results are not available. Sources consulted in an effort to find these results include the following: *Official Report*, *Sporting Life*, all major British and American newspapers, multiple Olympic record books, the Fédération Internationale de Gymnastique (FIG), the National Governing Bodies of gymnastics for every nation which competed in 1908 gymnastics, Olympic historians for every country which competed in 1908 gymnastics, the gymnastics historians of the United States, Canada, Great Britain, and Germany, and gymnastics magazines from 1908 in the United States, France, Great Britain, and Germany.

The results must exist somewhere, as is evident from Tony Bijkerk and Ruud Paauw's book on Dutch Olympians, *Gouden Boek van de Nederlandse Olympiers*, which contains the placements for all the Dutch gymnasts.[1]* Tony Bijkerk, Secretary-General of the International Society of Olympic Historians (ISOH) kindly provided us with the original Dutch article which gave these placements and scores for the Dutch gymnasts. Unfortunately, it contains no other placements or marks, and gives no source for its marks. In addition, places and marks are known for the gymnasts of Bohemia, Canada, Finland, and Hungary.

Site:	White City Stadium, Shepherd's Bush, London
Dates:	14–16 July
Events:	2
Competitors:	326
Nations:	13

*See Notes on pages 187–188.

Competitors		1st	2nd	3rd	Totals
Belgium	2	-	-	-	-
Bohemia	2	-	-	-	-
Canada	2	-	-	-	-
Denmark	24	-	-	-	-
Finland	31	-	-	1	1
France	59	-	-	1	1
Germany	11	-	-	-	-
Great Britain	65	-	1	-	1
Hungary	6	-	-	-	-
Italy	32	1	-	-	1
The Netherlands	23	-	-	-	-
Norway	30	-	1	-	1
Sweden	38	1	-	-	1
Totals	325	2	2	2	6
Nations[2]	13	2	2	2	6

Officials

Team Competition

Judges: John Adams, Lt. Grenfell, Lt. Lockhart Leith

Reserve Judge: Major C. Moore

Timekeepers: —— Cooker, —— Faith, —— French, —— Hall, —— Haskins, A. Holloway, —— Larchin, A. J. Perring, H. W. Rendell, —— Sandon, —— Syers, A. Fattorini

Chief Steward: H. E. Williams (Birmingham Athletic Club)

Deputy Chief Steward: F. W. Stevens (Southern Counties AGA)

English Stewards/Whips: —— Bath, —— Bass, —— Baxter, —— Booker, —— Dodd, —— English, Anthony Fattorini, T. E. Marr, A. Mosley, G. Mortimer, —— Partridge, H. W. Rendell, —— Rickards, —— Rodgers, G. F. Simmons, —— Taylor, W. T. Walton, —— Ward, W. O. Williams, —— Woodman

Scottish Stewards/Whips: —— Cullen, R. McGaw, —— McGregor, —— Scott, W. F. Wood

Welsh Stewards/Whips: —— Baker, —— Cowig, W. Fitt, —— Hawkins, C. V. Suderman, E. A. Watkins

Scorers: Harry J. Barclay (chief), —— Chesterton, —— Cole, —— Duffy, —— Keath, —— Lambert, —— Mortimer, —— Munroe, —— Parkinson, F. G. Perring, —— Ridout, —— Turner, —— Wilson

Medical Officers: Dr. J. A. Howard, Dr. —— Bell

Individual Competition

Judges—Horizontal Bar (swinging): J. Dallas (Midland Counties AGA), W. G. Millar (Scottish AGA), E. R. Rogers (Midland Counties AGA)

Judges—Horizontal Bar (slow): F. R. B. Emslie (Southern Counties AGA), B. M. Lloyd (Midland Counties AGA), T. White (Welsh AGA)

Judges—Parallel Bars (mixed): A. Barnard (Southern Counties AGA), D. C. Stuart (Scottish AGA), J. H. Tindall (Liverpool Gymnastic League)

Judges—Rings (steady): A. Grocock (Southern Counties AGA), S. Platt (Midland Counties AGA), S. Stewart (Midland Counties AGA)

Judges — Rings (flying): F. Jeans (Welsh AGA), W. Paterson (Scottish AGA), Dr. R. Ury (Liverpool District League)

Judges — Horse: H. L. Cain (Southern Counties AGA), A. F. Jenkin (Southern Counties AGA), E. Richardson (Southern Counties AGA)

Judges — Rope Climbing: D. Maule (Scottish AGA), G. Howells (Welsh AGA), E. Wilson (Yorkshire AGA)

Reserve Judges: -- Burfield, H. Cooke, -- Drury, Felix Graf, -- Perrott, H. C. Potts, E. F. Richardson, S. Stewart

Combined Exercises, Individual, Men

A: 95³; C: 11; D: 14 –15 July; T: 1430 both days; F: Horizontal Bar (swinging and slow movements), Parallel Bars, Pommelled Horse, Rings (stationary and swinging movements), Rope Climb.

The individual championship was known in the *Official Report* as "The Heptathlon" because it encompassed seven events, although they were conducted on only five apparatuses. The winner was the Italian Alberto Braglia, who had been runner-up in both individual events at the 1906 Olympics in Athens. Braglia used his Olympic fame to become a circus performer. Working on a trapeze, he sustained a serious injury from a fall in 1910. But he recovered from that setback to return in 1912 at Stockholm, where he defended his Olympic title in individual gymnastics. He then turned professional, returning to the circus as an acrobat. Braglia later returned to gymnastics and coached the Italian team at the 1932 Olympics.

1.	Alberto Braglia	ITA	317.00
2.	S. Walter Tysal	GBR	312.00
3.	Louis Ségura	FRA	297.00
4.	Curt Steuernagel	GER	273.50
5.	Friedrich Wolf	GER	267.00
6.	Samuel Hodgetts	GBR	266.00⁴
7.	Marcel Lalu	FRA	258.75
8.	Robert Diaz	FRA	258.50
9.	Edward Potts	GBR	252.50
10.	Jules Rolland	FRA	249.50
11.	François Nidal	FRA	249.00
=12.	George Bailey	GBR	246.00
	Karl Borchert⁵	GER	246.00
14.	Antoine Costa	FRA	241.75
15.	János Nyisztor	HUN	236.00
=16.	Franklin Dick	GBR	233.50
	Arthur Hodges	GBR	233.50
18.	Georges Thurnheer	FRA	232.00
19.	Guido Romano	ITA	230.00⁶
20.	Jean Castigliano	FRA	227.00
21-24.	gymnasts and marks not known		
25.	Josef Čada	BOH	⁷
26-33.	gymnasts and marks not known		
34.	Kálmán Szabó	HUN	209.00

35.	gymnast and mark not known		
36.	Bohumil Honzátko	BOH	20–.––[8]
37-38.	gymnasts and marks not known		
39.	Imre Géllert	HUN	202.00
40-44.	gymnasts and marks not known		
45.	Mihály Antos	HUN	198.00
46-48.	gymnasts and marks not known		
49.	Michel Biet	NED	187.50
50-59.	gymnasts and marks not known		
59.	Allan Keith	CAN	[9]
60.	Gerardus Wesling	NED	165.00
61.	Reiner Blom	NED	160.50
62.	I. Goudeket	NED	159.00
63.	Johannes Stikkelman	NED	159.00
64.	E. Brouwer	NED	158.00
65.	gymnast and mark not known		
66.	Johannes Posthumus	NED	155.50
67-68.	gymnasts and marks not known		
69.	Dirk Janssen	NED	153.50
70.	gymnast and mark not known		
71.	Cornelis Becker	NED	152.50
72.	Jan Janssen[10]	NED	150.50
73.	gymnast and mark not known		
74.	Jan Jacob Kieft	NED	149.50
75.	Richard "Riku" Korhonen	FIN	143.50
76-77.	gymnasts and marks not known		
78.	Abraham Mok	NED	141.00
79.	gymnast and mark not known		
80.	Orville Elliott	CAN	[11]
81-82.	gymnasts and marks not known		
83.	Hendricus Thijsen	NED	127.00
84-89.	gymnasts and marks not known		
90.	Johann Flemer	NED	118.50
91-92.	gymnasts and marks not known		
93.	Constantijn van Daalen	NED	116.50
94.	gymnast and mark not known		
95.	Herman van Leeuwen	NED	101.00
96.	Jonas Slier	NED	96.00
	Frigyes Gráf	HUN	DNF
AC.[12]	Antoine De Buck	BEL	
	Jean Van Guysse	BEL	
	Eetu Kosonen	FIN	
	Iivari Partanen	FIN	
	Jaska Saarivuori	FIN	
	David Teivonen	FIN	[13]
	Edouard Boisléve	FRA	
	Alfred Castille	FRA	
	Ferdinand Castille	FRA	
	Georges Charmoille	FRA	

Victor Dubois	FRA
Dominique Follacci	FRA
E. Gauthier	FRA
F. Lekim	FRA
Justinien Lux	FRA
G. Mounier	FRA
Georges Ratelot	FRA
E. Aspinall	GBR
Oliver Bauscher	GBR
Joseph Cook	GBR
S. Domville	GBR
E. Dyson	GBR
W. Fergus	GBR
A. Ford	GBR
J. Graham	GBR
R. Hanley	GBR
Leonard Hanson	GBR
G. Meade	GBR
C. H. Smith	GBR
J. A. Walters	GBR
W. Watters	GBR
August Ehrlich	GER
Paul Fischer	GER
Georg Karth	GER
Wilhelm Kaufmann	GER
Carl Körting	GER
Josef Krämer	GER
Heinrich Siebenhaar	GER
Wilhelm Weber	GER
Ferenc Szűts	HUN
Otello Capitani	ITA
Conrad Carlsrud	NOR
Petter Hol	NOR
Eugen Ingebretsen	NOR
Ole Iversen	NOR
Per Mathias Jespersen	NOR
Carl Klæth	NOR
Frithjof Olsen	NOR
John Skrataas	NOR

14

Combined Exercises, Team, Men

A: 254[15]; C: 8; D: 14-16 July; T: 14 July —1430 (Denmark), 1600 (Great Britain); 15 July —1430 (Finland), 1515 (France), 1600 (Sweden); 16 July —1430 (The Netherlands), 1515 (Norway), 1600 (Italy); F: Consisted of voluntary mass exercises, by teams of 16 to 40 competitors. The time limit for the exercise was 30 minutes per team. Team possible: 480 points.

1. Sweden   438.00
    (Gösta Åsbrink, Carl Bertilsson, Andreas Cervin, Hjalmar Cedercrona, Rudolf Degermark, Carl Folcker, Sven Forssman, Erik Granfelt, Carl Hårleman, Nils Hellsten, Gunnar Höjer, Arvid Holmberg, Carl Holmberg, Oswald Holmberg, Hugo Jahnke, Johan Jarlén, Gustaf Johnsson, Rolf Johnsson, Nils Kantzow, Sven Landberg, Olle Lanner, Axel Ljung, Osvald Moberg, Carl Norberg, Erik Norberg, Tor Norberg, Axel Norling, Daniel Norling, Gösta Olson, Leonard Peterson, Sven Rosén, Gustaf "Gösta" Rosenquist, Axel Sjöblom, Birger Sörvik, Haakon Sörvik, Karl-Johan Svensson (Sarland), Karl Gustaf Vindqvist, Nils Widforss)

2. Norway   425.00
    (Arthur Amundsen, Carl "Flisa" Andersen, Otto Authén, Hermann Bohne, Trygve Bøyesen, Oskar Bye, Conrad Carlsrud, Sverre Grøner, Harald Halvorsen, Harald Hansen, Petter Hol, Eugen Ingebretsen, Ole Iversen, Per Mathias Jespersen, Sigurd "Sigge" Johannessen, Nicolai Kiær, Carl Klæth, Thor Larsen, Rolf Lefdahl, Hans Lem, Anders Moen, Frithjof Olsen, Carl Pedersen, Paul Pedersen, John Skrataas, Harald Smedvik, Sigvard Sivertsen, Andreas Strand, Olaf Syvertsen, Thomas Torstensen)

3. Finland   405.00
    (Eino Forsström, Otto Granström, Johan Kemp, Iivari Kyykoski, Heikki Lehmusto, John Lindroth, Yrjö Linko, Edvard Linna, Matti Markkanen, Kaarle "Källe" Mikkolainen, Veli Nieminen, Källe Paasia, Arvi Pohjanpää, Aarne Pohjonen, Eino Railio, Heikki Riipinen, Arno Saarinen, Einar Sahlstein, Aarne Salovaara, Karl Viktor Sandelin, Elis Sipilä, Viktor Smeds, Kaarlo Soinio, Kurt Stenberg, Väinö Tiiri, Magnus Wegelius)

4. Denmark   378.00
    (Carl Andersen, Hans Bredmose, Jens Chiewitz, Arvor Hansen, Christian Hansen, Ingvardt Hansen, Einar Hermann, Knud Holm, Poul Holm, Oluf Husted-Nielsen, Charles Jensen, Gorm Jensen, Hendrik Johansen, Harald Klem, Robert Madsen, Vigo Meulengracht-Madsen, Lukas Nielsen, Oluf Olsson, Niels Petersen, Nicolai Philipsen, Hendrik Rasmussen, Viktor Rasmussen, Marius Thuesen, Niels Turin-Nielsen)

5. France   319.00
    (Lucien Bogart, Albert Borizée, Henri de Breyne, Nicolas Constant, Charles Courtois, Louis Delattre, A. Delecluse, Louis Delecluse, Georges Demarle, Joseph Derov, Charles Desmarcheliers, Claude Desmarcheliers, Étienne Dharaney, Gérard Donnet, Émile Duhamel, A. Duponcheel, Paul Durin, A. Eggremont, G. Guiot, L. Hennebicq, Henri Hubert, Daniel Hudels, E. Labitte, L. Lestienne, R. Lis, Victor Magnier, G. Nys, Joseph Parent, Louis Pappe, V. Polidori, Gustave Pottier, Antoine Pinoy, Louis Sandray, Émile Schmoll, Edouard Steffe, E. Vercruysse, Hugo Vergin, E. Vicogne, Jules Walmée, G. Warlouzer)

6. Italy   316.00
    (Alfredo Accorsi, Nemo Agordi, Umberto Agliorini, Adriano Andreani, Vincenzo Blo, Flaminio Bottoni, Bruto Buozzi, Giovanni Bonati, Pietro Borsetti, Adamo Bozzani, Gastone Calabresi, Carlo Celada, Tito Collevati, Antonio Cotichini, Guido Cristofori, Stanislao Di Chiara, Giovanni Gasperini, Amedeo Marchi, Carlo Marchiandi, Ettore Massari, Roberto Nardini, Gaetano Preti, Decio Pavani, Gino Ravenna, Massimo Ridolfi, Gustavo Taddia, Giannetto Termanini, Ugo Savonuzzi, Gioacchino Vaccari)

7.   The Netherlands   297.00
    (Cornelis Becker, Michel Biet, Jan de Boer, Reiner Blom, Jan Bolt, E. Brouwer, Constan-
    tijn van Daalen, Johann Flemer, Johannes Göckel, I. Goudeket, Dirk Janssen, Jan Jacob
    Kieft, Salomon Konijn, Herman van Leeuwen, Abraham Mok, Abraham de Oliveira,
    Johannes Posthumus, Johan Schmitt, Jonas Slier, Johannes Stikkelman, Hendricus Thi-
    jsen, Gerardus Wesling)

8.   Great Britain   196.00
    (P. A. Baker, W. F. Barrett, R. Bonney, J. H. Catley, M. Clay, E. Clough, J. Cotterell, W.
    Cowy, G. C. Cullen, F. Denby, Herbert Drury, W. Fitt, H. Gill, A. S. Harley, Arthur
    Hawkins, William Hoare, J. A. Horridge, H. J. Huskinson, J. W. Jones, E. Justice, N. J.
    Keighley, R. Laycock, R. McGaw, J. McPhail, W. Manning, W. G. Merrifield, C. J.
    Oldaker, G. Parrott, E. Parsons, E. F. Richardson, J. Robertson, George Ross, D. Scott,
    J. F. Simpson, W. R. Skeeles, J. Speight, H. Stell, C. V. Suderman, William Tilt, Charles
    Vigurs, E. Walton, H. Waterman, E. A. Watkins, John Whitaker, F. Whitehead)
    [16]

Exhibitions

Gymnastic Exhibitions

A number of gymnastic exhibitions were conducted during the 1908 Olympic Games. They
were as follows:

Date   *Time*   *Teams*

13 July   1630   Teams from Denmark, Norway and Sweden.

15 July   1630   Female gymnasts from Denmark, the Northern Polytechnic Institute, and the
                   ladies' section of the Yorkshire Amateur Gymnastic Association. The Dan-
                   ish gymnasts were led by Hann Lønborg Nielsen, and the team members
                   were: Ann Bork, Agnes Boserup, Inger Briehm-Hansen, Astrid Dalberg,
                   Elise Dujardin, Erna Gad, Laura Gad, Sara Hansen, Sigrid Hertel, Emma
                   Køster, Gerda Liebetrau, Marie Michelsen, Camilla Neve, Anna Nielsen,
                   Estrid Nielsen, Margrethe Nielsen, Sophie Otterstrøm, Ingeborg Randrup,
                   Inger Rubin, Ester Schrøder, Ellen Tscherning, and Ellen Wolfhagen.

15 July   1800   Groups from the Metropolitan and Southern Counties Amateur Gymnastic
                   Association. The clubs taking part were as follows: Boys' Brigade 1st South
                   Essex Company, Bowes' Gymnastic Society, Bowes' Ladies' Gymnastic Soci-
                   ety, Bromley Gymnastic Club, Camden Gymnastic Club, City of London
                   College Gymnastic Club, Christ Church Gymnastic Club, German Gym-
                   nastic Society, Marylebone Youths' Gymnastic Club, Northampton Insti-
                   tute Gymnastic Club, Northampton Institute Women's Gymnastic Club,
                   Orion Gymnastic Club, Perry Hill Gymnastic Club, Surrey Commercial
                   Docks Athletic Club, St. Andrews (Newington), St. Alban's Gymnastics
                   Club (Rotherhithe), St. Matthew's (Bayswater), St. Paul's (Canonbury),
                   St. Paul's (Paddington), Woodsrange Gymnastic Club, Wood Green Gym-
                   nastic Club, and West Ham League.

16 July	1645	Dutch Team.
16 July	1730	Norwegian Team.
16 July	1800	Battersea Polytechnic Team.
17 July	1800	Exibitions were given by the Borough Polytechnic, the Woolwich Polytechnic, and the Regent Street Polytechnic.
18 July	1800	Gymnasts from the Bristol Secondary Schools.
18 July	1900	Gymnasts from the Yorkshire Amateur Athletic Association.

NOTES

1. The source was a 1908 magazine published by the Dutch Gymnastic Association.

2. It is often mentioned that Turkey had a competitor in 1908 gymnastics, Aleko Mulos, who would have been the first Olympic competitor from Turkey (excluding the unusual situation involving 1906 Turkish Olympians — see the 1906 book in this series). However, although he was entered, there is no evidence that Mulos actually competed.

3. DW, EK, and FW have 12 nations. VK has 106 starters. OSVK has 93 starters, however, he does list a ninety-fifth and ninety-sixth place and a DNF after that. In addition, his results actually include 94 gymnasts, although one is listed twice. The OR has 95 starters listed, and we have those 95 included below. The OR had 128 entrants, listing them all, and noted which did not start by brackets.

It is probable that there were actually 97 starters and that two of the gymnasts we list as non-starting entrants did actually compete. The reason for that is that Bijkerk and Paauw, in their book on Dutch Olympians, list two of their athletes as finishing ninety-fifth and ninety-sixth. There is also a Hungarian (Gráf) known to have competed without finishing, which would make him the ninety-seventh gymnast.

OSVK lists a P. A. Lemaire as competing, with no mark or place. Lemaire is listed in the OR as not competing. He also listed among those who also competed, with no mark or place, S. Walter Tysal, and listed him as Norway. Tysal was British and finished second in this event, and was also correctly listed by OSVK in that position. OSVK did not list the above competitors who were listed as competing in the OR: Gerardus Wesling (NED), Jan Janssen (NED), and Ferenc Szűts (HUN).

4. FW, and VK/OSVK have 265.00.

5. Borchert was not in the original entry lists.

6. Not listed in OSVK, who has Castigliano in nineteenth place. Romano is listed as nineteenth with 230.00 in SL and SLR. OR also does not list Romano, which is likely an error, as it usually copied SL and SLR.

7. Mark not known.

8. Exact mark not known but is must be between 200 and 209.

9. Per Lewis R. Waller, Canadian gymnastics historian. His source is *A History of Competitive Gymnastics in Canada*, by Reet Nurmberg, a research thesis done for a masters degree at the University of Edmonton (Alberta, Canada). Mark not known.

10. Jan Janssen was not in the original entry lists.

11. Per Lewis R. Waller, Canadian gymnastics historian. His source is *A History of Competitive Gymnastics in Canada*, by Reet Nurmberg, a research thesis done for a masters degree at the University of Edmonton (Alberta, Canada). Mark not known.

12. The following 49 gymnasts also competed and should fill the "gaps" listed above where we are uncertain of the exact placements.

13. Per Markku Siukonen, Finnish sources note that the others finished "about the same as Korhonen" (seventy-fifth). Presumably Korhonen was the top placing Finn, so we suspect the others finished between 76-90.

14. There were 128 entrants. The following 33 athletes were entered but did not compete: E. Franta (BOH), P. A. Lemaire (FRA), R. Behme (GER), Otto Franke (GER), Rudolf Kallmeyer (GER), M. Rank (GER), R. Schönecker (GER), K. Schwarz (GER), W. Simon (GER), C. Trippel (GER), W. Weser (GER), E. Dahinten (HUN), Béla Erődy (HUN), A. Gerhauser (HUN), Boldizsár Horváth (HUN), E. Spécz (HUN), A. Andreotti (ITA), E. Bacchelli (ITA), Rodrigo Bertinotti (ITA), P. Borghi (ITA), Emilio Brambilla (ITA), Cino Civinini (ITA), A. Fedi (ITA), C. Gualeni (ITA), Mario Gubiani (ITA), Filiberto Innocenti (ITA), Vitaliano Masotti (ITA), Serafino Mazzarocchi (ITA), Quintilio Mazzoncini (ITA), Spartaco Nerozzi (ITA), ... Racchetta (ITA), Romolo Tuzzi (ITA), and Hans Lem (NOR).

15. FW has 280 competitors. OSVK has 255.

16. Germany was also entered but did not compete.

Hockey (Field)

The English Hockey Association initially proposed that a combined team from England, Ireland, Scotland and Wales should represent Great Britain at the Games. The Irish did not take kindly to the suggestion, rejecting the proposal at an emergency committee meeting on 21 November 1907, and after Scotland and Wales followed the Irish line, four separate British teams took part. They were joined by a German team from the Uhlenhorster Hockey Club of Hamburg and a French team made up of players from Club Athletique International, Racing Club de France, and the Stade Français.

The first match of the tournament was between Germany and Scotland, who were unable to call on a number of their leading players because of injuries. A last minute inclusion in the Scottish team was Ivan Laing, who opened the scoring against Germany and has the distinction of scoring the first-ever goal in Olympic hockey. But after playing in Scotland's second Olympic match against England, Laing never represented his country again. Scotland defeated Germany 4–0, France lost to England 10–1, and the following morning the first round losers met in a "friendly" match with victory going to the Germans, who scored the only goal of the match. It is possible that this France/Germany match should probably not be considered as part of the Olympic tournament, but we have included it below for reference.

In the semi-finals played that afternoon Ireland beat Wales (3–1) and England enjoyed a comfortable victory over Scotland (6–1). The final was the sixth match to be played on the same pitch within three days and, understandably, the playing surface was not in the best of condition. Accurate passing and related skills became something of a lottery but England was clearly the better team and won, 8–1.

In view of their clear superiority it came as no surprise that England provided the outstanding player of the tournament. Reggie Pridmore individually scored 10 goals in three games, just one short of the combined total of 11 goals scored by all the other five competing nations.

When the England versus Ireland match ended, late in the afternoon of 31 October, the Games of the IVth Olympiad also ended, with virtually no fanfare. The "closing ceremony" had taken place months earlier, on 25 July, at the end of the Stadium events. There is no record of any ceremony on 31 October denoting the closing of the 1908 Olympic Games at the end of the match. However, *The Times* did note that this marked the end of the Olympics and the final official function of the 1908 Olympic Games came that night with a banquet at the Holborn Restaurant for Olympic officials and any remaining competitors.

Site:	White City Stadium, Shepherd's Bush, London
Dates:	29–31 October
Events:	1
Competitors:	68
Nations:	3 [6]

	Competitors	*1st*	*2nd*	*3rd*	*Totals*
France	12	-	-	-	-
Germany	11	-	-	-	-
Great Britain	45	1	1	2	4
GBR/Ireland	12	-	1	-	1
GBR/England	11	1	-	-	1
GBR/Scotland	11	-	-	1	1
GBR/Wales	11	-	-	1	1
Totals	68	1	1	2	4
Nations	3 [6]	1	1	1 [2]	1 [4]

Final Standings

A: 68[1]; C: 3; D: 29–31 October.

		W	*T*	*L*	*Pts*	*GF*	*GA*
1.	GBR/England	3	0	0	6	24	3
2.	GBR/Ireland	1	0	1	2	4	9
=3.	GBR/Scotland	1	0	1	2	5	6
	GBR/Wales	0	0	1	0	1	3
5.	Germany	1	0	1	2	1	4
6.	France	0	0	2	0	1	11

Team Rosters

Great Britain/England
(Harry Freeman, Harvey Wood, Louis Baillon, John Robinson, Edgar Page, Alan Noble, Percy Rees, Gerald Logan, Stanley Shoveller, Reginald Pridmore, Eric Green)

Great Britain/Ireland
(Edward Holmes, Henry Brown, Walter Peterson, Jack Peterson, William Graham, Walter Campbell, Henry Murphy, Charles Power, Richard Gregg, Edward Allman-Smith, Frank Robinson, Robert Kennedy)

Great Britain/Scotland
(John Burt, Hugh Neilson, Charles Foulkes, Hew Fraser, Alexander Burt, Andrew Dennistoun, Norman Stevenson, Ivan Laing, James Harper-Orr, Hugh Walker, William Orchardson)

*See Notes on page 193.

Great Britain/Wales
 (Bertrand Turnbull, Edward Richards, Llewellyn Evans, Charles Shephard, Richard Lyne, Frederick Connah, Frederick Phillips, Arthur Law, Philip Turnbull, James Williams, Wilfred Pallott)

Germany (Uhlenhorster Hockey Club, Hamburg)
 (Albert Stüdemann, Friedrich Rahe, Alfons Brehm, Elard Dauelsberg, Franz Diederichsen, Carl Ebert, Mauricio Galvao, Raulino Galvao, Fritz Möding, Friedrich Uhl, Jules Fehr)

France
 (René Salarnier, L. Saulnier, F. Roux, R. P. Aublin, L. Gautier, R. Benoit, D. Baidet, D. M. Girard, L. Poupon, André Bonnal, C. Pattin, F. Versini²)

Tournament Summary

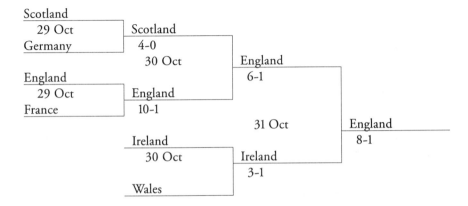

Extra Match

Germany
  30 Oct   Germany
France   1-0

Match Summaries

29 October

GBR/Scotland   4   Germany   0
    Time: 1345
    Halftime: 3–0
    Umpires: E. Fletcher, J. A. Kirkwood
    Goals: Scotland: Burt (2), Laing, Walker.
    Scotland (J. Burt [G], H. Neilson [FB], C. Foulkes [FB], H. Fraser [HB], A. Burt [HB], A. Dennistoun [HB], N. Stevenson [F], I. Laing [F], J. Harper-Orr [F], H. Walker [F], W. Orchardson [F])
    Germany (C. Ebert [G], E. Dauelsberg [FB], A. Stüdemann [FB], R. Galvao [HB], A. Brehm

[HB], M. Galvao [HB], F. Möding [F], F. Rahe [F], F. Diederichsen [F], J. Fehr [F], F. Uhl [F])

GBR/England   10   France   1
Time: 1500
Halftime: 4–0
Umpires: E. P. Denny, T. Burman
Goals: England: Pridmore (3), Shoveller (3), Logan (2), Rees, Green; France: Poupon.
England (H. Wood [G], H. Freeman [FB], L. Baillon [FB], J. Robinson [HB], E. Page [HB], A. Noble [HB], P. Rees [F], G. Logan [F], S. Shoveller [F], R. Pridmore [F], E. Green [F])
France (R. Salarnier [G], L. Saulnier [FB], F. Roux [FB], R. Aublin [HB], L. Gautier [HB], R. Benoit [HB], D. Baidet [F], D. Girard [F], L. Poupon [F], A. Bonnal [F], C. Pattin [F])

30 October

Germany   1   France   0
Time: Morning
Halftime: 1–0
Umpires: not known
Goal: Germany: Möding.
Germany (C. Ebert [G], E. Dauelsberg [FB], A. Stüdemann [FB], M. Galvao [HB], A. Brehm [HB]. R. Galvao [HB], J. Fehr [F], F. Möding [F], F. Uhl [F], F. Diederichsen [F], F. Rahe [F])
France (R. Salarnier [G], L. Saulnier [FB], R. Benoit [FB], R. Aublin [HB], L. Gautier [HB], F. Versini [F], D. Girard [F], L. Poupon [F], F. Roux [F], A. Bonnal [F], C. Pattin [F])

GBR/Ireland   3   GBR/Wales   1
Time: 1345
Halftime: 2-1
Umpires: G. H. Lings, H. J. Greening
Goals: Ireland: Robinson, Power, Gregg; Wales: Williams.
Ireland (E. Holmes [G], H. Brown [FB], W. Peterson [FB], W. Graham [HB], W. Campbell [HB], H. Murphy [HB], C. Power [F], R. Gregg [F], E. Allman-Smith [F], F. Robinson [F], R. Kennedy [F]);
Wales (B. Turnbull [G], E. Richards [FB], L. Evans [FB], C. Shephard [HB], R. Lyne [HB], F. Connah [HB], F. Phillips [F], A. Law [F], P. Turnbull [F], J. Williams [F], W. Pallott [F])

GBR/England   6   GBR/Scotland   1
Time: 1500
Halftime: 2–0
Umpires: Henry M. Tennent, E. T. S. Wilson
Goals: England: Pridmore (3), Shoveller (2), Logan; Scotland: Walker.
Rosters: *England* (H. Wood [G], H. Freeman [FB], L. Baillon [FB], J. Robinson [HB], E. Page [HB], A. Noble [HB], P. Rees [F], G. Logan [F], S. Shoveller [F], R. Pridmore [F], E. Green [F]);
Scotland (J. Burt [G], H. Neilson [FB], C. Foulkes [FB], H. Fraser [HB], A. Burt [HB], A. Dennistoun [HB], N. Stevenson [F], I. Laing [F], J. Harper-Orr [F], H. Walker [F], W. Orchardson [F])

31 October

GBR/England   8   GBR/Ireland   1
   Time: 1500
   Attendance: 5,000
   Halftime: 3–0
   Umpires: M. Baker, G. H. Morton[3]
   Goals: England: Pridmore (4), Shoveller (2), Logan (2); Ireland: Robinson.
   England (H. Wood [G], H. Freeman [FB], L. Baillon [FB], J. Robinson [HB], E. Page [HB], A. Noble [HB], P. Rees [F], G. Logan [F], S. Shoveller [F], R. Pridmore [F], E. Green [F])
   Ireland (E. Holmes [G], J. Peterson [FB],[4] W. Peterson [FB], W. Graham [HB], W. Campbell [HB], H. Murphy [HB], C. Power [F], R. Gregg [F], E. Allman-Smith [F], F. Robinson [F], R. Kennedy [F])

     Goal Scoring Summary

Reginald Pridmore [ENG]	10	Percy Rees [ENG]	1
Stanley Shoveller [ENG]	7	Eric Green [ENG]	1
Gerald Logan [ENG]	5	Richard Gregg [IRL]	1
Alexander Burt [SCO]	2	Fritz Möding [GER]	1
Frank Robinson [IRL]	2	L. Poupon [FRA]	1
Hugh Walker [SCO]	2	Charles Power [IRL]	1
Ivan Laing [SCO]	1	James Williams [WLS]	1

NOTES

1. EK, FW, and VK/OSVK have 66. The new athletes we include are the Irish player Jack Peterson and the French player F. Versini. See footnotes below concerning those players. Disputing the inclusion of Versini is certainly understandable.

2. Versini's status as an Olympian depends on the interpretation of the "friendly" match played between France and Germany. He competed only in that match. If it is not considered as part of the Olympic tournament he is not considered an Olympic competitor by the strict definition of actually having competed.

3. The OR lists Baker and ETS Wilson, but *Times* and TF give GH Morton in place of Wilson.

4. In this match against Wales, Jack Peterson replaced Henry Brown at fullback. Per *Hockey in Ireland* by TSC Dagg (1944) and confirmed by *Times,* 2 Nov 1908. The OR does not mention this and has Brown at fullback.

Jeu de Paume
(Tennis [Court/Real Tennis])

Jeu de Paume, also known by the names of court tennis, royal tennis, real tennis, or in 1908, simply "tennis," is the original racket sport. It is played indoors on a dédan, with a very complicated system of scoring. Finesse and strategy count for far more than power compared to what was then called lawn tennis.

Professional tennis has crowned a world champion since the mid-eighteenth-century in a series of challenge matches, not unlike professional boxing or chess. The greatest professional players of the era were British, Peter Latham and Cecil "Punch" Fairs. Latham had claimed the title in 1895, and defended it in 1898 and 1904, but lost it in 1905 to Fairs, who again defeated him in 1906. Latham regained the championship in 1907 and 1908, with Fairs claiming the championship again later in 1908 and winning his final championship in 1910. Because of the amateur restrictions, neither could compete in the Olympics.

Among the amateurs, the top British player in 1908 was Eustace Miles who was Amateur Tennis Champion in 1899–1903, 1905–1906, and 1909–1910. He had also been American champion in 1900. But the top player of the era was an American, the youthful Jay Gould, the son of the well-known robber baron of the Gilded Age of the late nineteenth century. Gould won the American championship in 1906–1917 and 1920–1925. He was also British champion in 1907 and 1908 and would later become world professional champion in 1914 and 1916.

The entries were all from Great Britain and the United States. The *Official Report* and *The Times* expressed regret that the top French "*paumiers*" did not enter, notably M. A. de Luze and M. Basin. Both Miles and Gould entered the Olympic tournament, setting up a match between the top amateur players of the era. The only other non-British entrant was Charles Sands, who had been U.S. champion in 1905, and won the gold medal in men's golf at the 1900 Olympics in Paris.

Gould and Miles were the class of the tournament. Miles got to the final by winning three matches by 3–0, and Gould, who had received an opening round bye, won two matches by 3–0. In the final, Gould also won all three sets, but it was a well-fought match, the set scores being close at 6–5, 6–4, and 6–4. Miles actually led every set, but could not close out Gould. Miles had a 4–1 and 5–2 advantage in the first set, but lost the last four games of that set. He likewise lost the last three games of the second set after leading 4–3, and with the third set even at 4-4, Gould closed out the match by winning the last two games.

194

The precise scoring of the final was as follows, Gould always listed first: Set 1: 4-2 (1-0), 4-6 (1-1), 3-5 (1-2), 5-7 (1-3), 1-4 (1-4), 4-1 (2-4), 2-4 (2-5), 4-2 (3-5), 4-2 (4-5), 5-2 (5-5), 4-1 (6-5); Set 2: 4-0 (1-0), 3-5 (1-1), 4-0 (2-1), 2-4 (2-2), 2-4 (2-3), 4-1 (3-3), 0-4 (3-4), 4-2 (4-4), 5-3 (5-4), 4-2 (6-4); and Set 3: 2-4 (0-1), 2-4 (0-2), 6-4 (1-2), 2-4 (1-3), 5-3 (2-3), 4-1 (3-3), 4-1 (4-3), 2-4 (4-4), 4-2 (6-4), 5-3 (6-4).

Site:	Queen's Club, West Kensington, London			
Dates:	18–21, 23, 28 May			
Events:	1			
Competitors:	11			
Nations:	2			

	Competitors	1st	2nd	3rd	Totals
Great Britain	9	–	1	1	2
United States	2	1	–	–	1
Totals	11	1	1	1	3
Nations	2	1	1	1	2

Gentlemen's Singles

A: 11; C: 2; D: 18–21, 23, 28 May; F: Single-elimination.

1.	Jay Gould	USA
2.	Eustace Miles	GBR
3.	Neville Lytton	GBR
4.	Arthur Page	GBR
=5.	Edwin Biedermann	GBR
	Arthur Palmer	GBR
	Evan Noel	GBR
	Vane Pennell	GBR
=9.	Charles Tatham	GBR
	William Cazalet	GBR
	Charles Sands	USA

Tournament Draw

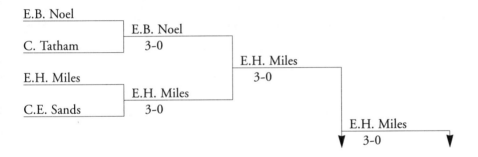

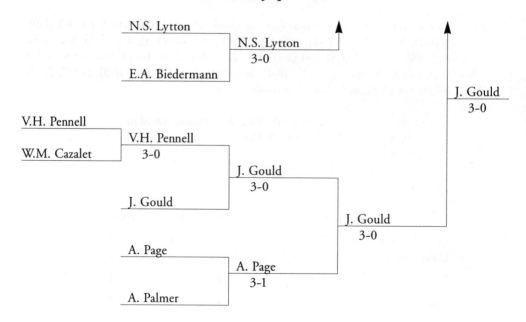

Match Summaries

Round One A: 6; C: 2; D: 18 May.

Noel d. Tatham	6-2, 6-3, 6-3
Miles d. Sands	6-3, 6-3, 6-3
Pennell d. Cazalet	6-1, 6-4, 6-1

Quarter-Finals A: 8; C: 2; D: 19-20 May.

Lytton d. Biedermann	6-5, 6-1, 6-2	(D: 19 May; T: 1230)
Page d. Palmer	5-6, 6-4, 6-5, 6-1	(D: 19 May; T: 1400)
Miles d. Noel	6-5, 6-1, 6-5	(D: 19 May; T: 1530)
Gould d. Pennell	6-3, 6-3, 6-2	(D: 20 May; T: 1430)

Semi-Final A: 4; C: 2; D: 21 May.

Gould d. Page	6-1, 6-0, 6-0	(T: 1430)
Miles d. Lytton	6-4, 6-1, 6-3	(T: 1600)

Finals A: 2; C: 2; D: 23 May; T: 1430.

Gould d. Miles	6-5, 6-4, 6-4

Third-Place Match A: 2; C: 1; D: 28 May.

Lytton d. Page	6-2, 6-4, 6-4

Lacrosse

Following the withdrawal of South Africa, only one match was played in the lacrosse tournament with Canada facing Great Britain for Olympic honors. The match was started at 1:00 P.M. (1300), immediately before the soccer final which resulted in a large crowd present for the lacrosse game. The vast majority of the spectators knew little of lacrosse and even those familiar with the game were often confused, as some rules had been modified to bring together certain differences in the Canadian and English laws. The goal crease was enlarged and special restrictions prevented an opponent from entering it. The ball was intermediate in weight between the lighter English ball and the heavier Canadian ball. Play was also divided into four quarters instead of two halves.

At the end of the first quarter Canada led 5–1 and then 6–2 at half-time after which some brilliant play by England tied the game at 9–9, before Canada rallied to win an excellent game, 14–10. Excellent sportsmanship was demonstrated during the match. When Canada's Angus Dillon broke his stick and was having difficulty finding a replacement, England's R. G. Martin agreed to stay out until Dillon returned. At the end of the game, the players exchanged sticks, shook hands and congratulated each other on a well-played match.

Previous Canadian lacrosse teams to visit England had been known simply as "The Canadians" and were usually from the Toronto area, but the Olympics marked the first time that a Canadian team had been selected on a nation-wide basis. Several trial games were held before team members from clubs as far apart as New Westminster in the west and Montreal in the east were finally chosen. The eventual make-up of the squad saw all parts of Canada represented: four members were from the Montreal Shamrocks, two from the Montreal Amateur Athletic Association, one from the Montreal Nationals, and two were from New Westminster. One player each came from Calgary, Ottawa, Cornwall, Toronto, St. Catharine's, and Orangeville. The British also took unusual care with selection and the painstaking selection process adopted by both countries resulted in a game of the highest quality.

Site:	White City Stadium, Shepherd's Bush, London
Date:	24 October
Events:	1
Competitors:	24
Nations:	2

	Competitors	1st	2nd	3rd	Totals
Canada	12	1	-	-	1
Great Britain	12	-	1	-	1
Totals	24	1	1	-	2
Nations	2	1	1	-	2

Final Standings

A: 24[1];* C: 2; D: 24 October; T: 1300; F: Single match between the two teams.

1. Canada
    (Frank Dixon, George "Doc" Campbell, Angus Dillon, Richard Duckett, George Rennie, Clarence McKerrow, Alexander Turnbull, Henry Hoobin, Ernest Hamilton, John Broderick, Thomas Gorman, Patrick Brennan [captain])

2. Great Britain
    (Charles Scott, G. Mason, H. W. Ramsey [captain], E. O. Dutton, J. Parker-Smith, Wilfrid Johnson, Norman Whitley, George Buckland, S. N. Hayes, Gustav Alexander, R. G. Martin, Edward Jones)

Match Summary

24 October

Canada	5	1	3	5	14
Great Britain	1	1	5	3	10

Time: 1300
Referee: A. Norris
Goal Judges: H. H. Allingham, V. Barker
Timekeepers: G. Nield, C. W. S. Crawley
Canada (F. Dixon [goal], G. Campbell [point], A. Dillon [cover point], R. Duckett [3rd man], G. Rennie [defense field], C. McKerrow [defense field], A. Turnbull [center/attack field], H. Hoobin [attack field], E. Hamilton [attack field/center], J. Broderick [3rd home], T. Gorman [2nd home], P. Brennan [1st home]);
Great Britain (C. Scott [goal], G. Mason [point], H. W. Ramsey [cover point], E. O. Dutton [3rd man], J. Parker-Smith [defense field], W. Johnson [defense field], N. Whitley [center], G. Buckland [attack field], S. Hayes [attack field], G. Alexander [3rd home], R. G. Martin [2nd home], E. Jones [1st home]).

Scoring Summary

Canada	-	unknown (first period, shortly after one minute)	1-0
Great Britain	-	Buckland (first period, about 2 minutes)	1-1

*See note on page 199.

Canada	–	Turnbull (first period)	2-1
Canada	–	Brennan (first period)	3-1
Canada	–	Brennan (first period)	4-1
Canada	–	unknown (first period)	5-1
Great Britain	–	Jones (second period)	5-2
Canada	–	unknown (second period)	6-2
Great Britain	–	Jones (third period)	6-3
Great Britain	–	Jones (third period)	6-4
Canada	–	Turnbull (third period)	7-4
Canada	–	Turnbull (third period)	8-4
Great Britain	–	Buckland (third period)	8-5
Great Britain	–	Buckland (third period)	8-5
Canada	–	unknown (third period)	9-6
Great Britain	–	Buckland (third period)	9-7
Great Britain	–	Jones (fourth period)	9-8
Great Britain	–	unknown (fourth period)	9-9
Canada	–	Brennan (fourth period)	10-9
Canada	–	Turnbull (fourth period)	11-9
Canada	–	Brennan (fourth period)	12-9
Canada	–	unknown (fourth period)	13-9
Canada	–	unknown (fourth period)	14-9
Great Britain	–	unknown (fourth period)	14-10

NOTES

1. OSVK incorrectly has 30.

Motorboating

The Olympic motorboat racing was originally scheduled to be held in mid-July but as the dates did not suit the Duke of Westminister or Lord Howard de Walden, they were postponed for more than a month. On the original date, these two influential figures were in America making an unsuccessful challenge for the "British International Cup."

The Olympic races were held under the auspices of the Motor Yacht Club from their club ship *Enchantress* in Southampton Water. All races consisted of five laps of a course of approximately eight nautical miles, for a total distance of 40 nautical miles. The competitions were marred by extremely poor weather conditions. In addition to the three Olympic events, there were several handicap events held concurrently at Southampton.

Motorboating never again appeared on the Olympic program and, in fact, it is not even permitted by the *Olympic Charter*. The current version of the *Olympic Charter* contains Rule 52.4.2, which states, "Sports, disciplines or events in which performance depends essentially on mechanical propulsion are not acceptable."

Site:	Southampton Water, Southampton, Southern Coast of England
Dates:	28–29 August
Events:	3 [2 Men; 1 Mixed]
Competitors:	14 [13 Men; 1 Woman]
Nations:	2 [2 Men; 1 Women]

Total	Competitors	1st	2nd	3rd	Totals
France	1	1	–	–	1
Great Britain	13	2	–	–	2
Totals	14	3	–	–	3
Nations	2	2	–	–	2

Women	Competitors	1st	2nd	3rd	Totals
Great Britain	1	–	–	–	–
Totals	1	–	–	–	–
Nations	1	–	–	–	–

A-Class (Open)

A: 7^{1*}; C: 2; D: 28–29 August; F: Two races, both of five laps of a course of approximately eight nautical miles for a total distance of 40 nautical miles. Open to boats of any length or power.

The winner, *Camille*, did not start in the race which, on the previous day, was abandoned after three laps due to adverse weather conditions. *Dylan*, who started in the abandoned race, did not compete in the re-scheduled race. The *Daily Telegraph* (31 August) refers to "Mr. Thubron and *his crew*," but the names of his crew members are not known. The report also mentions that "Mr. Thubron's boat was variously described during the day as *Camille*, *X*, and *Tréfle-à-Qua-tre*." In race two, the *Wolseley-Siddeley* ran aground and did not finish, giving the victory to *Camille*.

The "Yachting and Boating" volume (1916) in the *British Sports & Sportsmen* series states that Emile Thubron was British and that he entered his French-built boat for France in order to give an international flavor to the competition. Judging by his name, Emile Thubron's connection with France was probably stronger than the mere fact that *Camille* had been built there.

Race One A: 6; C: 1; D: 28 August.

AB. Great Britain   DNF   *[Wolseley-Siddeley]*
(Duke of Westminster, Winchester St. George Clowes, Joseph Frederick Laycock, G. H. Atkinson)

Great Britain   DNF   *[Dylan]*
(Lord Howard de Walden, A. G. Fentiman)

Race Two A: 5; C: 2; D: 29 August.

1. France   2-26:53   *[Camille]*
(Emile Thubron)

Great Britain   DNF   *[Wolseley-Siddeley]*
(Duke of Westminster, Winchester St. George Clowes, Joseph Frederick Laycock, G. H. Atkinson)

2

B-Class (Under 60 feet)

A: 5; C: 1; D: 28 August; F: five laps of a course of approximately eight nautical miles for a total distance of 40 nautical miles.

This class was limited to motorboats less than 60 feet in length, and with a total piston area not exceeding that of four cylinders, each of 106 mm. bore. It has not previously been published in a book that women competed in this sport, but *The Times* noted, "... it is worthy of special remark as an example of feminine endurance that Mrs. Gorham was also on board."

*See Notes on page 204.

1.   Great Britain   2-28:58.8[3]   *[Gyrinus]*
(Thomas Thornycroft, Bernard Redwood, John Field-Richards)

    Great Britain   DNF   *[Quicksilver]*
(John Marshall Gorham, Mrs. John Marshall Gorham)
[4]

C-Class

A: 5; C: 1; D: 29 August; F: five laps of a course of approximately eight nautical miles for a total distance of 40 nautical miles.

This class was limited to motorboats exceeding 6½ meters but less than 8 meters in length, weighing not less than 800 kg. without fuel or crew, and with a total piston area not exceeding that of four cylinders, each of 106 mm. bore. This race was very close until the *Sea Dog* was forced to stop due to a "hot bearing."[5]

1.   Great Britain   2-28:26   *[Gyrinus]*
(Thomas Thornycroft, Bernard Redwood, John Field-Richards)

    Great Britain   DNF   *[Sea Dog]*
(Warwick Wright, Thomas D. Wynn Weston)
[6]

NON-OLYMPIC (HANDICAP) EVENTS

Handicap Race #1

A: ?; C: 1; D: 28 August; F: Motorboats exceeding eight knots but not exceeding 15 knots. Three laps of the course, or about nine nautical miles in all.

1.   Great Britain   won by 3 minutes   *[Maudslay I]*   hdcp — 13:08
(C. C. Maudslay)

2.   Great Britain   *[Napier IV]*
[-- Hearman]
[7]

Handicap Race #2

A: ?: C: 1; D: 28 August; F: Motorboats not exceeding eight knots. Three laps of the course, or about nine nautical miles in all.

1.   Great Britain   1-02:50.4   *[Napier Major]*   hdcp — 5:03
(-- Hearman [owned by S. F. Edge])

2.   Great Britain   1-04:22.6   *[Cid]*   hdcp — 3:12
(unknown crew [owned by Commander Mansfield Cummings])

3.   Great Britain   1-06:19.6   *[Commander]*   hdcp — 1:55
(unknown crew [owned by Commander Mansfield Cummings])

Handicap Race #3

A: ?; C: 1; D: 29 August; F: Motorboats not exceeding eight knots.

1.   Great Britain   *[Commander]*
(crew unknown [owned by Commander Mansfield Cummings])
2.   Great Britain   *[Cannibal]*
(crew unknown [owned by Mr. H. S. Benzice])
3.   Great Britain   1:21 bh1   *[Napier Major]*
(crew unknown [owned by Mr. S. F. Edge])
     Great Britain   *[Microbe]*
(crew unknown [owned by Mr. G. H. Atkinson])
     Great Britain   *[Squirt]*
(crew unknown [owned by Mr. T. S. Winan])
     Great Britain   *[Solace]*
(crew unknown [owned by Mr. Francis P. Armstrong])
     Great Britain   *[Cid]*
(crew unknown [owned by Commander Mansfield Cummings])
     Great Britain   *[Mynonia]*
(crew unknown [owned by Mr. C. Priestley Foster])

Handicap Race #4

A: ?; C: 1; D: 29 August; F: Motorboats of all classes.

1.   Great Britain   29:05   *[Gyrinus]*   hdcp — 1:40
(crew unknown [owned by Thomas Thornycroft])
2.   Great Britain   31:35   *[Quicksilver]*   hdcp — scratch
(crew unknown [owned by Mr. John Marshall Gorham])
3.   Great Britain   *[Napier IV]*   hdcp — 12:27
(crew unknown [owned by Mr. S. F. Edge])
4.   Great Britain   *[Maudslay I]*
(crew unknown [owned by Mr. C. C. Maudslay])
8

Handicap Race #5

A: ?; C: 1; D: 29 August; F: Motorboats exceeding 15 knots. Length about 12½ nautical miles.

1.   Great Britain   *[Quicksilver]*
(crew unknown [owned by Mr. John Marshall Gorham])

2.   Great Britain   *[Sea Dog]*
(crew unknown [owned by Mr. Warwick Wright])

Great Britain   DNF   *[Gyrinus]*
(crew unknown [owned by Mr. Thomas Thornycroft])

Handicap Race #6

A: ?; C: 1; D: 29 August; F: Length about 6 nautical miles.

1.   Great Britain   29:34   *[Camille]*   hdcp — scratch
(crew unknown [owned by Mr. R. N. Fairbanks])

2.   Great Britain   30:40   *[Cid]*   hdcp — 0:20
(crew unknown [owned by Commander Mansfield Cummings])

3.   Great Britain   *[Maudslay I]*
(crew unknown [owned by Mr. C. C. Maudslay])

4.   Great Britain   *[Carreerma]*
(crew unknown [owned by Mr. Grahame Wright])

NOTES

1. OSVK has 10 competitors.
2. Also entered in Race Two, but not starting, were *Daimler II* of Great Britain, owned by Lord Howard de Walden; and *Trident* of Great Britain, owned by P. G. Westmacott.
3. DW, and EK have the time as 2-28:58.0, but the only 1908 source giving the time has it as 2-28:58.8, which time is correctly seen in FM, VK, and OSVK.
4. Also entered in B-Class, but not starting, was *Pastime* of Great Britain, owned by P. G. Westmacott.
5. Times, 30 August 1908.
6. Also entered in C-Class, but not starting, were *Lotus II* of Great Britain, owned by H. W. Hutchinson; and Emile Thubron's boat, which went variously by the name of *Camille*, *X*, and *Tréfle-à-Quatre*.
7. *Lotus II* (steered by Mr. H. W. Hutchinson) and *Camilla* (steered by Mr. R. N. Fairbanks) did not start.
8. *Napier Major* (owned by Mr. S. F. Edge) was entered but did not start.

Polo

The Olympic matches had little relevance in the overall context of the 1908 international polo season. From May to August there was a non-stop round of tournaments in such fashionable places as London, Paris, Ostend, and Cannes, and Olympic polo held no special place in this social and sporting calendar. Fewer than 30 high-handicapped players formed the core of the variously styled teams who played both with and against each other throughout the summer and all the Olympic players had been both teammates and opponents in recent weeks.

For the Olympic tournament an entry of only three teams, two from England and one from Ireland, meant that just two matches were played. The English teams entered under the names of their respective clubs and it was appropriate that the brothers Charles and George Miller, who owned and founded the Roehampton club, were on the winning team.

Contrary to certain reports this was not a round-robin tournament. The Irish team never played Hurlingham and qualified for the final by drawing a bye in the first round. The winning Roehampton team was awarded the Hurlingham Trophy, in addition to their gold medals.

	Site:	Hurlingham Polo Grounds, London
	Dates:	18, 21 June
	Events:	1
	Competitors:	12
	Nations:	1

	Competitors	1st	2nd	3rd	Totals
Great Britain	12	1	2	-	3
England	8	1	1	-	2
Ireland	4	-	1	-	1
Totals	12	1	2	-	3
Nations	1	1	1	-	1

Final Standings

A: 12; C: 1; D: 18, 21 June.

1. Great Britain   (Roehampton)
    (Charles Miller, Patteson Nickalls, George Miller, Herbert Wilson)
=2. Great Britain   (Hurlingham)
    (John, Lord Wodehouse, Walter Buckmaster, Frederick Freake, Walter Jones)
       Great Britain/Ireland[1]*
    (Percy O'Reilly, Hardress Lloyd, John McCann, Auston Rotherham)

Tournament Summary

Match Summaries

18 June

GBR/Roehampton   4   GBR/Hurlingham   1
    Site: Hurlingham Polo Grounds, London
    Time: 1600
    Umpires: Major MacLaren, Captain Fagan.
    Halftime: GBR/Roehampton, 2–1.
    Goals: GBR/Roehampton: Wilson (2), Nickalls, G. Miller; GBR/Hurlingham: Buckmaster.
    GBR/Roehampton C. Miller, P. Nickalls, G. Miller, H. Wilson
    GBR/Hurlingham Lord Wodehouse, W. Buckmaster, F. Freake, W. Jones

21 June

GBR/Roehampton   8   GBR/Ireland   1
    Site: Hurlingham Polo Grounds, London
    Time: unknown
    Umpires: Major MacLaren, Captain Fagan.
    Halftime: GBR/Roehampton, 7-0.
    Goals: GBR/Roehampton: G. Miller (4), Wilson (2), Nickalls (2); GBR/Ireland: McCann.
    GBR/Roehampton C. Miller, P. Nickalls, G. Miller, H. Wilson
    GBR/Ireland P. O'Reilly, H. Lloyd, J. McCann, A. Rotherham

Goal Scoring Summary

George Miller (GBR)	5	Walter Buckmaster (GBR)	1
Herbert Wilson (GBR)	4	John McCann (GBR/IRL)	1
Patteson Nickalls (GBR)	3		

*See Notes on page 207.

NOTES

1. FM does not mention the Irish team as joint second.

2. EK, FW, and VK/OSVK have the score incorrectly as 3–1. All 1908 sources, including SLR, OR, and Times have the score as 4–1.

3. EK, FW, and VK have the score incorrectly as 5–1. All 1908 sources, including SLR, OR, and Times have the score as 8–1.

Racquets

The 1908 Olympic Games began on the afternoon of 27 April 1908, when Evan Noel defeated Cecil Browning in the first round of the racquets tournament. Racquets is another racket sport, somewhat similar to squash rackets, which is a modern, now more popular variant. In 1908 racquets was primarily popular in Great Britain. In fact, there were no entrants or competitors from any other nation. The *Official Report* noted, "Racquets, it may be noted, is always so expensive a game that, except at the public schools, the number of players is always so restricted and, out of the United Kingdom, India and the United States of America are the only countries where the game is played, which may be a reason for not including it in future programmes for the Olympic Games."

Professional racquets was quite popular in 1908 and the greatest player ever was Britain's Peter Latham, who had won the championship in 1887 and held it until 1903 when India's J. Jamsetjhi became the holder. The top amateur player of the era was Edgar Maximilian Baerlein, who entered both events, but did not compete in either. Baerlein was British Amateur champion in 1903, 1905, 1908–1911, and 1920–1921. He was also British champion at court tennis (jeu de paume) from 1914–1927 and again in 1929–1930. He had won the 1908 amateur title by defeating Evan Noel in the final and with Baerlein not competing, Noel had a relatively easy time of it, losing only one of 10 games en route to the singles' final. The singles' final was not held as Henry Leaf had to scratch because of an injury he had received during the doubles. Noel won one British Amateur championship, that in 1907.

The 1908 doubles champions of Great Britain were Vane Pennell and F. Dames Longworth. Longworth did not enter for the Olympic tournament. Pennell joined up with John Jacob Astor, whose father was later a victim of the *Titanic* disaster, and they won two closely fought matches, narrowly defeating Noel and Leaf in the semi-finals.

Site:	Queen's Club, West Kensington, London
Dates:	27 April–1 May
Events:	2
Competitors:	7
Nations:	1

	Competitors	1st	2nd	3rd	Totals
Great Britain	7	2	2	3	7
Totals	7	2	2	3	7
Nations	1	1	1	1	1

Gentlemen's Singles

A: 6[1]*; C: 1; D: 27-29 April; F: Single elimination.

1.	Evan Noel	GBR
2.	Henry Leaf	GBR
=3.	Henry Brougham	GBR
	John Jacob Astor[2]	GBR
5.	Vane Pennell	GBR
6.	Cecil Browning	GBR

Gentlemen's Singles Draw

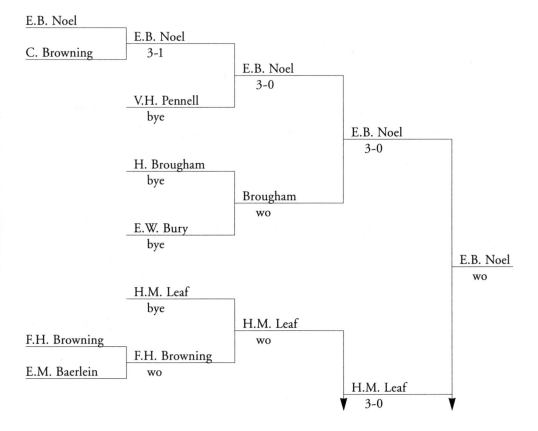

*See Notes on page 211.

B.S. Foster
bye
                    J.J. Astor
J.J. Astor
bye

Match Summaries

Round One A: 2; C: 1; D: 27 April; T: Afternoon.

Noel d. Browning   18-13, 8-15, 15-8, 15-9   (56-40)

Quarter-Finals A: 2; C: 1; D: 28 April; T: 1400.

Noel d. Pennell   15-11, 15-7, 15-5   (45-23)
Brougham d. Bury (scratched)   wo

Semi-Finals A: 4; C: 1; D: 29 April; T: 1400.

Noel d. Brougham   15-4, 15-12, 15-6   (45-22)
Leaf d. Astor   15-8, 15-5, 15-4   (45-17)

Final D: 1 May (scheduled).[3]

Noel d. Leaf (scratched)   wo

Gentlemen's Doubles

A: 6[4]; C: 1; D: 30 April–1 May; F: Single elimination.

1. Vane Pennell–John Jacob Astor   GBR
2. Edmund Bury–Cecil Browning   GBR
3. Henry Leaf–Evan Noel   GBR[5]

Gentlemen's Doubles Draw

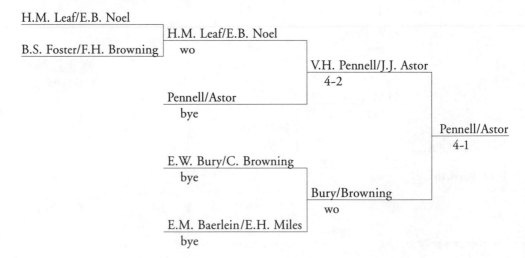

H.M. Leaf/E.B. Noel
                          H.M. Leaf/E.B. Noel
B.S. Foster/F.H. Browning   wo
                                          V.H. Pennell/J.J. Astor
                                              4-2
                          Pennell/Astor
                          bye
                                                          Pennell/Astor
                                                              4-1
                          E.W. Bury/C. Browning
                          bye
                                          Bury/Browning
                                              wo
                          E.M. Baerlein/E.H. Miles
                          bye

Match Summaries

Semi-Finals A: 4; C: 1; D: 30 April; T: 1430.

Pennell/Astor d. Leaf/Noel   15-11, 0-15, 15-7, 9-15, 18-14, 17-15   (74-77)

Final A: 2; C: 1; D: 1 May; T: 1430.

Pennell/Astor d. Bury/Browning   6-15, 15-7, 16-15, 15-6, 15-7   (67-50)

NOTES

1. There were 10 entrants as listed below in the draw chart. OSVK incorrectly has 7 starters.
2. FM listed Astor as sole third.
3. The exact date of the final is not mentioned specifically in any sources. But Leaf competed in the doubles on 30 April, and in describing the final the OR noted, "As Leaf had injured his hand on the previous day, he was obliged to scratch, … "
4. There were 10 entrants of 5 teams, as listed below in the draw chart.
5. FM did not list a third-place team.

Rowing & Sculling

The 1908 Olympic rowing events were held at Henley, long the site of the famous Henley Regatta. A fairly good international field appeared, with rowers from eight nations competing.

From a statistical point of view, the most difficult question deals with which medals were awarded. It seems likely that only gold medals, and no silver or bronze medals, were given. The rules, as given in the *Official Report*[1]*, note, "The Winners or Winner of the events will each receive the British Olympic Council's Gold Medal for the Olympic Games of 1908." And on another page of the Official Report[2], one finds under Rowing, "Prizes:— Gold Olympic Medals to the winners in each Event." There is no mention of silver or bronze medals in either place. In the results section of the *Official Report*[3] the four rowing events are listed, with only the winners listed under gold medals. No silver or bronze medal placements are listed.

Because of the organization of the Henley course, only two crews or sculls competed at any one time. Thus the semi-finals and finals consisted of only two crews or single scullers. Certainly the losing finalist would seem to be considered the "silver medalist" although we do not know if those rowers actually received such a medal. In addition, it would seem natural, and consistent with other Olympic sports such as boxing and tennis, to consider the losing semi-finalists as "bronze medalists." Again, there is no evidence if these rowers received any bronze medals.

Olympic statisticians vary on the listing of these results. Erich Kamper, in his *Encyclopaedia of the Olympic Games*, listed the losing semi-finalists in the single sculls and eights as finishing third, but he did not list the losing semi-finalists that way in the coxed pairs or coxed fours. Both Volker Kluge (*Die olympischen Spiele von 1896 bis 1980*) and David Wallechinsky (*The Complete Book of the Summer Olympics*) consider all the losing semi-finalists as finishing in third place. But in his more recent book, *Olympische Sommerspiele: Die Chronik I*, Kluge listed the results exactly as they occurred, and they are listed below — by rounds and heats, and he did not describe the losing semi-finalists as bronze medalists.

In the statistical section, we have considered the losing finalists as silver medalists (second place) and both the losing semi-finalists as bronze medalists (third place). It is, however, debatable whether they should be considered bronze medalists.

The rowers started at either Berks (Berkshire) Station or Bucks (Buckinghamshire) Station, referring to whether the boat began on the Berkshire (south) or Buckinghamshire (north) side of Temple Island. We have indicated the starting position below in all cases.

See Notes on page 218.

Site:	Henley on Thames				
Dates:	28–31 July				
Events:	4				
Competitors:	81				
Nations:	8				

	Competitors	*1st*	*2nd*	*3rd*	*Totals*
Belgium	10	–	1	–	1
Canada	13	–	–	3	3
Germany	3	–	–	2	2
Great Britain	30	4	3	1	8
Hungary	11	–	–	1	1
Italy	1	–	–	–	–
The Netherlands	4	–	–	1	1
Norway	9	–	–	–	–
Totals	81	4	4	8	16
Nations	8	1	2	5	6

Officials

Judge: Frederick Fenner
Umpires: Frederick Pitman (Cambridge University Boat Club), William Fletcher (Oxford University Boat Club)
Timekeepers: Theodore Andrea Cook (Oxford University Boat Club), Victor Mansell
Committee: H. T. Steward, R. S. Bradshaw, W. A. L. Fletcher, Stanley Muttlebury, R. Philipson, Frederick Pitman, S. le Blanc Smith, C. T. Steward, J. F. Cooper (Assistant Secretary)

Single Sculls

A: 9; C: 6; D: 28–31 July; F: 1½ miles.

This was probably the first great international sculling competition. Both the finalists, Harry Blackstaffe and Alexander McCulloch, were champions of the Diamond Challenge Sculls at Henley — Blackstaffe winning in 1906 and McCulloch holding the title in 1908. One of the first round losers, Lou Scholes, was the top Canadian sculler and had won the Diamond Sculls in 1904. The only top scullers not present were Britain's Frederick Kelly, Henley Diamond champion in 1902–03 and 1905, but now retired as a sculler (he competed in the eights at the 1908 Olympics), and America's Frank Greer, U.S. champion in 1903–05 and 1908 and the 1904 Olympic champion.

In the qualifying rounds, Blackstaffe and McCulloch were not challenged at all. In the final, McCulloch, starting out of Bucks Station, took the early lead, but started by pulling fewer strokes than Blackstaffe. McCulloch opened up as much as 1½ lengths and led through 1,200 yards before being caught by Blackstaffe. Shortly after 1 mile though, Blackstaffe had pulled ahead by ¾ of a length, and McCulloch could not close the gap.

Final A: 2; C: 1; D: 31 July; T: 1430.

1.	Harry Blackstaffe (Berks)	GBR	9:26.0
2.	Alexander McCulloch (Bucks)	GBR	at 1¼ lengths

Semi-Finals A: 4; C: 3; D: 30 July; F: Winners of each heat advanced to the final.

Heat 1 A: 2; C: 2; T: 1230.

1.	Alexander McCulloch (Bucks)	GBR	10:22.0
2.	Károly Levitzky (Berks)	HUN	won easily

Heat 2 A: 2; C: 2; T: 1645.

1.	Harry Blackstaffe (Bucks)	GBR	10:14.0
	Bernhard von Gaza (Berks)	GER	DNF

4

Round Two A: 8; C: 6; D: 29 July; F: Winners of each heat advanced to the semi-finals.

Heat 1 A: 2; C: 2; T: 1230.

1.	Bernhard von Gaza (Bucks)	GER	9:47.0
2.	Louis Scholes (Berks)	CAN	at 1½ lengths

Heat 2 A: 2; C: 2; T: 1500.

1.	Károly Levitzky (Bucks)	HUN	10:08.0
2.	Gino Ciabatti (Berks)	ITA	won easily

Heat 3 A: 2; C: 2; T: 1600.

1.	Harry Blackstaffe (Bucks)	GBR	10:03.0
	Walter Bowler (Berks)	CAN	DNF

Heat 4 A: 2; C: 2; T: unknowm.

1.	Alexander McCulloch (Bucks)	GBR	10:08.0
2.	Joseph Hermans (Berks)	BEL	won easily

Round One A: 2; C: 2; D: 28 July; F: Winner of heat advanced to round two.

Heat 1 A: 2; C: 2; T: 1500.

1.	Bernhard von Gaza (Bucks)	GER	9:35.0
	Ern Killer (Berks)	HUN	DNF

5

Coxless Pairs

A: 8; C: 3; D: 28, 30–31 July; F: 1½ miles.

Only four pairs entered, two British and one each from Canada and Germany. From 1905–1911, the European championship was always won by a Belgian or Italian pair, although with coxswain, but neither nation entered a pair in the 1908 Olympics. At Henley, the event for coxless pairs is the Silver Goblets and Nickalls Challenge Cup. It was won in 1906–1907 by Banner Johnstone and Ronald Powell, and in 1908 by Harold Barker and Albert Gladstone, but neither pair entered the Olympic event. Johnstone and Gladstone competed at the Olympics for Leander in the winning eight-oared crew, while Barker competed for the gold-medal winning Leander four.

The Olympic final came down to the two British pairs, both representing the Leander Club. Fenning and Thomson opened on 38 strokes and opened ¾ length lead by the time they passed Temple Island. They continued to pull away and were never really challenged.

Final A: 2; C: 1; D: 31 July; T: 1230.

1.	Great Britain (Leander Club) (Berks) (Reginald Fenning [bow], Gordon Thomson [stroke])	9:41.0
2.	Great Britain (Leander Club) (Bucks) (George Fairbairn [bow], Philip Verdon [stroke])	at 2½ lengths

Semi-Finals A: 8; C: 3; D: 28, 30 July; F: Winner of each heat advanced to the final.

Heat 1 A: 4; C: 2; D: 28 July; T: 1630.

1.	Great Britain (Leander Club) (Berks) (Reginald Fenning [bow], Gordon Thomson [stroke])	9:46.0
2.	Canada (Argonaut Rowing Club) (Bucks) (Frederick Toms [bow], Norwey Jackes [stroke])	won easily

Heat 2 A: 4; C: 2; T: 1515.

1.	Great Britain (Leander Club) (Bucks) (George Fairbairn [bow], Philip Verdon [stroke])	11:05.0
	Germany (Berliner Ruderclub) (Berks) (Martin Stahnke [bow], Willy Düskow [stroke]) 6	DNF

Coxless Fours

A: 16; C: 3; D: 28, 30–31 July; F: 1½ miles.

The Magdalen College (Oxford) Boat Club had won the Stewards' Challenge Cup at Henley in both 1907 and 1908. The winners in 1905–06 had been a four representing the Leander Club, so the final of this event brought the two top fours from Britain over the past few years. European championships in this era were only held for coxed fours, and Belgium and Italy dominated this class, but did not enter for the Olympics.

In the final, the Magdalen four opened at 38 strokes and was a length ahead at the halfway point. The Oxonian crew gradually increased their lead to win by a margin described variously as 1½ or 2 lengths.

Final A: 8; C: 1; D: 31 July.

1. Great Britain (Magdalen College Boat Club) (Berks)   8:34.0
   (C. Robert Cudmore [bow], James Gillan [2], Duncan Mackinnon [3], Robert Somers-Smith [stroke])

2. Great Britain (Leander Club) (Bucks)   at 1½ lengths
   (Philip Filleul [bow], Harold Barker [2], Reginald Fenning [3], Gordon Thomson [stroke])

    Semi-Finals A: 16; C: 3; D: 28, 30 July; F: Winner of each heat advanced to the final.

    Heat 1 A: 8; C: 2; D: 28 July; T: 1545.

1. Great Britain (Magdalen College Boat Club[7]) (Bucks)   8:34.0
   (C. Robert Cudmore [bow], James Gillan [2], Duncan Mackinnon [3], Robert Somers-Smith [stroke])

2. Canada (Argonaut Rowing Club[8]) (Berks)   at 2¼ lengths
   (Gordon Balfour [bow], Becher Gale [2], Charles Riddy [3], Geoffrey Taylor [stroke])

    Heat 2 A: 8; C: 2; D: 30 July; T: 1615.

1. Great Britain (Leander Club[9]) (Bucks)   9:04.0
   (Philip Filleul [bow], Harold Barker [2], Reginald Fenning [3], Gordon Thomson [stroke])

2. The Netherlands (Amstel Amsterdam) (Berks)
   (Hermannus Höfte [bow], Albertus Wielsma [2], Johan Burk [3], Bernardus Croon [stroke])
   [10]

Coxed Eights

    A: 54; C: 5[11]; D: 29–31 July; F: 1½ miles.

The greatest eight in the world in 1908 was considered to be the Belgian crew representing the Royal Club Nautique de Gand. They had won the European championship from 1906–1908 and a Belgian eight had won that title every year from 1897–1910 with the exception of 1905 and 1909. At Henley, the Royal Club Nautique de Gand won the Grand Challenge Cup (for eights) in 1906–07 and 1909. Leander Club had an eight win the Grand Challenge Cup in 1903–05, while the 1908 title went to an Oxford crew representing the Christ Church College Boat Club. The top American eight was the team from Vesper Boat Club in Philadelphia, which had won the Olympic championship in 1900 and 1904, but Vesper did not enter the 1908 Olympic rowing regatta.

The two favored crews came through to the final, although both had reasonable competition in the early rounds. Leander went out at 42 strokes and Gand at 43 strokes. Leander went ahead by ½-length as they passed Temple Island. Shortly after one mile, Gand pulled even and may have even led briefly but it was a futile effort which exhausted them. Leander pulled away easily after passing Phyllis Court and won by 2 lengths. All the members of the Leander crew had rowed for either Oxford or Cambridge.

Final A: 18; C: 2; D: 31 July; T: 1515.

1. Great Britain (Leander Club) (Bucks)   7:52.0
   (Albert Gladstone [bow], Frederick Kelly [2], Banner Johnstone [3], Guy Nickalls [4], Charles Burnell [5], Ronald Sanderson [6], Raymond Etherington-Smith [7], Henry Bucknall [stroke], Gilchrist Maclagan [cox])

2. Belgium (Royal Club Nautique de Gand) (Berks)   at 2 lengths
   (Oscar Taelman [bow], Marcel Morimont [2], Rémy Orban [3], Georges Mijs [4], François Vergucht [5], Polydore Veirman [6], Oscar de Somville [7], Rodolphe Poma [stroke], Alfred Van Landeghem [cox])

   Semi-Finals A: 36; C: 3; D: 30 July; F: Winner of each heat advanced to the final.

   Heat 1 A: 18; C: 2; T: 1315.

1. Great Britain (Leander Club) (Bucks)   8:12.0
   (Albert Gladstone [bow], Frederick Kelly [2], Banner Johnstone [3], Guy Nickalls [4], Charles Burnell [5], Ronald Sanderson [6], Raymond Etherington-Smith [7], Henry Bucknall [stroke], Gilchrist Maclagan [cox])

2. Canada (Argonaut Rowing Club) (Berks)   at 1 length
   (Irvine Robertson [bow], Joseph Wright [2], Julius Thomson [3], Walter Lewis [4], Gordon Balfour [5], Becher Gale [6], Charles Riddy [7], Geoffrey Taylor [stroke], Douglas Kertland [cox])

   Heat 2 A: 18; C: 2; T: 1545.

1. Belgium (Royal Club Nautique de Gand[12]) (Berks)   8:22.0
   (Oscar Taelman [bow], Marcel Morimont [2], Rémy Orban [3], Georges Mijs [4], François Vergucht [5], Polydore Veirman [6], Oscar de Somville [7], Rodolphe Poma [stroke], Alfred Van Landeghem [cox])

2. Great Britain (Cambridge University Boat Club[13]) (Bucks)   at 1⅓ lengths
   (Frank Jerwood [bow], Eric Powell [2], Oswald Carver [3], Edward Williams [4], Henry Goldsmith [5], Harold Kitching [6], John Burn [7], Douglas Stuart [stroke], Richard Boyle [cox])

   Round One A: 36; C: 4; D: 29 July; F: Winner of each heat advanced to the semi-final.

   Heat 1 A: 18; C: 2; T: 1300.

1. Canada (Argonaut Rowing Club[14]) (Bucks)   8:06.0
   (Irvine Robertson [bow], Joseph Wright [2], Julius Thomson [3], Walter Lewis [4], Gordon Balfour [5], Becher Gale [6], Charles Riddy [7], Geoffrey Taylor [stroke], Douglas Kertland [cox])

2. Norway (Norwegian Rowing Association[15]) (Berks)   at 2¾ lengths
   (Otto Krogh [bow], Erik Bye [2], Ambrosius Høyer [3], Gustav Hæhre [4], Emil Irgens [5], Hannibal Feght [6], Wilhelm Hansen [7], Annan Knudsen [stroke], Einar Tønsager [cox])

Heat 2 A: 18; C: 2; T: 1520.

1. Great Britain (Leander Club[16]) (Bucks)   8:10.0
   (Albert Gladstone [bow], Frederick Kelly [2], Banner Johnstone [3], Guy Nickalls [4],
   Charles Burnell [5], Ronald Sanderson [6], Raymond Etherington-Smith [7], Henry
   Bucknall [stroke], Gilchrist Maclagan [cox])

2. Hungary (Pannonia RC/National RC[17]) (Berks)   at 2 lengths
   (Sándor Klekner [bow], Lajos Haraszthy [2], Antal Szebeny [3], Róbert Éder [4], Sándor Hautzinger [5], Jenő Várady [6], Imre Wampetich [7], Ferenc Kirchknopf [stroke],
   Kálmán Vaskó [cox])
   [18]

NOTES

1. OR, p. 528.
2. OR, p. 37.
3. OR, p. 358.
4. FM listed von Gaza as sole third.
5. A sculler, not named in SL, was also entered from the Netherlands.
6. An Italian pair was also entered but did not compete.
7. The Magdalen reserves, who did not compete in this event, were Robert Philip Stanhope and Evelyn Herbert Lightfoot Southwell.
8. The Argonaut reserves, who did not compete in this event, were Julius A. Thomson and C. G. Toms.
9. The Leander reserves, who did not compete in this event, were Edouard Majolier and Guy Nickalls.
10. Hungary and Italy also entered fours, but they did not compete.
11. VK/OSVK incorrectly have nine nations.
12. The Gand reserves, who did not compete in this event, were Guillaume Visser, –– Urbain, –– Molmans, Ferdinand Bauwens, Georges Desenfaus, and Rodolphe Colpaert.
13. The Cambridge reserves, who did not compete in this event, were Philip Verdon, George E. Fairbairn, Gordon L. Thomson, A. F. Kindersley, and Bertie Garfield Alma Scott.
14. The Argonaut reserves, who did not compete in this event, were Frederick B. Toms, Norwey B. Jackes, and C. G. Toms.
15. The Norwegian reserves, who did not compete in this event, were Jacob Jacobsen, Knut C. Langaard, and Ludwig Mstue (cox).
16. The Leander reserves, who did not compete in this event, were Philip R. Filleul, Harold R. Barker, Albert C. Gladstone, R. C. Bourne, and Arthur William Fishburn Donkin.
17. The Pannonia reserves, who did not compete in this event, were Károly Levitzky and Ernő Killer.
18. An Italian eight was also entered, but did not compete.

Rugby Union Football

After a rather informal tournament in 1900, rugby football was accorded full Olympic status in 1908 but the entries fell well short of expectations. South Africa and New Zealand declined their invitations and Ireland, Scotland, and Wales completely ignored theirs. This left just Australia, England, and France as the participating nations. England was originally scheduled to meet France with the winners taking on Australia, but one week before the match France withdrew on the grounds that they could not raise a representative team and the two remaining teams, Australia and England, met in the only rugby match of the 1908 Games.

The Australians had no difficulty in selecting their team as their top players were already touring in England. By the time of the Olympic rugby match, Australia had played eight matches, winning seven of them. Conversely, the best Anglo-Welsh players were on tour in Australia and New Zealand and the Olympic match was scheduled to take place shortly after their return home. A letter was sent to the touring team asking if they would be prepared to accept an Olympic commitment so soon after an arduous tour but the letter was never received. In the ensuing silence it was decided that Cornwall, who had won the English County Championship in March, should be Great Britain's Olympic representatives. During the course of their tour the Australians had already beaten Cornwall (18–5) three weeks before the Games and they scored a more emphatic victory (32–3) in the Olympic match. The match was played on a dismal day, described by *The Times* as, "… a dark afternoon in a Scotch mist. The ground was slippery and the footballs in a perpetual state of greasiness."[1]*

Notable among the Australians were Danny Carroll, who won a second gold medal representing the United States in 1920, and Syd Middleton, who rowed in the Australian eight at the 1912 Games. The Australian team continued to tour Great Britain and finished their tour with 26 wins and 5 losses, scoring 438 points, while conceding only 146. The other members of the touring Australian rugby team, who did not play at the Olympics, were William Dix, H. Daly, Edward Mandible, Esmend Parkinson, Warden Prentice, J. M. Stevenson, Frederick Wood, Dr. Herbert M. Moran (the captain, who had injured his shoulder the previous Saturday), E. McIntyre, Kenneth Gavin, Peter H. Burge, Albert P. Burge, Norman E. Row, Peter Flanagan, and C. A. Hammons. C. Murnin was also to be a touring member but had been taken ill in Naples on the trip to England and returned to Australia.[2] The captain, Dr. Moran, in his autobiography,

*See Notes on page 221.

Viewless Winds, noted that his greatest achievement as captain was to get the team home after five months away without a single player contracting venereal disease.[3]

	Site:	White City Stadium, Shepherd's Bush, London
	Date:	26 October
	Events:	1
	Competitors:	30
	Nations:	2

	Competitors	1st	2nd	3rd	Totals
Australia	15	1	-	-	1
Great Britain	15	-	1	-	1
Totals	30	1		-	2
Nations	2	1	1	-	2

Final Standings

A: 30; C: 2; D: 26 October; T: 1515; F: Single match between the two teams.

1. Australia
   (Phillip Carmichael, Charles Russell, Daniel Carroll, John Hickey, Frank Bede Smith, Christopher McKivat, Arthur McCabe, Thomas Griffin, John "Jumbo" Barnett, Patrick McCue, Sydney Middleton, Thomas Richards, Malcolm "Mannie" McArthur, Charles McMurtrie, Robert Craig)

2. Great Britain
   (Edward Jackett, John "Barney" Solomon, Bert Solomon, L. F. Dean, J. T. Jose, Thomas Wedge, James "Maffer" Davey, Richard Jackett, E. J. Jones, Arthur Wilson, Nicholas Tregurtha, A. Lawry, C. R. Marshall, A. Wilcocks, John Trevaskis)

Match Summary

26 October

Australia	32	Great Britain	3

Time: 1515
Attendance: Less than 3,000
Halftime: 13–0
Referee: F. C. Potter-Irwin[4]
Australia (P. Carmichael [FB], C. Russell [B], D. Carroll [B], J. Hickey [B], F. Bede Smith [B], C. McKivat [HB], A. McCabe [HB], T. Griffin [F], J. Barnett [F], P. McCue [F], S. Middleton [F], T. Richards [F], M. McArthur [F], C. McMurtrie [F], R. Craig [F]);
Great Britain (E. Jackett [FB], J.C. Solomon [B], B. Solomon [B], L.F. Dean [B], J.T. Jose [B], T. Wedge [HB], J. Davey [HB], R. Jackett [F], E.J. Jones [F], A. Wilson [F], N. Tregurtha [F], A. Lawry [F], C.R. Marshall [F], A. Wilcocks [F], J. Trevaskis [F]).

Australia	Tries	Convs	Penalty	Dropped	Points
Carmichael [FB]	–	4	1	–	11
Carroll [B]	2	–	–	–	6
McCabe [HB]	2	–	–	–	6
Hickey [B]	1	–	–	–	3
McKivat [HB]	1	–	–	–	3
Richards [F]	1	–	–	–	3
Totals	7	4	1	–	32

Great Britain	Tries	Convs	Penalty	Dropped	Points
B. Solomon [B]	1	–	–	–	3
Totals	1	–	–	–	3

NOTES

1. *Times*, 27 October 1908.
2. Lester, p. 46.
3. Moran H.M., *Viewless Winds*, quoted in Buchanan I, "Rugby Football at the Olympic Games," *J Olympic History*, 5(1); (Spring 1997),1–14.
4. Potter-Irwin was the referee listed in *The Times*. Cartwright is listed as a second referee in Lester's book, *Australians at the Olympics*, but rugby football usually has only one referee.

Shooting

The Bisley rifle range was the home of British shooting and it proved a suitable location for the 1908 Olympic shooting. The trap shooting events were the only ones held elsewhere—at the Uxendon School Shooting Club. The trap shooting took place over four days—8–11 July, while the other shooting events took place over 3 days, 9–11 July. The shooting events were basically separated into five categories: (1) long-range rifle shooting, (2) small-bore rifle shooting, (3) pistol shooting, (4) running deer shooting, and (5) trap shooting.

The weather was clear and good on Wednesday, 8 July, the first day of trap shooting. But otherwise, the weather was noted to be poor and very difficult on the shooters. It was windy, cool, cloudy, dark, and rainy throughout the last three days of the competition.

Site:	Bisley Rifle Range (rifle, pistol, and running deer shooting) and Uxendon School Shooting Club (trap shooting)
Dates:	8–11 July
Events:	15
Competitors:	215
Nations:	14

	Competitors	1st	2nd	3rd	Totals
Australia	1	-	-	-	-
Belgium	10	1	2	-	3
Canada	22	1	2	1	4
Denmark	10	-	-	-	-
Finland	9	-	-	-	-
France	20	-	-	2	2
Germany	1	-	-	-	-
Great Britain	67	6	7	8	21
Greece	7	-	-	-	-
Hungary	2	-	-	-	-
The Netherlands	17	-	-	-	-
Norway	13	2	-	1	3

Sweden	19	2	2	1	5
United States	17	3	2	1	6
Totals	215	15	15	14	44
Nations	14	6	5	6	7

Officials

Rifle/Pistol Committee: Major-General Lord Cheylesmore, CVO; Rt. Honorable Earl Walde-grave, VD; Colonel the Honorable T. F. Fremantle, VD; A. P. Humphry, G. Mortimer, Major J. S. Oxley, VD; Captain Thomas "Ted" Ranken; Major P. W. Richardson, VD; Walter Winans; Charles W. Wirgmann.

Clay Bird Committee: The Right Honorable Lord Westbury (Chairman); The Honorable Arthur Bligh, A. Brampton, J. Newton Hayley, W. R. Hillsdon, A. F. Kemp, Dr. W. Mitchell, H. W. Newton, Percy Newton, E. H. Stone (Honorary Secretary)

Clay Bird Referees: N. Coopmans, W. R. Hillsdon, H. W. Newton, Captain Pellier Johnson, Dr. W. Mitchell.

Long-Range Rifle Shooting

Free Rifle, Three Positions (300 meters)

A: 51; C: 10; D: 11 July; F: 120 shots (40 standing, 40 kneeling, 40 prone). Target 1 meter in diameter, with 60 cm. bullseye, worth 10 points. Individual possible 1,200. Any rifle allowed.

			Standing	Kneeling	Prone	Total
1.	Albert Helgerud	NOR	277	292	340	909
2.	Harry Simon	USA	228	294	365	887
3.	Ole Sæther	NOR	272	284	327	883
4.	Gustav-Adolf Sjöberg	SWE	251	285	338	874
5.	Johan "Janne" Gustafsson	SWE	265	283	324	872
6.	Julius "Jul" Braathe	NOR	257	291	303	851
7.	Axel Jansson	SWE	235	296	312	843
8.	Léon Johnson	FRA	250	282	303	835
9.	Olaf Sæter	NOR	240	291	299	830
10.	Jesse Wallingford	GBR	201	303	324	828
11.	Maurice Blood	GBR/IRL	201	290	334	825
12.	Per-Olof Arvidsson	SWE	236	277	310	821
13.	Georg Erdmann	NOR	234	277	310	821
14.	Lars Jørgen Madsen	DEN	236	294	283	813
15.	Gustaf Adolf Jonsson	SWE	226	267	319	812
16.	Edward Green	USA	190	276	326	792
17.	Voitto Kolho	FIN	231	269	288	788
18.	Christian Pedersen	DEN	191	278	311	780
19.	Kolbjørn Kvam	NOR	234	267	276	777
20.	Alexander Jackson	GBR	187	249	335	771

			Standing	Kneeling	Prone	Total
21.	Hans Christian Schultz	DEN	223	257	289	769
22.	Pieter van Waas	NED	188	285	295	768
23.	Fredrik Mossberg	SWE	174	288	299	761
24.	Olivius Skymoen	NOR	206	240	314	760
25.	Paul Colas	FRA	231	233	293	759
26.	R. Hawkins	GBR	189	273	301	752
27.	Per Olaf Olsen	NOR	222	237	293	752
28.	Erik Ohlsson	SWE	174	271	306	751
29.	John Hessian	USA	176	233	337	746
30.	Frans Nässling	FIN	221	244	268	733
31.	Maurice Lecoq	FRA	196	280	254	730
32.	Petrus ten Bruggen Cate	NED	216	238	271	726
33.	Niels Laursen	DEN	202	224	286	712
34.	André Angelini	FRA	154	247	305	706
35.	Ernest Ista	BEL	169	232	300	701
36.	Fernand Rey	BEL	169	245	284	698
37.	Huvi Tuiskunen	FIN	193	246	256	697
38.	Heikki Huttunen	FIN	204	212	270	686
39.	Lauri Kolho	FIN	171	236	265	672
40.	Henry Chaney	GBR	140	240	291	671
41.	Emil Nässling	FIN	204	234	219	657
42.	Poul Liebst	DEN	187	197	261	645
43.	Sándor Prokopp	HUN	144	236	247	627
44.	Gustav Nyman	FIN	200	166	249	615
45.	Karl Reilin	FIN	217	174	193	584
46.	Heikki Hallamaa	FIN	165	181	230	576
47.	Mathias Glomnes	NOR	––	250	313	563
48.	Christian Christensen	DEN	202	––	299	501
49.	István Móricz	HUN	122	179	189	490
50.	Ossian Jörgensen	SWE	––	112	308	420
51.	Lorents Jensen	DEN	46	––	275	321

1*

Free Rifle (1,000 yards)

A: 50^2; C: 8; D: 9 July; F: 20 shots. Bullseye worth 5 points and 36 inches (91.44 cm.) in diameter. Any rifle allowed. Any position allowed.

Joshua Millner was 61 years old, having started his shooting career in 1871 and distinguishing himself on the first British Palma team in 1876. Representing the Irish Ulster Rifle Association, he used a match rifle based on a Mannlicher action with a British service barrel and a Blood telescopic sight. He used a British .303 cartridge with a pointed 225-grain bullet at a muzzle velocity of 2,200 feet/second (670.5 mps). Millner shot in the "back position," lying on his back with his feet pointed at the target, knees drawn up and the rifle supported by his feet.[3]

*See Notes on pages 238–241.

Tie Shots

1.	Joshua Millner	GBR/IRL	98								
2.	Kellogg Casey	USA	93								
3.	Maurice Blood	GBR/IRL	92	5	5	5	5	5	5	5
4.	Richard Barnett	GBR/IRL	92	4	5	5	4			
5.	Thomas "Ted" Ranken[4]	GBR	92	4	4					
=6.	Thomas Caldwell[5]	GBR	91							
	John Sellars	GBR/IRL	91							
	S. Harry Kerr	CAN	91							
=9.	Frank Utton	CAN	90							
	Charles Crowe	CAN	90							
=11.	William Leuschner	USA	89							
	Stanley Brown	CAN	89							
=13.	Charles Jeffers	USA	88							
	Ivan Eastman	USA	88							
	Charles Benedict	USA	88							
=16.	Charles Winder	USA	87							
	Dugald McInnis	CAN	87							
	Thomas Fremantle	GBR	87							
=19.	Peter Whitehead	GBR	86							
	Raoul de Boigne	FRA	86							
	Frank Morris	CAN	86							
	Harry Simon	USA	86							
23.	André Angelini	FRA	85							
=24.	John Hopton	GBR	84							
	Edward Green	USA	84							
	John Hessian	USA	84							
27.	James Freeborn	CAN	83							
=28.	Alexander Rogers[6]	GBR	82							
	Paul Colas	FRA	82							
	Fred Elmitt	CAN	82							
	James Jones	CAN	82							
	Jrgen Bru	NOR	82							
33.	Arthur Martin	CAN	79							
34.	Ossian Jörgensen	SWE	77							
=35.	George Rowe	CAN	75							
	Léon Hecht	FRA	75							
37.	J. Arthur Steele	CAN	74							
38.	Daniel Mérillon	FRA	69							
39.	Léon Moreaux	FRA	67							
40.	Georg Erdmann	NOR	61							
=41.	Asmund Enger	NOR	58							
	Kolbjørn Kvam	NOR	58							
43.	Erik Ohlsson	SWE	54							
44.	Fredrik Mossberg	SWE	48							
45.	Alexandros Theofilakis	GRE	30							
46.	Ernst Rosell[7]	SWE	27							
47.	Mathias Glomnes	NOR	26							

48.	Léon Tétart[8]	FRA	21
49.	Erich Wagner-Hohenlobbese	GER	12
AC.	Olivius Skymoen	NOR	0 [9]

[10]

Free Rifle, Team (300 meters)

A: 54; C: 9; D: 9-10 July; F: 6-man teams. 120 shots (40 standing, 40 kneeling, 40 prone) per shooter. 720 shots (240 standing, 240 kneeling, 240 prone) per team. Target 1 meter in diameter, with 60 cm. bullseye, worth 10 points. Individual possible 1,200. Team possible 7,200. Any rifle allowed.

This was the first shooting event contested at the 1908 Olympics. The match began on 9 July in clear but windy weather. The wind quartered against the shooters from the left and teams using light rifles, especially Finland, were hampered. A variety of rifles were used. Finland used the light Mofferd rifle; Sweden used the Mauser government issue; Denmark used the Crag-Jørgensen; Greece and the Netherlands used the Mannlicher; France used the Swiss Martini rifle. The wind died down during the afternoon and the shooting improved. Darkness fell, however, and the match could not be finished. It was concluded the next day in very wet, windy weather. The winning Norwegian team used private match rifles.

		Standing	Kneeling	Prone	Totals
1.	Norway	1,549	1,651	1,855	5,055
	Albert Helgerud	259	303	312	874
	Ole Sæther	274	281	310	865
	Gudbrand Skatteboe	247	277	317	841
	Olaf Sæter	237	283	320	840
	Julius "Jul" Braathe	249	272	305	826
	Einar Liberg	283	235	291	809
2.	Sweden	1,267	1,566	1,878	4,711
	Gustaf Adolf Jonsson	238	289	313	840
	Per-Olof Arvidsson	233	268	311	812
	Axel Jansson	228	263	310	801
	Gustav-Adolf Sjöberg	210	238	312	760
	Claës Rundberg	160	265	334	759
	Johan "Janne" Gustafsson	198	243	298	739
3.	France	1,250	1,539	1,863	4,652
	Léon Johnson	225	313	298	836
	Eugène Balme	230	250	321	801
	André Parmentier	206	264	303	773
	Albert Courquin	203	235	330	768
	Maurice Lecoq	222	240	294	756
	Raoul de Boigne	164	237	317	718
4.	Denmark	1,244	1,534	1,765	4,543
	Niels Andersen	163	249	313	725
	Lars Jørgen Madsen	240	297	279	816
	Ole Olsen	214	257	283	754

		Standing	Kneeling	Prone	Totals
	Christian Christensen	209	249	294	752
	Christian Pedersen	227	224	297	748
	Hans Christian Schultz	191	258	299	748
5.	Belgium	1,220	1,496	1,747	4,509
	Charles Paumier du Verger	217	296	313	826
	Paul Van Asbroeck	222	237	328	787
	Ernest Ista	224	270	292	786
	Henri Sauveur	206	241	319	766
	Joseph Geens	215	259	266	740
	Edouard Poty	145	204	255	604
6.	Great Britain	999	1,519	1,837	4,355
	Jesse Wallingford	188	284	317	789
	Harold Hawkins	201	268	307	776
	Charles Churcher	162	270	328	760
	Thomas Raddall	195	246	313	754
	John Bostock	126	246	296	668
	Robert Brown	127	205	276	608
7.	The Netherlands	965	1,427	1,738	4,130[11]
	Gerard van den Bergh	176	273	302	751
	Christiaan Brosch	179	234	295	708
	Cornelis van Altenburg	149	249	291	689
	Antonie de Gee	164	254	266	684
	Uilke Vuurman	145	231	277	653
	Pieter Brussaard	152	186	307	645
8.	Finland	1,182	1,324	1,456	3,962
	Frans Nässling	222	253	242	717
	Gustav Nyman	199	249	252	700
	Heikki Huttunen	184	221	239	644
	Voitto Kolho	209	216	217	642
	Emil Nässling	181	190	266	637
	Huvi Tuiskunen	187	195	240	622
9.	Greece	848	1,311	1,630	3,789
	Ioannis Theofilakis	162	248	302	712
	Matthias Triantafilladis	149	227	277	653
	Alexandros Theofilakis	160	216	269	645
	Georgios Orfanidis	117	242	263	622
	Deukal. Rediadis	155	190	274	619
	Frangiskos Mauromatis	105	188	245	538

12

"The International"; Military Rifle, Team (200/500/600/800/900/1,000 yards)

A: 48; C: 8; D: 10–11 July (200, 500, and 600 yards on 10 July; 800, 900, and 1,000 yards on 11 July; F: Individual possible 75 at each distance. Total individual possible of 450. Team possible of 450 at each distance. Total team possible of 2,700. Fifteen shots at each distance with a maximum score of 5 on each shot. Bullseye 6 inches (15.24 cm.) at 200 yards; 20 inches (50.8 cm.) at 500 and 600 yards; and 36 inches (91.44 cm.) at 800, 900, and 1,000 yards. The rifle was required to be the "National Military Arm of any country." Any position allowed for shooting.[13]

Although nine teams were entered, only eight competed. The ninth team was Russia which never withdrew and actually tried to compete. In 1908, as today, most nations in the world used the Gregorian Calendar, but unlike today, a few nations used the older Julian Calendar. Russia was one of the nations using the Julian Calendar, which differed by 13 days from the Gregorian Calendar. The Russian shooters, thinking that the International team match was to begin on 10 July in the Julian Calendar, arrived shortly before that date, which equated to 23 July by the Gregorian Calendar. Unfortunately, they found that the International team match had been completed and all the shooters had by now left Bisley.[14]

This was a very closely fought contest on the first day with the United States team holding a narrow lead over the British team —1,291 to 1,281. But on the second day, the U.S. shooters continued to post marginally better scores than the British and won by 34 points. The weather was terrible on both days, but especially so on the second with wind varying from 12–20 mph (5.3-8.9 mps), low cloud cover and rain showers off and on all day.

		200y	*500y*	*600y*	*800y*	*900y*	*1000y*	*Total*
1.	United States	428	438	425	436	405	399	2,531
	William Leuschner	71	75	73	73	67	71	430
	William Martin	71	74	72	73	71	69	430
	Charles Winder	69	74	72	73	72	69	429
	Kellogg Casey	74	71	69	73	67	69	423
	Ivan Eastman	70	74	70	71	67	60	412
	Charles Benedict	73	70	69	73	61	61	407
2.	Great Britain	419	436	426	433	399	383	2,497
	Harcourt Ommundsen	68	74	73	72	70	67	424
	Fleetwood Varley	72	75	71	71	67	67	423
	Arthur Fulton	71	70	71	75	65	65	417
	Philip Richardson	68	73	70	72	64	66	413
	William Padgett	70	73	69	71	68	59	410
	John Martin	70	71	72	72	66	59	410
3.	Canada	412	418	414	434	394	367	2,439
	William Smith	71	72	70	75	72	61	421
	Charles Crowe	69	66	71	74	65	70	415
	Bruce Williams	71	74	70	74	67	58	414
	Dugald McInnis	68	73	73	74	65	60	413
	William Eastcott	69	63	65	70	64	61	392
	S. Harry Kerr	64	70	65	67	61	57	384
4.	France	397	417	378	401	373	306	2,227[15]
	Raoul de Boigne	70	72	65	67	60	51	385
	Albert Courquin	67	68	68	62	58	60	383
	Eugène Balme	70	71	65	65	65	43	379
	Daniel Mérillon	59	65	60	68	61	50	376[16]
	Léon Hecht	64	70	63	72	65	55	376
	André Parmentier	67	71	57	67	64	47	373

		200y	500y	600y	800y	900y	1000y	Total
5.	Sweden	423	425	381	378	337	269	2,213
	Claës Rundberg	72	75	64	66	57	54	388
	Ossian Jörgensen	68	73	61	67	56	57	382
	Johan "Janne" Gustafsson	70	69	63	64	59	51	376
	Per-Olof Arvidsson	72	74	66	68	50	44	374
	Axel Jansson	69	69	61	59	58	35	351
	Gustaf Adolf Jonsson	72	65	66	54	57	28	342
6.	Norway	396	391	386	394	329	296	2,192
	Ole Sæther	65	69	68	67	63	53	385
	Einar Liberg	70	70	70	65	54	46	375
	Gudbrand Skatteboe	63	61	61	67	58	59	369
	Albert Helgerud	65	63	60	67	49	58	362
	Mathias Glomnes	69	58	63	59	52	51	352
	Jørgen Bru	64	70	64	69	53	29	349
7.	Greece	384	385	357	316	282	275	1,999
	Ioannis Theofilakis	70	68	59	65	48	47	357
	Frangiskos Mauromatis	66	63	62	60	60	38	349
	Alexandros Theofilakis	64	71	65	64	32	53	349
	Georgios Orfanidis	60	62	59	40	48	56	325
	Matthias Triantafilladis	62	60	56	50	51	35	314
	Deukal. Rediadis	62	61	56	37	43	46	305
8.	Denmark	375	359	369	307	279	220	1,909
	Niels Andersen	65	60	63	68	53	43	352
	Christian Christensen	67	67	64	49	42	44	333
	Lorents Jensen	60	56	59	57	48	46	326
	Niels Laursen	56	52	58	64	43	36	309
	Julius Hillemann-Jensen	65	60	62	48	45	27	307
	Ole Olsen	62	64	63	21	48	24	282

17

Small-Bore Rifle Shooting

Small-Bore Rifle, Prone [50 and 100 yards] (English Match)

A: 19[18]; C: 5; D: 11 July; F: Prone position. 50 yards with a 1½-inch (3.8 cm.) bullseye worth 5 points. 100 yards with a 3-inch (7.6 cm.) bullseye worth 5 points. 40 shots at each distance. 200 possible at each distance, 400 total possible. Maximum bullet weight of 140 grains. Maximum velocity of 1,450 feet/second. Any breech-loading rifle shooting miniature ammunition as described was allowed.

In a very controversial event, Arthur Carnell eventually led a British sweep of the first nine places. But Carnell did not have the highest score in this event. That honor was left to British shooter Philip Plater, who is not actually considered to have even taken part.

The limit for entrants per nation in all individual shooting events was 12. But the entry forms for George Barnes, the eventual bronze medalist, were lost, and Plater was named as the twelfth British entrant in his place. However, an extension of the deadline for entries was made and Barnes' application was eventually accepted. On the day of the competition, the British team officials lost count of the number of British shooters who had competed in this event. With only half an hour to go before the time limit, they called on Plater to shoot, thinking he was the twelfth British shooter in the small-bore rifle when, in fact, he was the thirteenth — one beyond the limit. In varying light, a gusty wind, and fine drizzle, he fired his 80 rounds in less than 30 minutes, scoring 391, the leading score and a new world record. In the initial results issued by the National Rifle Association, and published in *The Sporting Life*, Plater was listed as the winner.[19]

But the error of Britain having 13 competitors was then discovered and it took several days to sort out the error. It was not certain if Plater's or Barnes' mark would be deleted from the official results; eventually Plater was declared an unofficial entrant and not given an Olympic medal. But in October 1908, Philip Plater was presented a special gold medal and a record diploma by the British Olympic Council.

			50y	*100y*	*Totals*
1.	Arthur Carnell	GBR	192	195	387
2.	Harold Humby	GBR	197	189	386
3.	George Barnes[20]	GBR	189	196	385
4.	Maurice Matthews	GBR	195	189	384
5.	Edward Amoore	GBR	194	189	383
6.	William Pimm	GBR	192	187	379
7.	Albert Taylor	GBR	189	187	376
8.	Harold Hawkins	GBR	185	189	374
9.	Jack Warner	GBR	191	182	373
=10.	Vilhelm Carlberg	SWE	184	186	370
	Arthur Wilde	GBR	194	176	370
12.	James Milne	GBR	182	186	368
13.	André Mercier	FRA	178	188	366
14.	William Milne	GBR	183	180	363
15.	Georgios Orfanidis	GRE	180	177	357
16.	William Hill[21]	AUS	183	171	354
17.	Léon Tétart	FRA	176	174	350
18.	Johan Hübner von Holst	SWE	172	177	349
19.	Henri Bonnefoy	FRA	147	157	304
	Philip Plater[22]	GBR	195	196	391

23

Small-Bore Rifle (25 yards–Moving Target)

A: 22; C: 5; D: 11 July; F: Moving target 4 inches (10.16 cm.) in height, and 1½ inches (3.81 cm.) wide. The target appeared over a 10 foot (3.05 meters) run for four seconds, during which time 15 shots were to be fired. The upper third of the target was worth three points, the lower third was worth one point. Individual possible 45. Ammunition of .22 or .297/.230 calibre only. Any breech-loading rifle shooting miniature ammunition as described was allowed.

Four British shooters tied for first in this event and the places were decided by examination of the targets. The winner, John Fleming, was a long-time member of the City Rifle Club and from 1914–1918 was an instructor at the National Rifle Association's (NRA) School of Musketry. He was in the King's Hundred in 1934 and was a life member of the NRA.

1.	John Fleming	GBR	24
2.	Maurice Matthews	GBR	24
3.	William Marsden	GBR	24
4.	Edward Newitt	GBR	24
5.	Philip Plater	GBR	22
6.	William Pimm	GBR	21
7.	William Milne	GBR	21
8.	Otto von Rosen	SWE	18
9.	William Styles	GBR	17
=10.	Arthur Wilde	GBR	13
	Walter Winans	USA	13
	Léon Johnson	FRA	13
13.	James Milne	GBR	12
14.	André Mercier	FRA	10
=15.	Léon Tétart	FRA	9
	Eric Carlberg	SWE	9
	Vilhelm Carlberg	SWE	9
	Johan Hübner von Holst	SWE	9
=19.	Harold Hawkins	GBR	3
	Edward Amoore	GBR	3
	William Hill[24]	AUS	DNF
	Frans-Albert Schartau [25]	SWE	DNF

Small-Bore Rifle (25 yards–Disappearing Target)

A: 22; C: 5; D: 11 July; F: Moving target 4 inches (10.16 cm.) in height, and 1½ inches (3.81 cm.) wide. 15 shots. The target appeared 15 times for three seconds each, with five second intervals between appearances. The upper third of the target was worth three points, the lower third was worth one point. Individual possible 45. Ammunition of .22 or .297/.230 calibre only. Any breech-loading rifle shooting miniature ammunition as described was allowed.

Eight athletes tied for first with perfect scores in this event. The places were decided by a count-back and examination of the targets. The winner, William Styles, returned as a member of the 1912 British Olympic shooting team and won a silver medal in the small-bore rifle team event.

1.	William Styles	GBR	45
2.	Harold Hawkins	GBR	45
3.	Edward Amoore	GBR	45
4.	William Milne[26]	GBR	45
5.	James Milne	GBR	45
6.	Arthur Wilde	GBR	45
7.	Vilhelm Carlberg	SWE	45
8.	Harold Humby	GBR	45
=9.	Maurice Matthews	GBR	42
	Otto von Rosen	SWE	42
	Eric Carlberg	SWE	42
	John Fleming	GBR	42

	Frans-Albert Schartau	SWE	42
	Edward Newitt	GBR	42
=15.	William Pimm	GBR	39
	Johan Hübner von Holst	SWE	39
	Philip Plater	GBR	39
18.	William Hill[27]	AUS	36
=19.	André Mercier	FRA	30
	Walter Winans	USA	30
21.	Léon Johnson	FRA	24
22.	Léon Tétart	FRA	21

28

Small-Bore Rifle, Team (50 and 100 yards)

A: 12; C: 3; D: 11 July; F: Prone position. 50 yards with a 1½-inch (3.8 cm.) bullseye worth 5 points. 100 yards with a 3-inch (7.6 cm.) bullseye worth 5 points. 20 shots at each distance per shooter; 80 shots at each distance per team. Individual possible 100 per distance, 200 total. Team possible 400 per distance, 800 total. Maximum bullet weight of 140 grains. Maximum velocity of 1,450 feet/second. Any breech-loading rifle shooting miniature ammunition as described was allowed.

		50y	*100y*	*Totals*	
1.	Great Britain	387	384		771
	Maurice Matthews	98	98	196	
	Harold Humby	97	97	194	
	William Pimm	99	93	192	
	Edward Amoore	93	96	189	
2.	Sweden	373	364		737
	Vilhelm Carlberg	95	92	187	
	Frans-Albert Schartau	96	90	186	
	Johan Hübner von Holst	94	90	184	
	Eric Carlberg	88	92	180	
3.	France	359	351		710
	Paul Colas	96	93	189	
	André Regaud	91	95	186	
	Léon Lécuyer	85	84	169	
	Henri Bonnefoy	87	79	166	

29

Pistol Shooting

Free Pistol (50 yards)

A: 43; C: 7; D: 10 July; F: 60 shots per shooter. 50 centimeter target. Individual possible 600. Any pistol or revolver with open sights allowed.

This competition came down to Paul Van Asbroeck and James Gorman, who would also post the highest individual scores in the team free pistol event, with Gorman besting Van Asbroeck in that event. Gorman was the last man to shoot but came in behind Van Asbroeck and his teammate, Réginald Storms. After the scores were announced, Gorman protested, claiming a double, noting that one of his bullets had gone through a previous hole. The protest was considered but disallowed the next day, and Van Asbroeck won the gold medal, Gorman the bronze.

1.	Paul Van Asbroeck	BEL	490
2.	Réginald Storms	BEL	487
3.	James Gorman	USA	485
4.	Charles Axtell	USA	480
5.	Jesse Wallingford	GBR	467
6.	André Barbillat	FRA	466
7.	Walter Ellicott	GBR	458
8.	Irving Calkins	USA	457
9.	John Dietz	USA	455
10.	André Regaud	FRA	451
11.	Geoffrey Coles	GBR	449
12.	Jacob van der Kop	NED	447
13.	Henry Lynch-Staunton	GBR	443
14.	William Lane-Joynt	GBR/IRL	442
15.	René Englebert	BEL	441
16.	William Newton	GBR	440
17.	Léon Moreaux	FRA	438
18.	Frans-Albert Schartau	SWE	436
19.	Thomas LeBoutillier, II	USA	436
20.	Vilhelm Carlberg	SWE	432
21.	Reginald Sayre	USA	430
22.	Jean Depassis	FRA	427
23.	Charles Wirgmann	GBR	425
24.	Petrus ten Bruggen Cate	NED	421
25.	Frangiskos Mauromatis	GRE	419
26.	Alexandros Theofilakis	GRE	409
27.	Johan Hübner von Holst	SWE	408
28.	Peter Jones	GBR	407
29.	Ioannis Theofilakis	GRE	406
30.	Léon Lécuyer	FRA	401
31.	James Le Fevre	GBR	399
32.	Deukal. Rediadis	GRE	397
33.	Eric Carlberg	SWE	396
34.	Maurice Robion du Pont	FRA	391
35.	Otto von Rosen	SWE	386
36.	Jan Johannes de Blécourt	NED	381
37.	Jacques Pinchart	BEL	372
38.	Walter Winans	USA	368
39.	Henry Munday	GBR	358
40.	Gerard van den Bergh[30]	NED	343
41.	Christiaan Brosch	NED	337
42.	John Bashford	GBR	329
43.	Antonie de Gee[31]	NED	226

[32]

Free Pistol, Team (50 yards)[33]

A: 28; C: 7; D: 11 July; F: Four man teams. 60 shots per shooter; 240 shots per team. 50 centimeter target. Individual possible 600. Team possible 2,400. Any pistol or revolver with open sights.

The United States' team won with relative ease. The captain of the U.S. pistol team, Dr. Reginald Sayre, commented, "The weather conditions were bad, and I should say that the shooting was only up to our average practice. Gorman's victory over Van Asbroeck today was a source of great satisfaction to us, however. The Continentals certainly had the advantage over us. Most of them used longer barrels than are permitted in the United States and also hair triggers. We have to pull at least two pounds in excess of them. The continental weapons are very superior for such a match as was shot today, but the better marksmanship of our team counteracted everything." Sayre also expressed gratitude at the reception accorded the American shooters in London.[34]

1.	United States		1,914
	James Gorman	501	
	Irving Calkins	473	
	John Dietz	472	
	Charles Axtell	468	
2.	Belgium		1,863
	Paul Van Asbroeck	493	
	Réginald Storms	477	
	Charles Paumier du Verger	462	
	René Englebert	431	
3.	Great Britain		1,817
	Jesse Wallingford	477	
	Geoffrey Coles	459	
	Henry Lynch-Staunton	446	
	Walter Ellicott	435	
4.	France		1,750
	André Barbillat	463	
	André Regaud	440	
	Léon Moreaux	436	
	Jean Depassis	411	
5.	Sweden		1,732
	Vilhelm Carlberg	471	
	Eric Carlberg	462	
	Johan Hübner von Holst	416	
	Frans-Albert Schartau	383	
6.	The Netherlands		1,632
	Jacob van der Kop	449	
	Gerard van den Bergh	401	
	Jan Johannes de Blécourt	398	
	Petrus ten Bruggen Cate	384	
7.	Greece		1,576
	Frangiskos Mauromatis	419	
	Alexandros Theofilakis	401	

Ioannis Theofilakis	398
Georgios Orfanidis	358

35

Running Deer Shooting

Running Deer, Single Shot, Individual

A: 16[36]; C: 4; D: 9 July; F: 110 yards distance. 10 shots in one run of the deer. 40 possible. The deer run occurred over 75 feet (22.9 meters). Bullseye of 6 inches (15.24 cm.) worth 4 points. Any single, double, or repeating rifle, of any calibre, with open sights, and minimum of 3-pound. pull.

Oscar Swahn was 60 years, 263 days old when he won this event. This would make him the oldest individual gold medalist in Olympic history except that, on the same day, Britain's Joshua "Jerry" Millner won the 1,000 yard Free Rifle event, aged 61 years, 4 days.

1.	Oscar Swahn	SWE	25
2.	Thomas "Ted" Ranken	GBR	24
3.	Alexander Rogers	GBR	24
4.	Maurice Blood	GBR/IRL	23
5.	Albert Kempster[37]	GBR	22
=6.	William Lane-Joynt[38]	GBR/IRL	21
	Walter Winans	USA	21
	James Cowan	GBR	21
9.	Joshua Millner	GBR/IRL	20
10.	Charles Nix	GBR	19
11.	Ernst Rosell	SWE	17
12.	Walter Ellicott	GBR	16
13.	Léon Tétart	FRA	11
14.	Maurice Robion du Pont	FRA	6
15.	André Barbillat	FRA	3
AC.	John Bashford	GBR	0[39]

40

Running Deer, Double Shot, Individual

A: 15; C: 4; D: 9-10 July; F: 110 yards distance. 20 shots in two runs of the deer, 10 per run. 80 possible. The deer run occurred over 75 feet (22.9 meters). Bullseye of 6 inches (15.24 cm.) worth 4 points. Any single, double, or repeating rifle, of any calibre, with open sights, and minimum of 3-pound pull.

This event started on 9 July and almost finished on that day as well. But Walter Winans and "Ted" Ranken tied for first place with 46 and it was too dark for them to shoot off the tie. They did so the next day, with Winans winning.

Winans was an American who had been born in Russia of American parents but lived most of his life in England. His eligibility was questioned and he had to swear his allegiance to the U.S. Consul General in England and expressed his intention to return to the United States after the Olympics and eventually resume his duties of citizenship. To our knowledge, this never occurred. It is not recorded that Winans ever set foot in the United States. He was a renowned equestrian sculptor, exhibiting 14 times at the British Royal Academy.

July 10, 1908 turned out to be quite a day for Walter Winans. Just after winning the shoot-off he received two envelopes. The first contained a telegram announcing that his horses had won three firsts, two seconds, and five thirds at the English Royal Counties Show. The other was a cablegram from Vienna noting his horse Samers had won the local trotting contest.[41]

1.	Walter Winans	USA	46	44
2.[42]	Thomas "Ted" Ranken	GBR	46	41
3.	Oscar Swahn	SWE	38	
4.	Maurice Blood	GBR/IRL	34	
5.	Albert Kempster[43]	GBR	34	
=6.	Walter Ellicott[44]	GBR	33	
	Alexander Rogers	GBR	33	
8.	Ernst Rosell	SWE	27	
9.	John Bashford	GBR	25	
10.	James Cowan	GBR	24	
11.	Charles Nix	GBR	22	
12.	Léon Tétart	FRA	21	
13.	William Lane-Joynt	GBR/IRL	20	
14.	Maurice Robion du Pont	FRA	18	
15.	Joshua Millner	GBR/IRL	15	

[45]

Running Deer, Single Shot, Team

A: 8; C: 2; D: 10 July; F: 110 yards distance. Ten shots in one run of the deer. 40 possible per shooter. Four shooters per team for a team possible of 160. The deer run occurred over 75 feet (22.9 meters). Bullseye of 6 inches (15.24 cm.) worth 4 points. Any single, double, or repeating rifle, of any calibre, with open sights, and minimum of 3-pound. pull.

1.	Sweden		86
	Alfred Swahn	26	
	G. Arvid Knöppel	22	
	Oscar Swahn	21	
	Ernst Rosell	17	
2.	Great Britain/Ireland		85
	Charles Nix	27	
	William Lane-Joynt (Ireland)	22	
	Walter Ellicott	18	
	Thomas "Ted" Ranken	18	

[46]

Clay Trap Shooting

Trap Shooting

A: 31[47]; C: 6[48]; D: 8-9, 11 July; L: Uxendon Shooting School Club; F: First stage (8-9 July)—30 clays at known traps and unknown angles in two rounds of 15 clays; Second stage (9

July)—20 clays at known traps and unknown angles in two rounds of 10 clays; Third stage (11 July)—30 clays, 20 at known traps and unknown angles in two rounds of 10 clays, followed by 10 clays at unknown traps and unknown angles. Shot limit = 1.125 ounces (31.96 gms.).

The *Official Report* noted that "wretched weather conditions prevailed" for this event, describing heavy rain, high winds, and poor light. The shooting area had been constructed so that July sunlight would not be in the eyes of the shooters. But in the poor light, it was difficult to see the dark shooting clays, so they were marked with white, giving them a "magpie appearance."

The competition began on Wednesday, 8 July with the first stage. A three-way tie for first place resulted after that stage between Charles Palmer, Richard Hutton, and John Postans. The next day, the Canadians lodged an objection against the previous day's scores and were allowed to shoot again. Postans subsequently withdrew, and did not shoot the second or third stages. The reason is not given in the shooting magazines, but it was presumably in anger over the Canadians being allowed to re-shoot. Canada's Walter Ewing scored 27 in the re-shoot of the second day to take a lead he never relinquished. He had the top score in all three stages. Ewing used an American Lefever gun with Winchester factory-loaded Leader shells. For his victory, in addition to a gold medal, he was awarded Lord Westbury's Cup, which was presented specially for the winner of the individual clay trap shooting.

1.	Walter Ewing	CAN	27	18	27	72
2.	George Beattie	CAN	21	17	22	60
3.	Alexander Maunder[49]	GBR	21	14	22	57
4.	Anastasios Metaxas	GRE	21	14	22	57
=5.	Charles Palmer	GBR	23	12	20	55
	Arthur Westover	CAN	21	12	22	55
=7.	Richard Hutton	GBR/IRL	23	10	20	53
	John Wilson	NED	20	13	20	53
	Mylie Fletcher	CAN	22	9	22	53
10.	Frank Moore	GBR	21	11	20	52
11.	George Whitaker	GBR	18	9	24	51
=12.	Donald McMackon	CAN	19	14	17	50
	James Pike	GBR	22	12	16	50
14.	Cornelis Viruly	NED	18	13	17	48
=15.	Eduardus van Voorst tot Voorst	NED	18	14	15	47
	Franciscus van Voorst tot Voorst	NED	19	13	15	47
=17.	Harold Creasey	GBR	22	9	15	46
	Peter Easte	GBR	18	11	17	46
19.	Gerald Merlin	GBR	18	10	17	45
=20.	George Vivian	CAN	16	10	18	44
	William Morris	GBR	10	12	22	44
22.	Romain de Favauge	NED	18	11	—	29
23.	Emile Béjot	FRA	18	10	—	28
24.	John Butt	GBR	15	11	—	26
25.	Alfred Swahn	SWE	13	9	—	22
26.	Jacob Laan	NED	13	8	—	21
=27.	Frank Parker	CAN	14	5	—	19
	Edward Benedicks	SWE	13	6	—	19
AC.	John Postans[50]	GBR	23	—	—	

Ernst Rosell	SWE	—	—
Baron Rudolf van Pallandt	NED	—	—

Trap Shooting, Team

A: 24[51]; C: 3; D: 9–11 July; L: Uxendon Shooting School Club; F: Six-man teams. First stage — 30 birds per shooter; Second stage — 20 birds per shooter; Third stage — 50 birds per shooter. 100 possible per shooter, 600 possible per team.

		9 July	*10 July*	*11 July*	*Total*
1.	Great Britain	127	96	184	407
	Alexander Maunder	25	18	40	83
	James Pike	23	22	32	77
	Charles Palmer	25	12	34	71
	John Postans	16	14	31	61
	Frank Moore	22	15	23	60
	Peter Easte	16	15	24	55
2.	Canada	114	95	196	405
	Walter Ewing	24	19	38	81
	George Beattie	20	18	35	73
	Arthur Westover	22	15	35	72
	Mylie Fletcher	18	13	34	65
	George Vivian	18	12	28	58
	Donald McMackon	12	18	26	56
3.	Great Britain/Ireland	106	84	182	372
	George Whitaker	15	18	37	70
	Gerald Skinner	17	16	30	63
	John Butt	19	12	31	62
	William Morris	18	12	32	62
	Harold Creasey	20	14	25	59
	Richard Hutton (Ireland)	17	12	27	56
4.	The Netherlands	90	84	---	174
	John Wilson	17	17	—	34
	Eduardus van Voorst tot Voorst	15	13	—	28
	Cornelis Viruly	14	14	—	28
	Franciscus van Voorst tot Voorst	18	16	—	34
	Baron Rudolf van Pallandt	14	12	—	26
	Romain de Favauge	12	12	—	24

52

NOTES

1. Entry lists are given in SL. However, there appear to be several problems with the lists for this event. Notably, Norway's and France's entries are all listed twice. No entrants are listed for Denmark, although seven Danes competed in this event. Of the entrants, there were 63 who did not compete in the event, nationally as follows: The Netherlands (10), Belgium (8), France (8), Hungary (8), Italy (8), Greece (7), Great Britain (6), United States (6), Australia (1), and Canada (1). Notably, no shooters from Italy, Greece, Australia, or Canada competed in this event.

2. DW, EK, FW, and VK have 49 starters, certainly omitting Skymoen (see below).

3. OS, p. 44.

4. VK has Barnett and Ranken tied for fourth. The tie-breaking shots are given in SLR.

5. DW has Caldwell sixth, Sellars seventh, and Kerr eighth. EK has Caldwell as lone sixth. There is no evidence of any tie-breaking shoot-offs after fifth.

6. Rogers was not listed among the original entrants in this event.

7. Rosell was not listed among the original entrants in this event.

8. Tétart was not listed among the original entrants in this event.

9. Skymoen is not listed in the OR as competing in this event, but he is noted as competing in AATM and SL. It is likely that he took a few shots and missed and subsequently withdraw without taking the full complement of shots.

10. There were 66 other entrants in this event who did not compete. Nationally, they were as follows: Denmark (12), Italy (12), Hungary (10), Norway (8), France (6), Greece (6), Sweden (6), Great Britain (3), Australia (1), Belgium (1), and the United States (1). Notably, no shooters from Denmark, Hungary, Italy, Australia and Belgium competed in this event.

11. OSVK has 4,140, an obvious typo.

12. Also entered in this event, but not competing, were Canada, Italy, and the United States.

13. OR, p. 536.

14. This story is described in Cornfield.

15. VK/OSVK have 2,272, which is certainly a transposition.

16. Scores per OR. The total given in OR was 2,227, and the individual scores do add up to 2,227. However, the scores for Mérillon total 363, while those for Hecht total 389, and both are credited with 376 in the OR. There must be a transposition of 13 points for two scores at one of the distances, but it is uncertain which is wrong. Supporting this point is that they are listed in OR between Balme and Parmentier (as we do), which indicates that their totals were between 379 and 373. Unfortunately, SL, TF, and AATM gave individual scores only for the medal-winning teams in this event so we cannot identify nor correct the error.

17. Italy was also entered but did not compete.

18. There were actually 20 competitors, but only 19 were considered official. See the following discussion.

19. TRS, July 1908.

20. As noted above, in the original entry lists, as given in SL, Barnes was not entered in this event.

21. Hill was not entered in this event. The only Australian entered in shooting, and he was entered in every individual event, was Sgt. S. A. Green.

22. Not considered an official entrant. See text at the start of this event for the reasoning. Plater is not listed in OSVK.

23. Per SL, there were 62 other entrants, listed nationally as follows: Norway (13), Denmark (12), Hungary (10), Sweden (10), France (9), Greece (6), Australia (1), and Germany (1). Notably, Norway, Denmark, and Hungary did not have any shooters compete in this event. Also, per the regulations and as discussed in the summary of this event, only 12 entrants were allowed per nation, although Norway definitely had 13 in SL.

24. Hill was not entered in this event. The only Australian entered in shooting, and he was entered in every individual event, was Sgt. S. A. Green.

25. According to SL, there were 58 other entrants, listed nationally as follows: Norway (13), Denmark (12), Hungary (10), France (9), Sweden (7), Greece (6), and Australia (1). Notably, Norway, Denmark, Hungary, and Greece did not have any shooters compete in this event. Again, the limit for entrants in shooting was 12 from any nation in any individual event, and it is unknown why Norway had 13 entrants.

26. VK has W. Milne, J. Milne, Wilde, Carlberg, Humby as tied for fourth. However, SLR notes that the 45 scorers participated in a shoot-off, so presumably, places 4–8 were also decided by that shoot-off.

27. Hill was not entered in this event. The only Australian entered in shooting, and he was entered in every individual event, was Sgt. S. A. Green.

28. Per SL, there were 59 other entrants, listed nationally as follows: Norway (13), Denmark (12), Hungary (10), France (9), Sweden (7), Greece (6), and Australia (1). Notably, Norway, Denmark, Hungary, and Greece did not have any shooters compete in this event. Again, the limit for entrants in shooting was 12 from any nation in any individual event, and it is unknown why Norway had 13 entrants.

29. Also entered in this event, but not competing, were Denmark, Greece, and Norway.

30. Gerard van den Bergh was not entered in this event.

31. Antonie de Gee was not entered in this event.

32. There were 41 other entrants who did not compete, nationally as follows: Italy (12), Hungary (10), France (6), Belgium (3), Greece (3), The Netherlands (2), the United States (2), Great Britain (1), Norway (1), and Sweden (1). Notably, no shooters from Hungary or Italy competed in this event.

33. DW and EK list this as "Military Revolver, Teams," but in the OR, the rules stated, "Any Revolver or Pistol with open sights."

34. *AATM, XLIV(15)*, p. 346.

35. Italy was also entered but did not compete.

36. DW, EK, FW, and VK/OSVK have 15 starters, certainly omitting Bashford (see below).

37. Kempster was not entered in this event.

38. DW has Lane-Joynt sixth, Winans seventh, and Cowan eighth. There is no evidence of a shoot-off for lower places.

39. Bashford is not listed in the OR, but he almost certainly competed. He is listed as competing with a score of 0 in SL, and is also listed as competing, with no score given, in TF. It is likely that he missed his first few shots and then withdrew, not taking the full complement of shots.

40. There were 40 other entrants who did not compete, given nationally as follows: Norway (11), Hungary (10), France (8), Greece (7), Sweden (3), and Australia (1). Notably, Norway, Hungary, Greece, and Australia had no starters in this event.

41. AATM, 16 July 1908, Vol. XLIV(15), p. 347.

42. FM listed this event as a dead-heat for first between Walter Winans and "Ted" Ranken, not mentioning the shoot-off.

43. Kempster was not entered in this event.

44. DW has Ellicott sixth and Rogers seventh. There is no evidence of a shoot-off for lower places.

45. There were 40 other entrants who did not compete, given nationally as follows: Norway (11), Hungary (10), France (9), Greece (6), Sweden (3), and Australia (1). Notably, Norway, Hungary, Greece, and Australia had no starters in this event.

46. France and Norway were also entered but did not compete.

47. DW, EK, FW, and VK/OSVK have 61 starters. The OR only listed 28 finishers, but implies that 61 started. There are 61 shooters listed as "Individual Competitors" per the OR, and the rules of the competition suggest that they all actually started. The contest was shot in three stages, 30 birds in the first stage, 20 in the second stage, and 30 in the third stage. The rules noted that after each stage, the field was "effectively" cut in half. The OR stated, "The competitors in the nearest proportion of half of the original number, making the highest scores in the First Stage, will shoot in the Second Stage." We know that 28 shooters competed in the second stage, which would imply that approximately 55-60 shooters started, if the rules were followed precisely.

However, we believe that 61 is the number of entrants, and not competitors, as described, and that the rules were modified in some manner. First of all, the *Official Report*, in its report of this event, does mention that "In the Individual competition, there were also a number of withdrawals." The controversy concerning the re-shoot after the first day may have led to the officials allowing everybody to advance to the second stage who wished to continue, which is what appears to have occurred.

We have checked numerous sources and cannot come close to finding 61 shooters. This includes the best national Olympic record books published in the various nations, most of the important newspapers of the United States and Great Britain, several sports journals from 1908, and several shooting magazines from 1908. Possibly the very poor weather on the first day discouraged many of the entrants from actually starting.

TF notes that 31 started, while ST lists 33 starters. We have been able to identify 31 starters. It is uncertain whether we are missing two shooters or have identified them all, and only 31 started.

For the record, the other "starters," as listed in the OR, were as follows: M. Bucquet (FRA), Cornelis Abraham Adriaan Dudok de Wit (NED), E. Fesingher (BEL), Count de Fontenay (FRA), A. Fleury (FRA), L. Gernaert (BEL), Robert Waldemar Huber (FIN), E. Herrmann (BEL), Baron Jaubert (FRA), J. A. C. Knöppel (SWE), G. Arvid Knöppel (SWE), Axel Fredrik Londen (FIN), A. G. E. Ljungberg (SWE), Léon de Lunden (BEL), Pierre Louis Lucassen (NED), P. Levé (FRA), P. Lefébvre (FRA), Frangiskos Mauromatis (GRE), Christiaan Nicolaas Jacob Moltzer (NED), Georgios Orfanidis (GRE), Henri L. R. Quersin (BEL), Count S. de Rouville (FRA), Baron A. de Roest d'Alkemade (BEL), Oscar Swahn (SWE), E. Soufart (BEL), Réginald Storms (BEL), K. Tazer (FIN), Lt. L. Van Tilt (BEL), Gerard Jan van der Vliet (NED), and Pieter Wilhelm Waller (NED). SL listed 64 entrants, the 31 starters, the 30 other entrants just given, and three additional Canadian entrants: P. Wakefield, G. M. Dunk, and J. E. Overholt.

48. OSVK incorrectly has eight nations.

49. In most sources (OR, DW, EK, FM, FW, VK, OSVK), Maunder and Metaxas are listed as tied for third. We think this is wrong, but the source for this is obviously the OR, which lists them in that manner on both pages 280 (results) and 380 (medalist lists). But the rules of the event, given on p. 275 of the OR, called for a shoot-off, "Ties to be shot off at ten birds each shooter at known traps and unknown angles, on the continuous fire principle." SL lists Maunder as the only bronze medalist, noting that he "won in the ties." OS also lists only Maunder as the bronze medalist. Further, TF and Times concur with Maunder as the only third-place finisher, without giving the specific results of a shoot-off.

50. Postans is not listed as having competed in this event by the OR. However, STBS noted that the Canadian shooters asked to shoot the first round again on the second day, and that Walter Ewing posted his first round score of 27 on the second day (Thursday, 9 July). It also notes of the second day, "J. M. Postans, who had made the top score overnight, declined to shoot again." The reason for his withdrawal is not known for certain although we speculate above.

51. FW had 36 from 6 nations. VK has 42 from 6 nations. EK has 18 shooters.

52. Also entered in this event, but not competing, were Belgium, France, and Sweden.

Swimming

This was likely the best international swimming meet to this date. All of the top swimmers of Britain, Australia, Sweden, the United States, and Hungary were present. The races were held in the 100 meter long pool which was built in the infield of the White City Stadium, just inside the running track, on the west side of the stadium.

The quality of competition was excellent. Although at this time world records were not ratified by any organized group, in all six races, the winning time was considered to be a world record. During the 1908 Olympics, however, specifically on 19 July, representatives from England, Ireland, Wales, Belgium, Sweden, Germany, Finland, Hungary, France and Denmark gathered and formed the international swimming federation which has since become known as the Fédération Internationale de Natation Amateur (FINA).

Site: White City Stadium, Shepherd's Bush, London
Dates: 13–18, 20–21, 23–25 July
Events: 6
Competitors: 100
Nations: 14

	Competitors	1st	2nd	3rd	Totals
Australia	5	-	1	1	2
Austria	1	-	-	1	1
Belgium	7	-	-	-	-
Canada	1	-	-	-	-
Denmark	5	-	1	-	1
Finland	3	-	-	-	-
France	4	-	-	-	-
Germany	5	1	-	-	1
Great Britain	28	4	2	1	7
Hungary	10	-	2	-	2
Italy	4	-	-	-	-
The Netherlands	7	-	-	-	-

Sweden	12	-	-	2	2
United States	8	1	-	1	2
Totals	100	6	6	6	18
Nations	14	3	4	5	8

Officials

Starters: W. M. Bull, H. E. Fern, A. Hudson, R. W. Jones, H. T. Johnson, H. Thomsett

Judges: W. N. Benjamin, Dr. W. J. Leighton, G. H. Roper, A. St. P. Cufflin, H. T. Bretton, W. S. Hankins, J. C. Hurd, W. N. Benjamin, A. E. Birch, W. J. Read, J. R. Mellody, G. A. Potter, R. H. Nicol, G. Marshall, R. Beattie

Referees: G. W. Hearn, A. Mosley, T. J. Hincks, George Pragnell, J. H. Fisher, H. Davenport

Timekeepers: J. C. Hurd, H. H. Griffin, J. Brogdon, W. Kendall, E. J. Plumbridge, M. Jefferson, E. J. Tackley, H. Crapper, F. Baxter, R. F. B. Cross, L. Meaden, G. T. Snow, J. S. Walker

Timekeepers for Second: R. F. B. Cross, H. Crapper, E. J. Tackley, W. E. Bull, F. Baxter

Turning Judges: A. W. Creasy, C. E. Macrae, G. H. Gray, F. Cordingley, W. H. M. Marx, G. T. Evershed, W. Beven, A. St. P. Cufflin, G. A. Potter

Stewards: H. E. Fern, W. G. Emery, R. W. Jones, F. O. Venning, G. Ludlam, T. Clegg, J. H. Phipps, A. G. Chalmers, H. B. Howard, G. H. Lee, A. W. Creasy, J. H. Buckle, H. Bolton, H. B. Martin, A. Freedman, H. T. Bretton, G. F. Simmons, H. J. Johnson, W. S. Hankins, M. Jefferson, Conway G. Warne, A. Richardson, H. T. Edney, T. Roe, R. S. Town, F. Harris, J. G. Coppock, A. Judkins, E. J. Plumbridge, J. E. Hopkinson, J. C. Richardson, G. A. Potter, J. S. Walker

Lap Scorers: Harry J. Barclay, A. E. Ormondroyd, T. Clegg, W. S. Hawkins

Costume Stewards: W. G. Emery, W. S. Hawkins, H. J. Johnson, R. W. Jones

Press Stewards: H. T. Bretton, G. F. Simmons, W. E. Bull, Conway G. Warne, A. Sinclair

Telegraph Steward: A. Freedman, E. A. Johns

100 Meter Freestyle

A: 34; C: 12; D: 17, 20 July.

The final brought together the two top sprinters in the world and the last two Olympic champions. Charles Daniels had won in 1906 at Athens, and in 1904 at St. Louis he had finished third behind Hungary's Zoltán von Halmay. Halmay was the recognized holder of the world record, having posted 1:06.8 in Vienna on 3 December 1905.

In the final, Halmay started quickly and led through 30 meters, when Daniels caught him. At 50 meters, Daniels had a very slight lead. At the finish he was ahead by ½ yard, while Halmay led Harald Julin by 2 yards. Both Daniels and Halmay broke the old world record.

Final A: 4; C: 3; D: 20 July; T: 1430.

1. Charles Daniels	USA	1:05.6	OR, WR
2. Zoltán von Halmay	HUN	1:06.2	

3. Harald Julin	SWE	1:08.0[1]*	
4. Leslie Rich	USA		

Semi-Finals A: 11; C: 6; D: 20 July; T: 1100; F: First two in each heat advanced to the final.

Heat 1 A: 6; C: 5; F: Winners of heats 1, 3, 4, 6, and 7 in the first round to compete.

1. Zoltán von Halmay	HUN	1:09.4	Q
2. Harald Julin	SWE	1:10.2	Q
3. Harry Hebner	USA	1:11.8	
4. Frank Beaurepaire	AUS		
AC. Wilfred Edwards	GBR		
Paul Radmilovic[2]	GBR		

Heat 2 A: 5; C: 3; F: Winners of heats 2, 5, 8, 9, and the fastest loser in the first round to compete.

1. Charles Daniels	USA	1:10.2	Q
2. Leslie Rich	USA	1:10.8	Q
3. George Dockrell	GBR/IRL	1:11.4	
4. Otto Scheff	AUT		
5. Addin Tyldesley	GBR		

Round One A: 34; C: 12; D: 17 July; T: 1615; F: Winners of heats and fastest loser advance to semi-finals.

Heat 1 A: 6; C: 6.

1. Zoltán von Halmay	HUN	1:08.2	Q
2. Theodore Tartakover	AUS	won easily	
AC. Bouke Benenga	NED		
Herman Meyboom	BEL		
Harald Klem	DEN		
Davide Baiardo	ITA		

Heat 2 A: 5; C: 5.

1. Otto Scheff	AUT	1:11.4	Q
2. Arthur Tyldesley	GBR	1:12.0	Q
AC. Gérard Meister	FRA		
József Munk	HUN		
Conrad Trubenbach	USA		

Heat 3 A: 5; C: 5.

1. Frank Beaurepaire	AUS	1:13.2	Q
2. Lambertus Benenga	NED	1:14.0	
AC. Poul Holm	DEN		
Henrik Hajós	HUN		
Robert Andersson	SWE		

Heat 4 A: 4; C: 4.

1.	Harald Julin	SWE	1:12.0	Q
2.	John Derbyshire	GBR	1:12.6	
AC.	Robert Foster	USA		
	Victor Boin	BEL		

3

Heat 5 A: 5; C: 5.

1.	Charles Daniels	USA	1:05.8	Q
2.	József Ónody	HUN	1:13.2	
3.	George Innocent	GBR		
AC.	René André	FRA		
	Hjalmar Saxtorph	DEN		

Heat 6 A: 4; C: 4.

1.	Harry Hebner	USA	1:11.0	Q
2.	Paul Radmilovic	GBR	1:12.0	Q
AC.	Fernand Feyaerts	BEL		
	Edward Cooke	AUS		

4

Heat 7 A: 2; C: 3.

1.	Wilfred Edwards	GBR	1:15.8	Q
2.	Robert Zimmerman	CAN	1:35.0	

5

Heat 8 A: 1; C: 2.

1.	George Dockrell	GBR/IRL	1:13.2	Q

6

Heat 9 A: 2; C: 2.

1.	Leslie Rich	USA	1:14.6	Q
2.	André Duprez	BEL	1:18.0	

7

400 Meter Freestyle

A: 25; C: 10; D: 13–16 July.

There was no official world record at this time. The two favorites were Henry Taylor and Frank Beaurepaire. Taylor had won the mile race and finished second in the 400 meters at the 1906 Athens Olympics. He had won the Amateur Swimming Association (ASA) title at 440 yards in 1906–1907, but in 1908, Beaurepaire took the championship. The defending Olympic champion at this distance was also present, the Austrian Otto Scheff. The top American swimmer, Charles Daniels, was entered in this event, but withdrew to save himself for the shorter distance sprint and the relay.[8]

In the final, Taylor had the fastest start. After one lap (100 meters in 1:15.0), Taylor, Beaurepaire, and Scheff were in a virtual dead heat. The 200 meters was passed in 2:35 by Taylor, leading Scheff, who was clocked at 2:37.0. Beaurepaire then came up quickly, and after 300 meters, he and Taylor were equal at 4:10.0. But the effort exhausted the Australian as Taylor drew away to win by at least 5 yards. Austria entered a protest in Scheff's behalf, claiming that he was fouled in the final, but it was disallowed.

Final A: 4; C: 3; D: 16 July; T: 1615.

1. Henry Taylor	GBR	5:36.8	OR, WR
2. Frank Beaurepaire	AUS	5:44.2	
3. Otto Scheff	AUT	5:46.0	
4. William Foster	GBR		

Semi-Finals A: 9; C: 4; D: 15 July; T: 1100; F: First two in each heat advanced to the final.

Heat 1 A: 5; C: 3; F: Winners of heats 1, 6, 7, 9, and fastest loser in the first round to compete.

1. Otto Scheff	AUT	5:40.6	Q	OR
2. Henry Taylor	GBR	5:41.0	Q	
3. Sydney Battersby	GBR	at 4 yards		
4. Béla Las Torres	HUN			
5. Henrik Hajós	HUN			

Heat 2 A: 4; C: 3; F: Winners of heats 2, 3, 4, 5, and 8 in the first round to compete.

1. Frank Beaurepaire	AUS	5:44.0	Q
2. William Foster	GBR	5:52.2	Q
3. Paul Radmilovic	GBR	at 8 yards	
4. Imre Zachár	HUN		

[9]

Round One A: 25; C: 10; D: 13-14 July; F: Winners of heats and fastest loser advance to semi-finals.

Heat 1 A: 5; C: 5; D: 13 July; T: 1600.

1. Sydney Battersby	GBR	5:48.8	Q
2. Béla Las Torres	HUN	5:52.2	Q
3. Leo "Budd" Goodwin	USA		
4. Vilhelm Andersson	SWE		
Henri Decoin	FRA	DNF	

[10]

Heat 2 A: 2; C: 2; D: 13 July; T: 1600.

1. William Foster	GBR	5:54.8	Q
2. Robert Andersson	SWE	6:28.0	

[11]

Heat 3 A: 1; C: 1; D: 13 July; T: 1600.

1. Theodore Tartakover   AUS   6:35.0   Q
    12

Heat 4 A: 4; C: 4; D: 14 July; T: 1645.

1. Frank Beaurepaire   AUS   5:49.2   Q
2. Sam Blatherwick   GBR   6:16.8
3. Conrad Trubenbach   USA
   Davide Baiardo   ITA   DNF
    13

Heat 5 A: 2; C: 2; D: 14 July; T: 1645.

1. Paul Radmilovic   GBR   6:10.0   Q
2. Aage Holm   DEN   8:08.8
    14

Heat 6 A: 3; C: 3; D: 14 July; T: 1645.

1. Henry Taylor   GBR   5:42.2   Q
2. Frederick Springfield   AUS   5:57.4
3. Mario Massa   ITA   at 50 yards
    15

Heat 7 A: 5; C: 5; D: 14 July; T: 1645.

1. Otto Scheff   AUT   5:51.0   Q
2. William Haynes   GBR   6:21.2
3. József Ónody   HUN
AC. Friedrich Meuring   NED
   Hjalmar Saxtorph   DEN

Heat 8 A: 1; C: 1; D: 14 July; T: 1645.

1. Imre Zachár   HUN   6:09.8   Q
    16

Heat 9 A: 2; C: 2; D: 14 July; T: 1645.

1. Henrik Hajós   HUN   6:19.8   Q
2. Arthur Sharp   GBR   7:00.4
    17

1,500 Meter Freestyle

A: 19; C: 8; D: 21, 23, 25 July.

The favorites were again Henry Taylor and Frank Beaurepaire. Taylor had won the ASA title over one mile in 1906–1907 but Beaurepaire claimed the 1908 championship. However, in the final, the second Briton, Sydney Battersby, led the race almost throughout. He went to the front immediately and led each lap through 1,300 meters. Taylor passed him shortly before the end of the fourteenth lap, and Beaurepaire was only a few yards behind, still in the race. But

Taylor hung on, and held off Battersby to win by 2½ yards over his countryman. Taylor then stopped, but Battersby continued to swim, as planned, and set a new world's record for one mile of 24:33.0, beating David Billington's (GBR) 1905 mark of 24:42.6.

Final A: 4; C: 3; D: 25 July; F: 1530.

1. Henry Taylor	GBR	22:48.4	OR, WR
2. Sydney Battersby	GBR	22:51.2	
3. Frank Beaurepaire	AUS	22:56.2	
Otto Scheff	AUT	DNF	

18

Semi-Finals A: 8; C: 3; D: 23 July; T: 1545; F: First two in each heat advanced to the final.

Heat 1 A: 4; C: 2; F: Winners of heats 2, 3, 6, and 7 in the first round to compete.

1. Henry Taylor	GBR	22:54.0	Q
2. Frank Beaurepaire	AUS	23:25.4	Q
3. William Foster	GBR		
4. Lewis Moist	GBR		

Heat 2 A: 4; C: 2; F: Winners of heats 1, 4, and 5 and the fastest loser in the first round to compete.

1. Sydney Battersby	GBR	23:23.0	Q
2. Otto Scheff	AUT	24:25.4	Q
AC. John Jarvis	GBR	DNF	
Paul Radmilovic	GBR	DNS	

Round One A: 19; C: 8; D: 21 July; T: 1430; F: Winners of heats and fastest loser advance to semi-finals.

Heat 1 A: 3; C: 3.

1. Paul Radmilovic	GBR	25:02.4	Q
2. Gunnar Wennerström	SWE	27:15.4	
3. Oreste Muzzi	ITA	28:52.8	

19

Heat 2 A: 4; C: 4.

1. Frank Beaurepaire	AUS	23:45.8	Q
2. Sam Blatherwick	GBR	25:15.4	
3. Pieter Ooms	NED	27:24.4	
4. Vilhelm Andersson	SWE	27:34.4	

20

Heat 3 A: 1; C: 1.

1. Lewis Moist	GBR	26:52.0	Q

21

Heat 4 A: 3; C: 3.

1. Sydney Battersby	GBR	23:42.8	Q
2. Frederick Springfield	AUS	24:52.4	
3. André Theuriet	FRA	32:37.0	

22

Heat 5 A: 3; C: 2.

1. John Jarvis	GBR	25:51.6	Q
2. James Green	USA	28:09.0	
3. Richard Hassell	GBR	28:14.8	

23

Heat 6 A: 4; C: 4.

1. Henry Taylor	GBR	23:24.4	Q
2. Otto Scheff	AUT	24:15.8	Q
3. Gustaf Wretman	SWE	28:40.8	
Eduard Meijer	NED	DNF	

24

Heat 7 A: 1; C: 1.

1. William Foster	GBR	24:33.4	Q

25

100 Meter Backstroke

A: 21; C: 11; D: 16-17 July.

The Germans were considered the top backstroke swimmers in the world and they placed two men in the finals — Arno Bieberstein and Gustav Aurisch. Bieberstein led the final from the start, with Britain's Herbert Haresnape second until 70 meters, at which time he was passed by Ludvig Dam (DEN). Bieberstein was German backstroke champion for 1905–07 and was also Austrian champion in 1907.

Final A: 4; C: 3; D: 17 July; T: 1700.

1. Arno Bieberstein	GER	1:24.6	OR, WR
2. Ludvig Dam	DEN	1:26.6	
3. Herbert Haresnape	GBR	1:27.0	
4. Gustav Aurisch	GER		

Semi-Finals A: 8; C: 3; D: 17 July; T: 1430; F: First two in each heat
advanced to the final.

Heat 1 A: 4; C: 3; F: Winners of heats 1, 2, and 5 and the fastest loser
in the first round to compete.

1. Arno Bieberstein	GER	1:25.2	Q
2. Ludvig Dam	DEN	at 1 yard	Q

3. Max Ritter	GER	at 6 yards	
4. Stanley Parvin	GBR		

Heat 2 A: 4; C: 2; F: Winners of heats 3, 4, 6, and 7 in the first round to compete.

1. Gustav Aurisch	GER	1:28.2	Q
2. Herbert Haresnape	GBR	1:28.8	Q
3. John Taylor	GBR		
4. Colin Lewis	GBR		

Round One A: 21; C: 11; D: 16 July; T: 1630; F: Winner of each heat and the fastest loser advanced to the semi-finals.

Heat 1 A: 3; C: 3.

1. Arno Bieberstein	GER	1:25.6	Q
2. Frederick Unwin	GBR	1:29.8	
3. Hugo Jonsson	FIN	"bad third"	

26

Heat 2 A: 3; C: 3.

1. Max Ritter	GER	1:33.4	Q
2. Sidney Willis	GBR	1:34.4	
3. John Henrikssen	FIN		

27

Heat 3 A: 3; C: 3.

1. Colin Lewis	GBR	1:31.0	Q
2. Bartholomeus Roodenburch	NED	1:36.2	
3. Robert Zimmerman	CAN		

28

Heat 4 A: 3; C: 3.

1. Herbert Haresnape	GBR	1:26.2	Q
2. Ludvig Dam	DEN	1:26.4	Q
3. Amilcare Beretta	ITA		

29

Heat 5 A: 1; C: 1.

1. Stanley Parvin	GBR	1:30.2	Q

30

Heat 6 A: 4; C: 4.

1. John Taylor	GBR	1:25.8	Q
2. Augustus Goessling	USA	1:29.0	
3. Gustaf Wretman	SWE		
Oscar Grégoire	BEL	DNF	

Heat 7 A: 4; C: 4.

1.	Gustav Aurisch	GER	1:27.4	Q
2.	Johan Cortlever	NED		
3.	Eric Seaward	GBR		
	Sándor Kugler	HUN	DQ [1:27.0 (1)]	

200 Meter Breaststroke

A: 27; C: 10; D: 15-16, 18 July.

In the final, Pontus Hanson took the lead and held a 2 meter margin through 50 meters. At 100 meters, William Robinson (GBR) and Hanson were equal first. By 150 meters, Hanson had faded to last, but he would recover slightly to get the bronze medal. Fred Holman did not take the lead until the last lap but pulled away to win by 2½ yards.

Holman never won a British breaststroke championship, as he could never defeat the top breaststroker of the era, Percy Courtman, who was ASA champion at 220 yards in 1907–09, and 1912–13. Courtman competed in this event, but in round one, he finished second to Belgium's Félicien Courbet, and did not qualify for the semi-finals.

Final A: 4; C: 3; D: 18 July; T: 1430.

1.	Fred Holman	GBR	3:09.2	OR, WR
2.	William Robinson	GBR	3:12.8	
3.	Pontus Hanson	SWE	3:14.6	
4.	Ödön Toldi	HUN	3:15.2	

Semi-Finals A: 8; C: 5; D: 16 July; F: First two in each heat advanced to the final.

Heat 1 A: 4; C: 3; T: 1430.

1.	Fred Holman	GBR	3:10.0	Q
2.	Ödön Toldi	HUN	3:16.4	Q
3.	Erich Zeidel	GER	at 1½ yds.	
4.	József Fabinyi	HUN		

Heat 2 A: 4; C: 3; T: 1430.

1.	William Robinson	GBR	3:11.8	Q
2.	Pontus Hanson	SWE	3:13.0	Q
3.	Wilhelm Persson	SWE		
4.	Félicien Courbet	BEL		

Round One A: 27; C: 10; D: 15 July; F: Winner of each heat and the fastest loser advanced to the semi-finals.

Heat 1 A: 3; C: 3; T: 1430.

1.	Fred Holman	GBR	3:10.6	Q
2.	Richard Rösler	GER	3:18.0	
3.	Max Gumpel	SWE		

31

Heat 2 A: 5; C: 5; T: 1430.

1. Wilhelm Persson	SWE	3:17.6		Q
2. András Baronyi	HUN	3:18.0		
3. Augustus Goessling	USA			
AC. Herman Cederberg	FIN			
Frank Naylor	GBR			

Heat 3 A: 4; C: 4; T: 1430.

1. Erich Seidel	GER	3:17.2	Q
2. Hjalmar Johansson	SWE	3:21.2	
3. Arthur Davies	GBR	at 10 yds.	
4. Pierre Strauwen	BEL		

32

Heat 4 A: 4; C: 4; T: 1430.

1. Ödön Toldi	HUN	3:14.4	Q
2. Pontus Hanson	SWE	3:15.0	Q
3. Sidney Gooday	GBR	at 2½ yards	
4. Amilcare Beretta	ITA		

33

Heat 5 A: 4; C: 4; T: 1430.

1. William Robinson	GBR	3:13.0	Q
2. Per Fjästad	SWE	3:31.4	
3. John Henrikssen	FIN		
Edward Cooke	AUS	DNF	

34

Heat 6 A: 4; C: 4; T: 1430.

1. József Fabinyi	HUN	3:23.4	Q
2. Torsten Kumfeldt	SWE	3:24.6	
3. Harald Klem	DEN		
Hugo Jonsson	FIN	DNF	

35

Heat 7 A: 3; C: 3; T: 1430.

1. Félicien Courbet	BEL	3:16.4	Q
2. Percy Courtman	GBR	3:18.4	
3. Adolf Andersson	SWE		

36

4 × 200 Meter Freestyle Relay

A: 24; C: 6; D: 24 July.

The finals saw four nations competing, all with rich swimming traditions, and all with a chance to win the relay gold medal. After one leg, Hungary's József Munk led by four yards in

2:40.8. Frank Beaurepaire (AUS) was second with John Derbyshire third (GBR) and Harry Hebner (USA) in last. Imre Zachár swam the second leg for Hungary and increased the lead, reaching 400 meters in 5:27.2, 8 yards ahead of Paul Radmilovic of Britain.

The third leg saw Hungary maintain its lead, with Béla Las Torres finishing 600 meters in 8:10.0, leading by 6 yards. But now in second was the United States, as Charles Daniels swam a great leg to pass Britain's William Foster. They finished their legs, respectively, in 8:15.2 and 8:18.6. The race appeared to be over, with Hungary's redoubtable Zoltán von Halmay swimming their anchor leg. But mainly a sprinter, he went out far too fast, leading Leslie Rich (USA) by 15 yards after 700 meters, with Britain's Henry Taylor another 5 yards back. Taylor caught Rich with 50 meters left and pulled away from him. Halmay was now a shambles and swam into the wall only 20 meters from the finish, allowing Taylor to pass him and win by 3 yards.

Final A: 16; C: 4; D: 24 July; T: 1620.

1.	Great Britain	10:55.6	OR, WR

   (John Derbyshire, Paul Radmilovic, William Foster, Henry Taylor)

2. Hungary 10:59.0
   (József Munk, Imre Zachár, Béla Las Torres, Zoltán von Halmay)

3. United States 11:02.8
   (Harry Hebner, Leo "Budd" Goodwin, Charles Daniels, Leslie Rich)

4. Australia[37] 11:14.0
   (Frank Beaurepaire, Frederick Springfield, Reginald "Snowy" Baker, Theodore Tartakover)

Semi-Finals A: 24; C: 6; D: 24 July; T: 1430; F: Winner of each heat
   and the fastest loser advanced to the semi-finals.

Heat 1 A: 8; C: 2.

1. Australia 11:35.0 Q
   (Frank Beaurepaire, Frederick Springfield, Reginald "Snowy" Baker, Theodore Tartakover)

2. Denmark 12:53.0
   (Poul Holm, Harald Klem, Ludvig Dam, Hjalmar Saxtorph)
   [38]

Heat 2 A: 12; C: 3.

1. Great Britain 10:53.4 Q
   (William Foster, Paul Radmilovic, John Derbyshire, Henry Taylor)

2. United States 11:01.4 Q
   (Harry Hebner, Leo "Budd" Goodwin, Charles Daniels, Leslie Rich)

3. Sweden
   (Gustaf Wretman, Gunnar Wennerström, Harald Julin, Adolf Andersson)

Heat 3 A: 4; C: 1.

1. Hungary [39] Q
   (József Munk, Imre Zachár, Béla Las Torres, Zoltán von Halmay)
   [40]

NOTES

1. FM has 1:08.8.

2. There were 6 starters in this heat, and 11 in the semi-finals because Paul Radmilovic and Arthur Tyldesley tied as the fastest losers in the first round with 1:12.0.

3. G. Hornung (HUN) was also entered in this heat, but did not compete.

4. J. Hegner (HUN) was also entered in this heat, but did not compete.

5. Also entered in this heat, but not competing, were Géza Kiss (HUN), Leo "Budd" Goodwin (USA), and —— Gentilly (FRA).

6. Also entered in this heat, but not competing, were R. A. Lagergren (SWE), Alajos Bruckner (HUN), Reginald "Snowy" Baker (AUS), and Paul Vasseur (FRA).

7. Also entered in this heat, but not competing, were L. Apor (HUN), Axel Persson (SWE), and Sándor Ádám (HUN).

8. NYH, 13 July 1908.

9. Theodore Tartakover (AUS) apparently did not start in the semi-final. That is the listing in SL but OR has him competing and DNF.

10. Edward Cooke (AUS) was also entered in this heat, but did not compete.

11. Also entered in this heat, but not competing, were E. Renou (FRA), L. Apor (HUN), Harry Hebner (USA), and V. de Stephanis (ITA).

12. Also entered in this heat, but not competing, were Charles Daniels (USA), T. Zoltán (HUN), Frederick Unwin (GBR), Gunnar Wennerström (SWE), and C. Regal (FRA).

13. Also entered in this heat, but not competing, were J. Hegner (HUN) and F. Roux (FRA).

14. Also entered in this heat, but not competing, were Max Gumpel (SWE), Géza Kiss (HUN), Leslie Rich (USA), and Victor Boin (BEL).

15. Also entered in this heat, but not competing, were Sándor Ádám (HUN), and André Theuriet (FRA).

16. Also entered in this heat, but not competing, were Fernand Feyaerts (BEL), Robert Foster (USA), Zoltán von Halmay (HUN), and Reginald "Snowy" Baker (AUS).

17. Also entered in this heat, but not competing, were Sigfrid D. Larsson (SWE), Alajos Bruckner (HUN), and A. Gonzani (ITA).

18. The meter splits were as follows: 100—1:20.8 (Battersby); 200—2:50.0 (Battersby); 300—4:02.6 (Battersby); 400—5:54.2 (Battersby); 500—7:27.8 (Battersby); 600—9:00.0 (Battersby); 700—10;34.0 (Battersby); 800—12:07.4 (Battersby); 900—13:42.0 (Battersby); 1,000—15:14.2 (Battersby); 1,100—16:47.0 (Battersby); 1,200—18:19.4 (Battersby); 1,300—19:51.4 (Battersby); 1,400—21:22.8 (Taylor); 1,600—24:25 (Battersby).

19. Also entered in this heat, but not competing, were Paul Vasseur (FRA), Theodore Tartakover (AUS), and Fernand Feyaerts (BEL).

20. Also entered in this heat, but not competing, were G. Drigny (FRA) and V. Bronner (ITA).

21. Also entered in this heat, but not competing, were Herman Cederberg (FIN), Mario Massa (ITA), E. Renou (FRA), and Henrik Hajós (HUN).

22. Also entered in this heat, but not competing, were Friedrich Meuring (NED), and F. Negri (ITA).

23. Also entered in this heat, but not competing, were A. Mans (BEL) and H. Jenault (FRA).

24. Also entered in this heat, but not competing, was —— Taube (FRA).

25. Also entered in this heat, but not competing, were Reginald "Snowy" Baker (AUS), F. de Pasquale (ITA), Béla Las Torres (HUN), and —— Baubiat (FRA).

26. Also entered in this heat, but not competing, were József Ónody (HUN), and Axel Persson (SWE).

27. Also entered in this heat, but not competing, were S. Eruber (HUN), and H. A. Gosnell (USA).

28. Also entered in this heat, but not competing, were Sándor Ádám (HUN), and Walter Brack (GER).

29. K. Fulop (HUN) was also entered in this heat, but did not compete.

30. Also entered in this heat, but not competing, were F. Kellner (AUT), Edward Cooke (AUS), and Herman Cederberg (FIN).

31. Also entered in this heat, but not competing, were J. Vaczi (HUN) and G. Petit (ITA).

32. Also entered in this heat, but not competing, was G. Bowidon (FRA).

33. Georg Zacharias (GER) was also entered in this heat, but did not compete.

34. H. A. Gosnell (USA) was also entered in this heat, but did not compete.

35. A. Frick (FRA) was also entered in this heat, but did not compete.

36. Also entered in this heat, but not competing, were Walter Brack (GER) and F. Negri (ITA).

37. Usually listed in sources as Australasia or Australia & New Zealand, all four members of the team were Australian, according to Australian and New Zealand source books.

38. Belgium was also entered in this heat but did not compete.

39. No time is listed either in SL or OR.

40. Italy and the Netherlands were also entered in this heat but did not compete.

Tennis (Lawn)

There were three different sets of events held in the sport we now call tennis. In 1908, "tennis" usually referred to the specific indoor game often called court tennis, real tennis, royal tennis, or jeu de paume, and which was contested at the 1908 Olympics. In those days, "tennis," as we now know it, was usually contested on grass courts, and was termed "lawn tennis." However, in addition, an indoor version of the sport was also on the 1908 Olympic program, termed covered court tennis.

The lawn tennis events of the 1908 Olympics were held at that renowned facility, the All-England Lawn Tennis & Croquet Club, better known to the rest of the world as Wimbledon. The covered court events were held at Queen's Club in West Kensington, which also hosted the jeu de paume and racquets events of the 1908 Olympics.

The 1908 Olympic events were basically European and British Empire championships. No Americans or Australian tennis players competed in London. The only players from outside Europe were from Canada and South Africa. In the covered court events, the representation was even more limited; only tennis players from Great Britain and Sweden took part.

Site:	All-England Lawn Tennis & Croquet Club (Wimbledon), London [Lawn Tennis]; Queen's Club, West Kensington, London [Covered Court Tennis]
Dates:	6–9, 11 May [Covered Court Tennis]; 6–11 July [Lawn Tennis]
Events:	6 [4 Men, 2 Women] (3 Lawn Tennis [2 Men, 1 Women]; 3 Covered Court Tennis [2 Men, 1 Women])
Competitors:	50 [40 Men, 10 Women] (39 Lawn Tennis [34 Men, 5 Women], 17 Covered Court Tennis [10 Men, 7 Women], 6 Both [4 Men, 2 Women])
Nations:	10 [10 Men, 2 Women] (9 Lawn Tennis [9 Men, 1 Women], 2 Covered Court Tennis [2 Men, 2 Women], 1 Both [1 Men, 1 Women])

Overall

	Total	Competitors Lawn	Covered	1st	2nd	3rd	Totals
Austria	3	3	-	-	-	-	-
Bohemia	4	4	-	-	-	-	-
Canada	3	3	-	-	-	-	-
France	1	1	-	-	-	-	-
Germany	5	5	-	-	1	-	1
Great Britain	22	15	13	6	5	4	15
Hungary	3	3	-	-	-	-	-
The Netherlands	2	2	-	-	-	-	-
South Africa	3	3	-	-	-	-	-
Sweden	4	-	4	-	-	2	2
Totals	50	39	17	6	6	6	18
Nations	10	9	2	1	2	2	3

Men

	Total	Competitors Lawn	Covered	1st	2nd	3rd	Totals
Austria	3	3	-	-	-	-	-
Bohemia	4	4	-	-	-	-	-
Canada	3	3	-	-	-	-	-
France	1	1	-	-	-	-	-
Germany	5	5	-	-	1	-	1
Great Britain	14	10	8	4	3	3	10
Hungary	3	3	-	-	-	-	-
The Netherlands	2	2	-	-	-	-	-
South Africa	3	3	-	-	-	-	-
Sweden	2	-	2	-	-	1	1
Totals	40	34	10	4	4	4	12
Nations	10	9	2	1	2	2	3

Women

	Total	Competitors Lawn	Covered	1st	2nd	3rd	Totals
Great Britain	8	5	5	2	2	1	5
Sweden	2	-	2	-	-	1	1
Totals	10	5	7	2	2	2	6
Nations	2	1	2	1	1	2	2

Officials

Honorary Referee: W. H. Collins
Honorary Manager: George W. Hillyard
Committee: E. R. Clarke, W. H. Collins, S. A. E. Hickson, George W. Hillyard, R. B. Hough, R. J. McNair, George Richmond Mewburn

MEN

Men's Singles

A: 31; C: 9; D: 6–11 July; F: Single-elimination.

The outdoor version of men's singles attracted a meager field, lacking the top British, American, and Australian players. The best British player of the era was Arthur "Wentworth" Gore, but he competed only in the covered court events. The top American player was Bill Larned, and the top Australasians were Norman Brookes (AUS) and Tony Wilding (NZL), but they did not compete.

In their absence, Josiah Ritchie won the gold medal, taking the final in four sets over the German, Otto Froitzheim. Ritchie was a good player but never the top player in the world. His other career titles include: 1903–1906 and 1908 German singles, 1909 and 1914 British covered court singles, 1907 Irish singles, 1902, 1904, 1906, and 1909 London singles, 1908 and 1910 Wimbledon doubles (with Tony Wilding), 1907–07 British covered court doubles (with Tony Wilding), and the 1904 and 1906 German doubles.

1.	Josiah Ritchie	GBR
2.	Otto Froitzheim	GER
3.	Wilberforce Eaves	GBR
4.	John Richardson[1]*	SAF
=5.	Charles Brown	CAN
	George Caridia	GBR
	Charles Dixon	GBR
	Maurice Germot	FRA
=9.	Walter Crawley	GBR
	Bohuslav "Černý" Hvkš	BOH
	Moritz von Bissing	GER
	James Parke	GBR/IRL
	Richard Powell	CAN
	James Foulkes	CAN
	Karel "Sláva" Robětín	BOH
=16.	Heinrich Schomburgk	GER
	Vincent Gauntlett	SAF
	Dezső Lauber	HUN
	Jenő Zsigmondy	HUN
	Arthur Zborzil	AUT
	Ede Tóth	HUN
	Oscar Kreuzer	GER
	Ladislav "Rázný" Žemla	BOH
	Harald Kitson	SAF
	Roelof van Lennep	NED
=26.	Friedrich Wilhelm Rahe	GER
	Rolf Kinzl	AUT
	Josef Gruss (Mičovský)	BOH

*See Notes on page 267.

Fritz Felix Piepes	AUT
Kenneth Powell	GBR
Christiaan van Lennep	NED

2

Tournament Draw

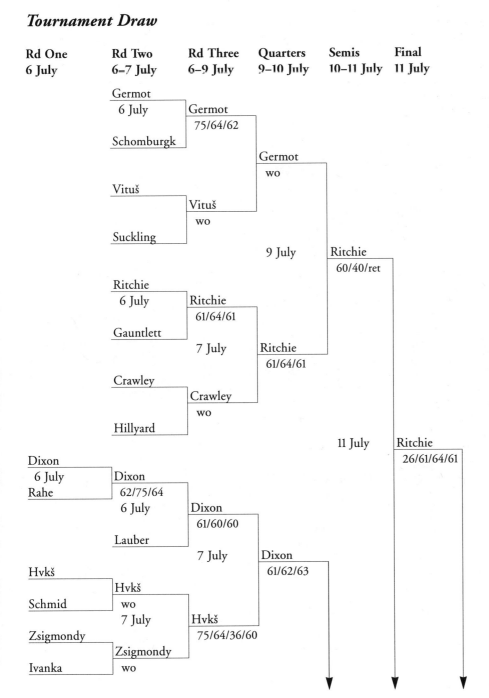

Rd One 6 July	Rd Two 6–7 July	Rd Three 6–9 July	Quarters 9–10 July	Semis 10–11 July	Final 11 July

Germot
6 July
Schomburgk

Germot
75/64/62

Vituš
Suckling

Vituš
wo

Germot
wo

Ritchie
6 July
Gauntlett

Ritchie
61/64/61

Crawley
Hillyard

Crawley
wo

9 July

Ritchie
61/64/61

7 July

Ritchie
60/40/ret

Dixon
6 July
Rahe

Dixon
62/75/64

6 July

Lauber

Dixon
61/60/60

Hvkš
Schmid

Hvkš
wo

7 July

Zsigmondy
Ivanka

Zsigmondy
wo

Hvkš
75/64/36/60

Dixon
61/62/63

7 July

11 July

Ritchie
26/61/64/61

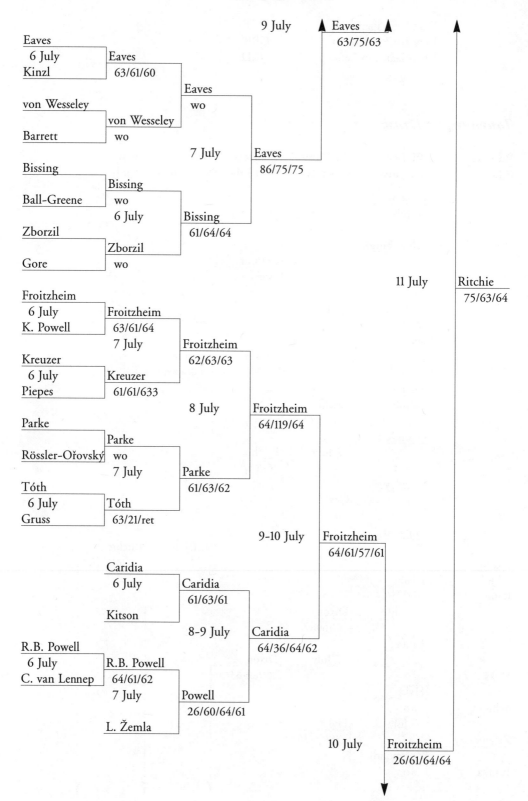

9 July ▲ Eaves ▲
          63/75/63

Eaves
 6 July   Eaves
Kinzl   63/61/60
                          Eaves
                          wo
von Wesseley
               von Wesseley
Barrett   wo
                          7 July   Eaves
Bissing   86/75/75
               Bissing
Ball-Greene   wo
                6 July   Bissing
Zborzil   61/64/64
               Zborzil
Gore   wo

                                                        11 July   Ritchie
                                                                  75/63/64

Froitzheim
 6 July   Froitzheim
K. Powell   63/61/64
                7 July   Froitzheim
                          62/63/63
Kreuzer
 6 July   Kreuzer
Piepes   61/61/633
                          8 July   Froitzheim
                                    64/119/64
Parke
               Parke
Rössler-Ořovský wo
                7 July   Parke
                          61/63/62
Tóth
 6 July   Tóth
Gruss   63/21/ret

                                    9–10 July   Froitzheim
                                                64/61/57/61

Caridia
 6 July   Caridia
               61/63/61
Kitson
                8–9 July   Caridia
                           64/36/64/62
R.B. Powell
 6 July   R.B. Powell
C. van Lennep 64/61/62
                7 July   Powell
                           26/60/64/61
L. Žemla

                                    10 July   Froitzheim
                                              26/61/64/64

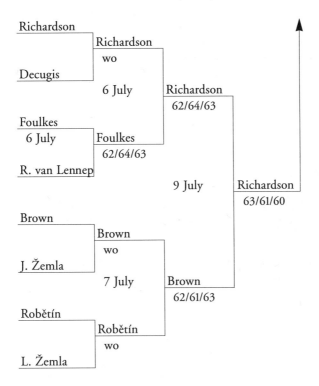

Men's Doubles

A: 24; C: 8⁴; D: 6-7, 9-11 July; F: Single-elimination.

By 1908 there was no dominant doubles team in England or in world tennis. The Doherty brothers, Reggie and Laurie, had been the top pair, winning eight Wimbledon titles from 1897-1905. But Laurie retired in 1906 because of health problems. However Reggie played on, partnering various players. He and George Hillyard won the 1908 Olympic doubles. In addition to his doubles titles with his brother, Reggie Doherty won the Wimbledon singles in 1897-1900. He played eight Davis Cup rubbers, losing only one match, and that against the top American of the era, Bill Larned.

George Hillyard was Secretary of the All-England Club for 17 years, 1907–1924, and was married to the great British female player, Blanche Bingley. At 44 years of age, he was beyond his prime at the 1908 Olympics. He had won the British covered court doubles in 1890–91 with Harry Scrivener and again in 1904–05 with Laurie Doherty. He was German singles champion in 1897 and 1900. He was also quite accomplished at cricket and golf. Together, Hillyard and Reggie Doherty also won the 1909 South African doubles, their only other title together.

1.	George Hillyard–Reginald Doherty	GBR
2.	Josiah Ritchie–James Parke (Ireland)	GBR/IRL
3.	Clement Cazalet–Charles Dixon	GBR
=4.	Walter Crawley–Kenneth Powell	GBR
	Vincent Gauntlett–Harald Kitson	SAF
	Arthur Zborzil–Fritz Felix Piepes	AUT

=7.   James Foulkes–Richard Powell   CAN
        Christiaan van Lennep–Roelof van Lennep   NED
        Otto Froitzheim–Heinrich Schomburgk   GER
        Jenő Zsigmondy–Ede Tóth   HUN
=11.   Oscar Kreuzer–Friedrich Wilhelm Rahe   GER
        Bohuslav "Černý" Hvkš–Karel "Sláva" Robětín   BOH
        5

Tournament Draw

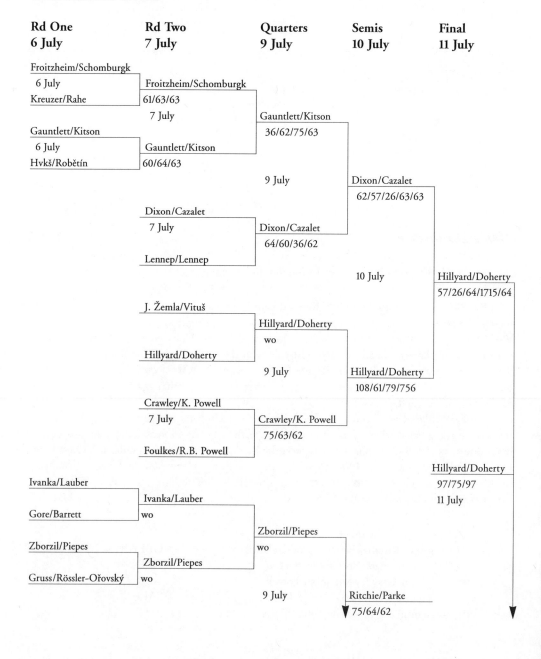

Rd One 6 July	Rd Two 7 July	Quarters 9 July	Semis 10 July	Final 11 July
Froitzheim/Schomburgk 6 July Kreuzer/Rahe	Froitzheim/Schomburgk 61/63/63 7 July	Gauntlett/Kitson 36/62/75/63		
Gauntlett/Kitson 6 July Hvkš/Robětín	Gauntlett/Kitson 60/64/63		Dixon/Cazalet 62/57/26/63/63	
	Dixon/Cazalet 7 July Lennep/Lennep	Dixon/Cazalet 64/60/36/62 9 July		Hillyard/Doherty 57/26/64/1715/64
	J. Žemla/Vituš Hillyard/Doherty	Hillyard/Doherty wo 9 July	10 July	
	Crawley/K. Powell 7 July Foulkes/R.B. Powell	Crawley/K. Powell 75/63/62	Hillyard/Doherty 108/61/79/756	
Ivanka/Lauber Gore/Barrett	Ivanka/Lauber wo	Zborzil/Piepes wo		Hillyard/Doherty 97/75/97 11 July
Zborzil/Piepes Gruss/Rössler-Ořovský	Zborzil/Piepes wo	Ritchie/Parke 75/64/62 9 July		

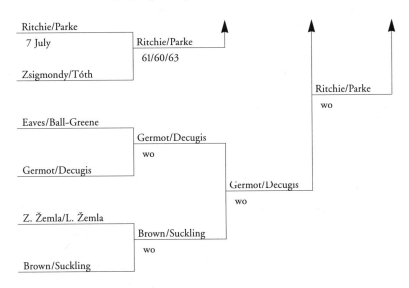

Men's Singles, Covered Courts

A: 6[7]; C: 2; D: 6–9, 11 May; F: Single-elimination.

There were only six players who ended up competing in this event, but it was significant in that the top singles player in the world was one of them, Arthur "Wentworth" Gore. He survived a very difficult semi-final against Josiah Ritchie, who would win the Olympic lawn tennis outdoors later in the year, and then won easily in the final, winning in three sets over George Caridia, representing Britain although he was of Greek origin (né Georgios Karidias).

Arthur "Wentworth" Gore had one of the longest careers of any tennis player. He played at Wimbledon every year from 1888 to 1927 and won the Wimbledon singles title three times — 1901, 1908, and 1909. He is still the oldest Wimbledon singles' finalist, losing in 1912 to Tony Wilding at the age of 44.

1.	Arthur "Wentworth" Gore	GBR	
2.	George Caridia	GBR	
3.	Josiah Ritchie	GBR	
4.	Wilberforce Eaves	GBR	
=5.	Gunnar Setterwall	SWE	
	Wollmar Boström	SWE	

Tournament Draw

Rd One 6 May	Quarters 7–8 May	Semis 8–9 May	Final 11 May

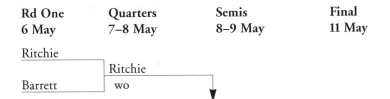

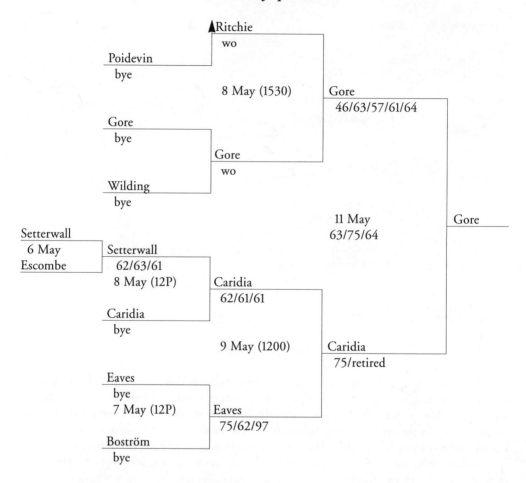

Men's Doubles, Covered Courts

A: 10; C: 2; D: 6–7, 9 May; F: Single-elimination.

This was likely the weakest of the tennis tournaments in 1908. Arthur "Wentworth" Gore and H. Roper Barrett would win the 1909 British covered court title as well. They won a four-set final over George Simond and George Caridia, who had been forced to play 13 sets in their three matches.

1.	Arthur "Wentworth" Gore–H. Roper Barrett	GBR
2.	George Simond–George Caridia	GBR
3.	Gunnar Setterwall–Wollmar Boström	SWE
4.	Josiah Ritchie–Lionel Escombe	GBR
5.	George Hillyard–Wilberforce Eaves	GBR

Tournament Draw

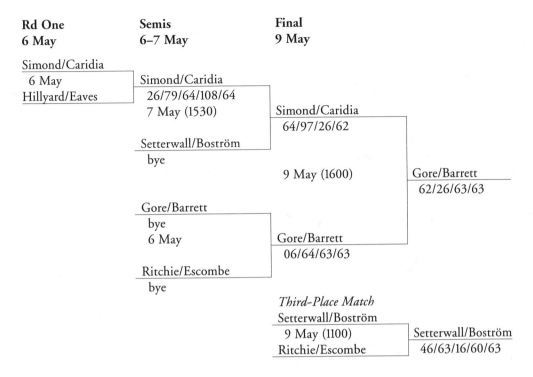

Rd One 6 May	Semis 6–7 May	Final 9 May

Simond/Caridia
6 May
Hillyard/Eaves

Simond/Caridia
26/79/64/108/64
7 May (1530)

Setterwall/Boström
bye

Simond/Caridia
64/97/26/62

9 May (1600)

Gore/Barrett
bye
6 May

Ritchie/Escombe
bye

Gore/Barrett
06/64/63/63

Gore/Barrett
62/26/63/63

Third-Place Match
Setterwall/Boström
9 May (1100)
Ritchie/Escombe

Setterwall/Boström
46/63/16/60/63

WOMEN

Women's Singles

A: 5; C: 1; D: 7, 9–11 July; F: Single-elimination.

In this unusual tournament, all of the players in the lower half of the draw scratched, leaving the tournament essentially as a series of challenge matches against Dorothy Lambert Chambers. She was more than up to the task. After Agnes Morton defeated Alice Greene in round one, she faced Lambert Chambers, who won three consecutive matches without the loss of a set to win the title.

As Dorothea Douglass, Mrs. Lambert Chambers had won the Wimbledon title in 1903–1904 and 1906. Following her 1907 marriage to Robert Lambert Chambers, she again won Wimbledon in 1910–1911, and 1913–1914, giving her seven titles in all. The runner-up at the 1908 Olympics, Penelope Boothby, would go on to win at Wimbledon in 1909.

1.	Dorothy Lambert Chambers	GBR
2.	Penelope Boothby	GBR
3.	Joan Winch	GBR
4.	Agnes Morton	GBR
5.	Alice Greene	GBR

8

Tournament Draw

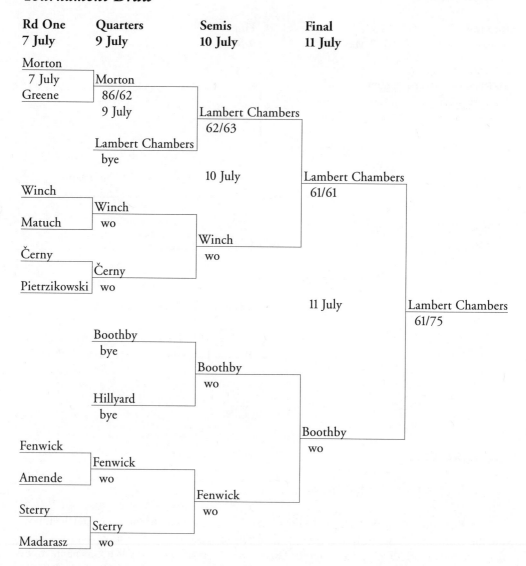

Rd One 7 July	Quarters 9 July	Semis 10 July	Final 11 July

Morton
  7 July   Morton
Greene   86/62
            9 July   Lambert Chambers
                            62/63
          Lambert Chambers
          bye
                            10 July   Lambert Chambers
                                             61/61
Winch
          Winch
Matuch   wo
                            Winch
                            wo
Černy
          Černy
Pietrzikowski wo
                                             11 July   Lambert Chambers
                                                              61/75
          Boothby
          bye
                            Boothby
                            wo
          Hillyard
          bye
                                             Boothby
                                             wo
Fenwick
          Fenwick
Amende   wo
                            Fenwick
                            wo
Sterry
          Sterry
Madarasz wo

Women's Singles, Covered Courts

A: 7; C: 2; D: 7-9, 11 May; F: Single elimination.

When Dorothy Lambert Chambers scratched in the first round to Märtha Adlerstråhle, this tournament became wide open with no clear favorite. The eventual winner, Gladys Eastlake-Smith, claimed only one other major title, that also under covered courts, when she won the 1907 British title for women.

1.   Gladys Eastlake-Smith   GBR
2.   Alice Greene[9]   GBR
3.   Märtha Adlerstråhle   SWE

4.	Elsa Wallenberg	SWE
=5.	Penelope Boothby	GBR
	Violet Pinckney	GBR
	Mildred Coles	GBR

Tournament Draw

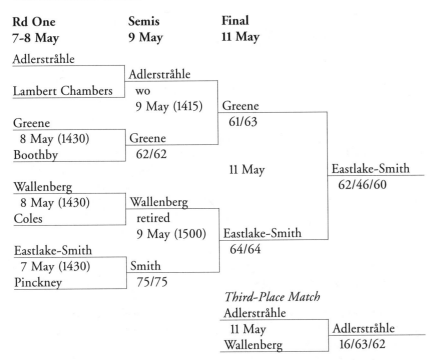

Rd One 7-8 May	Semis 9 May	Final 11 May

Adlerstråhle

Adlerstråhle

Lambert Chambers — Adlerstråhle / wo / 9 May (1415) — Greene / 61/63

Greene / 8 May (1430) / Boothby — Greene / 62/62

11 May — Eastlake-Smith / 62/46/60

Wallenberg / 8 May (1430) / Coles — Wallenberg / retired / 9 May (1500) — Eastlake-Smith / 64/64

Eastlake-Smith / 7 May (1430) / Pinckney — Smith / 75/75

Third-Place Match
Adlerstråhle
11 May
Wallenberg — Adlerstråhle / 16/63/62

NOTES

1. Listed as Ivie Richardson in DW and Ivie John Richardson in EK, VK, and OSVK. This is incorrect and the reasons are discussed in the South African index of athletes.

2. Also entered in this event, but not competing, were — Moritz (GER), G. C. Ball-Greene (GBR/IRL), Arthur "Wentworth" Gore (GBR), George Hillyard (GBR), H. Roper Barrett (GBR), H. Laurie Doherty (GBR), O. Schmid (HUN), L. Ivanka (HUN), Zdenek "Janský" Žemla (BOH), Jaroslav Žemla (BOH), Károly Vituš (BOH), Jiří Rössler-Ořovský (BOH), H. M. Suckling (CAN), and Max Decugis (FRA).

3. Listed as a walkover in OR, the score of the match was given in *The Times*.

4. VK has seven nations.

5. There were other entries listed from South Africa, Austria, Great Britain, Hungary, Bohemia, Canada, and France, but they were not listed as teams and it is not possible to be precise as to which players were paired together.

6. The 1908 OR lists the score of the second set as an obvious typo, 5-1.

7. FW, VK incorrectly have seven athletes.

8. Also entered in this event, but not competing, were M. Amende (AUT), E. Matuch (AUT), F. Pietrzikowski (AUT), Mrs. Blanche Hillyard (GBR), Mrs. Charlotte R. Sterry (GBR), M. Madarasz (HUN), K. Černy (HUN), and C. Fenwick (FRA).

9. Listed as Angela Greene in GBOG, which is incorrect.

Tug-of-War

There were seven teams entered in tug-of-war, but Germany and Greece scratched. Three teams of British policemen then competed against teams from the United States and Sweden in what was a very controversial competition. In the first round the Liverpool Police team pulled the U.S. team "in a rush," winning easily, with the *Daily Graphic* noting, "The United States remained as competitors for the shortest time on record. The Liverpool Police pulled them over the line almost as soon as they threw their weight on the rope."[1]*

The Americans then protested, claiming that the British were wearing illegal boots. The Liverpool team offered to pull again barefooted but the American team, which was composed of specialists in the "heavy" field events, made no response and withdrew. In the semi-finals Liverpool defeated Sweden, but were then easily defeated by a team of London City Policemen in the final.

The American protest did not die and received significant play in the press and, eventually, in the American and British responses to the multiple protests and criticisms made by the United States' officials. The American protest concerned the Liverpool footwear, which they considered illegal. The pertinent rule, as listed in the program, was the following, "No competitor shall wear prepared boots or shoes or boots or shoes with any projecting nails, tips, sprigs, points, hollows, or projections of any kind."[2] However, the policemen were wearing standard police boots, with metal rims, but no projecting studs or other items. The protest must have considered this footwear as "prepared boots or shoes," but it seemed to have little basis and was disallowed.

On 21 July 1908, *The Sporting Life* published the following letter directed to the American Olympic team.

> Sir,-In connection with the complaint made by the American tug-of-war team regarding the boots worn by the Liverpool Police team, I should like to state that the City of London Police team are prepared to make a match with the Americans before they return home, in which both teams shall pull in stockinged feet. The match might take place at the Stadium on Wednesday or Thursday, and the City Police would be willing to pull for anything the Americans like in the way of a prize, or for nothing at all. We do not wish the Americans to go back home dissatisfied

*See Notes on page 271.

with their beating, and we therefore give them this opportunity of showing if they are as capable "tuggers" as they claim to be.-I am, &c.,

H. DUKE
Captain City Police Team
London, July 20.[3]

The next day, *The Sporting Life* ran the following short paragraph, which should have closed out the discussion, "Mr. Duke, who captained the winning team in the tug-of-war, has been provoked into issuing a challenge in reply to the complaint about the boots of the men of whom he is so proud. They are sportsmen to the backbone, but the incident must be considered closed by the statement of a member of the U.S.A. team that they were satisfied with the result, and they knew that they had met better men at the game than themselves. 'We know really nothing about tug-of-war,' he said, 'and before we can hope to hold our own with such a clockwork team as you can put in the field we must have considerable practice. Your men won easily, and they would win easily again, and what more need be said. I have nothing to say, at any rate, and there will be no more pulling by us.'"[4]

But certain American athletes surely considered the Liverpool footwear as illegal. In the *New York Evening World*, the great American athlete Martin Sheridan wrote a column during the Olympics. In one edition (18 July), his article was as follows: "The American team was handed a real sour lemon here this afternoon when the tug-of-war event was announced. When our men went into the Stadium for the event they wore regulation shoes, without spikes or projecting nails or tips, as laid down in the rules for the contest. What was our surprise to find the English team wearing shoes as big as North River ferryboats, with steel-topped heels and steel cleats in the front of the soles, while spikes an inch long stuck out of the soles. The Englishmen had to waddle out on the field like a lot of County Mayo ganders going down to the public pond for a swim. The shoes they wore were the biggest things over here and were clearly made for the purpose of getting away with the event by hook as well as crook."

The secretary of the Liverpool Police Athletic Society finally addressed the question of "prepared boots" in a letter to the British Olympic Association.

The policemen who pulled in the tug-of-war against the American team in the Olympic Games wore their ordinary duty boots, as it is their invariable custom to pull in such boots which have gone too shabby to be worn on street duty. The boots were not prepared or altered in any way.

Yours faithfully,
[Signed] J. PARK
October 26, 1908

Hon. Secretary: Liverpool Police Athletic Society[5]

Much of the American attitude must be attributed to James E. Sullivan, who was in charge of the American Olympic team, and who lodged the official protest. In an article in *The New York Herald*[6] he described "... the prepared shoes worn by the Liverpool policemen in the tug-of-war, and the work that dishonest officials did in the committee rooms." However, in A Reply to Certain Criticisms[7], it was noted, "The American athletes never wished, for instance, to protest against the tug-of-war. They knew that they had been fairly pulled over in a game of which they were completely ignorant, and for which their manager should never have entered them."

Site:	White City Stadium, Shepherd's Bush, London				
Dates:	17–18 July				
Events:	1				
Competitors:	40				
Nations:	3				

	Competitors	*1st*	*2nd*	*3rd*	*Totals*
Great Britain	24	1	1	1	3
Sweden	8	-	-	-	-
United States	8	-	-	-	-
Totals	40	1	1	1	3
Nations	3	1	1	1	1

Final Standings

A: 40[8]; C: 3[9]; D; 17–18 July; F: Single-elimination tournament.

1. Great Britain/Ireland   (London City Police Team)
2. Great Britain/Ireland   (Liverpool Police Team)
3. Great Britain   ("K" Division Metropolitan Police Team)
4. Sweden   (National Team)
5. United States   (National Team)

Team Rosters

Great Britain/Ireland (London City Police Team)
(Edward Barrett [Ireland], Frederick Goodfellow, William Hirons, Frederick Humphreys, Albert Ireton, Frederick Merriman, Edwin Mills, James Shepherd)

Great Britain/Ireland (Liverpool Police Team)
(Thomas Butler, James Clark [Ireland], William Greggan, Alexander Kidd, Daniel McLowry, Patrick Philbin, George Smith, Thomas Swindlehurst)

Great Britain ("K" Division Metropolitan Police Team)
(Walter Chaffe, Joseph Dowler, Ernest Ebbage, Thomas Homewood, Alexander Munro, William Slade, Walter Tammas, James Woodget)

Sweden
(Albrekt Almqwist, Frans Fast, Carl-Emil Johansson, Emil Johansson, Knut Johansson, Karl Krook, Karl-Gustaf Nilsson, Anders Wollgarth)

United States
(Wilbur Burroughs, Wesley Coe, Arthur Dearborn, John Flanagan, Marquis "Bill" Horr, Matt McGrath, Ralph Rose, Lee Talbott)

Tournament Summary

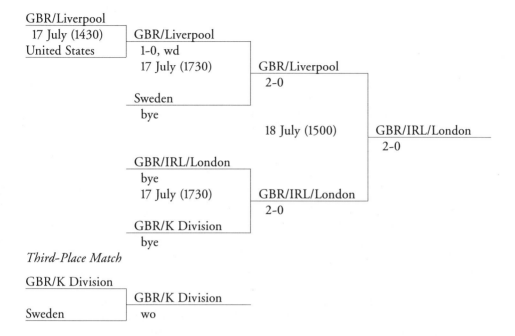

GBR/Liverpool
17 July (1430)
United States

GBR/Liverpool
1-0, wd
17 July (1730)

Sweden
bye

GBR/Liverpool
2-0

18 July (1500)

GBR/IRL/London
bye
17 July (1730)

GBR/K Division
bye

GBR/IRL/London
2-0

GBR/IRL/London
2-0

Third-Place Match

GBR/K Division

Sweden

GBR/K Division
wo

NOTES

1. DG, 18 July 1908.
2. OR, p. 408.
3. SL, 21 July 1908.
4. SL, 22 July 1908.
5. ARCC, p. 20.
6. NYH, 9 August 1908.
7. ARCC, p. 20.
8. VK/OSVK have 44, although OSVK only lists 40 athletes.
9. There were originally seven teams entered from five nations. Germany and Greece also entered teams but did not compete.

Water Polo

The withdrawal of Hungary and Austria reduced the number of competing teams to four. After beating the Netherlands (8–1) and Sweden (8–4), Belgium met Great Britain in the final. Having drawn a bye in the first round and having received a walkover against Austria in the semi-final, the final was the only match that Great Britain was called on to play during the tournament.

In the final, Britain scored the first four goals and led at the half by 5–2. They scored four goals in the second half and shut out Belgium to win, 9–2. The final was a re-match of the 1900 Olympic final, also won by Great Britain over Belgium. Britain's leading goal scorer, George Wilkinson, had played on the winning team in 1900 and for the Belgians, Fernand Feyaerts and Oscar Grégoire had also played in the 1900 final. Whereas in 1900, the British team had all hailed from Manchester, representing the Osborne Swimming Club, the 1908 team was a true conglomerate. Three of the players were from the Salford Swim Club, two from Weston-Super-Mare Swim Club, and one each from Hyde Seal Swim Club and Inverness Swim Club.

Site:	White City Stadium, Shepherd's Bush, London
Dates:	15, 20, 22 July
Events:	1
Competitors:	28
Nations:	4

	Competitors	1st	2nd	3rd	Totals
Belgium	7	-	1	-	1
Great Britain	7	1	-	-	1
The Netherlands	7	-	-	-	-
Sweden	7	-	-	1	1
Totals	28	1	1	1	3
Nations	4	1	1	1	3

Officials

Referees: Rev. G. W. Brodribb, W. Beattie, F. Baxter

Goal Judges: W. G. Emery, A. Judkins, L. Lyons, W. M. Bull, R. E. Claridge, Richard H. Hassell, A. R. Ingersoll

Timekeepers : R. F. B. Cross

Final Standings

A: 28[1]*; C: 4; D: 15, 20, 22 July; F: Single-elimination tournament.

	W	L	Goals For	Goals Against
1. Great Britain	1	0	9	2
2. Belgium	2	1	18	14
3. Sweden	0	1	4	8
4. Netherlands	0	1	1	8

Team Rosters

Great Britain

(Charles Smith, George Nevinson, George Cornet, Thomas Thould, George Wilkinson, Paul Radmilovic, Charles Forsyth)

Belgium

(Albert Michant, Herman Meyboom, Victor Boin, Joseph Pletincx, Fernand Feyaerts [captain], Oscar Grégoire, Herman Donners)

Sweden

(Torsten Kumfeldt, Axel Runström, Harald Julin, Pontus Hanson, Gunnar Wennerström, Robert Andersson, Erik Bergvall)

Netherlands

(Johan Rühl, Johan Cortlever, Jan Hulswit, Eduard Meijer, Karel Meijer, Pieter Ooms, Bouke Benenga)

Tournament Summary

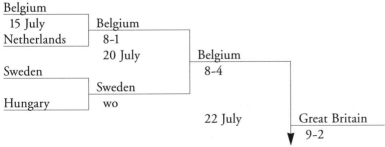

See Notes on page 275.

Match Summaries

15 July

Belgium   8   Netherlands   1
   Time: 1700
   Referee: Rev. G. W. Brodribb
   Halftime: Belgium, 3-1.
   Goals: Feyaerts (1-0), K. Meijer (1-1), Feyaerts (2-1), Feyaerts (3-1); Feyaerts (4-1), Feyaerts
      (5-1), Feyaerts (6-1), Pletincx (7-1), Donners (8-1). *Summary:* Feyaerts [6], Pletincx [1],
      Donners [1]; K. Meijer [1]
   Belgium (A. Michant [goal], V. Boin [back], H. Meyboom [back], J. Pletincx [halfback], F.
      Feyaerts [captain], O. Grégoire [forward], H. Donners [forward])
   Netherlands (J.H.W. Rühl [goal], J. G. Cortlever [back], F. J. Hulswit [back], E. Meijer [for-
      ward], K. Meijer [forward], P. L. Ooms [forward], B. Benenga [forward])

20 July

Belgium   8   Sweden   4
   Time: 1615
   Referee: W. Beattie
   Halftime: Belgium, 4-2.
   Goals: Meyboom (1-0), Hanson (1-1), Grégoire (2-1), Pletincx (3-1), Pletincx (4-1), Run-
      ström (4-2); Grégoire (5-2), Feyaerts (6-2), Andersson (6-3), Grégoire (7-3), Meyboom
      (8-3), Hanson (8-4). *Summary:* Grégoire [3], Meyboom [2], Pletincx [2]; Feyaerts [1]; Han-
      son [2], Runström [1], Andersson [1].
   Belgium (A Michant [goal], V. Boin [back], H. Meyboom [back], J. Pletincx, [halfback], F.
      Feyaerts [captain], O. Grégoire [forward], H. Donners [forward])
   Sweden (T. Kumfeldt [goal], A. Runström [back], H. Julin [back], P. Hanson [captain], G.
      Wennerström [forward], R. Andersson [forward], E. Bergvall [forward])

22 July

Great Britain   9   Belgium   2
   Time: 1600
   Referee: F. Baxter
   Halftime: Great Britain, 5–2.
   Goals: Wilkinson (1-0), Forsyth (2-0), Wilkinson (3-0), Radmilovic (4-0), Grégoire (4-1),
      Feyaerts (4-2), Forsyth (5-2); Radmilovic (6-2), Forsyth (7-2), Wilkinson (8-2), Wilkin-
      son (9-2). *Summary:* Wilkinson [4], Forsyth [3], Radmilovic [2]; Grégoire [1], Feyaerts [1].
   Great Britain (C.S. Smith [goal], G. Nevinson [back], G. Cornet [back], T. Thould [half-
      back] G. Wilkinson [forward], P. Radmilovic [forward], C. E. Forsyth [forward])
   Belgium (A. Michant [goal], V. Boin [back], H. Meyboom [backs], J. Pletincx [halfback],
      F. Feyaerts [captain], O. Grégoire [forward], H. Donners [forward])

Goal Scoring Summary

Fernand Feyaerts (BEL)	8	Herman Meyboom (BEL)	2
Oscar Grégoire (BEL)	4	Paul Radmilovic (GBR)	2
George Wilkinson (GBR)	4	Robert Andersson (SWE)	1
Joseph Pletincx (BEL)	3	Herman Donners (BEL)	1
Charles Forsyth (GBR)	3	Karel Meijer (NED)	1
Pontus Hanson (SWE)	2	Axel Runström (SWE)	1

Exhibitions

Two water polo exhibitions were given. On Saturday, 18 July, an exhibition match was held between the English Reserves and a team representing the "British Isles." The "British Isles" team won the match, 5–1, after leading 2–0 at the half. Rosters were as follows: English Reserves — A. Judkins (captain), Arthur E. Hill, P. Shaw, J. Hodgson, F. Woods, William H. Dean, Stanley Parvin; and British Isles — Charles Smith (captain), George Nevinson, George Cornet, Thomas Thould, George Wilkinson, George S. Dockrell, Charles Forsyth. Except for G. S. Dockrell taking the place of Paul Radmilovic, the "British Isles" was exactly the same as the winning British team in the Olympic tournament. Wilkinson scored four of the team's five goals, the fifth going to Thould. The Reserves' goal was scored by Dean.

A second water polo exhibition was given on Saturday, 25 July at 2:30 PM (1430). Further details of this exhibition are not known.

NOTES

1. FW, and VK/OSVK have 30. However, OSVK listed all competitors, and has only 28.

Wrestling

The wrestling competition was held on mats laid out in the infield of the White City Stadium. This was the first time that both Greco-Roman and freestyle-type competitions were held at the same Olympics. It would not occur again until 1920, at which time it became standard for future Olympic Games. In 1908, only Great Britain and Sweden entered wrestlers in both styles.

Favorites could really only be chosen in Greco-Roman as, up until 1908, world and European championships had only been conducted in that class. The matches were the best of one fall, except for the finals and bronze-medal matches, which were the best two of three falls. Time limit was 15 minutes in catch-as-catch-can and 20 minutes in Greco-Roman.

Site:	White City Stadium, Shepherd's Bush, London
Dates:	20–24 July (Catch-as-Catch-Can), 20–25 July (Greco-Roman)
Events:	9 (5 Catch-as-Catch-Can, 4 Greco-Roman)
Competitors:	115 (58 Catch-as-Catch-Can, 72 Greco-Roman, 15 Both)
Nations:	15 (5 Catch-as-Catch-Can, 12 Greco-Roman, 2 Both)

Overall	Competitors	1st	2nd	3rd	Totals
Belgium	4	–	–	–	–
Bohemia	4	–	–	–	–
Canada	1	–	–	1	1
Denmark	10	–	–	3	3
Finland	4	1	1	1	3
Germany	1	–	–	–	–
Great Britain	53	3	4	4	11
Hungary	7	1	–	–	1
Iceland	1	–	–	–	–
Italy	1	1	–	–	1

	Competitors	1st	2nd	3rd	Totals
The Netherlands	9	-	-	-	-
Norway	1	-	1	-	1
Russia	4	-	2	-	2
Sweden	9	1	1	-	2
United States	6	2	-	-	2
Totals	115	9	9	9	27
Nations	15	6	5	4	10

Catch-Catch-Can	*Competitors*	*1st*	*2nd*	*3rd*	*Totals*
Canada	1	-	-	1	1
Great Britain	48	3	4	4	11
Norway	1	-	1	-	1
Sweden	2	-	-	-	-
United States	6	2	-	-	2
Totals	58	5	5	5	15
Nations	5	2	2	2	4

Greco-Roman	*Competitors*	*1st*	*2nd*	*3rd*	*Totals*
Belgium	4	-	-	-	-
Bohemia	4	-	-	-	-
Denmark	10	-	-	3	3
Finland	4	1	1	1	3
Germany	1	-	-	-	-
Great Britain	19	-	-	-	-
Hungary	7	1	-	-	-
Iceland	1	-	-	-	-
Italy	1	1	-	-	1
The Netherlands	9	-	-	-	-
Russia	4	-	2	-	2
Sweden	8	1	1	-	2
Totals	72	4	4	4	12
Nations	12	4	3	2	5

Officials

Greco-Roman

> *Chairman NAWA:* A. H. Sutherland
> *Referees:* F. Klein, Percy Longhurst
> *Judges (Mat #1):* G. H. Wheeldon, E. P. Gruhn, A. R. Nielson
> *Judges (Mat #2):* C. Helgesson, J. J. Kenzi, Alfred Brüll
> *Timekeeper:* Albert E. Taylor
> *Scorekeeper:* H. W. Keen

Judges' Steward (Mat #1): M. E. Tredwell, F. W. Knight
Judges' Steward (Mat #2): F. G. Crust
Competitors Steward: P. Cain, F. G. Crust, C. Spital, A. White

Catch-as-Catch-Can

Chairman NAWA: A. H. Sutherland
Referees: W. H. Levy
Judges (Mat #1): F. Emslie, T. Merry, H. C. Potts
Judges (Mat #2): T. Merry, C. Spital, H. C. Potts, E. P. Gruhn
Timekeeper: Capt. D. Bremner, G. de G. Griffith, W. Lawrence Smith
Scorekeeper: J. W. Wheeldon, S. Haines, B. Sansom
Judges' Steward (Mat #1): J. W. Burch, H. C. Potts, F. G. Crust, F. Turner
Judges' Steward (Mat #2): S. Haines, A. White
Competitors' Steward: P. Cain, F. Emslie, T. Merry, C. Spital, F. Turner, J. W. Wheeldon
Doctors: Dr. J. C. McCarroll, Dr. J. McNamara, Dr. H. P. Potter

CATCH-AS-CATCH-CAN WRESTLING

Bantamweight Class (≦54 kg. [118.8 lbs.])

A: 13; C: 3; D: 20 July; T: 1000–1800; F: Single elimination.

George Mehnert had won the flyweight class gold medal at St. Louis in 1904. He won all his matches by falls. He had won U.S. championships each year from 1902-1908, with the exception of 1907. Mehnert easily defeated William Press (GBR) in straight falls in the final. It was noted, "At the end the victor offered to shake hands with the vanquished man, but the latter refused and went off grumbling."[1]*

1.	George Mehnert	USA
2.	William Press	GBR
3.	Aubert Coté	CAN
4.	Frederick Tomkins	GBR
=5.	Frank Davis[2]	GBR
	Bruce Sansom	GBR
	George Saunders	GBR
	Harry Sprenger[3]	GBR
=9.	Harold Witherall	GBR
	George Schwan	GBR
	William Cox	GBR
	James Cox	GBR
	Frank Knight	GBR
	4	

*See Notes on page 292.

Draw Summary

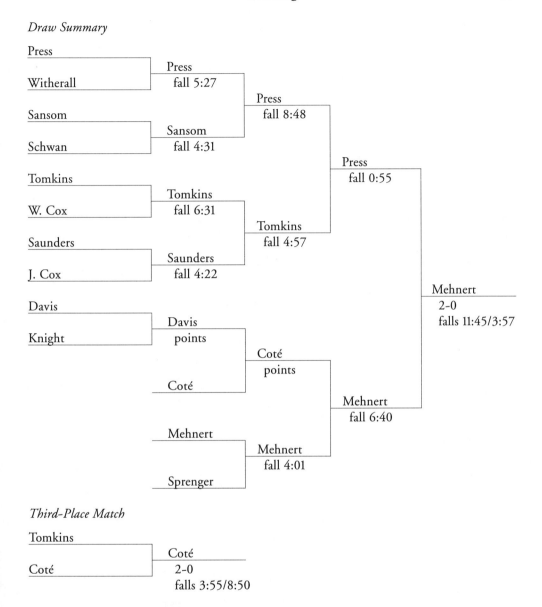

Press
Witherall
— Press fall 5:27

Sansom
Schwan
— Sansom fall 4:31

Press fall 8:48

Tomkins
W. Cox
— Tomkins fall 6:31

Saunders
J. Cox
— Saunders fall 4:22

Tomkins fall 4:57

Press fall 0:55

Davis
Knight
— Davis points

Coté
— Coté points

Mehnert
Sprenger
— Mehnert fall 4:01

Mehnert fall 6:40

Mehnert 2-0 falls 11:45/3:57

Third-Place Match

Tomkins
Coté
— Coté 2-0 falls 3:55/8:50

Featherweight Class (≦60.3 kg. [132.7 lbs.])

A: 12; C: 2; D: 22 July; T: 1000–1800; F: Single elimination.

George Dole, representing Yale, had won the IC4A wrestling championship for four consecutive years. He also won three AAU crowns—at 125 lbs. in 1907, and at both 125 lbs. and 135 lbs. in 1908. He was the only non-British wrestler in this class.

1.	George Dole	USA
2.	James Slim	GBR
3.	William McKie	GBR

4.	William Tagg	GBR
=5.	James Webster	GBR
	James White	GBR
	Arthur Goddard	GBR
	Sidney Peake[5]	GBR
=9.	Percy Cockings	GBR
	William Adams	GBR
	William Jones	GBR
	Richard Couch	GBR

[6]

Draw Summary

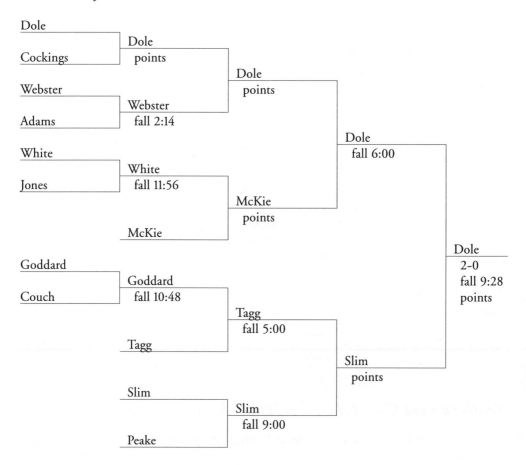

Third-Place Match

Lightweight Class (≦66.6 kg. [146.5 lbs.])

A: 11; C: 2; D: 24 July; T: 1000–1800; F: Single elimination.

George de Relwyskow was the British lightweight and middleweight champion in both 1907 and 1908. He was the only wrestler to compete in two classes in catch-as-catch can wrestling at the 1908 Olympics, as he also competed, and won a silver medal, in the middleweight class.

1.	George de Relwyskow	GBR
2.	William Wood	GBR
3.	Albert Gingell	GBR
4.	George MacKenzie	GBR
=5.	John Krug	USA
	James McKenzie	GBR
	William Shepherd	GBR
	Herbert Baillie	GBR
=9.	Joseph Hoy	GBR
	George Faulkner	GBR
	William Henson	GBR
	7	

Draw Summary

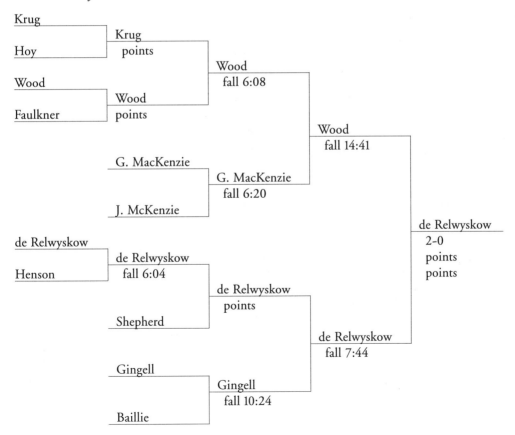

Third-Place Match

Gingell

Gingell

G. MacKenzie

Gingell
2-0
falls 6:44/3:20

Middleweight Class (≤73 kg. [160.6 lbs.])

A: 12; C: 3; D: 21–22 July[8]; T: 1000–1800 (21 July), 1500 (22 July); F: Single elimination.

Stanley Bacon was the most successful of five wrestling brothers. Stanley Bacon won 15 British championships, and his other brothers brought the family total to 30. He later competed at both the 1912 and 1920 Olympics, with less success. In the semi-finals, George de Relwyskow (GBR) defeated Carl Andersson (SWE) on points, but the Swedish officials protested the decision, stating that Andersson had been the more aggressive wrestler. The controversy while the protest was being considered pushed the final match to the next day. Andersson then withdrew and refused to compete for the bronze medal.

1.	Stanley Bacon	GBR
2.	George de Relwyskow	GBR
3.	Frederick Beck	GBR
4.	Carl Andersson	SWE
=5.	Edgar Bacon	GBR
	Aubrey Coleman	GBR
	Frederico Narganes[9]	USA
	John Craige[10]	USA
=9.	Arthur Wallis	GBR
	Henry Chenery	GBR
	George Bradshaw	GBR
	Harry Challstorp	SWE

[11]

Draw Summary

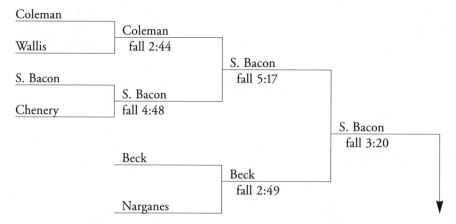

Coleman

Coleman
fall 2:44

Wallis

S. Bacon

S. Bacon
fall 5:17

S. Bacon

S. Bacon
fall 4:48

Chenery

S. Bacon
fall 3:20

Beck

Beck
fall 2:49

Narganes

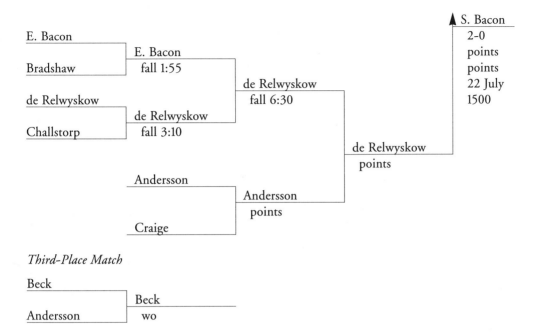

E. Bacon
Bradshaw — E. Bacon fall 1:55

de Relwyskow
Challstorp — de Relwyskow fall 3:10

de Relwyskow fall 6:30

Andersson
Craige — Andersson points

de Relwyskow points

S. Bacon
2-0
points
points
22 July
1500

Third-Place Match

Beck
Andersson — Beck wo

Heavyweight Class (Unlimited Weight)

A: 11; C: 3; D: 23 July; T: 1000–1800; F: Single elimination.

The Irish-born George "Con" O'Kelly had been British heavyweight champion in 1907, but had lost the 1908 title to Edward Barrett. At the Olympics, O'Kelly and Barrett met in the semi-finals and O'Kelly turned the tables with a quick fall. O'Kelly's son, Cornelius, boxed for Great Britain at the 1924 Olympics and later turned professional.

1.	George "Con" O'Kelly	GBR/IRL
2.	Jacob Gundersen[12]	NOR
3.	Edward Barrett	GBR/IRL
4.	Edward Nixson	GBR
=5.[13]	Lawrence Bruce	GBR
	Frederick Humphreys	GBR
	Harold Foskett	GBR
	Charles Brown	GBR
=9.	Leander Talbott	USA
	Arthur Banbrook	GBR
	Walter West	GBR

[14]

Draw Summary

Bruce
Banbrook — Bruce fall 3:25 ↓

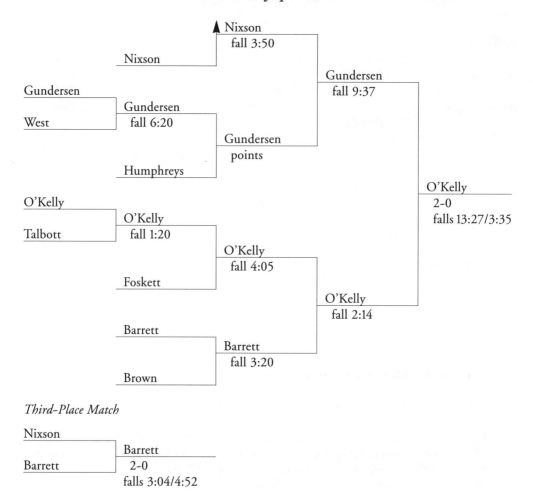

Third-Place Match

GRECO-ROMAN WRESTLING

Lightweight Class (≦66.6 kg. [146.5 lbs.])

A: 25; C: 10; D: 23, 25 July; T: 1000–1800 (23 July), 1000 (25 July); F: Single elimination.

This was the largest class of the 1908 Olympic wrestling competition. Gustaf Malmström (SWE) was European champion in 1907 at 75 kg., and he would win again in 1909 at 67½ kg., but at London he lost in the quarter-finals to the Italian, Enrico Porro. Porro went on to win the gold medal. He competed at the Olympics again, in both 1920 and 1924, failing to medal both times. But none of the three medalists ever competed at a world or European championship.

1. Enrico Porro   ITA
2. Nikolay Orlov   RUS
3. Arvo Lindén   FIN

4.	Gunnar Persson	SWE
=5.	Anders Møller	DEN
	Ödön Radvány	HUN
	Gustaf Malmström	SWE
	József Maróthy	HUN
=9.	Carl Carlsen	DEN
	George Faulkner	GBR
	Carl Erik Lund	SWE
	Arthur Hawkins	GBR
	József Téger	HUN
	Ulferd Bruseker	NED
	Edward Blount	GBR
	William Wood	GBR
=17.	Lucien Hansen	BEL
	Fernand Steens	BEL
	Andrew Whittingstall	GBR
	William Ruff	GBR
	Christian Carlsen	DEN
	Jacob van Moppes	NED
	George MacKenzie	GBR
	Arthur Rose	GBR
	Karel Halík	BOH

Draw Summary

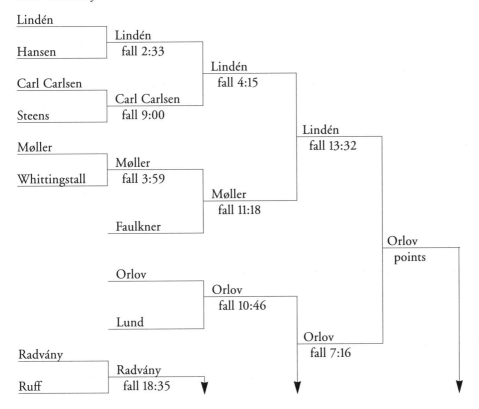

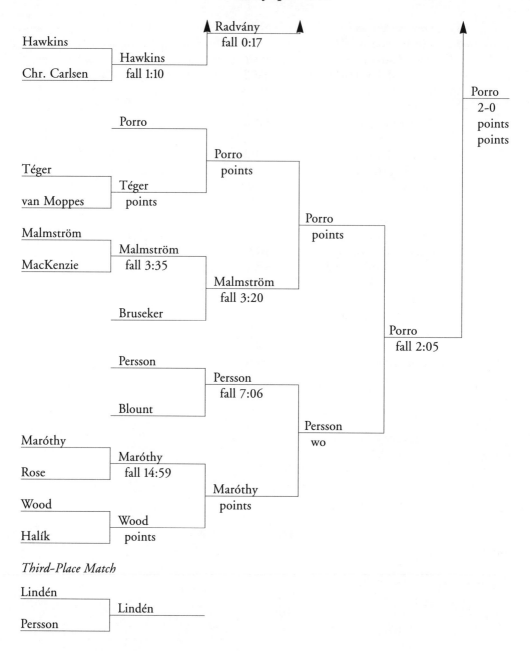

Third-Place Match

Lindén
      Lindén
Persson

Middleweight Class (≦73 kg. [160.6 lbs.])

A: 21; C: 9; D: 20, 24–25 July; T: 1000–1800 (20, 24 July), 1000 (25 July); F: Single elimination.

The top eight wrestlers in this class all hailed from Scandinavia. The fourth-place finisher, Jóhannes Jósepsson of Iceland, which is considered a part of Scandinavia, technically represented Denmark at the Olympics, as Iceland was still a Danish province. He forfeited the third-place match due to a broken arm which he had sustained in the semi-finals.

The final between the two Swedes, Frithiof Mårtensson and Mauritz Andersson, was also postponed overnight because of an injury sustained by Mårtensson in the semis. But he overcame that injury to win two successive bouts in the final against his countryman, the first on points and the second by a fall in 6:25. Mårtensson would also win the 1909 European championship at 75 kg.

1.	Frithiof Mårtensson	SWE
2.	Mauritz Andersson	SWE
3.	Anders Andersen	DEN
4.	Jóhannes Jósepsson	ISL
=5.[15]	Johannes Eriksen	DEN
	Axel Frank	SWE
	Axel Larsson	DEN
	Jacob "Jaap" Belmer	NED
=9.	Frederick Beck	GBR
	Edgar Bacon	GBR
	Miklós Orosz	HUN
	Georgy Demin[16]	RUS
	George Bradshaw	GBR
	Aäron Lelie	NED
	Jacobus Lorenz	NED
	Jaroslav Týfa	BOH
=17.	Stanley Bacon	GBR
	Harry Challstorp[17]	SWE
	Josef "Jakoubek" Bechyně	BOH
	Gerrit Duijm	NED
	Wilhelm Grundmann	GER

18

Draw Summary

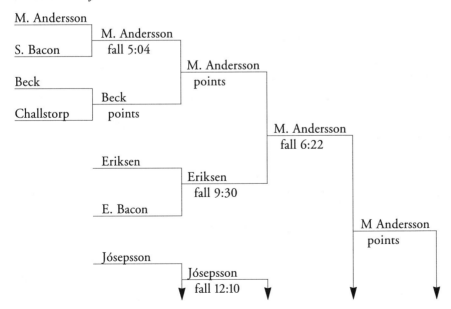

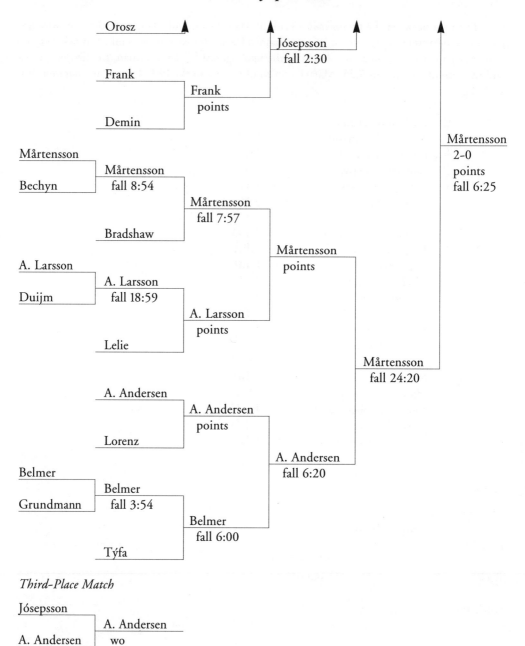

Third-Place Match

Jósepsson
                 A. Andersen
A. Andersen   wo

Light-Heavyweight Class (≦73 kg. [160.6 lbs.])

A: 21; C: 9; D: 22 July; T: 1000–1800; F: Single elimination.

This class brought together two recent champions. Verner Weckman (FIN) had been world heavyweight champion in 1905, and Carl Jensen (DEN) was the 1907 European heavyweight champion. In addition, Weckman had won the middleweight gold medal at the 1906 Olympics.

Weckman barely escaped with his second gold medal, winning the final over Yrjö Saarela (FIN) by two falls to one, taking the deciding fall in 16:10.

Weckman was not able to see the Finnish flag raised at the awards ceremony, but only a placard bearing the name "Finland." This was because Finland was still a province of Russia and the Russian authorities refused to allow Finland to display its flag.

1.	Verner Weckman	FIN
2.	Yrjö Saarela	FIN
3.	Carl Jensen	DEN
4.	Hugó Payr	HUN
=5.	Fritz Larsson[19]	SWE
	Jacob van Westrop	NED
	Marcel Dubois	BEL
	Arthur Banbrook	GBR
=9.	Douwe Wijbrands	NED
	Walter West	GBR
	Yevgeny Zamotin	RUS
	Jussi Kivimäki	FIN
	Edward Nixson	GBR
	Charles Brown	GBR
	Leendert van Oosten	NED
	August Meesen	BEL
=17.	Harald Christiansen	DEN
	Miroslav Šustera	BOH
	Henri Nielsen	DEN
	Harold Foskett	GBR
	György Luntzer	HUN

[20]

Draw Summary

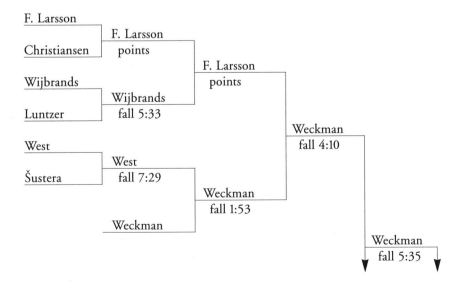

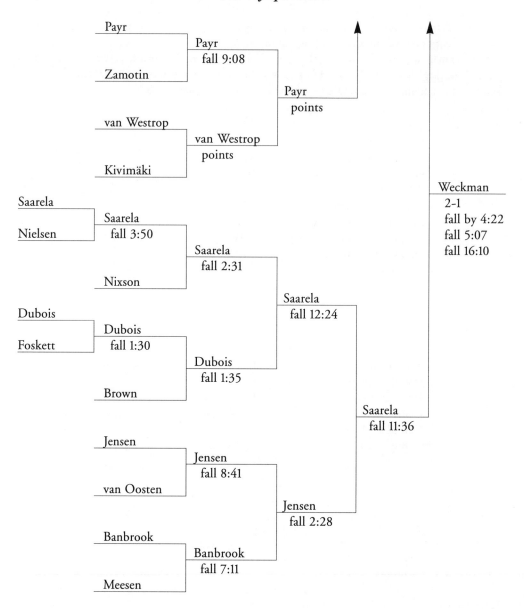

Payr

Payr
fall 9:08

Zamotin

Payr
points

van Westrop

van Westrop
points

Kivimäki

Weckman
2-1
fall by 4:22
fall 5:07
fall 16:10

Saarela

Saarela
fall 3:50

Nielsen

Saarela
fall 2:31

Nixson

Saarela
fall 12:24

Dubois

Dubois
fall 1:30

Foskett

Dubois
fall 1:35

Brown

Saarela
fall 11:36

Jensen

Jensen
fall 8:41

van Oosten

Jensen
fall 2:28

Banbrook

Banbrook
fall 7:11

Meesen

Third-Place Match

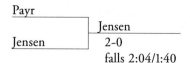

Payr

Jensen
Jensen

2-0
falls 2:04/1:40

Heavyweight Class (Unlimited Weight)

A: 7; C: 4; D: 21, 24 July; T: 1000–1800 (21 July); 1700 (24 July); F: Single elimination.

Of the most recent world champions, only Søren Marinus Jensen (DEN), champion in 1905, competed. He was also the defending Olympic champion in this event, having won at Athens in 1906. His countryman, Carl Jensen (DEN), had been 1907 European champion. Both lost to the Hungarian Richárd Weisz. Weisz was a remarkably versatile athlete, having won Hungarian championships in hammer throw, fencing, and weightlifting, as well as the national heavyweight wrestling title five times—1905–09.

1.	Richárd Weisz	HUN
2.	Aleksandr Petrov	RUS
3.	Søren Marinus Jensen	DEN
4.	Hugó Payr	HUN
=5.[21]	Frederick Humphreys	GBR
	Edward Barrett	GBR/IRL
	Carl Jensen	DEN
22		

Draw Summary

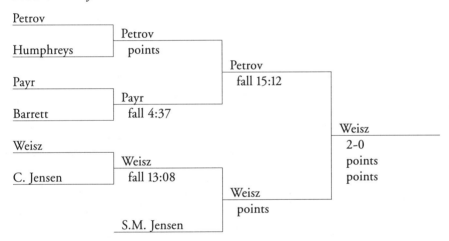

Third-Place Match

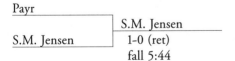

EXHIBITION

Glíma, Cumberland, and Westmoreland Wrestling

On the last day of the stadium competitions, exhibitions of both Glíma (Icelandic) and Cumberland and Westmoreland wrestling were given in the infield of the stadium. These were held on Saturday, 25 July at 3 P.M. (1500). The Cumberland and Westmoreland events took place on the North Platform of the infield, while the Glíma events were held on the South Platform.

NOTES

1. NYHP, 21 July 1908.
2. Listed as sole fifth in VK.
3. DW did not list Sprenger as tied for fifth or among the top eight.
4. G. H. Sealey (GBR) was also entered but did not compete.
5. DW did not list Peake as tied for fifth or among the top eight.
6. A. Holloway (GBR) was also entered but did not compete.
7. Also entered, but not competing, were H. J. Collett (GBR), Edward J. Blount (GBR), and A. Struby (SUI).
8. Only the finals were held on 22 July.
9. DW did not list Narganes as tied for fifth or among the top eight.
10. DW did not list Craige as tied for fifth or among the top eight.
11. H. Gerig (USA) was also entered but did not compete.
12. Gundersen was not in the original entry lists.
13. DW listed Lawrence Bruce as sole fifth and did not mention Humphreys, Foskett, or Brown.
14. Also entered, but not competing, were F. H. Harman (GBR), Harry Challstorp (SWE), and Carl Andersson (SWE).
15. DW, and VK have Marcel Dubois (BEL) as fifth alone. He did not compete in this event, but in the light-heavyweight class.
16. Demin was not entered in this event.
17. Challstorp was not entered in this event.
18. Also entered in this event, but not competing, were J. Jvisak (BOH), George de Relwyskow (GBR), J. Baddeley (GBR), J. Gelok (NED), C. A. de Haan (NED), J. Sint (NED), C. H. D. Tugt (NED), A. F. W. Pofinger (NED), J. Barrette (NED), C. van Ederen (NED), Carl G. Andersson (SWE), C. Jørgensen (DEN), W. Petersen (DEN), B. Csudor (HUN), and A. Horwath (HUN).
19. VK has Larsson has sole fifth.
20. The entrants are not listed separately in SL. They appear to be listed at the end of the Middleweight entrants but some nations' entrants are obviously omitted. Thus we cannot be precise about who was or was not entered in this event. It can be noted that the following wrestlers competed, as noted above, but are not listed as entered in the SL lists: Hugó Payr (HUN), Jacob van Westrop (NED), Marcel Dubois (BEL), Douwe Wijbrands (NED), Yevgeny Zamotin (RUS), Leendert van Oosten (NED), August Meesen (BEL), and Miroslav Šustera (BOH). In addition, there were a few entrants who definitely did not compete, as follows: Frederick Beck (GBR), C. Sandberg (SWE), F. F. Svam (DEN), Josef "Jakoubek" Bechyně (BOH), A. Andreoli (ITA), and A. Heessen (BEL).
21. VK has Barrett fifth and Jensen and Humphreys as tied for sixth. All lost in the first round.
22. Also entered, but not competing, were George "Con" O'Kelly (GBR/IRL), Jacob Gundersen (NOR), Miroslav Šustera (BOH), and 12 Dutch (NED) wrestlers, as follows: Jacob van Westrop, W. J. Eijling, J. F. Onatfass, P. A. van Dougen, Leendert van Oosten, J. Tuyt, H. Heersma, Douwe Wijbrands, J. E. van Tol, J. H. van Boyen, H. Kleingold, and L. Dinger.

Yachting

Races for the 6 meter, 7 meter, and 8 meter classes were held from the Royal Victoria Yacht Club in Ryde, Isle of Wight. The races for the 12 meter class were held on the River Clyde in Glasgow. There were no entries for the 15 meter class.

As there were no foreign entries in the 12 meter class and both the British entries were racing on the River Clyde in Glasgow that summer, the British Olympic Council agreed that no good purpose would be served by asking the owners to transport their vessels from Glasgow to the south coast of England solely for the Olympic races. The 12 meter class is the only Olympic event ever to be held in Scotland and the arrangements were made by the Clyde Corinthian Yacht Club and the Royal Clyde Yacht Club.

Placings were decided solely by the number of victories. An official points system was used only in the event of a tie for first or second place. The official tie-breaking system provided 3 points for first place, 2 for second place and 1 for third.

Site:	Royal Victoria Yacht Club, Ryde, Isle of Wight (6 meter, 7 meter and 8 meter classes); Royal Clyde Yacht Club, Hunter's Quay, Glasgow, Scotland (12 meter class).
Dates:	27–29 July (6 meter, 7 meter and 8 meter classes); 11–12 August (12 meter class)
Events:	4 [3 Men, 1 Mixed]
Competitors:	64 [63 Men, 1 Woman][1]
Nations:	5 [5 Men, 1 Women]

Total	*Competitors*	*1st*	*2nd*	*3rd*	*Totals*
Belgium	3	–	1	–	1
France	3	–	–	1	1
Great Britain	40	4	1	1	6
Norway	5	–	–	–	–
Sweden	13	–	1	–	1

See Notes on page 297.

293

Totals	64	4	3	2	9
Nations	5	1	3	2	4

Men	*Competitors*
Belgium	3
France	3
Great Britain	39
Norway	5
Sweden	13
Totals	63
Nations	5

Women	*Competitors*
Great Britain	1
Totals	1
Nations	1

Officials

Committee: Charles Newton-Robinson, Brooke Heckstall-Smith, G. Flemmich, G. H. Harrison

6 Meter Class

A: 15; C: 4; D: 27–29 July; T: Each race started at 1230; F: Three races, each over two circuits of a course in the Solent. Total distance, 13 miles. Each race started and finished at the Ryde Pier, Isle of Wight.

	27 July Race 1		28 July Race 2		29 July Race 3		Wins	Pts
1. Great Britain *(Dormy)*	1	3-52:14	1	4-17:23	3	4-19:33	2	7

(Gilbert Laws [helmsman], Thomas McMeekin, Charles Crichton)
[Owner: Thomas McMeekin; Designer: Gilbert Laws; Rig: Gaff sail]

2. Belgium *(Zut)*	3	3-56:20	4	4-19:17	1	4-13:46	1	4

(Léon Huybrechts [helmsman], Louis Huybrechts, Henri Weewauters)
[Owner: R. Osterrieth; Designer: Linton Hope (GBR); Rig: Gunter sail]

3. France *(Guyoni)*	4	4-03:21	2	4-17:55	2	4-15:16	-	4

(Henri Arthus [helmsman], Louis Potheau, Pierre Rabot)
[Owner: R. Delagrave; Designer: unknown; Rig: Gaff sail]

4. Great Britain *(Sibindi)*	2	3-54:06	3	4-18:19	4	4-19:47	-	3

(John Leuchars [helmsman][2], William Leuchars, Frank Smith)
[Owner: John Leuchars[3]; Designer: Alfred Mylne; Rig: Gaff sail]

5. Sweden *(Freja)*   5   4-24:0   5   4-36:48   5   4-59:51   -   0
(Karl-Einar Sjögren [helmsman], Birger Gustafsson, Jonas Jonsson)
[Owner: Royal Swedish YC; Designer: unknown; Rig: Lug]
4

7 Meter Class

A: 4; C: 1[5]; D: 27–28 July; T: Each race started at 1215; F: Three races each over two circuits of a course in the Solent. Total distance, 13 miles. Each race started and finished at the Ryde Pier, Isle of Wight.

Captain R. Sloane Stanley's entry, *Mignonette*, did not start and *Heroine* completed one circuit in each of the first two races on 27 & 28 July to claim the Olympic title. The third race, scheduled for 29 July, was cancelled.

	27 July Race 1		28 July Race 2		29 July Race 3		Wins	Pts
1. Great Britain *(Heroine)*	1	2-11:54	1	2-11:33	not held		2	6

(Charles Rivett-Carnac [helmsman], Richard Dixon, Norman Bingley, Frances Rivett-
    Carnac)
[Owner: Charles Rivett-Carnac; Designer: John Odgers; Rig: Lug]

8 Meter Class

A: 25[6]; C: 3; D: 27–29 July; T: Each race began at 1200; F: Three races, each over two circuits of a course in the Solent. Total distance, 16 miles. Each race started and finished at the Ryde Pier, Isle of Wight.

The British boat *Cobweb* won the first two races, clinching the gold medal. Some controversy concerns the make-up of the third-place crew of the boat *Sorais*, owned by the Duchess of Westminster. Some sources indicate that she was a passenger on the boat during the races, while in his report on the yacht races, published 27 February 1909, Charles Newton-Robinson, the Yacht Racing Association representative on the British Olympic Council, refers to the Duchess as "the pilot."

	27 July Race 1		28 July Race 2		29 July Race 3		Wins	Pts
1. Great Britain *(Cobweb)*	1	4-01:41	1	4-35:56	4	4-57:46	2	6
2. Sweden *(Vinga)*	5	4-55:56	4	5-16:21	1	4-52:31	1	3[7]

(Blair Cochrane [helmsman], Arthur Wood, Hugh Sutton, John Rhodes, Charles Campbell)
[Owner: Blair Cochrane; Designer: W. Fife; Rig: Cutter]

(Carl Hellström [helmsman], Edmund Thormählen, Erik Wallerius, Eric Sandberg, Harald
    Wallin)
[Owner: Royal Gothenburg YC; Designer: unknown; Rig: Sloop]

3. Great Britain *(Sorais)*   2   4-02:14   3   4-35:15   2   4-56:29   -   5
   (Philip Hunloke[8] [helmsman], Collingwood Hughes, Frederick Hughes, George Ratsey, William Ward)
   [Owner: Duchess of Westminster; Designer: W. Fife; Rig: Cutter]

4. Norway *(Fram)*   3   4-07:30   2   4-39:15   3   4-57:10   -   4
   (Johan Anker [helmsman], Einar Hvoslef, Hagbart Steffens[9], Magnus Konow, Eilart Fach Lund)
   [Owner: C. Wisbech; Designer: Johan Anker; Rig: Cutter]

5. Sweden *(Saga)*   4   4-46:11   dnf   5   5-00:45   -   0
   (John Carlsson [helmsman], Edvin Hagberg, Hjalmar Lönnroth, Karl Ljungberg, August Olsson)
   [Owner — Royal Swedish YC. Designer ———Rig — Sloop]
   10

12 Meter Class

A: 20[11]; C: 1; D: 11–12 August; T: Each race began at 1130; F: Three races[12], each over two circuits of a course on the Clyde. Total distance, 26 miles. Each race and started and finished at the clubhouse of the Royal Clyde Yacht Club, Hunter's Quay, Glasgow.

The event was not held in London, nor even in England, but took place in Glasgow, Scotland. It is one of the very few times in Olympic history that an event was not only held outside the host city, but was not even contested in the host country. In 1920 yachting, this occurred again. The 1920 Olympic games took place in Antwerp, Belgium, although the yachting competition was primarily held in Ostend, Belgium, during July. In the 12-foot dinghy class the first two races were split between two Dutch boats, the *Boreas* and the *Beatrijs III*. The deciding race was held in their home country, in September, at the Buiten-Y, a water near Amsterdam.

As neither of the two 1908 12 meter class entries were based in the South of England it was agreed that the owners should not be put to the trouble and expense of transporting their boats and crews from Glasgow and Liverpool to the Isle of Wight where the other Olympic races were held. The majority of the crew of *Mouchette* were members of the Royal Mersey Yacht Club (Liverpool) and *Hera* was crewed entirely by members of the Royal Clyde Yacht Club (Glasgow).

After *Hera* won the first two races, it was not necessary to hold a third race, and race three, scheduled for 13 August, was cancelled.

	11 August Race 1		*12 August* Race 2		*13 August* Race 3	*Wins*	*Pts*
1. Great Britain *(Hera)*	1	3-19:41	1	4-47:40	not held	2	6

(Thomas Glen-Coats [helmsman], Arthur Downes, John Downes, John Buchanan, David Dunlop, John Mackenzie, Gerald Tait, James Bunten, Albert Martin, R. B. Aspin[13])
[Owner: Thomas Glen-Coats; Designer: Thomas Glen-Coats]

| 2. Great Britain *(Mouchette)* | 2 | 3-21:21 | 2 | 4-48:42 | not held | 0 | 4 |

(Charles MacIver [helmsman], Cecil R. MacIver, James Baxter, William Davidson, John Spence, Thomas Littledale, John Jellico, McLeod Robertson, James Kenion, J. A. Gardiner[14])
[Owner: Charles MacIver; Designer: Alfred Mylne]

15 Meter Class[15]

NOTES

1. In a sport where professional and amateur crews often sailed together it was stressed in the OR (pp. 624–5) that only amateurs could take part in the Olympic races. Apparently, only those who were professional crew members were debarred and those who earned their living as yacht designers were eligible, e.g. Gilbert Laws (6 meter) and Alfred Mylne (possibly 12 meter).

2. Although invariably listed as being British, Leuchars was, in fact, South African. He was born in Durban, served as Mayor of the City in 1892 and was elected to the Legislative Assembly of Natal the following year.

3. See previous footnote

4. Neither the French nor Swedish yachts were among the original entrants. Both British boats and the Belgian boat were entered. A second Belgian yacht, *Kimone*, was also entered, but did not compete.

5. The only other entrant, a crew raised by Captain R. Sloane Stanley (GBR), failed to put in an appearance.

6. EK, FW, and VK/OSVK incorrectly have 24. There were definitely 25 sailors, 5 for each of 5 crews.

7. Vinga (SWE) was placed second by virtue of her one win (Race 3). Had the points scoring system, which was only to be used officially to resolve a tie, been the decisive factor in determining places throughout the entire competition, Vinga would have been placed fourth.

8. Incorrectly listed as Himloke in OR.

9. The OR has Christian Jensen, but the Norwegian Olympic Committee lists him only as a reserve and lists Hagbart Steffens as the crew member competing.

10. Both British yachts and the Norwegian boat were entered, but neither Swedish yacht was on the original entry lists.

11. FW incorrectly has 18.

12. *Hera*, sailing in home waters, won the first two races and the third race was, therefore, cancelled.

13. The OR shows John Aspin as the tenth crew member but of all the sources consulted, the OR is the only publication which lists him. His brother, R. B. Aspin, appears in a photograph of the crew and is listed in YM although he is only shown as a reserve in YW, SF and GH. He is not mentioned at all in the OR. Mainly on the evidence of the crew photograph, we have listed R. B. Aspin as the tenth crew member although the fact that he is only listed as a reserve in the two local (i.e., Scottish) sources consulted must cast some doubt on this assumption.

The only other realistic possibility is Alfred Mylne who is listed as a crew member in YW, SF and GH. He is not mentioned, even as a reserve, in the OR or YM and does not appear in the crew photograph.

14. John Adam is listed as the tenth crew member in the OR but this is the only source to do so. YW, SF and GH only show him as a reserve and in these three sources J. A. Gardiner is shown as the crew member. Although Gardiner is not shown as a competitor in the OR the available evidence indicates that he was far more likely than Adam to have been the tenth crew member.

15. This class was scheduled but was cancelled as there were no entries.

Other Sports and Events

Airplane Racing

Airplace racing was not conducted at the 1908 Olympics, either as a medal sport or a demonstration. However, in his book *The Evolution of the Olympic Games—1829 BC–1914 AD*, Frederick Webster discussed the plans for the 1908 Olympic Games in some detail. On page 206, he listed the preliminary program which was drawn up, including as the sixth event "flying machines (it was added that models should be included)." But no further mention of such events can be found.

Automobile Racing

Automobile racing was also not conducted at the 1908 Olympics, either as a medal sport or a demonstration. However, in the above mentioned book Webster describes the thirteenth event as "motor racing." No further mention of such events can be found.

Bicycle Polo

Bicycle polo was probably invented in 1891 by R. J. Mecredy who was then editor of the *Irish Cyclist*. The first Bicycle Polo Association was formed in London in 1901 and the first international match took place at the Crystal Palace in London in 1901 when Ireland beat England 10–1. The next major international encounter was the demonstration event at the 1908 Olympics when Ireland beat Germany 3–1. The two nations were represented by the Irish Bicycle Polo Association and the Deutscher Radfahrerbund. It is not known whether the Germans developed the game independently or imported it from Ireland. Teams consisted of four players but the names of the Germans who took part in the 1908 "Olympic" match are not recorded. The Irish team was as follows: L. R. Oswald-Sealy (captain/Rathclaren Rovers), H. E. Oswald (Rathclaren Rovers), A. S. Oswald (Rathclaren Rovers), and R. J. Mecredy, Jr. (Ohne Hast).

Diving Exhibitions

Several diving exhibitions were given. The first was held on Monday, 13 July at 5:00 P.M. (1700). Another was held on the last day of the stadium competition, Saturday, 25 July, this at 2:30 P.M. (1430).

On Saturday, 18 July at 4:30 P.M. (1630), a diving exhibition was also held between Miss Valborg Florström (FIN) and Miss Ebba Gisico (SWE). This was the first time women have appeared at the Olympics in either swimming or diving.

Equestrian Events

Equestrian events, other than the polo tournament, were never held at the 1908 Olympics, either as medal events or demonstrations. Webster (see above) listed the fourteenth event on the preliminary program as "Military riding (referred to a committee, which requested Count von Rosen [SWE] to look into the matter and report to the British Olympic Council)." We are not aware of any further definitive attempts to include equestrian events at the 1908 Olympics.

Fencing–Foil

An exhibition of foil fencing was also included on the Olympic program. Foil fencing was considered by the British as not suitable for competition, but more of an art form. Details of the exhibition are given at the end of the "Fencing" section.

Golf

Golf is a very popular sport in the British Isles and it seemed natural for the 1908 Olympic organizers to include golf on the program. They actually planned a 108-hole (6 rounds) stroke play event at three courses — Royal St. George's and Prince's Golf Clubs, both in Sandwich, and Cinqueports Golf Club, in nearby Deal. Both individual and team events were on the original schedule.

The Royal and Ancient Golf Club of St. Andrews, however, is the governing body of golf in Britain and they became embroiled in a dispute over eligibility with the Olympic organizing committee and all the British entrants withdrew. Some measure of how the Royal and Ancient Golf Club felt about golf in the Olympics can be gleaned from their action after receiving a letter sent by the London Olympic organizers. They did not reply. Eventually, however, the organizing committee gained some support and planned the Olympic golf event. W. Ryder Richardson, Esquire, secretary of Royal St. George's, was on the Council of the British Olympic Association in 1908, and was placed in charge. In the individual medal round 20 players from each country were permitted to enter but neither the individual or team event were ever held because the British Olympic Association and the Royal and Ancient Golf Club, failed to reach agreement on a number of matters. Despite the absence of golf from the program, the *Official Report* still included 15 pages of Rules of the Game. The defending Olympic golf champion from 1904, Canada's George Lyon, had actually sailed for Britain prior to the event's cancellation. He was offered a symbolic gold medal but declined.

Gymnastics Exhibitions

In addition to the medal events in gymnastics, several exhibitions were given in the main stadium. On the first day of the stadium events, Monday, 13 July, a display by teams from Denmark, Norway, and Sweden was given at 4:30 P.M. (1630).

On Wednesday, 15 July, the ladies' gymnastics exhibition took place at 4:30 P.M. (1630), representing female gymnasts from Denmark, the Northern Polytechnic Institute, and the ladies' section of the Yorkshire Amateur Gymnastic Association. Later that day, a men's gymnastics exhibition was given by groups from the Metropolitan and Southern Counties Amateur Gymnastic Association a 6 P.M. (1800).

On Thursday, 16 July, several groups performed. These were a display by the Dutch team at 4:45 P.M. (1645), by the Norwegian team at 5:30 P.M. (1730), and by the Battersea Polytechnic at 6 P.M. (1800).

On Friday, 17 July at 6 P.M. (1800), exibitions were given by the Borough Polytechnic, the Woolwich Polytechnic, and the Regent Street Polytechnic.

Two further exhibitions were held on Saturday, 18 July. At 6 P.M. (1800) a display was given by gymnasts from the Bristol Secondary Schools while at 7 P.M. (1900) gymnasts from the Yorkshire Amateur Athletic Association performed.

Motorboating

In addition to the three Olympic events, six handicap motorboat races were conducted at Southampton Water on the same days as the Olympic events. The handicap results are given at the end of the Motorboating section.

Water Polo Exhibitions

Two water polo exhibitions were given. On Saturday, 18 July, an exhibition match between the English Reserves and a team representing the "British Isles" was held. On the last day of the stadium competitions, a water polo exhibition was given in the pool at the White City Stadium. It was held on Saturday, 25 July at 2:30 P.M. (1430).

Wrestling — Glíma, Cumberland, and Westmoreland

On the last day of the stadium competitions, exhibitions of both Glíma (Icelandic) and Cumberland and Westmoreland wrestling were given in the infield of the stadium. These were held on Saturday, 25 July at 3 P.M. (1500). The Cumberland and Westmoreland events took place on the North Platform of the infield, while the Glíma events were held on the South Platform. The Icelandic Glíma wrestlers entered were as follows: Hallgrimur Benediktsson, Pall Guttormsson, Johannes Jósefsson, Jon Palsson, Sigurjon Petursson, Petur Sigfusson, and Gudmundur Sigurjonsson.

Yachting–15 meter class

This event was scheduled but not held. See the "Yachting" chapter for details.

Banquets and Festivities

Date	Time	Site	Event (Participants)
29 May		Queen's Club	Dinner for foreign representatives and competitors in tennis, racquets, and covered court tennis
11 July	2100	Grafton Galleries	Reception for the Olympic athletes (3,000)
11 July			Dinner for foreign representatives and competitors in lawn tennis
13 July	2100	Mansion House	Reception by the Sir John Bell, the Right Honorable Lord Mayor of London for representatives of all nations and the IOC (800)
14 July	1900	Holborn Restaurant	Opening Banquet in the King's Hall for Olympic officials and competitors (520)
15 July	2000	Fishmongers' Hall	Court of Assistants of the Worshipful Company of Fishmongers for IOC and British Olympic Council
16 July	1900	Holborn Restaurant	Second Banquet in the King's Hall for Olympic officials and competitors (400)
17 July	1900	Holborn Restaurant	Third Banquet in the King's Hall for Olympic officials and competitors (525)
18 July		Holborn Restaurant	Dinner of the Amateur Swimming Association (250)
19 July		St. Paul's Cathedral	Special service for Olympic competitors arranged by the Ven. Archdeacon of London, with the sermon preached by Ethelbert Talbott, the Bishop of Central Pennsylvania
20 July		Lyceum Club	Dinner of the Lyceum Club
21 July	1900	Holborn Restaurant	Fourth Banquet in the King's Hall for Olympic officials and competitors (525)
22 July		Trocadero	Dinner of the Amateur Athletic Association
23 July		Holborn Restaurant	Banquet in the King's Hall by His Majesty's Government for Olympic cycling competitors and officials (497)
24 July		Grafton Galleries	Dinner given for dignitaries attending the Games on behalf of foreign governments (120)
24 July		Holborn Restaurant	Ball in the King's Hall for all competitors and officials (1,575)
24 July		Henley Town Hall	Municipal reception of Olympic rowing competitors and officials
25 July		Phyllis Court Club	Open-air concert
25 July		White City Stadium	Awards Ceremonies; officials and athletes
26 July		Taplow Court	Luncheon for Olympic rowing competitors and officials

Date	Time	Site	Event (Participants)
27 July		Phyllis Court	Luncheon and excursion to Sonning
28 July		Henley-on-Thames	Sir Frank Crisp's luncheon for Olympic rowing competitors and officials
29 July		Greenlands	The Hon. W. F. D. Smith's dinner at Henley
30 July		Greenlands	Luncheon for Olympic rowing competitors and officials
31 July		Lawns Club (Henley)	Municipal Banquet for Olympic rowing competitors and officials
31 July		Henley Town Hall	Ball for Olympic rowing competitors and officials
1 Aug.		Bourne End, Henley	Banquet given by Mr. G. A. Kessler
2 Aug.		Strawberry Hill, Henley	Garden party given by Lord Michelham
20 Oct.		Holborn Restaurant	Banquet for Olympic officials and competitors in autumn sports (349)
31 Oct.		Holborn Restaurant	Closing Banquet in the King's Hall for Olympic officials and competitors (497)

Ninth Session of the International Olympic Committee

The ninth session of the International Olympic Committee was held during the Games of the IVth Olympiad in London on 13 and 16 July at the Imperial Sports Club. The session on 13 July was opened at 1000 and three sessions were held on that day—1000–1030, 1045–1200, and 1430–1700. British newspapers do not discuss this opening day of the session at all, and Wolf Lyberg notes that no written report exists, only a printed report in *The Olympic Review*[1]*. Thus, it is not possible to be certain which members were present on 13 July nor what actually occurred at the meetings on that day. Some items had to be decided on the 13 July, however, notably the co-option of new members Captain Johan Sverre of Norway and Baron Reinhold von Willebrand of Finland. The previous Norwegian member, Thomas Heftey, also resigned on this date.

The Opening Ceremony of the Olympics, however, must have constituted the bulk of 1430–1700 meeting of the IOC on 13 July, as that coincides exactly with the first day's events at the White City Stadium. In addition, *The Sporting Life* does mention that the following IOC members were present at the Opening Ceremony: Dr. Jiří Guth-Jarkovský (BOH), Captain Torben Grut (DEN), Count Albert de Bertier de Sauvigny (FRA), Count Egbert von der Asseburg (GER), Count von Wartensleben (GER), Count Alexandros Merkati (GRE), Baron van Tuyll van Serooskerken (NED), Count Eugenio Brunetta d'Usseaux (ITA), Colonel Viktor Balck (SWE), Count Clarence von Rosen (SWE), Baron Godefroy de Blonay (SUI), and William Milligan Sloane (USA).[2] Not mentioned, but definitely present were Lord Desborough and Reverend Robert de Courcy Laffan, who were likely included as members of the British Olympic Council, the proper name of the organizing committee. Pierre de Coubertin was also not specifically mentioned, although he was there.

In contrast, the IOC Session on 16 July was fully reported in *The Times*.[3] In attendance on

16 July were the following members of the IOC: Baron de Coubertin (President/FRA), Lord Desborough (Chairman of the British Olympic Council/GBR), Reverend de Courcy Laffan (GBR), General von der Asseburg (GER), Count von Wartensleben (GER), Baron van Tuyll van Serooskerken (NED), Count de Bertier de Sauvigny (FRA), Colonel Balck (SWE), Count von Rosen (SWE), Captain Sverre (NOR), Captain Grut (DEN), Count Merkati (GRE), Baron von Willebrand (FIN), Count Brunetta d'Usseaux (ITA), Dr. Guth-Jarkovský (BOH), and Count Albert Gautier Vignal (MON).[4]

On this second day of the session, Baron de Coubertin moved for a vote of thanks to King Edward VII for his help in organizing the 1908 Olympic Games. A tribute was also paid to Sir Howard Vincent, IOC Member from Great Britain, who had recently died (7 April 1908). The IOC conferred the Olympic Medal to the Company of Fishmongers in Britain. The Olympic Cup was given for 1909 to the Deutscher Turnerschaft. The host city for the 1912 Olympics was also considered, but the decision was postponed to the next meeting in Berlin in 1909.

NOTES

1. pp. 103-105, quoted in Lyberg, p. 40.
2. SL, 14 July 1908, found in BOADW.
3. Times, 17 July 1908.
4. Counting both days of the Session, we can confirm Lyberg's numbers (p. 40) in which he stated that there were 18 IOC Members present in London in 1908.

Appendix I
The 1908 Olympic Program

Date	Time	Site	Event
27 April	Afternoon	Queen's Club	Racquets — singles, round one
28 April	1400	Queen's Club	Racquets — singles, quarter-finals
29 April	1400	Queen's Club	Racquets — singles, semi-finals
30 April	1430	Queen's Club	Racquets — doubles, semi-finals
1 May	1430	Queen's Club	Racquets — doubles, final
6 May		Queen's Club	Covered-court tennis — men's singles, round one, 1 match
		Queen's Club	Covered-court tennis — men's doubles, round one, 1 match
		Queen's Club	Covered-court tennis — men's doubles, semi-finals, 1 match
7 May	1200	Queen's Club	Covered-court tennis — men's singles, quarter-finals, 1 match
	1430	Queen's Club	Covered-court tennis — ladies' singles, round one, 1 match
	1530	Queen's Club	Covered-court tennis — men's doubles, semi-finals, 1 match
8 May	1200	Queen's Club	Covered-court tennis — men's singles, quarter-finals, 1 match
	1430	Queen's Club	Covered-court tennis — ladies' singles, round one, 2 matches
	1530	Queen's Club	Covered-court tennis — men's singles, semi-finals, 1 match
9 May	1200	Queen's Club	Covered-court tennis — men's singles, final
	1415	Queen's Club	Covered-court tennis — ladies' singles, semi-final #1

Date	Time	Site	Event
	1500	Queen's Club	Covered-court tennis — ladies' singles, semi-final #2
	1600	Queen's Club	Covered-court tennis — men's doubles, final
11 May		Queen's Club	Covered-court tennis — ladies' singles, final
18 May		Queen's Club	Jeu de paume — round one
19 May	1230	Queen's Club	Jeu de paume — quarter-finals #1
	1400	Queen's Club	Jeu de paume — quarter-finals #2
	1530	Queen's Club	Jeu de paume — quarter-finals #3
20 May	1430	Queen's Club	Jeu de paume — quarter-final #4
21 May	1430	Queen's Club	Jeu de paume — semi-final #1
	1600	Queen's Club	Jeu de paume — semi-final #2
23 May	1430	Queen's Club	Jeu de paume — final
28 May		Queen's Club	Jeu de paume — third-place match
18 June		Hurlingham Polo Club	Polo — Roehampton v. Hurlingham
21 June		Hurlingham Polo Club	Polo — Roehampton v. Ireland
6 July		Wimbledon	Lawn Tennis — men's doubles, round 1
		Wimbledon	Lawn Tennis — men's singles, rounds 1–3
7 July		Wimbledon	Lawn Tennis — ladies' singles, round 1
		Wimbledon	Lawn Tennis — men's doubles, round 2
		Wimbledon	Lawn Tennis — men's singles, rounds 2 and 3
8 July		Uxendon Shooting Club	Shooting — trap shooting, individual
		Wimbledon	Lawn Tennis — men's singles, round three
9 July		Bisley	Shooting — free rifle, 1,000 yards
		Bisley	Shooting — free rifle, team
		Bisley	Shooting — running deer, double shot
		Bisley	Shooting — running deer, single shot
		Uxendon Shooting Club	Shooting — trap shooting, individual
		Uxendon Shooting Club	Shooting — trap shooting, team
		Wimbledon	Lawn Tennis — ladies' singles, quarter-finals
		Wimbledon	Lawn Tennis — men's doubles, quarter-finals
		Wimbledon	Lawn Tennis — men's singles, rounds 3and 4
10 July		Bisley	Shooting — free pistol
		Bisley	Shooting — free rifle, team
		Bisley	Shooting — international military rifle, team
		Bisley	Shooting — running deer, double shot
		Bisley	Shooting — running deer, single shot, team
		Uxendon Shooting Club	Shooting — trap shooting, team
		Wimbledon	Lawn Tennis — ladies' singles, semi-finals

Date	Time	Site	Event
		Wimbledon	Lawn Tennis — men's doubles, semi-finals
		Wimbledon	Lawn Tennis — men's singles, quarter- and semi-finals
11 July		Bisley	Shooting — free pistol, team
		Bisley	Shooting — free rifle, 3 positions
		Bisley	Shooting — international military rifle, team
		Bisley	Shooting — small-bore rifle, disappearing target
		Bisley	Shooting — small-bore rifle, moving target
		Bisley	Shooting — small-bore rifle, prone
		Bisley	Shooting — small-bore rifle, team
		Uxendon Shooting Club	Shooting — trap shooting, individual
		Uxendon Shooting Club	Shooting — trap shooting, team
		Wimbledon	Lawn Tennis — ladies' singles, final
		Wimbledon	Lawn Tennis — men's doubles, final
		Wimbledon	Lawn Tennis — men's singles, semis and final
13 July	1549	White City Stadium	Opening Ceremony
	1600	White City Stadium	Athletics — 1,500 meters, round one
	1600	White City Stadium	Swimming — 400 meter freestyle, round one, heat 1-3
	1615	White City Stadium	Cycling — tandems, round one, heats 1-4
	1630	White City Stadium	Gymnastics — team exhibition
	1700	White City Stadium	Diving — exhibition
	1715	White City Stadium	Cycling — tandems, round one, heats 5-7
14 July	1000	White City Stadium	Athletics — hammer throw, qualifying round
	1000–1600	White City Stadium	Cycling — 20 km., round one
	1100	White City Stadium	Athletics — 3,500 meter walk, round one
	Noon	White City Stadium	Athletics — hammer throw, final
	1430	White City Stadium	Diving — fancy diving, round one, heats 1-2
	1430	White City Stadium	Gymnastics — individual combined events
	1430	White City Stadium	Gymnastics — team combined event (Denmark)
	1530	White City Stadium	Athletics — 3,500 meter walk, final
	1555	White City Stadium	Athletics — 3-mile team race, round one
	1600	White City Stadium	Cycling — one lap match sprint — round one
	1600	White City Stadium	Gymnastics — team combined event (Great Britain)
	1645	White City Stadium	Swimming — 400 meter freestyle, round one, heats 4-9
	1720	White City Stadium	Athletics — 1,500 meters, final
	1730	White City Stadium	Cycling — 20 km., final
15 July	1000	White City Stadium	Athletics — javelin, freestyle, qualifying round
	1000	White City Stadium	Cycling — 100 km., round one, heat 1
	1100	White City Stadium	Swimming — 400 meter freestyle, semi-finals
	1130	White City Stadium	Athletics — 3-mile team race, final
	1130	White City Stadium	Diving — fancy diving, round one, heat 3

Date	Time	Site	Event
	Noon	White City Stadium	Athletics — javelin, freestyle, final
	1430	White City Stadium	Athletics — 5 miles, round one
	1430	White City Stadium	Gymnastics — team combined event (Finland)
	1430	White City Stadium	Swimming — 200 meter breaststroke, round one
	1515	White City Stadium	Gymnastics — team combined event (France)
	1530	White City Stadium	Cycling — one lap match sprint, semi-finals
	1545	White City Stadium	Diving — fancy diving, round one, heat 4
	1600	White City Stadium	Gymnastics — team combined event (Sweden)
	1630	White City Stadium	Cycling — one lap match sprint, final
	1630	White City Stadium	Gymnastics — women's team exhibitions
	1700	White City Stadium	Cycling — tandems, semi-finals
	1700	White City Stadium	Water Polo — Belgium v. Netherlands
	1745	White City Stadium	Cycling — tandems, final
	1800	White City Stadium	Gymnastics — team exhibitions
16 July	1000	White City Stadium	Athletics — 10-mile walk, round one
	1000	White City Stadium	Athletics — discus throw, qualifying round
	1000	White City Stadium	Cycling — 100 km., round one, heat 2
	Noon	White City Stadium	Athletics — discus throw, final
	1430	White City Stadium	Athletics — shot put, qualifying round
	1430	White City Stadium	Gymnastics — team combined event (Netherlands)
	1430	White City Stadium	Swimming — 200 meter breaststroke, semi-finals
	1500	White City Stadium	Cycling — 1 km. match sprint, round one
	1500	White City Stadium	Diving — fancy diving, round one, heat 5
	1515	White City Stadium	Gymnastics — team combined event (Norway)
	1600	White City Stadium	Gymnastics — team combined event (Italy)
	1615	White City Stadium	Swimming — 400 meter freestyle, final
	1630	White City Stadium	Swimming — 100 meter backstroke, round one
	PM	White City Stadium	Athletics — shot put, final
	1645	White City Stadium	Cycling — 1 km. match sprint, semi-finals
	1645	White City Stadium	Gymnastics — team exhibition (Netherlands)
	1730	White City Stadium	Cycling — 1 km. match sprint, final
	1730	White City Stadium	Gymnastics — team exhibition (Norway)
	1800	White City Stadium	Gymnastics — team exhibition (Battersea Polytechnic)
17 July	1000	White City Stadium	Archery — men's double York round
	1100	White City Stadium	Archery — ladies' double national round
	AM	Fencing Ground	Fencing — sabre, individual, round one, pools 1-4
	1430	White City Stadium	Athletics — 10-mile walk, final
	1430	White City Stadium	Athletics — javelin, middle, qualifying round
	1430	White City Stadium	Swimming — 100 meter backstroke, semi-finals
	1430	White City Stadium	Tug-of-War — round one
	1525	White City Stadium	Diving — fancy diving, semi-finals
	1530	White City Stadium	Tug-of-War — semi-finals
	1600	White City Stadium	Cycling — 5,000 meters, round one
	1615	White City Stadium	Swimming — 100 meter freestyle, round one
	PM	White City Stadium	Athletics — javelin, middle, final
	1700	White City Stadium	Athletics — 3,200 meter steeplechase, round one

Date	Time	Site	Event
	1700	White City Stadium	Cycling — team pursuit, round one
	1700	White City Stadium	Swimming — 100 meter backstroke, final
	1745	White City Stadium	Cycling — team pursuit, semi-finals
	1800	White City Stadium	Gymnastics, team exhibitions
	1815	White City Stadium	Cycling — team pursuit, final
	PM	Fencing Ground	Fencing — épée, individual, round one, pools 1-8
18 July	1000	White City Stadium	Archery — men's double York round
	1030	Fencing Ground	Fencing — épée, individual, round one, pools 9-13
	1100	White City Stadium	Archery — ladies' double national round
	1430	Fencing Ground	Fencing — sabre, individual, round one, pools 5-7
	1430	White City Stadium	Athletics — 3,200 meter steeplechase, final
	1430	White City Stadium	Swimming — 200 meter breaststroke, final
	1440	White City Stadium	Athletics — discus throw, classical, qualifying round
	1445	White City Stadium	Cycling — 5,000 meters, final
	1455	White City Stadium	Diving — fancy diving, final
	1500	White City Stadium	Tug-of-War — final
	1530	White City Stadium	Cycling — 100 km., final
	1600	Fencing Ground	Fencing — sabre, individual, round one, pools 8-11
	1630	White City Stadium	Diving — women's exhibition
	PM	White City Stadium	Athletics — discus throw, classical, final
	1730	Fencing Ground	Fencing — sabre, individual, round one, pools 12-13
	1730	White City Stadium	Athletics — 5 miles, final
	1800	White City Stadium	Gymnastics — team exhibition
	1900	White City Stadium	Gymnastics — team exhibition
20 July	1000–1800	White City Stadium	Wrestling — bantamweight catch-as-catch can
	1000–1800	White City Stadium	Wrestling — middleweight Greco-Roman, rounds 1-2
	1030	Fencing Ground	Fencing — épée, individual, round two, pools 1-4
	1100	White City Stadium	Swimming — 100 meter freestyle, semi-finals
	1130	Fencing Ground	Fencing — sabre, individual, round two, pools 1-4
	1130	White City Stadium	Diving — plain high diving, round one, heat 1
	1430	White City Stadium	Athletics — standing long jump, qualifying round
	1430	White City Stadium	Swimming — 100 meter freestyle, final
	1455	White City Stadium	Diving — plain high diving, round one, heat 2
	1500	Fencing Ground	Fencing — épée, team, rd. one, GBR v. NED
	1500	White City Stadium	Athletics — 100 meters, round one
	1530–1730	White City Stadium	Athletics — 800 meters, round one
	1615	Fencing Ground	Fencing — sabre, individual, round two, pools 5-8
	1615	White City Stadium	Water Polo — Belgium v. Sweden
	PM	White City Stadium	Athletics — standing long jump, final
	1645	White City Stadium	Athletics — 400 meter hurdles, round one
	1715	Fencing Ground	Fencing — épée, individual, round two, pools 5-8
		White City Stadium	Archery — men's Continental Style
21 July	1000–1800	White City Stadium	Wrestling — heavyweight Greco-Roman
	1000–1800	White City Stadium	Wrestling — middleweight catch-as-catch-can
	1030	White City Stadium	Athletics — high jump, qualifying round

Date	Time	Site	Event
	1100	White City Stadium	Athletics — 200 meters, round one
	1130	White City Stadium	Diving — plain high diving, round one, heats 3-4
	1430	White City Stadium	Athletics — high jump, final
	1430	White City Stadium	Swimming — 1,500 meter freestyle, round one
	1500	Fencing Ground	Fencing — épée, team, quarter-final, ITA v. BOH
	1500	Fencing Ground	Fencing — sabre, team, quarter-final, FRA v. BEL
	1500	White City Stadium	Athletics — 400 meters, round one
	1530	White City Stadium	Athletics — 110 meter hurdles, round one
	1535	White City Stadium	Athletics — 100 meters, semi-finals
	1600	Fencing Ground	Fencing — épée, team, quarter-final, FRA v. DEN
	1600	Fencing Ground	Fencing — épée, team, quarter-final, FRA v. DEN
	1600	Fencing Ground	Fencing — sabre, team, quarter-final, ITA v. GBR
	1600	White City Stadium	Athletics — 400 meter hurdles, semi-finals
	1700	Fencing Ground	Fencing — épée, team, quarter-final, BEL v. SWE
	1700	White City Stadium	Athletics — 800 meters, final
22 July	1000	Fencing Ground	Fencing — sabre, team, quarter-final, BOH v. NED
	1000	Fencing Ground	Fencing — sabre, team, quarter-final, HUN v. GER
	1000–1800	White City Stadium	Wrestling — featherweight catch-as-catch can
	1000–1800	White City Stadium	Wrestling — light-heavyweight Greco-Roman
	1015	White City Stadium	Athletics — 200 meters, semi-finals
	1030	White City Stadium	Athletics — long jump, qualifying round
	1130	White City Stadium	Athletics — 110 meter hurdles, semi-finals
	1430	White City Stadium	Diving — plain high diving, round one, heat 5
	1500	White City Stadium	Wrestling — middleweight catch-as-catch-can final
	1500	Fencing Ground	Fencing — épée, team, semi-final, BEL v. ITA
	1500	Fencing Ground	Fencing — sabre, team, semi-final, BOH v. FRA
	1530	White City Stadium	Athletics — 400 meter hurdles, final
	1530	White City Stadium	Athletics — long jump, final
	1600	White City Stadium	Water Polo — Great Britain v. Belgium
	1615	White City Stadium	Athletics — 100 meters, final
	1630	Fencing Ground	Fencing — épée, team, semi-final, FRA v. GBR
	1630	Fencing Ground	Fencing — sabre, team, semi-final, HUN v. ITA
	1730	White City Stadium	Athletics — 400 meters, semi-finals
23 July	1000–1800	White City Stadium	Wrestling — heavyweight catch-as-catch-can
	1000–1800	White City Stadium	Wrestling — lightweight Greco-Roman
	1030	Fencing Ground	Fencing — épée, individual, semi-final, pool 1
	1030	Fencing Ground	Fencing — sabre, individual, semi-final, pool 1
	1130	White City Stadium	Diving — plain high diving, semi-finals
	1445	Fencing Ground	Fencing — épée, team, final, FRA v. BEL
	1445	Fencing Ground	Fencing — sabre, team, final, HUN v. BOH
	PM	White City Stadium	Athletics — standing high jump
	1545	White City Stadium	Swimming — 1,500 meter freestyle, semi-finals
	1600	Fencing Ground	Fencing — épée, individual, semi-final, pool 2
	1600	Fencing Ground	Fencing — sabre, individual, semi-final, pool 2
	1600	White City Stadium	Athletics — 200 meters, final
	1730	White City Stadium	Athletics — 400 meters, final (original)
	2100	Prince's Galleries	Fencing — foil exhibitions

Date	Time	Site	Event
24 July	1000–1800	White City Stadium	Wrestling — heavyweight Greco-Roman final
	1000–1800	White City Stadium	Wrestling — lightweight, catch-as-catch-can
	1000–1800	White City Stadium	Wrestling — middleweight Greco-Roman, quarter- and semi-finals
	1030	Fencing Ground	Fencing —épée, team, third-place semi, GBR v. DEN
	1100	White City Stadium	Athletics — pole vault, qualifying round
	1200	White City Stadium	Athletics — 1,600 meter relay, round one
	1430	White City Stadium	Swimming — 4 × 200 meter freestyle relay, semi-finals
	1433	White City Stadium	Athletics — marathon
	1445	Fencing Ground	Fencing —épée, individual, final
	1445	Fencing Ground	Fencing — sabre, individual, final
	1515	White City Stadium	Diving — plain high diving, final
	1620	White City Stadium	Swimming — 4 × 200 meter freestyle relay, final
	1730	Fencing Ground	Fencing —épée, team, third-place final, GBR v. BEL
	1730	Fencing Ground	Fencing — sabre, team, third-place final, ITA v. GER
	1730	White City Stadium	Athletics — pole vault, final
25 July	1000	White City Stadium	Athletics — triple jump, qualifying round
	1000	White City Stadium	Wrestling — lightweight Greco-Roman final
	1000	White City Stadium	Wrestling — middleweight Greco-Roman final
	1130	White City Stadium	Athletics — 110 meter hurdles, final
	1200	White City Stadium	Athletics — 400 meters, final (re-run)
	Noon	White City Stadium	Athletics — triple jump, final
	1230	White City Stadium	Athletics — 1,600 meter relay, final
	1530	White City Stadium	Swimming — 1,500 meter freestyle, final
	1600	White City Stadium	Closing Ceremony and Prize Presentations
27 July	1200	Isle of Wight	Yachting — 8-meter class, race 1
	1215	Isle of Wight	Yachting — 7-meter class, race 1
	1230	Isle of Wight	Yachting — 6-meter class, race 1
28 July	1200	Isle of Wight	Yachting — 8-meter class, race 2
	1215	Isle of Wight	Yachting — 7-meter class, race 2
	1230	Isle of Wight	Yachting — 6-meter class, race 2
	1500	Henley-on-Thames	Rowing — single sculls, round one, heat 1
	1545	Henley-on-Thames	Rowing — coxless fours, semi-finals, heat 1
	1630	Henley-on-Thames	Rowing — coxless pairs, semi-finals, heat 1
29 July	1200	Isle of Wight	Yachting — 8-meter class, race 3
	1215	Isle of Wight	Yachting — 7-meter class, race 3
	1230	Henley-on-Thames	Rowing — single sculls, round two, heat 1
	1230	Isle of Wight	Yachting — 6-meter class, race 3
	1300	Henley-on-Thames	Rowing — coxed eights, round one, heat 1
	1500	Henley-on-Thames	Rowing — single sculls, round two, heat 2
	1520	Henley-on-Thames	Rowing — coxed eights, round one, heat 2
	1600	Henley-on-Thames	Rowing — single sculls, round two, heat 3
		Henley-on-Thames	Rowing — single sculls, round two, heat 4

Date	Time	Site	Event
30 July	1230	Henley-on-Thames	Rowing — single sculls, semi-finals, heat 1
	1315	Henley-on-Thames	Rowing — coxed eights, semi-finals, heat 1
	1515	Henley-on-Thames	Rowing — coxless pairs, semi-finals, heat 2
	1545	Henley-on-Thames	Rowing — coxed eights, semi-finals, heat 2
	1615	Henley-on-Thames	Rowing — coxless fours, semi-finals, heat 2
	1645	Henley-on-Thames	Rowing — single sculls, semi-finals, heat 2
31 July	1230	Henley-on-Thames	Rowing — coxless pairs, final
	1430	Henley-on-Thames	Rowing — single sculls, final
		Henley-on-Thames	Rowing — coxless fours, final
	1515	Henley-on-Thames	Rowing — coxed eights, final
11 Aug.	1130	Hunter's Quay, Glasgow	Yachting — 12-meter class, race 1
12 Aug.	1130	Hunter's Quay, Glasgow	Yachting — 12-meter class, race 2
13 Aug.	1130	Hunter's Quay, Glasgow	Yachting — 12-meter class, race 3
28 Aug.		Southampton Water	Motorboating — Classes A, B, and C
29 Aug.		Southampton Water	Motorboating — Class A, second race
19 Oct.	1500	White City Stadium	Football — round one, Denmark v. France "B"
20 Oct.	1500	White City Stadium	Football — round one, Great Britain v. Sweden
22 Oct.	1300	White City Stadium	Football — semi-final, Great Britain v. The Netherlands
	1500	White City Stadium	Football — semi-final, Denmark v. France "A"
23 Oct.	1500	White City Stadium	Football — third-place semi-final, The Netherlands v. Sweden
24 Oct.	1300	White City Stadium	Lacrosse — final, Canada v. Great Britain
	1500	White City Stadium	Football — final, Great Britain v. Denmark
26 Oct.	1515	White City Stadium	Rugby Football — final, Australia v. Great Britain
27 Oct.	1125–2230	Northampton Institute	Boxing tournament — all classes, all matches
28 Oct.	1000	Prince's Skating Club	Figure Skating — ladies' compulsory figures
	1500	Prince's Skating Club	Figure Skating — men's compulsory figures
29 Oct.	1000	Prince's Skating Club	Figure Skating — special figures competition
	1345	White City Stadium	Hockey — round one, Scotland v. Germany
	1500	Prince's Skating Club	Figure Skating — men's and ladies' free skating, pair skating
	1500	White City Stadium	Hockey — round one, England v. France
30 Oct.	AM	White City Stadium	Hockey — friendly, Germany v. France
	1345	White City Stadium	Hockey — semi-final, Ireland v. Wales
	1500	White City Stadium	Hockey — semi-final, England v. Scotland
31 Oct.	1500	White City Stadium	Hockey — final, England v. Ireland

Appendix II
Controversies and Protests

The 1908 Olympic Games were marked by constant bickering and protestations by the American team against the British officials. But the Americans were not the only team which lodged protests against the British officials. Following is a list of all known protests and controversies which occurred during the 1908 Olympic Games, with brief summaries. In some of the more famous examples (400 meters, tug-of-war, marathon race), more explanation is given in the text of the event.

We have also tried to correct the historical record with this listing. Since the 1908 Olympics, all manner of misconceptions have sprung up concerning some of these controversial events and much of what has been written about them has been incorrect.

The Opening Ceremony and the Flags

During the opening ceremonies, the flags of the competing nations flew around the White City Stadium. In addition, the Chinese and Japanese flags were also present, even though neither country was competing at the 1908 Olympic Games. But two nations' flags were missing — those of Sweden and the United States, and the officials of both countries were upset by this oversight, for which the British Olympic Council later apologized.

It was noted in the British newspapers, "Commissioner [James] Sullivan has received a reply to the letter he sent to Lord Desborough, Chairman of the Council of the British Olympic Association, protesting against certain of the rules governing the contests and referring to other matters in connection with the games.

"In his reply Lord Desborough opens with an apology to the Americans for the failure to use a single American flag in the decoration of the Stadium on the opening day, the omission to do which, he says, has been remedied."[1*]

Many writers have credited the problems at the Opening Ceremony with being the catalyst for the remainder of the controversies throughout the 1908 Olympics. In particular, James R. Coates has noted, "Anglo-American friction had begun with the opening day ceremonies,

*See Notes on pages 325–326.

313

when the American, Swedish, and Finnish flags were not displayed. In protest, some Swedes left the games. Finland, under Russian domination, could not afford to do much in protest. When Ralph Rose, a shot-putter and flag bearer, refused, as a customary courtesy, to dip the American flag when passing before King Edward, the remaining activities were held with open animosity."[2]

William Johnson also has noted, "The Games of 1908 featured a very nasty feud between Americans and Englishmen that apparently began when the U.S. team arrived at the stadium in London, gazed around and suddenly realized that, within the full fluttering forest of flags on display, Old Glory was nowhere to be seen. As it turned out, the Swedes had no flag there either, and they quit the Games, and the Finns had none either, but they simply marched (albeit grimly) anyway."[3]

But there are several problems with these analyses. First of all, it is not true that Sweden left the Olympics. They competed throughout the Olympics, represented by 175 athletes who won 25 medals, and 8 gold medals. Sweden later lodged a protest over a wrestling decision (see below) and it has been stated that, upset by the flag incident at the Opening Ceremony, and angered by the decision in wrestling, they then withdrew from the Olympics. That is also not true. That decision took place on 21 July, and Swedish athletes competed throughout the remainder of the Olympics.

Further, it is not precisely true that no Finnish flag was present and the Finns were upset by this "oversight." In fact, in 1908, Finland was considered a part of Russia. Finland was conquered by Alexander I of Russia in 1809 and remained under the control of that country until the Finnish Diet (legislature) proclaimed Finnish independence on 20 July 1917, at the time of the Bolshevik revolution. This became complete independence by 6 December 1917.

In 1908, Russia refused to allow Finland to compete as an independent nation and carry the Finnish flag, demanding instead that the Finns compete under the Russian flag. It was noted, "Finland has her own delegation which attracts much attention. The Finns were anxious to parade with the Finnish flag, but as their request to be allowed to carry it was vetoed by the Russian officials, the Finnish contingent was the only one that appeared yesterday in the procession without a flag, as they would not display the Russian colors."[4]

Further nationalistic problems occurred with England's neighbor in the British Isles, the Irish. England had claimed control of Ireland many times throughout the centuries, but absolute control under the British monarch occurred in the seventeenth century. By the Act of Union of 1801, England and Ireland became the "United Kingdom of Great Britain and Ireland." Anti-British sentiment was strong, however, and eventually led to the Easter Rebellion in Dublin (24-29 April 1916) in which Irish nationalists attempted to claim independence. Guerrilla warfare continued until the rebels proclaimed an Irish republic in 1919. The Irish Free State was established as a Dominion of the crown on 6 December 1922, with the six northernmost countries remaining part of the United Kingdom. Complete independence occurred after World War II with the formation of the Republic of Ireland on 18 April 1949.

But 1908 was still a time in which Irish nationalism was high and the Irish athletes also preferred to compete as an independent nation. This was likewise denied, this time by the British Olympic Council, the organizing committee of the Olympics, certainly influenced by their government's wishes.

It was noted in BOADW, "The Irish athletes have expressed dissatisfaction because the Olympic Committee has refused to permit them to enter a separate team on the ground that Ireland is not a nation, thereby compelling them to compete as a part of the British team."

Further problems concerning flags at the Opening Ceremony concerned the American team and the failure of their flag bearer to dip the American flag in the presence of King Edward VII. Perhaps more apocrypha has been written about this incident than any single Olympic moment, so we will deal with this in some detail, including discussion of the 1908 reports, later reports, and attention to the various errors.

There should have been little doubt as to what was expected of the flag bearers at the 1908 Olympic Opening Ceremony. The protocol was published in multiple British newspapers for several days before the Olympic Games. The protocol was given specifically as follows:

1. That all teams should assemble at 2 o'clock in their respective dressing rooms at the Stadium on Monday, the 13th inst.

2. On the parade it is expected that every athlete taking part will be in the athletic costume of his country, or of the sport in which he intends to compete. In the event of it being a wet day, it is left entirely to the discretion of the manager of each team as to what precaution should be taken for the protection of the various members.

3. All teams will parade in the rear of the Stadium facing Wood-lane at 2.45 promptly and behind their respective representatives, who will bear the flag and entablature of their country.

4. Each nationality will be formed up in sections of four, and will be headed eight paces in front by the bearer of the entablature or name of the country, and four paces between the entablature and the front column by the bearer of the flag of the country.

5. On the sounding of the bugle the columns will march off in alphabetical order.

6. Each team on entering the Stadium will wheel either to right or left on to the centre of the cinder track and march to its special flag, which will be placed off the side of the track, then wheeling on the flag march straight forward into its proper position in front of the Royal Box, which will be indicated by another flag.

7. On arriving in position facing the Royal Box the entablature bearer will fall back to the right side of the leading section of his team. The flag bearer to stand six paces in front of column.

8. The International Committee and Representatives will next parade before his Majesty, who will then declare the Stadium open. The National Anthem will then be performed by the band, *all flags being lowered to the salute* and three cheers will be called from the whole of the teams for His Majesty.

9. On the signal being given by Mr. H. Elliott, the Chief Marshal, the columns will wheel to the right, and march off in alphabetical order with the exception that America will immediately precede the British Colonial Contingents, which will precede Great Britain, who will bring up the rear.

10. On the march the entablature bearer will march four paces in front of the flag bearer, who will also be four paces in front of the leading section of his column.

11. An interval of at least four paces should be kept between the entablature bearer and the rear rank of the preceding column.

12. *Each column on passing the Royal Party will salute*, afterwards marching right round the track and make its exit.

13. A full meeting of managers and (as far as possible) the team, will be held at the Stadium, on Saturday, 11th, at 11.30; also, on Monday, 13th, at 12 o'clock, for rehearsal. (emphasis ours)

There are three main controversies: (1) Who was the American flag bearer? (2) Did the American flag bearer refuse to dip the flag? and (3) Were the British upset by this affront?

Three different American athletes are often mentioned as the American flag bearer in 1908 — Ralph Rose, Martin Sheridan, and Johnny Garrells. But it was Ralph Rose, without a doubt, who carried the American flag. It was also Ralph Rose who apparently did not dip the flag. However, it is not so certain that the British were decidedly upset by this action.

Concerning the identity of the flag bearer, we will examine the most commonly quoted sources. Among recent works we have Richard Schaap, who noted, "When the Olympians marched before King Edward, each nation dipped its flag in tribute — but, to the outrage of the crowd, not the Americans. 'This flag dips to no earthly king,' snapped Martin Sheridan, the weight thrower. The tradition has persisted; the United States still does not dip its flag in Olympic parades."[5]

Alexander Weyand also has described the event as follows, "The honor of bearing the Stars and Stripes went to Johnny Garrels, the famous University of Michigan football player. The British were somewhat perturbed at the opening ceremonies, too. Most nations do not attach a great deal of importance to their national flags. All of the flags were dipped to King Edward except ours [USA]. Regulations prescribe that the United States flag should never be dipped. Some of the athletes thought that this might indicate a stiff-necked attitude, and there was some talk of following the example of other nations. Martin Sheridan has been quoted as silencing the argument with the laconic assertion, 'This flag dips to no earthly king.'"[6]

Finally, among more recent works, both Johnson and the Associated Press have claimed the flag bearer was Martin Sheridan. Johnson wrote, "When the opening ceremonial parade commenced, the American shot putter Martin Sheridan was leading the United States forces, carrying a particularly large and brilliant flag. Flag-bearers from all other nations obeyed the gentle protocol of the day by dipping their flags in tribute to the head of state, King Edward, as they passed his seat of honor. Not the Americans. The burly, hot-tempered Sheridan muttered, 'This flag dips to no earthly king.' The crowd gasped, but Sheridan held his flag erect when he stomped past the king."[7]

In *Pursuit of Excellence: The Olympic Story*, we find, "It was expected that each of the 22 participating nations' flag bearers would dip his flag as the delegation marched past King Edward VII. The Americans, however, refused to dip theirs. Discus thrower Martin Sheridan, an Irish-American who needed no encouragement when it came to balking the English, asserted 'this flag dips to no earthly king.' He started a U.S. tradition that continues even today."[8]

So who was the flag bearer? Most of the 1908 evidence supports Rose, although a few contemporary sources state that it was Johnny Garrells, notably *The New York Times*, which was most likely Weyand's source. Looking at the 1908 papers we find the following:

> *New York Sun*, 14 July 1908 — "Ralph Rose, the giant shot putter of the Olympic Athletic Club of San Francisco was at the head of the little body of Americans, carrying the Stars and Stripes."

> *New York Herald (Paris Edition)*, 14 July 1908 — "Then came the Americans, Garrell carrying the sign, and big Ralph Rose the flag, and the manager, 'Mat' Halpin, in top hat and frock coat, heading about seventy of the team."

> *The Sportsman*, 14 July 1908 — "Several of the nations dipped their flag as they arrived opposite the Royal party, while others contented themselves with a military salute.... Next came the United States, whose flag was borne by Ralph Rose, the giant shot putter, and it was a thousand pities that the large squad of competitors should not have been in their athletic costumes."

> *The Sporting Life*, 14 July 1908 — " ... the next body of athletes being the Americans, led by the gigantic Rose, as standard-bearer."

Amos Alonzo Stagg writing in the *Chicago Tribune*, 14 July 1908 — "Ralph Rose, carrying the American flag and leading the American contingent, failed to dip the flag in passing the royal box."

Martin Sheridan writing in the *Chicago Record-Herald*, 14 July 1908 — "Ralph Rose, carrying an American flag in the parade in the Stadium, failed to lower it when passing the king's stand, as those of all other nations did. Rose did not give any reason for not lowering his flag."

New York Herald, 14 July 1908 — "The procession was formed in alphabetical order, Austria leading with the exception that the English speaking athletes came last. The latter section was led by the American team with Garrels, of the Chicago Athletic Association, at its head carrying the Stars and Stripes."

Obviously the flag bearer was not Sheridan, who wrote a column about the incident, and described the bearer as Rose and did not mention himself. Garrells is described as the flag bearer only in *The New York Times* and the *New York Herald*. Garrells was described elsewhere as the "standard bearer," i.e., carrying the name placard for the United States. We think the reference to him as flag bearer is a mistake confusing the standard bearer and flag bearer.

Photographic evidence exists to support this thesis. Pictures of the American flag bearer can be found in *Outing Magazine*, the British newspaper, *The Daily Mirror*, and the *Chicago Daily News*. In all three photos, one thing is obvious — the American flag bearer is the tallest and largest American in the contingent. This guarantees it to be Rose, who stood 2 meters in height (6-6¾) and weighed upwards of 125 kg. (275 lbs.) Garrells was not small, standing 1.88 meters (6-2), but weighed only about 84 kg. (185 lbs.) and he was dwarfed by Rose, who was gargantuan for the era.

Rose was a somewhat unusual choice and Sheridan, multiple Olympic champion in 1904 and 1906, and hugely popular among American athletes, would have been a better one. Dyreson noted the following:

> *The Bookman* criticized the choice of Rose as flag-bearer. "Now Ralph Rose is unquestionably an athlete of considerable ability, but beyond that one cannot truthfully go," opined the editor, recalling Rose's indiscreet challenge to fight world heavyweight boxing champion James J. Jeffries after the 1904 Olympics, and the rowdy behavior that ended his scholastic career at the University of Michigan. "All this was perfectly well known to those in charge of the American team," observed *The Bookman*. "Yet this young man was selected to carry the American flag in the march of competing athletes past the Royal Box," the editor marveled. "He deliberately chose to insult the English people by his failure to salute King Edward." *The Bookman* castigated those who had supported Rose's defiant gesture. "'Boyish patriotism!' 'The Spirit of 1776!' Nonsense. Sheer, caddish, boorish manners," lectured the editor. "It was an incident of which Americans should be heartily ashamed."[9]

Amos Alonzo Stagg, a member of the American Olympic Council, wrote that Rose "was not 'relished' as a fellow student by the better class of his colleagues at the University of Michigan." Ralph Rose claimed that no one had told him what to do during the ceremony and while this might well be true it is strange that he chose to do nothing rather than be guided by the actions of all the other standard bearers around him.

Rose's remark that he was not told what to do has also been repeated by Lucas[10]. However, given the above description of the Opening Ceremony, published in every British paper we have seen, it is hard to see how Rose could not know he was supposed to dip the American flag. In addition, the above protocol describes two salutes to be made to the Royal Box, although the second salute does not specifically mention lowering the flag. And seeing the other flag bearers lower their staffs, most likely twice, what could Rose have been thinking?

Did Rose refuse to dip the flag as has been reported continuously since 1908? We think he did refuse, but the evidence for this is not as definite as that for his identity. Note the following from 1908 reports:

> *New York Sun*, 14 July 1908 — "As each contingent passed the royal box the standard bearer dipped the flag of his country ..."

> *New York Herald (Paris Edition)*, 14 July 1908 — " ... the other countries lined up on either side and *the standard bearer of each nation* lowered his flag in salute."

> British Olympic Association/Wallechinsky File (source uncertain) — "All heads were turned towards the Royal pavilion, and each nation saluted the King according to its custom. Then in unison, all brought their hands to the salute, military fashion. *All the flags were dipped in passing.*"

> *The Sporting Life* noted in three different sections — "All previous contingents had passed the Royal box at attention, with eyes right and colours lowered; ..." " ... as each contingent passed the Royal box the flags were dipped, caps removed and hands brought to the salute." and "The standard bearers, carrying the national flags, stepped a few paces to the front, taking up their dressing along the edge of the swimming tank. In the meantime the members of the International Olympic Committee, the British Olympic Council, and members of the Comité d'Honneur, headed by Lord Desborough, had passed in front of the Royal box. Flags were lowered to the salute, and Lord Desborough, stepping forward, requested His Majesty to declare the Fourth International Olympiad open."

> *The Sportsman*, 14 July 1908 — "The cheering had scarcely subsided when the band of the Grenadier Guards played the National Anthem, and *the standard-bearers of all the nations dipped their flags in salute.*" (emphasis ours)

From these reports it would appear that Rose did lower the flag in unison with all the other flag bearers. But other sources, notably Stagg and Sheridan, as noted above, disagree. Given these reports, especially Sheridan's, who was presumably marching with the U.S. team, it is difficult to assume any conclusion other than the oft stated fact that Rose did not dip the American flag, although this brings us to the final question — why was there so little British furor over this affront to their King?

No British newspaper that we have seen describes anything about the American flag not being lowered at the Opening Ceremony. Certainly no furor existed concerning Rose's breach of etiquette. It is not described, even after the fact, in *A Reply to Certain Criticisms*, and there is little that the British held back in that report.

Stagg, writing from England, noted in the above report, "There is one incident of the games *which has received little comment in this country*, but which may explain in part the markedly noticeable unpopularity of the Yankees with the spectators aside from the fact that they were winning a majority of the events. That incident took place in the parade of the athletes of all nations on opening day. Ralph Rose, carrying the American flag and leading the American contingent, failed to dip the flag in passing the royal box."

The New York Herald also noted that no opprobrium accompanied the American actions during the Opening Ceremony, "As the procession came into the Stadium each country received applause, that for America and the Colonies being particularly enthusiastic."[11]

However, Tait[12] described the results of the action, stating that it was an affront to the British, "To the English officials this alone was a terrible slight, but as they scurried across the grass to demand an explanation, they found that, not only was Rose instructed to take the action he took[13], but that his teammates considered him to be a hero for having the pluck to follow the instructions through."[14]

Thus in North America, Rose's defiant act was well known, while the British appear not to have been overly concerned by it. The American attitude seems to have been one of "We'll show them!" while the British seemed to have had too much restraint and gallantry to trouble themselves with it, and respond to it in the media.

Even after weighing all the foregoing evidence certain aspects remain unresolved. While the British press might not have noticed, or chosen to ignore the fact, that Rose had failed to dip their flag during the march past, it is difficult to fathom that the press would have shown the same insouciance if the action was repeated when the teams lined up in front of the Royal Box. If the Stars and Stripes remained held aloft while all the other flag bearers in the line lowered their Standards, the effect would have been so striking that comment would surely have been passed. But no such comment can be found in the British press.

One other possibility exists which will likely never be resolved but would explain the problem. Perhaps Rose failed to dip the flag during the march past, to which Sheridan and Stagg referred, but which was of little consequence to the British media, but then he did dip it while in line with the other flag bearers, so that no comment was made by the British media.

Thus we make the following conclusions. The American flag bearer was Ralph Rose, it seems likely that at least one time, he did not dip the American flag to King Edward, but the British made very little public comment about this breach of protocol.

The Marathon Footrace

The marathon generated tremendous amounts of publicity and controversy both before and after the event. Prior to the start of the race the bulk of the media attention focused on Tom Longboat, a Canadian and Native American of the Onodaga Tribe of Iroquois Nation. Longboat had won the 1907 Boston Marathon and was definitely one of the top long-distance runners in the world. But the Americans considered him a professional in 1908 and protested his entry into the Olympic marathon.

Bruce Kidd, the Canadian sports historian and former Olympic distance runner himself, has written a biography of Longboat, entitled simply *Tom Longboat*. In it, he discusses in detail the circumstances which led to the American protest of Longboat's amateur status, noting:

> Longboat joined the Irish-Canadian Athletic Club (ICAC) in July 1907, after winning the Boston Marathon. It was managed by Tom Flanagan, who favored professional sport and tried to capitalize on sport whenever possible. He set up Longboat's schedule, gave him expense money, arranged for his room and board at the Grand Hotel in Toronto when he visited that city, but still managed to keep his amateur standing in the eyes of the Canadian AAU (CAAU). In February 1908, Longboat and three other ICAC runners ran a 10-mile exhibition in Boston. One week later, the New England AAU, suspecting that the four were paid more than expenses, declared them all professionals.[15]

During the controversy, the publisher of the *Montreal Star*, Hugh Graham, convinced Longboat to remain an amateur. His telegram is quoted in Kidd[16]:

> Canadians are proud of what you have done in the field of sport. Your own victories may gratify your personal ambition, but that should not be the end of it. Your country can be not a little served by a continued example of clean sport.
>
> If at the end of five years you are still in the athletic field and it can be truthfully said of you that you have resisted temptations, kept temperance and managed yourself always on the side of clean sport, I shall be most pleased to hand you a check for $2,000.

But Kidd notes that Graham's offer was interpreted by the Americans as further evidence against Longboat. An inquiry followed, and Flanagan was able to present enough evidence in Longboat's favor so that he was declared eligible for amateur competition by the CAAU.[17]

But this was not enough for the Americans, in particular James Sullivan, who vehemently protested Longboat's participation. Sullivan was quoted in the *New York Evening Sun*, discussing the problem, "I have learned that Mr. Boyd, the Canadian Olympic delegate, is preparing a similar protest against Longboat, who has been declared a professional by the Canadian Amateur Athletic Union. The Canadian protest will undoubtedly be of considerable importance as reinforcing ours."

In England, during the week of the Olympics, *The Sportsman* reported, "At the last moment yesterday afternoon it was officially given out that Tom Longboat's entry in the Marathon race had been protested against. The official statement was as follows: 'Longboat runs in Marathon race under protest of the Committee from the United States and the L.A. of Canada, who desire to protect their own registered athletes in America.'"

The *Official Report* gave significant attention to the Longboat question. They reported as follows:

> At the meeting of the Canadian Central Olympic Committee, held at Ottawa on April 21, 1908, the following resolution was adopted:—"That the Board of Governors of the Canadian Amateur Athletic Union be requested to formally certify to this Committee the amateur status of Thomas Longboat, and his complete eligibility to compete in the Olympic Races in England under all the regulations and qualifications governing that contest, copies of same to be forwarded.
>
> A letter was received by Mr. F. L. C. Pereira, Hon. Secretary of the Canadian Central Olympic Committee, signed by Mr. William Stark, President, and Mr. H. H. Crow, Secretary-Treasurer of the Canadian Amateur Athletic Union, dated April 29, 1908 from Toronto, as follows:—"I beg to inform you that Longboat is registered as an amateur with the C.A.A.U. (No. 1488), and that he is an athlete of good standing, not only according to the amateur definition of the C.A.A.U., but under the regulations and qualifications laid down by the British Olympic Committee to govern entries of amateur athletes. Trusting that this assurance will be satisfactory to you, on behalf of the Canadian Amateur Athletic Union, we beg to remain, &c...."
>
> Letter of May 4, 1908 from J. Hanbury Williams, Chairman of the Canadian Central Olympic Committee (and later IOC Member) to the Chairman of the British Olympic Council, "You will observe that the Association deem Longboat to be eligible in every particular to participate in the Games as an amateur. The C.A.A.U. is one of two great bodies which control all sport in the Dominion, and has a

membership of some 750 to 800 clubs, and its Board of Governors is composed of men of high standing in athletics. One hears a great deal in conversation, and one reads a great deal in the Press, but we have to be guided by clubs of good standing, and the decision seems clear.'

Based on the above, the BOC noted that it was impossible to deny Longboat entry.

Sullivan's formal protest to Percy L. Fisher, Esq., Honorary Secretary of the AAA, read:

Dear Sir,—Mr. Gustavus T. Kirby informs me that our protest against Thomas Longboat should be sent to you as Secretary, and should be accompanied by £1.

I enclose you herewith £1 1s., and you can consider the communication from our Committee men as our official protest against professional Thomas Longboat.

Yours truly,

(Signed) James Edward Sullivan[18]

Sullivan was asked for further evidence of Longboat's professionalism, and replied to Rev. R. S. de Courcy Laffan:

Dear Sir,—Your communication of July 20 has been received and noted.

The A.A.U. of the United States through its officials now in London desire to acquaint you with the fact that, as a matter of record, Thomas Longboat has been declared as professional by the A.A.U. of the United States for an act committed in the United States. This is merely a matter of record.

May I suggest that you call upon Mr. Percy L. Fisher, Secretary of the A.A.A., to furnish you with all the information and evidence that he has received in relation to Thomas Longboat's doings in the United States and also in Canada? I feel confident that Mr. Percy L. Fisher and the other officials of the A.A.A. can give you information in relation to one Percy Sellen, who has been competing with this Thomas Longboat in America.

Yours truly,

(Signed) James Edward Sullivan[19]

But the British Olympic Council then correctly noted that Sullivan had not at all answered their request for evidence against Longboat, merely citing innuendo, and basically evading the questions they had posed. They denied Sullivan's protest and allowed Longboat to compete.

Longboat ran in the 1908 Olympic Marathon, but did not finish, dropping out at around 20 miles. The race eventually saw one of the most dramatic finishes in Olympic history when the Italian marathoner, Dorando Pietri, collapsed after he entered the White City Stadium in the lead. He was helped by the British officials, finishing with their assistance. Naturally he was disqualified, the victory going to the next finisher, American Johnny Hayes. Further details of the race are given in the description of the marathon event.

However, three protests eventually occurred as a result of the controversy surrounding Pietri's finish. First, the Americans protested Pietri being initially declared the winner—the British ran the Italian flag up the victory pole. The American protest was upheld, the official statement reading, "That, in the opinion of the judges, M. P. Dorando would have been unable to finish the race without the assistance rendered on the track, and so, therefore, the protest of the U.S.A. is upheld, and the second man, Mr. J. Hayes, is the winner, the protest being made by the South African team being withdrawn."[20]

The South African protest had been lodged similarly to the American one, protesting the aid given to Pietri. South African Charles Hefferon was the third runner to finish, eventually receiving the silver medal. But Hefferon wanted nothing to do with the protest, believing Pietri should have been declared the winner, "Such a race as this I will either win by being first past the post, or I will not win at all. Dorando has won; he deserves the great victory, and I will not do anything to rob him of it, nor will I seek to gain second place on a protest. Dorando was the best man; let the best man have the honour. No protests for me."[21] However, after the American protest was upheld, the official statement noted that "… the protest being made by the South African team being withdrawn."[22]

The next day, after his disqualification, Pietri and Count Brunetta d'Usseaux, Italian member of the IOC, protested his disqualification and the final result. Newspaper reports noted, "In his protest [Pietri] sets forth that he did not ask for or desire assistance in completing the race. This assistance, he says, was given by committeemen and members of the Olympic council who were grouped about the finish. He says again that he could have finished the race unaided, and he protests against being penalized for what he terms 'official interference.'"[23] This protest was not upheld and Pietri's disqualification remained intact.

400 Meter Race in Athletics

In the final, John Carpenter (USA) fouled Wyndham Halswelle (GBR) by bearing out of his lane coming into the final straight. The British officials disqualified Carpenter, which the American team protested. The protest was disallowed. A second final took place, but Carpenter was not allowed to participate. The two remaining American runners refused to participate and Halswelle walked over for the gold medal.

Complete details are found in the description of the 400 meter race, and in the American and British responses to the controversy — see Appendix III.

The Method of Drawing Heats in Athletics

During the first few days of the track & field athletics events, the American team protested the method of drawing for the early heats. In most events, only the winner of the heats advanced to the next round and the Americans felt that their runners were being drawn together, which would give only one American per heat a chance to advance. There is little evidence that this occurred deliberately but in one instance in which two Americans were drawn together — the 800 meters, Mel Sheppard was allowed to run in a different heat after he and John Halstead were drawn in the same heat. Otherwise the method of drawing heats and qualifying was not changed. One British newspaper[24] noted:

> With regard to the question of heat drawings Lord Desborough pointed out in his letter that the drawings had already been made in the various heats and could not be altered, although this had not been asked for. The Athletic Association, he said, had invited the American committee to have a man in the arena during the progress of the events in which America was interested, and Mr. Halpin, the American manager, had been appointed to this post.
>
> After reading Lord Desborough's letter Commissioner Sullivan replied that if the drawings were already made the Americans would like to see them before the day on which the events were to be contested, a privilege which heretofore had not been accorded them.

In the 800 meters, the United States specifically protested the drawing of the heats for round one. American Olympic officials noted that in the original draw Sheppard and Halstead were drawn in the same heat and that no American was in heat 6 and asked that one of them be changed to that heat. The Swedes also protested the original draw as in two heats, two Swedes were to compete against one another. This dual protest was eventually upheld as the heat line-ups were adjusted slightly.

High Jump

As in the pole vault, the Americans protested that no softened landing pit was available for the high jump. This protest was allowed, as noted below in the description of the pole vault landing pit problem.

During the event itself, the Americans made another protest. Pool 1 was held at the south end of the stadium, but under very slippery conditions. The remaining three pools were then moved to another jumping area at the north end of the stadium. Herbert Gidney (USA), who had not qualified in pool 1, then lodged a protest, claiming that the original results of the first pool should be declared void and the competition held again under more favorable conditions at the north end. Rather surprisingly, the judges upheld Gidney's protest, despite the fact that all the jumpers had been equally affected by the original adverse conditions.

Otto Monsen (NOR) and Edward Leader (GBR) had originally shared first place in pool 1, but Monsen refused to take part in the re-scheduled pool. Leader failed to match the height he had achieved in the less favorable conditions, thus the only beneficiary of the protest was Gidney himself.

Pole Vault

The American team protested against the fact that no hole or box was provided for placement of the pole. The protest was disallowed. The *New York Sun*[25] gave the fullest description of this protest:

> The American athletes were somewhat downcast over the decision of the international committee ruling against them in their protest relative to the placing of the pole in the vaulting competition. They believe that the ruling, which compels them to adopt a new method at the last moment, will mean the loss of at least a foot in their distance. Even with this loss, however, they may be able to distance their English competitors, all of whom are 9 and 10 foot men.
>
> The Americans said that they should be allowed to dig a hole for their pole, so as to prevent its slipping in the earth, with the attendant menace of a dangerous fall, and they further requested that the turf on the opposite side of the mark be dug up so as to break their fall. Both these requests the international committee ruled against.
>
> The pole vault arrangement is the same as at the English championships for years. No vaulter ever has been permitted to dig a hole in front of the uprights for his pole, nor has a loose pit been ever dug at the other side of the uprights for the man to drop into.
>
> Many years ago in the English championships held at Crewe the ground was frightfully hard and the late T[homas] Ray of Ulverston asked that a bed of straw

be placed at the other side of the bar. The officials of the games granted the request, and this has been the only case where a concession was made in the way of a plan to soften the jar of the competitor when alighting.

Cycling Protests

On the cycling track, there were three protests that took place. The first occurred on Wednesday, 15 July, in the final of the tandem match sprint event. Colin Brooks and Walter Isaacs (GBR), who finished third, lodged a protest against the winning French tandem of Maurice Schilles and André Auffray, for "boring." Boring was a British term then common for swinging out of line to cut off a rider or runner behind oneself. The protest was disallowed.

In heat 2 of the 100 kilometer event, held on Thursday, 16 July, Canada's Harry Young was originally not advanced to the final, as it was ruled that he had been lapped and had not finished with the main group. Canada protested this ruling, stating that Young had not been lapped. The protest was upheld, and Young was allowed to compete in the final.

In the 5,000 meter track race, the runner-up, Maurice Schilles (FRA), entered a protest, claiming that the winner, Benjamin Jones (GBR), had collided with him at the turn entering the backstretch on the last lap, but the protest was not allowed.

Plain High Diving

In the semi-finals, George Gaidzik of the United States, one of the favorites, finished third and did not originally qualify for the final. He was actually briefly disqualified, as one of the judges felt he was receiving signals (coaching) from a teammate on the ground. The judges' scores for Gaidzik were as follows: one gave him an 8, a 6, and a 9½; one gave him a 9 for each dive; while the third judge scored him 0 for each dive, and disqualified him, based on the above reasoning. The Americans protested, and after consideration by the judges, the protest was upheld and Gaidzik was advanced as an extra diver to the final.[26]

Rugby Football

In rugby football, the British were soundly beaten by the Australians. During the match, the British complained that the Australians were wearing spikes because of the wet turf. Australian captain, Herbert Moran, who did not play because of an injury, commented on this in his autobiography, "We were leading easily when an important official of the Cornish side came to me to lay a complaint that our men were using running spikes; at half-time they had found some scratches on the body of one of their players.... A moment's reflection would have convinced anyone of the folly of using running spikes in Rugby, but somebody's mortification at being so severely defeated had to find an outlet. I insisted at once on an examination of the boots of all the players as they came off the field at full time, and I nominated an English doctor to carry out the task.... There was not a trace of a spike!... I expected at least a graceful withdrawal of the accusation. Nothing of the kind happened."[27]

400 Meter Freestyle Swimming

In the final of the 400 meter freestyle swimming, Otto Scheff of Austria finished third behind Henry Taylor (GBR) and Frank Beaurepaire (AUS). Austria claimed a foul against Otto Scheff in the final, and protested the result of the race. The protest was disallowed and the result stood as listed.

Tug-of-War

The American team protested the footwear worn by the Liverpool Police team in their first round match, and refused to finish the match after losing the first pull. The protest was disallowed. See the description of the tug-of-war event for complete details.

The Swedish Wrestling Protest

In the semi-finals of the middleweight catch-as-catch-can class, George de Relwyskow (GBR) defeated Carl Andersson (SWE) on points, but the Swedish officials protested the decision, stating that Andersson had been the more aggressive wrestler. The delay during consideration of the protest led to the final match being held the next day. The protest was later disallowed, which caused Andersson to withdraw, refusing to compete for the bronze medal.

It is not true that this protest, combined with the Swedes being upset about the failure of the British to have a Swedish flag flying at the Stadium during the Opening Ceremony, caused the Swedes to withdrew from the 1908 Olympic Games in protest. The Andersson–de Relwyskow match took place on Tuesday, 21 July. But Swedish wrestlers continued to compete on 22–25 July, and Swedes also competed in the stadium in athletics (track and field) from 22–25 July.

NOTES

1. BOADW source uncertain.
2. Coates, p. 37.
3. Johnson, p. 128.
4. BOADW source uncertain.
5. Schaap, p. 106.
6. Weyand, p. 82–83.
7. Johnson, p. 128.
8. POE, p. 60. Interestingly, although the Sheridan quote is repeated almost *ad nauseum*, we can find no source for it in 1908 newspapers.
9. Referenced to "Chronicle and Comment: The Olympic Muddle," *The Bookman*, 28, pp. 104–105, October 1908, in Dyreson, p. 321–322.
10. JAL, p. 59.
11. NYH, 14 July 1908.
12. Tait, p. 40.
13. Referenced to JAL, p. 59, but Lucas's text (above) says the exact opposite.
14. Referenced to Good HJ. "The Modern Olympics," *The Canadian Magazine*, 32(8), 1908.
15. Kidd, p. 35–37.
16. Kidd, p. 38.

17. *Ibid.*
18. OR, p. 81
19. OR, p. 82.
20. SL, 25 July 1908.
21. SL, 25 July 1908.
22. SL, 25 July 1908.
23. BOADW source uncertain.
24. BOADW source uncertain.
25. NYS, 13 July 1908.
26. NYH (Paris), 24 July 1908.
27. Quoted in Harry Gordon, *Australia and the Olympic Games*, St. Lucia, Queensland; University of Queensland Press, 1994, p. 68, referenced to H. Moran, *Viewless Winds*, London: Peter Davies, 1939; p. 63.

Appendix III
The British and
American Responses to
"The Battle of Shepherd's Bush"

If the athletes and officials at the 1908 Olympic Games thought that the controversies would end when the events did, they were sadly mistaken. Both the Americans and the British decided to continue their verbal gymnastics in the press for several months. In this Appendix we are including complete reprints of the most pertinent press commentaries by the major players, many of which were published as pamphlets or short monographs.

The first significant salvo in the press battle was fired by Gustavus Kirby, a member of the American Olympic Committee, who gave a speech in New York on 8 September to the Inter-collegiate Association of Amateur Athletes of America (ICAAAA). In one of his later salvos, a small six-page pamphlet published in February 1909 and criticizing the British officials, Kirby stated that the September speech was published. Despite extensive efforts, we have been unable to find the published version of this speech, and the New York newspapers contained only short quotes from it. Kirby's February 1909 pamphlet was entitled *To the Inter-Collegiate Association of Amateur Athletes of America: An answer to statements of the Amateur Athletic Association of Great Britain concerning the Olympic games of 1908*, which is reproduced below.

Kirby's September talk was shortly followed by an American criticism of his comments in the Boston newspapers. It was written by Francis Peabody, Jr., a Boston lawyer, but one who held no official function in the Olympic Movement in 1908 or at any later date. He was simply a spectator at the 1908 Olympics, a lawyer, and a former athlete of some renown in Boston.

Despite Peabody having no official Olympic status, his critique of Kirby aroused quick and pronounced resentment, and led to the publication of *The Olympic Games: An Answer to Mr. Francis Peabody, Jr., and "A Member of the British Olympic Committee"* by "A Member of the American Olympic Committee." Although the author of this 35-page rejoinder is never officially mentioned, it was likely either Kirby or James E. Sullivan.

It was then left to the British to respond to the attacks by Kirby and other members of the American press. They produced a pamphlet entitled *The Olympic Games of 1908 in London: A*

Reply to Certain Criticisms, edited by Theodore Andrea Cook, who also edited the Official Report in 1908. The pamphlet contained an official response from the Amateur Athletic Association of Great Britain.

Concurrent with these publications, Caspar Whitney, an influential American sportswriter of the time, and a former member of the International Olympic Committee (1900–1904), wrote several columns in the sporting journal *Outing Magazine* which discussed the controversies and especially Kirby's comments. We have included these especially because they contain quotes from Kirby's original September tirade which, as noted, we have been unable to locate.

All of the above are reproduced in full as follows.

TO THE INTER-COLLEGIATE ASSOCIATION OF AMATEUR ATHLETES OF AMERICA: AN ANSWER TO STATEMENTS OF THE AMATEUR ATHLETIC ASSOCIATION OF GREAT BRITAIN CONCERNING THE OLYMPIC GAMES OF 1908

by Gustavus T. Kirby

It is with great regret that I again refer to the Olympic games; but certain statements set down in the "Official Statement of the Amateur Athletic Association of Great Britain" make it necessary that some answer should be made to the end that upon the documents of the case the Chairman of your Advisory Committee should not go down in history as a lying scoundrel who is seeking to make trouble and accomplish no good result.

In my report to the Association under date of September the 8th, 1908, I stated that on my return from the Olympic Games I had found much uncertainty among university men as to just what had or had not taken place at the Games; especially as some newspaper reports had made it appear that at times there had been ungentlemanly or unbecoming conduct on the part of the American Team. The object of my report was to inform the members of the Inter-Collegiate Association just what the Chairman of its Advisory Committee had personally observed and knew to have happened at the Games and to show how, under circumstances which were often, to say the least, provoking, the members of the American Team had behaved with a forbearance much to be commended, and at no time either in a manner ungentlemanly or unworthy of a representative of the United States.

As important as the effort to have the members of the Association know just what had happened at London, was also the desire to arrest as much as possible certain sensational and alarming stories in the press, which could have no object in view except to arouse a bitter antagonism on the part of the people of the United States against those of England, and it was hoped that the athletic authorities and the press, both in Great Britain and at home, would unite to allay such bad feeling as had arisen, and that it would be understood that the criticism of the management and officials of the Games had been made not to be nasty, but to the end that the American athlete be commended for his forbearance and good behavior, and that from the errors of the past there might be found profit for the future.

In my report I made criticisms under the following headings:

The acceptance of the Longboat entry;

The absence of the American flag within the Stadium on the opening day of the Games;

The unwise arrangement of the programme;

The method of drawing the heats;

The system of running the Field Events in sections;

The rules relating to the Pole Vault;

The rules relating to the High Jump;

The coaching by the British officials;

The absence of any representative of the American Team upon the field;

The conduct of the British officials towards the American Committee;

The decision in the 400-Meter Race;

The team work by British athletes; and

The Marathon Race.

The replies of the British Association to these charges amount to nothing more than implied admittances, excuses or half-hearted apologies, with the exception of those to the absence of any representative of the American Team upon the field, and as to the decision in the 400-Meter Race. As to the former, the reply states: "The badges of the Committee d'Honneur admitted after the second day of the Games." If this means what it infers; that is, that these badges admitted to the field within the Stadium, so far as it concerns the American Committee d'Honneur it is an unqualified falsehood, and known to be such by the Secretary of the British Association and other officials of the Games.

The reply of the British Association to the charges relating to the 400-Meter decision is one which, if true, would discredit not only my report but myself as well, for it calls the interview with the Referee "bogus," and infers that all my statements in reference thereto are false. That the interview was "bogus" is untrue; that it did take place is a fact; that a protest was lodged is admitted by the very official of the Association who called "bogus" the interview leading up to the lodgement of the protest. There is certainly a mystery here. It cannot be in reference to the interview having taken place, as not only did the American Committee and other Americans know and notice it, but also many others in the grand stand or at the gate opening to the inner field must have noticed that a conference of some kind was going on. The mystery must be in the identity of the official. Who was he? Certainly not David Scott Duncan, if he be an honest man; for he states that the interview was not with him. Was it with Mr. Abraham; who is stated by Mr. Hugh Goble, the Starter, to have been the Referee of the race? I think not; but I do not know.

The Honorable Percy L. Fisher, Secretary of the British Association, could and would clear up this mystery if he were an honorable man — but is he? Under date of December 12, 1908, Mr. Fisher on the letter head of the Amateur Athletic Association of Great Britain sent, addressed to me, the following communication:

G. T. Kirby, Esq., 2 Wall Street, New York, U.S.A.

DEAR SIR: I am in receipt of your favor of the 17th ult., and in reply thereto would point out that you made a specific statement that you had a conversation with the referee, which is proved not to be the case.

I can give you no information on the matter, and have nothing further to add.

Yours truly,

PERCY L. FISHER.

The "favor of the 17th ult." referred to by him being a letter from me, and which in part reads as follows:

Heretofore I have paid no attention whatever to any newspaper articles or statements having to do with my report; but inasmuch as the article referred to must in some manner have the approval of your Government, assuming that it was issued by the British Embassy from Washington, I feel out of justice to myself, primarily, and also to Mr. David Scott Duncan, who states that he was the sole Referee of the 400-Meter Race, an effort should be made to set me straight as to the name and identity of the official with whom I had my conversation as set down in my report, and which you quote … As to the facts in reference to that part of my report quoted by you, you probably are even better informed than I, or at least better informed as to the identity and official title of the man with whom Mr. Weeks and I had our conversation. In my report I did not give this man's name; neither did I then, nor do I now know his name. In fact, the only two officials whom I knew by name were Lord Desborough and yourself. I am confident that I would know the man if I saw him again. You should remember who it was with whom I was conversing. That he was the Referee I certainly believed, and this for the reason that when Mr. Sullivan, Mr. Weeks and I came to the gate and failed to obtain permission from the officer stationed thereat to go upon the field (although we showed to that officer our badges as members of the American Committee d'Honneur), we requested of some one of the officials (was it you?) that he request the Referee of the event to come to the gate and there receive our protest in reference to his decision and to inform us as to the reasons therefor. Mr. Sullivan, offended by reason of the treatment which we had received, refused to wait for the Referee whom some one had gone to bring to us, and went back to the Grand Stand. Presently a gentleman appeared conducted by another official (was that other official you?) and this man — whoever he was — either in name of position certainly held himself out to Mr. Weeks and me as the Referee, and indulged with us in the conversation set down by me.

Now, my dear sir, I do not object to anyone taking issue with me as to the rights or wrongs of anything; but I certainly do object to being proclaimed a liar, even though it may be inferentially, and certainly the statement of Mr. David Scott Duncan would lead a reader to believe that not only had I not had any conversation with him such as set down in my report, but that I have never had any conversation of that kind with anyone, and I certainly feel — and I think that in this you will agree with me — that it is unfair, unsportsmanlike and dishonorable for anyone on that field at the time of the finish of the 400-Meter Race who knows with whom it was that I had the conversation, to stand silent and not inform me and the British public that while Mr. Duncan was undoubtedly speaking the truth in his letter to the *Sporting Life*, that it was another and not he with whom I conversed, and who received our protests in reference to the decision of the 400-Meter final.

From your report it would certainly seem that it would have been a very easy matter for more than one person to have held himself out to me, and with honesty, as the Referee of that race. The letter from your starter states that he received instructions from a Referee whose name is one other than Mr. Duncan. I do not believe the Mr. Abraham referred to was the one with whom I conversed, as I am informed Mr. Abraham has a beard. The gentleman with whom I had my conversation did not at the time wear a beard.

Mr. Fisher replies that I "made a specific statement" and that he "can give no further information." He stands silent and inactive; he wants the "bogus" interview to remain "bogus"; and yet is this a proper and honest reply? Is not one who stands silently by when a mere word or action on his part could set all right, a despicable character and unworthy of any honor in his community? And yet Mr. Fisher is Secretary of the Amateur Athletic Association of Great Britain!

Can it be that the excitement of the 400-Meter Race has driven either all honesty or all memory from all of the officials on the field during that race? I cannot believe that such is the case, and rest confident that sooner or later some official who is not trying to make trouble and does not delight in the use of the ugly term of "liar" and the like; some one with respect for himself, for his country and for us, will answer my inquiries to Mr. Fisher, even if *he* will not. The whole attitude of the Amateur Athletic Association of Great Britain, and, in fact, a large part of the London press, seems to be to stir up trouble; to justify anything done by the officials and the management, and to burn their bridges behind them; so that to go on in their campaign of vituperation and trouble-making is imperative, and getting together for the sake of international good feeling and future competition impossible.

What is the Amateur Athletic Association of Great Britain trying to do? Is it endeavouring to break down that deep feeling of friendship and regard between the two countries which has taken so long to build? If so, it is fast succeeding. Is it pleasant for any man to have either himself or his friends call him a liar? Is such an attitude on the part of those who hold themselves out as representatives of Great Britain calculated to engender good feeling? Is the giving out by the British Embassy at Washington of such a report of the Amateur Athletic Association of Great Britain directed towards that end? Is it diplomatic or bombastic? Is the Britisher so perfect that he cannot err? Is he not big enough to be criticized? Is he going to be a "won't-play" child because his games were found fault with?

How foolish it all is; how unnecessary! There was lots of good in the Games; lots to commend; lots to admire. Let us hope for the future and strive to bring peace and profit out of discord and demerit.

That the British Association cannot discredit in this country the members of the American Olympic Committee has been plainly shown by the action of the various governing bodies of athletics in America towards these men and towards the reports on the Games, which they have made. That the athletes in this country and the thousands of those who are interested in their welfare desire to do all that within them lies to be friendly with the athletes of every other country in the world, and to have friendly and properly conducted international competition with them, has been clearly shown by the action of the Amateur Athletic Union in appointing a committee to endeavour to bring about this end; not through independent action of its own, but by coöperation with committees existing, or which may be created, for the purposes and ends sought by those in America to be attained for the sake of friendly sport and the good and furtherance of international peace.

Respectfully submitted,

GUSTAVUS T. KIRBY

THE FRANCIS PEABODY, JR., ARTICLE

In September 1908, one Francis Peabody, Jr., wrote a letter which was published in the *Boston Daily Globe.*[1]* The letter basically condemned the American behavior during the 1908 Olympic Games and Gustavus Kirby's published support of that behavior, and it eventually elicited much response and discussion from the principals involved. Peabody was described in the article as follows:

*See Notes on page 405.

Francis Peabody Jr. one of Boston's best known lawyers and an enthusiastic follower of all contests that test athletic skill and prowess, has sent to the Globe an interesting answer to the pamphlet recently issued by Gustavus T. Kirby, a member of the American committee that managed the American team of athletes who competed in the Olympic games.

Mr. Peabody is a member of a well-known New England family. He was prepared for Harvard in Salem, then went for two years to Cheltenham college, a big English public school; was four years at Trinity college, Cambridge, and later returned to America and was for a year at the Harvard law school.

He was in his school crew two years and on its football team and while at Cheltenham went in for every form of athletics. For five years he was constantly racing in eights, fours, pairs and sculls. He was the first captain of the Trinity boat club, and rowed for that club and afterwards for Leander in the Henley regatta.

During the year 1879, when at the Harvard law school, he rowed three in one of Gen. Bancroft's famous Harvard crews, which won from Yale by 1m 43s. He has kept in close touch with university rowing and all other sports, both here and in England.[2]

Peabody was in London during the 1908 Olympic Games and did not agree at all that the British had been biased towards the American athletes and officials. His letter to the *Boston Daily Globe* was as follows:

How tired the American public is of the endless bickerings over the Olympic games, and what a bore a man becomes who insists on discussing them I fully realize. One must, therefore, have some valid excuse for again alluding to them, and I think there is not only such valid excuse, but that a duty is imposed on some one to make a further attempt to clear the air by the publication of a pamphlet by Gustavus T. Kirby, one of the three members of the American committee of honor, addressed to the Intercollegiate association of amateur athletes of America. Mr. Sullivan has also again broken out, charging the British officials with "dishonesty." Moreover, as one of our greatest Americans has said, "Nothing is ever settled until it is settled right."

Since the publication of Mr. Kirby's pamphlet, I have waited hoping some worthier pen would take up the issues raised therein, and especially in his account of the 400-meter race; but now, as no one has appeared, I will do my best to clear up the situation, assuming that we are not so much interested in finding out whether the words and actions of the British were proper, as whether the words and actions of our representatives were fair and sportsmanlike, for we are in a sense responsible for the former.

We all want to know who is to blame for this bitter feeling. I was in London during the Olympic week, followed the races and the accounts thereof in the daily papers with close interest, was not present at the Stadium on Thursday, when the 400-meter race was run, but was present and saw the finish of the Marathon race on Friday, and got the full details of the 400-meter race from both English and American friends.

A resume of Mr. Kirby's charges appeared in the press on Saturday, Sept. 12, and it is with this resume alone that we shall deal. From this resume Mr. Kirby's pamphlet would seem to be of great value, because, among other reasons, it assumes to be a sort of official statement of the contention of the American committee as to the 400-meter race.

From this and the English statement we can form a fair idea of exactly what happened and make up our mind for ourselves whether, as the English judges and public unanimously believe, there was a flagrant, open and defiant disregard of the English rule, or whether the contention of our American managers that the decision of the English judges was a glaring injustice, is true. The English rule is as follows:

> Any competitor willfully jostling or running across or obstructing another competitor so as to impede his progress, shall forfeit his right to be in the competition, and shall not be awarded any position or prize that he would otherwise have been entitled to.

This rule was read to every man entered in the sports before the competition began, was printed in full at the head of every program, and when the three Americans, Carpenter, Robbins and Taylor, and Halswelle, the Englishman, were on their marks at the start of the 400-meter race, the starter, by order of the referee, warned them that if this rule was broken the race would be declared no race, the offender disqualified and the race re-run without him; and that umpires were posted at the head to see that the rule was observed.

In judging the merits of this controversy it is of great importance to remember that Mr. Carpenter had drawn the inside next the curb. Halsewelle [sic] came next Robbins next and Taylor on the outside.

I now append portions of the English official statement and portions of Mr. Kirby's statement.

English Statement

> Dr. Badger, one of the umpires, said:

> At the bend just before entering the straight Robbins was leading Carpenter, they being in such a position as to compel Halswelle to run very wide round the bend.

> As they came into the straight Halsewelle [sic] made a big effort and was gaining fast, but the farther they went the wider Carpenter went out from the edge of the track, keeping his right shoulder sufficiently in front of Halswelle to prevent his passing.

> In fact, when they had run about 30 yards up the straight, Carpenter was only about 18 inches from the outside of the track. The track is 24 feet wide. Photographs were immediately ordered to be taken of the footprints, which conclusively corroborate this evidence.

> The referee said that he took up his position opposite the winning post, where he watched the race very carefully in the straight. He stated that on swinging into the straight Halswelle commenced to gain on the man in front, whereupon Carpenter went straight to the outside edge of the track, while Robbins nipped through on the inside. The boring by Carpenter continued, and the umpires held up their hands to signal the foul.

Mr. Kirby's Statement

> Robbins, the third from the curb at the start, gained the curb before 20 yards were run. At 300 yards Carpenter was right behind Robbins and next

him from the curb. Halswelle some four strides back and next the curb, and Taylor fully 10 yards behind Robbins and Carpenter, and in the rear of and further from the curb than Halswelle.

At 300 yards Carpenter passed Robbins. He did not take the curb, but ran with each stride further and further from the curb, leaving between Robbins and himself a gap large enough to drive a car through, and through which (...) Halswelle should have endeavored to pass.

Halswelle, however, endeavored to pass Carpenter on the outside. Try as he would, he could not get up. At no time was he within better than half a stride of Carpenter, and at no time did Carpenter strike or in any manner foul him.

At all times there was never less than four feet between Carpenter and the outside of the track, and through this gap Halswelle could and would have come if he had had the speed to do so.

At 350 yards he was a beaten man. Thereafter it was either Carpenter's or Robbins' race, both of these moving away and leaving Halswelle further behind at every stride. Carpenter crossed the finish line first, with Robbins and Halswelle some two strides behind.

There is no doubt whatever but that Carpenter ran Halswelle wide at the turn, but there is also no doubt that Carpenter in doing so ran the same diameter as Halswelle, and not only gained no advantage on Halswelle, but for more than 20 yards of the race gave Halswelle an opportunity to come through on the inside and thereby gain the curb and point of advantage on gaining the homestretch.

Kirby's Statement Analyzed

Thus the English and American official statements do not differ very materially, except as to the distance which Carpenter ran Halswelle out. Kirby claiming, without measuring, that it was 20 feet, and the British claiming, after measuring, that it was 22 feet 6 inches, and the American public can now judge of the merits of the controversy.

Let us carefully consider Mr. Kirby's account in detail. He says that "Robbins gained the curb before 20 yards were run," which means that Robbins made a rush at the start and ran across both Halswelle and Carpenter, a clear violation of the rule, for which many who saw it thought that Robbins ought to have been disqualified.

Kirby's description shows that Robbins went out to make the running, which he did for 300 yards at a tremendous pace; that at this point Carpenter passed Robbins and instead of taking the curb, which was his plate, "ran with each stride further and further from the curb"; that is, he proceeded to cross, bore or run out Halswelle, in an obvious violation of the rule, for it increased the distance which Halswelle, who was entitled to be unobstructed, had to go.

Between the 300 and the 350 yards (if Kirby is right in saying that Halswelle was four strides behind at 300 yards) Halswelle gained three and one-half strides on Carpenter, being within half a stride of him at 350 yards; meanwhile Carpenter, having carried him, according to Kirby, 20 feet out of his course, was of course so near as necessarily to obstruct Halswelle so as to impede his progress.

Assertions That Conflict

Then follow the extraordinary and inconsistent statements that "thereafter it was either Carpenter's or Robbins'" race, both of these moving away and leaving Halswelle further behind at every stride; and yet Carpenter crossed the finish line first, with Robbins and Halswelle only some two strides behind.

There is no doubt whatever but that Carpenter ran Halswelle wide at the turn which is just the very thing the rule is intended to prevent. I venture to think that every fair-minded person of ordinary intelligence, whether an expert or not, will say that this was a flagrant, open and defiant violation of a plain rule, evidently intended to secure to each runner immunity, not only from intentional jostling, but also from being crossed or obstructed so as to impede his progress.

The minute he "ran Halswelle wide at the turn" he broke the rule. "Halswelle, however, endeavored to pass Carpenter on the outside." This, of course, it was his duty to do, and he had a right to do it without being forced out of his course or crossed by Carpenter.

Mr. Kirby's argument is ingenious but not convincing, for he forgets that the question is not what Halswelle might or could have done, but what Carpenter did.

But whether the judges were right or wrong, though important, is not of the first importance.

The judges in this case, with evident sincerity and equal justice, disqualified Carpenter, ordered the race to be re-run between tapes on Saturday, and according to every rule of sportsmanlike conduct, Robbins and Taylor should have appeared and run that race.

From Taylor's statement that the judges were quite right in their decision, it would seem that Taylor and Robbins would have appeared and ran if they had not been interfered with by this so-called committee of honor, by Mr. Halpin, or by some professional trainer.

Whoever was responsible for this, whether it was the manager, Mr. Halpin, Mr. Sullivan or the other members of the committee of honor, placed our runners in an indefensible and mortifying position, suggesting the idea that Carpenter and the others had been in collusion, and unsportsmanlike and unmanly to the last degree.

Mr. Kirby and his committee, disliking a decision of the judges, and claiming for themselves the right to act as judges refused to play the game.

Mr. Kirby's statement, instead of making the contention of the American managers better, makes it infinitely worse. The belief in London was that our athletes were honest and sportsmanlike, but that their actions and conduct were constantly hampered and misdirected by the American managers — the so-called committee of honor — and the professional trainers, and Mr. Kirby's statement only tends to confirm this view.

The Marathon Race

As to the Marathon race, which I saw from a front seat in the grandstand, within 100 feet of the finish, the facts appeared to me as follows:

Dorando arrived at the Stadium dazed and apparently almost dying. If he could have been told to simply walk for the one-third of a mile on the track to the finish he could have done so. But some excited individuals rushed up to him and shouted to him to run, which he attempted to do, and the result was that he collapsed in a heap on the track and was at once surrounded by a crowd of 50 or 60, whom two policeman tried in vain to keep back.

There is no doubt that of the 80,000 people there, every generous soul hoped that this man, without regard to his nationality, might win, especially as it became apparent as the minutes slipped by, that the next man had been beaten to the Stadium by about four minutes.

Dorando was helped to his feet three times, and finally, half led and half carried to the finish in a perfectly public and open way. Every one who was not too excited realized that the moment he was helped his chance of winning the race was gone. The man who had hold of his right arm when he passed me was the announcer, dressed in a livery and with a megaphone in his right hand.

After Dorando, Hayes and one or two others had crossed the line, the Italian flag was run up, but when a protest was lodged with the judges they at once declared that Hayes had won.

The act of the announcer in helping Dorando was inexcusable and stupid to the last degree, but the judges were in no way responsible for it and could not have prevented it. When Dorando was receiving the outside help, which resulted in his disqualification, all of us who were waiting in the Stadium thought that an Englishman from South Africa, named Hefferon (who, according to the latest bulletin was leading) was second, and that Dorando was being helped to beat him.

I could see in the events of this finish nothing but an intense desire to help a man who seemed on the brink of death, and who had run 26 miles four minutes faster than any of his opponents, attempts which were properly made fruitless by the inevitable disqualification of Dorando.

Other Charges Considered

Mr. Kirby makes the very serious charge that "British officials coached the British contestants." I saw no case of this during the many races I witnessed, and never heard this charge made before. Such action might well have elicited from our managers a formal and forcible protest.

Instead of a protest against this, we heard only complaints that too many Americans were drawn together in the preliminary heats — although these drawings were by lot — that the British team of Liverpool policemen who won the tug-of-war wore "especially prepared" boots, although they wore their ordinary boots provided by the city, and, when a protest was made, offered to pull over again without any boots, and finally of the decision of the judges in the 400-meter race.

This letter is written simply to show how groundless are the charges of "dishonesty" against the judges; that our managers and committees — not our athletes or the English judges — precipitated the trouble, and since then have done all they can to keep alive hatred of England. It would seem that even an Englishman is entitled to fair treatment, to be judged on the facts, and may be painted even blacker than he is.

What we all desire to see in our universities, colleges, and schools is a keen but sportsmanlike spirit, a determination to win, but only by honorable and fair means. We want no tricks, no undue elation in victory, and no undue dejection in defeat; in short, "good winners" and "good losers."

Mr. Kirby's pamphlet will not hasten this desirable condition. On the contrary his complaints of personal affronts and trivial indignities are hardly worth publishing, but only show an angry and prejudiced state of mind and prove, unfortunately, that bad losers are to be found even out of England.

It would be interesting to know who defined the functions of this committee with its modest but appropriate name, and whether the actual contestants expected and agreed to be governed by these men. If it was the duty of this committee to make protests or complaints with little or no reason, to criticise, kick and finally usurp the functions of the judges, they did their duty thoroughly, but they must indeed have suffered, for surely they could not enjoy stirring up and keeping alive dissensions between the two greatest English-speaking nations.

THE OLYMPIC GAMES: AN ANSWER TO MR. FRANCIS PEABODY, JR., AND "A MEMBER OF THE BRITISH OLYMPIC COMMITTEE"

by A Member of the American Olympic Committee

Mr. Francis Peabody, Jr., in the opening paragraph of his remarkable communication of September 19, hits the nail so hard on the head that it is reproduced herewith:

> How tired the American public is of the endless bickerings over the Olympic games, and what a bore a man must become who insists on discussing them I fully realize. One must, therefore, have some valid excuse for again alluding to them, and I think there is not only such valid excuse, but that a duty is imposed on someone to make a further attempt to clear the air by the publication of a pamphlet by Gustavus T. Kirby, one of the three members of the American "Committee of Honor," addressed to the Intercollegiate Association of Amateur Athletes of America. Mr. Sullivan has also again broken out, charging the British officials with "dishonesty." Moreover, as one of our greatest Americans has said.

> *Nothing is ever settled until it is settled right.*

The American public is tired of hearing of the unfairness of the athletic officials who managed the Olympic games, but as nothing is ever settled until it is settled right, and as I presume Mr. Peabody, on account of his British affiliations, desires very much to have this settled right, let us hope that it will be.

In the first place, it is contended by many that the officials who conducted the athletic portion of the Olympic Games were unfair, athletically, that through their ignorance and stupidity they did not give to each contestant a fair chance. A stupid athletic official can justly be accused of unfairness in athletics.

Mr. Peabody says:

> Since the publication of Mr. Kirby's pamphlet I have waited, hoping that some worthier pen would take up the issues raised therein, and especially in his account of the 400-meter race; but now, as no one has appeared, I will do my best to clear up the situation assuming that we are not so much interested in finding out whether

the words and actions of the British were proper as whether the words and actions of our representatives were fair and sportsmanlike, for we are in a sense responsible for the latter, but in no sense responsible for the former. We all want to know who is to blame for this bitter feeling.

It is indeed very modest of Mr. Peabody to have waited for a worthier pen than his to take up the issues raised in Mr. Kirby's pamphlet. I do not know that we could have got a worthier one; but, on athletic matters, particularly on the Olympic Games of 1908, I certainly do not think we could have got one more unfamiliar with the conditions. I do not think Mr. Peabody means to be unfair, but the little pamphlet he has issued shows conclusively that he is in a class with some of the officials who served at the Olympic Games from July 13 to July 25, 1908.

We all agree with him that it is perfectly fair to find out who is to blame for the bitter feeling that was brought about by the Olympic games; certainly if it was the American Committee and the American athletes they are not fit to occupy the position they do in athletics. Mr. Peabody further says:

> I was in London during the Olympic week, followed the race and the accounts thereof in the daily papers with close interest, was not present at the Stadium when the 400-meter race was run.

The above is certainly a gem and shows what a remarkable man Mr. Francis Peabody, Jr., is. He devoted a column or more to discussing the 400-meter race and then very calmly states that he was not present when that event was run. Well, if that is not worthy of a stupid English official I have nothing further to say; of course, having witnessed the 400-meter race, I absolutely refuse to discuss it with one who was not in the Stadium when the race was run.

Mr. Peabody in discussing the race nevertheless seems to have lost sight entirely of the fact that the race as conducted in England, eliminating the Halswelle-Carpenter claim of foul, was unfair.

He acknowledges he did not witness the contest. Well, perhaps it as well that he did not; but is it not a positive fact that the officials were prepared to claim a foul and break the race up? Did not "The Sportsman" publish in advance a notice to the effect that the race was to be watched, that foul work was expected? Is it not a matter of record that the race was broken up, and that there was really no finish? Is it not true that an individual was stationed at a certain point, and if at that point anything that looked like a foul occurred he was to signal the judges and they would break the tape, declare it "no race," and not announce the time? Is not that a matter of record? Was there ever an incident like this in the history of athletic sport throughout the world? Where and when have we a record of an amateur competition being broken up by officials before the race was finished? Is it not a fact that the officials acted in a manner unbecoming their positions? Did they not lose their heads? Did they not inflame the audience by acts unheard of at an amateur contest? Did not the announcer immediately take a megaphone and announce it "no race"? Did not the officials put the sign, "NO RACE," on the bulletin board? Did not Mr. Davidson announce that the race would be run over in half an hour? Did not someone, with or without authority, hold a meeting and an hour later announce that Carpenter was disqualified and the race ordered re-run? Is it not a fact that in arriving at this decision the officials broke their own rules, that were supposed to govern foot racing in England? They informed us that an umpire was placed at a certain point to watch for foul work and that he gave the signal to break the tape. In the "Laws of Athletics," as printed by the Amateur Athletic Association of Great Britain, there is no such official as an umpire. Therefore, is it not true that in arriving at this conclusion the Amateur Athletic Association broke its own law?

It is apparent that Mr. Peabody is not very familiar with the manner of conducting athletic meetings, either in this country or in Great Britain, and I am convinced that he has never read the laws of athletics that govern track and field sport in this country or the laws that govern athletics in Great Britain.

Mr. Peabody, however, is perfectly willing to let the public have his views on the Marathon Race, so I herewith reproduce some extracts from his remarkable letter.

> Dorando arrived at the Stadium dazed and apparently almost dying.

Now that is a remarkable statement from one who wants to be so fair, and who is willing to quote rules and talk about rules. For his benefit I append herewith a few rules of the Marathon Race:

> Rule 3. A competitor must retire from the race if ordered to do so by a member of the medical staff appointed by the British Olympic Council to patrol the course.
>
> Rule 4. No competitor, either at the start or during the progress of the race, may take or receive any drug. The breach of this rule will operate as an absolute disqualification.
>
> Rule 8. Upon arrival at the Stadium the attendants must leave the competitors and enter at a different gate. No attendant will be allowed on the track.

I would state that there was not the slightest desire on the part of the British officials, as represented by the doctors, to order Dorando from the race, as they should have done when he fell exhausted outside the Stadium in the lane; they permitted him to enter the stadium — with one object in mind, that of beating an American.

The photographs show that when Dorando was brought on the track it was done by British officials, held by them and they turned him in the right way to the finish line.

> But some excited individuals rushed up to him and shouted to him to run, which he attempted to do.

They were not excited individuals but very anxious officials. The photographs show that there were three British officials on the track when Dorando was started toward the winning post. They were Mr. Andrews, Dr. Bulger, and the groundsman, Mr. Perry; these were showing Dorando the way to go.

> Dorando was helped to his feet three times, and finally half led and half carried to the finish in a perfectly public and open way. Every one who was not too excited realized that the moment he was helped his chance of winning the race was gone.

This statement is as near the truth as the others. Dorando was helped to his feet positively four times and perhaps five. The men who did this were not excited individuals, they were not his handlers, not outsiders, but British Olympic officials, and the photographs tell the tale.

> The man who had hold of his right arm when he passed me was the announcer, dressed in a livery with a megaphone in his right hand.

This is on a par with all of the other statements made by Mr. Peabody. The man, or the two men, who lifted Dorando up when he fell thirty yards from the tape were Mr. Andrews, a

British Olympic official, who had charge of the Marathon Race, and Dr. Bulger. The photographs show Mr. Andrews carrying him across the line and breaking the tape. He did not have a livery on at all; Mr. Peabody has mixed up two different Olympic officials; the official announcer was the man who usually presides at functions of the Lord Mayor — the City Toastmaster — he wore a uniform; Mr. Andrews did not wear a uniform.

> When Dorando was receiving this outside help, which resulted in his disqualification, all of us who were waiting in the Stadium thought that an Englishman from South Africa, named Hefferon (who, according to the latest bulletin, was leading), was second and that Dorando was being helped to beat him.

Was there ever anything more unfair than the contents of this paragraph? What does Mr. Peabody mean by outside help? The only help he received was from the British officials: five photographs, taken each time Dorando was down, show that he received inside help, help from the officials who were appointed to see that the race would be conducted fairly. If Mr. Peabody is such a fair man and he was convinced that the Americans in the Stadium received fair treatment and the American athletes were so very well treated, how does he then account for the non-appearance of Hayes' name on the bulletins, that were sent around the Stadium during the race? Is it not a fact, Mr. Peabody, that at twenty-one miles Hayes was in third position? Is it not a matter of record that after the announcement was telephoned to the Stadium the leaders in the race were Nos. 19, 16, and 26? And is not the record of the race positive that after the twenty-first mile Hayes was from that point always one of the first three? Is it not also true, Mr. Peabody, that after the announcement at the twenty-first mile Hayes' number was never put on the bulletin board? Was this fair to the Americans who were in the Stadium? Was it fair to deceive them? Was it fair play not to let the Americans who had paid to get in the Stadium know where the American entry was? What object could they have had in leaving Hayes' name off the bulletin board on which the names of the leaders were posted? If Mr. Peabody was in the Stadium and was at all interested in the success of the American entry he would have been one of those who were more than anxious to know where Hayes was during the last part of the race.

> I could see in the events of this finish nothing but an intense desire to help a man who seemed on the brink of death and who had run twenty-six miles four minutes faster than any of his opponents — attempts which were properly made fruitless by the inevitable disqualification of Dorando.

Well, of the babyish statements this certainly takes the premier position, and it only goes to show what a few years abroad will do to one, even though he has been brought up in an American atmosphere. So Mr. Peabody could see nothing whatever in the unfair actions of British officials but an intense desire to help a man who seemed on the brink of death? Isn't that a remarkable statement to come from a man who is trying to defend the British Olympic officials? Again I ask him to read the Marathon rules in relation to the duties of the doctors. Was it not their duty to order him from the race when he fell in the lane outside the Stadium? Was it not their duty when he fell, after going thirty yards in the Stadium, to have taken him out of the race? There is a photograph showing the fourth time Dorando fell; it is on the bend as he entered the home stretch. What do we find? Dorando on the track, helpless, Dr. Bulger is holding him up and testing his heart, and another doctor is massaging him. Standing on the track, not watching Dorando but watching the entrance where Hayes at that moment entered, are Mr. Davidson and Mr. Andrews, two British Olympic officials, and on the infield, close by, Secretary Fisher.

The doctors worked hard on the poor, apparently dying man, who should have been taken out of the race; they got him on his feet, and started him off; after going about twenty yards the Italian fell again; Hayes was near him, and it was then that Mr. Andrews took him up and rushed him across the finish line, breaking the tape.

If in a race of this kind, where the rules are printed in the programme clearly, the British officials would permit a race being won in such a manner, is it a wonder that some pronounced Americans might term it a stupid act?

> After Dorando, Hayes and one or two others had crossed the line, the Italian flag,
> was run up, but when a protest was lodged with the judges they at once decided
> that Hayes had won.

Mr. Peabody did not witness the 400-meter race, but he was in the Stadium at the finish of the Marathon and occupied a seat in the grandstand within one hundred yards of the finish, and one of the facts he wants the American people to believe is that after Dorando, Hayes and one or two others had crossed the line the Italian flag was run up, but when a protest had lodged with the judges they at once decided that Hayes had won.

Mr. Peabody, who, I believe, has had four years training at Trinity, will kindly pardon me if I pronounce the above statement ridiculous, and I am now convinced that he not only did not witness the 400-meter race but was not in the Stadium during the finish of the Marathon Race. Why a man of good standing in a community would publish such an untrue statement, particularly when it is one affecting the rights of an American, I cannot understand. The moment Dorando finished, the Italian flag was raised and as soon as Hayes finished the American flag was placed in second position. The American Committee did not for an instant believe that it would have been necessary to make a protest, because the assistance the officials gave Dorando was of such a character that a novice in athletics would know that Dorando never won. The raising of the Italian flag was a deliberate insult, and the American Committee entered the arena and protested that the raising of the Italian flag in first place was an insult to the United States and a demand was made to lower the Italian flag until such time as the protest from the American Committee was settled. The American Committee cared not what the British officials did with the protest, but as Dorando had not won the race it was an insult to let the Italian flag be raised, indicating that he had won. The officials were asked to settle the protest immediately, and if it was decided in favor of Dorando to then raise the Italian flag. This they refused to do. The American Committee was forced to write out the protest. While the members of the American Committee were talking to the officials, one British official distinctly stated to a member of the American Committee, "Why, my dear sir, Dorando was not assisted." This member then pointed to Mr. Andrews and said: "There is the man who picked up Dorando and carried him across the finish." This Mr. Andrews denied. The officials then came back to another member of the American Committee and informed him that Hayes had been protested. This member of the American Committee told him that he cared nothing about that; that it was simply ridiculous and that the American Committee wanted the protest on Dorando settled.

After many minutes of discussion, which I might say was conducted in a gentlemanly and correct manner, one British Olympic official, a large fellow with a gray suit, standing near the finish line, used foul language to one member of the American Committee and ordered another member off the track, telling him he was in the way.

A few minutes later the officials came to a member of the American Committee and informed him that there would be a meeting, and invited the American Committee to the conference, as they were going to take evidence in relation to the Marathon race. The American Committee absolutely refused to present evidence or to enter into any conference, but left the matter entirely to the British officials. The English officials then went into executive session and the American Committee were requested to wait until they were finished, which they did, at the Imperial Sports Club, and after *two hours* or more, a decision was rendered, which read as follows:

> That, in the opinion of the judges, M. P. Dorando would have been unable to finish the race without the assistance rendered on the track, and therefore, the United States of America is upheld, and the second man, Mr. J. J. Hayes, is declared the winner, the protest made on behalf of the South African team being withdrawn.

Now, Mr. Peabody, does not the above official decision that was handed to the American Committee prove that your statement that "when a protest was lodged with the judges they at once decided that Hayes had won" is untrue?

One more question I would like to ask you, Mr. Peabody, in connection with this. Did you ever in your life or in the history of sport throughout the world hear of the judges of an athletic meeting leaving the field and debating for two hours before rendering their decision? There is no recollection among the oldest followers of athletics of any such action on the part of any judges except in England during the Olympic games. They did the same thing in the Carpenter case — they made one decision on the field and then went into a private room and made another decision.

Perhaps this may strike you as being just the way to conduct amateur sport; perhaps, after spending so much time in England, you can give us other instances similar to the acts referred to above.

Now why in the world would Mr. Peabody make such a statement as the above, i.e., "but when a protest was lodged with the judges they at once decided that Hayes had won"? That is a misstatement. However, it is on a par with many other statements made by this remarkable gentleman and the more I read his pamphlet the more convinced I am that he was not at the Olympic Games.

> Mr. Kirby might well drop these childish complaints and remember that this hostility may be accounted for by the fact that Mr. Sullivan announced to the press on the opening day that the British were "more than one hundred years behind us in managing sports," and that the American managers followed this up by a succession of kicks and "knocks."

This statement is as near right as any other made by Mr. Peabody. Mr. Sullivan did not make that statement on the opening day, nor at any other time.

Mr. Sullivan did say during the week, however, to several prominent English athletic authorities, after having watched the arrangements of the heats and observed under what rules they conducted the field events and observed with what stupidity they arranged the order of events, that they were twenty-five years behind America, and not only are they twenty-five years behind America, but they are twenty-five years behind England. English officials, twenty-five years ago, would never have been guilty of the mismanagement of the games as were the officials at the recent Olympic Games.

The fact that they were twenty-five years behind England and American is responsible for their stupid rules in shot putting, high jumping and pole vaulting; their stupid rules account for the fact that England has not got a champion shot putter, high jumper or pole vaulter.

The fact that England is twenty-five years behind America was proven in the Marathon Race, where they simply relied on traditions and expected to win the race, when their records show they have not had a Marathon Race in dozens of years up to 1908. Furthermore, the attitude assumed by the A.A.A. at their last meeting, as published by "Sporting Life," proves that they are still willing to be behind the times. Some energetic member of the A.A.A. suggested that the A.A.A. give annually a long distance run of twenty-six miles. The report tells us the committee were not in favor of holding this championship race under its auspices. That would be all right if they had in the past any clubs in England giving twenty-five-mile runs, but they have not. I repeat, they are more than twenty-five years behind America, and if Mr. Peabody desires proof of this he can get it right from English records; not from American records.

> Mr. Kirby does, however, make the very serious charge that "British officials coached the British contestants." I saw no case of this during the many races I witnessed and never heard this charge made before. Such action might well have elicited from our managers a formal and forcible protest.

The above paragraph further convinces me that Mr. Peabody was not in the Stadium and did not witness the Olympic Games, and if he did witness the Olympic games he is a man who never saw a foot race before and who certainly does not understand what the word coaching means, but we must give him credit for at least stating that if they did coach, that it might well elicit from our managers a formal and forcible protest.

Fine! He has at last really found one thing that is worthy of a forceful and formal protest. What does he mean by "forcible"? Formal is all right, but what does he mean by "forcible"? Can it be possible — but wait, for his information I will give him a few facts. On the opening day the officials on the infield deliberately coached the English runners. Mr. Andrews ran along with a megaphone, coaching the runner for fully ninety yards, and the only thing that stopped him was that if he continued he would probably have taken a header into the tank. The American Committee very justly protested, and the Chairman of the British Olympic Council said that he would stop it and have the official removed from the infield. The offender was not removed from the arena but his megaphone was taken away from him for one day, thus handicapping him. The next day the same official was on the backstretch, coaching the English runners again, and two members of the American Committee will make an affidavit to that effect. Is it not a fact that one English paper published an editorial objecting to British coachers? Any one who followed athletics and was present at the Olympic Games must have seen the coaching that was done there by the British Olympic officials during the two weeks. We will let the American people decide as to whether it is the American Committee's fault, the American athletes' or the British Officials'. Let me say that it is men of the type of F. Peabody, Jr., who will keep alive the hatred for England by the publication of such a letter as his.

> It would seem that even an Englishman is entitled to fair treatment, to be judged on the facts, and may be painted even blacker than he is.

The Englishman or any other man in sport is certainly entitled to fair treatment, and America has always given the visiting English athlete fair treatment when he comes to this country; and if we do a wrong in sport we are always ready to apologize for it; the American papers would not permit us to do wrong. Not so in England in athletics. They cannot do anything wrong, and if they did they would never admit it, and all of this controversy would have been over long ago if they had only admitted, man fashion, that their officials were stupid, and that they mismanaged the Olympic Games. Poor Mr. Peabody. He really writes enough copy to fill an eight-page circular, and I doubt if there is another man who claims to have a knowledge of athletic matters who could display so much ignorance on subjects that are perfectly clear to even a novice.

It would be interesting to know who defined the functions of this committee, with its modest but appropriate name, and whether the actual contestants expected and agreed to be governed by these men. If it was the duty of this Committee to make protests or complaints with little or no reason, to criticize, kick and finally usurp the functions of the judges, they did their duty thoroughly, but they must indeed have suffered, for surely they could not enjoy stirring up and keeping alive dissensions between the two greatest English-speaking nations.

The above shows conclusively just how much Mr. Peabody knows, and it is a pity that one is forced to answer him. For his information it may be stated that the Committee of Honor was created by the British Olympic Council, a fact he might easily have ascertained if he had referred to page 5, rule 14, of the book issued by the Council, the rule in question being as follows:

An Honorary Committee will be formed, consisting of three representatives from each competing country to be nominated by the Olympic Committee in that country. Special seats will be reserved for them as for the members of the International Olympic Committee, at all contests and all festivities connected with the Olympiad, and they will be distinguished by a separate badge. (N. B.— In the case of competitors not represented on the Honorary Committee, the British Olympic Council will appoint three members to act on behalf of such competitors.)

It was the duty of this Committee to make protests; an athlete could not make a protest; therefore, the Committee had to make the protests for the athletes, and the Committee did not make a protest affecting the rights of the athletes until they were requested to do so by the athletes.

That the British team of Liverpool policemen who won the tug-of-war wore "specially prepared" boots, although they wore their ordinary boots provided by the city, and when a protest was made offered to pull over again without any boots.

The above shows the absolute ignorance of the writer and his desire to be unfair. For his benefit we quote the following clause from the rules:

"No competitor shall wear prepared boots or shoes or boots or boots shoes with any projecting nails, tips, sprigs, points, hollows or projections of any kind."

The members of the American tug of war team claimed that the British team wore prepared boots; the captain of the team and the manager of the team demanded that the American Committee protest the prepared boots and the American Committee did, and they feel convinced that the boots the Liverpool policemen wore were prepared. One member of the American Committee went to one of the largest shoe dealers in the city of London and asked to be shown a policeman's boot and they showed him one which was not like the ones the Liverpool policemen wore and a certificate to that effect was given to this member of the American Committee and is now in his possession. The statement that they offered to pull over again without boots is made without the knowing the facts. It was the members of the American team who offered to pull without boots, and three days later when two members of the tug of war team, McGrath and Flanagan, had gone to Ireland a public challenge was issued and declined for the above reason.

Instead of a protest against this we heard only complaints that too many Americans were drawn together in the preliminary heats, although these drawings were by lot.

Mr. Peabody has well suggested that a worthier pen than his might have taken up the issues raised by Mr. Kirby in relation to these Olympic games, for certainly his ignorance of what occurred at the Stadium during the recent Olympic Games is apparent to all. He does not even know how the drawings were made. It is a well known fact that in the 1,500-meter race the placing put together four of America's fastest men at that distance in two heats — Halstead, Sheppard, Lightbody, and Sullivan. This would have been all right if they had allowed the second men to run over again and given the fastest second man a chance in the final heat, which could have been done and which showed that they did not want to be fair by not doing. The second fastest man in this race was undoubtedly Lunghi of Italy, who would undoubtedly have been the first, second, or third in the final heat. That is a matter of record. His running in the half mile showed conclusively that he was one of the fastest men at that distance. Furthermore, we in America think that Halstead would have been third, and the finish of the 1,500-meter race should have been Sheppard, Lunghi, and Halstead. I doubt if Wilson would have been placed.

The drawing together of the best Americans in two heats in the 1,500-meter race might have been, as the English term it, "the luck of the draw," but what do we find in the 800-meter race the following Monday? What did the American Committee find? They again found four of their fastest men in two heats — Sheppard, Halstead, Ramey, and Bromilow. Sheppard won the Eastern try-outs and Ramey won the Western try-outs. Halstead was regarded as the find of the season in college athletic circles, and Bromilow was the second fastest man to Sheppard in the Eastern try-outs at Philadelphia. Naturally, the American Committee objected and they asked the secretary, one of the men who were responsible for the heats, how they fixed the heats. He told us that an American was placed in each heat; the Committee then drew his attention to the fact that in the sixth heat, Mr. Just, the English champion, did not have a single American against him; however, they took Halstead out of the heat with Sheppard and put him in another, but not in the one with Just. In this way Halstead won his heat, which he would never had done had he remained in the heat with Sheppard. Now, Mr. Peabody, if you understand athletics what would you call that but unfair, bungling or stupid?

Now, Mr. Peabody, you seem to feel that the Americans should have been simply delighted at the way the heats were arranged. Apparently to you it was all right to have four of the fastest 1,500 meter men in American placed in two heats, winners only to count. Perhaps to you it was all right to have the second fastest man in America, perhaps the second fastest man in the race, barred. If that is the kind of fair racing you want, then it would be useless to argue with you. Perhaps, Mr. Peabody, it was all right on the following Monday to have the four fastest 800 meter men in America placed in two heats, second men not to count. Perhaps that's the kind of fair racing that you have been used to, but it is not the kind of racing we have in America. In America we endeavor to give to each contestant entered a fair chance to win one of the prizes.

Mind you, Mr. Peabody, we would not have objected to two of our best men being placed in one heat if the English officials were fair enough to admit that the second man should have a chance to run over to get a place in the final, but they would not allow that. They stated it was contrary to their laws and customs to permit the second men in the 1,500 meter race and 800 meter race or the 400 meter hurdle race to run over again, in order to qualify for the final; that it was against their laws, against their customs. Now, the members of the American Committee investigated this claim and found that it was not against their rules or customs, but they wanted to be unfair to the Americans in these events, because it was believed that in these three events America had men who would get first, second and third places. They wanted to discriminate, and they did discriminate, against the Americans. They had no law at all that barred the second man in the 1,500 meter, 800 meter and 400 meter hurdle races from trying for a place in final; they deliberately made misstatements. To my way of thinking they were deliberately unfair, because in this same meeting they allowed the second men in the five-mile race, in which particular race England seemed to have a chance to get first, second and third places, to run in the final. In both walks, where England seemed to have a chance to get first, second and third places, they allowed the second men and third men to walk in the final. Now, Mr. Peabody, if that was a fair athletic meeting how do you account for that? They would not allow the Americans who got second to run in the finals, but in the events in which the British excelled, they allowed the second and even third men to compete in the final.

In order to make it clear to men of the type of Mr. Peabody and to those who frequently claim that the heats as printed and announced were the luck of the draw we give the following facts. Perhaps the statement that four of the best men in American at 1,500 meters were placed in two heats might be doubted if we did not have records. Let us look at the records. Who won the 1,500-meter run at the try-outs at Philadelphia to select men to go to the Olympic Games? J. P. Halstead. Who finished second to Mr. Halstead? J. P. Sullivan. Who was the intercollegiate champion at one mile? J. P. Halstead. Who was admitted to be the fastest miler in America on his past record? M. W. Sheppard. Who won the Western try-outs at 1,500 meters, to select men for the Olympic Team? J. D. Lightbody. Therefore, a child could take the reports of the spring games and pick the four fastest milers in America. These four men were in two heats! It may have been, "the luck of the draw," but when they barred second men and wouldn't let the second men have a chance, to which they were entitled, to compete in the finals, then it was very hard luck of the draw.

On Monday, July 20, the four fastest half-milers in America were placed in two heats. Any child who followed athletics could take the papers and tell you who were the four fastest half-milers in America on records made last spring up to about the time the team was selected. Who won the 800-meter try-out at Philadelphia? M. W. Sheppard. Who was second to Sheppard? J. Bromilow. Who won the 800-meter run at the Western try-outs? H. P. Ramey. Who was admitted by such men as J. Moakley to be the athletic find of the year? J. P. Halstead. Who would any novice select, if he had the records, as the four fastest half-milers in America? And these were placed in two heats on July 20, second man not to have the chance of running over for the prize. It may have been "the luck of the draw," but it would be interesting for any man to try and draw out of a hat the heats as they were drawn on July 13 and 20.

Some day, however, perhaps the truth will be told about how the heats were arranged. The American Committee was told that the selections were made in the usual way. Well, the usual way is to start the fastest men in different heats. The old way was to put the numbers in a hat and take a chance on getting the fastest men in one heat, but we in America have no recollection of ever having barred the second man from having a chance to get a place in the finals.

If the drawings were made in the usual way, or if it was their intention to put an American in each heat, as it was claimed, how was it that when the programme was printed on July 20 we found that Mr. Just, the English champion, was in a heat with the Hungarians and not a single American with him? They put Mr. Just with the foreigners, who were not his equal, although in another heat two Americans were forced to run against each other.

Mr. Peabody classes the insults to the American flag as trivial and by insinuation tries to make one believe that these were little incidents that should not be noticed. These were the very incidents that caused the Americans to sit up and take notice. The non-appearance of the American flag on the opening day was an "oversight." A good joke. The pulling down of the American flag in one section of the grandstand. Another good joke. The attempt to take away an American flag from one college boy by British athletes. Another joke. The placing of the American athletes in the gallery with the Finlanders and the press at one of the banquets. Another good joke. A very good joke, in fact, when we remember that one athlete who asked why the Finns were put in the gallery was told that they were despised by the Russians, who would not eat on the same floor with them. This athlete is still wondering who despised the Americans. Then the time it took to raise the American flag when an American won a victory — on one occasion it took thirteen minutes. A good joke.

Does Mr. Peabody know that in the standing high jump the American athletes were hooted and booed at so violently that one of the officials in a laughing way had to ask the crowd to desist or the competition would be postponed. Mr. Peabody apparently has looked at the Olympic Games through British official glasses.

I am convinced that Mr. Francis Peabody, Jr., has written on a subject about which he has not the slightest conception. I doubt if the statement is true that he saw the finish of the Marathon Race; it does not seem possible that such a communication would be issued and signed by a man who had the slightest athletic knowledge, because he proves that he is absolutely ignorant of athletic matters.

Of course it was a rare good joke to have an Englishman get up in the stand and shout, "Semi-pros, semi-pros." Why that was a great joke. Of course, it was a good joke when a man waved an American flag, to hear them yell. "Take it down, put it down." Great joke.

Of course the American Committee is to blame for all of this for trying to get for the athletes they brought over a fair field and no favors.

Apparently the British Olympic officials feel a great deal like Mr. Peabody; they don't want to let the subject drop, they want to find out. The following remarkable letter was published in "Sporting Life" on September 28:

> THE PRESIDENT OF THE BRITISH OLYMPIC ASSOCIATION,
> LONDON.
> SIR: I am instructed by the Swedish Olympic Committee of 1908 to express to you their sincere thanks for the great hospitality and kindness shown to the Swedish Olympic competitors, and to state at the same time how greatly they appreciated the good will and fair play which governed the spirit in which the Games were conducted.
>
> My Committee earnestly hopes that, as a result of the competitions, the strong ties of friendship already existing between British and Swedish sportsmen may serve as an inducement to British sportsmen and athletes to visit Sweden in the near future, where at all times they will be assured of a hearty welcome.
> I have the honour to be, sire,
Your obedient servant,
VIKTOR BALCK

This would be all right if "Sporting Life" had not published on July 23 the following protest from Mr. Edstrom of Sweden:

> ### THE WRESTLING COMPETITIONS.
> #### A PROTEST FROM SWEDEN
>
> The following letter was handed to one of our representatives at the Stadium yesterday with the request that it be made public through the columns of the "Sporting Life":
>
> TO THE BRITISH OLYMPIC COUNCIL:
> SIRS: I hereby beg to protest against the decision of the National Amateur Wrestling Association this afternoon, when deciding about the protest given in by me to Mr. Sutherland. The protest was caused by the decision of the

referee in the semi-final of the catch-as-catch-can wrestling. Mr. de Relwoy-skow of England, met Mr. C. G. Anderson, of Sweden, who is champion wrestler of U.S.A. in his class.

Mr. Anderson attacked all the time during the bout; he walked the Englishman all over the mat, threw him down, and attacked. The bout gave no definite result. The judges differed, and the referee decided in favor of the Englishman. I immediately raised a protest, and called all the members of the honorary committee that happened to be present as witnesses.

The following gentlemen are willing to state that the Swede was the better man on points — Mr. Weeks, Hon. Com. U.S.A.; Baron Hillebrand, Hon. Com. Finland; Mr. Sayers, Member of Olympic Council; Mr. Knight, official of wrestling. Besides, all the wrestlers surrounding share our opinion.

Mr. Sutherland heard the referee, and decided that the wrestling should be continued for another fifteen minutes. Mr. Relwyskow, however, refused to wrestle again and brought the matter up before the board of the National Wrestling Association. The board upset Mr. Sutherland's decision, and decided that there should be no new wrestling.

As our first protest was decided by Mr. Sutherland, I maintain that his decision ought to be final, and I therefore appeal to you to uphold the decision given in the first instance and accepted by us, as protesters. I am, etc.

J. T. EDSTROM
Member Honorary Committee
Hon. Sec. Swedish Olympic Council

London, July 21.

Now why this change of heart? What can the British Olympic officials gain by this controversy? Perhaps they agree with Mr. Peabody that a thing is not settled until it is settled right.

In connection with the letter from Mr. Viktor Balck it might be interesting to give to our readers the story of how the Americans found there was not an American flag displayed in the Stadium on the opening day.

The American Committee noticed Mr. Edstrom and several other Swedes rushing frantically across the infield, come through the barrier and in an indignant manner explain to the American Committee the terrible insult that had been heaped upon Sweden. "What do you think," said Mr. Edstrom, "there is not a Swedish flag on the poles around the Stadium." The American Committee replied, "That is impossible; there must be some mistake." "Then," said Mr. Edstrom, "what do you think they told me when I called the matter to their attention? They told me to 'go get a flag and they will put it up.'"

In the meantime it was discovered that the American flag was not to be found on the poles either, and one member of the American Committee went to a member of the British Olympic Council, whose name is set forth prominently in all their booklets, and explained to him that there was not an American flag among the decorations. In the brutal manner for which he is noted, the member of the British Olympic Council said: "Go and get a flag and we will put it up." The American Committeeman started to search for one, but could not find any. So it is interesting to know that Sweden's flag as well as America's was left out of the decorations on the opening day.

In relation to the 400-meter race, I for one will refuse to discuss that contest with a man who writes a column about it and admits that he did not see the race; certainly a man who was not in the Stadium and did not see the race is incompetent to discuss Mr. Kirby's version or any other version of it.

ANOTHER ONE.

The "Sporting Life" of London evidently believes with Mr. Francis Peabody of Boston that nothing is ever settled until it is settled right, and this particular paper has not allowed a week to pass since July 20th without some reference to the Olympic Games and the American protests. We quote the following from "Sporting Life" of October 14:

> The American contingent, however, were not satisfied with their share of the spoils. Petty protests were the order of the day, and the culmination came when they protested against the right disqualification of J. C. Carpenter in the now historic 400-meter race, and thus accepted the onus of justifying a foul so deliberate that the A.A.A. have permanently disqualified the athlete named. From every other country our officials' conduct of the athletic events received almost unequalled praise. That there would be little hitches in connection with an unrehearsed gathering of this nature was a certainty, but the method of management, and the organization generally will serve as a pattern for the government of future international athletic contests. The U.S.A. representatives were alone in their protests, and are equally isolated in the charges of unfairness and partisanship which they have since published broadcast. We do not think that the reputation of the A.A.U. for sportsmanship will be enhanced by the action of its leading officers and the athletes under its charges in uttering wholesale slanders against our officials. It is only too evident that nothing short of the entire control of the games would have appeased Yankee officials, and judging from what we have heard since, they would not have been an improvement on our own leaders of athleticism.

The American Committee did protest, and rightfully, against the disqualification of J. C. Carpenter, on the ground that the decision as arrived at was illegal according to the British Olympic laws. The breaking up of that race was done on the strength of the announcement of a man that, according to the Amateur Athletic Association's laws, had no authority, and there is only one other record in amateur sport of a race being broken up, and that was when Eugene Merrill of American was robbed of a victory in a walking match against Raby at Birmingham, England; more about that later. A careful reading of the above, however, satisfies the Americans that it is the intention of the English to bluff it out, and if possible to convince the world that everything "as just as it should in connection with the recent Olympic Games."

It is very clever indeed of the "Sporting Life" writer to say that every other country praises the conduct of the officials in the athletic events; that is very clever, because it must be admitted that the athletes from the other countries had very little to find fault with. It is true that the Swedes did find fault with the javelin throwing. Of course the Italians did not know that Lunghi was illegally and unjustly barred out of the 1,500-meter race, final heat, and they did not care, because they have not been long enough in athletics to know just what was going on. It would be well if the writer in "Sporting Life" would sit down and figure out just what interest the other countries had in the athletic events. He must know, and we know, that it was anything to beat the Americans. It was not "anything to beat the Norwegians," or "anything to beat the Swedes," because they did not figure in the Olympic Games, athletically speaking. The records answer that question.

So "Sporting Life" tells us that there would be little hitches in connection with an unrehearsed gathering of this nature. What a remarkable statement. Do you mean to tell me that the British officials did not know their own rules and that it was necessary to have a rehearsal? Was it necessary to have a rehearsal of the finish of the Marathon Race? Is it possible that such a thing is now claimed?

So the method of management of the recent Olympic Games is to be a pattern for the government of future Olympic or international athletic contests? I hope not; I doubt it; I do not think there will ever be another set of Olympic Games managed as were the ones at Shepherd's Bush, London, in 1908. By continuing this controversy, and by your weekly article and flings at the United States and its representatives you will of course have the subject continued, but we feel confident that at the next international contest the athletes will at least know under just what rules they are going to compete. They will not have to rely on customs.

STILL ANOTHER

The following from the "Sporting Chronicle" is a gem:

> One gathers that they were on the "protest" bright and early. Longboat, the Indian, was objected to in connection with the Marathon Race on the score of professionalism a fortnight before the games commenced. Presumably the Committee did not consider the charges proven, but in any case it is obvious that Mr. Kirby felt in this matter he was treading on delicate ground. He knows as well as anybody that the ethics of American amateurism are "sketchy" in the extreme, and while I am not to be taken as arguing that two wrongs make a right, the fact that Hayes had scarcely got back to his own country before he became an avowed professional; that Cameron, the cyclist who represented them at the Stadium, has since been declared a professional (let no one say because he was beaten), and that their Olympic winners have been "starring" the States like a troupe of strolling players, does not allow of Mr. Kirby taking on a very strong position on the Longboat matter. So he drops the subject very quickly.

Another illustration of the conceit, impudence and arrogance of an Englishman when he writes of amateur athletics when it affects the standing of an Englishman. It was not necessary for Mr. Kirby to devote a great deal of space to the running of Longboat as an amateur. The world at large will never forget the fact that the Amateur Athletic Association, with its much-talked-of desire to have purity in athletics, allowed a professional to compete with amateurs, so it is well for them to sit down and keep quiet when pure amateurism is discussed. Of course, the Committee did not consider the charges proven; here was an opportunity to get someone in who could possibly beat the Americans, someone who had really gone twenty-five miles on more than one occasion. We on this side of the water did not think it was delicate ground at all, we thought it was a brazen attempt on the part of the A.A.A. officials to inject professionalism into amateur sport.

The cowardly fling at Hayes is just like an English writer, Hayes returned to America and left the amateur ranks in a manly way; he was told in manly fashion by the governing body of amateurism in athletics that he could not accept the position on the stage and still retain his amateur status. How different in the case of Dorando! The Amateur Athletic Association acted in the most weak-kneed manner possible. Dorando accepted music hall engagements and the British A.A.A. did not have the nerve to declare him a professional. The A.A.U. had the necessary nerve. In England Dorando is still an amateur, I suppose, and is still eligible to compete in amateur events under the rules of the A.A.A. of Great Britain.

Cameron was an amateur when he returned to this country and he was afterwards transferred to the professional ranks for reasons well known to the National Cycling Association. This must strike the Englishmen as being very peculiar, because it is a well-known fact that it takes them a very long time to transfer a man from the amateur ranks to the professional. Will the "Sporting Chronicle" tell us a little about W. G. George, Bredin, Bacon, Downer, Shrubb, and dozens of others who posed as amateurs for years in Great Britain? The starring that several Olympic winners did was at important games in and around New York City, where expense money such as they give in England is unheard of, where bookmakers who control meets are unknown. What the Olympic winners did in this country was done for the good of the sport, and if the "Sporting Chronicle" would like to have some more discussion of the Longboat matter I guess they can have it. Certainly those who had control of the Olympic Games in London knew of the Longboat affair in the United States, and their acceptance of his entry was an absolute defiance of the body controlling amateur sport in America.

> It would have been better if after the fashion of the good Prince George of Greece at the previous Games, held in Athens, the British Committee had handed over the entire control to the talented impresario, Mr. Matt Halpin, or some member of the American Committee d'Honneur, Mr. Kirby, for instance.

Was there ever in the history of sport such a cowardly attack on one of the best sportsmen who ever officiated at an athletic meeting, Prince George of Greece? One is led to believe from reading this paragraph that Prince George was as stupid as some of the officials who served at the recent Olympic Games in London. The above is a typical example of the fair play one receives from writers of sport in England when it affects English interests. They cannot be fair.

As for the games at Athens, it is quite true that the Americans won the majority of the events, but there was no reason to object, because the decisions were honest and the meeting was well managed, the officials were sportsmen and no one tried to take an unfair advantage of a competitor. Is it not true that the two gentlemen who were the English representatives to the games at Athens, Mr. J. Fowler-Dixon and Mr. G. B. Robertson, are not good enough to come forward and tell the truth about Prince George and the games? They were there; there never was a Committee meeting that they did not attend; there never was a decision of the Committee that they were not acquainted with; the entire arrangement of the programme, the arrangement of the heats was known to them; there was nothing that took place during the games in which the English representatives did not have a voice. As a matter of fact the only change made in the programme was one that was made at the suggestion of Mr. Robertson. Perhaps that gentleman has forgotten, but the writer has not.

Why do they not come out and tell the truth in relation to the 400-meter race and the statement that Halswelle was bored when Pilgrim beat him? It would be a good idea to get a few of the photographs that are in the possession of the French photographers, showing the race. Of course, the English must have some excuse for their defeats and they keep on creating them. Are they good losers? We will let the English writers answer that. No one else can. Read the results of the track and field events at the recent Olympic games at London and see what rapid strides England has made in athletics under the mismanagement of the Amateur Athletic Association.

Prince George's reputation for being a true sportsman is known the world over and his keen knowledge of athletics is appreciated by all, and any attacks on the Athens management will not serve to distract attention from the incompetence of the British officials. The Olympic Games at Athens were conducted in a manner that was ideal; they were conducted by Greek sportsmen, and in future let us consider the Greek sportsmen as the ideal one in sport, and we cannot be far wrong. After comparing the Olympic Games held in France, the United States and England, we can only remark that there is just one place to hold the Olympic Games, and that is at Athens.

Of course, the insinuation that the Americans ran the Olympic games at Athens is merely a British excuse for defeat. Go over the history of the Olympic Games; pick out how many Englishmen were winners, or secured second or third place. Go back to the winners of the first international meet, at Athens, in 1896, and one will understand why it is necessary for English writers to defend England's athletic degeneracy. When, at the Olympic Games at Paris, where, even after changing the rules so that a colonial could represent England, they still lost, the writers at that time stated that England was not represented; that they took no interest in the games, merely looked out for their development at home. Development at home is good. When English interests are defeated, naturally "they were not properly represented" or "did not take interest."

The statement that appeared in one English paper in connection with the recent Olympic Games that English athletes were not acquainted with the use of the javelin and discus, is on a par with the other statements. Did not one member of the Olympic Games Committee of 1908 compete in the discus throw at the Olympic Games at Athens? So how can you account for that statement?

"Sporting Life's" comment at the recent one-mile fiasco at the A.A.U Championships at Travers Island is right; it was a stupid blunder, but how differently the American papers handled it. Some claimed it was unfair, that the officials were dishonest, but one thing pleased the A.A.U officials. On the day following the championships every paper in New York denounced the mistake, called it stupid and handled it as such matters are handled in America.

The whole Kirby pamphlet is laughed at, and passed over; in fact, the "Sporting Chronicle" is a good deal like the "Sporting Life"; it admits Mr. Kirby's charges but apparently did not like the language of same. Of course, the "Sporting Chronicle" could not for a moment imagine that any official appointed by the great A.A.A. would ask Mr. Kirby "who in –– he was." Well, we in America know Mr. Kirby, and it is a positive fact that a distinguished gentlemen, very large, with a grey suit, standing at the finish line of the Marathon race, did ask Mr. Kirby "who in –– he was." This individual was the same one who in a gross, brutal manner also told another member of the American Committee to get off the field, that he was in the way, when the member of the American Committee was speaking to Lord Desborough in relation to the American flag not being raised when the Marathon Race was won.

In relation to the reputation of the leading officials of the Amateur Athletic Union for sportsmanship, we will let the world at large decide, certainly not those who were guilty of the unsportsmanlike acts that one found at the Stadium at Shepherd's Bush. When the proper time comes, when the photographs are published, when the programmes are reproduced, when the protests that we made are made public I do not think any one will accuse the American officials of being wholesale slanderers.

"Sporting Life" is quite wrong in thinking that the American officials wanted to control the games, or wanted to have anything to do with them. They did feel at one time that perhaps it would be a good thing to have had some Yankee officials, but after what happened they can only look back and thank their stars that they were not officiating during the two weeks. That will certainly be always referred to as two weeks of blundering on the part of the English officials.

Apparently the Amateur Athletic Association of Great Britain believes in Mr. Francis Peabody's contention that nothing is ever settled until it is settled right, for the following remarkable letter has been received in New York:

AMATEUR ATHLETIC ASSOCIATION

London, October 6, 1908

J. E. SULLIVAN, ESQ.
 A.A.U. of America
  Warren Street, New York
   DEAR SIR: I beg to inform you that at a meeting of the General Committee of

this Association, held on Saturday last at Birmingham, Mr. J. C. Carpenter was permanently disqualified from competition.

Yours faithfully,

(Signed)P. L. FISHER

Hon. Sec.

The above will be considered at the Annual Meeting of the Amateur Athletic Union, on November 16, and it is another illustration of the impudence of some people. Apparently the Amateur Athletic Association will endeavor to bluff through on this proposition, as certain writers in "Sporting Life" are trying to do each week. It is strange, indeed, that Secretary Fisher should send such a communication to the A.A.U. after having, with his brother official, insulted the A.A.U. and all those throughout the world who recognized amateurism by allowing Thomas Longboat to compete with amateurs after he had been declared a professional by the Amateur Athletic Union of the United States. An association that will tolerate Longboat and defy the governing body of America by accepting his entry, after he had been declared a professional by said governing body, is entitled to very little consideration in relation to its decisions.

Therefore, it must be apparent to all that Mr. Francis Peabody, Jr., wants it settled right. "Sporting Life" wants it settled right, the A.A.A. wants it settled right, and the member of the British Olympic Council by his letter to the "Telegraph" shows he wants it settled right, so it is now up to the American Committee to let the world at large know what protests it made, publish the photographs, the programmes, the arrangements of the heats, the photographs of the Marathon Race, etc.

The "London Sportsman" likewise believes in keeping everlastingly at it and the following appeared in its issue of October 7:

> It was a meeting full of interest and good work which the General Committee of the Amateur Athletic Association held at Birmingham last Saturday. In permanently suspending the American, J. C. Carpenter, from competing under A.A.A. Laws the committee did the only thing possible after the disgraceful exhibition of foul play which had been witnessed in the 400-meter race at the Olympic Games.
>
> Henceforth Carpenter is out of amateurism for good and all, so far as Great Britain and British athletes are concerned. Nor is he wanted in the new professionalism, for it is only by discouraging such unsportsmanlike conduct as that of which Carpenter was guilty and by setting their faces against trickery that the professionals have a chance of bringing about a permanent and honest revival.
>
> What view the Americans will take of the matter is impossible to say, but there has been so much misrepresentation on the other side of the Atlantic as to the unsavoury disqualification that one must be prepared for another lot of "screeching."

It is quite true no one knows now what view the Americans will take of the matter; some feel that it ought to be treated with utter contempt, but as it is apparently the policy of the British to try to bluff it through, it might be a good idea for the American Committee to publish its protests and their reasons for objection to the management of the recent Olympic Games held in London.

BOSTON, October 15, 1908

MR. THOMAS RILEY,
Cambridge

DEAR TOM: Your letter of the 12th received. I have not the letter which I wanted to have sign of the American authorities in London. It was simply the written protest they was asked to sign.

About the javelin competition, I'll say that "Sweden" lost a second prize by English injustice or unknowledge of the game.

In Free Javelin throw, Hugo Wieslander of Sweden threw the second best throw, which was disqualified, because he in the run (not when throwing) supported the javelin by the left, as he later threw it by the right hand.

Nothing in the English temporary rules said something about this, and certainly the most stupid official, you believe, ought to know that in free javelin as well as in free discus nothing hinders you to support with both hands.

Sweden, I think, did not protest to my knowledge, but that was because we Swedes never stick up for our right before it has gone considerable far.

Anyway, I hope you can get use of these things. I am doing fine in the Waltham schools, and hoping to see you soon, I remain now,

Yours very truly,
(Signed)CARL ANDERSON [sic]
206 W. Springfield Street.

P.S.— Besides me, Sweden had a wrestler, "Malmstrom," in the lightweight Græco-Roman, who threw his man six times, by sufficient falls, but as the judges thought he did not hold his man down long enough he did not secure any of them, and after twenty minutes were up he lost the bout by "decision." The man who won such an easy victory was later the winner of first prize.

Carl Anderson [sic] was a member of the Swedish team.

*　　*　　*

Since the above answer to British slanders was written, another "Jim the Penman," one Theodore Cook, of press agency fame, has broken out with a characteristic English bluffing communication. His letter-writing ability, impudence and ignorance stick out on each page, and his ignorant, impudent and insulting reference on several occasions to the Hon. Theodore Roosevelt, President of the United States, shows his caliber. If he is the type of a British sportsman the I.C.O. and B.O.C put forward as their official spokesman, then we may expect fuller contributions from Messrs. Davidson, Fisher and Andrews and a few of the other choice spirits that grace the infield at Shepherd's Bush from July 13 to July 25. The American Committee will, at the proper time, answer the booklet that has been issued, apparently with the authority of the I.C.O. and B.O.C.

A writer in the Daily Telegraph (London) of Saturday, September 26, 1908, signing himself "A Member of the British Olympic Council," seeks to create the impression that the American officials undervalued the ability of their team and seemed to think that the latter had only a chance to win by resorting to tactics and continuous uproar. As the American officials, who have been in close touch with athletics for years, knew thoroughly the caliber of each member of the team, such a statement is absurd, and, speaking of tactics, anyone who watched the performance of the English stable of athletes during the two weeks of the Olympic games would have been greatly enlightened as to the meaning of the word in an athletic sense. The American officials and athletes conceded that their knowledge of tactics was greatly increased. They saw more tactics, more scheming, more jockeying, more team work — honorable and dishonorable — than they had ever witnessed. It was "stable work" from beginning to end, on the part of the British officials and committeemen as well as the athletes. The whole Olympic meeting just reeked with tactics, indoors and outdoors, and if the reader thinks this statement prejudiced he can refer to the references to tactics, taken from the English papers and quoted herewith, and judge for himself.

The Bystander, July 29, 1908 — "In one or two instances our men would have done even better if they could have been induced to subordinate their own interests to those of their countries."

The Sportsman, July 15, 1908 — "According to the programme the three-mile team race was to take place early in the afternoon, the final of the 1,500-meter race being scheduled for a later hour. These two events were interchanged, however, and the walk was succeeded by the mile, that being the approximate distance, according to English standards, to 1,500 meters."

NOTE.— And not for the Americans? More tactics from the committee room.

Daily Telegraph, July 15, 1908 — "The real reason for our defeat in a race which every one had considered a certainty for this country, was that our men did not run to suit themselves, but just exactly as the winner liked it, and the result must therefore be put down largely to bad generalship, which did not permit the best runners at the distance to produce their best efforts at the critical moment."

Daily Telegraph, July 15, 1908 — "It was a race [1,500 metres flat] of which a story worthy of notice has to be told. The Britishers, of whom H. A. Wilson, the light-footed little mile champion; J. E. Deakin, his runner-up in the race that bestowed this title, and the Oxford stayer, N. F. Hallows, had nothing to fear if a strong pace was set. The only danger lay in a slow, muddling race, as it was bound to suit M. W. Sheppard, the versatile American athlete, who is equally good over any distance from a hundred yards to a mile, with the quarter mile and half mile as his specialties. It was agreed by all that the British trio named required a fast-run mile, particularly in the first two of the three laps which had to be covered. To that end I. F. Fairbairn-Crawford and E. V. Loney unselfishly agreed, mutually, to carry a pacemaking mission, but their notions of what this duty involved were at fault.

"The willing Scot, Fairbairn-Crawford, went through the first with the lead. He certainly was pacemaking, but not at the higher pressure needed. The same defect was observed when Loney took up the running in the second lap. It was obvious that the time was going to be slow. Moreover, Sheppard, the one American to be feared, had still a reserve of power left to him. He was running easily within himself when the last lap was reached. Here Wilson soon worked himself into first place, closely attended by Hallows, with Deakin, who ran with the poorest judgment imaginable, and utterly regardless of any but his own purely personal interest, lying right away behind. Deakin is a stayer of the first water, and a runner of ripe experience, who should have long before this have gone up as a pioneer for the welfare of the British team. As it was Wilson had to make his own running with Hallows, and the two Americans, J. P. Sullivan and M. W. Sheppard, treading closely on his heels."

Daily Telegraph, July 25, 1908 — 1,500 METERS FLAT RACE.— "A race to be remembered. The pace was made very strong by Fairbairn-Crawford and Loney in the best interests of the other British competitors. This order was maintained into the last lap, when Wilson went to the front, followed by Hallows and Sheppard. Two hundred yards from the tape Wilson sprinted and looked all over the winner as he came into the finishing straight with a decided advantage. But with a marvellous and sustained sprint, Sheppard wore the British mile champion down, to win in meritorious fashion by a bare yard. Hallows was fifteen yards behind Wilson. Time 4 minutes 3 3-5 seconds, which equals the Olympic record."

Sporting Life, July 15, 1908 — UNITED KINGDOM WINS TEAM RACE. – "It was a grand exhibition of that spirit which was lacking in the 1,500 meters final, and the result causes one to regret that the British competitors in the shorter distance event were not instructed beforehand as to the tactics which they should adopt. The American runner, Eisele, did the performance of his life, keeping the front division in hand all the way up to the last lap, when Deakin came away with a brilliant spurt and took Robertson and Coales off with him. But Eisele was not done; he came again, and up the straight would certainly have passed Coales had not Robertson kept him in hand until the tape was reached. It was indeed a grand finish, and the Britishers were delighted to score in the team race, one of the most important events of the games."

Sporting Life, July 17, 1908 — "There was a welcome improvement yesterday in the tactics of the British cyclists. We understand that the view put forward by us that they were not riding for themselves, but for their country, was impressed upon them very strongly by those who had a right to speak on behalf of this phase of British sport. The advice thus tendered was received in the spirit in which it was given, and how immediately effective it was we had an example of in the 100 kilometers race (62.125 miles) in the morning. Unfortunately, the conditions were not satisfactory, as the showers which fell at frequent intervals made the dust on the track into liquid mud, which was transferred in turn to the cyclists, many of whom were colorable imitations at the finish of stokers on an Atlantic liner."

Sporting Life, July 28, 1908 — "We had previously learned the strength of M. W. Sheppard from the 1,500 meters, so, in the final of the 800, I. F. Fairbairn-Crawford set out to make the pace a cracker, and, if possible, take T. H. Just clear of the field. But the Cantab was not fast enough, and it was Sheppard who came along with a wet sail in the last 400 yards to win by about 8 yards from Lunghi in 1 minute 52 4-5 seconds. A second tape had been erected at the full half, and this Sheppard broke in 1 minute 54 seconds, knocking two-fifths of a second off the twenty-year-old record of F. J. K. Cross. It was a brilliant piece of running, the like of which we have never seen. Nor must Lunghi be forgotten, for he covered 800 meters in 1 minute 54 1-5 seconds, while Just could not go the pace in the straight, and was beaten by Braun and Bodor, who finished out together, the Geran struggling into third place.

"The British defeat was unquestionable, an American first, and three Continentals next. Some have drawn a line between Crawford's tactics in the half and those of the Americans in the quarter, but there was no comparison, for Crawford simply set a hot pace, to make sure that the race was fast, knowing that Just could not beat Sheppard in a fast finish. It was Crawford who got Sheppard the record, in point of fact, and the American athlete realizes that."

The Mail, July 15, 1908 — "This race was lost to Great Britain by an error of judgment, a foolish as it was quite unnecessary. The obvious was disregarded. The correct tactics undoubtedly were for one of our five representatives competing to take the field along at a fast pace, and so run Sheppard, who is known to be a speedy finisher, off his legs in the first two laps. It was consequently in the nature of a surprise to see the early laps being run at a pace entirely suited to the American."

The Sportsman, July 16, 1908 — "The arrangements were excellent, but once again the track was invaded by an army of officials and loiterers, the majority of whom had no business there at all. A police sergeant did his best and Lord Desborough himself asked several to leave, but it had little effect until near the end of the day, when there was a slight improvement."

NOTE.— Officials and loiterers! They were there for an object. No American was on the field on July 15.

Sporting Life, July 16, 1908 — "It was quickly made apparent that the United Kingdom did not intend to favor any loafing tactics. There was not to be any loafing. In the 1,500 meters the United Kingdom representatives played right into the hands of the States, but on this occasion they had evidently a pre-arranged plan of campaign, which included a determination that the pace should be a cracker from start to finish. The field soon began to spread-eagle, and the various incidents will be found detailed elsewhere. What gave profound satisfaction to the majority of onlookers was that the United Kingdom had four men in the first five. Eisele made more than one effort to take the lead, but this was a privilege which Robertson, Deakin & Co. had reserved for themselves, and they began to draw away. At last the States man was shaken off, but he was still full of running. Two hundred yards from the finish Deakin drew out and came up the straight as if he were finishing a quarter of a mile. Robertson showed a considerable amount of restraint. He was running second, but noticing that Coales was laboring somewhat, and that Eisele was overhauling him, he dropped back to Coales' shoulder and brought him up the straight, nursing him so carefully that try as Eisele would, he could not split the Britishers, who thus had the honor of furnishing the first three men home, and won, in a style that will always be remembered with pride and satisfaction, the great team race of the 1908 Olympiad."

Sporting Life, July 16, 1908 — "In the fourth heat another great disappointment for the United Kingdom occurred, as J. E. Deakin, one of the idols of the crowd, found himself unable to keep going after his hard race of the morning, and had to give up the race early on. Although J. Murphy, who forced the pace all the way, won comfortably, it is impossible to avoid an expression of regret at the arrangement of the programme which asked our distance men to run two severe races in one day."

Sporting Life, July 16, 1908 — "In the last lap Deakin came away with a fine spurt, and, running brilliantly, won with something to spare by eight yards. Eisele came up the stretch in good style, but Robertson, in a splendid spurt, kept Coales on the move instead of going up, so England was left with a bloodless victory."

Daily Telegraph, July 16, 1908 — "The turn of speed which Eisele had displayed overnight at the end of his qualifying heat *had to be taken from him*, and resolutely all set themselves to bring this about. The American was quite as good as he had seemed to be and he made a most plucky fight of it, hanging on to the heels of the British flying squad long after Wilson and Hallows had been left in the rear. In the last lap Eisele gamely strove to save one of the first places which were the objective of the British runners. *What is more, he would assuredly have beaten Coales for third place but for the very unselfish, and, indeed, most sportsmanlike action of Robertson.* This runner ran for his side. He coached the hardly pushed Coales all through the last lap, throwing away his own good chance of winning in doing so. His good offices caused the first three places to fall to the British team. The time of 14 minutes 39 3-5 seconds will tell how strongly the pace was set."

Daily Telegraph, July 16, 1908 — "Here our crack sprinter, V. L. Johnson, the dapper little Birmingham rider, carried the French crack, Demangel, for the best part of a half lap and still beat him comfortably and more easily than his half length advantage would indicate. Then the French tricolour saluted most fervently, and bringing the impulsive Frenchmen to their feet, greeted the success of the powerful tandem combination, Schilles and Auffroy, in the 2,000 meter race. If wobbling somewhat up the straight, they did nothing to call for the protest unbecomingly lodged by the second pair of riders. A notification to the effect that 'this protest is not upheld,' by the medium of the megaphone, was loudly applauded. The French riders well earned their brilliant success."

Daily Mail, July 17, 1908 — "It is a matter to be deplored that cyclists should be guilty of such ruinous tactics — for that such foolish methods as crawling at the start are greatly detrimental to cycling as a spectacular form of entertainment few will deny. And in an Olympic programme it is nothing short of outrageous that a race should be void — taken no account of whatsoever in the awarding of the prizes and in the records of the festival."

Sporting Life, Jul 20, 1908 — "I am not one of those who go so far as to say that the 1,500 meters race was thrown away, for after Sheppard's brilliant effort I would not like to say that he could not have hung on in faster time. But I do think that our chance was lost when the third quarter was run slow. I. F. Fairbairn-Crawford ran a fast lap, but E. V. Loney is not a sufficiently good man to take a field along, *and one of the others should have sacrificed his chances.* But it was not to be. The men ran along together, and not till the end of the back stretch did Wilson come along. Sheppard was lying back, but striding grandly, and 120 yards from home he came along like a lion, and won nicely. Time 4 minutes 3 2-5 seconds — and Wilson has beaten 4 minutes. There were many gloomy faces, and no wonder. Before the race I expressed my opinion to Wilson's mentor that unless he beat 4 minutes Sheppard would win, and so it proved. *Right here let me say that a mistake was made in attacking Deakin for not cutting out the pace in the 1,500 meters. He was instructed — or shall we say advised?— to hold back a bit, in view of the three miles later in the day. Personally, I think this was a great mistake, for he could never run a waiting race. The man, however, who might have shifted matters up a bit was N. F. Hallows who won his heat in precisely the same time as Sheppard won the final.*

"In the three miles our men fairly redeemed their reputation. The heat saw Deakin, Robertson, Wilson and Coales finish abreast, and in the final the leaders kept one another going until *the last lap when Deakin ran away and won comfortably, while Robertson took Coales right up to the tape and just kept him clear of a fine plucky young American in J. L. Eisele — so we had the first three.*"

The Sportsman, July 25, 1908 — "At the twentieth mile the name of Hayes cropped up for the first time, running third to Hefferon and Dorando. Thereafter the spectator heard no more of him, subsequent information being confined to the statement that Hefferon was still leading, with Dorando at his heels."

NOTE. — The above is a sample of the tactics of the few British officials that bungled the games. Why was Hayes heard of no more? More tactics to deceive the public.

Daily Telegraph, July 22, 1908 — "The Scot, Fairbairn-Crawford, dashed to the front after there had been a rare tussle on the northern bend for the leadership. Immediately he was at the head of affairs Crawford cut out such a pace as is seldom seen in what was practically a half mile. *There is no doubt but that he was sacrificing his own chance in the interest of the other Britisher, Just, and for the good of his country. It was a cut-throat policy aimed, without a doubt, at trying to find a weak spot in Sheppard, and bring out in the fullest degree the supposed extra staying power of Just. For about 460 yards Crawford led the way. Nothing loath to go as fast as any one called upon him to do, the American crack was well on the heels of the leader, attended by Just and Lunghi. The pace was such a cracker that the other four competitors were already left well behind.*"

ANOTHER GENTLEMAN HEARD FROM

The following remarkable speech is taken from the London Sportsman of Thursday, December 3, 1908, and was delivered at the annual dinner of the London A.C. by Mr. G. R. Robertson, a graduate of Oxford and a member of the British Olympic Council.

"Mr. G. S. Robertson then rose to propose 'The Visitors.' In doing so he paid a tribute to the unwearying efforts of the Olympic Council, of many of these he saw around him, and mentioned the extraordinary labors of the Hon. Secretary, the Rev. R. S. deCourcy Laffan. They had great pleasure in welcoming their visitors that night, but there had also been recently unwelcome visitors. Mr. Fisher had merely suggested, but he could say what he thought? Mr. Hawes, whose name he also coupled with the toast, had nothing to do with these visitors; fortunately, he had had to deal with gentlemen from Canada. (Applause.) But there had been other foreign individuals who had not always proved gentlemen. Those who read the official reply of the A.A.A. to the charges made would, he thought, agree that it was crushing and conclusive. This reply had been issued by the British Embassy at Washington and it was, he believed, the first time that such an official retort had been made. He had extracts from the New York papers which showed that the reply to the malicious slanders had so been made. The accusations especially affected the London A.C. because so many of their members were officials. He did not blame the American athletes as a whole — few of them said anything — but the trouble was caused by athletic managers. The athletes were as gentlemanly as the managers permitted them to be, and that was not saying much. They had actually had a suggestion made by the A.A.U. of the United States, by which the latter hoped to set up a special set of rules for Olympic Games, and naming five delegates, including Messrs. Sullivan, Maccabe and Kirby. He had asked Mr. Maccabe at his chambers why the trouble had arisen, and he had replied that they didn't think they had been treated with sufficient respect, and proceeded to point out the standing in the States of those who composed their party. He thought it would not matter if we in this country had no further 'truck' with them. If people were not sportsmen they knew what to do; if they were liars they also knew. But if both 'no sportsmen and liars,' then the lethal chamber at the Batterseas Dogs' Home was only fit for them. It was the first opportunity he had had since the Olympic Games had concluded and he had determined to speak freely."

The above remarkable tirade is not the vaporings of a denizen of the slums but an alleged gentlemen who prides himself on the fact that he is an Oxford graduate. That Mr. Robertson is correctly quoted can hardly be possible, but, if he is, it is a most remarkable contribution to the present controversy — in fact, *the* most remarkable — because in America Mr. Cook is not taken seriously, but Mr. Robertson has had a different reputation on this side of the water.

Mr. Robertson impeaches the veracity of the American committeemen. Truthful answers to the following questions would speedily prove Mr. Robertson's economy of the truth.

Is it not true that in the heat of the 800 meters run Mr. T. H. Just, the British champion, practically had a walk-over, and there was not an American placed in that heat as his opponent, while two Americans were forced to run against each other in another heat of the same race?

Is it not true that the British Olympic officials assisted Dorando in the lane outside the Stadium and that British Olympic officials assisted him on the track in the presence of thousands of people? Did not one British official carry him across the finish line, and after this remarkable exhibition of how not to finish a race legally, the judges awarded the race to Dorando?

Is it not true that several Englishmen tried to take an American flag from one of the young men in the section where the American contestants sat during the games?

Is it not true that the starting in the sprints was bad? "Bad" was the term used in the Manchester Athletic News?

Is it not true that British Olympic officials publicly coached the English athletes in their races?

Is it not true that the American Committee were kept from the field for several days while representatives of every other country had access to the same?

Is it not true that the officials ran on the track, obstructed the contestants and illegally broke up the 400 meters race?

Is it not true that when the British officials were measuring the discus throw they ordered the American manager away, and also ordered away one of the American contestants who desired to see the measurement?

Is it not true that when one American contestant was making his try in the standing high jump 20,000 people "booed" him? So much so, in fact, that he could not make his attempt, and one official had to take his megaphone and threaten to call the competition off if the spectators did not desist.

Is it not true that the management refused to entertain the American protests against the barring of second men in the 800 and 1,500 meter runs and then allowed second — and even third — men to compete in the finals of other events?

Is it not true that the London policemen were allowed to wear prepared boots in the tug-of-war?

Is it not true that the American pole vaulters were not permitted to dig a hole, a custom that has heretofore been always allowed in the international competition?

Is it not true that Dorando was brought on the field by a British Olympic official and started on his exhibition tour toward the royal box and was detained in front of the Committee stand until such time as he was brought forward to receive his consolation cup for the Marathon Race — which was presented before Hayes, the real winner, received the Marathon Trophy?

Is it not true that Daniels received a bad start in the 100 meters swim?

Is it not true that Narganes was not thrown in the wrestling bout when he was declared down by the official?

Is it not true that several remarks were made at the drawing of the wrestling competition that were not at all creditable to the wrestling committee?

Is it not true that a British Olympic official swore at one member of the American Committee, and immediately ordered another member of the American Committee off the field?

Is it not true that at one of the banquets no places were reserved on the main floor for the American athletes and they were sent to the gallery with the Finlanders and the press? When a prominent official was asked why the Finlanders were the only body of Continental athletes in the gallery, he replied that they were despised by the Russians, who would not attend the dinner if placed on the same floor with them.

Is it not true that when it was found that not a single American flag was flying on the opening day from one of the many flag poles and one member of the American Committee asked a member of the British Committee why it was, he was told to go and get a flag and they would put it up? Is it not true that an apology was sent for this omission?

Is it not true that the field events were conducted illegally, in sections, and that all the contestants did not receive athletic fair play?

The English claim America was the only nation that protested. Is it not true that the following protests were made during the two weeks:

France protested the 5,000 meters bicycle race. (The Sportsman, July 20, 1908.)

Sweden protested in wrestling bout between Anderson and Ralwyskow. (Sporting Life, July 22, 1908.)

Austria protest in 400 meters swim. (Sporting Life, July 17, 1908.)

French protest in 1,000 meters cycle race. (Sporting Life, July 17, 1908.)

Protest by Brooks and Isaacs (Great Britain and Ireland) in 2,000 meters tandem cycle race. (The Sportsman, July 16, 1908.)

Canada protested Thomas Longboat's entry in Marathon Race.

Is it not true that American was the only country that was compelled to write out its protests?

Is it not true that the Italian flag was kept at the masthead for an hour or more, indicating that Dorando had won, and did it not take the officials two hours to render their decision that Dorando had not won?

Is it not true that never before in the history of athletics has there been an occasion when an athlete has been carried across the finish and declared the winner?

Is it not true that someone in authority allowed a professional runner, Thomas Longboat, to compete with amateurs, when the fact of his disqualification by the Amateur Athletic Union of the United States had been forwarded to the governing body of athletics in Great Britain?

Is it not true that the A.A.A. of Great Britain thought so very little of the amateur standing of its own men that they did not even protect them by protesting Longboat, but relied on Canada and the United States to protect their amateurs?

Is it not true that the manager of the Marathon Race refused the American Committee the privilege of following their runners in an automobile?

Is it not true that in the steeplechase event the British officials annoyed an American entry and threatened to disqualify him because he had white pants on instead of black? Did they not allow divers and women to appear and perform daily in the Stadium with tight fitting clothes?

Is it not true, as one paper at least stated, that when Hayes came up to get his medal — not his trophy, but his medal — yells for Dorando were heard all over the Stadium?

* * *

TWO WAYS — THE FAIR AND UNFAIR
IN ENGLAND.

The Referee, July 26, 1908 — Pitiful Ending Great Struggle. — "To complicate the situation a second competitor arrived — Hayes, the American — the ultimate winner on an objection — and in their eagerness to get the fainting Italian to the stretch of worsted in front of the royal box, officials, attendants, and others helped him, half pushing and dragging him along. That was the great race that 100,000 people had come to see."

IN AMERICA.

New York Press, December 16, 1908 — "Madison Square Garden last night was the scene of another 'Dorando finish.' The same drama that thrilled a hundred thousand persons at Shepherds Bush last summer was re-enacted in New York's great indoor stadium before a crowd that packed the building from floor to roof. This time, however, the game little Italian who fell helpless on the track when within sight of his heart's desire, was not carried across the finish line. Weeping, half conscious, racked with pain, the swarthy little son of sunny Italy was borne off the track, and Tom Longboat, the great Canadian Indian, was left to finish the race alone."

THE OLYMPIC GAMES OF 1908 IN LONDON

I. A Reply to Certain Charges Made by Some of the American Officials
  (1) The Olympic Programme
  (2) Mr. Sullivan's Statements
  (3) The Four Hundred Metres (With Lieut. Halswelle's Letter)
  (4) The Value of Evidence
  (5) Mr. Kirby's Pamphlet

II. Official Statement of the Amateur Athletic Association

I. A Reply to Certain Charges Made by Some of the American Officials

by Theodore A. Cook
Member of the British Olympic Council, 1908

Some American Criticisms

The organisers of the Olympic Games of 1908 London were naturally anxious that the United States should be represented by as fine a team of athletes as possible, and, to that end, the British Olympic council did its best before the Games began to meet the wishes of the American officials, to whom we were very grateful for sending us over such magnificent competitors. Before the Stadium Sports began, American victories had been scored in Court Tennis, the National Rifle teams, the Revolver teams, and the Running Deer Double Shot. In the Stadium itself the American team won fifteen out of the twenty-seven events under the single heading of "Athletics," besides seven seconds and nine thirds; and during that same fortnight in July they won the 100 metres swimming and two classes in wrestling. Several of these events were not only victories over the world of amateur sport at the largest meeting of the kind ever held, but were also records of the very highest merit. As we had been ready to do all in our power before the Games, so, after they had begun, were we anxious to show every hospitality to men who had done so well. We have been, therefore, all the more surprised to hear what some of the American officials are reported to have said on their return, and to read accounts in the American Press which give a grossly incorrect idea of what took place.

The American papers have been flooded with reports from those who accompanied the American team in an official capacity as to the unfairness, discourtesy, and dishonesty with which the Americans had in every respect been treated. After reading the statements attributed to Mr. Sullivan, which he has never contradicted, one might imagine that the American team, instead of being the finest body of athletes whoever visited this country, instead of having carried off the majority of the prizes in the events in which they specialised, were, as a matter of fact, a second-rate lot, who could only win by "tactics," and could only secure justice by continuous uproar. They were, as a matter of fact, a splendid team, and quite good enough to stand on their own merits; yet they will go down to history as the team on whose behalf more complaints were made than was the case with any other in the whole series of these Games, and as the only team which went away without a single acknowledgment of the hospitality which the British Olympic Council did its best to show them in this country. This is a most unfair weight for them to carry — a weight they will entirely owe to Mr. James Sullivan, Mr. Gustavus Kirby, Mr. McCabe, and their friends.

It is right to say that we are well aware that some of the newspaper reports were inaccurate. Mr. C. M. Daniels, for instance, was reported to have been ordered to start his swimming race while he was taking off his jersey. He hastened to contradict the suspicion of an unfairness that was manifestly absurd, and would have done so sooner had he not been abroad on the Continent when the report was published. In a letter to Mr. William Henry, a member of the British Olympic Council, he writes as follows:

"New York Athletic Club:
"Oct. 14.

"MY DEAR HENRY, — I have just written a letter to the 'Sportsman' regarding the article about me on Sept. 24, which said that on arriving here I stated, through the American newspapers, that I had my sweater on when the signal for the start of the 100 metres was given, and also that I received a bad start. Those reports were published here long before my return, and I have done my best to deny the first, which is decidedly untrue, and to corroborate the second, as you and all the others who saw the start will admit that I lost considerably on the start.

"Yours very truly,
"(Signed) C. M. DANIELS."

This single incident will be sufficient, for the moment, to indicate both the bias and the inaccuracy displayed by the informants of American newspapers as to the management of the Olympic Games. Mr. Daniels contradicted what concerned him, and in the "Sportsman" for October 27 he writes from New York over his signature to say: "I have always told everyone over here that I never wished to find better or fairer treatment than I have received in England during the three years I have competed there." Others, however, have allowed incorrect impressions to remain uncontradicted; and that is why it has become inevitable to reopen a question which, under other circumstances, would never have been raised on this side of the Atlantic. The Games of 1908 are over, and the time has now arrived to take notice of these matters; for the statements made have been of such a character that they cannot pass unchallenged. But before I deal more faithfully with Mr. Sullivan, Mr. Kirby, Mr. McCabe and others, it will be right to insert a short description of the way in which the Games in London were arranged, and I offer no excuse for doing so, because, as one of the greatest Americans has said, "Nothing is ever settled till it is settled right."

I. (2) MR. SULLIVAN'S STATEMENTS

Having said thus much as to the organisation of these Games, and our reasons for it, I pass on to Mr. Sullivan's opinions.

Mr. Sullivan, as soon as he landed from this country in America, is reported in the *New York Herald* for August 9, and other papers, to have said:

(1) "The attitude of Messrs. Davidson, Andrews, Fisher, and Dr. Bulger, the English officials of the Games, was not only outrageous to the Americans but contrary to their own rules ...

(2) "They [the English] taunted us in every conceivable way. They ridiculed our flag...

(3) "Their conduct [the English officials] was cruel, unsportsmanlike, and absolutely unfair...

(4) "On the day the prizes were being distributed these English officials hunted up Dorando, brought him out on the track, and escorted him around to the royal box. Hayes wouldn't have had a hand from even the fourth section had not word come down from the royal box that Hayes should be shown some courtesy...

(5) "Carpenter did not foul anyone. He simply out-ran Halswelle, who, in my opinion, was quitting as I have seen him quit before.... without the slightest hesitation I say that this race was deliberately taken away from us."

Considering what follows, it will not be necessary here to contradict these five untruths in detail. But with regard to No. (1) Dr. Bulger writes to say that he "did not come in conflict with any of the Americans and never spoke a word to Mr. Sullivan or any other American official," and as to No. (4) I may say, as the official to whom the arrangement of every detail in the prizegiving had been entrusted, that Mr. Sullivan is, to my personal knowledge, entirely incorrect in every word he says.

His fabrications have not even the advantage of corroboration by his own colleagues, or by the competitors concerning whom they have been made.

Mr. C. C. Hughes, one of the five delegates of the Amateur Athletic Union of America to the Olympic Games, has shown a laudable degree of impartiality and moderation; and, with regard to the offence and disqualification of Carpenter in the 400 metre race, he merely pleads that he cannot believe the former to have been intentional or the latter to have been merited. He admits the fact of a collision between the two runners, whereas Mr. Sullivan declares himself to be certain that Carpenter never touched Halswelle, and herein directly contradicts his colleague. Mr. Sullivan sees in the assistance given to Dorando a deliberate and official example of anti-Americanism, instead of a very natural feeling of admiration and sympathy for pluck and courage. This feeling did not, however, in any way affect Dorando's subsequent disqualification, in which Mr. Sullivan is unable to perceive any spirit of fairness whatsoever. Mr. Sullivan is reduced to the ridiculous contention on behalf of Carpenter that when he ran out to obstruct Halswelle he left his opponent "plenty of room to come through on the inside"- a statement which might possibly be made by one entirely ignorant of running, but which from Mr. Sullivan is even more detrimental to official American sportsmanship than Mr. Carpenter's *faux pas*. It is with pleasure also that I can quote another American opinion from a gentleman who sent some of his athletes to the Games in London, and who is well acquainted with athletics. Mr. Alonzo A. Stagg, athletic director of the University of Chicago and one of those who selected the American team, is in direct opposition to Mr. Sullivan, in the following statement, which he made in the *Mining Gazette*, of Houghton, Michigan:

> The English people are good sportsmen, and they showed it in the Olympic Games. The showered applause on every winner, whether he was English or not. I noticed this same spirit when I was in England before, and I believe I am right about their sportsmanlike qualities. The English officials did satisfactory work. I do not believe as good a bunch of officials could have been gathered in the United States or any other country to do the enormous amount of work accomplished by these men.

Another American authority who has been roused to contradict the assertions of Mr. Sullivan and Mr. Kirby is Mr. Francis Peabody, of Boston, who rowed in the winning crew of 1878 for Harvard against Yale, and was present during the Games in London. I shall quote later on from the pamphlet he published on September 19 in Boston.

With regard to the athletes themselves, I shall never believe either that they would endorse Mr. Sullivan's attitude, or that, left to themselves, they would ever have taken the line urged on them at the moment, and afterwards, by their representatives, and I am glad to find that Mr. Peabody is of the same opinion: for he writes, in the pamphlet just mentioned, that "the belief in London was that our [the American] athletes were honest and sportsmanlike, but that their actions and conduct were constantly hampered and misdirected by the American managers — the so-called Committee of Honour — and the professional trainers." The American athletes never wished, for instance, to protest against the tug-of-war. They knew that they had been fairly pulled over in a game of which they were completely ignorant, and for which their manager should never have entered them. A significant comment on this incident is the refusal of their manager to entertain the proposal, made by the British policemen at the first whisper of a protest, that they should pull against the Americans in their socks. The whole matter is dealt with in the Amateur Athletic Association's statement further on. I need only add here that the policemen wore, when they were pulling against the American team, exactly the same boots in which they had always pulled in previous contests of the kind. Sergeant Park, the Hon. Secretary of the Liverpool Police Athletic Society, writes to me on the subject as follows:

> The policemen who pulled in the tug-of-war against the American team in the Olympic Games wore their ordinary duty boots, as it is their invariable custom to pull in such boots which have gone too shabby to be worn on street duty. The boots were not prepared or altered in any way.
>
> Yours faithfully,
> October 26, 1908,   [Signed] J. PARK,
> Hon. Secretary: Liverpool Police Athletic Society.

Mr. R.C. Ewry is the only competitor whose signed statements are objectionable, as far as I have seen, and what he has said will not be forgotten. But I hope and believe he stands alone. Mr. Hayes, who has informed Mr. Sullivan of his resignation from the Amateur Athletic Union, and Mr. Halstead have given the lie to their "bosses" by bearing testimony to the fairness with which they were treated. I am certain that this is the general impression among the boys themselves.

But they have been used, most shamefully as I think, merely as the tools of some ulterior purpose best known to Mr. Sullivan himself; and until such men as Mr. Sullivan are no longer allowed to blacken the reputation of as fine a team of athletes as ever visited this country it is difficult to see how American competition can be welcomed in Europe.

For a long time — many will think for too long — we have remained silent under the calumny and abuse which have been heaped upon the management of the Olympic Games in the Stadium last July. But apparently our silence, which lasted until the games were brought to a conclusion on the 31st October, has been misinterpreted; and a limit was placed upon any further forbearance by the deliberate statements made at a public banquet in New York by Judge Victor Dowling, of the Supreme Court; by Mr. James Sullivan, the American Commissioner to the Games in London; and by Mr. Conway, President of the Irish-American Athletic Club. A pamphlet has also been published by Mr. Gustavus T. Kirby, an American member of the Comité d'Honneur, who was present at the Games. The other American members were General Drain, Mr. Bartow S. Weeks, and Mr. Sullivan; and I may add that General Drain is here entirely dissociated from anything said or done by his companions. I knew him at the Games; he was uniformly courteous, and he expressed himself as entirely satisfied with all that had come within his experience.

Mr. James Sullivan, however, is in a very different category. He has several times dilated on "the prepared shoes worn by the Liverpool policemen in the tug-of-war, and the work that dishonest officials did in the committee rooms."

This he repeated at the banquet of September 21; and he has now forfeited every shred of tolerance or consideration here by leaving uncontradicted what he knows to be untrue and by striving to shelter this unpardonable conduct under the pleas that he represents the President of the United States. From all that is represented by the honesty, the sportsmanship, the true patriotism of President Roosevelt and the best of his compatriots, Mr. Sullivan has put himself wide as the Poles asunder.

No one would imagine from his attitude since his return that it was owing entirely to Mr. Sullivan's urgent request that the American entries were at the last moment allowed to be made by cable, a course which may have given his team some advantage, and certainly doubled the work of the British Olympic Council.

When the question arose of fixing the date of the closing of the entries of the British Olympic Council had before it the request of the American Committee that the closing of entries be put as late as possible in order to give the American organisers the fullest possible opportunity of selecting their team. With great reluctance, knowing the mass of work to be got through, the Secretary of the British Olympic Council and his colleague in the office consented to the date of June 12 on the understanding that on that date all the entries should be on their table, and that they should be able on that day to begin immediately the work of registration and classification.

In order to meet the needs of competitors from beyond the Atlantic whether from the United States or from Canada, it was decided in March last that entries for any number of competitors might be received before the date fixed for the closing of the entries, but that a cable must on that date be sent reducing these entries to the number to which any country was entitled. This was done entirely out of consideration for Transatlantic competitors, and although it would have considerably added to the work of the British Olympic Council Offices, yet as we should have been able still to begin to deal with entries on June 13 it was felt that it was a concession which ought to be made.

Finally, about the middle of May, Lord Desborough received a letter from Mr. Sullivan pointing out the great difficulties under which the United States laboured in making their entry, as their last Try-Outs could not be held before June 6, and again requesting that cable entries should be allowed.

The Minute of the Council on this subject is dated May 25, and runs as follows: "After considerable discussion in view of the gravity of the case as affecting the participation of American competitors, it was decided that the Hon. Secretary should inform all Olympic Committees that cable entries would be accepted for all sports."

Accordingly the bare names of the American Competitors were received in the office of the British Olympic Council on June 10. The Entry Forms themselves for the Athletic events were received here some on June 22 and some as late as June 30, and in a large number of cases the rule that a separate form must be filled in for each event by each competitor (which is printed in leaded type on every form) was complied with after the arrival of the Manager of the American Team in London some two days before the Games began. Anyone who has had any experience of dealing with entries must know how immensely the work of this office was complicated and increased by the acceptance of cable entries, by the delay in sending in the entry forms, and by the irregularity in filling them up. Not is even this all. It was only by a special concession, which we were very glad to be able to make to so courteous a visitor as General Drain, that the American Rifle team, whose entries arrived too late, were permitted to compete at all.

All these difficulties, however, were accepted by the British Olympic Council and made the best of in our anxiety to make things easy for our American visitors. No one desires to claim for this Council that its work was perfect. We are very well aware that many shortcomings were apparent in the organisation of the most complicated international meeting that has ever taken place. But it is curious that, alone among our thousands of visitors, Mr. Sullivan and his friends should have left us not merely without a word of thanks, but with accusations of discourtesy, inhospitality, and deliberate dishonesty; alone, amongst them, he refused the invitation both of the Amateur Athletic Association and of the English Government to the dinners given to the more important of the foreign officials; alone, among the representatives of twenty nations, he and his friends continually protested against everything while the Games were in progress, and continued to misrepresent the facts after they were over.

The Americans were treated in every respect exactly as every other nation, and as our own athletes were treated. Every invitation extended to other nations was extended to them.

Various technical points raised by Mr. Sullivan, Mr. Kirby, and others are dealt with in their right place further on. But I may say here that Mr. Sullivan appeared to desire that his athletes should be divided up into various classes, according to their merit or published form, so that the best of them should not be drawn in preliminary heats together. Our own view of all the athletes sent in to these Games from every nation was that each was a picked Olympic representative; and we saw no reason to give either to the American team or to any other team a preferential treatment over the rest of the competitors by any such preliminary classification. Even if that classification had taken place, what guide does Mr. Sullivan see in previous form to such results as those of the Hundred or the Two Hundred Metres? Did he imagine that Walker of South Africa would win the one, or Kerr of Canada the other? Did he think that Lunghi, the Italian, would best every other Continental representative in the Half-mile or that Dorando would finish ahead of all the English long-distance racers, or that an American could safely be predicted to win the Marathon, or that Sheppard would win the mile as well as the half-mile? Mr. Sullivan knows perfectly well that all these results were contrary both to general expectation and to previous form, and sport in general would lose half its interest were not this so frequently the case. Mr. Sullivan, of course, raised the point with reference to the drawing of the heats, with which he has expressed grave discontent. Yet he is well aware that only when the total of competitors from any single nation was greater than the total of preliminary heats did two competitors from the same nation appear in the same preliminary heat. This double appearance happened as often with English athletes as with American. With other accusations in regard to the heats the Amateur Athletic Association have fully dealt in their official statement, given below.

We are not used either to making all our evidence public in cases of athletic disputes, or to interviewing our competitors and officials as to the facts of competitions with which they were personally concerned.

That is one reason why no detailed answer appeared, before now, to the malevolent mendacities uttered by some of our American visitors. But when American officials, who insisted that they represented President Roosevelt and the American nation at these games, repeatedly make inaccurate statements in public concerning the conduct of the sports, it is time to take notice of them in a way that has never been necessary before. And when the inevitable misunderstanding aroused by such accusations, among a population far from the events and generally unaware of the details, is recklessly exacerbated by Mr. Sullivan and his friends, it is time to show these gentlemen up in their true colours, and to demonstrate that they have deliberately deceived their countrymen by fabricating falsehoods for purposes best known to themselves.

We are under no delusion as to the real feeling of the best part of that great population which Mr. Sullivan has so frequently attempted to mislead, or even of the majority of those American athletes whose reputation he has done so much to harm. But however great our admiration and goodwill for American athletes as a whole, I cannot help thinking that it would be a matter for very serious consideration whether we should in future take part in any international contest in which a man who has so grossly abused his high representative position were again allowed to hold any responsible place.

I. (3) THE FOUR HUNDRED METRES
(With Lieut. Halswelle's Letter)

Though the official statement of the Amateur Athletic Association gives the complete record of the evidence concerning the Four Hundred Metre Race as it was taken at the official inquiry, I have a few words to say on certain points not covered by that official statement, the essential parts of which were first published on August 15.

Mr. Sullivan makes the ungenerous comment on Halswelle, that he "was quitting, as I have seen him quit before." This may be a reference to the Games of Athens in 1906, where, as Mr. Sullivan well knows, the corners make high speed impossible, and where an American won in 53⅕ seconds. But both from his trial heats and from other performances in 1908 (a year in which he has done the wonderful time of 48⅖ seconds in Scotland for the quarter-mile), it is abundantly clear that Halswelle was at the top of his form in the July Games in London. It is new to me, and it must be highly distasteful to many of his countrymen, to find their representative, Mr. Sullivan, not only accepting the onus of justifying a foul that has permanently disqualified his own candidate, but also belittling the powers and courage of the competitor of another nation.

For anyone to say for a moment, and it has been urged that such is the case, that the tactics Mr. Carpenter employed in the Four Hundred Metre Race would be permitted on any racing track in America is absurd. His disqualification would have taken place on any American racing track, and in some parts of America would have met with more serious treatment than disqualification.

Mr. David Scott Duncan wrote on this point, to the Field, on August 29, as follows:

> That Halswelle was badly bored and obstructed is, of course, beyond question, and the American rules as to such tactics are even more explicit than those obtaining in Britain. Here they are:
>
> > "Rule III. — The Referee. — When in a final heat a claim of four or interference is made, he (the referee) shall have power to disqualify the competitor

who was at fault if he considers the foul intentional or due to culpable carelessness, and he shall also have the power to order a new race between such competitors as he thinks entitled to such a privilege."

"Rule XVIII.— The Course.— Each competitor shall keep in his respective position from start to finish in all races on straightaway tracks, and in all races on tracks with one or more turns he shall not cross to the inner edge of the track except when he is at least six feet in advance of his nearest competitor. *After turning the last corner in to the straight in any race each competitor must keep a straight course to the finish line, and not cross, either to the outside or inside, in front of any of his opponents."*

In the face of the above rules of the Union of which Mr. Sullivan is president, he is surely left "without a leg to stand upon." I may add that I was referee of the Four Hundred Metres.

DAVID SCOTT DUNCAN.

In reply to a request from the Editor of the *Sporting Life* Lieutenant Halswelle authorised the publication of the following letter in that paper:

As regards the Four Hundred Metres Race, Carpenter did not strike me any vigorous blows with his elbow, nor were they any marks on my chest, nor did I say that Carpenter struck me or show the marks to any Press representative. I did not attempt to pass the Americans until the last corner, reserving my effort for the finishing straight. Here I attempted to pass Carpenter on the outside, since he was not far enough from the curb to do so on the inside, and I was too close up to have crossed behind him. Carpenter's elbow undoubtedly touched my chest, for as I moved outwards to pass him he did likewise, keeping his right arm in front of me.

In this manner he bored me across quite two-thirds of the track, and entirely stopped my running. As I was well up to his shoulder and endeavouring to pass him, it is absurd to say that I could have come up on the inside. I was too close after half way round the bend to have done this; indeed, to have done so would have necessitated chopping my stride, and thereby losing anything from two to four yards.

When about thirty to forty yards from the tape I saw the officials holding up their hands, so slowed up, not attempting to finish all out.

From the official Report of the Amateur Athletic Association given below, it will be seen that, even if the competitors had not read the rule as to obstructions which was printed in the day's programme now before me, they were each told exactly the rules under which the race was run and exactly the precautions taken to ensure the observance of those rules. I have also before me the photograph of the track during and after the race. They are unquestionably conclusive. I was present during this race and throughout the Games.

"When Carpenter ran Halswelle almost off the track," writes Mr. Francis Peabody, "the indignation was intense." It certainly was. Long before the officials had time to take action, a spontaneous howl of disgust went up from the stands near the corner, and from twenty thousand spectators all the way down the last straight to the finish.

I need only add that it is entirely unusual in this country to run the quarter-mile in strings. To have set out the strings on the first occasion when the final was run would have been little short of a direct accusation that a deliberate foul was contemplated.

Mr. Francis Peabody considers that the action of the American managers in refusing to let

Robbins and Taylor run in strings on the second occasion of the final was contrary to every rule of sportsmanlike conduct. The men had entered and agreed to be bound by the judge's decision. That decision was given, thinks Mr. Peabody, "with evident sincerity and equal justice." The conduct of the American officials, he goes on, "placed our runners [the Americans] in an indefensible and mortifying position, suggested the idea that Carpenter and the others had been in collusion, and was unsportsmanlike and unmanly to the last degree."

It is perhaps as well that, in these pages, such strong condemnation of the American officials should come from one of their own compatriots.

At the meeting of the General Committee of the Amateur Athletic Association held in Birmingham on October 3, it was unanimously decided to suspend Carpenter permanently, and he will be unable to compete again against British amateur athletes.

I. (4) THE VALUE OF EVIDENCE

Part of Mr. Kirby's pamphlet has been answered in detail by the officials of the Amateur Athletic Association. The more general charges have been brought to the notice of the Rev. R. S. de C. Laffan, Secretary of the British Olympic Council and member of the International Olympic Committee, who has been kind enough to give me the fullest assistance in what is written in the next section. I preface it with a short consideration of the value that may be attached to the evidence given by Mr. Kirby and his friends when considered as an account of what has occurred in London.

If I may judge from his pamphlet, Mr. Kirby seems to think that one of his duties as an American Representative was to teach us manners. It may therefore be well that, before giving Mr. Laffan's replies to his statements, I should throw some little light on the "forbearance and gentlemanly behaviour" on which Mr. Kirby prides himself. It is true that on one occasion during his presence in the Stadium, he spoke to Mr. William Henry, a member of the British Olympic Council, and expressed himself as "highly pleased with all the arrangements at the Stadium," an exaggerated courtesy which must have violated his real feelings to an extent only appreciable by those who have read the denunciations he published in New York. But he is also the gentleman who sat next to Mr. Laffan at the dinner given by His Majesty's Government; and he spent a considerable portion of his time at that dinner, to the great annoyance of those sitting near him, in dictating a very partisan account of the Carpenter incident to a newspaper correspondent. As will be seen from the facts concerning the race for the Four Hundred Metres published further on, Mr. Kirby's pamphlet contains so many misstatements on this one point alone that he destroys all possibility of credence in the rest of it.

As Mr. Francis Peabody has pointed out, Mr. Kirby in one sentence speaks of Carpenter as "leaving Halswelle further behind at every stride," and in another says that Carpenter finished "only some two strides" in front of Robbins and Halswelle, a description of foot-racing which can only be paralleled in the same writer's work on another page, which relates how Hayes entered the arena at the end of the marathon Race and "came on with a burst of speed which seemed as if he fairly flew." That excellent and courageous runner would himself be the first to modify Mr. Kirby's inflated periods.

Mr. Peabody is equally pertinent in his criticism of Mr. Kirby's suggestion that Halswelle might have cut in on the inside. "Mr. Kirby's argument is ingenious, but not convincing, for he forgets that the question is not what Halswelle might or could have done, but what Carpenter did."

It may possibly be that Mr. Kirby never saw the testimony laid before the judges in the Four Hundred Metres Race, though it was published in several hundred newspapers a month before he issued his pamphlet and announced that this testimony "is not known." It is also possible that he never saw Mr. Peabody's letter in the *Boston Transcript* of September 9. But the long conversation (which he prints) between himself (with other Americans) and the referee in this race turns out to be a fabrication of his own from beginning to end, for which there is no excuse whatsoever. This is shown by the signed testimony of the referee given later on; and in order that there may be no mistake, I append here a further signed statement from another official.

In reply to a request from the Editor of the *Sporting Life*, Mr. T. M. Abraham (a vice-president of the A.A.A.) authorised the publication of the following letter in that paper:

> With reference to your inquiry of the 23rd inst. Although nominally one of the racing referees on the Four Hundred Metres day, my colleague, Mr. David Duncan, by arrangement, undertook the responsibilities of the position, while I was simply a looker-on, and certainly had no conversation either with G. T. Kirby or any other foreigner respecting the disqualification of Mr. Carpenter.
>
> You invite me to comment upon the subject, and, briefly, I should like to state that the decision given by the judges was the only one possibly under the circumstances.
>
> From the winning post I had an excellent view of the race from start to finish, and never before during my thirty years' experience as a judge and referee have I witnessed anything approaching such a disgraceful exhibition.

By the production, as evidence in support of his contentions, of a conversation with an English official who never spoke a word to him, Mr. Kirby places himself in the same category with Mr. Sullivan; and I am inclined to the opinion that, if Mr. Sullivan, Mr. Kirby, or Mr. McCabe are accepted as American Representatives at any Olympic Games in the future, it is very doubtful whether the Associations of Great Britain would take any part. Those Associations will of course preserve their entire liberty of action in the future.

I might be inclined to leave Mr. Kirby's literary labours to the tender mercies of Mr. Dooley, if they were not so evidently calculated to do injury. His peroration is as follows:

> All blame and censure for bad feeling, unpleasant memories, and disquieting fears must be and is laid at the feet of and upon the officials of the Games, and such condemnation as can be made [*sic*] Lord Desborough and the British Olympic Council, is his or its error of judgment in permitting other than a fair and impartial body of men to act as officials, and in delegating to incompetent and dishonourable men powers which were used in an unfair effort to advance the interest of their own country, and which resulted in naught but its everlasting disgrace.

These be brave words, and I need not repeat the reasons of the Council for delegating the duties of detailed management to such bodies as our Athletic or Swimming Associations, who manage several international meetings every year, and who have more experience in this direction than any similar associations in any other country. But from Mr. Kirby's righteous horror it would never be realised that Mr. Sullivan was carefully informed several months before the Games took place that the actual control of the different divisions of sport would be handed over to recognised Associations governing these sports in this country. Could anyone imagine, after hearing Mr. Sullivan or Mr. Kirby dilate on the iniquities of our officials, that as early as last March Mr. Sullivan wrote to acquiesce in our arrangements and to approve of our Associations?

Mr. Kirby's pamphlet is addressed to the Inter-Collegiate Association of Amateur Athletes of America, and a copy has been mailed to every college paper in the United States. I trust these papers will give an equal prominence to the English reply. Such Universities as Yale and Harvard, for instance, are not likely to be taken in by Mr. Kirby; but Americans as a whole should clearly realise what harm is being done to themselves and all their athletic representatives by such malignant falsehoods as those published by Mr. Sullivan, Mr. Kirby, or Mr. McCabe.

It will be seen that if such methods as those displayed by Mr. Sullivan and his friends are to become common, American athletic competition against British athletes will be limited, in this country and elsewhere, to such meetings as those between combined teams of Yale and Harvard against Oxford and Cambridge. This would, in my opinion, be most unjust to American national representation as far as all forms of athletics are concerned. But there seems no alternative in this country if international meetings in the future are to be followed by such campaigns of misrepresentation and bitterness; and I do not imagine that other countries in Europe can have been unmindful of the attitude of these American officials.

I will only express the hope that all into whose hands this reply may fall will do their best to see that the American public are no longer allowed to imagine that the slanderous untruths to which Mr. Kirby, Mr. McCabe, and Mr. Sullivan have given such wide circulation, are the only evidence available as to the conduct of the Olympic Games. The American people are rightly slow in suspecting their appointed representatives. But it is my belief that they will be far from slow in expressing their resentment when they realise how disgracefully their confidence — in these three instances especially — has been betrayed. "If it was the duty," writes Mr. Francis Peabody concerning Mr. Sullivan and Mr. Kirby, "of this [American] Committee to make protests or complaints with little or no reason, to criticise, kick, and finally usurp the functions of the judges, they did their duty thoroughly." I am glad to think that the best of their countrymen evidently do not endorse their actions.

Mr. Laffan's reply to Mr. Kirby's pamphlet contains several expressions of official opinion from Continental competing nations. I will add one more here.

In the *Expansion Belge* for September 1908 the Baron de Laveleye, the chief Belgian representative at the Olympic Games of London, writes as follows:

> Each association was exclusively charged, with full powers, with the organisation in these games of the particular sport which it controls in England; and, thanks to this principle, the organisation of every contest may be affirmed to have been, from the point of view of sport, absolutely faultless.... The British Olympic Council, in choosing this method, was only obeying the decisions, with reference to organisation, which had been passed by the International Olympic Committee, and no other course was possible.... The rules of these various associations were printed, translated into three languages, and distributed six months before the Games began, and it must be admitted that those who did not know them were most ungracious in critcising them.... It is quite possible to find certain errors in the verdicts rendered by various judges, or to object to various regulations as either faulty or superannuated; but the author of these lines followed the Games very closely, and he is able to affirm in all sincerity that though errors may have been committed (and it is impossible for humanity never to err) the good faith and impartiality of the judges can never be questioned for a single moment.... In the Four Hundred Metres, according to the expression of two Belgian competitors who were particularly well placed for observing the incident. Halswelle "was bored in the most odious way possible" ("aussi odieusement balance qu'il est possible de l'être"), and this, although the runners had all been *officially* warned at the start that any infraction of the rules would be followed by a fresh race from which those guilty of illegality would be excluded.

It is only fair, also, to the Amateur Athletic Association, which Mr. Sullivan has preferred to attack instead of approaching the British Olympic Council, to add what happened at their last General Committee Meeting on October 3.

Communications were read from the Swedish Governing Athletic Association, expressing appreciation of the courtesy and fairness shown its representatives at the recent Olympic Games by the British officials, and asking the A.A.A. to arrange a match between British and Swedes in various forms of athleticism during the present month, and under the same rules as governed the Olympic Games. The Committee, whilst heartily approving the idea, felt that, owing to the shortness of the notice given and to the late period of the year, it was by no means easy now to make arrangements for the proposed match. They, therefore, regretfully could not see their way to accede to the application, but expressed a wish to arrange for an international contest next year, if the Swedish authorities still thought well of the proposal for such a meeting.

The U.S.F.S.A. (the recognised French governing body) also wrote expressing a wish to meet the representatives of the A.A.A. in international friendly rivalry, the match to take place either at Whitsuntide or on July 14 next year. Owing to the late sitting, however, the Committee whilst cordially approving the idea, decided to defer the matter for further consideration at their next meeting.

Finally, a well-earned and unanimously voted testimonial was awarded by his colleagues to Mr. Percy Fisher, who has so ably represented the Amateur Athletic Association on the British Olympic Council, and who so capably and successfully supervised the numerous details of the Stadium meeting. How difficult such details may be the severest of our foreign critics have only quite recently discovered; for, as I have already had occasion to point out, the officials of the Amateur Athletic Union of the United States, of which Mr. James Sullivan is President, not only counted the laps wrong in a mile once, in their championships this September at the Travers Island Meeting, but made exactly the same mistake again in the same race later in the day, and the contest had to be postponed. Mr. James Sullivan was the referee. It is difficult to imagine what Mr. Sullivan would have said if such mistakes had occurred in England.

I. (5) MR. KIRBY'S PAMPHLET

A pamphlet published on September 8 at 8 Wall Street, New York by Mr. Gustavus T. Kirby, purports to set forth "a few incidents chosen for the purpose of showing clearly the attitude of the British Press, public and officials, and the good behaviour, courage, and sportsmanship of the American competitors" during the Olympic Games of London.

Mr. Kirby says "the officials of the Games did make it hard for the Americans to win, or, for that matter, hard for any competitor to win who was not a member of the team known as that of Great Britain and Ireland. The results of such an unwise and shortsighted policy was not only American but universal dissatisfaction...."

In order to make out his case for universal dissatisfaction, Mr. Kirby drags in a reference to the disqualification of Dorando. I should like to ask what the American comments would have been if the Amateur Athletic Association had declined to disqualify Dorando. Mr. Kirby also seems to think that the action of the officials who assisted Dorando was "cruel, unwise, and unfair," and suggests that they were ready to do anything rather than let an American win. But, as Mr. Peabody points out, "when Dorando was receiving this outside help, which resulted in his disqualification, all of us who were waiting in the Stadium thought that an Englishman from South Africa, named Hefferon (who, according to the latest bulletin, was leading), was second, and that Dorando was helped to beat him. I could see in the events of this finish nothing but an intense desire to help a man who seemed on the brink of death.... There is no doubt that of the 80,000 people there every generous soul hoped that this man, without regard to his nationality, might win .... Everyone who was not too excited realised that the moment he was helped his chance of winning was gone."

This seems to me a fair and straightforward account of a most unfortunate incident which has been given a very different complexion by Mr. Sullivan and his friends.

Mr. Kirby goes on, in his pamphlet, to quote an article which states that German, Danish, and Spanish comments were on the whole unfavourable to this country. But he does not think it necessary to state that no single Spanish representative attended the Games, and that therefore the Spanish comments, if there were any, are not likely to prove of great value. As to the Germans the letter sent to the Olympic Council by Dr. Martin, the Secretary of their Olympic Committee, is as follows:

"Permit me to congratulate you on the carefully elaborated organisation of the Games and on their splendid success." I can quote no letter from the Danes, for we have not made it any part of our business to tout for appreciation; but it is hardly likely they would have returned to London for the October Games if they had been dissatisfied with those held in July.

Mr. Kirby is kind enough to state that it is not the object of his report "to set forth the causes for French, Swedish, Italian, German, and Danish grievances. The representatives of those countries are well able to speak, and have spoken, for themselves." That is quite correct. Colonel Viktor Balck, Vice-President of the Swedish Olympic Committee, has sent an official letter to the Chairman of the British Olympic Council, in which he says:

Brunkebergstorg 12,
Stockholm:
14*th August*, 1908.

To the President of the British
    Olympic Association, London.

Sir,— I am instructed by the Swedish Olympic Committee of 1908 to express to you their sincere thanks for the great hospitality and kindness shown to the Swedish Olympic Competitors, and to state at the same time how greatly they appreciated the goodwill and fair play which governed the spirit in which the games were conducted.

My Committee earnestly hope that, as a result of the Competitions, the strong ties of friendship already existing between British and Swedish sportsmen may have been further strengthened, and that it may serve as an inducement to British sportsmen and athletes to visit Sweden in the near future, where at all times they will be assured of a hearty welcome.

I have the honour to be, Sir,

Your obedient servant,
(signed)VIKTOR BALCK.

Mr. Laffan also provides me with a few typical examples of other letters and messages he has received.

(1) The Secretary of the Italian Olympic Committee, Count Brunetta d'Usseaux, writes of—

"La gloire de l'Angleterre, qui a pu confirmer, dans un époque qui restera mémorable, sa supériorité incontestable et une double supériorité en courtoisie."

(2) The following official letter was received from the Greek Olympic Committee:

Rue de l'Université, 3,
Athènes:
11-24 *Août*, 1908.

MONSIEUR LE PRÉSIDENT,—A l'occasion de la clôture de vos Jeux Athlétiques j'ai l'honneur de vous exprimer à vous, ainsi qu'aux honorables membres du British Olympic Council et aux officiels, les vifs remerciments de notre Comité de l'acceuil courtois dont vous avez fait preuve en faveur de nos représentants officiels et des attentions dont vous avez comblé les participants hellènes.

Nous saisissons l'occasion pour vous exprimer nos sincères félicitations du succès qui a couronné votre brillante réunion sportive.

Veuillez agréer, Monsieur le Président, l'assurance de notre consideration la plus distinguée.

Par ordre de S.A.R. le Prince Royal des Hellènes, Duc de Sparte, Président du Comité des Jeux Olympiques.

LE SECRÉTAIRE GENERAL, p.o.

Rt. Hon Lord Desborough,
President du Council of
British Olympic Association
108 Victoria Street, S.W.

(3) Toronto: *Sept.* 21*st*, 1908.

Rev. R. S. de Courcy Laffan,
Hon. Sec. British Olympic Association,
108 Victoria Street, London, S.W.

DEAR SIR,—I desire to express my thankfulness and appreciation for, the kind and hospitable treatment while in England with the Canadian Olympic Team.

Faithfully yours,
(Signed)   JOHN L. TAIT.

(4) Telegram from Mons. Georges Berger, Secretary of the French Olympic Committee:

Equipe française Epée de retour adresse chaleureux souhaits et renouvelle remerciments pour accueil sympathique.

BERGER.

(5) Telegram from Baron Reinhold von Willebrand, Finnish Representative:

Leaving hospitable shores of England beg you to accept my and all Finlanders' warmest thanks.

(6) Letter from Dr. Jiri Guth, Bohemian Representative:

V praze, dne 26te Oct., 1098.

To the British Olympic Council
108 Victoria St.
London, S.W.

GENTLEMEN.—By the festival meeting of the Bohemian Olympic Committee the 24th of October, 1908, it was unanimously decided to express to the British Olympic Council our best thanks for the hospitality to the Bohemian Olympic expedition at London in July last, and at the same time to congratulate you for the excellent success and arrangement of the Olympic Games.

The Bohemian Olympic Committee regret only that it was impossible to participate in the Winter Games.

Yours truly,

(Signed)   Dr. JIRI GUTH,

President of the Bohemian Olympic Committee in Prague.

(7) Extract from letter from Baron de Laveleye, President of the Belgian Olympic Committee:

May I ask you to act as my interpreter to all the members of your Committee and tell them that I shall never forget the manner in which myself and the Belgian contingent were greeted in London?

(8) Letter from Mons. Negropontes, the Greek Representative:

Comité des Jeux Olympiques à Athènes sous la présidence de
S.A.R. le Prince Royal de Grèce,
le 28 Juillet, 1098.

Monsieur,— Comme délégué du Comité des Jeux Olympiques à Athènes j'ai l'honneur de vous exprimer mes plus sincères remerciments de la bonté et des aimables attentions dont vous avez comblé ses représentants et les athletes helléniques.

Veuillez agréer, Monsieur, l'assurance de ma haute considération.

(Signed)   MILT. M. NEGROPONTES.

(9) Letter from the President of the Italian Committee:

Paris, le 21 Octobre, 1908.

MY DEAR COLLEAGUE AND FRIEND,— I transmit herewith a letter that the Marquis Compans de Brichanteau, President of the Italian Committee, for the IVth Olympiade is begging me to send to you.

I have nothing to add to the feelings he is expressing in the name of His Majesty the King of Italy, in the name of the Italian People, of the Committee and the Athletes that came to London: and I associate with by sending to you and the Committee my best thanks for his cordial hospitality.

With the President of our Committee I acknowledge kindly that the B.O.C. was always guided by the highest mind of justice and impartiality in the organisation and unfolding of the IVth Olympiade.

May I beg you will kindly accept, my dear friend, for you and for our dear colleague, the Rev. R. S. de Courcy Laffan, as for all your colleagues of the B.O.C., the feelings of my grateful and affectionate remembrance.

(Signed)   COMTE EUGÉNE BRUNETTA D'USSEAUX,

Commissaire Général d'Italie à la IVeme Olympiade.

Lord Desborough of Taplow.

Translation.   Rome
                                  October 12th, 1908.
To His Excellency Lord Desborough of Taplow, K.C.V.O.,
       President of the British Olympic Council,
             London.

With my heart still full of the grateful recollection of the many proofs of sympathy and good-will lavished upon the Italian Committee, over which I had the honour to preside, permit me, Your Excellency, in view of the approaching end of the IVth Olympiad to fulfill the pleasant duty of offering you the homage of our most cordial thanks in the name of all my colleagues.

The manifestation of esteem and fraternity with which the Italian Competitors were at all times surrounded during their unforgettable sojourn in London, but more especially in the moments when they felt the most need of comfort, help, and protection, will for ever remain engraved on their hearts and ours: that high spirit of equity and justice which at all times and with so much serenity inspired your governing Committee will never, we assure your Excellency, cease to be remembered and admired by us.

Of such manifestations we comprehend all the high value inasmuch as they go beyond our own personalities, and afford fresh confirmation of the traditional generous hospitality of Great Britain, and strengthen more and more those bonds of solidarity which, independently of our excellent international relations — and it is the good fortune we most desire — draw together as brothers in all circumstances the English and Italian people.

The echo of these cordial testimonies has reached and from every point of view delighted His August Majesty our beloved King, whose enlightened thought and nobility of whose soul always stir with enthusiasm whenever the hearts of Italians beat. The King has followed with lively interest — and he was informed on our arrival in our country of all the particulars and of all your kindness — the development of the magnificent and splendidly impressive proof of International prowess and of the rapid progress which is so full of promise and assurance for the physical education of the younger generations.

Permit me once more to address to you, illustrious President, the warm expression of the emotion of my heart, while at the same time I ask you to act as interpreter of our unanimous feelings of devoted gratitude towards the unsurpassable Rev. de Courcy Laffan and the sympathetic Captain Jones, who loaded us with delicate and affectionate courtesies.

With profoundest respect to Your Excellency,
       I remain

       The President of the Italian Committee,
    (Signed)   MARQUIS CARLO COMPANS DI BRICHANTEAU.
       Member of the National Parliament.

That during the course of the Games different nations at different times found reason to object to some arrangements and decisions is no more than has happened in every athletic gathering since international sport began; but the fact that all the nations mentioned by Mr. Kirby entered for the Winter Games is a fairly conclusive testimony to the fact that they do not share his opinion of the character of English Judges. I might even add that his opinions cannot be shared by all the competitors of his own nation, for an American skater was among those who entered for the Winter Games, and I have at present heard no complaint concerning his treatment at a meeting he is not likely to have attended had he believed Mr. Kirby's pamphlet. He competed at a time when Sweden, Russia, the Argentine, Germany, Holland, Denmark, and France were among the various nations who were content to accept the same organisation which had been enforced when Mr. Kirby was with us in July.

To come now to some of Mr. Kirby's definite charges.

(I) The first is as follows:

"The acceptance of the entry of one Thomas Longboat, the Canadian who had made himself a professional runner by competing for a money prize in the city of Boston, Mass. Longboat was permitted to run in the Marathon Race representing Canada when under protest by America and the Amateur Athletic Federation of Canada: and this notwithstanding the fact that there were two weeks time prior to the race within which evidence in his case could have been given and a decision reached."

Enquiries as to the eligibility of Longboat began as soon as it was realised that his previous performances entitled him to representation in the Canadian team; and these enquiries did not come from American sources alone. At the meeting of the Canadian Central Olympic Committee, held at Ottawa on April 21, 1908, the following resolution was adopted:

> That the Board of Governors of the Canadian Amateur Athletic Union be requested to formally certify to this Committee the amateur status of Thomas Longboat and his complete eligibility to compete in the Olympic Races in England under all the regulations and qualifications governing that contest, copies of same to be forwarded.

> In reply to this resolution a letter was received by Mr. F. L. C. Pereira, Hon. Secretary of the Canadian Central Olympic Committee, signed by Mr. William Stark, President, and Mr. H.H. Crow, Secretary-Treasurer of the Canadian Amateur Athletic Union, as follows:

> I beg to inform you that Longboat is registered as an amateur with the C.A.A.U. (No. 1488), and that he is an athlete of good standing, not only according to the amateur definition of the C.A.A.U., but under the regulations and qualifications laid down by the British Olympic Committee to govern entries of amateur athletes. Trusting that this assurance will be satisfactory to you, on behalf of the Canadian Amateur Athletic Union, we beg to remain, &c....

This letter is dated from Toronto on April 29, 1908.

On May 4 Colonel J. Hanbury-Williams, Chairman of the Canadian Central Olympic Committee, wrote from Ottawa as follows to the Chairman of the British Olympic Council in London, pointing out that the Canadian Amateur Athletic Union controlled the Irish-Canadian Amateur Athletic Club, of which Longboat is a member. "You will observe that the Association deem Longboat to be eligible in every particular to participate in the Games as an amateur. The C.A.A.U. is one of two great bodies which control all sport in the Dominion, and has a membership of some 750 to 800 clubs, and its Board of Governors is composed of men of high standing in athletics. One hears a great deal in conversation, and one reads a great deal in the Press, but we have to be guided by clubs of good standing, and the decision seems clear."

After this correspondence it was evidently impossible for the British Olympic Council to refuse Longboat as a Canadian entry without the most careful consideration of any new evidence that might be subsequently produced.

However, two days after the Games in London had begun, the following communication was sent to Mr. Fisher, of the Amateur Athletic Association, a course, by the way, which was entirely contrary to rules in the possession both of Mr. Sullivan and Mr. Kirby months before. But I need not insist on the lesser inaccuracies of Mr. Kirby's mind. The letter is as follows:

American Committee, Olympic Games London.
"2-3 Hind Court, Fleet Street, E.C.
July 15, 1908.

P.L. Fisher, Esq.,
10 John Street, Adelphi, W.C.

Dear Sir,—Mr. Gustavus T. Kirby informs me that our protest against professional Thomas Longboat should be sent to you as Secretary, and should be accompanied by £1.

I enclose you herewith £1 1s., and you can consider the communication from our Committee men as our official protest against professional Thomas Longboat.

Yours truly,
(Signed)   JAMES EDWARD SULLIVAN.

Mr. Laffan, to whom, as Secretary of the British Olympic Council, this letter was handed, replied that as Longboat's status had been guaranteed by the Canadian Amateur Athletic Union and the Canadian Central Olympic Committee, the British Olympic Council found themselves in presence of a conflict of statements between governing associations, and it was therefore necessary to ask for the evidence on which Longboat had been disqualified in the United States, in order that this evidence might be laid before the British Olympic Council.

Mr. Laffan received the following reply:

American Committee, Olympic Games.
London, England, 1908.
2-3 Hind Court, Fleet Street., E.C.

The Rev. R.S. de Courcy Laffan,
108 Victoria Street, S.W.

DEAR SIR,—Your communication of July 20 has been received and noted.

The A.A.U. of the United States through its officials now in London desire to acquaint you with the fact that, as a matter of record, Thomas Longboat has been declared a professional by the A.A.U. of the United States for an act committed in the United States. This is merely a matter of record.

May I suggest that you call upon Mr. Percy L. Fisher, Secretary of the A.A.A., to furnish you with all the information and evidence that he has received in relation to Thomas Longboat's doings in the United States and also in Canada? I feel confident that Mr. Percy L. Fisher and the other officials of the A.A.A. can give your information in relation to one Percy Sellen who has been competing with Thomas Longboat in America.

Yours truly,
(Signed)   J. E. SULLIVAN.

It will be observed that Mr. Sullivan's reply disregards the request for evidence, and gives none of the facts upon which he charges Mr. Thomas Longboat has having been disqualified as amateur; and it will hardly be believed that the allegations in Mr. Kirby's pamphlet of September 8 are the first suggestion of evidence to the Secretary of our Council. The representatives of Canada declared themselves to have a complete answer to the charge hinted at in Mr.

Sullivan's reply, and it is obvious that under such circumstances the burden of proof lies on the person who challenges the amateur qualification of an athlete duly entered by his national governing body. I am still wondering why Mr. Kirby rakes up the question at all about a runner who was too ill to finish. However, as he had done so, I must point out that when the governing body which enters a competitor vouches for his amateur status, and that amateur status is contested by a foreign governing body, the mere assertion of the latter body cannot be considered as concluding the case against a competitor.

All that the British Olympic Council could do under the circumstances was to notify the Canadian manager that Longboat would run under a protest from the manager of the American team. This notification we duly made. Having no evidence offered them, the British Olympic Council could not possibly have given a definite decision before the race, and would not have given one at any time without the full inquiry which would no doubt have taken place had Longboat won.

The facts, I think, may be left to speak for themselves in the judgment of any unprejudiced or sane-minded person.

(II.) Mr. Kirby's second charge is as follows:

> The opening day found no flag of the United States flying within the Stadium. This, it was afterwards said, was due to the carelessness of the decorator. If it were mere carelessness, certainly the carelessness was gross, for not only was there no American flag among those of the other nations of the world flying from the stands in the Stadium, but there was none even on the grounds, for when the American Committee d'Honneur requested the 'decorator' to hoist the American flag he said they had none, and did not know where there was one, but would hoist one if the Committee could find one, which the Committee could not do outside of those carried by the Americans in the stand.

On this point I will begin by saying that if by any unfortunate accident the American flag had been absent from the decorations of the Stadium no one would have regretted it more sincerely than members of the British Olympic Council; but it is also well to point out that Mr. Kirby is perfectly well aware that an American flag was provided by us for his team to carry in the procession, and it is therefore curious that he should say our Committee could not find one, for it was presented to him as a souvenir by the very organisers whom he is abusing, and we shall hear more of his adventures with it later on.

The best reply to his statement that no American flag was to be found in the Stadium or the grounds will be the following letter, which I quote with the preliminary explanation that the British Olympic Council had nothing whatever to do with the decoration of the Stadium, which was provided and paid for by the Franco-British Exhibition. Mr. Imre Kiralfy, Commissioner-General of that exhibition, writes as follows on this subject:

> Franco-British Exhibition, London, 1908.
> Shepherd's Bush, W.:
> *August* 5, 1908.

> Dear Lord Desborough, — There were on the opening day of the Olympic Games two complete sets of emblems on the facade of the Stadium bearing the American coat-of-arms, with seven American flags, three on each side, and one on top above the height of the Stadium. As to the rest Messrs. Pain & Sons, who furnished these, received instructions that the flags of all nations who took part in the Games should

be put up. If those of the United States were not put up on the opening day it was a stupid blunder committed by one of the men who had charge of it.

Yours faithfully,

(Signed)   IMRE KIRALFY.

The British Olympic Council are quite prepared to admit that the flag decorations of the Stadium, having been got up rather hurriedly, were not well carried out. For although there were Scotch and Irish flags, there was no English flag among the decorations, the whole time, while Japan and China (who were not competing) had standards flying all the while. Further, the arrangements for the Stadium decoration were to a large extent, in the able hands of Mr. Kiralfy's three sons, who were all born in New York, and are all American citizens, one of them in fact being a member of Mr. Kirby's American team for the Hundred Metres. So that if any animus can be discovered in the matter of flags it certainly cannot be traced to the handiwork of British officials, and I think that Mr. Kiralfy's family may also be exonerated from any desire to insult the country to which they are proud to belong. Whatever involuntary mistake there may have been was rectified, as concerns the American flag, on the day after it was noticed: and it could only have been a malevolent feeling towards his hosts of last July which would have distorted the incident into the petty spite suggested by Mr. Kirby.

Finally, I may say that if Mr. Kirby confines his objections to the flags used for decorative purposes with no other significance, there were as I have shown, fourteen American flags of this kind on the exhibition side of the Stadium; if his complaint is meant to have any international significance, I must tell him that in the line of the flags of the competing nations, flown in the most prominent position opposite the Royal Box the American flag was the third from the middle, on the right as you looked across the grass from the Royal Box; and Mr. Kirby might have observed that it was close to the stand chiefly occupied by his own countrymen during these Games.

(III.) Mr. Kirby quotes an English newspaper of July 20 concerning the Hundred Kilometres Cycle Race and the finish between the three Englishmen (Denny, Pett, and Bartlett) and the Frenchman (Lapize):

> A beautiful piece of generalship followed. Denny and Pitt looked round and steered their machines in front of the Frenchman. Bartlett crept up at the rear. Lapize, riding for dear life, was completely boxed in. Assuming that he had nothing to beat except what was in front of him, Lapize allowed the riders to carry him to the top of the last bank; Bartlett, who had kept at the bottom of the trap, darted past like a torpedo and won by two lengths.

Mr. Kirby adds the comment: "Poor, fair-minded, fair-running, fair-riding Englishmen!" My own observation on this would be that no one who has any experience of sport at all quotes the rules of one game to illustrate those of another. You might as well say that, since it is fair to ride off a man in polo, it is also fair for one jockey to bore another in the Derby or the St. Leger. It is impossible to generalise from a race on a hard cement track with banked-up corners to another race (without machines) on a flat cinder-path of the same dimensions all round. But I recognise my practical ignorance of cycling, and I have therefore written to Mr. James Blair, one of the cycling representatives (with Mr. T. W. J. Britten of the N.C.U.) on the British Olympic Council, for information concerning the paragraph quoted by Mr. Kirby.

In reply Mr. Blair writes as follows:

> The account quoted from the *Daily Mail* is not correct; the reporter evidently had an insufficient knowledge of cycle-racing, for if any deliberate "pocketing" such

as the *Daily Mail* describes, had really taken place in the Hundred Kilometres Race the offenders would have been disqualified.

"What happened was as follows: Two laps to go; Lapize sprinted along the back straight, Denny, Pett, and Bartlett being just behind him. At about the middle of the semicircle of the far banking he rode up the banking to the outer side of the track and slowed, so as to force the other riders to go in front, the others followed up the banking, all slowing down to a crawl, Denny in front, Lapize outside. Just before entering the straight for the last lap Bartlett 'jumped' down the banking, from the rear of Denny and Lapize, and made a bee line for the winning straight. Leading at the bell he finished a length in front of Denny. No protest of any kind was made by Lapize. No comparison can be made between running and cycling. In cycle racing finessing for positions is permissible: more races are won by clever head work than by sheer speed. "Cutting in or out" when going at full speed is not permissible, but when "crawling" and "finessing" the question does not arise. Riding up the banking and slowing down is a tactic imported from the Continent, the object being to force the other riders to go in front and give a lead before a finish.

(Signed)   JAS. BLAIR.

From what Mr. Blair says it is evident that Mr. Kirby would have done well to verify the truth of the account and the justice of the opinions which he quotes as a proof of the unfairness of the English. I think it may be said that he is a little reckless as to the value of such evidence as he does not manufacture for himself.

(IV.) The technical points which Mr. Kirby raises as to the arrangement of the programme, drawing of heats, running of field events in sections, &c., have been dealt with elsewhere. It may, however, be desirable that I should note one thing, namely, that the arrangement of the programme was very largely determined by the fact that we were continually reminded by the European committees that their men could not remain during the whole period of the Games. This made it necessary that the sprints should be put in one week and the long-distance races in another.

This was another reason why it was so important to get the entries here in good time, so as to enable Continental competitors to make arrangements to be in London for their particular event; for, unlike the American team, the majority of our foreign visitors were unable to be here during the whole fortnight of the Stadium Games.

(V.) I come now to Mr. Kirby's next general complaint:

> Until the third day of the meet not an invitation was issued to an American representative to be upon the field, and no American other than the competitors in the events taking place was permitted on the field, and this when from time to time were on the field not only unnecessary officials, but dozens who were not officials.

The original regulation laid down by the British Olympic Council was that none but officials actually engaged in conducting the various events or members of the British Olympic Council who were responsible for the whole conduct of the Games should be allowed to enter the arena. This is a regulation which we have been very severely blamed for not maintaining. The *Revue Olympique*, the official organ of the International Olympic Committee, in its leading article of August 1908 on the Olympic Games, writes as follows:

> "Beaucoup trop de monde y avait accès; seulement il est à remarquer que tous les étrangers réclamaient pour y être admis et que plus d'un tempêtait des qu'on faisait

mine de lui fermer la barrière. N'importe. Ce fut une grande erreur d'autoriser une pareille circulation."

It was because of these demands on the part of the Foreign, and especially American, Representatives to be admittted into the arena that on the second day of the meeting Mr. Laffan brought before the Council the question of relaxing the rule, and was authorised to admit representatives of foreign countries where necessary. From that time, to the best of my belief, there was not a single instance in which an American Representative, were he a member of the Comité d'Honneur, trainer, or official applying for permission to go on the track was refused permission to do so. To say that there were on the field dozens who were not officials is simply untrue.

(VI) Mr. Kirby complains that:

> When the writer, on the last day of the Games, carried with him in a taxicab from the Stadium to his hotel the American flag which had been used to indicate the American victories, not flying it to the winds in exultation of victory, but having with modesty and dignity furled it around its staff, that boys and girls and even men and women cried out "Put it away" and "Throw it out," and cursed it out with vile words.

It is difficult to take such a passage as this very seriously: and it leads Mr. Kirby into further outbursts concerning "the American Revolution" and other matters; but I may, perhaps, be allowed to remind him of one small point he conveniently forgets. The flag was the one I mentioned as having been presented to him by the officials he so gallantly attacks; and, unless we are to understand the incident as being on the same plane as his "conversation" with gentlemen who never spoke to him, I am inclined to accept it as a remarkable, though perhaps involuntary testimony to the acuteness of London's juvenile population, who seem gifted with the extraordinary power of detecting the nationality of a flag after Mr. Kirby had "with modesty and dignity furled it around its staff." We regret, of course, if some rude boy in the street cried "Put it away" as Mr. Kirby passed by: but probably this is only what little boys in any country would do if they saw anyone carrying a flag in a taxicab, even if his modesty and dignity were as conspicuous as Mr. Kirby describes his own to have been.

It would be unnecessary to quote such observations were it not that Mr. Kirby describes himself on his first page as "one of the three members of the American Comité d'Honneur present at the Games, and as one who, either as a member of the Executive Committee, President or Chairman of the Advisory Committee of the I.C.A.A.A.A., has been for the past fifteen years identified and in close touch with the best and the straightest athletes in the world." I am sure we all congratulate Mr. Kirby on these facts in his past career: but I am inclined to think that his energies will be better displayed in future in some more congenial atmosphere than that of the comparatively untutored scenes in which he suffered so much last July.

(VII.) Lastly, it is only necessary to repeat for Mr. Kirby's benefit that Lord Desborough did *not* "entrust the direct control of the Olympic Games of 1908 to a body known as 'The Amateur Athletic Association of Great Britain.'" Out of the twenty divisions of these Games, the Amateur Athletic Association controlled one.

It is much to be regretted, and we regret with Mr. Kirby, that these Games should have in any way failed as a means of bringing the nations of the world into a closer bond: but, from all the evidence before us, that failure applies only to the nation on behalf of which Mr. Kirby poses as a representative, and only to the small, though noisy, portion of that nation which has hitherto believed him. Perhaps the best comment to make upon that is to quote once more from the *Revue Olympique*, which speaks of the Games as having for one result "cette constatation, qu'il n'est au pouvoir d'aucun groupement national, si puissant soit-il ou se figure-t-il être, de contrecarrer sans raison l'action combinée des autres."

This concludes that portion of my subject to which Mr. Laffan has been kind enough to contribute the documents and the special knowledge in his possession; and I may translate his last quotation by the phrase: "No single nation, however powerful it may be, can upset without good reason the combined action agreed upon by other nations."

I may add that no single nation's representatives, however reckless they may be, can discredit without good reason the officials whose appointment for an athletic meeting has been sanctioned by all the nations taking part.

Nothing that has occurred this year inspires me with the assurance that Mr. Sullivan, Mr. Kirby, or Mr. McCabe are the sole repositories of those sentiments of honesty, courtesy, and athletic experience which are not unknown upon the continent of Europe. These gentlemen seem to have stifled their own feelings long enough to keep their team in the Stadium until the prize-giving was over. But if one quarter of the accusations they have subsequently levelled at us had been true, I cannot imagine that any of our visitors would have given our meeting the support of their presence for a single day. Not only, however, did nineteen other nations compete with British athletes under British officials throughout the Stadium programme, but many of them competed again this October; as I have shown, they have even asked for further opportunities of competition; and neither indirectly nor directly have they ever endorsed a single word of the blame so freely showered upon us by some of the American officials.

I now conclude with the official statement of the Amateur Athletic Association. For this their own officials are responsible. It needs no further comment.

London, England: October 31, 1908.

II. OFFICIAL STATEMENT OF THE AMATEUR ATHLETIC ASSOCIATION

The Amateur Athletic Association, in view of the unfair and untrue statements published in a section of the American Press concerning the conduct of the Olympic Games, have decided to issue the following statement, answering in detail the various matters complained of. They would not have adopted this course had it been simply newspaper comment, but in view of the speeches made by prominent American officials present at the Games, and in view of the pamphlet published by one of them, they now think it right emphatically to refute these charges.

The statements particularly referred to are those which appeared in the Boston *Globe* of August 26, 1908, purporting to have emanated from the Hon. Joseph B. McCabe, who is described as having represented U.S.A. at the Olympic Games as a Commissioner, others attributed to Mr. J. E. Sullivan, President of the A.A.U. of America, and also those published in a pamphlet by Mr. Gustavus T. Kirby, one of the American members of this Comité d'Honneur.

The following are the specific charges made by the Hon. J.B. McCabe, and the replies of the A.A.A.:

1. "In the first place they drew the heats to suit themselves. They had a lot of green slips representing English athletes, and white ones representing all the others. Instead of putting them all in the hat and drawing them, the green slips were kept separate. This resulted in the Englishmen getting all walk overs, and when we protested no attention was paid to us."

1. The American members of the Comité d' Honneur twice wrote to ask the method of drawing the preliminary heats, and were fully informed. They were drawn in the usual manner. Except for these preliminary heats, all heats were drawn in the presence of and with the assistance of Mr. B. S. Weeks, an American member of the Comité d'Honneur, with the exception of the draw for the Team Race and the Marathon Race, which were drawn by

Mr. C. O. Lowenadler, a Swedish member of the Comité d'Honneur, whose signed statement is in the possession of the A.A.A. No green slips were ever used, and the statement made is a deliberate lie.

2. "Some of the officials actually swore at our men."

2. That is absolutely untrue.

3. The disqualification of Carpenter in the Four Hundred Metres Race. "Some of them (the Englishmen) actually pulled Taylor off the track by force."

3. Taylor was not interfered with in any way, neither did he have anything to do with this deplorable incident.

On August 15, Mr. Percy Fisher, Secretary of the Amateur Athletic Association, authorised a statement for publication concerning the final heat of the Four Hundred Metres.

The inquiry into the final heat of the Four Hundred Metres Race was held at the Garden Club, Franco-British Exhibition, on the evening of the day of the race. Among those present were Mr. Duxfield, Vice-President of the Amateur Athletic Association, in the chair; Sir Lees Knowles (British Olympic Council), Mr. G. S. Roberston (British Olympic Council), Mr. Percy Fisher, Mr. Pennycook (Scottish Amateur Athletic Association) Mr. E. W. Parry, Dr. M. J. Bulger (British Olympic Council), Mr. David Scott Duncan (Hon. Secretary, Scottish Amateur Athletic Association), Mr. W. J. Basan (London Athletic Club), Mr. E. H. Pelling (Hon. Secretary, London Athletic Club) and others.

The evidence, written and signed is as follows:

Olympic Games. Quarter mile Race.

Inquiry into the allegations of unfair competition by which Mr. W. Halswelle was said to be willfully obstructed.

Dr. Bulger, a member of the British Olympic Council and an umpire said: I took up a position on the back stretch 100 yards from the start. I saw No. 3 in the draw-*i.e.* No. 3 position from the verge.

At this point Mr. Moss, the Assistant Secretary, explained that No. 1, T. C. Carpenter, drew the first position next to the verge; No. 2 W. Halswelle, drew the second position; No. 4,

W. C. Robins [*sic*], drew the third position; and No. 3, J. B. Taylor, drew the fourth position.

Mr. Bulger proceeded: About 50 yards from the start I saw No. 3, W. C. Robins [*sic*], go right across Halswelle and take Halswelle's position as No. 2. Halswelle then seemed to drop back, and came more on the outside of Robins, and in that position he rounded the first bend. That is as far as I know of the matter.

MICHAEL J. BULGER.

Mr. Harry Goble's Evidence.

I am a member of the Manchester A.C., and on this occasion I acted as starter in the final heat of the Four Hundred Metres Flat Race at the Olympic Games. I was instructed by the referee, Mr. Abraham, and other officials to caution the competitors against willful jostling, and did so while they were on their marks. I said in case of any willful jostling the race will be declared void, and when the race is re-run the offender will not be allowed to take part. I told them that officials were posted every few yards to notice any such jostling.

HARRY GOBLE.

July 23, 1908.

Dr. Badger, a vice-president of the A.A.A., said: I acted as an umpire, and took up a position on the bend just before entering the straight. The position of Robins [*sic*] at that point was that he was leading and about a yard in front of Carpenter. Robins [*sic*] and Carpenter were in such a position as to compel Halswelle to run very wide all round the bend, and as they swung into the straight Halswelle made a big effort and was gaining hard; but running up the straight the further they went the wider Carpenter went out from the verge, keeping his right shoulder sufficiently in front of Mr. Halswelle to prevent his passing. When they had run 30 yards up the straight Carpenter was about 18 inches off the outside edge of the track. I at once ran up the track, waving my hands to the judges to break the worsted.

A. ROSCOE BADGER.
Vice-President, A.A.A.

Mr. David Basan: I am a member of the A.A.A. and the London Athletic Club, and I acted as an umpire in the Four Hundred Metres Flat Race final heat. I was standing beside Dr. Badger at the bend entering the straight. I corroborate the evidence of Dr. Badger in every particular. As the competitors passed me I called the attention of the next umpire further on to the running of the competitors. In my opinion Carpenter willfully obstructed Halswelle.

Mr. Halswelle is not a personal friend of mine, and I only know him as a competitor.

D. BASAN.

Mr. David Scott Duncan.

I am a member of the British Olympic Council and Secretary of the Scottish Amateur A.A. I acted as referee in the final heat of the Four Hundred Metres Flat Race at the Olympic Games. I took up my position on the cycle track immediately behind Mr. Pennycook, one of the judges, and opposite the winning post. I watched the race carefully, and saw that thirty yards after the start Halswelle had been dispossessed of second position by Robins [sic]. Swinging into the straight Halswelle commenced to gain on the two men in front whereupon Carpenter made straight for the outside edge of the track, while Robins [sic] nipped through on the inside. The boring by Carpenter continued, and the umpires held up their hands and signalled a foul. The worsted was broken, but I do not know by whom. Three of the judges, Messrs. Parry, Pennycook, and Fisher, consulted with me, and on the evidence of the umpires the race was declared void, and the words "No race" were signalled on the telegraph board and announced by megaphone.

DAVID SCOTT DUNCAN.
July 23, 1908.

We, the undersigned, being Judges of the Final of the Four Hundred Metres, declare the race void, and order same to be re-run on Saturday next without Carpenter, he being disqualified, and further order that the race be run in strings.

PERCY L. FISHER.
C. PENNYCOOK.
E. W. PARRY.

4. *Re:* Marathon Race: "These same men (Andrews and the Surgeon) hit Hayes when he was coming to the tape."

4. This is a disgraceful falsehood.

5. *Re:* Tug-of-War.-"The English team had specially prepared shoes, which are not allowed under the rules. They had prongs at the toe, and heel-plates like small horseshoes in the heel."

5. The English teams had in some instances heel-tips, but these were sunk level with the leather, and are clearly permissible, as will be seen from the following extract from the competition rule: "No competitor shall wear prepared boots or shoes, or boots or shoes with any projecting nails, tips, sprigs, points hollows, or projections of any kind." There were no prongs at the toes, and the boots worn absolutely complied with the conditions of the contest.

McCabe's statement concludes with the following—"After the Marathon, spectators would yell every day: "Who won the Marathon? Dorando. Who got the prize? America." To this we need only reply that the Marathon Race took place on the last day but one of the Games, and the phrase "every day" is quite in keeping with the other untrue and unfair charges.

Mr. J. E. Sullivan charges the officials with being the most prejudiced and unfair in the world.

An ample and sufficient reply to this is the fact that no protest or objection as to the conduct of the Games was made by any of the other twenty nations; but, on the contrary, very many letters have been received by the A.A.A. congratulating them on the success of the Games, and on the efficient manner in which they were carried out, and expressing thanks for the generous treatment accorded the competitors.

Mr. Gustavus T. Kirby published a pamphlet in New York, dated September 8, in which he states that the American Committee complain of the following:

1. The acceptance of the entry of T. Longboat, the Canadian.

1. The question of the eligibility of any competitor was a matter for the British Olympic Council to settle.

2. He complains that the officials refused to permit Mr. Sherman to compete in the Broad Jump because he was not present at roll call, when during roll call he was actually running in the Two Hundred Metres dash.

2. Mr. Sherman was informed that if he had notified the judges that he was competing in the Two Hundred Metres he would have been transferred to another section in the Jump.

3. "The system of running the field events

3. In view of the large entries sections

in sections — that is, to divide the athletes up so that some compete in the morning and some in the afternoon, and some from one take-off and some from another, was also unwise and unfair."

He complains that in the Pole Vault a hole was not allowed for the pole.

4. Further, he complains that the High Jumpers would have been required to land on the hard turf unless complaint and suggestion had been made by the American Committee.

5. "Until the third day of the Meeting not an invitation was made to an American Representative to be upon the field."

6. Four Hundred Metres Race.— He makes a statement that the American members of the Comité d'Honneur after the finish went to the entrance of the field, and, "not being permitted thereon, sent for the Referee, who after considerable time came; then the following conversation took place":

American Committee: We desire to formally protest against your declaring the Four Hundred Metres Race final as "no race."

The Referee: Your protest will be noted.

American Committee: In compliance with the rules we will submit our protest in writing.

The Referee: Have the same sent to the Secretary.

Mr. Kirby: We would like to know on just what grounds you have declared the final as "no race."

The Referee: It was because Lieutenant Halswelle was fouled.

Mr. Kirby: How and by whom?

The Referee: By being elbowed by the American Carpenter.

had to compete morning and afternoon, but they only did so from one take-off. In the first section of the High Jump objection was raised to the take-off, and the contestants were allowed to jump again from a fresh take-off.

This is contrary to our rule and also to that of other nations competing.

4. It is usual in this country to land on the turf, but in deference to the wishes of the American officials, it was arranged that the competitors should alight into the sandpit.

5. The badges of the International Committee admitted to the centre of the ground. The badges of the Comité d'Honneur admitted after the second day. No distinction whatever was made in this respect, between the American representatives and those of any other nation. The invitation mentioned was sent because the A.A.A. understood that difficulty had been experienced in passing through the barrier.

6. The following letter from the Referee is a complete answer to this bogus interview.

In answer to a request from the Editor of the *Sporting Life*, Mr. David Scott Duncan (British Olympic Council, Hon. Secretary of the Scottish Amateur Athletic Association, and Referee in this race) wrote the following letter, which appeared in the *Sporting Life* for September 30:

DEAR SIR,— Absence on holiday in North Wales has prevented my replying sooner to your letter of the 22nd inst.

I shall not attempt to characterise Mr. Kirby's pamphlet, which I return, but shall content myself by saying that I was sole Referee of the Four Hundred Metres Race, and that I had no conversation of any kind whatever with any American officials either before or after our decision was arrived at that the race be re-run.

Yours very truly,
DAVID SCOTT DUNCAN.
118 Craiglea Drive, Edinburgh.
September 28, 1908.

Mr. Kirby: How could that be when Mr. Carpenter was always leading Lieutenant Halswelle? The only way for Halswelle to be elbowed by Carpenter was for Halswelle to run into Carpenter, and in which case it would be Halswelle, and not Carpenter, who fouled.

The Referee: I was mistaken when I said Carpenter. I meant the other American.

Mr. Kirby: Who? Robins [*sic*] or Taylor?
The Referee: The white man.

Mr. Kirby: Then, Mr. Referee, to the end that there may be no misunderstanding, are we to believe that the final is declared "no race" because Mr. Robins [*sic*] fouled Lieut. Halswelle by elbowing him?
The Referee: That is the case.

Mr. Weeks: Do you not think, Mr. Referee, it would be wise to call your Judges together, and take and consider testimony before disposing of the American protest?
The Referee: We will do so.

Mr. Weeks: And at once?
The Referee: At once.
"And then, for the first time, the judges got together," continued Mr. Kirby. "What testimony they took is not known."

A further statement appears in the *San Francisco Chronicle*, amongst other papers, dated August 28, in which it stated:

> "The A.A.U. of the United States will break off athletic relations with the British A.A.A. because of the spirit shown by the Britons towards the American athletes in the Olympic Games. This action will be taken following a mail vote. It is almost unanimously in favour of severing connection with the British organisation. As soon as Bartow S. Weeks returns from abroad a meeting will be held and final action taken."

To this it is sufficient to say that, although the A.A.U. of America have repeatedly asked to enter into a working agreement with the A.A.A, the latter body have always respectfully declined. There are, therefore, no athletic relations to break off.

Signed on the behalf of the General Committee of the Amateur Athletic Association.

(Signed)T. M. ABRAHAM
E. B. HOLMES
PERCY L. FISHER
Hon. Sec.
October 12, 1908.

OUTING MAGAZINE:
THE VIEW-POINT
by Caspar Whitney[3]

"And if you win or if you lose,
Be each, pray God, a gentleman."

Reflections

Long after its unhappy dissensions have been forgotten the brilliant achievements of the American athletes at the fifth revival of the Olympic Games will be remembered. Let us embrace that solace now while highly colored and partisan "interviews" are being battledored and shuttlecocked across the Atlantic. Let us on the American side also rest content in the belief that however suggestive of unfairness some of their acts many have appeared, the English officials did the best of which they were capable; and did their best honestly.

Let me, also assure the sportsmen of the other side that the hearts of our athletes are of prime quality even though their manners may not be an invariably correct index. Indeed I may pursue the thought further and out of my own experience and observation affirm for the information of both sides of the Atlantic — that, class for class, and apart from the universities, American athletes have the heart and British athletes the manner.

And while the reflective mood is on me I wish likewise to say that had it not been for the Amateur Athletic Union, had it not been for the indefatigable efforts, the technical knowledge, and the experience of James E. Sullivan, there would have been no such winning team from America at the Olympic Games. Put that in your pipes and smoke it all ye little Americans with petty spites who seized every opportunity to say something unkind and unjust about the A.A.U. or its president.

And had it not been for the wisdom and the sportsmanship of Lord Desborough, England would have been unequal to the task of handling the Games.

Finally, I add that the American contribution to Stadium controversy should be attributed to variance in custom (rules), to absence of tradition, and to a mistaking of violent gloriation for patriotism by the younger element.

In the Band Wagon

As one of the members of the committee which struggled so long and so desperately to raise the money to send these American athletes to London, it affords me some emotion (I suppress its description) to note now the hurrahing and ostentatious caperings of those who either kept silent or refused to help at the time when, for lack of funds, it looked as if we would be unable to send a representative team. I observe with languid gratification the patriotic efforts making in New York to give the returning champions an "elegant" reception; also that Alfred Gwynne Vanderbilt has given $2,500 to the British Olympic entertainment fund, and that Kessler, the wine tout, has contributed an equal amount to the same English committee for a like purpose.

Of course one does not expect service from a wine tout which is not to return him newspaper notoriety — but from Vanderbilt! Yet when I review the experiences of our American

Olympic Committee, I recall that no Vanderbilt offered a dollar's worth of help, nor an Astor—however, the latter is not a familiar name on such lists.

Where all are so deserving of credit, it is a blunder to discriminate among the returning athletes in matter of tribute. They all did nobly—the most notable performances being those of Sheppard, Smithson and Sheridan.

American Victory in Speed, Agility, Endurance

Success for the American team was counted on by their countrymen, but the results in detail are surprising on account of the strength developed in hitherto weak directions and because of the team's open pre-eminence in so large a proportion of the track and field events. And this was the most important international contest in the history of track and field athletics, for here were gathered the cream of the world's athletes; the champions of champions.

The United Kingdom, which included England, Ireland, Scotland and Wales, had upwards of five hundred men entered for the various contests. America was represented by about eighty. Yet American captured 15 firsts, 9 seconds, and 6 thirds, to the United Kingdom's 8 firsts, 6 seconds, and 3 thirds.

Naturally English-speaking athletes dominated the meeting though I had hoped to see both Germany and France show more prominently in the strictly track events. Perhaps the greatest surprise, however, was absence of German competitors in either the rifle or revolver matches.

France made something of a showing in bicycling, and attained to the most satisfactory display of continental nations in track events.

Sweden gave an unexpectedly excellent all-round exhibition—better, in fact, than Canada, which was not on the cards' and Italy, with whose sunny skies and languorous temperament we have not in our thoughts associated the strenuous, furnished two of the most brilliant athletes of the entire galaxy in Lunghi (who gave Sheppard a very close race in the 800 meter event) and plucky Dorando, who, reaching the Stadium first on the last stage of the Marathon race, struggled on and on only to collapse finally, with victory but forty yards away, when his strength was utterly spent. It was a dramatic scene and appeared near to being a literal revival of the legendary finish of this classic footrace.

South Africa, also, was represented by two surpassing athletes; Walker, who captured the 100 meter from Rector, to America's astonishment; and Hefferon, who finished second in the Marathon.

Canada disclosed its one really high-rank man, in Kerr, and his class is undoubted, though he was lucky in racing Cartmell when the latter was not at his best. I shall look with interest to the next meeting of these two first-grade sprinters.

Altogether, from first to last, it was a remarkable exhibition of high-class athletics, not the least noteworthy feature being the impressive superiority of the Americans over the full strength of the United Kingdom—noteworthy as we consider it to be within the memory of Americans still comparatively young when a visiting team to England did well in winning one or two or three events on the British programme.

It was a victory of training, of methods, as well as of performance. It was a triumph in all the games that make for speed, for agility, and for endurance. Ten Olympic records were equaled or broken.

Practice Not Stamina Needed

Certainly the most exulting triumph of the Games came in the Marathon, and for the sufficient reason that distance-running has never occupied a prominent place in our athletic curriculum. Our comparatively poor showing in the longer running events tempted foreigners to vote us deficient in stamina, and led uninformed Americans to agree with them. England has always been pre-eminent in these events, because from time immemorial cross country running has been an established and a popular feature of athletic England. Since the last Olympic Games at Athens in 1906, we have been giving some attention to cross country running—with what results this year's Marathon rather convincingly illustrates.

America had seven men in the Marathon race, five of whom finished (Hayes) first, (Forshaw) third, (Welton) fourth, (Tewanina) ninth, and (Hatch) fifteenth respectively; the other two didn't finish. England had twelve men in the race of whom only four finished, and the first of these four was thirteenth to cover the Marathon distance, or, in time, twenty-two minutes behind Hayes and seven minutes behind Welton. The Canadians entered twelve men, of whom seven finished in fifth, sixth and seventh places. In 1906, a Canadian won the Athens Marathon in 2 hours, 51 minutes, 23 3-5 seconds.

Of the twenty-four point winners on America's team, one is Irish-born and American by adoption; five are American-born of Irish parents; one is American-born of German parents; the balance are of American-born parents. This is apropos of the English Magazine, Outlook, statement that "the pick of American athletes are of Irish stock."

Lessons for England and America

Unhappy as have been the controversies and the recriminations attending some of the rulings and methods that obtained in the London Stadium, yet instruction has resulted; and if both England and America profit by the lessons which these disputes have provided, the unpleasantness will not have been without fortunate outcome. And Americans need to be told at once that the lessons awaiting their attention are as important as those for the English.

The first lesson for us both to commit thoroughly, is need of reorganizing the whole International Olympic Committee in personnel and in method of conduct. At present it is a clumsy affair, composed largely of inexperienced men, chosen quite after the fashion that obtains in nomination patronesses to smart garden parties — by the well-meaning if capricious gentlemen who appear to view the "Comité Athlétique" as a kind of social board-walk.

The International Olympic Committee should be rearranged on practical working lines, with an official structure competent individually and collectively to handle such a big business as these Olympic Games have become. Its membership should be restricted to the countries which support the meetings. Its present scope is ridiculous, as may be judged from the fact that Turkey and Spain and Russia and Peru are all represented, whereas Canada has no member on the Committee!

The present Committee should be allowed to die of inanition, and a new one organized. That is the first step of the first lesson.

The second step is appointment by this International Olympic Committee of an experienced sub-committee to manage the Games; and this Committee should appoint the officials who are to have the actual conduct of the contests in charge.

There should, of course, be international rulings to reconcile local differences of custom or regulation, such for example, as those which brought the pole vault, the 400 meter, and the drawing for heats into discussion this year.

Incompetent Not Dishonest

The indisputable incompetence of the local management at the London Stadium emphasized the urgent necessity for a management of international character. We see now that it was an unfortunate mistake for the British Olympic Council, of which Lord Desborough was chairman, to give the management of these Games into the hands of the Amateur Athletic Association. Yet it was but following established precedent, and the only thing that could well be done.

Had, however, custom permitted of the British Council creating its own officials, I am confident no friction would have resulted, because Lord Desborough is a thorough-going sportsman, and would not surround himself with men of whom he did not approve.

Certainly American sportsmen will deplore as sincerely as do English sportsmen the inadequacy of the officials in charge. And I know that American sportsmen deplore sincerely the highly colored comment of some of the American newspaper correspondents and representatives. Englishmen may be assured that such reckless statement does not represent the sentiment of American sportsmen.

Of course it is outrageous to charge the unfitness of the officials to downright dishonesty. However much, and quite naturally so, they may have desired English victory, it is insulting to say there was "underhanded work" in the drawing for heats, or "highway robbery" in the disqualification of Carpenter in the 400 meters.

It was indeed a dire misfortune that, in addition to being incapable, the officials were also stupid, losing their heads so completely as to establish a record for incompetency which is not likely to be surpassed in many years to come.

To begin with, the programme of events was badly arranged; for instance, the 3-mile team and the 5-mile trials were run on the same afternoon. The enclosure swarmed with unnecessary officials. The track in the 400-meter race was not marked in lanes at the time of the race; but after the disqualification of Carpenter, when Halswelle ran alone, the path was carefully laned throughout!

The action of the judges in the final of the 400 meter was unprecedented, and so extraordinary as to lay them open to a charge of rank prejudice in addition to incompetence. Their breaking the tape and rushing hysterically about shouting "foul," was extraordinary to say the least. The place of those judges was at the finish to decide who first broke the tape. That was their business. They had nothing whatever to do with the protest, which was a matter for the Inspector and Referee.

Again, the action of the officials at the finish of the Marathon race, in helping the exhausted Italian, Dorando, across the tape, and then announcing him the winner by raising the Italian flag, and thus making a protest necessary from America — was so astonishing a proceeding, that it is small wonder some of the less-balanced Americans were provoked to proclaim the English management unfair.

"Luck of the Draw"

Of course the squabble about digging holes for the vaulting pole, and the method of drawing for heats, were annoying, but these were questions that should have been decided before the Games began, and the decision accepted in sportsmanlike spirit, and without dispute.

Personally, I believe that in any championship event, the drawing for heats should be so arranged that two men of the same nation or club do not fall into the same heat. Of course it is fair for one nation or club as for another, but "the luck of the draw" is a term that should not be heard in so important a meeting as the Olympic Games, or in any set of championship games, in fact, where the first and seconds count.

The Old, Old Story of the Shield

Whether the English runner Halswelle was fouled in the final of the 400 meters will probably never be settled to the mutual satisfaction of Englishmen and Americans. And as time goes on, each party to the contention will increase in number and positiveness. That is the usual course. Nothing in this disputatious world affords me quite so among observation, as the certainty with which people assert themselves on subjects of which they have no knowledge. And is there any place on this earth where conflicting opinions are upheld with greater vehemence, with less actual knowledge to support them — than at any kind of athletic entertainment.

In the case of three men going around a corner into the stretch at a 48-second gait, nobody not directly at the turn and by the track is qualified to express an opinion of what happened. The only man qualified to say whether or not a foul was committed in that 400 meter, was the inspector who stood at the turn. There may have been a few spectators sufficiently near, or so fortunately placed as to accurately determine what occurred, but of course, they are beside the question. The only man's word that counts was the inspector's, and as he declared a foul, such is the judgment which we must all accept. Such is the judgment that should have been accepted in dignity and in sportsmanly spirit.

In my opinion this is a case of conflicting custom (rule). The American rule permitted Carpenter to cross in front of Halswelle if he was two yards in the lead; the English rule prohibits such crossing under any conditions. As the race was under English rules, Carpenter's disqualification was just, if he crossed in front of Halswelle at the turn into the final stretch.

It is true also that the English rule forbidding all tricks to impede a competitor's progress is a righteous one, and ought to be adopted in America without delay.

The English had a great team; apparently they thought it unbeatable, especially in the 400, the 800 and the 1,500 meters. To have two, the 800 and the 1,500 taken by the same American shocked British equilibrium and an upheaval resulted when Carpenter showed his seeming superiority to their crack, Halswelle, in the 400.

Halswelle has been living on the reputation he made in 1906, when he ran a quarter mile (440 yards) in 48 4-5 seconds. He has not approached that time since.

An unbiased view seems to indicate that Halswelle had spent his effort at about the three-quarter pole; that he had been run off his feet by Carpenter, who went on and finished in unofficial time, said to range from 47 4-5 to 48 2-5 — the slowest clocking being faster than the best Halswelle ever did for the distance.

In his walk-over, Halswelle did not do better than 50, although he ran it out to the finish, evidently with the idea of making a new Olympic record and thereby putting some bloom on faded bay.

Play or Pay

Sportsmen will always regret that the Americans refused to run the race over as ordered by the Referee. No matter how incensed they may have been; no matter how sure they may have felt of the injustice of the decision, when they entered the Games they subscribed to its rules and agreed to abide by the decisions of the judges; the decision of the judges in this case was final, and the Americans should have kept their mouths shut and abided by that decision. It was up to them to accept the ruling; to play the game It was the sportsmanly thing to do.

May I take this occasion of calling to the minds of our athletes the mystic initials which their great granddaddies — a fine type of sportsmen they were — incorporated in every sporting venture set to paper — *viz.*, "P.P." — which mean: "Play or pay."

Play or pay — that means, young gentlemen, play the game, take your medicine; be generous in victory, take defeat gallantly. Play like a gentleman, which means like a sportsman for the word sportsman, you know, does not refer to the quality of play but to the quality of conduct in play. Win like a thoroughbred and lose like a man. Trying to rattle opponents in a desire to lessen the strength of their effort is not playing the game — is not playing like gentleman; and trying to bulldoze umpires and judges out of making decisions unfavorable to you, or sulking when an unfavorable decision is made against you, is not losing like a man; and, above all things it is best to be a MAN.

Two Habits That Discredit America

There are two habits of the American in his play, that are unhappy enough at home, but are certain to result in unfortunate friction when he is brought into contact with foreigners — these are (1) his disposition to "kick" at decisions, and (2) his training to beat the rules.

We in America understand the American. We know that his "kicking" and his endeavors to be too smart for the rule makers are by no means evidence of dishonest intent, but an expression of his frenzy to win. To him such tactics represent one means of "getting there." Thus it has come about that to beat the rules, to protest adverse decisions, to disregard the minor regulations of the game — are so characteristic of us and so widely in evidence as to have become a by-word with sportsmen outside of this country. And yet, in honest fact, the American sportsman is the fairest fighter, and the gamest loser in all the world; the best sportsman on earth when he is a sportsman.

Now there is nothing the matter with the "get there" spirit, *per se*; it is the spirit of the land that has made us what we are — a spirit which, let us hope, will never be quenched; but it needs direction. It requires control in our sport as it does in our business.

A letter from an American, who was intimately connected with the late Games, to me says, in referring to the English officials: "they look with distrust upon us."

Of course they did, and I honestly do not see how we can blame them. They have had several bitter experiences with American smartness, from the special rifle barrel which we slickly used at the 1904 Palma Trophy shoot in England, down to the team work of our runners. They do not know us well enough to understand that our smartness does not go to the length of the stolid dishonesty which is on view in their own club track athletics.

We do things in Wall Street that would put a man behind the bars if he was not ranked as being smart. The slickness which enters into high finance has a tendency to creep into our athletics. The mad passion for money-making — anything to make money — and the placing of money-making as the highest expression of one's endeavors, one's brain, one's skill, is reflected in athletics by the passion for victory which ignores sport for sport's sake. Among average Americans there is no love for the sport itself. It is increasing among a portion, but the majority have only the thought of winning. And this is not to say anything against that spirit, but to express gratification at the growing numbers of the men who do have the sporting spirit, and to explain why it is that the English distrust us. Add to this, that no people in the world so constantly and so conspicuously air their soiled linen in public, and there will not be so much cause for wonder that Englishmen look askance at athletes who so repeatedly befoul their own nest.

English Phlegm

It was a sweet, womanly thought that prompted the Queen's gracious donation of a consolation cup to the Italian who had so nearly won the Marathon, but the subsequent lionizing of the man was a maudlin, not to say amusing exhibit of Cockney England gone daft.

They had the poor man receiving bracelets stripped from the arms of women, and exhibiting himself on the stage of a music hall, within twenty hours of his collapse on the Stadium. And yet we refer to English phlegm!

OUTING MAGAZINE: THE VIEW-POINT
by Caspar Whitney[4]

"The creature we call a gentleman lies deep in the hearts of thousands that are born without a chance to master the outward graces of this type."

Olympic Games American Committee Report

Much as I would prefer to dismiss the unhappy controversy which has raged around the Olympic Games since they were decided, it is a discussion too far reaching and one bearing too many lessons to be closed without full hearing. That is why I give space here to some of the official report made by Mr. Gustavus T. Kirby of the American Olympic Committee:

> So much comment and criticism has been made in reference to the Olympic Games of 1908 and there seems to be so much uncertainty, especially among university men, as to just what did or did not happen at London during the Games, that I take this, my first opportunity, and immediately upon returning from abroad, to state to the Inter-Collegiate Association, and through it to all who may be interested, my observations as one of the three members of the American Committee d'Honneur present at the Games, and as one who, either as a member of the Executive Committee, President or Chairman of the Advisory Committee of the I.C.A.A.A.A., has been for the past fifteen years identified and in close touch with the best and straightest athletics in the world.
>
> WHAT THE AMERICAN COMMITTEE COMPLAINED
> OF OR PROTESTED AGAINST:
>
> The acceptance of the entry of one Thomas Longboat, a Canadian who had made himself a professional runner by competing for a money prize in the city of Boston, Mass. Longboat was permitted to run in the Marathon race, representing Canada, when under protest by America and the Amateur Athletic Federation of Canada; and this notwithstanding the fact that there were two weeks time prior to the race within which evidence in his case could have been given and a decision reached.

* * *

The opening day found no flag of the United States flying within the Stadium. This, it was afterwards said, was due to the carelessness of the decorator. If it were mere carelessness, certainly the carelessness was gross; for not only was there no American flag among those of the other nations of the world flying from the stands in the Stadium, but there was none even on the grounds, for when the American Committee d'Honneur requested the "decorator" to hoist the American flag he said they had none and did not know where there was one, but would hoist one if the Committee could find one; which the Committee could not do outside of those carried by the Americans in the stand.

*   *   *

The arrangement of the programme was such as to make it impossible or unwise for men to compete in both of the sprints, as in the Inter-Collegiate programme, and in certain other races, such as the individual and team distance races. Such an arrangement was to the advantage of the home team. It may have been done with no intent to injure or aid; but certainly there is no excuse in rules or in manners for the officials refusing to permit Mr. Sherman, of Dartmouth, to compete in the broad jump because he was not present at roll call, when during roll call he was actually running in the 200-meter dash.

*   *   *

The method of drawing the heats in the various events was such as to include all entrants, whether present at the Games or at home, and disregarded the respective abilities of the athletes, thereby producing heats where there were no contestants; heats which were walk-overs for one contestant, and heats in which were the fastest contestants, with the result that several fast second men were eliminated, as only first ran in the final, and second, third and fourth places in the final went to men who most assuredly would have been unplaced if second had also run or if the "fastest second" had been in the final. This method of drawing was especially hard on the American team and favored the British team. Until complaint was made by the American Committee, the drawings were in secret and made by British officials.

*   *   *

The system of running the field events in sections — that is, to divide the athletes up so that some would compete in the morning and some in the afternoon, and some from one circle or take-off and some from another — was also unwise and unfair. Certainly if it had not been for the tremendous superiority of the American competitors the system used would have lost to them many places and points. Imagine Ralph Rose not being at a disadvantage as to all others when he, as the last man in the last section, was called upon to put the shot from a circle (and one without a toe-board) which, dry for the first section, had been rained upon and was at the time of his trial an absolute mudhole.

*   *   *

The rule, taken from nowhere — not found in the A.A.A. of Great Britain rules — and contrary to Olympic precedent, that there should be no hole for the pole in the pole vault, was as foolish as improper. It can only be understood on the ground that it was made to place the American competitors at a disadvantage. But why complaint and suggestion had to be made by the American Committee, to have a pit dug so that the high jumpers would not have to land on the hard turf, and the pole-vaulting pit widened and lengthened for the same purpose, can only be answered by those who made these absurd arrangements and were loath to change them until they were made to realize their responsibility and liability for broken legs and sprained ankles.

*   *   *

The British officials openly coached the British contestants, not only by shouting to them with and without megaphones, but by running alongside of the track with them. This abuse became so flagrant that complaint was made by the American Committee. The reply was that there would be no more of it, and yet, in spite of such promises, the objected-to coaching probably lost to Eislee [*sic*] of Princeton second place in the three-mile team race.

*   *   *

When an English runner finished, every attention was given to him. If necessary, he was assisted from the field. Until the third day of the meet, not an invitation was issued to an American representative to be upon the field, and no American other than the competitors in the events taking place was permitted on the field; and this when from time to time there were on the field not only unnecessary officials but dozens who were not officials. At last an invitation came to the American Committee d'Honneur to have on the field one of its number or someone representing it, but did not come until the writer pointed out to the secretary of the A.A.A. the absolute necessity of there being someone at or near the finish line to help an American runner from the field if he finished in distressed condition.

*   *   *

Had these "trivial" instances been all, much could and would have been forgiven and charged to mismanagement and inexperience. One would have pardoned those Englishmen who hooted at you to "Sit down" when you stood during the playing of "The Star-Spangled Banner," and forgiven the others of the same breed who endeavored to take away a small American flag from a boy in the "American section" of the grand stand, on the ground that these acts were not characteristic of the British, but committed by a few who lacked manners. But when one looks to the 400-meter race and the Marathon, events of importance are being considered, and in considering these I here state only what I personally saw, heard and know of my own knowledge.

In the final of the 400-meters there were Carpenter of Cornell, Taylor of Pennsylvania, Robbins of the Boston Y.M.C.A., and the Englishman Halswell [*sic*][5]. The race was on a third-of-a-mile track and was around one run and without lanes. Robbins, the third from the curb at the start, gained the curb before 20 yards were run and set the pace for 300 yards close to, if not actually under, even time. At this point, Carpenter was right behind Robbins and next him from the curb, Halswell[e], some four strides back and next the curb, and Taylor fully ten yards behind Robbins and Carpenter and in the rear of and farther from the curb than Halswell[e]. At no part did Taylor prove a factor in the race. At 300 yards Carpenter passed Robbins; he did not take the curb, but — as is his custom, and to my mind a most unwise and unsafe custom, throughout used by him so as the better to keep his stride — ran with each stride farther and farther from the curb, leaving between Robbins and himself a gap large enough to drive a car through, and through which gap Halswell[e] should have endeavored to pass. Halswell[e], however, with what, I was told by a Cambridge athlete, was characteristic dumbness, in making his spurt endeavored to pass Carpenter on the outside. Try as he would, he could not get up. At no time was he within better than half a stride of Carpenter; and at no time did Carpenter strike him or in any manner foul him. If he was elbowed by Carpenter, it was because he ran into Carpenter. But Halswell[e] never made any such claim, nor has there been evidence other than newspaper talk to substantiate such a charge. At all times there was never less than four feet between Carpenter and the outside of the track, and through this gap Halswell[e] could and would have to come if he had had the speed to do so. The truth is that he was stale from his unnecessarily and foolishly fast trials of too few days before, and the fast 300 yards had killed him off. At 350 yards he was a beaten man. Thereafter, it was either Carpenter's or Robbins' race, both of these moving away and leaving Halswell[e] farther behind at every stride. Carpenter crossed the finish line first, with Robbins and Halswell[e] some two strides behind. There is no doubt whatever but that Carpenter ran Halswell[e] wide at the turn, but there is also no doubt that Carpenter in doing so ran on a circle of practically the same diameter as Halswell[e] and not only gained no advantage on Halswell[e] but, for more than 20 yards of the race, gave Halswell[e] an opportunity to come through on the inside and thereby gain the curb and point of advantage on entering the home stretch. There is no rule, A.A.A. of Great Britain or other, forbidding Carpenter from running the race in the manner in which he did. The A.A.A. rule stated in the press as that invoked to base Carpenter's disqualifications upon reads as follows: "Any competitor willfully jostling or running across or obstructing another competitor so as to impede his progress, shall forfeit his right to be in the competition and shall not be awarded any decision or prize that he would otherwise have been entitled to."

This rule can only mean that a man coming from the rear must not change his course so as to interfere with any competitor whom he has passed. If we interpret it to apply to one in the lead, that one of necessity must always run in the course in which he starts, as if he were running in a lane; for, if otherwise, one starting on the outside could never take the curb, for in so doing he would have to cross in front of the others, and such would impede them more or less, depending on the distance he was in the lead. The American rule states that one must not cross in front of another until he is two strides ahead of that one. Carpenter at no time crossed in front of Halswell[e]. If Halswell[e] had kept his course, Carpenter would have crossed in front of him, or rather Halswell[e] would have crossed the path Carpenter had taken and, for 20 or more yards, Halswell[e] could have and should have so done without interfering with Carpenter or impeding himself by having to break his stride to change is direction and get from behind Carpenter. But Halswell[e] did not keep to his course any more than did Carpenter. They both ran on concentric circles, with a slightly greater disadvantage to Halswell[e] because his was a greater diameter, but with a disadvantage due to no other cause whatever than that he ran only with his heels and not also with his head.

The race was declared "no race," and in what manner? At 350 yards Halswell[e] began to fall back, lacking speed in his final spurt and failing to pass Carpenter on the outside. Immediately the judges and referee, a hundred yards away, ran out on the track and one of them ran toward the inspector at the last part of the turn. This inspector called something to him. What it was could not be heard in that part of the grand stand opposite the finish line. It is to be presumed, however, that it was that Halswell[e] had been fouled. In the meantime, with unslackened speed, Carpenter, Robbins and Halswell[e] came down the stretch. Within twenty yards of the finish an official without authority of rule or reason broke the tape and held up his hand. If by so doing he meant to stop the race, his object was not accomplished, for they all came on, Halswell[e] "digging" stride by stride to get up. What it all meant no one knew, but they did not have long to wait, for, without even the semblance of a consultation or meeting of any kind, the judges and other officials rushed around like madmen. Some grabbed up megaphones and shouted into the stand, "No race." "Foul work on the part of the Americans," "Halswell[e] fouled", etc. Immediately sentiment framed itself against the American and a howl went up to "disqualify the dirty runners." And all the while the officials kept calling into and exciting the crowd, and one of them actually came outside the track and stood amidst a mob of excited Englishmen and started to harangue them as to the race being a good example of how the damned Yankees always tried to win.

* * *

The American Committee d'Honneur went to the entrance of the field and, not being permitted thereon, sent for the Referee, with whom they lodged a protest.

And then for the first time the judges go together. What testimony they took is not known. Certainly no American testimony was requested or given. Their decision was that the American protest was disallowed; that it was Carpenter and not Robbins who had fouled Halswell[e]; that the race was to be run over in lanes, but without Carpenter, for he was disqualified and his case was to be reported to the A.A.A. for its further action.

* * *

THE MARATHON: A huge placard was paraded around the field, showing to the 100,000 persons present in the Stadium the relative positions of the three leading men, as mile after mile of the race was finished. At 20 miles, for the first time, the number of an American contestant was shown. It was that of Hayes and he was in third place. Certainly America now had a chance, for Hayes could always be counted upon to make the last five miles the fastest five miles. At 21 miles, the placard showed Heff[e]ron and Dorando leading, but no third man. Had Hayes dropped by the wayside — was he down and out? So it would seem to those in the Stadium. Actually, Hayes was coming on, and fast, and at between 24 and 25 miles passed Heff[e]ron; but at 25 miles the placard showed Dorando in first place and no number for second or third place.

A few hundred yards before entering the Stadium, Dorando fell. He was examined by a physician and found to be in a condition of physical exhaustion, so serious, in fact, that he was given a hypodermic of digitalis or strychnine. He was assisted to his feet and staggered into the Stadium a horrible, sickening sight of an exhausted, done-up, almost dying man with the courage and desperation of his race stamped on his ashen features. Four times within the Stadium he fell, and four times by British officials he was assisted up and on. The last time he fell was but 30 yards from the finish and directly beneath and within 20 yards of the writer. He lay inert and all but lifeless. At this moment, Hayes entered the arena and came on with a burst of speed which seemed as if he fairly flew. In a minute he would be up to and past the helpless Dorando. But a victory such as this was to be denied him, for as he came on, those British officials who had theretofore helped Dorando, picked the Italian up, put him on his feet, and carried, pushed and pulled him over the line. Cruel, unwise and unfair, and as unfair to the Italian as it was cruel, for immediately he broke the tape, they gave him the race and hoisted the Italian flag to the top of the "victory staff," indicating that to his country went the greatest honor of the games, and then were forced to take away what should never had been given.

*   *   *

The rules of the race, among other things, stated that a competitor would be disqualified who, during the race, took or received any drug[6]; that at all periods of the race a competitor should be physically fit to proceed, and that a competitor should not be paced by his attendants, who must keep in his rear. The rules did not state that he should run the race unaided or only on his own legs and with his own strength. To state such a rule would be as absurd as to say that in a 100-yard dash the runner must not use an automobile; and yet, after the American Committee were forced into the unbecoming position of having to protest against the awarding of the race to a runner as courageous as any the world has ever seen, the English judges asked me to find a rule covering the point and were disgusted when I suggested that they might award the race to Longboat who had finished ahead of them all — in an automobile.

*   *   *

The judges met and the American Committee waited. The Italian flag still flew at the head of the staff. Minutes lengthened into hours — two long, anxious hours — and then Lord Desborough appeared and handed the American Committee d'Honneur the decision, reading as follows: "That in the opinion of the judges Mr. P. Dorando would have been unable to have finished the race without the assistance rendered on the track and so, therefore, the protest of the United States of American is upheld and the second man, John Hayes, is the winner; the protest made by the South-African team being withdrawn."

Put the Blame Where it Belongs

This is a severe arraignment which Mr. Kirby has lodged against the Olympic Games officials, and allowing for some natural feeling and righteous resentment, it must in the main be accepted as entitled to respectful consideration.

In publishing this statement of Mr. Kirby's, I have no wish or intention to indulge further in criticism or controversy. I believe there were also faults on our side in the beginning, but there is nothing to be gained now by retrospective argument. Let us stop recrimination; it is profitless and harassing. What I desire to point out and what Mr. Kirby's report illustrates, is, that the fundamental fault was lack of a real international committee. America must share the blame for this omission. We should long ago have insisted on reconciliation of conflicting rules and upon the appointment of an international body competent to handle such an important event. With feeling running so high and competition so keen, and an international committee so inconsequential, friction was, in the circumstances, inevitable.

It is unfair to lay all censure for the unfortunate dénouement upon England. The responsibility must be divided among all of us who have tolerated the casual Olympic organization which provided so incompetent an international committee.

There is reason other than athletic rivalry for much of English suspicion and prejudice. The disclosures of American "frenzied finance" have had their effect on the foreign mind. Undoubtedly American reputation abroad has suffered. The average Englishman believes alertness to be only another name for slickness. Much of England considers "frenzied finance" methods typical of all America. Thus the credit of the average American has been hurt. England is frankly prejudiced; they look for something dishonest in everything we do. If we are too smart for them if we are too fast for them, if we are too strong for them they cannot believe it superior prowess, but cast about instanter for some underhand advantage we have employed to beat them. This impression I am bound to say is helped out by the ill manners of some traveling Americans and by their tendency to brag and their insolent exultation in victory.

This is written in common fairness and not at all to relieve the British officials of any of the onus that belongs rightfully to them for their mean-spirited and obviously biased conduct, but it does go to show perhaps some of the reasons why prejudices have formed in unintelligent English heads.

The British A.A.A. is welcome to the credit of having established a record which will probably never be equaled, for its share of the Olympic Games provided the worst-managed athletic meeting the world has yet seen.

Let Us Forget

The thing to be done now is to get together for organization on proper lines. My suggestion is dismissal of the present so-called International Olympic Committee and formation of a new one composed of the representative of the countries which support the games, and that the presidency of the new committee be offered to Lord Desborough, the English sportsman who did so much to clear the atmosphere in London.

How They Love Us

It is not complimentary, certainly, yet quite the most convincing evidence of the violent prejudice ruling the British mind where we are concerned, is furnished by the following excerpts from that usually conservative and always stolid *Academy* in its issue of August first:

> It is a very unfortunate thing that the man who came in second at the Marathon Race last week happened to be an American. If he had been an Englishman it may be safely assumed that he would have brought no objection against Dorando. Of course, Hayes was rightly given the race as soon as he had made his protest, but by making this protest he lost the opportunity of his life. If he had been a sufficiently good sportsman to allow Dorando to retain the prize he would have been the most popular man in England, and he would have done much to wipe out the feeling of disgust which had been generated by the conduct of the American athletes and their rowdy supports. The sort of feeling which prompts a sculler in a race at Henley when his opponent runs in to the piles to wait for him instead of going on and taking a long lead is apparently unknown to a citizen of the United States. He would look upon such an act as one of sheer stupidity. America seems to have adopted the old professional maxim which was supposed to have distinguished a certain set of "sportsmen," "Win, tie, or wrangle." It is a spirit which is fatal to amateur athletics,

and for this reason we are delighted to see that no American crew is competing in the Olympic Regatta at Henley.

*   *   *

A correspondent who was present at the Stadium throughout the proceedings confirms our impression that the Americans behaved "odiously" from first to last. He points out that the American spectators and competitors alike sat in a great mass together and made disgusting noises and cries. No other nation behaved in this way, and if the other nations had adopted similar tactics the whole Exhibition would have been turned into a revolting pandemonium. The Americans ran all their races in collusion with each other, it being decided beforehand which of them was to win, the other men being told off to impede as far as possible the other runners. We sincerely hope that this is the last time we shall see American amateur athletes in this country, and we can get on very well without a great many other Americans who are not athletes. Of course it would be absurd not to admit that among Americans there are some good sportsmen and agreeable people, but they are in such a small minority that it is almost impossible to trace them.

These statements are so amazingly prejudiced as to be interesting for their audacity.

The balderdash concerning the Marathon Race reaches the ludicrous. The Marathon Race is a test of endurance. Whether a man wins in the last thirty yards or in the last five miles, is beside the question; added to which Dorando violated the plain rules of the race prohibiting any contestant to receive assistance or stimulants; all the world now knows the Italian would never have been able to stay on his feet in the Stadium without the help of strychnine injections and the British officials who held him up and supported him across the line.

As to Americans running races in "collusion" read the following praise of such work by English athletes in the *Telegraph* of July 15th, which refers to the 1500-meter event:

> It was agreed by all that the British trio named required a fast-run mile, particularly in the first two of the three laps which had to be covered. To that end J. F. Fairbairn-Crawford and E. V. Loney unselfishly agreed mutually to carry a pacemaking mission. But their notions of what this duty involved were at fault.
>
> The willing Scot Fairbairn-Crawford went through the first with the lead. He certainly was pacemaking, but not at the higher pressure needed. The same defect was observed when Loney took up the running in the second lap. It was obvious that the time was going to be slow. Moreover, Sheppard, the only American to be feared, had still a reserve of power left to him. He was running easily within himself when the last lap was reached. Here Wilson soon worked himself into first place, closely followed by Hallows, with Deakin, who ran with the poorest judgment imaginable and utterly regardless of any but his own purely personal interests, lined right away behind. Deakins is a stayer of the first water and a runner of ripe experience, who should long before this have gone up as a pioneer for the welfare of the British team. As it was, Wilson had to make his own running, with Hallows and the two Americans, J. P. Sullivan and M. W. Sheppard, treading closely on his heels.

And then read this from the *Mail* of July 20th with regard to the 100-kilometer cycle race:

> Then came the moment of the Olympic games, so far as they have gone. The three Englishmen in the first flight — Denny, Pitt and Bartlett — realizing that their

chance had come, dashed ahead with a swoop. At the time that the Texier had mounted his new machine, they were half a lap ahead and were out of danger from that source. But Lapize was with them — his strong face set hard, his stout legs caked with mud, his tri-colored costume drenched out of recognition by the rain.

A beautiful piece of generalship followed. Denny and Pitt looked around and steered their machines in front of the Frenchman. Bartlett crept up at the rear. Lapize, riding for dear life, was completely boxed in. Assuming that he had nothing to beat except what was in front of him, Lapize allowed the riders to carry him to the top of the last bank. Barlett, who had kept at the bottom of the trap, darted past like a torpedo and, amid a whirl of delirious excitement, won by two lengths, beating [Capelle]'s record by nearly eight minutes. Denny was second; the Frenchman a length behind, was third.

Barlett rode once more around the course, his face wreathed in smiles, the air full of tumultuous cheers.

And by the way of illustrating the intelligence and ken of the English sporting press, I publish below a paragraph taken from the editorial column of the *Sporting and Dramatic*, the leading British weekly of its kind, under date of August 15th:

Messrs. Belmont and J. R. Keene propose to remove themselves and their horses from the jurisdiction of Governor Hughes, of New York, and to come and race in England. This rather looks like abandoning the fight on behalf of the American Turf, and will, I suppose, be much regretted by lovers of racing on the other side; but it is not for use to criticise Messrs. Belmont and Keene's ideas of patriotism. They are both owners of a class that is welcome here. It will annoy Hughes to know that Mr. Belmont is having a good time in England, for, as I noted some time since, it was personal antagonism to the own of Norman III., a wish to worry and injure him, which induced Hughes to take up his present attitude.

Isn't this rich! Fancy Governor Hughes impelled to duty by his dislike of Mr. Belmont!

I am printing these not for sake of argument, but to illustrate why international games should have international rules and a competent international committee.

NOTES

1. BDG, 24 September 1908. ARCC also stated that it was published in the *Boston Transcript* on 19 September 1908. No such newspaper existed in Boston in 1908, the *Transcript* having become the *Boston Evening Transcript*. A thorough search of that newspaper failed to reveal any evidence of Peabody's letter in September 1908. It is possible ARCC was mistakenly referring to the BDG article, which was kindly provided by John A. Lucas, Ph.D. of Penn State University.

2. BDG, 24 September 1908, p. 7.

3. *Outing Magazine, 52(6),* (September 1908), p. 761–766.

4. *Outing Magazine, 53(2),* (November 1908), p. 244–249.

5. Whitney misspelled Halswelle's name throughout the text. We have not noted *sic* after all the following instances, but suffice to say that the misspelling is from the original text in all cases.

6. This actually was a rule in the 1908 *Official Report,* #4 in the marathon rules. However, it was broken by virtually all competitors in marathon racing in this era, when it was commonplace for the runners to be given stimulants.

Appendix IV
Maps of Olympic Sites

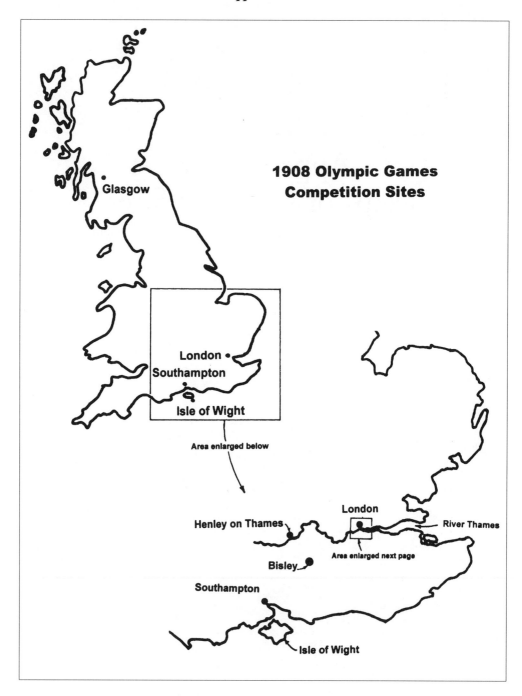

**1908 Olympic Games
Competition Sites**

Glasgow

London •
Southampton

Isle of Wight

Area enlarged below

London

Henley on Thames   River Thames

Area enlarged next page

Bisley

Southampton

Isle of Wight

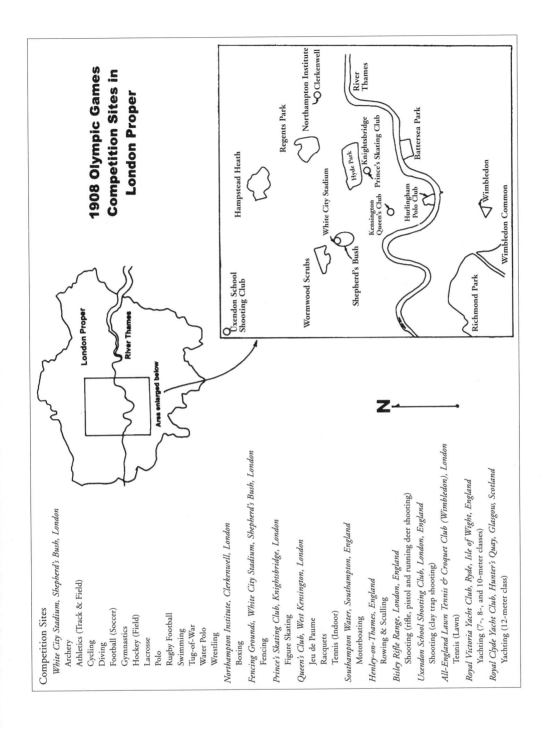

Competition Sites

White City Stadium, Shepherd's Bush, London
  Archery
  Athletics (Track & Field)
  Cycling
  Diving
  Football (Soccer)
  Gymnastics
  Hockey (Field)
  Lacrosse
  Polo
  Rugby Football
  Swimming
  Tug-of-War
  Water Polo
  Wrestling

Northampton Institute, Clerkenwell, London
  Boxing

Fencing Grounds, White City Stadium, Shepherd's Bush, London
  Fencing

Prince's Skating Club, Knightsbridge, London
  Figure Skating

Queen's Club, West Kensington, London
  Jeu de Paume
  Racquets
  Tennis (Indoor)

Southampton Water, Southampton, England
  Motorboating

Henley-on-Thames, England
  Rowing & Sculling

Bisley Rifle Range, London, England
  Shooting (rifle, pistol and running deer shooting)

Uxendon School Shooting Club, London, England
  Shooting (clay trap shooting)

All-England Lawn Tennis & Croquet Club (Wimbledon), London
  Tennis (Lawn)

Royal Victoria Yacht Club, Ryde, Isle of Wight, England
  Yachting (7-, 8-, and 10-meter classes)

Royal Clyde Yacht Club, Hunter's Quay, Glasgow, Scotland
  Yachting (12-meter class)

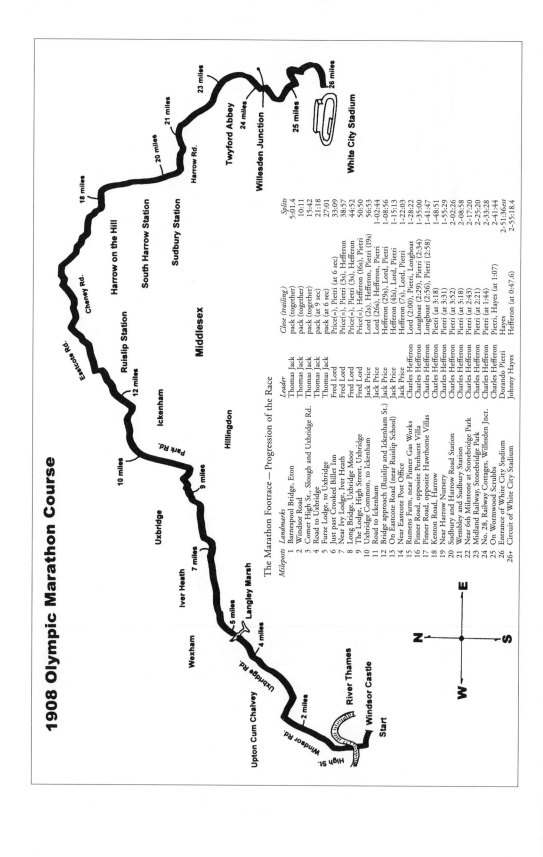

1908 Olympic Marathon Course

The Marathon Footrace — Progression of the Race

Mileposts	Landmarks	Leader	Close (trailing)	Splits
1	Barnespool Bridge, Eton	Thomas Jack	pack (together)	5:01.4
2	Windsor Road	Thomas Jack	pack (together)	10:11
3	Corner High St., Slough and Uxbridge Rd.	Thomas Jack	pack (together)	15:42
4	Road to Uxbridge	Thomas Jack	pack (at 9 sec)	21:18
5	Furze Lodge, to Uxbridge	Thomas Jack	pack (at 6 sec)	27:01
6	Just past Crooked Billet Inn	Fred Lord	Price(=), Pietri (at 6 sec)	33:09
7	Near Ivy Lodge, Iver Heath	Fred Lord	Price(=), Pietri (3s), Hefferon	38:57
8	Long Bridge, Uxbridge Moor	Fred Lord	Price(=), Pietri (3s), Hefferon	44:52
9	The Lodge, High Street, Uxbridge	Fred Lord	Price(=), Hefferon (16s), Pietri	50:50
10	Uxbridge Common, to Ickenham	Jack Price	Lord (2s), Hefferon, Pietri (19s)	56:53
11	Road to Ickenham	Jack Price	Lord (26s), Hefferon, Pietri	1-02:44
12	Bridge approach (Ruislip and Ickenham St.)	Jack Price	Hefferon (29s), Lord, Pietri	1-08:56
13	On Eastcote Road (near Ruislip School)	Jack Price	Hefferon (41s), Lord, Pietri	1-15:13
14	Near Eastcote Post Office	Jack Price	Hefferon (7s), Lord, Pietri	1-22:03
15	Rumens Farm, near Pinner Gas Works	Charles Hefferon	Lord (2.00), Pietri, Longboat	1-28:22
16	Pinner Road, opposite Penhurst Villa	Charles Hefferon	Longboat (2.29), Pietri (2.34)	1-35:00
17	Pinner Road, opposite Hawthorne Villas	Charles Hefferon	Longboat (2.56), Pietri (2.58)	1-41:47
18	Kenton Road, Harrow	Charles Hefferon	Pietri (at 3:18)	1-48:51
19	Near Harrow Nursery	Charles Hefferon	Pietri (at 3:31)	1-55:29
20	Sudbury and Harrow Road Station	Charles Hefferon	Pietri (at 3:52)	2-02:26
21	Wembley and Sudbury Station	Charles Hefferon	Pietri (at 3:18)	2-08:58
22	Near 6th Milestone at Stonebridge Park	Charles Hefferon	Pietri (at 2:43)	2-17:20
23	Midland Railway, Stonebridge Park	Charles Hefferon	Pietri (at 2:21)	2-25:20
24	No. 28, Railway Cottages, Willesden Jnct.	Charles Hefferon	Pietri (at 1:44)	2-33:28
25	On Wormwood Scrubs	Dorando Pietri	Pietri, Hayes (at 1:07)	2-41:44
26	Entrance of White City Stadium	Johnny Hayes	Hayes	2-51:36est
26+	Circuit of White City Stadium		Hefferon (at 0:47.6)	2-55:18.4

Appendix V
"Dorando" by Irving Berlin

Dorando
Words and Music by Irving Berlin

I feel-a much-a bad, like anything;
All the night I nunga canna sleep;
It's a my pizon Pasquale,
He say we take da car
And see Dorando race a "Long-a ship;"
Just like da sport, I sell da barber shop,
And make da bet Dorando he's a win.
Then to Madeesa Square, Pasquale and me go there,
And just-a like-a dat, da race begin.

CHORUS
Dorando! Dorando! He run-a, run-a, run-a,
Run like anything.
One-a, two-a hundred times around da ring,
I cry, "Please-a nunga stop!"
Just then, Dorando he's a drop!
Good-bye, poor old barber shop.
It's no fun to lose da mon,
When de sun-of-a-gun no run,
Dorando, He's good-a for not!

Dorando, he's a come around next day,
Say, "Gentlemen, I wanna tell-a you,
It's a one-a bigga shame,
I forgot da man's a-name,
Who make me eat da Irish beef-a stew;
I ask-a him to give me da spagett,
I know it make me run a-quick-a-quick,

But I eat da beef-a stew, And now I tell-a you,
Just like da pipps it make me very sick."

CHORUS

From Hamm, Charles, ed. *Irving Berlin. Early Songs. I. 1907-1911.* Volume 2, Part I of *Music of the United States of America*, Richard Crawford, editor-in-chief; Jeffrey Magee, executive editor. Madison, Wisconsin: A-R Editions, 1994. pp. 16-19.

5. DORANDO

Words and Music
by IRVING BERLIN

Appendix VI
Competitors (By Country)

In the following we have tried to give precise biographical information concerning full, complete names, and complete dates of birth and death (where known). Also given are all events in which the competitors competed and their placement. In events where competitors were eliminated prior to a final, the following notations serve as examples to explain the results:

4h3rl1/2 = 4th in heat 3, round 1 of 2.
ach4rl1/3 = also competed in heat 4, round 1 of 3.
dnfplr2/4 = did not finish, pool 1, round 2 of 4.
=13 = tied for 13th

Argentina (Total: 1; Men: 1; Women: 0)

Figure Skating (Total: 1; Men: 1; Women: 0)
Torromé, Horatio. Men's Individual [7].

Australasia (Australia and New Zealand) (Total: 30 [27 Australia, 3 New Zealand]; Men: 30; Women: 0)[1]*

Athletics (Track & Field) (Total: 9; Men: 9; Women: 0)
Aitken, William Victor. (b.1889) Marathon [dnf].
Blake, George B. 5 miles [3h1r1/2]; Marathon [dnf].
Hutcheon, Ernest Henry[2] (b.17 June 1889–d.9 June 1937) Standing High Jump [ac].
Kerr, Henry Edward "Harry" (b.28 January 1879–d.1951) (New Zealand) 3,500 meter walk [3].

*See Notes on pages 484–485.

Lynch, Joseph M. (b.22 April 1878–d.10 March 1952) 5 miles [dnfh5r1/2]; 1,500 meters [5h2r1/2]; Marathon [dnf].

Murray, Henry Steven Aubyn. (New Zealand) (b.14 January 1886–d.12 April 1943) 110 meter hurdles [2h1r1/3]; 400 meter hurdles [2h3r1/3].

Rowland, Arthur Edward M. (New Zealand) (b.1879) 3,500 meter walk [5]; 10 mile walk [5h1r1/2].

Sutton, Harvey Vincent. (b.18 February 1882–d.21 June 1963) 800 meters [3h8r1/2].

Swain, Charles Edward. (b.16 January 1885–d.5 February 1974) 1,500 meters [dnfh3r1/2].

Boxing (Total: 1; Men: 1; Women: 0)

Baker, Reginald Leslie "Snowy." (b.8 February 1884–d.1 December 1953) Middleweight [2]. [See also Diving and Swimming].

Diving (Total: 1; Men: 1; Women: 0)

Baker, Reginald Leslie "Snowy." (b.8 February 1884–d.1 December 1953) Fancy High Diving [6h4r2/3]. [See also Boxing and Swimming].

Rugby Union Football (Total: 15; Men: 15; Women: 0)

Barnett, John Thomas, "Jumbo." (b.19 January 1886–d.1951) [1].

Carmichael, Phillip P. (b.25 January 1884–d.1 September 1973) [1].

Carroll, Daniel Brendan. (b.17 February 1887–d.5 August 1956) [1].[3]

Craig, Robert Robertson. (b.1 September 1881–d.5 March 1935) [1].

Griffin, Thomas Sydney. (b.1884–d.1950) [1].

Hickey, John Joseph. (b.4 January 1887–d.15 May 1950) [1].

McArthur, Malcolm "Mannie." (b.30 July 1884) [1].

McCabe, Arthur John Michael. (b.1887–d.1 May 1925) [1].

McCue, Patrick Aloysius. (b.1 June 1883–d.10 September 1962) [1].

McKivat, Christopher Hobart. (b.27 November 1879–d.4 May 1947) [1].

McMurtrie, Charles H. (b.1880–d.1951) [1].

Middleton, Sydney Albert. (b.24 February 1884–d.1945) [1].

Richards, Thomas James. (b.1887–d.September 1935) [1].

Russell, Charles Joseph. (b.1884–d.May 1957) [1].

Smith, Francis Bede "Frank." (b.1886–d.1954) [1].

Shooting (Total: 1; Men: 1; Women: 0)

Hill, William. Small-Bore Rifle, Disappearing Target [18]; Small-Bore Rifle, Moving Target [=19]; Small-Bore Rifle, Prone [16].

Swimming (Total: 5; Men: 5; Women: 0)

Baker, Reginald Leslie "Snowy." (b.8 February 1884–d.1 December 1953) 4 × 200 meter relay [4]. [See also Boxing and Diving].

Beaurepaire, Francis Joseph Edmund.(b.13 May 1891–d.29 May 1956) 100 meter freestyle [4h1r2/3]; 400 meter freestyle [2]; 1,500 meter freestyle [3]; 4 × 200 meter relay [4].

Cooke, Edward J. L. 100 meter freestyle [ach6r1/3]; 200 meter breaststroke [dnfh5r1/3].

Springfield, Frederick William. 400 meter freestyle [2h6r1/3]; 1,500 meter freestyle [2h4r1/3]; 4 × 200 meter relay [4].

Tartakover, Theodore B. 100 meter freestyle [2h1r1/3]; 4 × 200 meter relay [4].

Austria (Total: 7; Men: 7; Women: 0)

Athletics (Track & Field) (Total: 2; Men: 2; Women: 0)
Rath, Emmerich. (b.5 November 1883–d.21 December 1962) Marathon [25]; 10 mile walk [8h2r1/2].
Schönecker, Erich Eduard "Emi" (b.21 January 1885–d.6 April 1963) 100 meters [4h13r1/3]; 200 meters [3h12r1/3].

Fencing (Total: 1; Men: 1; Women: 0)
Flesch, Siegfried.(b.11 March 1872–d.11 August 1939) Sabre, Individual [=3p6r2/4].

Swimming (Total: 1; Men: 1; Women: 0)
Scheff, Otto.[4] (b.12 December 1889–d.26 October 1956) 100 meter freestyle [4h2r2/3]; 400 meter freestyle [3]; 1,500 meter freestyle [dnf].

Tennis (Total: 3; Men: 3; Women: 0)
Kinzl, Rolf. (b.19 October 1878) Singles (Lawn) [=26].
Piepes, Fritz Felix. (b.15 April 1887) Singles (Lawn) [=26]; Doubles (Lawn) [=4].
Zborzil, Arthur. (b.15 July 1885–d.15 October 1937) Singles (Lawn) [=16]; Doubles (Lawn) [=4].

Belgium (Total: 70; Men: 70; Women: 0)

Athletics (Track & Field) (Total: 6; Men: 6; Women: 0)
Celis, François. Marathon [dnf].
Delloye, François. (b.16 September 1888–d.1958) 1,500 meters [5h8r1/2].
Dupont, Léon. (b.18 May 1881–d.6 October 1956) High Jump [=16]; Standing High Jump [=8]; Standing Long Jump [ac].
Halbart, Fernand.200 meters [5h10r1/3].
Jacquemin, Victor. (b.12 March 1892) 100 meters [2h6r1/3]; 400 meters [dnf/h10r1/3].
Konings, Jean. (b.4 March 1886–d.29 May 1974) 100 meters [2h4r1/3].

Cycling (Total: 6; Men: 6; Women: 0)
Coeckelberg, Guillaume. 100 km. [dnf-final]; 5,000 meters [ach7r1/2].
Coeckelberg, Léon. 20 km. [dqh6r1/2]; One Lap Match Sprint [2h15r1/2]; Tandem Sprint [4h1r2/3].
Patou, Jean. (b.28 December 1878) One Lap Match Sprint [2h4r1/2]; Tandem Sprint [4h1r2/3].
Renard, Lucien. One Lap Match Sprint [2h4r2/3].
Van Benthem, Jean. 20 km. [ach2r1/2]; One Lap Match Sprint [3h12r1/2].
Werbrouck, Joseph. (b.10 January 1882–d.3 June 1974) One Lap Match Sprint [2h8r1/2]; 20 km. [3].

Diving (Total: 1; Men: 1; Women: 0)
Huketick, Joseph. Plain High Diving [dnf/h2r1/3].

Fencing (Total: 18; Men: 18; Women: 0)

Anspach, Paul. (b.1 April 1882–d.28 August 1981) Épée, Individual [=5]; Épée, Team [3]; Sabre, Individual [5p5r2/4].

Beaurain, Désiré. (b.2 September 1881–d.1 September 1954) Épée, Team [3].

Bosmans, Fernand.(b.29 June 1883–d.30 July 1960) Épée, Individual [8p1r3/4]; Épée, Team [3].

de Montigny, Fernand.(b.5 January 1885–d.2 January 1974) Épée, Individual [=3p7r2/4]; Épée, Team [3].

du Bosch, André. Sabre, Individual [=4p9r1/4]; Sabre, Team [=5].

Feyerick, Ferdinand.(b.1870) Épée, Team [3].

Grade, Etienne. (b.12 March 1875) Sabre, Individual [=3p1r2/4]; Sabre, Team [=5].

Le Blon, Pierre. Épée, Individual [8p2r3/4].

Renard, Gaston Gérard. (b.27 March 1868). Épée, Individual [=5p1r3/4].

Rom, François. (b.1869–d.1953) Épée, Individual [=5p1r3/4]; Épée, Team [3].

Sarens, André. Épée, Individual [=7p4r1/4].

Simonson, Alexis. Sabre, Individual [5p12r1/4].

Six, Henri Émile Albert. (b.4 May 1872). Sabre, Individual [=5p1r1/4].

Stuyck, François. Épée, Individual [4p1r2/4].

Van der Voodt, Joseph. Sabre, Individual [7p2r3/4]; Sabre, Team [=5].

Van Langenhove, Marcel. Épée, Individual [=3p6r2/4].

Van Tomme, Antoine. Sabre, Individual [4p6r1/4]; Sabre, Team [=5].

Willems, Victor. (b.1877–d.1918) Épée, Team [3].

Gymnastics (Total: 2; Men: 2; Women: 0)

De Buck, Antoine. Combined Exercises, Individual [ac].

Van Guysse, Jean. Combined Exercises, Individual [ac].

Rowing & Sculling (Total: 10; Men: 10; Women: 0)

de Somville, Oscar Charles. (b.19 August 1876–d.30 August 1938) Coxed Eights [2].

Hermans, Joseph. Single Sculls [2h4r2/4].

Mijs, Georges. (b.1881) Coxed Eights [2].

Morimont, Marcel. (b.1886) Coxed Eights [2].

Orban, Rémy. (b.5 April 1880–d.1951) Coxed Eights [2].

Poma, Rodolphe. (b.1885–d.1954) Coxed Eights [2].

Taelman, Oscar. (b.1878) Coxed Eights [2].

Van Landeghem, Alfred.Coxed Eights [2].

Veirman, Polydore. (b.23 February 1881–d.1951) Coxed Eights [2].

Vergucht, François. (b.1887) Coxed Eights [2].

Shooting (Total: 10; Men: 10; Women: 0)

Englebert, René. Free Pistol [15]; Free Pistol, Team [2].

Geens, Joseph. Free Rifle, Team [5].

Ista, Ernest. Free Rifle, 3 Positions [35]; Free Rifle, Team [5].

Paumier du Verger, Charles. Free Pistol, Team [2]; Free Rifle, Team [5].

Pinchart, Jacques. Free Pistol [37].

Poty, Edouard. Free Rifle, Team [5].

Rey, Fernand Robert. Free Rifle, 3 Positions [36].

Sauveur, Henri. Free Rifle, Team [5].

Storms, Réginald. Free Pistol [2]; Free Pistol, Team [2].

Van Asbroeck, Paul. (b.1 May 1874–d.1959) Free Pistol [1]; Free Pistol, Team [2]; Free Rifle, Team [5].

Swimming (Total: 7; Men: 7; Women: 0)
   Boin, Victor. (b.28 February 1886–d.31 March 1974) 100 meter freestyle [ach4r1/3]. [See also Water Polo].
   Courbet, Félicien. (b.25 February 1888–d.1967) 200 meter breaststroke [4h2r2/3].
   Duprez, André. 100 meter freestyle [2h9r1/3].
   Feyaerts, Fernand.(b.1880–d.1927) 100 meter freestyle [ach6r1/3]. [See also Water Polo].
   Grégoire, Oscar. (b.27 March 1877–d.1947) 100 meter backstroke [dnfh6r1/3]. [See also Water Polo].
   Meyboom, Herman. (b.23 August 1889) 100 meter freestyle [ach1r1/3]. [See also Water Polo].
   Strauwen, Pierre. 200 meter breaststroke [4h3r1/3].

Water Polo (Total: 7; Men: 7; Women: 0)
   Boin, Victor. (b.28 February 1886–d.31 March 1974) [2]. [See also Swimming].
   Donners, Herman. (b.5 August 1888–d. 1915) [2].
   Feyaerts, Fernand.(b.1880–d.1927) [2]. [See also Swimming].
   Grégoire, Oscar. (b.27 March 1877–d.1947) [2]. [See also Swimming].
   Meyboom, Herman. (b.23 August 1889) [2]. [See also Swimming].
   Michant, Albert. [2].
   Pletincx, Joseph. (b.13 June 1888–d.1971) [2].

Wrestling (Total: 4; Men: 4; Women: 0)
   Dubois, Marcel. (b.27 August 1886–d.19 February 1955) Light-Heavyweight, Greco-Roman [=5].
   Hansen, Lucien. Lightweight, Greco-Roman [=17].
   Meesen, August. Light-Heavyweight, Greco-Roman [=9].
   Steens, Fernand.Lightweight, Greco-Roman [=17].

Yachting (Total: 3; Men: 3; Women: 0)
   Huybrechts, Léon. (b.11 December 1876–d.9 February 1956) 6-meter class [2].
   Huybrechts, Louis. (b.21 February 1875–d.1963) 6-meter class [2].
   Weewauters, Henri. (b.8 November 1875) 6-meter class [2].

Bohemia (Total: 18; Men: 18; Women: 0)

Athletics (Track & Field) (Total: 3; Men: 3; Women: 0)
   Nejedlý, Arnošt. (b.1883–d. 1917) 5 miles [3h6r1/2]; Marathon [18].
   Souček, František. (b.1878) Discus Throw (freestyle) [ac]; Javelin Throw (freestyle) [ac].
   Šustera, Miroslav. (b.15 March 1878–d.15 December 1961) Discus Throw (freestyle) [ac]; Discus Throw (classical) [ac]. [See also Wrestling].

Fencing (Total: 6; Men: 6; Women: 0)
   Goppold von Lobsdorf, Vilém. (b.28 May 1869–d.12 June 1943) Épée, Individual [3p3r2/4]; Épée, Team [=5]; Sabre, Individual [3]; Sabre, Team [3].
   Lada, Otakar. (b.22 May 1883–d.12 July 1956) Épée, Individual [6p5r1/4]; Épée, Team [=5]; Sabre, Individual [3p5r2/4]; Sabre, Team [3].

Lada-Sázavský, Vlastimil. (b.31 March 1886–d.20 April 1956) Épée, Individual [5p5r2/4]; Épée, Team [=5]; Sabre, Individual [=4p7r2/4]; Sabre, Team [3].

Schejbal, Bedřich. (b.1874) Sabre, Team [3]; Sabre, Individual [3p4r2/4]; Épée, Individual [=5p6r1/4].

Tvrzský, Vilém. (b.1880) Épée, Team [=5]; Épée, Individual [=3p4r2/4]; Sabre, Individual [4p4r2/4].

Šourek, Jaroslav "Tuček." (b.24 August 1882) Épée, Individual [5p7r2/4]; Épée, Individual [7p8r1/4]; Sabre, Individual [=5p1r1/4 and =5p13r1/4]; Sabre, Team [3].

Gymnastics (Total: 2; Men: 2; Women: 0)

Honzátko, Bohumil. (b.1875) Combined Exercises, Individual [36].

Čada, Josef. Combined Exercises, Individual [25].

Tennis (Total: 6; Men: 6; Women: 0)

Gruss, Josef "Mičovský." (b.8 July 1884–d.21 May 1968) Singles (Lawn) [=26].

Hvkš, Bohuslav "Černý." (b.7 May 1889) Singles (Lawn) [=9]; Doubles (Lawn) [=11].

Robětín, Karel "Sláva." Singles (Lawn) [=9]; Doubles (Lawn) [=11].

Žemla, Ladislav "Rázný." (b.6 November 1887–d.17 June 1955) Singles (Lawn) [=16].

Wrestling (Total: 4; Men: 4; Women: 0)

Bechyně, Josef "Jakoubek." Middleweight, Greco-Roman [=17].

Halík, Karel. (b.21 December 1883) Lightweight, Greco-Roman [=17].

Šustera, Miroslav. (b.15 March 1878–d.15 December 1961) Light-Heavyweight, Greco-Roman [=17]. [See also Athletics (Track & Field)].

Týfa, Jaroslav. Middleweight, Greco-Roman [=9].

Canada (Total: 87; Men: 87; Women: 0)

Athletics (Track & Field) (Total: 27; Men: 27; Women: 0)

Archibald, Edward Blake. (b.29 March 1884–d.1960) Pole Vault [=3].

Barber, George H. (b.23 August 1884) High Jump [=10]; Long Jump [19]; Standing High Jump [ac]; Standing Long Jump [ac].

Beland, David.100 meters [3h5r1/3].

Bricker, Calvin David.(b.3 November 1885–d.24 April 1963) Long Jump [3]; Triple Jump [4].

Buddo, Donald Smith. (b.6 October 1886–d.27 July 1965) 400 meters [2h6r1/3]; 800 meters [3h5r1/2]; 1,600 meter medley relay [3h2r1/2].

Burn, Arthur. Marathon [24].

Caffrey, John Peter. (b.21 May 1879–d.2 February 1919) Marathon [11].

Cotter, Edward V. (b.27 December 1887) Marathon [dnf].

Fitzgerald, John Ebenezer. (b.8 September 1886) 5 miles [7]; 1,500 meters [7h8r1/2]; 3,200 meter steeplechase [dnf h6r1/2].

Galbraith, William B. 1,500 meters [3h7r1/2]; 3,200 meter steeplechase [6].

Goldsboro, William L. Marathon [16].

Goulding, George Henry. (b.16 November 1884–d.3 February 1966) Marathon [22]; 3,500 meter walk [4]; 10 mile walk [dnf h2r1/2].

Kerr, Robert. (b.9 June 1882–d.12 May 1963) 100 meters [3]; 200 meters [1].

Lawson, Harry. (b.1888) Marathon [7].

Lister, George Andrew. (b.6 November 1888) Marathon [27].

Longboat, Thomas Charles "Tom." (b.4 June 1887–d.9 January 1949) Marathon [dnf].

Lukeman, Frank L. (b.1887) 100 meters [2h13r1/3]; 200 meters [3h3r1/3]; 1,600 meter medley relay [3h2r1/2]; Long Jump [13].

MacDonald, John Garfield.(b.8 August 1881) High Jump [=13]; Long Jump [ac]; Triple Jump [2].

Meadows, Frederick. 1,500 meters [3h1r1/2].

Noseworthy, Frederick. Marathon [dnf].

Parkes, R. Irving. 800 meters [3h2r1/2]; 1,600 meter medley relay [3h2r1/2].

Savage, Frank E. B. 110 meter hurdles [3h5r1/3].

Sebert, Louis J. 100 meters [2h14r1/3]; 200 meters [2h10r1/3]; 400 meters [2h4r2/3]; 1,600 meter medley relay [3h2r1/2].

Simpson, Frederick. (b.1876–d.May 1945) Marathon [6].

Tait, John Lindsay. (b.25 September 1889–d.July 1971) 1,500 meters [4]; 5 miles [dnfh4r1/2]; Marathon [dnf].

Walsh, Cornelius E. (b.24 April 1886–d.1942) Hammer Throw [3].

Wood, William H. Marathon [5].

Cycling (Total: 5; Men: 5; Women: 0)

Anderson, William. 5,000 meters [3h7r1/2]; 20 km. [3h5r1/2]; 100 km. [ach1r1/2]; Team Pursuit [3].

Andrews, Walter. (b.1881) One Lap Match Sprint [4h1r2/3]; 5,000 meters [ach6r1/2]; 20 km. [ach2r1/2]; 100 km. [6]; Tandem Sprint [3h7r1/3]; Team Pursuit [3].

McCarthy, Frederick. One Lap Match Sprint [2h2r1/2]; 1,000 meters Match Sprint [4h4r1/3]; 5,000 meters [2h2r1/2]; 20 km. [6h1r1/2]; 100 km. [dnfh1r1/2]; Tandem Sprint [3h7r1/3]; Team Pursuit [3].

Morton, William. One Lap Match Sprint [3h14r1/2]; 1,000 meters Match Sprint [2h9r1/3]; 100 km. [dnfh2r1/2]; Team Pursuit [3].

Young, Harry R. L. 20 km. [3h3r1/2]; 100 km. [dnf-final].

Diving (Total: 1; Men: 1; Women: 0)

Zimmerman, Robert M. (b.2 December 1881) Fancy High Diving [3h1r1/3]. [See also Swimming].

Fencing (Total: 1; Men: 1; Women: 0)

Nobbs, Percy E. (b.1875–d.November 1964) Épée, Individual [=6p9r1/4].

Gymnastics (Total: 2; Men: 2; Women: 0)

Elliott, Orville. (b.15 September 1885) Combined Exercises, Individual [80].

Keith, George Allan. (b.22 February 1889) Combined Exercises, Individual [59].

Lacrosse (Total: 12; Men: 12; Women: 0)

Brennan, Patrick "Paddy." [1].

Broderick, John. [1].

Campbell, George H., "Doc." [1].

Dillon, Angus. [1].

Dixon, Frank J. [1].

Duckett, Richard Louis. [1].

Gorman, Thomas Patrick. (b.9 June 1886–d.15 May 1961) [1].
Hamilton, Ernest. [1].
Hoobin, Henry Francis "Henny." (b.15 February 1879) [1].
McKerrow, Clarence D. "Clary." [1].
Rennie, George H. [1].
Turnbull, Alexander T., "Sandy." (b.6 December 1883–d.27 August 1956) [1].

Rowing & Sculling (Total: 13 Men: 13; Women: 0)
Balfour, Gordon Bruce. (b.25 December 1882) Coxless Fours [2h1r1/2]; Coxed Eights [2h1r2/3].
Bowler, Walter. Single Sculls [dnf h3r2/4].
Gale, Becher Robert. (b.14 August 1887) Coxless Fours [2h1r1/2]; Coxed Eights [2h1r2/3].
Jackes, Norwey Baldwin. Coxless Pairs [2h1r1/2].
Kertland, Douglas Edwin. (b.23 November 1886) Coxed Eights [2h1r2/3].
Lewis, Walter Aken. (b.17 July 1885) Coxed Eights [2h1r2/3].
Riddy, Charles. (b.3 March 1885) Coxless Fours [2h1r1/2]; Coxed Eights [2h1r2/3].
Robertson, Irvine Geale. (b.9 July 1883) Coxed Eights [2h1r2/3].
Scholes, Louis. (b.1880–d.1942) Single Sculls [2h1r2/4].
Taylor, Geoffrey Barron. (b.4 February 1890) Coxless Fours [2h1r1/2]; Coxed Eights [2h1r2/3].
Thomson, Julius A. (b.4 September 1882) Coxed Eights [2h1r2/3].
Toms, Frederick B. Coxless Pairs [2h1r1/2].
Wright, Joseph W. H. (b.14 January 1864–d.18 October 1950) Coxed Eights [2h1r2/3].

Shooting (Total: 22; Men: 22; Women: 0)
Beattie, George. (b.28 May 1877) Trap Shooting, Individual [2]; Trap Shooting, Team [2].
Brown, Stanley S. Free Rifle, 1,000 yards [=11].
Crowe, Charles Robert. (b.12 October 1867) Free Rifle, 1,000 yards [=9]; Military Rifle, Team [3].
Eastcott, William Merrill. (b.22 September 1883) Military Rifle, Team [3].
Elmitt, Fred F. Free Rifle, 1,000 yards [=28].
Ewing, Walter Henry. (b.1880) Trap Shooting, Individual [1]; Trap Shooting, Team [2].
Fletcher, Mylie E. Trap Shooting, Individual [=7]; Trap Shooting, Team [2].
Freeborn, James C. Free Rifle, 1,000 yards [27].
Jones, James M. Free Rifle, 1,000 yards [=28].
Kerr, S. Harry. Free Rifle, 1,000 yards [=6]; Military Rifle, Team [3].
Martin, Arthur. Free Rifle, 1,000 yards [33].
McInnis, Dugald.Free Rifle, 1,000 yards [=16]; Military Rifle, Team [3].
McMackon, Donald.Trap Shooting, Individual [=12]; Trap Shooting, Team [2].
Morris, Frank H. Free Rifle, 1,000 yards [=19].
Parker, Frank A. Trap Shooting, Individual [=27].
Rowe, George J. Free Rifle, 1,000 yards [=35].
Smith, William Albert. Military Rifle, Team [3].
Steele, J. Arthur. Free Rifle, 1,000 yards [37].
Utton, Frank W. Free Rifle, 1,000 yards [=9].
Vivian, George L. Trap Shooting, Individual [=20]; Trap Shooting, Team [2].
Westover, Arthur W. Trap Shooting, Individual [=5]; Trap Shooting, Team [2].
Williams, Bruce M. Military Rifle, Team [3].

Swimming (Total: 1; Men: 1; Women: 0)
Zimmerman, Robert M. (b.2 December 1881) 100 meter backstroke [3h3r1/3]; 100 meter freestyle [2h7r1/3]. [See also Diving].

Tennis (Total: 3; Men: 3; Women: 0)
Brown, Charles R. Singles (Lawn) [=5].
Foulkes, James F. Singles (Lawn) [=9]; Doubles (Lawn) [=7].
Powell, Richard B. Singles (Lawn) [=9]; Doubles (Lawn) [=7].

Wrestling (Total: 1; Men: 1; Women: 0)
Coté, Aubert. (b.1881) Bantamweight, Catch-as-Catch-Can [3].

Denmark (Total: 78; Men: 78; Women: 0)

Athletics (Track & Field) (Total: 8; Men: 8; Women: 0)
Agger, Harald.(b.11 April 1889–d.20 May 1954) Hammer Throw [ac].
Hansen, Rudy Constantin. (b.13 November 1888) Marathon [26].
Højme, Arne Halfdan Sigurd.(b.14 June 1884–d.17 April 1967) 3,500 meter walk [6h1r1/2]; 10 mile walk [dnfh1r1/2].
Jørgensen, Ferdinand Julius. (b.20 June 1880–d.3 October 1937) 5 miles [3h3r1/2]; Marathon [23].
Langkjær, Svend.(b.23 August 1886–d.2 May 1948) Standing High Jump [=8]; Standing Long Jump [ac].
Nielsen, Kjeld.(b.26 July 1887–d.14 February 1910) 1,500 meters [6h2r1/2]; 5 miles [4h2r1/2].
Petersen, Axel Johannes. (b.14 November 1880–d.23 May 1962) 100 meters [2h9r1/3].
Vestergaard, Charles Peter Martin. (b.10 April 1884–d.3 May 1956) 3,500 meter walk [6]; 10 mile walk [dnfh2r1/2].

Boxing (Total: 2; Men: 2; Women: 0)
Hansen, Hemming Emil. (b.2 May 1884–d.2 September 1964) Lightweight [=7].
Holberg, Valdemar. (b.29 May 1883–d.18 May 1927) Lightweight [=7].

Fencing (Total: 8; Men: 8; Women: 0)
Becker, Otto Christian. (b.31 December 1887–d.30 March 1970) Épée, Individual [=4p4r1/4]; Épée, Team [=5].
Jørgensen, Frantz Oscar. (b.3 August 1881–d.17 January 1973) Épée, Individual [5p9r1/4].
Krenchel, Harald.(b.28 May 1884–d.9 January 1922) Sabre, Individual [5p4r1/4].
Levison, Ejnar Herman. (b.15 May 1880–d.3 August 1970) Épée, Individual [5p1r2/4]; Épée, Team [=5].
Osiier, Ivan Joseph Martin. (b.16 December 1888–d.23 September 1965) Épée, Individual [=3p2r2/4]; Épée, Team [=5].
Østrup, Lauritz Christian. (b.6 June 1881–d.21 May 1940) Épée, Individual [=6p2r3/4]; Épée, Team [=5]; Sabre, Individual [6p2r3/4].
Sander, Herbert Stanley. (b.21 August 1879–d.18 November 1947) Épée, Individual [=4p2r1/4]; Épée, Team [=5].
Schwartz-Nielsen, Einar. (b.3 October 1883–d.10 March 1939) Sabre, Individual [4p8r2/4].

Football (Association Football [Soccer]) (Total: 13; Men: 13; Women: 0)

Andersen, Peter Marius. (b.25 April 1885–d.20 March 1972) [2].

Bohr, Harald August. (b.22 April 1887–d.22 January 1951) [2].

Drescher, Ludwig. (b.21 July 1881–d.14 July 1917) [2].

Gandil, Johannes. (b.21 May 1873–d.7 March 1956) [2].

Hansen, Harald.(b.14 March 1884–d.10 May 1927) [2].

Lindgren, August Ludvig. (b.1 August 1883–d.1 June 1945) [2].

Middelboe, Christian. (b.24 March 1881–d.20 May 1965) [2].

Middelboe, Nils. (b.5 October 1887–d.21 September 1976) [2].

Nielsen, Sofus Erhard.(b.15 March 1888–d.6 August 1963) [2].

Nielsen, Niels Christian Oscar. (b.4 October 1882–d.18 May 1941) [2]. (Later Niels Christian Oscar Nielsen-Nørlund [1914]).

Rasmussen, Bjørn Vilhelm Ravn. (b.19 May 1885–d.24 September 1962) [2].

von Buchwald, Charles. (b.22 October 1880–d.19 November 1951) [2].

Wolfhagen, Vilhelm. (b.11 November 1889–d.5 July 1958) [2].

Gymnastics (Total: 24; Men: 24; Women: 0)

Men

Andersen, Carl C. Combined Exercises, Team [4].

Bredmose, Hans. (b.28 March 1888–d.18 December 1958) Combined Exercises, Team [4].

Chiewitz, William Poul Jens. (b.1 January 1889–d.28 February 1965) Combined Exercises, Team [4].

Hansen, Arvor. (b.5 November 1886–d.19 June 1962) Combined Exercises, Team [4].

Hansen, Christian Marius. (b.24 September 1891–d.13 June 1961) Combined Exercises, Team [4].

Hansen, Ingvardt M. Combined Exercises, Team [4].

Hermann, Georg Richard Einar. (b.10 August 1878–d.7 September 1953) Combined Exercises, Team [4].

Holm, Knud Olaf. (b.2 January 1887–d.28 May 1972) Combined Exercises, Team [4].

Holm, Poul. (b.20 July 1888–d.29 October 1964) Combined Exercises, Team [4]. [See also Swimming].

Husted-Nielsen, Oluf. (b.9 December 1888–d.8 July 1972) Combined Exercises, Team [4].

Jensen, Charles Kristoffer Peter. (b.24 December 1885–d.5 June 1920) Combined Exercises, Team [4].

Jensen, Gorm Decem. (b.2 January 1886–d.1 January 1968) Combined Exercises, Team [4].

Johansen, Johan Hendrik. (b.19 April 1889–d.9 June 1948) Combined Exercises, Team [4].

Klem, Harald Robert Severin. (b.21 June 1884–d.24 July 1954) Combined Exercises, Team [4]. [See also Swimming].

Madsen, Robert Christian Klein. (b.13 December 1882–d.24 September 1954) Combined Exercises, Team [4].

Meulengracht-Madsen, Vigo. (b.13 November 1889–d.17 June 1979) Combined Exercises, Team [4].

Nielsen, Lukas Fredrik Christian. (b.23 December 1884–d.29 September 1964) Combined Exercises, Team [4].

Olsson, Oluf. (b.30 May 1873–d.25 June 1947) Combined Exercises, Team [4].

Petersen, Niels Knudsen. (b.12 July 1885–d.29 April 1961) Combined Exercises, Team [4].

Philipsen, Nicolai. (b.14 July 1880–d.3 March 1949) Combined Exercises, Team [4].

Rasmussen, Hendrik Andreas. (b.4 April 1887–d.5 August 1969) Combined Exercises, Team [4].

Rasmussen, Viktor Kristoffer. (b.10 January 1882–d.1 May 1956) Combined Exercises, Team [4].

Thuesen, Marius Laurits Theodor Jensen. (b.23 January 1878–d.12 July 1941) Combined Exercises, Team [4].

Turin-Nielsen, Niels Congo. (b.22 January 1889–d.25 December 1962) Combined Exercises, Team [4].

Women (Exhibition Only)

Bork, Anna Sofie. (b.6 March 1878–d.4 December 1949).

Boserup, Agnes Sofie. (b.4 June 1884–d.13 December 1970).

Briehm-Hansen, Inger Marie. (b.3 September 1887–d.12 January 1977).

Dalberg, Astrid Sciavitsky. (b.30 November 1881–d.27 April 1946).

Dujardin, Elise. (b.12 August 1885–d.26 April 1964).

Gad, Ernestine Georgia Gamél. (b.21 March 1884–d.8 April 1963).

Gad, Laura Gamél. (b.5 December 1880–d.16 May 1944).

Hansen, Sara.

Hertel, Sigrid Ingeborg. (b.13 May 1882–d.15 August 1975).

Køster, Emma Sofie. (b.22 June 1880–d.3 June 1944).

Liebetrau, Gerda. (b.29 September 1889–d.15 November 1938).

Michelsen, Marie. (b.8 April 1881–d.10 July 1954).

Neve, Clara Marie Camilla. (b.12 February 1886–d.31 August 1983).

Nielsen, Anna.

Nielsen, Estrid Agnete Ellen. (b.19 June 1882–d.21 November 1955).

Nielsen, Margrethe.

Otterstrøm, Caroline Sophie. (b.3 February 1880–d.24 September 1942).

Randrup, Ingeborg Johanne Louise. (b.7 September 1887–d.12 February 1955).

Rubin, Inger. (b.15 June 1884–d.18 May 1973).

Schrøder, Ester. (b.27 January 1876–d.18 March 1965).

Tscherning, Ellen Maggy. (b.13 May 1887–d.14 May 1953).

Wolfhagen, Ellen. (b.13 July 1885–d.30 March 1969).

Shooting (Total: 10; Men: 10; Women: 0)

Andersen, Niels. (b.14 May 1867–d.9 October 1930) Free Rifle, Team [4]; Military Rifle, Team [8].

Christensen, Niels Christian Olesen. (b.1 January 1871–d.18 May 1945) Free Rifle, 3 Positions [48]; Free Rifle, Team [4]; Military Rifle, Team [8].

Hillemann-Jensen, Julius. (b.27 October 1860–d.26 October 1930) Military Rifle, Team [8].

Jensen, Lorents Peter Martin. (b.16 November 1863–d.28 March 1928) Free Rifle, 3 Positions [51]; Military Rifle, Team [8].

Laursen, Niels. (b.11 April 1881–d.13 May 1944) Free Rifle, 3 Positions [33]; Military Rifle, Team [8].

Liebst, Poul Vilhelm. (b.13 November 1885–d.24 October 1984) Free Rifle, 3 Positions [42].

Madsen, Lars Jørgen. (b.19 July 1871–d.1 April 1925) Free Rifle, 3 Positions [14]; Free Rifle, Team [4].

Olsen, Ole. (b.7 July 1869–d.7 September 1944) Free Rifle, Team [4]; Military Rifle, Team [8].

Pedersen, Peter Christian. (b.18 August 1874–d.27 December 1957) Free Rifle, 3 Positions [18]; Free Rifle, Team [4].

Schultz, Hans Christian. (b.23 March 1864–d.26 June 1937) Free Rifle, 3 Positions [21]; Free Rifle, Team [4].

Swimming (Total: 5; Men: 5; Women: 0)

    Dam, Hans Peter Ludvig. (b.24 March 1884–d.29 March 1972) 100 meter backstroke [2]; 4 × 200 meter relay [2h1r1/2].

    Holm, Aage Vilhelm. (b.16 February 1890–d.4 October 1957) 400 meter freestyle [2h5r1/3].

    Holm, Poul. (b.20 July 1888–d.29 October 1964) 100 meter freestyle [ach3r1/3]; 4 × 200 meter relay [2h1r1/2]. [See also Gymnastics].

    Klem, Harald Robert Severin. (b.21 June 1884–d.24 July 1954) 100 meter freestyle [ach1r1/3]; 200 meter breaststroke [3h6r1/3]; 4 × 200 meter relay [2h1r1/2]. [See also Gymnastics].

    Saxtorph, Hjalmar Christen. (b.19 April 1883–d.24 April 1942) 100 meter freestyle [ach5r1/3]; 400 meter freestyle [ach7r1/3]; 4 × 200 meter relay [2h1r1/2].

Wrestling (Total: 10; Men: 10; Women: 0)

    Andersen, Anders Peter. (b.26 October 1881–d.19 February 1961) Middleweight, Greco-Roman [3].

    Carlsen, Carl Christian Peder. (b.1 July 1880–d.19 May 1958) Lightweight, Greco-Roman [=9].

    Carlsen, Christian Christoffer Schurmann. (b.18 September 1885–d.10 March 1961) Lightweight, Greco-Roman [=17].

    Christiansen, Jens Harald.(b.4 January 1884–d.1959) Light-Heavyweight, Greco-Roman [=17].

    Eriksen, Johannes Thorvald.(b.12 June 1889–d.25 June 1983) Middleweight, Greco-Roman [=5].

    Jensen, Carl Marinus. (b.13 September 1882–d.4 April 1942) Light-Heavyweight, Greco-Roman [3]; Heavyweight, Greco-Roman [=5].

    Jensen, Søren Marinus. (b.5 May 1879–d.6 January 1965) Heavyweight, Greco-Roman [3].

    Larsson, Karl Axel Andreas. (b.7 August 1885–d.30 June 1961) Middleweight, Greco-Roman [=5].

    Møller, Anders Carl Ferdinand.(b.22 February 1883–d.22 October 1966) Lightweight, Greco-Roman [=5].

    Nielsen, C. Henri. (b.*ca*1879) Light-Heavyweight, Greco-Roman [=17].

Finland (Total: 62; Men: 62; Women: 0)

Athletics (Track & Field) (Total: 15; Men: 15; Women: 0)

    Halme, Juho Waldemar. (né Juho Eliasson) (b.24 May 1888–d.1 February 1918) Triple Jump [ac]; Shot Put [ac]; Javelin Throw (freestyle) [9]; Javelin Throw (held in middle) [6].

    Jakobsson, Evert Brynolf. (b.16 February 1886–d.16 July 1960) Javelin Throw (freestyle) [ac]; Javelin Throw (held in middle) [ac].

    Jakobsson, Jarl Gustav Anian. (b.11 May 1880–d.28 January 1941) Standing Long Jump [ac]; Javelin Throw (freestyle) [ac]; Javelin Throw (held in middle) [ac].

    Järvinen, Verner. (b.4 March 1870–d.31 January 1941) Shot Put [ac]; Discus Throw (freestyle) [4]; Discus Throw (classical) [3]; Javelin Throw (freestyle) [ac].

    Kemp, Johan Valdemar. (b.1 July 1881–d.20 October 1941) Javelin Throw (freestyle) [ac]. [See also Gymnastics].

    Nieminen, Karl Maurits "Kalle." (b.26 April 1878–d.1946) Marathon [10].

    Niklander, Konstantin Elmer. (b.19 January 1890–d.12 November 1942) Shot Put [ac]; Discus Throw (freestyle) [ac]; Discus Throw (classical) [9].

    Pesonen, Armas Johannes. (b.25 March 1885–d.1947) Javelin Throw (freestyle) [6]; Javelin Throw (held in middle) [5].

Pihkala, Lauri "Tahko." (né Lauri Gummerus) (b.5 January 1888–d.20 May 1981) High Jump [=16]; Discus Throw (freestyle) [ac].

Salovaara, Aarne. (né Aarne Nylenius) (b.25 February 1887–d.11 September 1945) Discus Throw (freestyle) [ac]; Javelin Throw (freestyle) [ac]; Javelin Throw (held in middle) [4]. [See also Gymnastics].

Sauli, Jalmari Verner. (né Jalmari Saxolin) (b.17 August 1889–d.22 April 1957) Shot Put [7]; Discus Throw (freestyle) [ac]; Javelin Throw (freestyle) [8]; Javelin Throw (held in middle) [7].

Stenberg, Ragnar Olof Jakob. (b.14 June 1887–d.1954) 100 meters [5h7r1/3]; 200 meters [3h4r1/3].

Svanström, Aadolf Fredrik. (b.3 December 1885–d.17 April 1959) 800 meters [dnfh7r1/2]; 1,500 meters [3h5r1/2].

Wilskman, Lauri. (b.14 May 1887–d.25 November 1937) Discus Throw (freestyle) [ac].

Zilliacus, Bruno Wilhelm. (b.11 November 1877–d.3 July 1926) Shot Put [ac].

Diving (Total: 2; Men: 2; Women: 0)

Aro, Toivo Nestori. (b.9 February 1887–d.1962) Plain High Diving [3h1r2/3].

Wetzell, Oskar Wilhelm. (b.5 December 1888–d.1928) Plain High Diving [4h1r1/3]; Fancy High Diving [6h1r2/3].

Gymnastics (Total: 31; Men: 31; Women: 0)

Forsström, Eino Vilho. (b.10 April 1889–d.26 July 1961) Combined Exercises, Team [3].

Granström, Otto Emil. (b.4 October 1887–d.1 May 1941) Combined Exercises, Team [3].

Kemp, Johan Valdemar. (b.1 July 1881–d.20 October 1941) Combined Exercises, Team [3]. [See also Track & Field Athletics].

Korhonen, Aapeli Richard "Riku." (b.1883–d.1932) Combined Exercises, Individual [75].

Kosonen, Eetu. Combined Exercises, Individual [ac].

Kyykoski, Bert Ivar "Iivari." (b.16 February 1881–d.8 December 1959) Combined Exercises, Team [3].

Lehmusto, Heikki Heikinpoika. (b.30 August 1884–d.22 September 1958) Combined Exercises, Team [3].

Lindroth, John Hjalmar. (b.17 September 1883–d.24 July 1960) Combined Exercises, Team [3].

Linko, Yrjö. (b.1 February 1885–d.22 March 1934) Combined Exercises, Team [3].

Linna, Edvard Ferdinand.(b.26 August 1886–d.30 December 1974) Combined Exercises, Team [3].

Markkanen, Matti. (b.14 May 1887–d.2 April 1942) Combined Exercises, Team [3].

Mikkolainen, Kaarle "Källe." (b.9 January 1883–d.28 March 1928) Combined Exercises, Team [3].

Nieminen, Heikki Veli. (b.1 December 1886–d.1 April 1936) Combined Exercises, Team [3].

Paasia, Källe Kustaa. (b.28 August 1883–d.19 December 1961) Combined Exercises, Team [3].

Partanen, Ivar Aleksander "Iivari." (b.1880–d.1947) Combined Exercises, Individual [ac].

Pohjanpää, Arvi. (b.10 July 1887–d.21 December 1959) Combined Exercises, Team [3].

Pohjonen, Aarne Anders. (b.29 March 1886–d.22 December 1938) Combined Exercises, Team [3].

Railio, Johan Einar "Eino." (b.11 June 1886–d.3 February 1970) Combined Exercises, Team [3].

Riipinen, Heikki Aleksi "Åke." (b.28 May 1883–d.13 February 1957) Combined Exercises, Team [3].

Saarinen, Arno Aleksanteri. (b.11 September 1884–d.7 February 1970) Combined Exercises, Team [3].

Saarivuori, Johan Wilhelm "Jaska." (b.1888–d.1938) Combined Exercises, Individual [ac].

Sahlstein, Einar Werner. (b.30 May 1887–d.6 March 1936) Combined Exercises, Team [3].

Salovaara, Aarne. (b.25 February 1887–d.11 September 1945) Combined Exercises, Team [3]. [See also Athletics (Track & Field)].

Sandelin, Karl Viktor Torsten. (b.28 September 1887–d.8 May 1950) Combined Exercises, Team [3].

Sipilä, Elis Esaias. (b.2 March 1876–d.13 December 1958) Combined Exercises, Team [3].

Smeds, Viktor Reinhold.(b.18 September 1885–d.22 February 1957) Combined Exercises, Team [3].

Soinio, Kaarlo Kyösti. (b.28 January 1888–d.24 October 1960) Combined Exercises, Team [3].

Stenberg, Kurt Enoch. (b.11 July 1888–d.26 March 1936) Combined Exercises, Team [3].

Teivonen, David Toivo. (b.6 June 1889–d.1937) Combined Exercises, Individual [ac].

Tiiri, Väinö Edward.(b.31 January 1886–d.30 July 1966) Combined Exercises, Team [3].

Wegelius, Karl Magnus. (b.20 August 1884–d.9 December 1936) Combined Exercises, Team [3].

Shooting (Total: 9; Men: 9; Women: 0)

Hallamaa (Häyrén), Hugo Pietari "Heikki." (b.1867–d.1951) Free Rifle, 3 Positions [46].

Huttunen, Heikki. (b.26 September 1880–d.1947) Free Rifle, 3 Positions [38]; Free Rifle, Team [8].

Kolho (Saxberg), Lauri. (b.7 September 1886–d.1940) Free Rifle, 3 Positions [39].

Kolho (Saxberg), Voitto Valdemar. (b.6 February 1885–d.4 October 1963) Free Rifle, 3 Positions [17]; Free Rifle, Team [8].

Nässling, Emil Michael. (b.1864–d.1924) Free Rifle, 3 Positions [41]; Free Rifle, Team [8].

Nässling, Frans Reinhold.(b.1868–d.1933) Free Rifle, 3 Positions [30]; Free Rifle, Team [8].

Nyman, Gustav Rikhard.(b.12 October 1874–d.1952) Free Rifle, 3 Positions [44]; Free Rifle, Team [8].

Reilin, Karl Henrik Lorentz. (b.16 March 1874–d.1962) Free Rifle, 3 Positions [45].

Tuiskunen, Huvi Hjalmar. (b.22 July 1872–d.1930) Free Rifle, 3 Positions [37]; Free Rifle, Team [8].

Swimming (Total: 3; Men: 3; Women: 0)

Cederberg, Herman Edvard.(b.7 September 1883–d.1969) 200 meter breaststroke [ach2r1/3].

Henrikssen, John Gustav. (b.1883–d.1948) 100 meter backstroke [3h2r1/3]; 200 meter breaststroke [3h5r1/3].

Jonsson, Hugo Alarik. (b.1884–d.1949) 100 meter backstroke [3h1r1/3]; 200 meter breaststroke [dnfh6r1/3].

Wrestling (Total: 4; Men: 4; Women: 0)

Kivimäki, Johan Richard "Jussi." (b.1885–d.1976) Light-Heavyweight, Greco-Roman [=9].

Lindén (Linko), Arvo Leander. (b.27 February 1887–d.18 March 1941) Lightweight, Greco-Roman [3].

Saarela, Yrjö Erik Mikael. (b.13 July 1884–d.30 June 1951) Light-Heavyweight, Greco-Roman [2].

Weckman, Johan Verner. (b.26 July 1882–d.22 February 1968) Light-Heavyweight, Greco-Roman [1].

France (Total: 208; Men: 208; Women: 0)

Archery (Total: 15; Men: 15; Women: 0)
Aubras, Charles. Continental Style [4].
Baudoin, E. Double York round [25]; Continental Style [10].
Berton, H. Double York round [16]; Continental Style [8].
Cabaret, Gustave. Double York round [26]; Continental Style [3].
Dauchez, Albert. Double York round [23]; Continental Style [6].
de la Croix, L. S. Continental Style [14].
Fisseux, Émile. Continental Style [13].
Grisot, Eugène G. Double York round [19]; Continental Style [1].
Jay, O. Continental Style [17].
Poupart, A. Double York round [27]; Continental Style [16].
Quervel, Charles. Double York round [24]; Continental Style [5].
Richez, Eugène. (b.5 August 1864) Double York round [17]; Continental Style [9].
Salingne, L. A. Double York round [22]; Continental Style [7].
Vallie, C. Continental Style [11].
Vernet, Louis. Double York round [20]; Continental Style [2].

Athletics (Track & Field) (Total: 19; Men: 19; Women: 0)
André, Georges Ivan. (b.13 August 1889–d.4 May 1943) High Jump [=2]; Standing High Jump [=5].
Bonniot de Fleurac, Louis N. de L. (b.19 November 1876–d.23 March 1965) 1,500 meters [6h1r1/2]; 3,200 meter steeplechase [dnfh2r1/2]; 3-mile team race [3].
Bouin, Jean. (b.28 December 1888–d.29 September 1914) 1,500 meters [2h7r1/2]; 3-mile team race [3].
Dreher, Joseph. 1,500 meters [5h4r1/2]; 3-mile team race [3].
Dubois, O. Georges. 400 meter hurdles [dnfh6r1/3].
Fayollat, Armand Alexandre. (b.4 October 1889) 3-mile team race [2h2r1/2].
Guttierez, Henri. Long Jump [ac].
Jardin, Henri Alphonse. (b.23 June 1881) Standing High Jump [ac]; Standing Long Jump [ac].
Koeger, G. Pole Vault [=12].
Lagarde, Charles. (b.13 September 1878) Shot Put [ac]; Discus Throw (freestyle) [ac].
Lamotte, G. 100 meters [3h11r11/3].
Lescat, L. 100 meters [3h6r1/3].
Lizandier, Paul. (b.2 December 1884) 5 miles [4h4r1/2]; 3-mile team race [3].
Malfait, Georges W. (b.9 December 1878) 100 meters [2h3r1/3]; 200 meters [3h4r2/3]; 400 meters [4h3r2/3].
Meslot, Henri. (b.1884) 100 meters [3h13r1/3]; 200 meters [2h15r1/3]; 400 meter hurdles [2h12r1/3].
Motte, Alfred.(b.2 June 1887) Standing High Jump [=5]; Standing Long Jump [ac].
Pascarel, Robert. (b.1888) Pole Vault [=10].
Ragueneau, A. Gaston. (b.10 October 1881–d.14 July 1978) 1,500 meters [dnfh5r1/2]; 5 miles [dnfh1r1/2]; 3,200 meter steeplechase [dnfh1r1/2].
Tison, André. (b.26 February 1885) Shot Put [ac]; Discus Throw (freestyle) [8].

Boxing (Total: 7; Men: 7; Women: 0)
Aspa, Gaston. Middleweight [=6].
Bouvier, André. Lightweight [=7].

Constant, Louis. Featherweight [=5].
Doudelle, René. Middleweight [=6].
Mazior, Pierre. Bantamweight [=4].
Morard, Charles. Middleweight [=6].
Poillot, Etienne. Featherweight [=5].

Cycling (Total: 23; Men: 23; Women: 0)
Auffray, André. (b.1884–d.4 November 1953) One Lap Match Sprint [2h3r2/3]; 1,000 meters Match Sprint [3h4r2/3]; 5,000 meters [3]; Tandem Sprint [1]; Team Pursuit [5].
Avrillon, C. 20 km. [2h6r1/2]; 100 km. [dnfh2r1/2]; Tandem Sprint [2h3r1/3].
Baumler, Henri. 20 km. [5h4r1/2].
Bonnet, François. 20 km. [ac-final]; 100 km. [dnf-final]; Tandem Sprint [4h2r2/3].
Cunault, H. 20 km. [ach3r1/2]; 100 km. [dnfh2r1/2].
Delaplane, Gaston. (b.6 March 1882–d.13 December 1977) One Lap Match Sprint [3h8r1/2]; 1,000 meters Match Sprint [2h15r1/3]; 5,000 meters [ach5r1/2].
Demangel, Émile. (b.20 June 1882–d.20 October 1968) One Lap Match Sprint [2]; 1,000 meters Match Sprint [2h3r2/3]; 5,000 meters [dqh2r1/2]; Team Pursuit [5].
Dreyfus, G. One Lap Match Sprint [2h14r1/2]; 1,000 meters Match Sprint [4h8r1/3]; 5,000 meters [4h6r1/2]; Tandem Sprint [2h7r1/3].
Guyader, J. Tandem Sprint [2h3r1/3].
Hostein, Pierre. 20 km. [ach1r1/2]; 100 km. [dnfh2r1/2].
Lapize, André. 20 km. [4h1r1/2].
Lapize, Octave. (b.10 July 1889–d.14 July 1917) 20 km. [ac-final]; 100 km. [3]; Tandem Sprint [4h2r2/3].
Lepere, André. (b.1878) 100 km. [ach1r1/2].
Lutz, G. C. 20 km. [4h2r1/2]; 100 km. [dnf-final].
Madelaine, J. 100 km. [dnfh2r1/2].
Marechal, Émile One Lap Match Sprint [3h11r1/2]; 1,000 meters Match Sprint [2h12r1/3]; 5,000 meters [4]; Team Pursuit [5].
Perrin, G. One Lap Match Sprint [2h10r1/2]; 1,000 meters Match Sprint [dq-h16r1/3]; 5,000 meters [ach7r1/2].
Poulain, André. One Lap Match Sprint [2h12r1/2]; 1,000 meters Match Sprint [2h2r1/3]; 5,000 meters [ach4r1/2]; Tandem Sprint [2h7r1/3].
Schilles, Maurice. (b.25 February 1888–d.22 December 1950) One Lap Match Sprint [dnfh5r1/3]; 1,000 meters Match Sprint [dq-final]; 5,000 meters [2]; Tandem Sprint [1]; Team Pursuit [5].
Seginaud, Pierre. One Lap Match Sprint [3h2r1/2]; 1,000 meters Match Sprint [2h4r1/3]; 5,000 meters [4h1r1/2].
Texier, Maurice. Tandem Sprint [2h2r1/3].
Texier, Pierre. One Lap Match Sprint [3h1r2/3]; 1,000 meters Match Sprint [4h1r2/3]; 5,000 meters [3h4r1/2]; 20 km. [dnfh5r1/2]; 100 km. [5]; Tandem Sprint [2h2r1/3].
Villepontoux, R. One Lap Match Sprint [3h4r1/2]; 1,000 meters Match Sprint [2h7r1/3]; 5,000 meters [ach5r1/2].

Fencing (Total: 22; Men: 22; Women: 0)
Alibert, Gaston. (b.1883–d.26 December 1917) Épée, Individual [1]; Épée, Team [1].
Berger, Henri-Georges. Épée, Individual [=5p1r3/4]; Épée, Team [1].
Chapuis, Louis Émile. Sabre, Individual [4p12r1/4].
Collignon, Charles Henri. Épée, Individual [=3p6r2/4]; Épée, Team [1].

de la Falaise, Georges. (b.1870–d.1910) Sabre, Individual [=7]; Sabre, Team [4].

de Lesseps, Bernard.Sabre, Individual [8p1r3/4]; Sabre, Team [4].

de Lesseps, Ignace. Sabre, Individual [=5p7r1/4].

de Mas Latrie, Jean. (b.23 November 1879) Sabre, Individual [4p1r1/4].

de St. Brisson, Jacques. Sabre, Individual [6p9r1/4].

Dubordieu, Frédéric. Épée, Individual [=4p7r1/4].

Gravier, Bernard.Épée, Individual [=3p4r2/4]; Épée, Team [1].

Langevin, Georges Octave. Sabre, Individual [4p5r1/4].

Lateux, René. Sabre, Individual [5p1r2/4].

Lippmann, Alexandre. (b.1880) Épée, Individual [2]; Épée, Team [1].

Marais, Joseph Cyril. Épée, Individual [5p4r2/4].

Mikorski, Jean. Sabre, Individual [8p10r1/4].

Olivier, Eugène Victor. Épée, Individual [3]; Épée, Team [1].

Perrodon, Marc Marie Jean. (b.1878) Sabre, Individual [4p13r1/4]; Sabre, Team [4].

Quenessen, René. Épée, Individual [=3p8r2/4].

Renaud, Jean-Joseph. (b.1872–d.7 December 1953) Sabre, Individual [4p3r1/4]; Sabre, Team [4].

Rodocanachi, Jacques André. Épée, Individual [=3p2r2/4].

Stern, Jean. Épée, Individual [5p2r3/4]; Épée, Team [1].

Football (Association Football [Soccer]) (Total: 22; Men: 22; Women: 0)

Albert, Yves. [=5].

Bayrou, Georges. (b.21 December 1883) [=5].

Bilot, Charles. [=5].

Cypres, Gaston. [=5].

Dastarac, Serge. [=5].

Denis, Victor. [=5].

Desrousseaux, François. [=5].

Dubly, Jules. [=5].

Eucher, Marcel. [=5].

Fenouillere, Jean. [=5].

Filez, Adrien. (b.27 August 1885) [=5].

François, Albert. [=5].

Holgart, H. [=5].

Jenicot, Fernand.[=5].

Mathaux, P. [=5].

Morillon, E. [=5].

Renaux, C. [=5].

Sartorius, Émile. [=5].

Schubart, Roland.[=5].

Tillette, Maurice. [=5].

Verlet, Jules. [=5].

Wibaut, V. [=5].

Gymnastics (Total: 59; Men: 59; Women: 0)

Bogart, Lucien. Combined Exercises, Team [5].

Boisléve, Edouard E. Combined Exercises, Individual [ac].

Borizée, Albert. Combined Exercises, Team [5].

Castigliano, Jean. Combined Exercises, Individual [20].

Castille, Alfred.Combined Exercises, Individual [ac].

Castille, Ferdinand.Combined Exercises, Individual [ac].

Charmoille, Georges. Combined Exercises, Individual [ac].

Constant, Nicolas. Combined Exercises, Team [5].

Costa, Antoine. (b.23 October 1884) Combined Exercises, Individual [14].

Courtois, Charles Albert. Combined Exercises, Team [5].

de Breyne, Henri. Combined Exercises, Team [5].

Delattre, Louis. Combined Exercises, Team [5].

Delecluse, A. Combined Exercises, Team [5].

Delecluse, Louis. Combined Exercises, Team [5].

Demarle, Georges. Combined Exercises, Team [5].

Derov, Joseph. Combined Exercises, Team [5].

Desmarcheliers, Charles. Combined Exercises, Team [5].

Desmarcheliers, Claude. Combined Exercises, Team [5].

Dharaney, Étienne. Combined Exercises, Team [5].

Diaz, Robert. Combined Exercises, Individual [8].

Donnet, Gérard.Combined Exercises, Team [5].

Dubois, Victor. Combined Exercises, Individual [ac].

Duhamel, Émile. Combined Exercises, Team [5].

Duponcheel, A. Combined Exercises, Team [5].

Durin, Paul Joseph. (b.3 January 1890) Combined Exercises, Team [5].

Eggremont, A. Combined Exercises, Team [5].

Follacci, Dominique. (b.18 May 1879) Combined Exercises, Individual [ac].

Gauthier, E. Combined Exercises, Individual [ac].

Guiot, G. Combined Exercises, Team [5].

Hennebicq, L. Combined Exercises, Team [5].

Hubert, Henri. Combined Exercises, Team [5].

Hudels, Daniel. Combined Exercises, Team [5].

Labitte, E. Combined Exercises, Team [5].

Lalu, Marcel. (b.24 March 1882) Combined Exercises, Individual [7].

Lekim, F. Combined Exercises, Individual [ac].

Lestienne, L. Combined Exercises, Team [5].

Lis, R. Combined Exercises, Team [5].

Lux, Justinien. Combined Exercises, Individual [ac].

Magnier, Victor. Combined Exercises, Team [5].

Mounier, G. Combined Exercises, Individual [ac].

Nidal, François. Combined Exercises, Individual [11].

Nys, G. Combined Exercises, Team [5].

Pappe, Louis. Combined Exercises, Team [5].

Parent, Joseph. Combined Exercises, Team [5].

Pinoy, Antoine. Combined Exercises, Team [5].

Polidori, V. Combined Exercises, Team [5].

Pottier, Gustave. Combined Exercises, Team [5].

Ratelot, Georges. Combined Exercises, Individual [ac].

Rolland, Jules. Combined Exercises, Individual [10].

Sandray, Louis. Combined Exercises, Team [5].

Schmoll, Émile. Combined Exercises, Team [5].

Ségura, B.Louis. (b.23 July 1889) Combined Exercises, Individual [3].

Steffe, Edouard.Combined Exercises, Team [5].

Thurnheer, Georges. Combined Exercises, Individual [18].
Vercruysse, E. Combined Exercises, Team [5].
Vergin, Hugo. Combined Exercises, Team [5].
Vicogne, E. Combined Exercises, Team [5].
Walmée, Jules. Combined Exercises, Team [5].
Warlouzer, G. Combined Exercises, Team [5].

Hockey (Field) (Total: 12; Men: 12; Women: 0)
Aublin, R. P. [6].
Baidet, D.[6].
Benoit, R. [6].
Bonnal, André. [6].
Gautier, L. [6].
Girard, D.M. [6].
Pattin, C. [6].
Poupon, L. [6].
Roux, F. [6].
Salarnier, René. [6].
Saulnier, L. [6].
Versini, F. [6].

Motorboating (Total: 1; Men: 1; Women: 0)
Thubron, Emile B. Class A [1].

Shooting (Total: 20; Men: 20; Women: 0)
Angelini, André. Free Rifle, 3 Positions [34]; Free Rifle, 1,000 yards [23].
Balme, Eugène. Free Rifle, Team [3]; Military Rifle, Team [4].
Barbillat, André. Free Pistol [6]; Free Pistol, Team [4]; Running Deer, Single Shot, Individual [15].
Béjot, Emile. Trap Shooting, Individual [23].
Bonnefoy, Henri. Small-Bore Rifle, Prone [19]; Small-Bore Rifle, Team [3].
Colas, Paul René. (b.6 May 1880) Free Rifle, 3 Positions [25]; Free Rifle, 1,000 yards [=28]; Small-Bore Rifle, Team [3].
Courquin, Albert. (b.1875) Free Rifle, Team [3]; Military Rifle, Team [4].
de Boigne, Raoul. (b.25 December 1862) Free Rifle, 1,000 yards [=19]; Free Rifle, Team [3]; Military Rifle, Team [4].
Depassis, Jean. Free Pistol [22]; Free Pistol, Team [4].
Hecht, Léon. Free Rifle, 1,000 yards [=35]; Military Rifle, Team [4].
Johnson, Léon. (b.28 February 1876–d.1943) Free Rifle, 3 Positions [8]; Free Rifle, Team [3]; Small-Bore Rifle, Disappearing Target [21]; Small-Bore Rifle, Moving Target [=10].
Lecoq, Maurice. (b.26 March 1854) Free Rifle, 3 Positions [31]; Free Rifle, Team [3].
Lécuyer, Léon. (b.8 April 1855) Free Pistol [30]; Small-Bore Rifle, Team [3].
Mercier, André. Small-Bore Rifle, Disappearing Target [=19]; Small-Bore Rifle, Moving Target [14]; Small-Bore Rifle, Prone [13].
Mérillon, Daniel. (b.29 June 1852) Free Rifle, 1,000 yards [38]; Military Rifle, Team [4].
Moreaux, Léon. (b.1862) Free Pistol [17]; Free Pistol, Team [4]; Free Rifle, 1,000 yards [39].
Parmentier, André. (b.29 May 1876) Free Rifle, Team [3]; Military Rifle, Team [4].
Regaud, André. (b.13 February 1868) Free Pistol [10]; Free Pistol, Team [4]; Small-Bore Rifle, Team [3].

Robion du Pont, Maurice. Free Pistol [34]; Running Deer, Double Shot, Individual [14]; Running Deer, Single Shot, Individual [14].

Tétart, Léon. Free Rifle, 1,000 yards [48]; Running Deer, Double Shot, Individual [12]; Running Deer, Single Shot, Individual [13]; Small-Bore Rifle, Disappearing Target [22]; Small-Bore Rifle, Moving Target [=15]; Small-Bore Rifle, Prone [17].

Swimming (Total: 4; Men: 4; Women: 0)

André, René. 100 meter freestyle [ach5r1/3].

Decoin, Henri. (b.18 March 1890) 400 meter freestyle [dnfh1r1/3].

Meister, Gérard.(b.4 September 1889) 100 meter freestyle [ach2r1/3].

Theuriet, André A. G. (b.30 March 1887) 1,500 meter freestyle [3h4r1/3].

Tennis (Total: 1; Men: 1; Women: 0)

Germot, Maurice. (b.17 November 1882–d.6 August 1958) Singles (Lawn) [=5].

Yachting (Total: 3; Men: 3; Women: 0)

Arthus, Henri. 6-meter class [3].

Potheau, Louis A. 6-meter class [3].

Rabot, Pierre. 6-meter class [3].

Germany (Total: 83; Men: 81; Women: 2)

Athletics (Track & Field) (Total: 20; Men: 20; Women: 0)

Bechler, Carl. (b.15 February 1886) 100 meters [2h17r1/3]; Javelin Throw (held in middle) [ac].

Braun, Hanns. (b.26 October 1886–d.9 October 1918) 800 meters [3]; 1,500 meters [3h8r1/2]; 1,600 meter medley relay [2].

Breynck, Andreas. (b.4 July 1890–d.12 July 1957) 800 meters [2h6r1/2]; 1,500 meters [2h6r1/2].

Eicke, Hans. (b.1 December 1885–d.22 August 1947) 100 meters [3h7r1/3]; 1,600 meter medley relay [2].

Fischer, Paul. (b.1881–d.*ca.*1939–1945) 100 meters [dnfh10r1/3]. [See also Gymnastics].

Gunia, Paul. (b.27 February 1885–d.1 December 1954) 3,500 meter walk [4h1r1/2]; 10 mile walk [7h1r1/2].

Hesse, Arno. (b.1887) 1,500 meters [7h2r1/2].

Hoffmann, Arthur E. "Aute." (b.10 December 1887–d.4 April 1932) 100 meters [3h3r1/3]; 200 meters [2h13r1/3]; 1,600 meter medley relay [2]; Long Jump [15].

Kohlmey, Wilhelm "Willy." (b.19 July 1881–d.9 September 1953) 100 meters [3h15r1/3].

Mallwitz, Arthur. (b.15 June 1880–d.20 May 1968) Standing High Jump [=8]; Standing Long Jump [ac].

Nettelbeck, Franz Paul. (b.23 April 1889–d.14 August 1963) 5 miles [5h3r1/2].

Quarg, M. Oskar. (b.15 September 1887) 800 meters [4h5r1/2].

Rehder, Heinrich. (b.24 April 1887) 100 meters [3h8r1/3].

Reiser, Ferdinand "Fritz." (b.1875) Marathon [dnf].

Trieloff, Otto P. (b.17 November 1885–d.6 July 1967) 400 meters [2h14r1/3]; 1,600 meter medley relay [2].

Uettwiller, Octav Lucian "Ludwig." (b.28 November 1886–d.25 June 1949) Broad Jump [ac]; Standing High Jump [=17]; Discus Throw (freestyle) [ac]; Hammer Throw [ac]; Javelin Throw (freestyle) [ac].

von Bönninghausen, Hermann. (b.24 July 1888–d.26 January 1919) 100 meters [5h14r1/3]; Long Jump [ac].

Weinstein, George Albert "Berti." (b.13 October 1885–d.17 December 1969) Long Jump [7].

Welz, Emil. (b.5 April 1879) Discus Throw (freestyle) [11]; Javelin Throw (freestyle) [ac].

Wilhelm, Richard.(b.1888–d.1917) 3,500 meter walk [6].

Cycling (Total: 8; Men: 8; Women: 0)

Boldt, Alwin. (b.19 March 1884–d.1920) 20 km. [ach4r1/2]; 100 km. [ach1r1/2]; Tandem Sprint [2h1r1/3].

Götze, Bruno. (b.23 June 1882–d.28 May 1913) One Lap Match Sprint [3h10r1/2]; 1,000 meters Match Sprint [3h12r1/3]; 5,000 meters [4h3r1/2]; 100 km. [dnfh2r1/2].

Götze, Max. (b.13 October 1880–d.29 October 1944) 5,000 meters [ach5r1/2]; Tandem Sprint [3h1r2/3]; Team Pursuit [2].

Katzer, Richard.(b.1888) One Lap Match Sprint [2h3r1/2]; 5,000 meters [ach7r1/2]; 20 km. [ach1r1/2]; 100 km. [dnfh1r1/2]; Team Pursuit [2].

Martens, Hermann. (b.16 April 1877–d.1916) One Lap Match Sprint [2h7r1/2]; 1,000 meters Match Sprint [dq-h6r1/3]; 5,000 meters [2h3r1/2]; 20 km. [2h1r1/2]; 100 km. [dnfh2r1/2]; Team Pursuit [2].

Neumer, Karl. (b.23 February 1887–d.16 May 1984) One Lap Match Sprint [3]; 1,000 meters Match Sprint [2h1r2/3]; 5,000 meters [2h5r1/2]; Tandem Sprint [3h1r2/3]; Team Pursuit [2].

Schulze, Paul. One Lap Match Sprint [3h13r1/2]; 1,000 meters Match Sprint [3h4r1/3]; 20 km. [ach2r1/2]; 100 km. [dnfh2r1/2].

Triebsch, Max. (b.22 July 1885) 20 km. [5h3r1/2]; 100 km. [dnfh2r1/2]; Tandem Sprint [2h1r1/3].

Diving (Total: 5; Men: 5; Women: 0)

Behrens, Kurt. (b.26 November 1884–d.5 February 1928) Fancy High Diving [2].

Freyschmidt, Heinrich "Heinz." (b.20 July 1887) Fancy High Diving [4h1r2/3]; Plain High Diving [5h2r2/3].

Nicolai, Fritz. (b.11 February 1879–d.7 March 1946) Plain High Diving [5h5r1/3]; Fancy High Diving [3h2r2/3].

Walz, Gottlob. (b.29 June 1881–d.1943) Fancy High Diving [=3].

Zürner, Albert. (b.30 January 1890–d.18 July 1920) Fancy High Diving [1].

Fencing (Total: 10; Men: 10; Women: 0)

Adam, Johannes. (b.1871) Épée, Individual [=4p3r1/4]; Sabre, Individual [5p2r1/4].

Erckrath de Bary, Jacob. (b.10 March 1864–d.14 August 1938) Épée, Individual [=5p8r1/4]; Épée, Team [=5]; Sabre, Individual [=5p7r1/4]; Sabre, Team [=5].

Jack, Friedrich "Fritz." (b.26 December 1879–d. 15 May 1960) Épée, Individual [=6p2r1/4]; Sabre, Individual [5p2r2/4]; Sabre, Team [=5].

Krünert, Robert. Épée, Individual [=7p5r1/4]; Sabre, Individual [=4p8r1/4]; Sabre, Team [=5].

Lichtenfels, Julius. (b.19 May 1884–d.29 June 1968) Épée, Individual [=4p13r1/4]; Épée, Team [=5]; Sabre, Individual [4p4r1/4].

Moldenhauer, Ernst. Épée, Individual [=4p10r1/4]; Sabre, Individual [5p11r1/4].

Naumann, Albert. (b.1875) Épée, Individual [=5p6r1/4]; Sabre, Individual [6p12r1/4].

Petri, August. (b.1878) Épée, Individual [=6p9r1/4]; Épée, Team [=5]; Sabre, Individual [3p7r2/4]; Sabre, Team [=5].

Schön, Emil. (b.4 August 1872–d.29 January 1945) Épée, Individual [=4p7r1/4]; Sabre, Individual [4p5r2/4].

Stöhr, Georg. (b.25 August 1885–d.31 March 1977) Épée, Individual [6p1r1/4]; Épée, Team [=5]; Sabre, Individual [=6p10r1/4].

Figure Skating (Total: 3; Men: 1; Women: 2)

Women

Hübler, Anna. (b.2 January 1885–d.5 July 1976) Pairs [1].

Rendschimdt, Else. (b.11 January 1886–d.9 October 1969) Ladies' Individual [2].

Men

Burger, Heinrich. (b.31 May 1881–d.27 April 1942) Pairs [1].

Gymnastics (Total: 11; Men: 11; Women: 0)

Borchert, Karl. (b.1884) Combined Exercises, Individual [=12].

Ehrlich, August. (b.1883) Combined Exercises, Individual [ac].

Fischer, Paul. (b.1881–d.*ca*.1939–1940) Combined Exercises, Individual [ac]. [See also Track & Field Athletics].

Karth, Georg. (b.1884) Combined Exercises, Individual [ac].

Kaufmann, Wilhelm. (b.17 February 1872) Combined Exercises, Individual [ac].

Körting, Carl. (b.1881) Combined Exercises, Individual [ac].

Krämer, Josef. (b.4 May 1878–d.20 January 1954) Combined Exercises, Individual [ac].

Siebenhaar, Heinrich. (b.1883) Combined Exercises, Individual [ac].

Steuernagel, Curt. (b.1886–d.30 July 1918) Combined Exercises, Individual [4].

Weber, Wilhelm. (b.1880–d.28 April 1963) Combined Exercises, Individual [ac].

Wolf, Friedrich "Fritz." (b.21 January 1880–d.27 August 1961) Combined Exercises, Individual [5].

Hockey (Field) (Total: 11; Men: 11; Women: 0)

Brehm, Alfons. (b.16 July 1882–d. 7 December 1968) [5].

Dauelsberg, Elard.[5].

Diederichsen, Franz. [5].

Ebert, Carl. (b.3 February 1889) [5].

Fehr, Jules W. [5].

Galvao, Mauricio. (b.21 January 1890–d.March 1945) [5].

Galvao, Raulino. (d. circa 1960) [5].

Möding, Fritz. [5].

Rahe, Friedrich Wilhelm. (b.16 April 1888–d.18 February 1949) [5]. [See also Tennis (Lawn)].

Stüdemann, Albert. [5].

Uhl, Friedrich Conrad. (b.31 May 1882–d.6 June 1953) [5].

Rowing & Sculling (Total: 3; Men: 3; Women: 0)

Düskow, Willy. Coxless Pairs [2h2r1/2].

Stahnke, Martin. (b.11 November 1888) Coxless Pairs [2h2r1/2].

von Gaza, Bernhard.(b.6 May 1881–d.25 September 1917) Single Sculls [dnfh2r3/4].

Shooting (Total: 1; Men: 1; Women: 0)

Wagner-Hohenlobbese, Erich. (b.1873) Free Rifle, 1,000 yards [49].

Swimming (Total: 5; Men: 5; Women: 0)

Aurisch, Gustav. 100 meter backstroke [4].

Bieberstein, Arno. (b.17 October 1886–d.4 October 1918) 100 meter backstroke [1].

Ritter, Richard Max. (b.7 November 1886–d.24 May 1974) 100 meter backstroke [3h1r2/3].

Rösler, Richard.(b.1881–d.1969) 200 meter breaststroke [2h1r1/3].

Seidel, Erich. (b.1884) 200 meter breaststroke [3h1r2/3].

Tennis (Total: 5; Men: 5; Women: 0)

Froitzheim, Otto. (b.24 April 1884–d.29 October 1962) Singles (Lawn) [2]; Doubles (Lawn) [=7].

Kreuzer, Oscar. (b.14 June 1887–d.3 May 1968) Singles (Lawn) [=16]; Doubles (Lawn) [=11].

Rahe, Friedrich Wilhelm. (b.16 April 1888–d.18 February 1949) Singles (Lawn) [=26]; Doubles (Lawn) [=11]. [See also Hockey (Field)].

Schomburgk, Heinrich. (b.30 June 1885–d.29 March 1965) Singles (Lawn) [=16]; Doubles (Lawn) [=7].

von Bissing, Moritz F. (b.9 September 1886–d.18 March 1954) Singles (Lawn) [=9].

Wrestling (Total: 1; Men: 1; Women: 0)

Grundmann, Wilhelm. Middleweight, Greco-Roman [=17].

Great Britain (Total: 736; Men: 697; Women: 39)

Archery (Total: 41; Men: 16; Women: 25)

Men

Backhouse, Robert Ormston. (b.1854–d.10 April 1940) Double York round [13]; Continental Style [unofficial competitor].

Bagnall-Oakley, R. H. Double York round [21]; Continental Style [unofficial competitor].

Bridges, John Henry. (b.26 March 1852–d.12 February 1925) Double York round [5]; Continental Style [unofficial competitor].

Brooks-King, Reginald. (b.1861–d.19 September 1938) Double York round [2].

Coates, Charles Hutton. (b.4 May 1857–d.15 February 1922) Double York round [18].

Cornewall, Geoffrey. (b.7 May 1869–d.21 January 1951) Double York round [15]; Continental Style [unofficial competitor].

Dod, William. (b.18 July 1867–d.8 October 1954) Double York round [1].

Heathcote, Robert Webster. (b.28 December 1864) Double York round [14]; Continental Style [unofficial competitor].

James, Harold Vaughan. Double York round [6].

Keene, Charles John Perry. (b.1864–d.29 November 1926) Double York round [10].

Keyworth, John Bunyan. (b.9 May 1859–d.24 February 1954) Double York round [9]; Continental Style [12].

Nesham, Hugh Percy. (b.1877–d.26 June 1923) Double York round [8]; Continental Style [unofficial competitor].

Penrose, John. (b.5 May 1850–d.21 April 1932) Double York round [4].

Pownall, Capel George Pett. (b.1869–d.8 February 1933) Double York round [11]; Continental Style [unofficial competitor].

Robinson, Theodore. Double York round [7].

Stopford, John Thomas Sarsfield. Double York round [12]; Continental Style [unofficial competitor].

Women

Appleyard, Gertrude. (b.1865–d.9 June 1917) Double National round [=11].

Armitage, Mrs. S. H. Double National round [6].

Babington, Mrs. S. C. Double National round [18].

Cadman, Christine. Double National round [19].

Day, Doris E. Hermitage. (b.1878) Double National round [16].

Dod, Charlotte "Lottie." (b.24 September 1871–d.27 June 1960) Double National round [2].

Foster, Mrs. C. Priestley. Double National round [7].

Hill-Lowe, Beatrice Geraldine Ruxton. (Ireland) Double National round [3].

Honnywill, Mrs. G. W. H. Double National round [5].

Hyde, Martina Esther. (b.1866–d.17 May 1937) Double National round [20].

Leonard, Mrs. Everett. Double National round [21].

Mudge, K. G. Double National round [17].

Newall, Sybil Fenton "Queenie." (b.17 October 1854–d.24 June 1929) Double National round [1].

Nott Bower, Mrs. E.. Double National round [=11].

Robertson, Mrs. Norman. Double National round [13].

Rushton, Mrs. H. Double National round [24].

Thackwell, Albertine Anne. (b.1862–d.22 September 1944) Double National round [15].

Vance, J. Double National round [23].

Wadworth, Jessie Ellen. (b.1864–d.8 July 1936) Double National round [4].

Wadworth, Mary. Double National round [9].

Weedon, Margaret Kate. (b.1854–d.19 October 1930) Double National round [14].

Whetham, Mrs. Boddam. Double National round [10].

Williams, Hilda. Double National round [25].

Wilson, Lillian Sarah. (b.1864–d.1 March 1909) Double National round [8].

Wood, Ina. Double National round [22].

Athletics (Track & Field) (Total: 126; Men: 126; Women: 0)

Ahearne, Timothy J. (Ireland) (b.18 August 1885–d.December 1968) 110 meter hurdles [4h3r2/3]; Long Jump [8]; Triple Jump [1]; Standing Long Jump [ac].

Appleby, Frederick. (b.30 October 1879–d.7 April 1956) Marathon [dnf].

Ashford, Frederick Murray. (b.28 September 1886–d.29 September 1945) 800 meters [dnfh1r1/2].

Astley, Arthur. (d.1916) 400 meters [2h9r1/3]; 800 meters [2h5r1/2].

Barker, Henry. 3,200 meter steeplechase [dnfh3r1/2].

Barnes, Ernest. Marathon [13].

Barrett, Edward. (Ireland) (b.3 November 1880) Shot Put [5]; Discus Throw (freestyle) [ac]; Javelin Throw (freestyle) [ac]. [See also Tug-of-War and Wrestling].

Barrett, Henry Frederick. (b.30 December 1879–d.18 December 1927) Marathon [dnf].

Barrett, John James. (Ireland) (b.3 November 1880) Shot Put [ac]; Discus Throw (classical) [ac].

Beale, James George. (b.7 February 1881) Marathon [17].

Bellerby, Alfred Courthope Benson. (b.26 January 1888–d.10 April 1979) High Jump [20]; Long Jump [16].

Bleaden, Wilfred Harry. (b.6 March 1887–d.30 August 1965) Long Jump [17]; Standing Long Jump [ac].

Brown, William C. 3,500 meter walk [dqh1r1/2].

Buckley, Frank J. (Ireland) 3,200 meter steeplechase [dnfh2r1/2].

Burton, G. 400 meter hurdles [dnfh4r2/3].

Burton, Leslie Aubrey. (b.1883–d.10 June 1946) 400 meter hurdles [dnf-final].

Butler, John. (b.1871–d.3 October 1959) 3,500 meter walk [5]; 10 mile walk [dnfh2r1/2].

Butterfield, George. (b.1882–d.17 October 1917) 800 meters [2h1r1/2]; 1,500 meters [3h2r1/2].

Carter, Frank T. 10 mile walk [4].

Chapman, M. 100 meters [2h10r1/3].

Chavasse, Christopher Maude. (b.9 November 1884–d.10 March 1962) 400 meters [2h8r1/3].

Chavasse, Noel Godfrey. (b.9 November 1884–d.4 August 1917) 400 meters [3h7r1/3].

Clarke, William Thomas. (b.1873) Marathon [12].

Coales, William. (b.8 January 1886–d.19 January 1960) 5 miles [dnfh1r1/2]; 3-mile team race [1].

Collins, Michael. Discus Throw (freestyle) [ac].

Cornish, Lionel John. (b.25 December 1879–d.18 April 1939) Long Jump [ac]; Standing Long Jump [ac].

Davies, Charles C. 400 meters [2h1r2/3].

Deakin, Joseph Edmund. (b.6 February 1879–d.30 June 1972) 1,500 meters [6]; 5 miles [dnfh4r1/2]; 3-mile team race [1].

Densham, John Boon. (b.2 February 1880–d.8 January 1975) 400 meter hurdles [2h2r1/3].

Dineen, Michael D. (Ireland) Triple Jump [12].

Downing, Thomas. (Ireland) 3,200 meter steeplechase [dqh1r1/2].

Dugmore, Cyril Patrick William Francis Radclyffe. (Ireland) (b.20 May 1882–d.22 January 1966) Triple Jump [11].

Duncan, Alexander. (b.24 February 1884–d.21 January 1959) Marathon [dnf].

Duncan, Robert Cochran. (b.4 October 1887) 100 meters [4h3r2/3]; 200 meters [2h5r1/3].

English, Joseph C. 3,200 meter steeplechase [dnfh2r1/2].

Fairbairn-Crawford, Ivo Frank. (b.20 December 1884–d.24 August 1959) 800 meters [dnf-final]; 1,500 meters [5].

Flaxman, Alfred Edward. (b.1 October 1879–d.1 July 1916) Standing High Jump [ac]; Discus Throw (classical) [ac]; Javelin Throw (freestyle) [ac]; Discus Throw (freestyle) [ac].

Fyffe, Alan Herbert. (b.30 April 1884–d.5 March 1939) Hammer Throw [9].

George, John Phelps. (b.26 April 1882–d.26 November 1962) 100 meters [4h4r2/3]; 200 meters [3h3r2/3].

Gould, Edward Wyatt. (b.18 May 1879–d.9 February 1960) 400 meter hurdles [3h3r2/3].

Grantham, W. 3,200 meter steeplechase [dnfh6r1/2].

Groenings, Oswald Jacob. [later Oswald Birkbeck] (b.20 May 1880–d.24 March 1965) 110 meter hurdles [4h1r2/3]; 400 meter hurdles [dnfh2r2/3].

Halligan, Cyril Arthur W. (b.10 November 1886) 110 meter hurdles [2h2r1/3].

Hallows, Norman Frederic. (b.29 December 1886–d.16 October 1968) 1,500 meters [3]; 3-mile team race [1].

Halswelle, Wyndham. (b.30 May 1882–d.31 March 1915) 400 meters [1].

Hammond, Thomas Edgar. (b.18 June 1878–d.18 December 1945) 10 mile walk [6h1r1/2].

Harmer, Frederick William. (b.18 July 1884–d.13 March 1919) 400 meter hurdles [2h3r2/3].

Harmer, Henry Sutton. (b.8 July 1883–d.9 January 1958) 100 meters [dnfh5r1/3].

Harrison, Richard. 3,500 meter walk [dq]; 10 mile walk [dnf].

Hawkins, George Albert. (b.13 October 1883–d.22 September 1917) 200 meters [4]; 1,600 meter medley relay [2h3r1/2].

Healey, Alfred Hearn. (b.13 July 1879–d.12 September 1960) 110 meter hurdles [2h3r2/3].

Henderson, Walter Edward Bonhôte. (b.21 June 1880–d.2 September 1944) Standing High Jump [=8]; Standing Long Jump [ac]; Discus Throw (classical) [ac]; Discus Throw (freestyle) [ac]; Javelin Throw (freestyle) [ac].

Holdaway, Charles Guy. (b.28 February 1886) 3,200 meter steeplechase [4].

Holding, Harold Evelyn. (b.12 April 1883–d.20 July 1925) 800 meters [3h7r1/2].

Horgan, Denis. (Ireland) (b.18 May 1871–d.2 June 1922) Shot Put [2].

Hurdsfield, Samuel. 200 meters [4h3r2/3].

Hussey, Eric Robert James. (b.26 April 1885–d.19 May 1958) 110 meter hurdles [2h1r2/3].

Jack, Thomas. (b.5 February 1881–d.9 October 1960) Marathon [dnf].

Just, Theodore Hartman. (b.23 April 1886–d.13 February 1937) 800 meters [5]; 1,600 meter medley relay [2h3r1/2].

Kiely, Laurence A. (Ireland) 110 meter hurdles [3h3r2/3].

Kinahan, Cecil Edward. (Ireland) (b.15 April 1879–d.15 March 1912) 110 meter hurdles [2h4r2/3].

Kinchin, Joseph William. (b.11 June 1884–d.23 December 1969) 3,200 meter steeplechase [2h5r1/2].

Kitching, Frederick Overend. (b.7 July 1886–d. 1914) Standing Long Jump [ac].

Knott, Francis Arthur. (b.1883–d.24 March 1958) 1,500 meters [4h1r1/2].

Knyvett, William A. 110 meter hurdles [2h2r2/3].

Larner, Ernest Edward. (b.25 June 1880) 3,500 meter walk [4]; 10 mile walk [5].

Larner, George Edward. (b.7 February 1875–d.4 March 1949) 10 mile walk [1]; 3,500 meter walk [1].

Leader, Edward Eastlake. (b.28 August 1882–d.23 April 1959) 110 meter hurdles [2h13r1/3]; High Jump [10].

Leahy, Cornelius "Con." (Ireland) (b.27 April 1876–d.1921) High Jump [=2].

Leahy, Patrick Joseph. (Ireland) (b.20 May 1877–d.1926) High Jump [9].

Lee, John W. 800 meters [2h3r1/2]; 1,500 meters [4h2r1/2].

Leeke, Henry Alan. (b.15 November 1879–d.29 May 1915) Shot Put [ac]; Discus Throw (classical) [ac]; Discus Throw (freestyle) [ac]; Hammer Throw [ac]; Javelin Throw (freestyle) [ac]; Javelin Throw (held in middle) [ac].

Lindsay-Watson, Robert Hamilton. (b.4 October 1886–d.26 January 1956) Hammer Throw [ac].

Lintott, James Frederick. (b.29 March 1886–d.21 April 1963) 800 meters [2h2r1/2].

Loney, Ernest Vincent. (b.3 July 1882–d.27 August 1951) 1,500 meters [dnf-final].

Lord, Frederick Thomas. (b.11 February 1879) Marathon [15].

Manogue, L. J. 800 meters [ach4r1/2].

May, Ernest Edmund Bedford. (b.14 September 1878–d.5 January 1952) Discus Throw (freestyle) [ac]; Discus Throw (classical) [ac]; Hammer Throw [ac]; Javelin Throw (freestyle) [ac]; Javelin Throw (held in middle) [ac].

Mayberry, George Mahoney. (Ireland) (b.24 July 1884–d.21 November 1961) Triple Jump [ac].

McGough, John. (Ireland) (b.1887–d.1967) 1,500 meters [3h4r1/2].

Montague, Edwin Herbert. (b.18 March 1885–d.28 December 1937) 400 meters [2h2r2/3]; 1,600 meter medley relay [2h3r1/2].

Morphy, George Newcomen. (Ireland) (b.20 April 1884–d.1932) 800 meters [3h3r1/2].

Morton, John William. (b.13 February 1879–d.5 September 1950) 100 meters [3h2r2/3]; 200 meters [2h12r1/3].

Murphy, James. (Ireland) 5 miles [dnf-final].

Murray, Denis. (Ireland) (b.1881) 100 meters [3h4r1/3]; Long Jump [9].

Murray, George William. (Ireland) (b. 1885–d.24 March 1925) 100 meters [4h8r1/3].

Murray, John. (Ireland) (b.1881) Discus Throw (freestyle) [ac]; Hammer Throw [ac].

Nicol, George. (b.28 December 1886–d.28 January 1967) 400 meters [3h2r2/3].

Nicolson, Thomas Rae. (b.3 October 1879–d.18 April 1951) Shot Put [ac]; Hammer Throw [4].

Owen, Edward. (b.6 November 1886–d.24 September 1949) 5 miles [2].

Palmer, William James. (b.19 April 1882–d.21 December 1967) 3,500 meter walk [dnf]; 10 mile walk [dnf].

Pankhurst, Henry J. 100 meters [2h12r1/3]; 200 meters [3h10r1/3]; 1,600 meter medley relay [2h3r1/2].

Patterson, Alan. (b.12 March 1886–d.14 March 1916) 400 meters [2h11r1/3].

Powell, Kenneth. (b.8 April 1885–d.18 February 1915) 110 meter hurdles [2h5r1/3]. [See also Tennis (Lawn)].

Price, Jack T. (b.1884–d.November 1965) Marathon [dnf].

Quinn, Richard. (b.3 December 1882) 3,500 meter walk [dq].

Reed, Lionel James de Burgh. (b.31 December 1883) 200 meters [2h3r2/3].

Reid, John J. (Ireland) 3,500 meter walk [dq].

Robb, R. C. (Ireland) 400 meters [2h13r1/3].

Robertson, Arthur James "Archie." (b.19 April 1879–d.18 April 1957) 5 miles [5]; 3,200 meter steeplechase [2]; 3-mile team race [1].

Roche, James Patrick. (Ireland) (b.1886–d.7 June 1917) 100 meters [3h1r2/3]; 200 meters [2h4r2/3].

Russell, Arthur. (b.13 March 1886–d.23 August 1972) 3,200 meter steeplechase [1].

Ryle, Edward Hewish. (b.1 October 1885–d.5 April 1952) 400 meters [3h3r2/3].

Sarel, Sydney Lancaster. (b.18 June 1872–d.23 December 1950) 3,500 meter walk [5h1r1/2].

Schofield, Sydney Charles Apps. (b.1884–d.24 March 1956) 10 mile walk [6h2r1/2].

Sewell, Harry. 3,200 meter steeplechase [5].

Smith, Joseph M. 1,500 meters [5h1r1/2].

Spencer, Edward Adams. (b.1882–d.6 May 1965) 10 mile walk [3].

Stafford, Lancelot Henry Graham. (b.11 January 1887–d.15 June 1940) Standing High Jump [=17]; Standing Long Jump [ac].

Stark, James Primrose. (b.7 March 1885–d.16 June 1929) 100 meters [3h4r2/3]; 200 meters [3h11r1/3].

Stevenson, Samuel. 5 miles [3h5r1/2].

Thompson, Frederick Bertie. (b.4 August 1880–d.19 December 1956) Marathon [dnf].

Tremeer, Leonard Francis "Jimmy." (b.1 August 1874–d.21 October 1951) 400 meter hurdles [3]; Javelin Throw (held in middle) [ac].

Voigt, Emil Robert. (b.December 1882–d.16 October 1973) 5 miles [1].

Walters, David Wallis. (b.1878–d.10 February 1952) 110 meter hurdles [3h1r2/3].

Watson, Harold. (b.1883–d.15 February 1963) 100 meters [3h14r1/3].

Watt, William F. C. (Ireland) Long Jump [18].

Webb, Ernest James. (b.25 April 1874–d.24 February 1937) 3,500 meter walk [2]; 10 mile walk [2].

Williams, Charles Harold. (b.23 June 1887–d.15 December 1971) Long Jump [11].

Wilson, George Haswell. (b.13 May 1884–d.28 February 1951) High Jump [=10].

Wilson, Harold Allan. (b.22 January 1885–d.1916) 1,500 meters [2]; 3-mile team race [1].

Withers, Gadwin Robert James. (b.28 September 1884–d.5 February 1976) 10 mile walk [5h2r1/2].

Wyatt, Albert. Marathon [dnf].

Yeoumans, Alfred Thomas. (b.4 November 1876–d.29 September 1955) 10 mile walk [dqh1r1/2].

Yorke, Richard Francis Charles. (b.28 July 1885–d.22 December 1914) 3,200 meter steeplechase [dqh4r1/2].

Young, G. W. 400 meters [4h1r2/3].

Boxing (Total: 32; Men: 32; Women: 0)

Adams, Edward. Featherweight [=5].

Brewer, Harold. Heavyweight [=4].

Childs, William H. Middleweight [5].

Condon, John. (b.28 February 1889–d.21 February 1919) Bantamweight [2].

Dees, William J. Middleweight [=6].

Douglas, John William Henry Tyler. (b.3 September 1882–d.19 December 1930) Middleweight [1].

Evans, Sydney Charles H. (b.1881–d.8 January 1927) Heavyweight [2].

Fearman, Edward A. Lightweight [=7].

Fee, Patrick. Lightweight [=7].

Grace, Frederick. (b.29 February 1884–d.23 July 1964) Lightweight [1].

Gunn, Richard Kenneth. (b.16 February 1871–d.23 June 1961) Featherweight [1].

Holmes, Harold. Lightweight [=4].

Ireton, Albert. (b.15 May 1879–d.4 January 1947) Heavyweight [=4]. [See also Tug-of-War].

Jessup, George. Lightweight [=4].

Johnson, Harry H. Lightweight [3].

Lloyd, John. Featherweight [=5].

McGurk, Frank. Bantamweight [=4].

Morris, Charles W. Featherweight [2].

Murdoch, Arthur. Middleweight [=6].

Myrams, Ian. Heavyweight [=4].

Oldman, Albert Leonard. (b.18 November 1883) Heavyweight [1].

Osborne, Frank. Lightweight [=7].

Parks, Frederick Mostyn. (b.11 March 1885 — March 1945) Heavyweight [3].

Perry, Henry. Bantamweight [=4].

Philo, William. (b.5 March 1881) Middleweight [3].

Ringer, Thomas. (b.1883–d.1969) Featherweight [4].

Roddin, Hugh. Featherweight [3].

Spiller, M. Frederick. (b.22 February 1885) Lightweight [2].

Thomas, A. Henry. (b.1889) Bantamweight [1].

Warnes, Ruben Charles. (b.1875–d.16 January 1961) Middleweight [4].

Webb, William. (b.1882) Bantamweight [3].

Wells, Matthew. (b.14 December 1886–d.8 July 1953) Lightweight [=4].

Cycling (Total: 37; Men: 37; Women: 0)

Anderson, G. C. One Lap Match Sprint [4h14r1/2].

Bailey, Sydney Frederick. (b.1886) 100 km. [8].

Bailey, William James. (b.6 April 1888–d.12 February 1971) One Lap Match Sprint [3h2r2/3]; 1,000 meters Match Sprint [3h7r1/3]; 5,000 meters [dnfhr1/2].

Barnard, John Lewis. (b.25 February 1886–d.22 May 1977) Tandem Sprint [3h2r2/3].

Bartlett, Charles Henry. (b.6 February 1885–d.30 November 1968) 100 km. [1].

Bishop, J. H. 100 km. [dnf-final].

Bouffler, Herbert Clifford. (b.1881) 20 km. [4h3r1/2].

Brooks, Colin. 20 km. [2h2r1/2]; Tandem Sprint [3].

Calvert, A. E. 5,000 meters [ach6r1/2].

Clark, C. V. 5,000 meters [2h7r1/2].

Crowther, Herbert. (b.1882–d.1916) 1,000 meters Match Sprint [3h8r1/3].

Denny, Arthur J. One Lap Match Sprint [2h16r1/2]; 20 km. [ac-final].

Denny, Charles A. 100 km. [2].

Flynn, Daniel. One Lap Match Sprint [4]; 1,000 meters Match Sprint [ach2r2/3]; 5,000 meters [2h1r1/2]; 20 km. [dnfh1r1/2].

Hamlin, Frederick G. 20 km. [dnfh3r1/2]; Tandem Sprint [2].

Isaacs, Walter H. T. Tandem Sprint [3].

Johnson, Horace Thomas "Tiny." (b.1889–d.12 August 1966) Tandem Sprint [2].

Johnson, Victor Louis. (b.10 May 1883–d.23 June 1951) One Lap Match Sprint [1]; 1,000 meters Match Sprint [dq-final].

Jolly, R. 100 km. [dnfh2r1/2]; Tandem Sprint [2h6r1/3].

Jones, Benjamin. (b.1882) One Lap Match Sprint [3h4r2/3]; 1,000 meters Match Sprint [dq-final]; 5,000 meters [1]; 20 km. [2]; Team Pursuit [1].

Kingsbury, Clarence Brickwood. (b.3 November 1882–d.4 March 1949) One Lap Match Sprint [2h2r2/3]; 1,000 meters Match Sprint [dq-final]; 5,000 meters [5]; 20 km. [1]; Team Pursuit [1].

Lavery, J. L. (Ireland) One Lap Match Sprint [3h7r1/2]; 1,000 meters Match Sprint [3h3r2/3]; 5,000 meters [ach5r1/2].

Lower, W. 20 km. [dnfh4r1/2].

Magee, W. F. (Ireland) One Lap Match Sprint [2h11r1/2]; 1,000 meters Match Sprint [dq-h6r1/3]; 5,000 meters [2h4r1/2].

Matthews, Thomas John. (b.16 August 1884–d.20 October 1969) 1,000 meters Match Sprint [3h2r1/3]; Tandem Sprint [2h2r2/3].

McKaig, C. Tandem Sprint [3h3r1/3].

Meredith, Leon Lewis. (b.2 February 1882–d.27 January 1930) 20 km. [ac-final]; 100 km. [dnf-final]; Tandem Sprint [2h2r2/3]; Team Pursuit [1].

Morton, William. 5,000 meters [5h3r1/2].

Mussen, Harry. (Ireland) 100 km. [dnf-final].

Noon, David R. 100 km. [dnfh2r1/2].

Norman, J. 100 km. [ach1r1/2]; Tandem Sprint [2h6r1/3].

Payne, Ernest. (b.23 December 1884–d.10 September 1961) One Lap Match Sprint [4h3r2/3]; 1,000 meters Match Sprint [ach2r2/3]; 5,000 meters [dnfh2r1/2]; Team Pursuit [1].

Pett, William James. (b.25 August 1873–d.27 December 1954) 100 km. [4].

Piercy, E. C. Tandem Sprint [3h3r1/3].

Robertson, D. C. 20 km. [2h5r1/2]; 100 km. [7].

Rushen, Arthur. Tandem Sprint [3h2r2/3].

Summers, George F. One Lap Match Sprint [2h6r1/2]; 1,000 meters Match Sprint [2h13r1/3].

Diving (Total: 16; Men: 16; Women: 0)

Aldous, Henry James H. Plain High Diving [5h1r1/3].

Beckett, Anthony J. Fancy High Diving [5h1r2/3].

Bull, William J. (b.1886–d.1970) Fancy High Diving [3h4r2/3].

Cane, George F. Plain High Diving [3h4r1/3].

Clarke, Harold. (b.1888–d.23 October 1917) Fancy High Diving [4h2r2/3].

Collins, F. J. Plain High Diving [5h3r1/3].

Crank, Harry. (b.1885) Fancy High Diving [4h1r2/3].

Cross, Thomas A. (b.1887–d.1963) Fancy High Diving [4h5r2/3].

Errington, Frank E. (b.1890–d.April 1958) Fancy High Diving [5h1r2/3].

Goodworth, Harald. Plain High Diving [4h2r2/3].

Harrington, Thomas. Plain High Diving [6h5r1/3].

Hoare, William O. Plain High Diving [3h2r1/3]; Fancy High Diving [5h3r2/3]. [See also Gymnastics].

Pott, Herbert Ernest. (b.15 January 1883) Fancy High Diving [3h1r2/3].

Smyrk, Harold Nelson. (b.1889) Fancy High Diving [3h5r2/3].

Taylor, Anthony John. (b.17 June 1882–d.16 November 1932) Fancy High Diving [3h2r2/3].

Webb, William E. Plain High Diving [4h3r1/3].

Fencing (Total: 23; Men: 23; Women: 0)

Amphlett, Edgar Montague. (b.1 September 1867–d.9 January 1931) Épée, Individual [5p2r2/4]; Épée, Team [2].

Badman, Richard A. Sabre, Individual [4p2r2/4].

Blake, Jack Percy. (b.1874–d.19 February 1950) Épée, Individual [=4p3r1/4].

Brookfield, Edward Williams Hamilton. (b.1880) Sabre, Individual [=4p10r1/4].

Chalke, Anthony P. Sabre, Individual [7p13r1/4].

Chalmers, Ralph. (b.31 January 1891–d.10 May 1945) Épée, Individual [4p8r1/4].

Daniell, Charles Leaf. Épée, Individual [3p5r2/4]; Épée, Team [2].

Davids, Henry. Épée, Individual [5p3r2/4].

Davson, Percival May. (b.30 September 1887–d.5 December 1959) Épée, Individual [=4p5r1/4].

Fildes, Frederic Luke Val. (b.13 June 1879–d.22 April 1970) Épée, Individual [7p1r1/4].

Godfree, Douglas William. (b.16 October 1881–d.5 August 1929) Sabre, Individual [6p3r1/4].

Haig, Cecil Henry. (b.16 March 1862–d.3 March 1947) Épée, Individual [=5]; Épée, Team [2].

Holt, Martin Drummond Vesey. (b.13 January 1881–d.2 November 1956) Épée, Individual [8]; Épée, Team [2].

James, H. Evan. Sabre, Team [=5].

Keene, Alfred Valentine. Sabre, Individual [=4p9r1/4].

Leith, Lockhart. (b.2 June 1876–d.30 November 1940) Sabre, Individual [6p11r1/4].

Marsh, William Walter. (b.29 March 1877–d.12 February 1959) Sabre, Individual [3p3r2/4]; Sabre, Team [=5].

Martineau, Sydney. (b.6 January 1863) Épée, Individual [=3p7r2/4].

Montgomerie, Robert Cecil Lindsay. (b.15 February 1880–d.24 August 1939) Épée, Individual [4]; Épée, Team [2].

Murray, Arthur C. Sabre, Individual [4p2r1/4]; Sabre, Team [=5].

Notley, C. Barry. (b.1879) Sabre, Individual [7p1r3/4].

Seligman, Edgar Isaac. (b.14 April 1867–d.27 September 1958) Épée, Individual [=4p12r1/4]; Épée, Team [2].

Wilson, Charles A. Sabre, Individual [=4p8r1/4]; Sabre, Team [=5].

Figure Skating (Total: 11; Men: 7; Women: 4)

Women

Greenhough-Smith, Dorothy Vernon. (b.1875–d.9 May 1965) Ladies' Individual [3].

Johnson, Phyllis Wyatt. (b.8 December 1886–d.2 December 1967) Pairs [2].

Lycett, Gloria Gwendolyn. Ladies' Individual [5].

Syers, Florence Madeline "Madge." (b.1882–d.9 September 1917) Ladies' Individual [1]; Pairs [3].

Men

Cumming, Arthur Warren Jack. (b.8 May 1889–d.8 May 1914) Special Figures [2].

Greig, John Keiller. Men's Individual [4].

Hall-Say, George Norman Ernest. (b.27 April 1864–d.21 January 1940) Special Figures [3].

Johnson, James Henry. (b.1874–d.15 November 1921) Pairs [2].

March, Albert Arthur. Men's Individual [5].

Syers, Edgar Morris Wood. (b.18 March 1863–d.16 February 1946) Pairs [3].

Yglesias, Herbert Ramon. (b.1867–d.20 August 1949) Men's Individual [ac/dnf].

Football (Association Football [Soccer]) (Total: 11; Men: 11; Women: 0)

Bailey, Horace Peter. (b.3 July 1881–d.1 August 1960) [1].

Berry, Arthur. (b.3 January 1888–d.15 March 1953) [1].

Chapman, Frederick William. (b.10 May 1883–d.7 September 1951) [1].

Corbett, Walter Samuel. (b.26 November 1880–d.*ca*1955) [1].

Hardman, Harold Payne. (b.4 April 1882–d.9 June 1965) [1].

Hawkes, Robert Murray. (b.18 October 1880–d.12 September 1945) [1].

Hunt, Kenneth Reginald Gunnery. (b.24 February 1884–d.28 April 1949) [1].

Purnell, Clyde Honeysett. (b.14 May 1877–d.14 August 1934) [1].

Smith, Herbert. (b.22 November 1879–d.6 January 1951) [1].

Stapley, Henry. (b.29 April 1883–d.29 April 1937) [1].

Woodward, Vivian John. (b.3 June 1879–d.31 January 1954) [1].

Gymnastics (Total: 65; Men: 65; Women: 0)

Aspinall, E. Combined Exercises, Individual [ac].

Bailey, George. Combined Exercises, Individual [=12].

Baker, P. A. Combined Exercises, Team [8].

Barrett, W. F. Combined Exercises, Team [8].

Bauscher, Oliver. Combined Exercises, Individual [ac].

Bonney, R. Combined Exercises, Team [8].

Catley, J. H. Combined Exercises, Team [8].

Clay, M. Combined Exercises, Team [8].

Clough, E. Combined Exercises, Team [8].

Cook, Joseph. Combined Exercises, Individual [ac].

Cotterell, J. Combined Exercises, Team [8].

Cowy, W. Combined Exercises, Team [8].

Cullen, G. C. Combined Exercises, Team [8].

Denby, F. Combined Exercises, Team [8].

Dick, Franklin B. Combined Exercises, Individual [=16].

Domville, S. Combined Exercises, Individual [ac].

Drury, Herbert James. (b.5 January 1883–d.11 July 1936) Combined Exercises, Team [8].

Dyson, E. Combined Exercises, Individual [ac].

Fergus, W. Combined Exercises, Individual [ac].

Fitt, W. Combined Exercises, Team [8].

Ford, A. Combined Exercises, Individual [ac].

Gill, H. Combined Exercises, Team [8].

Graham, J. Combined Exercises, Individual [ac].

Hanley, R. Combined Exercises, Individual [ac].

Hanson, Leonard. (b.1 November 1887) Combined Exercises, Individual [ac].

Harley, A. S. Combined Exercises, Team [8].

Hawkins, Arthur E. Combined Exercises, Team [8]. [See also Wrestling].

Hoare, William O. Combined Exercises, Team [8]. [See also Diving].

Hodges, Arthur R. Combined Exercises, Individual [=16].

Hodgetts, Samuel. (b.28 October 1887) Combined Exercises, Individual [6].

Horridge, J. A. Combined Exercises, Team [8].

Huskinson, H. J. Combined Exercises, Team [8].

Jones, J. W. Combined Exercises, Team [8].

Justice, E. Combined Exercises, Team [8].

Keighley, N. J. Combined Exercises, Team [8].

Laycock, R. Combined Exercises, Team [8].

Manning, W. Combined Exercises, Team [8].

McGaw, R. Combined Exercises, Team [8].

McPhail, J. Combined Exercises, Team [8].

Meade, G. Combined Exercises, Individual [ac].

Merrifield, W. G. Combined Exercises, Team [8].

Oldaker, C. J. Combined Exercises, Team [8].

Parrott, G. Combined Exercises, Team [8].

Parsons, E. Combined Exercises, Team [8].

Potts, Edward William. (b.12 July 1881) Combined Exercises, Individual [9].

Richardson, E. F. Combined Exercises, Team [8].

Robertson, J. Combined Exercises, Team [8].

Ross, George James. (b.1 December 1887) Combined Exercises, Team [8].

Scott, D. Combined Exercises, Team [8].

Simpson, J. F. Combined Exercises, Team [8].

Skeeles, W. R. Combined Exercises, Team [8].

Smith, C. H. Combined Exercises, Individual [ac].

Speight, J. Combined Exercises, Team [8].

Stell, H. Combined Exercises, Team [8].

Suderman, C. V. Combined Exercises, Team [8].

Tilt, William. (b.8 February 1881) Combined Exercises, Team [8].

Tysal, Stanley Walter. Combined Exercises, Individual [2].

Vigurs, Charles Alfred. (b.11 July 1888–d.March 1917) Combined Exercises, Team [8].

Walters, J. A. Combined Exercises, Individual [ac].

Walton, E. Combined Exercises, Team [8].

Waterman, H. Combined Exercises, Team [8].

Watkins, E. A. Combined Exercises, Team [8].

Watters, W. Combined Exercises, Individual [ac].

Whitaker, John T. (b.9 April 1886) Combined Exercises, Team [8].

Whitehead, F. Combined Exercises, Team [8].

Hockey (Field) (Total: 45 [33 Great Britain, 12 Ireland]; Men: 45; Women: 0)

Baillon, Louis Charles. (b.5 August 1881–d.2 September 1965) [1].

Burt, Alexander Baird. (b.9 April 1884) [=3].

Burt, John. [=3].

Connah, Frederick. [=3].[5]

Dennistoun, Andrew G. [=3].

Evans, R. B. Llewellyn. (d.16 December 1963) [=3].

Foulkes, Charles Howard. (b.1 December 1875–d.6 May 1969) [=3].

Fraser, Hew Thomson. [=3].

Freeman, Harry Scott. (b.7 February 1876–d.5 October 1968) [1].

Green, Eric Hubert. (b.28 August 1878–d.23 December 1972) [1].

Harper-Orr, James. (b.18 October 1878–d.19 March 1956) [=3].

Laing, Ivan. (b.18 August 1885–d.30 November 1917) [=3].

Law, Arthur A. [=3].

Logan, Gerald. (b.29 December 1879) [1].

Lyne, Richard F. [=3].

Neilson, Hugh Edwin Beaumont. (b.5 May 1884–d.16 October 1930) [=3].

Noble, Alan H. [1].

Orchardson, William G. J. [=3].

Page, Edgar Wells. (b.31 December 1884–d.12 May 1956) [1].

Pallott, Wilfred James. (b.5 November 1884–d.7 November 1957) [=3].

Phillips, Frederick Gordon. (b.13 March 1884) [=3].

Pridmore, Reginald George. (b.29 April 1886–d.13 March 1918) [1].

Rees, Percy Montague. (b.27 September 1883–d.12 June 1970) [1].

Richards, Edward William Gruyffel. (b.15 December 1879–d.10 December 1930) [=3].

Robinson, John Yate. (b.6 August 1885–d.23 August 1916) [1].

Shephard, Charles W. [=3].

Shoveller, Stanley Howard. (b.2 September 1881–d.24 February 1959) [1].

Stevenson, Norman Lang. (b.1876) [=3].

Turnbull, Bertrand. (b.4 November 1880–d.17 November 1943) [=3].

Turnbull, Philip Bernard. (b.1879–d.20 October 1930) [=3].

Walker, Hugh Stewart. (b.2 February 1888–d.29 October 1958) [=3].

Williams, James Ralph. (b.28 July 1878) [=3].

Wood, Harvey Jesse. (b.10 April 1885) [1].

Ireland

Allman-Smith, Edward Percival. (b.3 November 1886–d.17 November 1969) [2].

Brown, Henry Joseph. (d.February 1961) [2].

Campbell, Walter Islay Hamilton. (b.14 October 1886–d.July 1967) [2].

Graham, William Ernest. (b.1874) [2].

Gregg, Richard George Stanhope. (b.9 December 1883–d.20 May 1945) [2].

Holmes, Edward Peter C. [2].

Kennedy, Robert L. [2].

Murphy, Henry Lawson. (b.12 December 1883–d.5 January 1942) [2].

Peterson, Jack. [2].

Peterson, Walter E. [2].

Power, Charles F. [2].

Robinson, Frank L. [2].

Jeu de Paume (Total: 9; Men: 9; Women: 0)

Biedermann, Edwin Anthony. (b.5 July 1877) Singles [=5]. (Later Edwin Best).

Cazalet, William Marshall. (b.8 July 1865–d.22 October 1932) Singles [=9].

Lytton, The Honorable Neville Stephen. (b.6 February 1879–d.9 February 1951) Singles [3].

Miles, Eustace Hamilton. (b.22 September 1868–d.20 June 1948) Singles [2].

Noel, Evan Baillie. (b.23 January 1879–d.22 December 1928) Singles [=5]. [See also Racquets].

Page, Arthur. (b.9 March 1876–d.1 September 1958) Singles [4].

Palmer, Arthur Nottage. (b.14 September 1886–d.27 November 1973) Singles [=5].

Pennell, Vane Hungerford. (b.16 August 1876–d.17 June 1938) Singles [=5]. [See also Racquets].

Tatham, Charles Edmund. (b.5 August 1864–d.27 February 1925) Singles [=9].

Lacrosse (Total: 12; Men: 12; Women: 0)

Alexander, Gustav Bernard Franck. (b.20 September 1881) [2].

Buckland, George Frederick. (b.13 April 1884–d.April 1937) [2].

Dutton, E. O. [2].

Hayes, S. N. [2].

Johnson, Wilfrid Alexander. (b.15 October 1885–d.21 June 1960) [2].

Jones, Edward Percy. (b.1880–d.17 November 1951) [2].

Martin, R. G. W. [2].

Mason, G. [2].

Parker-Smith, J. [2].

Ramsey, H. W. [2].

Scott, Charles Hubert. (b.1883–d.7 November 1954) [2].

Whitley, Norman Henry Pownall. (b.29 June 1883–d.12 April 1957) [2].

Motorboating (Total: 13; Men: 12; Women: 1)

Women

Gorham, Mrs. John Marshall. Class B [ac/dnf].

Men

Atkinson, G. H. Class A [ac/dnf].

Clowes, Winchester St. George. (b.4 October 1879) Class A [ac/dnf].

Howard de Walden, Lord. (b.9 May 1880–d.5 November 1946) Class A [ac/dnf].

Fentiman, A. G. Class A [ac/dnf].

Field-Richards, John Charles. (b.10 May 1878–d.18 April 1959) Class B [1]; Class C [1].

Gorham, John Marshall. (b.1853–d.12 January 1929) Class B [ac/dnf].

Laycock, Joseph Frederick. (b.12 June 1867–d.5 November 1952) Class A [ac/dnf].

Redwood, Bernard Boverton. (b.21 November 1874–d.28 September 1911) Class B [1]; Class C [1].

Thornycroft, Isaac Thomas. (b.22 November 1881–d.6 June 1955) Class B [1]; Class C [1].

Westminster, Duke of. (b.19 March 1879–d.19 July 1953) Class A [ac/dnf].

Weston, Thomas Douglas Wynn. Class C [ac/dnf].

Wright, Warwick. Class C [ac/dnf].

Polo (Total: 12 [8 Great Britain, 4 Ireland]; Men: 12; Women: 0)

Buckmaster, Walter Selby. (b.16 October 1872–d.30 October 1942) [=2].

Freake, Frederick Charles Maitland. (b.7 March 1876–d.12 December 1950) [=2].

Jones, Walter John Henry. (b.4 June 1866–d.14 April 1932) [=2].

Miller, Charles Darley. (b.23 October 1868–d.22 December 1951) [1].

Miller, George Arthur. (b.6 December 1867–d.21 February 1935) [1].

Nickalls, Patteson Wormesley. (b.23 January 1876–d.10 September 1946) [1].

Wilson, Herbert Haydon. (b.14 February 1875–d.11 April 1917) [1].

Wodehouse, Lord John. (b.11 November 1883–d.16 April 1941) [=2].

Ireland

Lloyd, John Hardress. (b.14 August 1874–d.28 February 1952) [=2].

McCann, John Paul. [=2].

O'Reilly, Percy Philip. (b.27 July 1870–d.2 July 1942) [=2].

Rotherham, Auston Morgan. (b.11 June 1876–d.24 February 1947) [=2].

Racquets (Total: 7; Men: 7; Women: 0)

Astor, John Jacob. (b.20 May 1886–d.19 July 1971) Singles [=3]; Doubles [1].

Brougham, Henry. (b.8 July 1888–d.18 February 1923) Singles [=3].

Browning, Cecil. (b.29 January 1883–d.23 March 1953) Singles [6]; Doubles [2].

Bury, Edmund William. (b.4 November 1884–d.4 December 1915) Doubles [2].

Leaf, Henry Meredith. (b.18 October 1862–d.23 April 1931) Singles [2]; Doubles [3].

Noel, Evan Baillie. (b.23 January 1879–d.22 December 1928) Singles [1]; Doubles [3]. [See also Jeu de Paume].

Pennell, Vane Hungerford. (b.16 August 1876–d.17 June 1938) Singles [5]; Doubles [1]. [See also Jeu de Paume].

Rowing & Sculling (Total: 30; Men: 30; Women: 0)

Barker, Harold Ross. (b.12 April 1886–d.29 August 1937)) Coxless Fours [2].

Blackstaffe, Henry Thomas "Harry." (b.28 July 1868–d.22 August 1951) Single Sculls [1].

Boyle, Richard Frederick Robert Pochin. (b.10 October 1888–d.6 February 1953) Coxed Eights [2h2r2/3].

Bucknall, Henry Cresswell. (b.4 July 1885–d.1 January 1962) Coxed Eights [1].

Burn, John Southerden. (b.25 June 1884–d.28 August 1958) Coxed Eights [2h2r2/3].

Burnell, Charles Desborough. (b.13 January 1876–d.3 October 1969) Coxed Eights [1].

Carver, Oswald Armitage. (b.2 February 1887–d.7 June 1915) Coxed Eights [2h2r2/3].

Cudmore, Collier Robert. (b.13 June 1885–d.16 May 1971) Coxless Fours [1].

Etherington-Smith, Raymond Broadley. (b.11 April 1877–d.19 April 1913) Coxed Eights [1].

Fairbairn, George Eric. (b.18 August 1888–d.20 June 1915) Coxless Pairs [2].

Fenning, John Reginald Keith. (b.23 June 1885–d.3 January 1955) Coxless Pairs [1]; Coxless Fours [2].

Filleul, Philip Rowland. (b.15 July 1885–d.29 July 1974) Coxless Fours [2].

Gillan, James Angus. (b.11 October 1885–d.23 April 1981) Coxless Fours [1].

Gladstone, Albert Charles. (b.28 October 1886–d.2 March 1967) Coxed Eights [1].

Goldsmith, Henry Mills. (b.22 July 1885–d.9 May 1915) Coxed Eights [2h2r2/3].

Jerwood, Frank Harold. (b.29 November 1885–d.17 July 1971) Coxed Eights [2h2r2/3].

Johnstone, Banner Carruthers. (b.11 November 1882–d.20 June 1964) Coxed Eights [1].

Kelly, Frederick Septimus. (b.29 May 1881–d.13 November 1916) Coxed Eights [1].

Kitching, Harold Edward. (b.31 August 1885–d.18 August 1980) Coxed Eights [2h2r2/3].

Maclagan, Gilchrist Stanley. (b.5 October 1879–d.25 April 1915) Coxed Eights [1].

McCulloch, Alexander. (b.25 October 1887–d.5 September 1951) Single Sculls [2].

Mackinnon, Duncan. (b.29 September 1887–d.9 October 1917) Coxless Fours [1].

Nickalls, Guy. (b.13 November 1866–d.8 July 1935) Coxed Eights [1].

Powell, Eric Walter. (b.6 May 1886–d.17 August 1933) Coxed Eights [2h2r2/3].

Sanderson, Ronald Harcourt. (b.11 December 1876–d.17 April 1918) Coxed Eights [1].

Somers-Smith, John Robert. (b.15 December 1887–d.1 July 1916) Coxless Fours [1].

Stuart, Douglas Cecil Rees. (b.1 March 1885) Coxed Eights [2h2r2/3].

Thomson, Gordon Lindsay. (b.27 March 1884–d.8 July 1953) Coxless Pairs [1]; Coxless Fours [2].

Verdon, Philip. (b.22 February 1886–d.18 June 1960) Coxless Pairs [2].

Williams, Edward Gordon. (b.20 July 1888–d.12 August 1915) Coxed Eights [2h2r2/3].

Rugby Union Football (Total: 15; Men: 15; Women: 0)

Davey, James "Maffer." (b.25 December 1880–d.18 October 1951) [2].

Dean, L. F. [2].

Jackett, Edward John. (b.4 July 1882–d.11 November 1935) [2].

Jackett, Richard. [2].

Jones, E. J. [2].

Jose, J. T. [2].

Lawry, A. [2].

Marshall, C. R. [2].

Solomon, Bert. (b.8 March 1885–d.30 June 1961) [2].

Solomon, John Charles, "Barney." (b.1883) [2].

Tregurtha, Nicholas Jacobs. (b.1884–d.14 May 1964) [2].

Trevaskis, John. [2].

Wedge, Thomas Grenfell. (b.1881–d.11 December 1964) [2].

Wilcocks, A. [2].

Wilson, Arthur James. (b.29 December 1886–d.1 July 1917) [2].

Shooting (Total: 67; Men: 67; Women: 0)

Amoore, Edward John. (b.20 March 1877–d.11 July 1955) Small-Bore Rifle, Disappearing Target [3]; Small-Bore Rifle, Moving Target [=19]; Small-Bore Rifle, Prone [5]; Small-Bore Rifle, Team [1].

Barnes, George. (b.1849–d.25 January 1934) Small-Bore Rifle, Prone [3].

Barnett, Richard Whieldon. (Ireland) (b.6 December 1863–d.17 October 1930) Free Rifle, 1,000 yards [4].

Bashford, John. Free Pistol [42]; Running Deer, Double Shot, Individual [9]; Running Deer, Single Shot, Individual [ac].

Blood, Maurice. (Ireland) (b.1870–d.31 March 1940) Free Rifle, 3 Positions [11]; Free Rifle, 1,000 yards [3]; Running Deer, Double Shot, Individual [4]; Running Deer, Single Shot, Individual [4].

Bostock, John. Free Rifle, Team [6].

Brown, Robert H. Free Rifle, Team [6].

Butt, John Hurst. (b.30 October 1852–d.1939) Trap Shooting, Individual [24]; Trap Shooting, Team [3].

Caldwell, Thomas. Free Rifle, 1,000 yards [=6].

Carnell, Arthur Ashton. (b.21 March 1862–d.11 September 1940) Small-Bore Rifle, Prone [1].

Chaney, Henry E. Free Rifle, 3 Positions [40].

Churcher, Charles W. Free Rifle, Team [6].

Coles, Geoffrey Horsman. (b.13 March 1871–d.27 January 1916) Free Pistol [11]; Free Pistol, Team [3].

Cowan, James Henry. (b.28 September 1856–d.7 August 1943) Running Deer, Double Shot, Individual [10]; Running Deer, Single Shot, Individual [=6].

Creasey, Harold P. Trap Shooting, Individual [=17]; Trap Shooting, Team [3].

Easte, Peter. Trap Shooting, Individual [=17]; Trap Shooting, Team [1].

Ellicott, Walter. Free Pistol [7]; Free Pistol, Team [3]; Running Deer, Double Shot, Individual [=6]; Running Deer, Single Shot, Individual [12]; Running Deer, Team [2].

Fleming, John Francis. (b.26 August 1881–d.9 January 1965) Small-Bore Rifle, Disappearing Target [=9]; Small-Bore Rifle, Moving Target [1].

Fremantle, Thomas Francis. (b.5 February 1862–d.19 July 1956) Free Rifle, 1,000 yards [=16].

Fulton, Arthur George. (b.16 September 1877–d.26 January 1972) Military Rifle, Team [2].

Hawkins, Harold I. Free Rifle, Team [6]; Small-Bore Rifle, Disappearing Target [2]; Small-Bore Rifle, Moving Target [=19]; Small-Bore Rifle, Prone [8].

Hawkins, R. Free Rifle, 3 Positions [26].

Hopton, John Dutton. (né John Hunt) (b.30 December 1858–d.1 June 1934) Free Rifle, 1,000 yards [=24].

Humby, Harold Robinson. (b.8 April 1879–d.23 February 1923) Small-Bore Rifle, Disappearing Target [8]; Small-Bore Rifle, Prone [2]; Small-Bore Rifle, Team [1].

Hutton, Richard. (Ireland) Trap Shooting, Individual [=7]; Trap Shooting, Team [3].

Jackson, Alexander Townsend. Free Rifle, 3 Positions [20].

Jones, Peter H. (b.3 September 1879) Free Pistol [28].

Kempster, Albert Joseph. (b.23 August 1875) Running Deer, Double Shot, Individual [5]; Running Deer, Single Shot, Individual [5].

Lane-Joynt, William R. (Ireland) Free Pistol [14]; Running Deer, Double Shot, Individual [13]; Running Deer, Single Shot, Individual [=6]; Running Deer, Team [2].

Le Fevre, James N. Free Pistol [31].

Lynch-Staunton, Henry George. (b.5 November 1873–d.15 November 1941) Free Pistol [13]; Free Pistol, Team [3].

Marsden, William V. B. Small-Bore Rifle, Moving Target [3].

Martin, John E. Military Rifle, Team [2].

Matthews, Maurice Kershaw. (b.21 June 1880–d.20 June 1957) Small-Bore Rifle, Disappearing Target [=9]; Small-Bore Rifle, Moving Target [2]; Small-Bore Rifle, Prone [4]; Small-Bore Rifle, Team [1].

Maunder, Alexander. (b.3 February 1861–d.2 February 1932) Trap Shooting, Individual [3]; Trap Shooting, Team [1].

Merlin, Gerald Eustace. (b.3 August 1884–d.1945) Trap Shooting, Individual [19].

Millner, Joshua Kearney. (Ireland) (b.5 July 1847–d.16 November 1931) Free Rifle, 1,000 yards [1]; Running Deer, Double Shot, Individual [15]; Running Deer, Single Shot, Individual [9].

Milne, James Law. (d.20 July 1958) Small-Bore Rifle, Prone [12]; Small-Bore Rifle, Disappearing Target [5]; Small-Bore Rifle, Moving Target [13].

Milne, William. (b.23 March 1852) Small-Bore Rifle, Disappearing Target [4]; Small-Bore Rifle, Moving Target [7]; Small-Bore Rifle, Prone [14].

Moore, Frank W. Trap Shooting, Individual [10]; Trap Shooting, Team [1].

Morris, William B. Trap Shooting, Individual [=20]; Trap Shooting, Team [3].

Munday, Henry. Free Pistol [39].

Newitt, Edward J. D. Small-Bore Rifle, Disappearing Target [=9]; Small-Bore Rifle, Moving Target [4].

Newton, William J. Free Pistol [16].

Nix, Charles George Ashburton. (b.25 August 1873–d.8 May 1956) Running Deer, Double Shot, Individual [11]; Running Deer, Single Shot, Individual [10]; Running Deer, Team [2].

Ommundsen, Harcourt. (b.23 November 1878–d.1915) Military Rifle, Team [2].

Padgett, William G. Military Rifle, Team [2].

Palmer, Charles. (b.18 August 1869) Trap Shooting, Individual [=5]; Trap Shooting, Team [1].

Pike, James F. Trap Shooting, Individual [=12]; Trap Shooting, Team [1].

Pimm, William Edwin. (b.10 December 1864–d.1952) Small-Bore Rifle, Disappearing Target [=15]; Small-Bore Rifle, Moving Target [6]; Small-Bore Rifle, Prone [6]; Small-Bore Rifle, Team [1].

Plater, Philip Edward. (b.6 June 1866) Small-Bore Rifle, Disappearing Target [=15]; Small-Bore Rifle, Moving Target [5]; Small-Bore Rifle, Prone [dq].

Postans, John M. Trap Shooting, Individual [ac]; Trap Shooting, Team [1].

Raddall, Thomas W. Free Rifle, Team [6].

Ranken, Thomas "Ted." (b.18 May 1875–d.27 April 1950) Free Rifle, 1,000 yards [5]; Running Deer, Double Shot, Individual [2]; Running Deer, Single Shot, Individual [2]; Running Deer, Team [2].

Richardson, Philip Wigham. (b.26 January 1865–d.23 November 1953) Military Rifle, Team [2].

Rogers, Alexander Elliott. (b.14 April 1867) Free Rifle, 1,000 yards [=28]; Running Deer, Double Shot, Individual [=6]; Running Deer, Single Shot, Individual [3].

Sellars, John Christopher. (Ireland) Free Rifle, 1,000 yards [=6].

Skinner, Gerald H. Trap Shooting, Team [3].

Styles, William Kensett. (b.11 October 1874–d.8 April 1960) Small-Bore Rifle, Disappearing Target [1]; Small-Bore Rifle, Moving Target [9].

Taylor, Albert E. Small-Bore Rifle, Prone [7].

Varley, Fleetwood Ernest. (b.12 July 1862–d.26 March 1936) Military Rifle, Team [2].

Wallingford, Jesse Alfred. Free Pistol [5]; Free Pistol, Team [3]; Free Rifle, 3 Positions [10]; Free Rifle, Team [6].

Warner, Jack. Small-Bore Rifle, Prone [9].

Whitaker, George. (b.25 August 1864) Trap Shooting, Individual [11]; Trap Shooting, Team [3].

Whitehead, Peter K. Free Rifle, 1,000 yards [=19].

Wilde, Arthur W. (d.1916) Small-Bore Rifle, Disappearing Target [6]; Small-Bore Rifle, Moving Target [=10]; Small-Bore Rifle, Prone [=10].

Wirgmann, Charles Wynn. Free Pistol [23].

Swimming (Total: 28; Men: 28; Women: 0)

Battersby, Thomas Sydney. (b.18 November 1887) 400 meter freestyle [3h1r2/3]; 1,500 meter freestyle [2].

Blatherwick, Sam. (b.16 October 1888–d.2 January 1975) 400 meter freestyle [2h3r1/3]; 1,500 meter freestyle [2h2r1/3].

Courtman, Percy. (b.14 May 1888–d.2 June 1917) 200 meter breaststroke [2h7r1/3].

Davies, Arthur. 200 meter breaststroke [3h3r1/3].

Derbyshire, John Henry. (b.29 November 1878–d.30 July 1938) 100 meter freestyle [2h4r1/3]; 4 × 200 meter relay [1].

Dockrell, George Shannon. (Ireland) 100 meter freestyle [3h2r2/3].

Edwards, Charles Wilfred. (b.1890) 100 meter freestyle [ach1r2/3].

Foster, William. (b.10 July 1890–d.17 December 1963) 400 meter freestyle [4]; 1,500 meter freestyle [3h1r2/3]; 4 × 200 meter relay [1].

Gooday, Sidney H. 200 meter breaststroke [3h4r1/3].

Haresnape, Herbert Nickall. (b.2 July 1880–d.1968) 100 meter backstroke [3].

Hassell, Richard H. 1,500 meter freestyle [3h5r1/3].

Haynes, William H. 400 meter freestyle [2h7r1/3].

Holman, Frederick. (b.March 1885–d.23 January 1913) 200 meter breaststroke [1].

Innocent, George. (b.13 May 1885–d.4 April 1957) 100 meter freestyle [3h5r1/3].

Jarvis, John Arthur. (b.24 February 1872–d.9 May 1933) 1,500 meter freestyle [dnfh2r2/3].

Lewis, Colin. (b.1882 100 meter backstroke [4h2r2/3].

Moist, Lewis. (b.1881–d.14 April 1940) 1,500 meter freestyle [4h1r2/3].

Naylor, Frank H. 200 meter breaststroke [ach2r1/3].

Parvin, Stanley. 100 meter backstroke [4h1r2/3].

Radmilovic, Paul. (b.5 March 1886–d.29 September 1968) 100 meter freestyle [ach1r2/3]; 400 meter freestyle [3h2r2/3]; 4 × 200 meter relay [1]. [See also Water Polo].

Robinson, William Walker. (b.23 June 1870) 200 meter breaststroke [2].

Seaward, Eric. (b.1892) 100 meter backstroke [3h7r1/3].

Sharp, Arthur T. 400 meter freestyle [2h9r1/3].

Taylor, Henry. (b.17 March 1885–d.28 February 1951) 400 meter freestyle [1]; 1,500 meter freestyle [1]; 4 × 200 meter relay [1].

Taylor, John Robert. (b.25 January 1884 – d.22 October 1913) 100 meter backstroke [3h2r2/3].

Tyldesley, Addin. (b.1891) 100 meter freestyle [4h2r2/3].

Unwin, Frederick A. (b.1888–d.28 May 1965) 100 meter backstroke [2h1r1/3].

Willis, Sidney. 100 meter backstroke [2h2r1/3].

Tennis (Total: 22; Men: 14; Women: 8)

Women

Boothby, Penelope Dora Harvey. (b.2 August 1881–d.22 February 1970) Singles (Lawn) [2]; Singles (Covered Court) [=5].

Coles, Mildred. Singles (Covered Court) [=5].

Eastlake-Smith, Gladys Shirley. (b.14 August 1883–d.18 September 1941) Singles (Covered Court) [1].

Greene, Alice Nora G. (b.1879) Singles (Lawn) [5]; Singles (Covered Court) [2].

Lambert Chambers, Dorothea Katharine. (b.3 September 1878–d.7 January 1960) Singles (Lawn) [1].

Morton, Agnes Mary "Agatha." (b.6 March 1872–d.5 April 1952) Singles (Lawn) [4].

Pinckney, Violet M. Singles (Covered Court) [=5].

Winch, Ruth Joan. Singles (Lawn) [3].

Men

Barrett, Herbert Roper. (b.24 November 1873–d.27 July 1943) Doubles (Covered Court) [1].

Caridia, George Aristides. (né Georgios Aristidis Karidias) (b.20 February 1869) Singles (Lawn) [=5]; Singles (Covered Court) [2]; Doubles (Covered Court) [2].

Cazalet, Clement Haughton Langston. (b.16 July 1869–d.25 March 1950) Doubles (Lawn) [3].

Crawley, Walter Cecil. (b.29 March 1880) Singles (Lawn) [=9]; Doubles (Lawn) [=4].

Dixon, Charles Percy. (b.7 February 1873–d.29 April 1939) Singles (Lawn) [=5]; Doubles (Lawn) [3].

Doherty, Reginald Frank. (b.14 October 1872–d.29 December 1910) Doubles (Lawn) [1].

Eaves, Wilberforce Vaughan. (b.10 December 1867–d.12 February 1920) Singles (Lawn) [3]; Singles (Covered Court) [4]; Doubles (Covered Court) [5].

Escombe, Lionel Hunter. (b.1875–d.15 October 1914) Doubles (Covered Court) [4].

Gore, Arthur William Charles "Wentworth." (b.2 January 1868–d.1 December 1928) Singles (Covered Court) [1]; Doubles (Covered Court) [1].

Hillyard, George Whiteside. (b.6 February 1864–d.24 March 1943) Doubles (Lawn) [1]; Doubles (Covered Court) [5].

Parke, James Cecil. (Ireland) (b.26 July 1881–d.27 February 1946) Singles (Lawn) [=9]; Doubles (Lawn) [2].

Powell, Kenneth. (b.8 April 1885–d.18 February 1915) Singles (Lawn) [=26]; Doubles (Lawn) [=4]. [See also Athletics (Track & Field)].

Ritchie, Major Josiah George. (b.18 October 1870–d.28 February 1955) Singles (Lawn) [1]; Singles (Covered Court) [3]; Doubles (Lawn) [2]; Doubles (Covered Court) [4].

Simond, George Mieville. (b.23 January 1867–d.8 April 1941) Doubles (Covered Court) [2].

Tug-of-War (Total: 24; Men: 24; Women: 0)

Barrett, Edward. (Ireland) (b. 3 November 1880) [1]. [See also Athletics (Track & Field) and Wrestling].

Butler, Thomas. [2].

Chaffe, Walter. (b.2 April 1870–d.22 April 1918) [3].

Clark, James Michael. (Ireland) (b.6 October 1874–d.29 December 1929) [2].

Dowler, Joseph. (b.1 February 1879–d.13 February 1931) [3].

Ebbage, Ernest Walter. (b.1 August 1873–d.2 September 1943) [3].

Goodfellow, Frederick William. (b.7 March 1874–d.22 November 1960) [1].

Greggan, William. [2].

Hirons, William. (b.15 June 1871–d.5 January 1958) [1].

Homewood, Thomas. (b.25 September 1881) [3].

Humphreys, Frederick Harkness. (b.28 January 1878–d.10 September 1954) [1]. [See also Wrestling].

Ireton, Albert. (b.15 May 1879–d.4 January 1947) [1]. [See also Boxing].

Kidd, Alexander. [2].

McLowry, Daniel McDonald. (d.24 October 1921) [2].

Merriman, Frederick. (b.18 May 1873–d.27 June 1940) [1].

Mills, Edwin Archer. (b.17 May 1878–d.12 Novmber 1946) [1].

Munro, Alexander. (b.30 November 1870) [3].

Philbin, Patrick. [2].

Shepherd, John James. (b.2 June 1884–d.9 July 1954) [1].

Slade, William. (b.9 May 1873–d.30 September 1941) [3].

Smith, George. (b.1876–d.14 January 1915) [2].

Swindlehurst, Thomas. (b.21 May 1874–d.15 March 1859) [2].

Tammas, Walter Baldry. (b.23 August 1870–d.12 January 1952) [3].

Woodget, James Henry. (b.28 September 1874–d.3 October 1960) [3].

Water Polo (Total: 7; Men: 7; Women: 0)

Cornet, George Thomson. (b.15 July 1877–d.22 November 1952) [1].

Forsyth, Charles Eric. (b.10 January 1885–d.24 February 1951) [1].

Nevinson, George Wilfred. (b.3 October 1882–d.13 March 1963) [1].

Radmilovic, Paul. (b.5 March 1886–d.29 September 1968) [1]. [See also Swimming].

Smith, Charles Sydney. (b.26 January 1879–d.6 April 1951) [1].

Thould, Thomas Henry. (b.11 January 1886–d.15 June 1971) [1].

Wilkinson, George. (b.3 March 1879–d.7 August 1946) [1].

Wrestling (Total: 53; Men: 53; Women: 0)

Adams, William T. Featherweight, Catch-as-Catch-Can [=9].

Bacon, Edgar Hugh. (b.9 October 1887) Middleweight, Catch-as-Catch-Can [=5]; Middleweight, Greco-Roman [=9].

Bacon, Stanley Vivian. (b.13 August 1885–d.13 October 1952) Middleweight, Catch-as-Catch-Can [1]; Middleweight, Greco-Roman [=17].

Baillie, Herbert. Lightweight, Catch-as-Catch-Can [=5].

Banbrook, Arthur. Heavyweight, Catch-as-Catch-Can [=9]; Light-Heavyweight, Greco-Roman [=5].

Barrett, Edward. (Ireland) (b.3 November 1880) Heavyweight, Catch-as-Catch-Can [3]; Heavyweight, Greco-Roman [=5]. [See also Athletics (Track & Field) and Tug-of-War].

Beck, Frederick. Middleweight, Catch-as-Catch-Can [3]; Middleweight, Greco-Roman [=9].

Blount, Edward J. Lightweight, Greco-Roman [=9].

Bradshaw, George A. Middleweight, Catch-as-Catch-Can [=9]; Middleweight, Greco-Roman [=9].

Brown, Charles H. Heavyweight, Catch-as-Catch-Can [=5]; Light-Heavyweight, Greco-Roman [=9].

Bruce, Lawrence. Heavyweight, Catch-as-Catch-Can [=5].

Chenery, Henry E. Middleweight, Catch-as-Catch-Can [=9].

Cockings, Percy Horatius. (b.19 December 1885) Featherweight, Catch-as-Catch-Can [=9].

Coleman, Aubrey. (b.1888) Middleweight, Catch-as-Catch-Can [=5].

Couch, Richard. Featherweight, Catch-as-Catch-Can [=9].

Cox, James E. Bantamweight, Catch-as-Catch-Can [=9].

Cox, William J. Bantamweight, Catch-as-Catch-Can [=9].

Davis, Frank. Bantamweight, Catch-as-Catch-Can [=5].

de Relwyskow, George Frederick William. (b.18 June 1887–d.9 November 1942) Lightweight, Catch-as-Catch-Can [1]; Middleweight, Catch-as-Catch-Can [2].

Faulkner, George A. Lightweight, Catch-as-Catch-Can [=9]; Lightweight, Greco-Roman [=9].

Foskett, Harold J. Heavyweight, Catch-as-Catch-Can [=5]; Light-Heavyweight, Greco-Roman [=17].

Gingell, Albert. Lightweight, Catch-as-Catch-Can [3].

Goddard, Arthur J. Featherweight, Catch-as-Catch-Can [=5].

Hawkins, Arthur E. Lightweight, Greco-Roman [=9]. [See also Gymnastics].

Henson, William J. P. Lightweight, Catch-as-Catch-Can [=9].

Hoy, Joseph. Lightweight, Catch-as-Catch-Can [=9].

Humphreys, Frederick Harkness. (b.28 January 1878–d.10 August 1954) Heavyweight, Catch-as-Catch-Can [=5]; Heavyweight, Greco-Roman [=5]. [See also Tug-of-War].

Jones, William F. Featherweight, Catch-as-Catch-Can [=9].

Knight, Frank W. Bantamweight, Catch-as-Catch-Can [=9].

MacKenzie, George. Lightweight, Catch-as-Catch-Can [4]; Lightweight, Greco-Roman [=17].

McKenzie, James. Lightweight, Catch-as-Catch-Can [=5].

McKie, William. (b.1886) Featherweight, Catch-as-Catch-Can [3].

Nixson, Edward E. Heavyweight, Catch-as-Catch-Can [4]; Light-Heavyweight, Greco-Roman [=9].

O'Kelly, George "Con." (Ireland) (b.29 October 1886–d.3 November 1947) Heavyweight, Catch-as-Catch-Can [1].

Peake, Sidney J. Featherweight, Catch-as-Catch-Can [=5].

Press, William J. Bantamweight, Catch-as-Catch-Can [2].

Rose, Arthur E. Lightweight, Greco-Roman [=17].

Ruff, William. (b.30 January 1883) Lightweight, Greco-Roman [=17].

Sansom, Bruce. Bantamweight, Catch-as-Catch-Can [=5].

Saunders, George J. Bantamweight, Catch-as-Catch-Can [=5].

Schwan, George H. Bantamweight, Catch-as-Catch-Can [=9].

Shepherd, William H. Lightweight, Catch-as-Catch-Can [=5].

Slim, James P. Featherweight, Catch-as-Catch-Can [2].

Sprenger, Harry Osmond. (b.1882–d.1957) Bantamweight, Catch-as-Catch-Can [=5].

Tagg, William. Featherweight, Catch-as-Catch-Can [4].

Tomkins, Frederick. Bantamweight, Catch-as-Catch-Can [4].

Wallis, Arthur E. Middleweight, Catch-as-Catch-Can [=9].

Webster, James A. Featherweight, Catch-as-Catch-Can [=5].

West, Walter. Heavyweight, Catch-as-Catch-Can [=9]; Light-Heavyweight, Greco-Roman [=9].

White, James G. Featherweight, Catch-as-Catch-Can [=5].

Whittingstall, Andrew J. Lightweight, Greco-Roman [=17].

Witherall, Harold F. Bantamweight, Catch-as-Catch-Can [=9].

Wood, William. (b.1888) Lightweight, Catch-as-Catch-Can [2]; Lightweight, Greco-Roman [=9].

Yachting (Total: 40; Men: 39; Women: 1)

Women

Rivett-Carnac, Frances Clytie. (b.1875–d.1 January 1962) 7-meter class [1].

Men

Aspin, R. B. 12-meter class [1].

Baxter, James. (b.8 June 1870–d.4 July 1940) 12-meter class [2].

Bingley, S. S. Norman. 7-meter class [1].

Buchanan, John. (b.1 January 1884–d.25 November 1943) 12-meter class [1].

Bunten, James Clark. (b.28 March 1875–d.3 January 1935) 12-meter class [1].

Campbell, Charles Ralph. (b.14 December 1881–d.19 April 1948) 8-meter class [1].

Cochrane, Blair Onslow. (b.11 September 1853–d.7 December 1928) 8-meter class [1].

Crichton, Charles William Harry. (b.7 July 1872–d.8 November 1958) 6-meter class [1].

Davidson, William Phythian. 12-meter class [2].

Dixon, Richard Travers. (b.20 November 1865–d.14 November 1949) 7-meter class [1].

Downes, Arthur Drummond. (b.23 February 1883–d.12 September 1956) 12-meter class [1].

Downes, John Henry. (b.18 October 1870–d.1 January 1943) 12-meter class [1].

Dunlop, David. 12-meter class [1].

Gardiner, J. A. 12-meter class [2].

Glen-Coats, Thomas Coats Glen. (b.5 May 1878–d.7 March 1954) 12-meter class [1].

Hughes, Alfred Collingwood. (b.1868–d.17 February 1935) 8-meter class [3].

Hughes, Frederick St. John. (b.22 February 1866–d.3 November 1956) 8-meter class [3].

Hunloke, Philip. (né Percival Hunloke) (b.1868–d.1 April 1947) 8-meter class [3].

Jellico, John F. 12-meter class [2].

Kenion, James G. 12-meter class [2].

Laws, Gilbert Umfreville. (b.6 January 1870–d.3 December 1918) 6-meter class [1].

Leuchars, John W. (b.1852–d.8 September 1920) 6-meter class [4].

Leuchars, William. 6-meter class [4].

Littledale, Thomas A. R. 12-meter class [2].

MacIver, Cecil R. 12-meter class [2].

MacIver, Charles. (b.28 November 1866–d.21 February 1935) 12-meter class [2].

Martin, Albert. 12-meter class [1].

Mackenzie, John. (b.21 September 1876–d.9 December 1949) 12-meter class [1].

McMeekin, Thomas D. 6-meter class [1].

Ratsey, George Ernest. (b.1875–d.25 December 1942) 8-meter class [3].

Rhodes, John Edward. (b.13 February 1870–d.6 February 1947) 8-meter class [1].

Rivett-Carnac, Charles James. (b.18 February 1853–d.9 September 1935) 7-meter class [1].

Robertson, McLeod. 12-meter class [2].

Smith, Frank B. 6-meter class [4].

Spence, John F. D. 12-meter class [2].

Sutton, Hugh. (b.26 September 1868–d.24 May 1936) 8-meter class [1].

Tait, Thomas Gerald. (b.7 November 1866–d.19 December 1938) 12-meter class [1].

Ward, William Dudley. (b.14 October 1877–d.11 November 1946) 8-meter class [3].

Wood, Arthur Nicholas Lindsay. (b.29 March 1875–d.1 June 1939) 8-meter class [1].

Greece (Total: 20; Men: 20; Women: 0)

Athletics (Track & Field) (Total: 12; Men: 12; Women: 0)
  Banikas, Georgios. (b.19 May 1888–d.9 April 1956) Pole Vault [=6].
  Dimitrios, Stefanos. 800 meters [ach4r1/2]; 1,500 meters [4h4r1/2].
  Dorizas, Mikhail M. (b.16 April 1888–d.21 October 1957) Shot Put [ac]; Discus Throw (classical) [5]; Discus Throw (freestyle) [ac]; Javelin Throw (freestyle) [2].
  Georgantas, Nikolaos. (b.12 March 1880–d.23 January 1958) Shot Put [ac]; Discus Throw (freestyle) [ac]; Discus Throw (classical) [6]; Javelin Throw (freestyle) [ac].
  Koulouberdas, Nikolaos. 5 miles [dnfh2r1/2]; Marathon [dnf].
  Kountouriotis, Stefanos. Pole Vault [9].
  Koutoulakis, Anastasios. Marathon [dnf].
  Muller, Dimitrios. Triple Jump [15].
  Paskhalidis, Mikhail. 100 meters [4h6r1/3]; 200 meters [2h9r1/3].
  Skoutaridis, Georgios. 100 meters [2h1r1/3]; 110 meter hurdles [2h3r1/3].
  Tsiklitiras, Konstantinos. (b.30 October 1888–d.10 February 1913) Standing High Jump [=2]; Standing Long Jump [2].
  Zouras, Kharalambos. Javelin Throw (freestyle) [4]; Javelin Throw (held in middle) [ac].

Cycling (Total: 1; Men: 1; Women: 0)
  Santorinaios, Ioannis. 20 km. [dnfh5r1/2]; 100 km. [dnfh1r1/2].

Shooting (Total: 7; Men: 7; Women: 0)
  Mauromatis, Frangiskos. (b.13 January 1870) Free Pistol [25]; Free Pistol, Team [7]; Free Rifle, Team [9]; Military Rifle, Team [7].
  Metaxas, Anastasios. (b.27 February 1862–d.1937) Trap Shooting, Individual [4].
  Orfanidis, Georgios D. (b.1859) Military Rifle, Team [7]; Free Pistol, Team [7]; Free Rifle, Team [9]; Small-Bore Rifle, Prone [15].
  Rediadis, Deukal. (b.2 February 1882) Free Pistol [32]; Free Rifle, Team [9]; Military Rifle, Team [7].
  Theofilakis, Alexandros. (b.1877) Free Pistol [26]; Free Pistol, Team [7]; Free Rifle, 1,000 yards [45]; Free Rifle, Team [9]; Military Rifle, Team [7].
  Theofilakis, Ioannis. (b.1879) Free Pistol [29]; Free Pistol, Team [7]; Free Rifle, Team [9]; Military Rifle, Team [7].
  Triantafilladis, Matthias. Free Rifle, Team [9]; Military Rifle, Team [7].

Hungary (Total: 65; Men: 65; Women: 0)

Athletics (Track & Field) (Total: 19; Men: 19; Women: 0)[6]
  Bodor, Ödön. (b.24 January 1882–d.22 January 1927) 800 meters [4]; 1,500 meters [8h1r1/2]; 1,600 meter medley relay [3].
  Drubina, István. (b.17 August 1884) 3,500 meter walk [5].
  Haluzsinszky, József. High Jump [=13].
  Holits, Ödön. (b.7 December 1886) Long Jump [14].
  Jesina, Ferenc. (né Ferenc Irmay) (b.19 August 1887) Discus Throw (freestyle) [ac]; Javelin Throw (freestyle) [ac].
  Kóczán, Mór. (b.8 January 1885–d.30 July 1972) Shot Put [ac]; Discus Throw (freestyle) [ac]; Discus Throw (classical) [ac]; Javelin Throw (freestyle) [ac].

Kováts, Nándor. (b.12 May 1881–d.4 April 1945) 110 meter hurdles [2h10r1/3]; 400 meter hurdles [dnfh2r2/3].

Kovesdy, Géza. Long Jump [ac].[7]

Lovas, Antal. (b.20 December 1884) 5 miles [dnfh6r1/2]; 3,200 meter steeplechase [dnfh2r1/2].

Luntzer, György. (b.23 August 1880) Discus Throw (freestyle) [7]; Discus Throw (classical) [ac]; Javelin Throw (freestyle) [ac]. [See also Wrestling].

Mezei Wiesner, Frigyes. (b.16 September 1887–d.27 March 1938) 100 meters [4h14r1/3]; 200 meters [2h6r1/3]; 1,600 meter medley relay [3].

Mudin, Imre. (b.8 November 1887–d.23 October 1918) Discus Throw (freestyle) [ac]; Discus Throw (classical) [ac]; Javelin Throw (freestyle) [7].

Mudin, István. (b.16 October 1881–d.22 July 1918) Shot Put [ac]; Discus Throw (classical) [7]; Hammer Throw [ac]; Javelin Throw (freestyle) [ac].

Nagy, József. (b.2 October 1881) 400 meters [2h7r1/3]; 800 meters [4h3r1/2]; 1,500 meters [2h5r1/2]; 1,600 meter medley relay [3].

Rácz, Vilmos. (b.31 March 1889–d.18 July 1976) 100 meters [2hr115/3]; 200 meters [2h4r1/3].

Radóczy, Károly. (b.31 August 1885) 200 meters [3h1r2/3].

Simon, Pál. (b.31 December 1890–d.25 February 1922) 100 meters [2h11r1/3]; 200 meters [4h10r1/3]; 1,600 meter medley relay [3].

Somodi, István. (b.22 August 1885–d.8 June 1963) High Jump [=2].

Szathmáry, Károly. (b.6 April 1890) Pole Vault [8].

Fencing (Total: 8; Men: 8; Women: 0)

Apáthy, Jenő. Sabre, Individual [3p8r2/4].

Földes, Desző. (b.30 December 1880–d.27 March 1950) Sabre, Individual [=5p1r3/4]; Épée, Individual [6p7r1/4]; Sabre, Team [1].

Fuchs, Jenő. (b.29 October 1882–d.14 March 1955) Sabre, Individual [1]; Sabre, Team [1].

Gerde, Oszkár. (b.8 July 1863–d.8 October 1944) Sabre, Individual [5p2r3/4]; Sabre, Team [1].

Szántay, Jenő. Sabre, Individual [4].

Tóth, Péter. (b.12 July 1882–d.28 February 1967) Épée, Individual [=4p13r1/4]; Sabre, Individual [5]; Sabre, Team [1].

Werkner, Lajos. (b.23 October 1883–d.12 November 1943) Sabre, Individual [6]; Sabre, Team [1].

Zulavszky, Béla. (b.23 October 1869–d.24 October 1914) Épée, Individual [=4p10r1/4]; Sabre, Individual [2].

Gymnastics (Total: 6; Men: 6; Women: 0)

Antos, Mihály. Combined Exercises, Individual [45].

Géllert, Imre. (b.24 July 1889–d.1981) Combined Exercises, Individual [39].

Gráf, Frigyes. Combined Exercises, Individual [dnf].

Nyisztor, János. Combined Exercises, Individual [15].

Szabó, Kálmán. Combined Exercises, Individual [34].

Szűts, Ferenc. (b.16 December 1891–d.28 November 1966) Combined Exercises, Individual [ac].

Rowing & Sculling (Total: 11; Men: 11; Women: 0)

Éder, Róbert. Coxed Eights [2h2r1/3].

Haraszthy, Lajos. Coxed Eights [2h2r1/3].

Hautzinger, Sándor. (b.1886) Coxed Eights [2h2r1/3].

Killer, Ernő. Single Sculls [dnfh1r1/4].

Kirchknopf, Ferenc. Coxed Eights [2h2r1/3].

Klekner, Sándor. Coxed Eights [2h2r1/3].

Levitzky, Károly. (b.1 May 1885–d.23 August 1978) Single Sculls [2h1r3/4].

Szebeny, Antal. (b.6 April 1886) Coxed Eights [2h2r1/3].

Várady, Jenő. Coxed Eights [2h2r1/3].

Vaskó, Kálmán. (b.23 November 1874) Coxed Eights [2h2r1/3].

Wampetich, Imre. Coxed Eights [2h2r1/3].

Shooting (Total: 2; Men: 2; Women: 0)

Móricz, István. (b.12 November 1849) Free Rifle, 3 Positions [49].

Prokopp, Sándor. (b.7 May 1887–d.4 November 1964) Free Rifle, 3 Positions [43].

Swimming (Total: 10; Men: 10; Women: 0)

Baronyi, András. (b.3 February 1891) 200 meter breaststroke [2h2r1/3].

Fabinyi, József. 200 meter breaststroke [4h1r2/3].

Hajós, Henrik. (b.21 July 1886–d.2 June 1963) 100 meter freestyle [ach3r1/3]; 400 meter freestyle [5h1r2/3].

Halmay, Zoltán von. (b.18 June 1881–d.20 May 1956) 100 meter freestyle [2]; 4 × 200 meter relay [2].

Kugler, Sándor. 100 meter backstroke [dqh7r1/3].

Las Torres, Béla. (b.20 April 1890–d.13 October 1915) 400 meter freestyle [4h1r2/3]; 4 × 200 meter relay [2].

Munk, József. (b.30 November 1890) 100 meter freestyle [ach2r1/3]; 4 × 200 meter relay [2].

Ónody, József. (b.12 September 1882–d.17 April 1957) 100 meter freestyle [2h5r1/3]; 400 meter freestyle [3h7r1/3].

Toldi, Ödön. (b.17 June 1892) 200 meter breaststroke [4].

Zachár, Imre. (b.11 May 1890–d.7 April 1954) 400 meter freestyle [4h2r2/3]; 4 × 200 meter relay [2].

Tennis (Total: 3; Men: 3; Women: 0)

Lauber, Dezső. (b.1879 — d.1966) Singles (Lawn) [=16].

Tóth, Ede. (b.11 March 1884) Singles (Lawn) [=16]; Doubles (Lawn) [=7].

Zsigmondy, Jenő. (b.4 July 1888) Singles (Lawn) [=16]; Doubles (Lawn) [=7].

Wrestling (Total: 7; Men: 7; Women: 0)

Luntzer, György. (b.23 August 1880) Light-Heavyweight, Greco-Roman [=17]. [See also Athletics (Track & Field)].

Maróthy, Ferenc József. (b.15 October 1887) Lightweight, Greco-Roman [=5].

Orosz, Miklós. (b.12 September 1882) Middleweight, Greco-Roman [=9].

Payr, Hugó. (b.11 April 1887) Light-Heavyweight, Greco-Roman [4]; Heavyweight, Greco-Roman [4].

Radvány, Ödön. (b.27 December 1888) Lightweight, Greco-Roman [=5].

Téger, József. Lightweight, Greco-Roman [=9].

Weisz, Richárd. (b.30 April 1879–d.4 December 1945) Heavyweight, Greco-Roman [1].

Iceland (Total: 1; Men: 1; Women: 0)

Wrestling (Total: 1; Men: 1; Women: 0)
Jósepsson, Jóhannes. (b.28 July 1883) Middleweight, Greco-Roman [4].

Ireland (Total: 53; Men: 52; Women: 1)

Ireland did not compete as an independent nation, its athletes representing Great Britain, as Ireland was still a dependency of the United Kingdom. Separate Irish teams were entered in hockey (field) and polo. For interest, we have listed all the Irish Olympians from 1908 below. Full details of their participation are found in the index for Great Britain.

Archery (Total: 1; Men: 0; Women: 1)
Hill-Lowe, Beatrice Geraldine Ruxton.

Athletics (Track & Field) (Total: 23; Men: 23; Women: 0)
Ahearne, Timothy J.
Barrett, Edward. (See also Tug-of-War and Wrestling)
Barrett, John James.
Buckley, Frank J.
Dineen, Michael D.
Downing, Thomas.
Dugmore, Cyril Patrick William Francis Radclyffe.
Horgan, Denis.
Kiely, Laurence A.
Kinahan, Cecil Edward.
Leahy, Cornelius "Con."
Leahy, Patrick Joseph.
Mayberry, George Mahoney.
McGough, John.
Morphy, George Newcomen.
Murphy, James.
Murray, Denis.
Murray, John.
Murray, George William.
Reid, John J.
Robb, R. C.
Roche, James Patrick.
Watt, W. F. C.

Cycling (Total: 3; Men: 3; Women: 0)
Lavery, J. L.
Magee, W. F.
Mussen, Harry.

Hockey (Field) (Total: 12; Men: 12; Women: 0)
Allman-Smith, Edward Percival.
Brown, Henry Joseph.

Campbell, Walter Islay Hamilton.
Graham, William Ernest.
Gregg, Richard George Stanhope.
Holmes, Edward Peter C.
Kennedy, Robert L.
Murphy, Henry Lawson.
Peterson, Jack.
Peterson, Walter E.
Power, Charles F.
Robinson, Frank L.

Polo (Total: 4; Men: 4; Women: 0)
Lloyd, John Hardress.
McCann, John Paul.
O'Reilly, Percy Philip.
Rotherham, Auston Morgan.

Shooting (Total: 6; Men: 6; Women: 0)
Barnett, Richard Whieldon.
Blood, Maurice.
Hutton, Richard.
Lane-Joynt, William R.
Millner, Joshua Kearney.
Sellars, John Christopher.

Swimming (Total: 1; Men: 1; Women: 0)
Dockrell, George Shannon.

Tennis (Lawn) (Total: 1; Men: 1; Women: 0)
Parke, James Cecil.

Tug-of-War (Total: 2; Men: 2; Women: 0)
Barrett, Edward. (See also Athletics (Track & Field) and Wrestling)
Clark, James Michael.

Wrestling (Total: 2; Men: 2; Women: 0)
Barrett, Edward. (See also Athletics (Track & Field) and Tug-of-War)
O'Kelly, George "Con."

Italy (Total: 66; Men: 66; Women: 0)

Athletics (Track & Field) (Total: 12; Men: 12; Women: 0)
Avattaneo, Umberto. (b.2 April 1883) Discus Throw (freestyle) [ac]; Discus Throw (classical) [10].
Barozzi, Umberto. (b.13 August 1881–d.13 July 1929) 100 meters [4h7r1/3]; 200 meters [2h8r1/3].
Blasi, Umberto. (b.12 October 1886–d.1 July 1938) Marathon [dnf].

Brambilla, Emilio. (b.26 June 1882–d.17 October 1938) 200 meters [5h11r1/3]; Javelin Throw (freestyle) [ac].

Cartasegna, Massimo. (b.30 June 1885–d.15 April 1963) 400 meters [2h10r1/3]; 1,500 meters [dnfh3r1/2]; 3,200 meter steeplechase [2h1r1/2]; 3-mile team race [dnfh1r1/2].

Giovanoli, Emilio. (b.1886) 3-mile team race [dnfh1r1/2].

Lunghi, Emilio. (b.16 March 1887–d.26 September 1925) 800 meters [2]; 1,500 meters [2h3r1/2]; 3-mile team race [dnfh1r1/2].

Pagliani, Pericle. (b.2 February 1883–d.4 October 1932) 5 miles [3h2r1/2]; 3-mile team race [dnfh1r1/2].

Penna, Roberto. (b.19 April 1886) 400 meters [2h4r1/3].

Pietri, Dorando. (b.16 October 1885–d.7 February 1942) Marathon [dq]; 3-mile team race [dnfh1r1/2].

Tarella, Giuseppe. (b.7 May 1883–d.17 January 1968) 400 meters [3h11r1/3].

Torretta, Gaspare. (b.1882–d.5 July 1910) 100 meters [2h16r1/3].

Cycling (Total: 4; Men: 4; Women: 0)

Arizini, Luigi. 100 km. [dnfh2r1/2]; 5,000 meters [3h5r1/2].

Malatesta, E. Guglielmo. 1,000 meters Match Sprint [3h1r1/3]; 5,000 meters [3h1r1/2]; 100 km. [dnfh2r1/2].

Morisetti, Walter Guglielmo. 1,000 meters Match Sprint [2h4r2/3]; 5,000 meters [2h6r1/2]; 20 km. [4h6r1/2].

Parini, Battista. 100 km. [dnfh2r1/2].

Diving (Total: 1; Men: 1; Women: 0)

Bonfanti, Carlo. (b.7 July 1875) Fancy High Diving [4h4r2/3].

Fencing (Total: 11; Men: 11; Women: 0)

Bertinetti, Marcello. (b.26 April 1885–d.31 July 1967) Épée, Individual [4p5r2/4]; Épée, Team [4]; Sabre, Individual [=5p1r3/4]; Sabre, Team [2].

Cagiati, Giulio. Épée, Individual [=3p8r2/4].

Ceccherini, Sante Lorenzo Minotti. (b.15 November 1863– d.9 August 1932) Sabre, Individual [dnfp2r3/4]; Épée, Individual [=4p5r1/4]; Sabre, Team [2].

Diana, Dino. Épée, Individual [=4p4r1/4]; Sabre, Individual [5p3r1/4].

Mangiarotti, Giuseppe. (b.27 May 1883) Épée, Individual [4p9r1/4]; Épée, Team [4].

Nowak, Riccardo. (b.25 December 1879–d.18 February 1950) Épée, Individual [=3p6r2/4]; Épée, Team [4]; Sabre, Individual [=4p3r2/4]; Sabre, Team [2].

Olivier, Abelardo. (b.9 November 1877–d.24 January 1951) Épée, Team [4]; Sabre, Team [2].

Pinelli, Aroldo N. S. Luigi. Sabre, Individual [4p11r1/4].

Pirzio Biroli, Alessandro. (b.23 July 1887–d.20 May 1962) Épée, Individual [=5p8r1/4]; Sabre, Individual [=4p7r2/4]; Sabre, Team [2].

Sarzano, Pietro. Épée, Individual [=4p10r1/4]; Sabre, Individual [=6p10r1/4].

Speciale, Pietro. (b.29 September 1876–d.9 November 1945) Épée, Individual [4p3r2/4].

Gymnastics (Total: 32; Men: 32; Women: 0)

Accorsi, Alfredo. (b.1871) Combined Exercises, Team [6].

Agliorini, Umberto. Combined Exercises, Team [6].

Agordi, Nemo. (b.10 January 1888) Combined Exercises, Team [6].

Andreani, Adriano. (b.14 September 1879) Combined Exercises, Team [6].

Blo, Vincenzo. (b.12 March 1888) Combined Exercises, Team [6].

Bonati, Giovanni. (b.28 February 1889) Combined Exercises, Team [6].

Borsetti, Pietro. (b.6 March 1882) Combined Exercises, Team [6].

Bottoni, Flaminio. (b.4 August 1881) Combined Exercises, Team [6].

Bozzani, Adamo. (b.8 September 1891) Combined Exercises, Team [6].

Braglia, Alberto. (b.23 April 1883–d.5 February 1954) Combined Exercises, Individual [1].

Buozzi, Bruto. (b.26 May 1885) Combined Exercises, Team [6].

Calabresi, Gastone. (b.6 April 1886) Combined Exercises, Team [6].

Capitani, Otello. (b.1890) Combined Exercises, Individual [ac].

Celada, Carlo. (b.15 February 1884) Combined Exercises, Team [6].

Collevati, Tito. (b.4 February 1891) Combined Exercises, Team [6].

Cotichini, Antonio. (b.28 July 1890) Combined Exercises, Team [6].

Cristofori, Guido. (b.12 April 1880) Combined Exercises, Team [6].

Di Chiara, Stanislao. (b.24 December 1891) Combined Exercises, Team [6].

Gasperini, Giovanni. (b.6 March 1886) Combined Exercises, Team [6].

Marchi, Amedeo. (b.8 February 1889) Combined Exercises, Team [6].

Marchiandi, Carlo. Combined Exercises, Team [6].

Massari, Ettore. (b.16 September 1883) Combined Exercises, Team [6].

Nardini, Roberto. (b.2 July 1891) Combined Exercises, Team [6].

Pavani, Decio. (b.15 June 1891) Combined Exercises, Team [6].

Preti, Gaetano. (b.28 February 1891) Combined Exercises, Team [6].

Ravenna, Gino. (b.30 August 1889) Combined Exercises, Team [6].

Ridolfi, Massimo. (b.24 December 1889) Combined Exercises, Team [6].

Romano, Guido. (b.31 January 1887–d.18 June 1916) Combined Exercises, Individual [19].

Savonuzzi, Ugo. (b.11 September 1887) Combined Exercises, Team [6].

Taddia, Gustavo. (b.23 November 1886) Combined Exercises, Team [6].

Termanini, Giannetto. Combined Exercises, Team [6].

Vaccari, Gioacchino. (b.1 May 1883) Combined Exercises, Team [6].

Rowing & Sculling (Total: 1; Men: 1; Women: 0)
Ciabatti, Gino. (b.1883) Single Sculls [2h2r2/4].

Swimming (Total: 4; Men: 4; Women: 0)
Baiardo, Davide. (b.11 May 1887–d.28 November 1977) 100 meter freestyle [ach1r1/3]; 400 meter freestyle [dnfh3r1/3].

Beretta, Amilcare. (b.15 March 1892) 100 meter backstroke [3h4r1/3]; 200 meter breaststroke [4h4r1/3].

Massa, Mario. (b.20 June 1892–d.16 February 1956) 400 meter freestyle [3h6r1/3].

Muzzi, Oreste. (b.7 July 1887) 1,500 meter freestyle [3h1r1/3].

Wrestling (Total: 1; Men: 1; Women: 0)
Porro, Enrico. (b.16 January 1885–d.4 May 1967) Lightweight, Greco-Roman [1].

The Netherlands (Total: 113; Men: 113; Women: 0)

Athletics (Track & Field) (Total: 19; Men: 19; Women: 0)
Braams, Wilhelmus Theodorus. (b.25 August 1886–d.3 July 1955) 5 miles [dnfh3r1/2]; Marathon [dnf]; 3-mile team race [dnfh1r1/2].

Buff, George Johan Marcel. (b.23 November 1874–d.3 March 1955) Marathon [dnf].

Evers, Brand "Bram". (b.16 July 1886–d.7 October 1952) 400 meters [3h15r1/3]; 800 meters [dnfh7r1/2]; 1,600 meter medley relay [h2r1/2]; Long Jump [ac]; Pole Vault [14]; Standing Long Jump [ac].

Goetzee, Johannes Elias "Jo." (b.8 March 1884–d.26 August 1935) 3,500 meter walk [7h1r1/2]; 10 mile walk [dnfh1r1/2].

Greven, Ernestus Johannes Christiaan. (b.8 September 1885–d.8 March 1924) 100 meters [ach4r1/3]; 200 meters [3h6r1/3].

Held, Cornelis Johannes den. (b.19 July 1883–d.12 September 1962) 200 meters [4h12r1/3]; 400 meters [2h12r1/3].

Henny, Victor. (b.30 October 1887–d.12 July 1941) 100 meters [3h1r1/3]; 200 meters [2h1r1/3]; 400 meters [4h7r1/3]; 1,600 meter medley relay [h2r1/2].

Hoogveld, Jacobus Johannes. (b.4 August 1884–d.17 February 1948) 100 meters [3h9r1/3]; 200 meters [3h15r1/3]; 400 meters [2h16r1/3]; 1,600 meter medley relay [h2r1/2]; Long Jump [ac]; Standing Long Jump [ac].

Huijgen, Johannes Hendrikus. (b.17 August 1888) 3,500 meter walk [7]; 10 mile walk [dnfh2r1/2].

Keyser, Jacques. (b.12 October 1885–d.21 March 1954) 1,500 meters [9h1r1/2]; 5 miles [dnfh4r1/2].

Koops, Evert. (b.2 January 1885–d.10 November 1938) 100 meters [4h3r1/3]; 200 meters [4h3r1/3]; 400 meter hurdles [dnfh1r2/3]; 1,600 meter medley relay [2h2r1/2]; Standing Long Jump [ac].

Leeuwen, Hermanus Nicolaas van "Herman." (b.8 June 1884–d.7 February 1926) High Jump [19]. [See also Gymnastics].

Ruimers, Petrus Adrianus Antonius. (b.21 October 1884–d.6 April 1945) 3,500 meter walk [6]; 10 mile walk [7h2r1/2].

Soudyn, Petrus Marie "Piet." (b.3 March 1880–d.18 September 1946) 10 mile walk [dnfh1r1/2].

Veenhuijsen, Coenraad van. (b.28 July 1886–d.8 December 1977) Pole Vault [13].

Vosbergen, Ary Carel Hugo. (b.10 June 1882–d.14 November 1918) 800 meters [dnfh6r1/2]; 1,500 meters [3h6r1/2]; 5 miles [dnfh5r1/2]; Marathon [dnf]; 3-mile team race [dnfh1r1/2].

Wakker, Willem Wouter. (b.8 December 1879) 5 miles [dnfh2r1/2]; Marathon [20]; 3-mile team race [dnfh1r1/2].

Wal, Hendrik Jacob van der. (b.20 August 1886–d.4 August 1982) 200 meters [3h2r1/3]; 400 meters [4h14r1/3]; 800 meters [dnfh1r1/2].

Winkelman, Wilhelmus Frederikus "Willem." (b.14 July 1887–d.1 July 1990) 3,500 meter walk [4]; 10 mile walk [dnfh1r1/2].

Cycling (Total: 5; Men: 5; Women: 0)

Bosch van Drakestein, Gerard Dagobert Henri. (b.24 July 1887–d.20 March 1972) One Lap Match Sprint [2h13r1/2]; 1,000 meters Match Sprint [2h1r1/3]; 5,000 meters [7]; 20 km. [5h2r1/2]; 100 km. [ach1r1/2]; Team Pursuit [4].

Damen, Georgius Bernardus. (b.18 June 1887–d.23 June 1954) One Lap Match Sprint [3h3r1/2]; 5,000 meters [ach5r1/2]; 20 km. [5h1r1/2]; 100 km. [ach1r1/2].

Gerrits, Antonie. (b.15 May 1885–d.22 January 1969) One Lap Match Sprint [4h11r1/2]; ; 1,000 meters Match Sprint [2h14r1/3]; 5,000 meters [3h2r1/2]; Team Pursuit [4].

Nijland, Dorotheus Magdalenus "Dorus." (b.26 February 1880–d.13 December 1968) One Lap Match Sprint [2h1r1/2]; 1,000 meters Match Sprint [2h5r1/3]; 5,000 meters [3h6r1/2]; 20 km. [ach3r1/2]; 100 km. [dnfh2r1/2]; Team Pursuit [4].

Spengen, Johannes Jacobus van. (b.20 February 1887–d.9 June 1936) One Lap Match Sprint

[2h1r2/3]; 1,000 meters Match Sprint [dq-h6r1/3]; 5,000 meters [6]; 20 km. [ach4r1/2]; Team Pursuit [4].

Fencing (Total: 13; Men: 13; Women: 0)

Beaufort, Jan Daniël Hendrik de. (b.2 December 1880–d.2 April 1946) Sabre, Individual [=5p13r1/4].

Doorman, Jetze. (b.2 July 1881–d.28 February 1931) Épée, Individual [3p1r2/4]; Épée, Team [9]; Sabre, Individual [=7]; Sabre, Team [=5].

Dwinger, Marcus "Max." (b.31 July 1870–d.12 August 1939) Épée, Individual [=4p3r1/4].

Hubert van Blijenburgh, Willem Peter. (b.11 July 1881–d.14 October 1936) Épée, Individual [7p7r1/4]; Sabre, Individual [=3p6r2/4].

Hulstijn, Gustaaf Adolf van. (b.24 August 1884 – d.22 April 1976) Sabre, Individual [2p11r1/4].

Jong, Adrianus Egbertus Willem de. (b.21 June 1882–d.23 December 1966) Épée, Team [9]; Sabre, Individual [=4p3r2/4]; Sabre, Team [=5].

Labouchere, Alfred Joan. (b.19 January 1867–d.24 January 1953) Épée, Individual [=5]; Sabre, Individual [=3p6r2/4]; Épée, Team [9].

Löben Sels, Maurits Jacob van. (b.1 May 1876–d.4 October 1944) Épée, Individual [=7p5r1/4]; Sabre, Individual [5p6r1/4]; Sabre, Team [=5].

Minden, Lion van. (b.10 June 1880–d.6 September 1944) Sabre, Individual [4p7r1/4].

Okker, Simon. (b.1 June 1881–d.6 March 1944) Épée, Individual [4p11r1/4].

Rossem, George van. (b.30 May 1882–d.14 January 1955) Épée, Individual [=7p4r1/4]; Épée, Team [9]; Sabre, Individual [3p2r2/4]; Sabre, Team [=5].

Schoemaker, Richard Leonard Arnold. (b.5 October 1886–d.3 May 1942) Sabre, Individual [=3p1r2/4].

Schreven, Johan Thomas Carel van. (b.17 September 1874–d.10 November 1924) Épée, Individual [=4p2r1/4]; Sabre, Individual [=4p10r1/4].

Football (Association Football [Soccer]) (Total: 12; Men: 12; Women: 0)

Beeuwkes, Reinier Bertus. (b.17 February 1884–d.1 April 1963) [3].

Bruyn Kops, George François de. (b.28 October 1886–d.22 November 1979) [3].

Heijting, Karel. (b.1 May 1883–d.1951) [3].

Kok, Johan Adolf Frederik. (b.9 July 1889–d.2 December 1958) [3].

Korver, Johannes Marius de "Bok." (b.27 January 1883–d.22 October 1957) [3].

Mundt, Emil Gustav. (b.30 May 1880–d.17 July 1949) [3].

Otten, Louis "Lou." (b.5 November 1883–d.7 November 1946) [3].

Reeman, Gerard Simon. (b.9 August 1886–d.16 March 1959) [3].

Snethlage, Everardus "Edu." (b.9 May 1886–d.12 January 1941) [3].

Sol, Johan Wilhelm Eduard. (b.10 June 1881–d.21 October 1965) [3].

Thomée, Johannes "Jan." (b.4 December 1886–d.1 April 1954) [3].

Welcker, Jan Herman "Cajus." (b.9 July 1885–d.13 February 1939) [3].

Gymnastics (Total: 23; Men: 23; Women: 0)

Becker, Cornelis Lambertus Josephus. (b.18 October 1886–d.26 November 1913) Combined Exercises, Individual [71]; Combined Exercises, Team [7].

Biet, Michel. (b.3 November 1883–d.25 November 1948) Combined Exercises, Individual [49]; Combined Exercises, Team [7].

Blom, Reiner Jan Cornelis. (b.31 March 1867–d.12 August 1943) Combined Exercises, Individual [61]; Combined Exercises, Team [7].

Boer, Jan de. (b.15 February 1859–d.8 June 1941) Combined Exercises, Team [7].

Bolt, Jan. (b.3 February 1876–d.7 May 1967) Combined Exercises, Team [7].

Brouwer, E. Combined Exercises, Individual [64]; Combined Exercises, Team [7].

Daalen, Constantijn van. (b.7 April 1884–d.5 September 1931) Combined Exercises, Individual [93]; Combined Exercises, Team [7].

Flemer, Johann Heinrich. (b.16 February 1888–d.12 August 1955) Combined Exercises, Individual [90]; Combined Exercises, Team [7].

Göckel, Johannes Cornelis Gerrit. (b.28 December 1886–d.6 June 1960) Combined Exercises, Team [7].

Goudeket, I. Combined Exercises, Individual [62]; Combined Exercises, Team [7].

Janssen, Dirk. (b.11 July 1881–d.22 November 1986) Combined Exercises, Individual [69]; Combined Exercises, Team [7].

Janssen, Jan. (b.6 December 1879–d.24 May 1953) Combined Exercises, Individual [72].

Kieft, Jan Jacob. (b.25 January 1877–d.2 April 1946) Combined Exercises, Individual [74]; Combined Exercises, Team [7].

Konijn, Salomon. (b.14 January 1874–d.15 March 1932) Combined Exercises, Team [7].

Leeuwen, Hermanus Nicolaas van "Herman." (b.8 June 1884–d.7 February 1926) Combined Exercises, Individual [95]; Combined Exercises, Team [7]. [See also Athletics (Track & Field)].

Mok, Abraham. (b.15 May 1888–d.29 February 1944) Combined Exercises, Individual [78]; Combined Exercises, Team [7].

Oliveira, Abraham de. (b.4 May 1880–d.26 March 1943) Combined Exercises, Team [7].

Posthumus, Johannes Jacobus. (b.24 September 1887–d.12 December 1978) Combined Exercises, Individual [66]; Combined Exercises, Team [7].

Schmitt, Johan Henri Antoine Gerrit. (b.31 August 1881–d.12 August 1955) Combined Exercises, Team [7].

Slier, Jonas. (b.22 March 1886–d.5 November 1942) Combined Exercises, Individual [96]; Combined Exercises, Team [7].

Stikkelman, Johannes. (b.16 June 1885–d.21 July 1953) Combined Exercises, Individual [63]; Combined Exercises, Team [7].

Thijsen, Hendricus Josephus Franciscus. (b.30 July 1881) Combined Exercises, Individual [83]; Combined Exercises, Team [7].

Wesling, Gerardus Jacobus. (b.21 November 1885–d.10 August 1954) Combined Exercises, Individual [60]; Combined Exercises, Team [7].

Rowing & Sculling (Total: 4; Men: 4; Women: 0)
Burk, Johan Frederik Karel Hendrik Jacob. (b.11 May 1887) Coxless Fours [2h2r1/2].
Croon, Bernardus Hermanus. (b.11 May 1886–d.30 January 1960) Coxless Fours [2h2r1/2].
Höfte, Hermannus. (b.5 August 1884–d.18 November 1961) Coxless Fours [2h2r1/2].
Wielsma, Albertus. (b.19 December 1883–d.26 March 1968) Coxless Fours [2h2r1/2].

Shooting (Total: 17; Men: 17; Women: 0)
Altenburg, Cornelis van. (b.24 July 1871–d.2 August 1953) Free Rifle, Team [7].
Bergh, Gerard Anne van den. (b.19 November 1882–d.22 October 1949) Free Pistol [40]; Free Pistol, Team [6]; Free Rifle, Team [7].
Blécourt, Jan Johannes de. (b.13 July 1860–d.20 March 1925) Free Pistol [36]; Free Pistol, Team [6].
Brosch, Christiaan Adolf Willem. (b.7 March 1878–d.29 June 1969) Free Pistol [41]; Free Rifle, Team [7].

Bruggen Cate, Petrus ten. (b.2 September 1870–d.15 November 1942) Free Pistol [24]; Free Pistol, Team [6]; Free Rifle, 3 Positions [32].

Brussaard, Pieter Johannes. (b.30 January 1875–d.28 December 1940) Free Rifle, Team [7].

Favauge, Romain Henri Theodor David de. (b.22 December 1872–d.8 October 1949) Trap Shooting, Individual [22]; Trap Shooting, Team [4].

Gee, Antonie Willem Jan de. (b.8 January 1872–d.19 January 1940) Free Pistol [43]; Free Rifle, Team [7].

Kop, Jacob van der. (b.25 July 1868–d.26 January 1945) Free Pistol [12]; Free Pistol, Team [6].

Laan, Jacob Adriaan. (b.31 March 1869–d.5 April 1939) Trap Shooting, Individual [26].

Pallandt, Baron Rudolph Theodorus van. (b.28 November 1868–d.15 March 1913) Trap Shooting, Individual [ac]; Trap Shooting, Team [4].

Viruly, Cornelis Marius. (b.11 November 1875–d.23 September 1938) Trap Shooting, Individual [14]; Trap Shooting, Team [4].

Voorst tot Voorst, Eduardus Ludovicus van. (b.17 November 1874–d.2 April 1945) Trap Shooting, Team [4]; Trap Shooting, Individual [=15].

Voorst tot Voorst, Franciscus Antonius Josephus Carel van. (b.19 May 1884–d.23 September 1955) Trap Shooting, Team [4]; Trap Shooting, Individual [=15].

Vuurman, Uilke. (b.2 October 1872–d.14 July 1955) Free Rifle, Team [7].

Waas, Pieter Marinus van. (b.30 December 1878–d.21 March 1962) Free Rifle, 3 Positions [22].

Wilson, John Waterloo. (b.1 September 1879–d.15 March 1940) Trap Shooting, Individual [=7]; Trap Shooting, Team [4].

Swimming (Total: 7; Men: 7; Women: 0)

Benenga, Bouke. (b.27 March 1888–d.4 January 1968) 100 meter freestyle [ach1r1/3]. [See also Water Polo].

Benenga, Lambertus. (b.17 February 1886–d.3 August 1963) 100 meter freestyle [2h3r1/3].

Cortlever, Johan George. (b.4 August 1885–d.14 April 1972) 100 meter backstroke [2h7r1/3]. [See also Water Polo].

Meijer, Eduard. (b.25 February 1878–d.20 March 1929) 1,500 meter freestyle [dnfh6r1/3]. [See also Water Polo].

Meuring, Friedrich Wilhelm. (b.6 June 1882–d.28 May 1973) 400 meter freestyle [ach7r1/3].

Ooms, Pieter Lodewijk "Piet." (b.11 December 1884–d.14 February 1961) 1,500 meter freestyle [3h2r1/3]. [See also Water Polo].

Roodenburch, Bartholomeus Adrianus. (b.29 June 1866–d.16 July 1939) 100 meter backstroke [2h3r1/3].

Tennis (Total: 2; Men: 2; Women: 0)

Lennep, Christiaan van. (b.3 January 1887–d.5 December 1955) Singles (Lawn) [=26]; Doubles (Lawn) [=7].

Lennep, Roelof van. (b.3 October 1876–d.13 September 1951) Singles (Lawn) [=16]; Doubles (Lawn) [=7].

Water Polo (Total: 7; Men: 7; Women: 0)

Benenga, Bouke. (b.27 March 1888–d.1 April 1968) [4]. [See also Swimming].

Cortlever, Johan George. (b.4 August 1885–d.14 April 1972) [4]. [See also Swimming].

Hulswit, Frederik Jan. (b.9 April 1885–d.2 May 1932) [4].

Meijer, Eduard. (b.25 February 1878–d.20 March 1929) [4]. [See also Swimming].

Meijer, Karel. (b.26 June 1884–d.29 December 1967) [4].

Ooms, Pieter Lodewijk "Piet." (b.11 December 1884–d.14 February 1961) [4]. [See also Swimming].

Rühl, Johan Hendrik Willem. (b.9 May 1885–d.4 December 1972) [4].

Wrestling (Total: 9; Men: 9; Women: 0)

Belmer, Jacob "Jaap." (b.22 January 1886–d.18 April 1936) Middleweight, Greco-Roman [=5].

Bruseker, Ulferd Onke. (b.21 March 1887–d.17 December 1968) Lightweight, Greco-Roman [=9].

Duijm, Gerrit Frederik. (b.5 December 1888–d.30 July 1942) Middleweight, Greco-Roman [=17].

Lelie, Aäron. (b.25 April 1886–d.25 March 1954) Middleweight, Greco-Roman [=9].

Lorenz, Jacobus. (b.22 December 1884–d.17 January 1969) Middleweight, Greco-Roman [=9].

Moppes, Jacob van. (b.18 August 1876–d.26 March 1943) Lightweight, Greco-Roman [=17].

Oosten, Leendert van. (b.7 November 1884–d.6 July 1936) Light-Heavyweight, Greco-Roman [=9].

Westrop, Jacob van. (b.7 November 1886) Light-Heavyweight, Greco-Roman [=5].

Wijbrands, Douwe. (b.9 October 1884–d.17 November 1970) Light-Heavyweight, Greco-Roman [=9].

New Zealand (Total: 3; Men: 3; Women: 0)[8]

Athletics (Track & Field) (Total: 3; Men: 3; Women: 0)

Kerr, Harry E. 3,500 meter walk [3].

Murray, Henry Steven Aubyn. 110 meter hurdles [2h1r1/3]; 400 meter hurdles [2h3r1/3].

Rowland, Arthur Edward Mackay. (b.26 October 1885–d.23 July 1918) 3,500 meter walk [5]; 10 mile walk [5h1r1/2].

Norway (Total: 69; Men: 69; Women: 0)

Athletics (Track & Field) (Total: 11; Men: 11; Women: 0)

Blystad, Wilhelm Arnt. (b.15 September 1881–d.4 July 1954) 110 meter hurdles [dnfh11r1/3]; Standing High Jump [=8].

Carlsrud, Conrad Maurentius. (b.9 February 1884–d.21 October 1973) Javelin Throw (freestyle) [ac]. [See also Gymnastics].

Dahl, Nils. (b.12 November 1882–d.17 July 1966) 1,500 meters [7h1r1/2].

Falchenberg, John. (b.12 September 1883–d.5 November 1960) Discus Throw (freestyle) [ac].

Guttormsen, Oscar. (b.27 March 1884–d.15 January 1964) 100 meters [2h2r1/3]; 200 meters [4h1r2/3]; 400 meters [2h5r1/3]; 110 meter hurdles [2h12r1/3]; Triple Jump [14].

Halse, Arne. (b.20 October 1887–d.3 July 1975) Shot Put [ac]; Javelin Throw (freestyle) [3]; Javelin Throw (held in middle) [2].

Johansen, C. E. John. (b.26 February 1883–d.15 October 1947) 100 meters [2h5r1/3]; Javelin Throw (freestyle) [ac]; Javelin Throw (held in middle) [ac].

Larsen, Edvard. (b.27 October 1881–d.11 September 1914) Triple Jump [3].

Larsen, Oscar. (b.11 September 1887–d.16 April 1975) 1,500 meters [4h8r1/2].

Monsen, Otto. (b.19 August 1887–d.14 December 1979) High Jump [wd/qr].

Olsen, Henry Martinus. (b.11 March 1887–d.24 August 1978) High Jump [=13]; Long Jump [ac]; Triple Jump [13].

Fencing (Total: 1; Men: 1; Women: 0)

Bergsland, Hans. (b.15 November 1878–d.9 June 1956) Épée, Individual [6p4r1/4].

Gymnastics (Total: 30; Men: 30; Women: 0)

Amundsen, Arthur M. (b.22 March 1886–d.1936) Combined Exercises, Team [2].

Andersen, Carl Albert "Flisa." (b.15 August 1876–d.28 September 1951) Combined Exercises, Team [2].

Authén, Otto Fredrik. (b.1 November 1886–d.7 July 1971) Combined Exercises, Team [2].

Bohne, Hermann. (b.22 September 1890–d.5 January 1949) Combined Exercises, Team [2].

Bøyesen, Trygve Carlsen. (b.18 February 1886–d.27 July 1963) Combined Exercises, Team [2].

Bye, Oskar Wilhelm. (b.3 June 1870–d.30 April 1939) Combined Exercises, Team [2].

Carlsrud, Conrad Maurentius. (b.9 February 1884–d.21 October 1973) Combined Exercises, Individual [ac]; Combined Exercises, Team [2]. [See also Athletics (Track & Field)].

Grøner, Sverre. (b.17 September 1890–d.3 February 1972) Combined Exercises, Team [2].

Halvorsen, Harald. (b.3 May 1887) Combined Exercises, Team [2].

Hansen, Harald. (b.30 October 1884–d.6 March 1956) Combined Exercises, Team [2].

Hol, Petter. (b.19 March 1883–d.22 June 1981) Combined Exercises, Individual [ac]; Combined Exercises, Team [2].

Ingebretsen, Eugen. (b.30 December 1884–d.1949) Combined Exercises, Individual [ac]; Combined Exercises, Team [2].

Iversen, Ole. (b.21 February 1884–d.9 March 1953) Combined Exercises, Individual [ac]; Combined Exercises, Team [2].

Jespersen, Per Mathias. (b.29 March 1888–d.13 July 1964) Combined Exercises, Individual [ac]; Combined Exercises, Team [2].

Johannessen, Sigurd Erhard Amanus "Sigge." (b.9 January 1884–d.7 February 1974) Combined Exercises, Team [2].

Kiær, Nicolai. (b.2 April 1888–d.29 May 1934) Combined Exercises, Team [2].

Klæth, Carl. (b.3 July 1887–d.16 August 1966) Combined Exercises, Individual [ac]; Combined Exercises, Team [2].

Larsen, Thor. (b.20 July 1886–d.3 September 1970) Combined Exercises, Team [2].

Lefdahl, Rolf. (b.13 August 1882–d.5 February 1965) Combined Exercises, Team [2].

Lem, Hans Schumann. (b.18 May 1875) Combined Exercises, Team [2].

Moen, Anders. (b.1 October 1887–d.5 July 1966) Combined Exercises, Team [2].

Olsen, Frithjof. (b.30 November 1882–d.22 February 1922) Combined Exercises, Individual [ac]; Combined Exercises, Team [2].

Pedersen, Carl Alfred. (b.5 May 1882–d.25 June 1960) Combined Exercises, Team [2].

Pedersen, Paul Andreas. (b.18 September 1886–d.16 August 1948) Combined Exercises, Team [2].

Sivertsen, Sigvard I. (b.27 February 1881–d.27 December 1963) Combined Exercises, Team [2].

Skrataas, John. (b.4 May 1890–d.12 February 1961) Combined Exercises, Individual [ac]; Combined Exercises, Team [2].

Smedvik, Harald J. (b.28 March 1888–d.1956) Combined Exercises, Team [2].

Strand, Andreas. (b.3 February 1889–d.19 April 1958) Combined Exercises, Team [2].

Syvertsen, Olaf. (b.23 August 1884–d.18 June 1964) Combined Exercises, Team [2].

Torstensen, Thomas. (b.18 May 1880–d.18 June 1953) Combined Exercises, Team [2].

Rowing & Sculling (Total: 9; Men: 9; Women: 0)

Bye, Erik O. (b.17 May 1883–d.1 March 1953) Coxed Eights [2h1r1/3].

Feght, Ole Hannibal Sommerfeldt. (b.27 August 1879–d.15 September 1967) Coxed Eights [2h1r1/3].

Hæhre, Gustav. (b.5 September 1878–d.25 September 1950) Coxed Eights [2h1r1/3].

Hansen, Wilhelm Emanuel. (b.15 March 1884–d.20 March 1931) Coxed Eights [2h1r1/3].

Høyer, Ambrosius. (b.August 1885–d.9 May 1919) Coxed Eights [2h1r1/3].

Irgens, Emil. (b.2 August 1883–d.13 July 1918) Coxed Eights [2h1r1/3].

Knudsen, Andreas Annan. (b.23 August 1887–d.11 February 1982) Coxed Eights [2h1r1/3].

Krogh, Otto Theodor. (b.29 February 1880–d.3 March 1952) Coxed Eights [2h1r1/3].

Tønsager, Einar. (b.12 April 1888–d.15 October 1967) Coxed Eights [2h1r1/3].

Shooting (Total: 13; Men: 13; Women: 0)

Braathe, Julius "Jul." (b.4 May 1876–d.8 July 1914) Free Rifle, 3 Positions [6]; Free Rifle, Team [1].

Bru, Jørgen Anders. (b.5 January 1881—17 December 1974) Free Rifle, 1,000 yards [=28]; Military Rifle, Team [6].

Enger, Asmund Johansen. (b.30 September 1881–d.11 April 1966) Free Rifle, 1,000 yards [=41].

Erdmann, Georg Marenus Gottlieb. (b.21 February 1875–d.22 February 1966) Free Rifle, 3 Positions [13]; Free Rifle, 1,000 yards [40].

Glomnes, Mathias. (b.2 February 1869–d.6 June 1956) Free Rifle, 3 Positions [47]; Free Rifle, 1,000 yards [47]; Military Rifle, Team [6].

Helgerud, Albert. (b.16 September 1876–d.27 June 1954) Free Rifle, 3 Positions [1]; Free Rifle, Team [1]; Military Rifle, Team [6].

Kvam, Kolbjørn. (b.20 October 1865–d.13 March 1933) Free Rifle, 3 Positions [19]; Free Rifle, 1,000 yards [=41].

Liberg, Einar. (b.16 October 1873–d.11 September 1955) Free Rifle, Team [1]; Military Rifle, Team [6].

Olsen, Per Olaf. Free Rifle, 3 Positions [27].

Sæter, Olaf. (b.1 July 1872–d.1 November 1945) Free Rifle, 3 Positions [9]; Free Rifle, Team [1].

Sæther, Ole Andreas. (b.23 January 1870–d.13 October 1946) Free Rifle, 3 Positions [3]; Free Rifle, Team [1]; Military Rifle, Team [6].

Skatteboe, Gudbrand Gudbrandsen. (b.18 July 1875–d.3 April 1965) Military Rifle, Team [6]; Free Rifle, Team [1].

Skymoen, Olivius Arntsen. (b.1857–d.19 August 1909) Free Rifle, 3 Positions [24]; Free Rifle, 1,000 yards [ac].

Wrestling (Total: 1; Men: 1; Women: 0)

Gundersen, Jacob. (b.29 October 1875–d.January 1968) Heavyweight, Catch-as-Catch-Can [2].

Yachting (Total: 5; Men: 5; Women: 0)

Anker, Johan August. (b.26 June 1871–d.2 October 1940) 8-meter class [4].

Hvoslef, Einar. (b.21 June 1876–d.1 December 1931) 8-meter class [4].

Konow, Magnus Andreas Thulstrup Clasen. (b.1 September 1887–d.25 August 1972) 8-meter class [4].

Lund, Eilart Fach. (b.27 January 1875–d.1960) 8-meter class [4].
Steffens, Hagbart. (b.1874–d.27 June 1932) 8-meter class [4].

Russia (Total: 6; Men: 6; Women: 0)

Athletics (Track & Field) (Total: 1; Men: 1; Women: 0)
Lind, Georg. Marathon [19].

Figure Skating (Total: 1; Men: 1; Women: 0)
Panin, Nikolay Aleksandrovich. (b.1 January 1874–d.19 January 1956) Men's Individual [ac/dnf];
Special Figures [1]. [Also competed under psuedonym of Nikolay Kolomenkin].

Wrestling (Total: 4; Men: 4; Women: 0)
Demin, Georgy. Middleweight, Greco-Roman [=9].
Orlov, Nikolay. Lightweight, Greco-Roman [2].
Petrov, Aleksandr. (b.1878) Heavyweight, Greco-Roman [2].
Zamotin, Yevgeny. Light-Heavyweight, Greco-Roman [=9].

South Africa (Total: 14; Men: 14; Women: 0)

Athletics (Track & Field) (Total: 6; Men: 6; Women: 0)
Baker, James Mitchell[9] (b.14 February 1878–d.14 December 1956) Marathon [dnf]
Duffy, Edward John. (b.6 June 1883–19 October 1918) 100 meters [3h3r2/3]; 200 meters
[2h2r1/3].
Hefferon, Charles Archie. (b.25 January 1878–d.15 March 1931) 5 miles [4]; Marathon [2].
Phillips, Herbert Thorne. (b.20 June 1883–d.5 August 1977) 100 meters [dnfh11r1/3].
Stupart, Douglas Annesley. (b.30 March 1882–d.6 May 1951) 110 meter hurdles [3h1r1/3];
Triple Jump [10].
Walker, Reginald Edgar "Reggie." (b.16 March 1889–d.5 November 1951) 100 meters [1].

Cycling (Total: 4; Men: 4; Women: 0)
Frylink, Philipus Thomas. (b.1886–d.15 Dec. 1908) One Lap Match Sprint [3h16r1/2]; 1,000
meters Match Sprint [2h8r1/3]; 5,000 meters [3h3r1/2]; Tandem Sprint [2h5r1/3].
Passmore, Thomas Henry Eddy. (b.19 June 1884–d.8 May 1955) One Lap Match Sprint
[2h9r1/2]; 5,000 meters [ach4r1/2]; 20 km. [3h4r1/2]; 100 km. [dnfh2r1/2].
Shore, Frank. (b.1887) One Lap Match Sprint [dnfh5r1/3]; 1,000 meters Match Sprint [dq-
h16r1/3]; 5,000 meters [ach5r1/2]; 20 km. [2h3r1/2].
Venter, Floris Daniel. (b.1886) One Lap Match Sprint [4h2r2/3]; 1,000 meters Match Sprint
[3h1r2/3]; 5,000 meters [ach7r1/2]; 20 km. [3h2r1/2]; Tandem Sprint [2h5r1/3].

Fencing (Total: 1; Men: 1; Women: 0)
Gates, Walter Percy. (b.1874) Épée, Individual [=6p2r1/4]; Sabre, Individual [6p8r1/4].

Tennis (Total: 3; Men: 3; Women: 0)
Gauntlett, Vincent R. Singles (Lawn) [=16]; Doubles (Lawn) [=4].
Kitson, Harald Austin. (b.17 June 1874) Singles (Lawn) [=16]; Doubles (Lawn) [=4].
Richardson, Reverend John C. Singles (Lawn) [4].[10]

Sweden (Total: 168; Men: 165; Women: 3)

Athletics (Track & Field) (Total: 31; Men: 31; Women: 0)

Andersson, E. Axel. (b.19 June 1887–d.17 August 1951) 1,500 meters [6h8r1/2].

Bengtsson, Allan. (b.30 June 1889–d.7 May 1955) Standing High Jump [=14].

Björn, Evert. (b.21 January 1888–d.21 December 1974) 800 meters [3h1r1/2]; 1,500 meters [dnfh3r1/2]; 1,600 meter medley relay [h1r1/2].

Dahl, Edward M. (b.3 August 1886–d.21 November 1961) 800 meters [dnfh5r1/2]; 1,500 meters [2h8r1/2]; 5 miles [dnfh2r1/2]; 3-mile team race [3h2r1/2].

Danielson, Frank Gösta. (b.17 November 1889) 800 meters [dnfh6r1/2].

Ekberg, O. Ragnar B. (b.12 August 1886) Standing Long Jump [5].

Fleetwood, Folke. (b.15 November 1890–d.4 February 1949) Discus Throw (freestyle) [ac]; Discus Throw (classical) [ac].

Fryksdahl, Karl. (b.22 June 1885–d.9 April 1944) 100 meters [3h12r1/3]; Triple Jump [7]; Standing High Jump [=14].

Hedenlund, Axel, Jr. (b.11 February 1888–d.18 April 1919) High Jump [8].

Hellstedt, Folke. (b.11 February 1891–d.13 June 1969) High Jump [=16].

Hellström, Kristian. (b.24 July 1880–d.14 June 1946) 800 meters [2h8r1/2].

Laftman, Sven. (b.16 December 1887–d.5 July 1977) 400 meters [3h4r1/3]; 1,600 meter medley relay [2h1r1/2].

Landqvist, Seth L. (b.8 August 1882–d.2 April 1945) 5 miles [9]; Marathon [dnf]; 3-mile team race [3h2r1/2].

Lemming, Eric Valdemar. (b.22 February 1880–d.5 June 1930) Discus Throw (freestyle) [ac]; Discus Throw (classical) [ac]; Hammer Throw [8]; Javelin Throw (freestyle) [1]; Javelin Throw (held in middle) [1].

Lemming, Oscar R. (b.11 October 1886–d.30 August 1979) 110 meter hurdles [dnfh6r1/3].

Lindberg, Knut. (b.2 February 1882–d.6 April 1961) 100 meters [2h8r1/3]; 200 meters [4h11r1/3]; 1,600 meter medley relay [h1r1/2]; Javelin Throw (freestyle) [ac].

Lindqvist, Johan. (b.29 August 1882–d.1958) Marathon [dnf].

Neijström, Theodor. (b.23 September 1883) Discus Throw (freestyle) [ac].

Nilsson, Otto. (b.26 September 1879–d.10 November 1960) Discus Throw (freestyle) [ac]; Javelin Throw (freestyle) [ac]; Javelin Throw (held in middle) [3].

Olsson, Carl Robert. (b.14 March 1883–d.21 July 1954) Hammer Throw [ac].

Peterson, J. Georg. (b.20 February 1883–d.23 November 1964) 5 miles [3h4r1/2]; 3-mile team race [3h2r1/2].

Ringstrand, K. Arvid. (b.3 February 1888–d.1 December 1957) 400 meters [3h14r1/3]; Long Jump [ac].

Ronström, Gunnar V. (b.25 January 1884–d.5 July 1941) Long Jump [10].

Rothman, Einar. (b.3 January 1888–d.3 September 1952) 3,500 meter walk [7]; 10 mile walk [dnfh2r1/2].

Silfverstrand, Carl. (b.9 October 1875–d.2 January 1975) Pole Vault [=10]; Long Jump [20].

Söderström, Bruno. (b.23 October 1881–d.1 January 1969) Pole Vault [=3]; Javelin Throw (freestyle) [ac].

Stenborg, Knut. (b.25 March 1890) 100 meters [2h7r1/3]; 200 meters [4h2r1/3]; 1,600 meter medley relay [h1r1/2].

Svanberg, Johan Fritiof. (b.1 May 1881–d.11 September 1957) 5 miles [3]; Marathon [8]; 3-mile team race [3h2r1/2].

Törnros, Gustaf. (b.18 March 1887–d.2 April 1941) Marathon [21].

Wiegandt, Axel J. A. (b.14 January 1888–d.8 April 1950) 5 miles [dnfh5r1/2]3-mile team race [3h2r1/2].

Wieslander, Karl Hugo. (b.11 June 1889–d.24 May 1976) Long Jump [ac]; Shot Put [ac]; Discus Throw (freestyle) [ac]; Javelin Throw (freestyle) [5]; Javelin Throw (held in middle) [ac].

Cycling (Total: 2; Men: 2; Women: 0)

Hansson, Andrew. (b.13 October 1882) One Lap Match Sprint [3h6r1/2]; 1,000 meters Match Sprint [2h3r1/3]; 20 km. [ac-final]; 100 km. [dnf-final]; Tandem Sprint [3h4r1/3].

Westerberg, Gustaf. (b.10 March 1884) 20 km. [3h6r1/2]; 100 km. [dnf-final]; Tandem Sprint [3h4r1/3].

Diving (Total: 10; Men: 10; Women: 0)

Adlerz, Erik "Loppan." (b.23 July 1892–d.8 September 1975) Plain High Diving [3h1r1/3].

Andersson, Robert "Robban." (b.18 October 1886–d.2 March 1972) Plain High Diving [4]. [See also Swimming and Water Polo].

Arbin, Harald Andersson. (b.4 August 1867–d.31 July 1944) Plain High Diving [5h1r2/3].

Johansson, Hjalmar. (b.20 January 1874–d.30 September 1957) Plain High Diving [1]. [See also Swimming].

Larsson, Sigfrid D. (b.1 January 1882–d.9 October 1968) Plain High Diving [3h3r1/3]; Fancy High Diving [5h4r2/3].

Löfberg, Hilmer. (b.22 July 1887–d.23 July 1940) Plain High Diving [4h1r2/3].

Malmström, Karl. (b.27 December 1875–d.6 September 1938) Plain High Diving [2]; Fancy High Diving [4h3r2/3].

Runström, Axel. (b.15 October 1883–d.10 August 1943) Plain High Diving [4h5r1/3]. [See also Water Polo].

Spångberg, Arvid "Sparven." (b.4 April 1890–d.19 October 1964) Plain High Diving [3].

Vindqvist, Karl Gustaf. (b.15 October 1883–d.19 November 1967) Plain High Diving [4h4r1/3].

Fencing (Total: 7; Men: 7; Women: 0)

Branting, Georg. (b.21 September 1887–d.6 July 1965) Épée, Individual [5p11r1/4].

Carlberg, Eric. (b.5 April 1880–d.14 August 1963) Épée, Individual [4p1r1/4]; Épée, Team [=5]. [See also Shooting].

Cnattingius, Birger A. (b.29 November 1875–d.19 February 1950) Épée, Individual [=4p12r1/4].

Lindblom, Gustaf. (b.19 August 1883–d.16 March 1976) Épée, Individual [=6p2r3/4]; Épée, Team [=5].

Olson, Gustaf "Gösta." (b.10 May 1883–d.23 January 1966) Épée, Individual [6p12r1/4]. [See also Gymnastics].

Peyron, Henry. (b.14 June 1883–d.18 February 1972) Épée, Individual [4p6r1/4]; Épée, Team [=5].

von Rosen, Pontus R. C. (b.21 November 1881–d.11 January 1951) Épée, Individual [5p1r1/4]; Épée, Team [=5].

Figure Skating (Total: 4; Men: 3; Women: 1)

Women

Montgomery, Elna. (b.23 October 1885) Ladies' Individual [4].

Men

Johansson, Richard. (b.18 June 1882–d.24 July 1952) Men's Individual [2].

Salchow, Karl Emil Julius Ulrich "Ulrich." (b.7 August 1877–d.18 April 1949) Men's Individual [1].

Thorén, Per. (b.26 January 1885–d.5 January 1962) Men's Individual [3].

Football (Association Football [Soccer]) (Total: 14; Men: 14; Women: 0)

Almkvist, Sune. (b.4 February 1886–d.8 August 1975) [4].

Andersson, Nils. (b.1887) [4].

Ansén, Karl. (b.26 July 1887–d.20 July 1959) [4].

Bengtsson, Oskar. (b.14 January 1885–d.12 October 1972) [4].

Bergström, Gustaf. (b.1884–d.9 February 1938) [4].

Fagrell, Arvid. (b.10 August 1886–d.6 December 1932) [4].

Fjästad, Åke. (b.16 December 1887–d.10 March 1956) [4].

Gustafsson, Karl "Köping." (b.16 September 1888–d.20 February 1960) [4].

Lidén, Valter. (b.10 March 1887) [4].

Lindman, Hans. (b.6 September 1884–d.24 January 1957) [4].

Malm, Teodor "Todde." (b.23 October 1889–d.2 October 1950) [4].

Ohlsson, Sven "Generalen." (b.1888) [4].

Olsson, Olle. (b.1884) [4].

Olsson, Sven "Bleddy." [4].

Gymnastics (Total: 38; Men: 38; Women: 0)

Åsbrink, Karl Gösta "Gösta." (b.18 November 1881–d.19 April 1966) Combined Exercises, Team [1].

Bertilsson, Carl. (b.18 October 1889–d.16 November 1968) Combined Exercises, Team [1].

Cedercrona, Hjalmar Axel Fritz. (b.23 December 1883–d.24 May 1969) Combined Exercises, Team [1].

Cervin, Andreas. (b.31 October 1888–d.14 February 1972) Combined Exercises, Team [1].

Degermark, Rudolf. (b.19 July 1886–d.21 May 1960) Combined Exercises, Team [1].

Folcker, Carl Wilhelm. (b.28 March 1889–d.2 July 1911) Combined Exercises, Team [1].

Forssman, Sven. (b.12 September 1882–d.1 March 1919) Combined Exercises, Team [1].

Granfelt, Erik G. (b.17 November 1883–d.18 February 1962) Combined Exercises, Team [1]. [See also Tug-of-War].

Hårleman, Carl. (b.23 June 1886–d.20 August 1948) Combined Exercises, Team [1].

Hellsten, Nils Erik. (b.19 February 1886–d.12 April 1962) Combined Exercises, Team [1]. [See also Fencing].

Höjer, Gunnar. (b.27 January 1875–d.13 March 1936) Combined Exercises, Team [1].

Holmberg, Arvid. (b.10 October 1886–d.11 September 1958) Combined Exercises, Team [1].

Holmberg, Carl. (b.9 March 1884–d.1 December 1909) Combined Exercises, Team [1].

Holmberg, Oswald. (b.17 July 1882–d.11 February 1969) Combined Exercises, Team [1].

Jahnke, Hugo. (b.6 March 1886–d.12 January 1939) Combined Exercises, Team [1].

Jarlén, Johan "John." (b.4 November 1880–d.18 April 1955) Combined Exercises, Team [1].

Johnsson, Harald Gustaf "Gustaf." (b.7 March 1890) Combined Exercises, Team [1].

Johnsson, Rolf. (b.1 December 1889–d.3 June 1931) Combined Exercises, Team [1].

Kantzow, Nils von. (b.30 August 1885–d.7 February 1967) Combined Exercises, Team [1].

Landberg, Sven. (b.6 December 1888–d.11 April 1962) Combined Exercises, Team [1].

Lanner, Olle. (b.30 December 1884–d.26 July 1926) Combined Exercises, Team [1].

Ljung, Axel. (b.31 March 1884–d.5 February 1938) Combined Exercises, Team [1].

Moberg, Osvald "Moppe." (b.14 September 1888–d.22 December 1933) Combined Exercises, Team [1].

Norberg, Carl Martin. (b.21 March 1886) Combined Exercises, Team [1].

Norberg, Erik. (b.30 September 1883–d.19 February 1954) Combined Exercises, Team [1].

Norberg, Tor. (b.17 December 1880) Combined Exercises, Team [1].

Norling, Axel. (b.16 April 1884–d.7 May 1964) Combined Exercises, Team [1].

Norling, Daniel. (b.16 January 1888–d.28 August 1958) Combined Exercises, Team [1].

Olson, Gustaf "Gösta." (b.10 May 1883–d.23 January 1966) Combined Exercises, Team [1]. [See also Fencing].

Peterson, Leonard. (b.30 October 1885–d.15 April 1956) Combined Exercises, Team [1].

Rosén, Sven. (b.10 March 1887–d.22 June 1963) Combined Exercises, Team [1].

Rosenquist, Gustaf "Gösta." (b.10 September 1887–d.22 December 1961) Combined Exercises, Team [1].

Sjöblom, Axel. (b.17 December 1882–d.10 October 1951) Combined Exercises, Team [1].

Sörvik, Birger. (b.4 December 1879–d.23 May 1978) Combined Exercises, Team [1].

Sörvik, Haakon. (b.31 October 1886–d.30 May 1970) Combined Exercises, Team [1].

Svensson (Sarland), Karl-Johan (né Svensson). (b.12 March 1887–d.20 January 1964) Combined Exercises, Team [1].

Vingqvist, Karl Gustaf. (b.15 October 1883–d.19 November 1967) Combined Exercises, Team [1].

Widforss, Nils. (b.3 November 1880–d.2 May 1960) Combined Exercises, Team [1].

Shooting (Total: 19; Men: 19; Women: 0)

Arvidsson, Per-Olof. (b.18 December 1864–d.30 August 1947) Free Rifle, 3 Positions [12]; Free Rifle, Team [2]; Military Rifle, Team [5].

Benedicks, Edward. (b.9 February 1879–d.24 August 1960) Trap Shooting, Individual [=27].

Carlberg, Eric. (b.5 April 1880–d.14 August 1963) Free Pistol [33]; Free Pistol, Team [5]; Small-Bore Rifle, Disappearing Target [=9]; Small-Bore Rifle, Moving Target [=15]; Small-Bore Rifle, Team [2]. [See also Fencing].

Carlberg, Vilhelm. (b.5 April 1880–d.1 October 1970) Free Pistol [20]; Free Pistol, Team [5]; Small-Bore Rifle, Disappearing Target [7]; Small-Bore Rifle, Moving Target [=15]; Small-Bore Rifle, Prone [=10]; Small-Bore Rifle, Team [2].

Gustafsson, Johan "Janne." (b.2 May 1883–d.24 September 1942) Free Rifle, Team [2]; Free Rifle, 3 Positions [5]; Military Rifle, Team [5].

Hübner von Holst, Johan. (b.22 August 1881–d.13 June 1945) Free Pistol [27]; Free Pistol, Team [5]; Small-Bore Rifle, Disappearing Target [=15]; Small-Bore Rifle, Moving Target [=15]; Small-Bore Rifle, Prone [18]; Small-Bore Rifle, Team [2].

Jansson, Axel. (b.24 April 1882–d.22 September 1909) Free Rifle, 3 Positions [7]; Free Rifle, Team [2]; Military Rifle, Team [5].

Jonsson, Gustaf Adolf. (b.26 June 1879–d.30 April 1949) Free Rifle, 3 Positions [15]; Free Rifle, Team [2]; Military Rifle, Team [5].

Jörgensen, Ossian. (b.26 June 1874–d.3 October 1948) Free Rifle, 3 Positions [50]; Free Rifle, 1,000 yards [34]; Military Rifle, Team [5].

Knöppel, G. Arvid. (b.7 March 1867–d.7 March 1925) Running Deer, Team [1].

Mossberg, Fredrik. (b.25 February 1874–d.14 August 1950) Free Rifle, 3 Positions [23]; Free Rifle, 1,000 yards [44].

Ohlsson, P. Erik F. "Pågen." (b.20 November 1884–d.19 September 1980) Free Rifle, 3 Positions [28]; Free Rifle, 1,000 yards [43].

Rosell, Ernst. (b.3 December 1881–d.26 July 1953) Running Deer, Double Shot, Individual [8]; Free Rifle, 1,000 yards [46]; Running Deer, Single Shot, Individual [11]; Running Deer, Team [1]; Trap Shooting, Individual [ac].

Rundberg, Claës. (b.14 November 1874–d.25 May 1958) Free Rifle, Team [2]; Military Rifle, Team [5].

Schartau, Frans-Albert. (b.13 July 1877–d.6 June 1943) Free Pistol [18]; Free Pistol, Team [5]; Small-Bore Rifle, Disappearing Target [=9]; Small-Bore Rifle, Moving Target [=19]; Small-Bore Rifle, Team [2].

Sjöberg, Gustav-Adolf. (b.22 March 1865–d.31 October 1937) Free Rifle, Team [2]; Free Rifle, 3 Positions [4].

Swahn, Alfred Gomer. (b.20 August 1879–d.16 March 1931) Running Deer, Team [1]; Trap Shooting, Individual [25].

Swahn, Oscar Gomer. (b.20 October 1847–d.1 May 1927) Running Deer, Double Shot, Individual [3]; Running Deer, Single Shot, Individual [1]; Running Deer, Team [1].

von Rosen, Otto. (b.11 May 1884–d.26 May 1963) Free Pistol [35]; Small-Bore Rifle, Disappearing Target [=9]; Small-Bore Rifle, Moving Target [8].

Swimming (Total: 12; Men: 12; Women: 0)

Andersson, Adolf "Ale." (b.23 June 1888–d.) 200 meter breaststroke [3h7r1/3]; 4 × 200 meter relay [3h2r1/2].

Andersson, Robert "Robban." (b.18 October 1886–d.2 March 1972) 100 meter freestyle [ach3r1/3]; 400 meter freestyle [2h2r1/3]. [See also Diving and Water Polo].

Andersson, Vilhelm. (b.11 March 1891–d.21 September 1933) 400 meter freestyle [4h1r1/3]; 1,500 meter freestyle [4h2r1/3].

Fjästad, Per. (b.15 March 1883–d.18 October 1955) 200 meter breaststroke [2h5r1/3].

Gumpel, Max. (b.23 April 1890–d.2 August 1965) 200 meter breaststroke [3h1r1/3].

Hanson, Pontus. (b.24 May 1884–d.4 December 1962) 200 meter breaststroke [3]. [See also Water Polo].

Johansson, Hjalmar. (b.20 January 1874–d.30 September 1957) 200 meter breaststroke [2h3r1/3]. [See also Diving].

Julin, Harald "Julie." (b.27 March 1890–d.31 July 1967) 100 meter freestyle [3]; 4 × 200 meter relay [3h2r1/2]. [See also Water Polo].

Kumfeldt, Torsten. (b.4 January 1886–d.2 May 1966) 200 meter breaststroke [2h6r1/3]. [See also Water Polo].

Persson, Wilhelm. (b.4 January 1886–d.27 May 1955) 200 meter breaststroke [3h2r2/3].

Wennerström, Gunnar. (b.27 June 1870–d.May 1931) 1,500 meter freestyle [2h1r1/3]; 4 × 200 meter relay [3h2r1/2]. [See also Water Polo].

Wretman, Gustaf. (b.10 August 1888) 1,500 meter freestyle [3h6r1/3]; 100 meter backstroke [3h6r1/3]; 4 × 200 meter relay [3h2r1/2].

Tennis (Total: 4; Men: 2; Women: 2)

Women

Adlerstråhle, Märtha. (b.16 June 1868–d.4 January 1956) Singles (Covered Court) [3].

Wallenberg, Elsa. (b.26 January 1877–d.17 October 1951) Singles (Covered Court) [4].

Men

Boström, Wollmar. (b.15 June 1878–d.7 November 1956) Singles (Covered Court) [=5]; Doubles (Covered Court) [3].

Setterwall, Gunnar. (b.18 August 1881–d.26 February 1928) Singles (Covered Court) [=5]; Doubles (Covered Court) [3].

Tug-of-War (Total: 8; Men: 8; Women: 0)
Almqwist, Albrekt. (b.14 November 1880–d.10 April 1961) [4].
Fast, Frans. (b.30 September 1885–d.29 June 1959) [4].
Johansson, Carl-Emil. (b.1886) [4].
Johansson, Emil. (b.13 January 1885) [4].
Johansson, Knut. (b.14 January 1888) [4].
Krook, Karl. (b.10 January 1887) [4].
Nilsson, Karl-Gustaf. (b.9 March 1879) [4].
Wollgarth, Anders. (b.29 April 1878–d.24 December 1950) [4].

Water Polo (Total: 7; Men: 7; Women: 0)
Andersson, Robert "Robban." (b.18 October 1886–d.2 March 1972) [3]. [See also Diving and Swimming].
Bergvall, Erik. (b.7 April 1880–d.4 February 1950) [3].
Hanson, Pontus. (b.24 May 1884–d.4 December 1962) [3]. [See also Swimming].
Julin, Harald "Julie." (b.27 March 1890–d.31 July 1967) [3]. [See also Swimming].
Kumfeldt, Torsten. (b.4 January 1886–d.2 May 1966) [3]. [See also Swimming].
Runström, Axel. (b.15 October 1883–d.10 August 1943) [3]. [See also Diving].
Wennerström, Gunnar. (b.27 June 1879–d.1931) [3]. [See also Swimming].

Wrestling (Total: 9; Men: 9; Women: 0)
Andersson, Carl G. (b.10 February 1884) Middleweight, Catch-as-Catch-Can [4].
Andersson, Mauritz. (b.22 September 1886–d.1 November 1997) Middleweight, Greco-Roman [2].
Challstorp, Harry. Middleweight, Catch-as-Catch-Can [=9]; Middleweight, Greco-Roman [=17].
Frank, Axel. (b.17 December 1882) Middleweight, Greco-Roman [=5].
Larsson, Fritz. (b.22 December 1882) Light-Heavyweight, Greco-Roman [=5].
Lund, Carl Erik. (b.23 September 1884–d.1940) Lightweight, Greco-Roman [=9].
Malmström, Gustaf. (b.4 July 1884) Lightweight, Greco-Roman [=5].
Mårtensson, Frithiof. (b.19 May 1884–d.20 June 1956) Middleweight, Greco-Roman [1].
Persson, Gunnar. (b.1889) Lightweight, Greco-Roman [4].

Yachting (Total: 13; Men: 13; Women: 0)
Carlsson, John. (b.5 January 1870–d.24 July 1935) 8-meter class [5].
Gustafsson, Birger. (b.15 January 1874–d.22 February 1969) 6-meter class [5].
Hagberg, Edvin. (b.31 July 1875–d.1 September 1947) 8-meter class [5].
Hellström, Carl Ludvig. (b.10 December 1864–d.4 July 1962) 8-meter class [2].
Jonsson, Jonas. (b.30 September 1873–d.14 March 1926) 6-meter class [5].
Ljungberg, Karl. (b.22 November 1868–d.11 July 1943) 8-meter class [5].
Lönnroth, Hjalmar. (b.11 September 1856–d.1917) 8-meter class [5].
Olsson, August "Möss-Olle." (b.18 August 1878–d.14 August 1943) 8-meter class [5].
Sandberg, Eric G. (b.19 December 1884–d.8 December 1966) 8-meter class [2].
Sjögren, Karl-Einar. (b.29 September 1871–d.6 May 1956) 6-meter class [5].
Thormählen, Edmund Gustaf. (b.21 July 1865–d.13 November 1946) 8-meter class [2].
Wallerius, Erik. (b.16 April 1878–d.7 May 1967) 8-meter class [2].
Wallin, J. Harald. (b.1883) 8-meter class [2].

Switzerland (Total: 1; Men: 1; Women: 0)

Athletics (Track & Field) (Total: 1; Men: 1; Women: 0)
    Wagner, Julius. (b.10 October 1882–d.2 March 1952) Hammer Throw [ac].

United States (Total: 122; Men: 122; Women: 0)

Archery (Total: 1; Men: 1; Women: 0)
    Richardson, Henry Barber. (b.19 May 1889–d.19 November 1963) Double York round [3]; Continental Style [15].

Athletics (Track & Field) (Total: 84; Men: 84; Women: 0)
    Adams, Platt. (b.23 March 1885–d.27 February 1961) Triple Jump [5]; Standing High Jump [=5]; Standing Long Jump [=6]; Discus Throw (freestyle) [ac]; Discus Throw (classical) [ac].
    Atlee, John Cox. (b.24 October 1882–d.2 August 1958) 400 meters [3h4r2/3].
    Bacon, Charles Joseph, Jr. (b.9 January 1885–d.15 November 1968) 400 meter hurdles [1].
    Beard, Clarke Briar. (b.29 November 1884–d.November 1978) 800 meters [dnf-final].
    Bellah, Samuel Harrison. (b.24 January 1887–d.January 1963) Pole Vault [=6]; Long Jump [12]; Triple Jump [17].
    Bellars, Frederick G. (b.2 January 1888–d.May 1971) 5 miles [8].
    Biller, John A. (b.14 November 1879–d.February 1960) Standing High Jump [=2]; Standing Long Jump [4].
    Bonhag, George V. (b.31 January 1882–d.30 October 1960) 3,200 meter steeplechase [dnfh4r1/2]; 3-mile team race [2].
    Brennan, John Joseph. (b.17 July 1879–d.February 1964) Long Jump [5]; Triple Jump [8].
    Bromilow, Joseph M., Jr. (b.20 October 1881–d.January 1972) 800 meters [2h7r1/2].
    Burroughs, Wilbur Gordon. (b.13 June 1884–d.6 August 1960) Shot Put [ac]; Discus Throw (freestyle) [10]; Discus Throw (classical) [8]. [See also Tug-of-War].
    Carpenter, John Conduit. (b.7 December 1884–d.4 June 1933) 400 meters [dq-final].
    Carr, Edward P. 3,200 meter steeplechase [dnfh1r1/2].
    Cartmell, Nathaniel John. (b.13 January 1883–d.23 August 1967) 100 meters [4]; 200 meters [3]; 1,600 meter medley relay [1].
    Cloughen, Robert. (b.26 January 1889) 200 meters [2].
    Coe, Harry Lee. (b.21 June 1885–d.April 1977) 800 meters [2h4r1/2]; 1,500 meters [2h4r1/2]; 400 meter hurdles [2h1r2/3].
    Coe, William Wesley, Jr. (b.8 May 1879–d.24 December 1926) Shot Put [4]. [See also Tug-of-War].
    Cohn, Harvey Wright. (b.4 December 1884–d.July 1965) 3-mile team race [2].
    Cook, Edward Tiffin, Jr. (b.27 November 1889–d.18 October 1972) Pole Vault [=1]; Long Jump [4].
    Dearborn, Arthur Kent. (b.27 May 1886–d.28 August 1941) Discus Throw (freestyle) [5]; Discus Throw (classical) [4]. [See also Tug-of-War].
    Dull, Gale Albert. (b.4 May 1883) 3,200 meter steeplechase [2h4r1/2]; 3-mile team race [2].
    Eisele, John Lincoln. (b.18 January 1884–d.30 March 1933) 3,200 meter steeplechase [3]; 3-mile team race [2].
    Ewry, Raymond Clarence "R. C." (b.14 October 1873–d.29 September 1937) Standing High Jump [1]; Standing Long Jump [1].

Flanagan, John Jesus. (b.9 January 1873–d.4 June 1938) Discus Throw (freestyle) [9]; Hammer Throw [1]. [See also Tug-of-War].

Forshaw, Joseph, Jr. (b.13 May 1880–d.26 November 1964) Marathon [3].

French, Charles Martin. (b.21 September 1886–d.24 June 1972) 800 meters [dnfh5r1/2].

Garrells, John Carlyle. (b.18 November 1885–d.21 October 1956) 110 meter hurdles [2]; Shot Put [3]; Discus Throw (freestyle) [ac]; Discus Throw (classical) [ac].

Gidney, Herbert Alfred. (b.16 November 1881–d.May 1963) High Jump [=5].

Giffin, Merritt Hayward. (b.20 August 1887–d.11 July 1911) Discus Throw (freestyle) [2].

Gilbert, Alfred Carleton "A. C." (b.15 February 1884–d.24 January 1961) Pole Vault [=1].

Gillis, Simon Patrick. (b.6 April 1880–d.14 January 1964) Discus Throw (freestyle) [ac]; Hammer Throw [7].

Hall, Charles Lincoln. (b.19 February 1887) 5 miles [4h3r1/2]; 3,200 meter steeplechase [4h5r1/2].

Halstead, John Preston. (b.15 August 1886–d.15 November 1951) 800 meters [6]; 1,500 meters [2h2r1/2].

Hamilton, William Frank. (b.1884) 200 meters [2h1r2/3]; 1,600 meter medley relay [1].

Hatch, Sydney H. (b.18 August 1883–d.January 1974) Marathon [14].

Hayes, John Joseph. (b.10 April 1886–d.23 August 1965) Marathon [1].

Hillman, Harry Livingston, Jr. (b.8 September 1881–d.9 August 1945) 400 meter hurdles [2].

Holmes, Francis LeRoy. (b.23 January 1885–d.February 1980) Standing High Jump [4]; Standing Long Jump [=6].

Horr, Marquis Franklin, "Bill." (b.1 July 1880–d.1 July 1955) Shot Put [6]; Discus Throw (freestyle) [3]; Discus Throw (classical) [2]; Hammer Throw [6]. [See also Tug-of-War].

Howe, Leonard Vernon. (b.10 December 1886–d.December 1974) 110 meter hurdles [3h2r2/3].

Huff, Harold J. (b.1881–d.April 1964) 100 meters [2h3r2/3]; 200 meters [3h2r2/3].

Irons, Francis C. (b.23 March 1886) Long Jump [1]; Triple Jump [16]; Standing High Jump [=8]; Standing Long Jump [ac].

Jackson, Thomas Marshall. (b.15 January 1884–d.22 February 1967) Pole Vault [=12].

Jacobs, Charles Sherman. (b.15 February 1872–d.February 1945) Pole Vault [=3].

Jones, Lloyd Peniston. (b.12 September 1884) 800 meters [3h4r1/2].

Kelly, Daniel Joseph. (b.1 September 1883–d.9 April 1920) Long Jump [2].

Kiralfy, Edgar Graham. (b.20 August 1884–d.17 May 1928) 100 meters [ach4r1/3].

Lightbody, James Davies. (b.15 March 1882–d.2 March 1953) 800 meters [4h1r1/2]; 1,500 meters [2h1r1/2]; 3,200 meter steeplechase [2h6r1/2].

May, William Wyman. (b.27 October 1886–d.October 1978) 100 meters [2h1r2/3]; 200 meters [2h11r1/3].

McGrath, Matthew John. (b.18 December 1878–d.29 January 1941) Hammer Throw [2]. [See also Tug-of-War].

Merriam, Ned Alvin. (b.26 October 1884–d.9 July 1956) 400 meters [3h1r2/3].

Moffitt, Thomas Robinson. (b.26 February 1884–d.2 May 1945) High Jump [=5].

Morrissey, Thomas Patrick. (b.2 September 1888–d.1 October 1968) Marathon [dnf].

Mount Pleasant, Frank. (b.1884–d.12 April 1937) Long Jump [6]; Triple Jump [6].

Muenz, Sigmund. Standing Long Jump [ac].

O'Connell, John F. V. Long Jump [ac].

Patterson, John Norman. (b.4 July 1889–d.20 December 1948) High Jump [7].

Pilgrim, Paul Harry. (b.26 October 1883–d.7 January 1958) 400 meters [2h1r1/3].

Porter, Harry Franklin. (b.31 August 1882–d.June 1965) High Jump [1].

Prout, William Christopher. (b.24 December 1886–d.4 August 1927) 400 meters [4h2r2/3].

Ramey, Horace Patton. (b.12 February 1885) 400 meters [2h3r2/3]; 800 meters [dnfh7r1/2].

Rand, William McNear. (b.7 April 1886–d.April 1981) 110 meter hurdles [4].

Rector, James Alcorn. (b.22 June 1884–d.10 March 1949) 100 meters [2].

Riley, Frank N. (b.3 July 1887–d.July 1961) 1,500 meters [dnfh3r1/2].

Robbins, William Corbett. (b.9 August 1885) 400 meters [dns-final2].

Robertson, Lawson N. (b.24 September 1883–d.22 January 1951) 100 meters [2h4r2/3]; 200 meters [2h3r1/3]; Standing High Jump [ac].

Rose, Ralph Waldo. (b.17 March 1885–d.16 October 1913) Shot Put [1]. [See also Tug-of-War].

Ryan, Michael J. (b.1 January 1889–d.December 1971) Marathon [dnf].

Selding, Frederick Monroe de. (b.22 June 1887–d.25 November 1971) 400 meters [2h15r1/3].

Shaw, Arthur Briggs. (b.28 April 1886–d.18 July 1955) 110 meter hurdles [3].

Sheehan, Francis Patrick. (b.11 May 1886–d.29 April 1953) 800 meters [4h8r1/2].

Sheppard, Melvin Winfield. (b.5 September 1883–d.4 January 1942) 800 meters [1]; 1,500 meters [1]; 1,600 meter medley relay [1].

Sheridan, Martin Joseph. (b.28 March 1881–d.27 March 1918) Triple Jump [9]; Standing High Jump [16]; Standing Long Jump [3]; Shot Put [ac]; Discus Throw (freestyle) [1]; Discus Throw (classical) [1].

Sherman, Benjamin Franklin. (b.5 April 1881) Hammer Throw [ac].

Sherman, Nathaniel Alden. (b.7 February 1888–d.4 August 1954) 100 meters [2h2r2/3]; 200 meters [2h2r2/3]; Triple Jump [ac].

Smithson, Forrest Custer. (b.26 September 1884–d.November 1962) 110 meter hurdles [1].

Spitzer, Roger Adelbert. (b.21 September 1885–d.20 March 1916) 3,200 meter steeplechase [3h5r1/2].

Stevens, Lester Barber. (b.28 February 1884–d.January 1972) 100 meters [4h1r2/3].

Sullivan, James Patrick. (b.28 February 1885–d.March 1964) 1,500 meters [dnf-final].

Talbott, Leander James, Jr., "Lee." (b.4 July 1887–d.16 September 1954) Shot Put [8]; Discus Throw (freestyle) [6]; Hammer Throw [5]. [See also Tug-of-War and Wrestling].

Taylor, John Baxter, Jr. (b.3 November 1882–d.2 December 1908) 400 meters [dns-final2]; 1,600 meter medley relay [1].

Tewanima, Lewis. (b.1888–d.18 January 1969) Marathon [9].

Trube, Herbert Lawrence. (b.3 September 1886–d.13 July 1959) 5 miles [dnfh5r1/2]; 3-mile team race [2].

Welton, Alton Roy. (b.1886–d.13 November 1958) Marathon [4].

Cycling (Total: 2; Men: 2; Women: 0)

Cameron, George Guthrie. One Lap Match Sprint [3h3r2/3]; 1,000 meters Match Sprint [ach2r2/3]; 20 km. [2h4r1/2].

Weintz, Louis J. (b.21 April 1885–d.February 1969) 1,000 meters Match Sprint [3h13r1/3]; 20 km. [4]; 100 km. [dnfh2r1/2].

Diving (Total: 2; Men: 2; Women: 0)

Gaidzik, George William. (b.22 February 1885) Plain High Diving [5]; Fancy High Diving [=3].

Grote, Harold C. Fancy High Diving [5h2r2/3]; Plain High Diving [3h5r1/3].

Figure Skating (Total: 1; Men: 1; Women: 0)

Brokaw, Irving. (b.1869–d.19 March 1939) Men's Individual [6].

Jeu de Paume (Total: 2; Men: 2; Women: 0)

Gould, Jay, Jr. (b.1 September 1888–d.26 January 1935) Singles [1].

Sands, Charles Edward. (b.22 December 1865–d.9 August 1945) Singles [=9].

Shooting (Total: 17; Men: 17; Women: 0)

Axtell, Charles Sumner. (b.1859–d.24 November 1932) Free Pistol [4]; Free Pistol, Team [1].

Benedict, Charles Sumner. (b.1857–d.15 April 1937) Free Rifle, 1,000 yards [=13]; Military Rifle, Team [1].

Calkins, Irving Romaro. (b.31 October 1875–d.26 August 1958) Free Pistol [8]; Free Pistol, Team [1].

Casey, Kellogg Kennon Venable. (b.17 September 1877–d.18 October 1938) Free Rifle, 1,000 yards [2]; Military Rifle, Team [1].

Dietz, John A. (b.24 November 1870–d.11 October 1939) Free Pistol [9]; Free Pistol, Team [1].

Eastman, Ivan L. (b.3 August 1883–d.September 1964) Free Rifle, 1,000 yards [=13]; Military Rifle, Team [1].

Gorman, James Edward. (b.30 January 1859) Free Pistol [3]; Free Pistol, Team [1].

Green, Edward Alonzo. Free Rifle, 3 Positions [16]; Free Rifle, 1,000 yards [=24].

Hessian, John William. (b.8 September 1877) Free Rifle, 3 Positions [29]; Free Rifle, 1,000 yards [=24].

Jeffers, Charles J. Free Rifle, 1,000 yards [=13].

LeBoutillier, Thomas, II. (b.18 January 1879–d.19 September 1929) Free Pistol [19].

Leuschner, William D. F. (b.27 November 1863–d.25 October 1935) Military Rifle, Team [1]; Free Rifle, 1,000 yards [=11].

Martin, William Franklin. (b.19 July 1863) Military Rifle, Team [1].

Sayre, Reginald Hall. (b.18 October 1859 —Â29 May 1929) Free Pistol [21].

Simon, Harry E. (b.1880–d.28 February 1930) Free Rifle, 3 Positions [2]; Free Rifle, 1,000 yards [=19].

Winans, Walter. (b.5 April 1852–d.12 August 1920) Free Pistol [38]; Running Deer, Double Shot, Individual [1]; Running Deer, Single Shot, Individual [=6]; Small-Bore Rifle, Disappearing Target [=19]; Small-Bore Rifle, Moving Target [=10].

Winder, Charles B. Free Rifle, 1,000 yards [=16]; Military Rifle, Team [1].

Swimming (Total: 8; Men: 8; Women: 0)

Daniels, Charles Meldrum. (b.24 March 1885–d.9 August 1973) 100 meter freestyle [1]; 4 × 200 meter relay [3].

Foster, Robert Bruce. 100 meter freestyle [ach4r1/3].

Goessling, Augustus M. (b.1879–d.22 August 1963) 100 meter backstroke [2h6r1/3]; 200 meter breaststroke [3h2r1/3].

Goodwin, Leo G. "Budd." (b.13 November 1883–d.25 May 1957) 400 meter freestyle [3h1r1/3]; 4 × 200 meter relay [3].

Green, James B. 1,500 meter freestyle [2h5r1/3].

Hebner, Harry J. (b.15 June 1891–d.12 October 1968) 100 meter freestyle [3h1r2/3]; 4 × 200 meter relay [3].

Rich, Leslie George. (b.29 December 1886) 100 meter freestyle [4]; 4 × 200 meter relay [3].

Trubenbach, Conrad Daniel. (b.4 November 1882–d.30 June 1961) 100 meter freestyle [ach2r1/3]; 400 meter freestyle [3h3r1/3].

Tug-of-War (Total: 8; Men: 8; Women: 0)

Burroughs, Wilbur Gordon. (b.13 June 1884–d.6 August 1960) [5]. [See also Athletics (Track & Field)].

Coe, William Wesley, Jr. (b.8 May 1879–d.24 December 1926) [5]. [See also Athletics (Track & Field)].

Dearborn, Arthur Kent. (b.27 May 1886–d.28 August 1941) [5]. [See also Athletics (Track & Field)].

Flanagan, John Jesus. (b.9 January 1873–d.4 June 1938) [5]. [See also Athletics (Track & Field)].

Horr, Marquis Franklin, "Bill." (b.1 July 1880–d.1 July 1955) [5]. [See also Athletics (Track & Field)].

McGrath, Matthew John. (b.18 December 1878–d.29 January 1941) [5]. [See also Athletics (Track & Field)].

Rose, Ralph Waldo. (b.17 March 1885–d.16 October 1913) [5]. [See also Athletics (Track & Field)].

Talbott, Leander James, Jr., "Lee." (b.4 July 1887–d.16 September 1954) [5]. [See also Athletics (Track & Field) and Wrestling].

Wrestling (Total: 6; Men: 6; Women: 0)

Craige, John Houston. (b.1886–d.14 August 1954) Middleweight, Catch-as-Catch-Can [=5].

Dole, George Stuart. (b.30 January 1885–d.6 September 1928) Featherweight, Catch-as-Catch-Can [1].

Krug, John H. (b.1 December 1886–d.June 1972) Lightweight, Catch-as-Catch-Can [=5].

Mehnert, George Nicholas. (b.3 November 1881–d.8 July 1948) Bantamweight, Catch-as-Catch-Can [1].

Narganes, Frederico. Middleweight, Catch-as-Catch-Can [=5].

Talbott, Leander James, Jr., "Lee." (b.4 July 1887–d.16 September 1954) Heavyweight, Catch-as-Catch-Can [=9]. [See also Athletics (Track & Field) and Tug-of-War].

NOTES

1. The New Zealand athletes are listed concurrently below, under Australasia, and in a separate listing for New Zealand. We have noted the New Zealanders below. If no "national" listing occurs after the name, the athlete was Australian.

2. Listed in some sources as a New Zealander, Australian Olympic experts' (notably Harry Gordon, who has researched his life) opinion is that he was Australian. Specifically, he was born and raised in Queensland. He is not listed n the New Zealand book on Olympic history by Palenski and Maddaford.

3. In 1920, Daniel Carroll competed in rugby football again at the Olympics, that time as a member of the United States team, and again won a gold medal. His date of birth is usually listed as 17 February 1892, but research by Buchanan and his British colleagues who study rugby history has shown this year to be incorrect. The 1892 year of birth made him only 16 in 1908 and one of the youngest gold medalists ever but again, this is not correct.

4. Otto Scheff was from what is now the Polish portion of the Austro-Hungarian Empire. He was born Sheff-Sochaczewski, but changed his name to the more German-like Scheff.

5. Year of birth listed as 1895 in WW. Buchanan disputes this and knows of no source confirming it.

6. Because Bohemia was a portion of the Austro-Hungarian Empire in 1908, some of these athletes are claimed by both the Hungarian Olympic Committee and the Czechoslovakian Olympic Committee (prior to its dissolution into Czech and Slovakia). Athletes listed by both sources, with their Bohemian spelling given, are as follows: Juraj Luntzer (ATH), František Ješina (ATH), Mór Koczán (ATH), Štefan Drubina (ATH), and Zoltán Halmaj (SWI).

7. Kovesdy is not listed among Hungarian Olympians in the best source for that information — *Az Olimpiai Játékokon Indult Magyar Versenyzők Névsora 1896-1980*. His full name was identified by Hungarian ATFS member Gabriel Szabó.

8. The New Zealand athletes are listed concurrently under Australasia and New Zealand.

9. Listed often as J. Mitchell-Baker, Baker was a well-decorated South African soldier who retired as a Lieutenant General after World War II. Later in his life, he signed his name James Mitchell-Baker, but as a youth he was known as J. M. Baker.

10. WW lists him as Ivie John Richardson, and a 1924 South African tennis player as L. John Richardson. DW, EK, OSVK, and VK all also give the name as either Ivie Richardson or Ivie John Richardson. According to Alan Little, tennis historian and honorary librarian at Wimbledon, Ivie J. Richardson was the 1924 tennis player who won the 1925 South African championship. The 1908 player was the Reverend John Richardson, who won the South African championship in 1906 and competed at Wimbledon in 1908 as well. Gillmeister also confuses them a bit, calling both the 1908 and 1924 player Reverend J. Richardson. SL entry lists for 1908 give the name only as the Rev. J. Richardson.

Index